ECONOMICS

ECONOMICS
A GENERAL INTRODUCTION

BY

FREDERIC BENHAM

Sir Henry Price Research Professor
of International Economics
Royal Institute of International Affairs

Formerly Professor of Commerce
(with special reference to International Trade)
in the University of London

SIXTH EDITION

LONDON
SIR ISAAC PITMAN & SONS, LTD.

First published 1938   *Reprinted*   1949
Reprinted   1939   *Reprinted*   1953
Second edition 1940   *Fifth edition*   1955
Third edition   1943   *Reprinted*   1957
Fourth edition 1948   *Sixth edition*   1960

SIR ISAAC PITMAN & SONS, Ltd.
PITMAN HOUSE, PARKER STREET, KINGSWAY, LONDON, W.C. 2
THE PITMAN PRESS, BATH
PITMAN HOUSE, BOUVERIE STREET, CARLTON, MELBOURNE
22-25 BECKETT'S BUILDINGS, PRESIDENT STREET, JOHANNESBURG
ASSOCIATED COMPANIES
PITMAN MEDICAL PUBLISHING COMPANY Ltd.
39 PARKER STREET, LONDON, W.C. 2
PITMAN PUBLISHING CORPORATION,
2 WEST 45TH STREET, NEW YORK
SIR ISAAC PITMAN & SONS (CANADA) Ltd.
(INCORPORATING THE COMMERCIAL TEXT BOOK COMPANY)
PITMAN HOUSE, 381–383 CHURCH STREET, TORONTO

PRINTED IN GREAT BRITAIN BY ROBERT MACLEHOSE AND CO. LTD
THE UNIVERSITY PRESS, GLASGOW
Fo—(B.293)

PREFACE TO SIXTH EDITION

THIS edition embodies only minor revisions, mainly to bring the facts and figures more up-to-date. Nevertheless the revisions have involved a considerable amount of rewriting, including the Note on the National Income of the United Kingdom 1958, at the end of Chapter IV; Chapter IX, Section 4 (The Population of the United Kingdom); Chapter XXV, Section 2 (The Share of Labour); Chapter XXIX, Section 2 (Profits in the United Kingdom); Chapter XXXV, Section 3 (The United Kingdom Balance of Payments, 1958); Chapter XXXVI, Section 4 (The European Monetary Agreement); and the last chapter, which has been expanded.

FREDERIC BENHAM

January, 1960

CONTENTS

PART II

PRODUCTION

CHAPTER V

CHAPTER VI

CHAPTER VII

PART III

DEMAND AND SUPPLY

CHAPTER XII

PART IV

THE WORKING OF THE PRICE SYSTEM UNDER CAPITALISM

PART V

THE DISTRIBUTION OF INCOMES

PART VII

INTERNATIONAL TRADE

PART I

INTRODUCTION

CHAPTER I

GENERAL SURVEY

1. THE GENERAL READER

"THE first thing I do when I come to a strange town," a tourist once told me, "is to climb the highest tower in the place in order to get a general view of the layout of the town and of the countryside round it." I suppose that nowadays, if he could afford it, he would take a flight by helicopter over the area.

Let us do the same. Here is a subject—economics—which is new to you. Let us spend the first chapter in having a general look at it.

The analogy between economics and a town, like most analogies, is far from perfect. We may as well begin by seeing what is wrong with it.

Each part of a town can be studied by itself. One could write quite a good account of, say, Chelsea, without much reference to the rest of London. But each part of economics is closely connected with every other; they all fit together, and you cannot understand one part properly without understanding the rest. This makes it difficult for a writer to plan a book on economics; he is always worried, and tempted to make long digressions, by constantly having to refer to something or other which he does not explain until later. In the same way, the reader is worried because questions keep occurring to him, as he reads, which are not answered at the time.

Some of them may not be answered at all. For another big difference between economics and a town is that the newcomer to a town knows little or nothing about it and accepts what he sees, while the newcomer to economics has read the papers and talked to people and therefore comes to the subject with quite a number of ideas. Some of his ideas may be right, and some may be wrong or partly wrong. It may well happen that a writer says nothing about some of the latter, either because his space is limited or because it just doesn't occur to him that anybody would believe them to be true.

I shall resist, for the moment, the temptation to give examples of widely-held beliefs on economic questions which can be shown to be wholly or partly false; such illustrations will fit in better when we discuss the particular subjects to which they relate. Nor shall I pursue further the analogy between economics and a town. I turn now to some remarks about the general tone of this book.

3

It is intended for the general reader. I have tried to write simply and to make it readable. It contains no mathematics apart from some easy diagrams and arithmetical illustrations and a few notes for the benefit of students (some of whom, I hope, will find the book useful) which I have tucked away in appendixes. Some technical "jargon" is essential, but I have avoided it as far as possible.

I think of the general reader as anybody from about sixteen years of age upwards who takes an intelligent interest in economic affairs. He, or she, wants to be able to follow the discussions on economic questions which take place in Parliament, in the Press, and elsewhere, and to be able to form and express views of his or her own based on something more than prejudice and intuition.

I can imagine such a general reader saying: "Yes, that's right. But why are you wasting time? Why not get on with the job? Chapter I on one problem, Chapter II on another problem, and so on until you have discussed twenty or thirty of the most important current economic problems, then finish."

There are two main answers to this. First, new economic problems are always cropping up, or at any rate old ones are presenting themselves in a different setting. A detailed discussion of many specific questions would soon get out of date; the facts and figures, and the relevant circumstances, would alter as time went on. The only way to cope with this is to try to give the reader a foundation of economic theory, an insight into the economic "method of approach" to a problem, and so to equip him to follow, and to form his own judgment on, the up-to-date discussions of current problems which he will find in the Press; I would especially recommend him to read the weekly *Economist*.

The second main answer is that it is almost impossible to explain anything properly, within the realm of economics, without explaining everything. If we started off bang on some particular question, we should have to keep pulling ourselves up for a long digression on this or that point of economic theory, which would have to be explained before we could resume the argument. The book would have no pattern at all.

What it comes to, then, is that after all this will be very like any other introduction to economics. Perhaps rather less accurate than some, because if a generalization is broadly true I shall seldom complicate the argument with exceptions and qualifications. Less methodology, less mathematics, less refinement of economic theory, less detail, and perhaps more stress on economic policy. But nevertheless just another text-book!

2. FACTS AND OPINIONS

The type of reader for whom I am writing has a critical mind. He thinks for himself. He wants to know enough about economics to form his own independent judgments. There are some students who regard economics merely as a subject in which they must pass an examination, and they hope to get through by learning by heart a few definitions and a few "economic laws." They will never be able to play their proper part as citizens, for they will never really understand the economic issues on which they should express their views or cast their votes. They will not even do well at their examinations, for examination questions tend to be framed to test whether or not the candidate has grasped the methods of economic analysis, and can apply them to new problems, rather than to test whether he has a good memory. This book is not for them; my advice to them is to take up another subject.

The reader should learn to distinguish at once between a statement of fact and a statement of opinion. I do not mean an opinion about what the facts are. "There's gold in them thar hills," says the Oldest Inhabitant. Maybe there is and maybe there isn't. He is expressing an opinion. But it is an opinion about a fact, and one day it may be proved either right or wrong. The kind of opinion which I mean is an opinion about what ought to be done, an opinion which by its nature is not capable of verification, can never be proved or disproved. This type of opinion is called a *value-judgment* because it is a judgment which springs from the general outlook and beliefs of the speaker, which reflects his views on what ends are the more desirable, and which therefore depends on his particular scale of values, in the philosophical sense of the word "values."

A value-judgment usually contains the word "ought" or "should" or speaks of the "right" course or the "best" policy. Some value-judgments are very widely accepted. For example, nearly everybody agrees that "the rich ought to be taxed more heavily than the poor." But it is a value-judgment all the same; it cannot be proved or disproved as a statement of fact (such as "Doubling the tax on spirits would yield little more revenue, if any, because people would switch to beer or give up drinking") can be proved or disproved.

This is not to belittle the significance of value-judgments. On the contrary, they can be of tremendous importance; they can shake the world. Millions have fought and died for beliefs that can never be "proved" true. It is very desirable, to my mind, that such beliefs should be discussed at length. In this way, the meaning of a belief, which is often rather vague even for people who hold it strongly, can be made more precise; some beliefs can be shown to be inconsistent with one another; arguments can be advanced in favour of one opinion or against another. Yet always, in the last resort, we may come up against a blank wall. If somebody declares that he does not agree with a particular value-judgment, and remains unmoved by all persuasions, there is nothing more to be done about it. There is no way on earth to prove that he is wrong.

I stress this point because so often in economic discussions somebody, perhaps somebody very eminent, will state an opinion, a value-judgment, as if it were beyond dispute, like the statement that the earth is round and not flat. The unwary listener may be tempted, especially perhaps if the speaker is himself an economist, to take the statement as an established fact of economic doctrine, like a "law" of physics or chemistry, instead of for what it is, a belief which the speaker happens to hold and with which others have every right to disagree.

This book will discuss, necessarily in somewhat general terms because the relevant details change as time goes on, quite a number of controversial issues. I shall try to give the arguments for and against the main opposing views. On a few subjects I may express my own opinion; in that event I shall warn the reader that I am doing so.

3. Economic Analysis

A book on economics, if it is to be alive, must contain a number of facts and figures in order to give a realistic setting to the questions which it discusses. But no amount of facts and figures will explain how the economic system works and why things happen as they do, nor will facts and figures by themselves enable us to discuss the probable effects of various proposals intended to improve our economic life.

Economics is concerned with explanation and discussion, with analysis rather than with description. It answers questions beginning with "why?" rather than with "how many?" or "how?" It does not answer questions on policy taking the form "what should be done about it?" but it does discuss the probable effects of doing this or doing that, and thereby helps people to form their own opinions.

The most satisfactory type of economic analysis, to my mind, is a discussion of some specific current problem. The relevant facts and figures can be set out, the reasons for the present situation can be explained, and the probable consequences of different proposals for improving it can be discussed. But there are many thousands of such specific problems, with new ones always cropping up and the relevant data always changing. The best we can do is to make our discussions rather general, with a few specific problems thrown in by way of illustration, and to hope that the reader will get a firm enough grasp of the methods of economic analysis to apply them himself to whatever particular questions interest him at the moment.

I shall assume that most people consider desirable certain aims: full employment, higher standards of living, improved working conditions, and a certain measure of economic equality and social security; the next chapter discusses these aims. On that assumption I shall consider what are the main influences affecting these aims, and the part which is played by public policy in helping to achieve them. I shall try to explain the working of what economists call the *price mechanism* and, always on the assumption that the aims mentioned above are desired, what are its advantages and defects, and how the latter might be remedied. But I must repeat that the discussions will be, inevitably, somewhat general. For example, I shall give a general explanation of why some prices are higher than others, but I cannot give a detailed explanation of why the price of, say, wool is what it is, for there are far too many commodities to consider them all, and even if I did, the discussions would be out of date by the time they were read.

One main feature of economic analysis is that it shows the whole picture. It takes the standpoint of the community as a whole and not of some particular section of it, and it takes into account the more distant as well as the more immediate consequences of economic action.

Let us take a simple example. Suppose that a shop window is broken. Somebody may say that it is hard luck for the shopkeeper, but that it is an ill wind that blows nobody any good, and at any rate it will make work for the glazier. But if the shopkeeper did not have to pay for a new window he would have been able to buy something else, perhaps a new suit, so that now the tailor loses an order. From the standpoint of the community, work must be done, materials and labour must be employed, on replacing the window which might otherwise have been employed in adding something to the assets of the country instead of merely making good this damage. If an unbreakable glass, just as easy to make and therefore just as cheap as our present glass, could be invented, the country as a whole would be better off. There would be less employment for glaziers, and some of them would have to find other jobs, but all the labour and material formerly employed in replacing windows could now be employed in producing something else that people want. It is quite wrong to think that the damage to buildings during a war is a good thing because it provides employment after the war. The labour and materials used in repairing past damage would have been used, had there been no war, to produce more and better houses for slum-dwellers and for the growing population, or some of it might have been diverted to other useful purposes; as things are, all this labour and material is tied up in merely making good the losses due to the war.

Another main feature of economic analysis is that it stresses alternatives. Every economic decision is a choice between alternatives. The cost of a thing, in the last resort, is not the money spent on it or the labour and materials employed on it, but the thing which was most nearly chosen instead, the alternative which was forgone. This economists call its *opportunity-cost*. The small boy with only sixpence to spend hesitates between chocolates and acid drops; the opportunity-cost to him of the chocolates he buys is the acid drops he goes without. The student goes without lunch to take his girl to the pictures; his opportunity-cost is the lunch he did not have. The same idea applies to production. A farmer decides to grow barley rather than oats; the opportunity-cost of the barley is the oats which he might have grown instead. The cost of rearmament is a somewhat lower standard of living than would otherwise be possible—more guns, less butter.

Economic analysis consists of logical reasoning like the reasoning in a theorem of Euclid. If there is a flaw in the reasoning, it can be exposed and has to be admitted. Hence no differences of opinion are possible about the reasoning, if it contains no flaws. The conclusions follow inevitably from the assumptions because they are implicit in the assumptions. For example, if we assume that a monopolist will maximize his profits and that we know what his total receipts would be and also what his total costs would be for any given weekly output, we can say exactly what output he would produce: it would be that output which maximized his profits (total receipts less total costs); and what price he would charge (total receipts divided by the number of units produced and, by assumption, sold).

Why, then, do economists sometimes disagree with one another? The main reason is that they disagree about what assumptions are true of the real world and should be applied, therefore, to the problem under discussion. By applying flawless logic to wrong assumptions you can arrive at some very odd conclusions. I am reminded of the man who, on the advice of a friend, took off his shoes, tied the laces together, carried the shoes in his mouth, and went up the stairs on all fours, in order not to wake his wife. His procedure was quite correct, but when he came to the top he found himself on Waterloo Station. Some economists appear to me sometimes to get to Waterloo Station by logic or mathematics in which there is no flaw. It is their assumptions which I think are wrong, and as their assumptions are about the way people behave, or would behave in certain circumstances, there is plenty of room for disagreement.

Another possible reason why economists may disagree on issues of policy is that they have different scales of values. They may agree on the assumptions and on the analysis, but not on what should be done.

Suppose, for example, that a proposal were made that the Government should pay, out of its revenue from taxation, £5 a week to every adult. Some economists might think that a good many people would take their £5 a week and would not bother to do any paid work, and that the high rates of tax needed to provide the money would induce other workers to do less work than before. Others might think that there would be very little loafing and that higher taxation might lead people to work harder. This is a disagreement about assumptions. Now suppose that two economists agreed with one another that there would be quite a substantial fall in output and therefore in general standards of living. Nevertheless one might favour the proposal and the other oppose it, because the former thought the consequent "social security" for all, due to the minimum guaranteed income of £5 a week, would be worth having at the cost of lower standards of living, and the latter did not. They would make different value-judgments.

There are many matters on which nearly all economists are in agreement but on which the general public, through sheer ignorance, holds opposite views or has no view at all. On questions about which economists disagree it is surely both interesting and important for the ordinary citizen to understand exactly what the problems are and why some economists are in opposite camps. Economics does not offer cut-and-dried solutions for every problem. It can help you, however, to see a problem in all its aspects, to look for the hidden or remote consequences as well as for the obvious and immediate ones, and to understand the arguments for all the conflicting opinions in so far as they are based on knowledge and reason.

4. ACTIVITY AND WANTS

The world is at work. The farm labourer is in the fields, tending the cattle or sowing the seed or gathering the harvest. The factory worker is controlling the machines, feeding them with the raw materials which they transform into manufactured goods. The miner is extracting mineral deposits from beneath the surface of the earth. The clerk is recording transactions in the office. The doctor is advising patients in his consulting room. The teacher is instructing pupils in the school. Transport workers are moving persons and goods from one place to another, by land or sea or air. By telegraph and telephone, by cable and wireless, orders and instructions are transmitted with amazing speed. The wheels of economic activity are whirling round.

Why does all this activity take place? Every wage-earner, for example, knows well enough why he goes to work. He may like his job, or he may not; in any event, he goes to work in order to earn wages. But he does not want the money which his employer pays him for its own sake; he wants it for what it will buy. He wants it in order to satisfy, as far as possible, his wants for what I shall call consumers' goods—that is, for food, clothing, house-room, and all the other things the consumption of which constitutes his standard of living. If he had no such wants, or if his wants could be satisfied without any effort on his part, he would not go to work. He works that he may eat, or, more generally, that he may consume.

This is equally true of everybody who contributes towards economic activity, whether by his personal exertion or by investing his money or permitting others to use his property, It may be that a man will choose a job that he prefers rather than one that is better paid; it may be that a business man will sometimes sell cheaply, from motives of charity, to a poor customer. But the vast majority of people engage in economic activity mainly in order to get a money income, and they want the money to purchase consumers' goods. I may remark, in passing, that this by no means implies that most people are selfish or sordid or base. A person's character will show itself in the way he disposes of his income. He may spend most of it upon his wife or children or other dependants; he may give largely to charity. But he wants a money income to provide himself and his family with consumers' goods; it is the wants which consumers' goods satisfy that give the main stimulus to economic activity.

If we turn from the motives of an individual to the functions performed by different kinds of economic activity, we find that the whole productive apparatus is directed towards producing consumers' goods. Only a small part of the work of the world consists of giving the final touches to consumers' goods and delivering them to the final consumer. Behind the shopkeeper who sells, let us say, a cotton shirt there stretches a vast army of workers, all of whom, aided by natural resources and buildings and machinery and means of transport, have played their part in making possible the presence of the shirt in the shop. There are the workers on the cotton plantation, in the ginning works, in the spinning mill, in the weaving shed, and in the works which bleaches or prints or dyes the cloth, and in the factory which makes the shirt. There are the transport workers—lorry-drivers, railwaymen and seamen. There are the bankers and merchants, and their clerks. And even so, the catalogue is far from complete. The miners who hewed the coal to make the coke to feed the blast furnace which made the pig-iron which made the steel which made the spindles contributed only a very tiny part indeed towards the shirt. But it was a necessary part, and the ultimate object (from the standpoint of the community) of their labour was achieved by the consumption of the shirts which it helped to produce.

It is easy to see that the whole economic apparatus depends upon sales and, ultimately, upon sales to the final consumers. A worker in, say, a spinning mill works in order to get wages. Why does his employer pay him wages? Because he hopes that his receipts from the sale of the yarn will exceed his various expenses, including the wages that he pays, and will thus yield him an income for himself. And why do other firms buy his yarn? Clearly for the same reason: they hope to sell the cloth at a price which will give them a profit. But, in general, yarn and cloth are not wanted for their own sakes; they are intermediate products in a chain of processes that culminates and has its purpose in the consumption of cotton clothing. One intermediary buys from another in the hope that, after transforming the commodity into a form more suitable for satisfying wants, he in turn will be able to sell it at a profit. The chain may be very long, but always at the end of it stands the final consumer who buys the consumers' goods.

I conclude, therefore, that the rationale of economic activity is to satisfy human wants by producing consumers' goods.

5. SPECIALIZATION AND MONEY

If we ask what people in Great Britain [1] are doing, the answer is, in round figures, as follows. At the close of 1959, the total population was 50·7 million, of whom some twelve million were children under fifteen, and some six million were over sixty-four years old. The working population—which by convention excludes housewives and others doing unpaid work—consisted of 16·1 million males and 8·1 million females. It was divided among industries as shown below—

WORKING POPULATION OF GREAT BRITAIN: END-1959

	Millions
Armed Forces	0·5
Agriculture, Forestry, and Fishing . . .	1·0
Coal Mining (and other mining and quarrying) .	0·8
Manufacturing	9·3
Building and Contracting	1·5
Transport and Communication	1·7
Distributive Trades	3·0
National and Local Government Service . .	1·3
Other	4·7
Unemployed	0·4
	24·2

The two biggest groups under "Manufacturing" were Metals, Engineering etc., including Shipbuilding and Vehicles (4·6 million) and Textiles and Clothing, including Footwear (1·5 million).

Of course much more detailed figures are available; they are given from time to time in the monthly *Ministry of Labour Gazette*. The above summary is reproduced only to give the reader a very broad general picture of what people are doing.

One fact that stands out from this table is that hardly any workers except farmers produce for themselves more than a small fraction of the goods and services which they consume. By tending a machine or driving a lorry or serving behind a counter or writing figures in a ledger a man can make food appear in his larder, clothing in his wardrobe, and furniture in his home. Even the farmer who grows, say,

[1] The United Kingdom consists of Great Britain and Northern Ireland. The latter had a population of 1·4 million.

wheat usually leaves it to others to mill the wheat into flour, to make
the flour into bread, and to deliver the bread to his home. The bread
will probably be made from flour containing mainly imported wheat,
it will contain other ingredients, such as sugar and yeast, and the
farmer will spend only a small part of his income on bread. This is
an age of specialization. Make a list of the different things which your
family buys in a week. Trace where they come from, where their
ingredients came from, how they were made, how much "transport
and distribution" was needed to get them to you, and you will find
that many thousands of workers have made some contribution, however small, to providing you with them.

The rest of the world plays its part in providing us with goods.
About half our food, a large part of the materials used in our industries,
and some of the manufactured goods we buy, are imported. In order
to pay for them, millions of our workers, especially in the manufacturing industries, assist in one way or another in producing goods for
export.

All the thousands of people who co-operate, in effect, to provide
your household with the goods which it consumes do not know one
another, nor do they know you. The whole complex system by which
we are provided with consumers' goods is impersonal. It works through
the use of money. The workers are paid in money and do not need
to know anything about all the other workers who contribute towards
the finished product that finally reaches your home. You pay money
for it, and do not need to know anything about the network of specialized effort which gets it to your door.

I discuss money at length later in this book. But its importance
should be appreciated at once. It is a generally accepted means of
payment. In itself it may be paper or metal worth very little, but
people will accept it at its face value in payment for their services or
products because they know that they can pass it on and buy with it
whatever they want. As long as people will accept it, all is well.
When for any reason they lose confidence in it and refuse it, something
acceptable must be used instead.

We probably think of money as cash—paper notes or cupro-nickel
and copper coins. Many of the payments made by final consumers
are made in cash. But a much greater value of transactions takes
place between firms, to pay for the materials which they buy, for
goods changing hands in bulk, and for other business dealings. Such
payments, as well as some payments by final consumers, are made by
cheque. However, cheques are accepted because they can be turned
into cash if necessary, so that these remarks apply to cheques as well as
to cash, with the proviso that you will not usually part with goods to a
stranger until after his cheque had been paid by the bank and credited
to your account.

Another purpose served by money is to act as a unit of account. Prices are expressed in money. Without money as a common measure of value it would be impossible to compare the costs of different possible methods of production or to judge whether receipts would cover costs.

Only a primitive system of self-supporting villages, with perhaps some barter transactions with the rest of the world, could survive without the use of money. Our present complex system, with its high degree of specialization, depends on money as a generally acceptable means of payment, and on prices for the purpose of making economic calculations.

6. ECONOMIC DECISIONS AS CHOICES

People are constantly deciding how they will use their time and energy and property and how they will spend their money. Millions of such decisions are made every day. It is these decisions which determine the nature and extent of economic activity. They are the motive force which operates the price mechanism. The decisions taken by some people today may affect prices and thereby induce other people to act differently tomorrow, or at least as soon as they can manage to respond to the changed conditions registered by the consequent changes in prices.

We may divide economic decisions into private decisions and business decisions. There are four important kinds of private decisions:

1. A man must decide how he will divide his time between remunerative work and leisure.

2. He must decide how much of his income he will spend, upon present consumption, and how much he will save, in order to provide for the future.

3. He must decide in what form he will hold his assets: how he will distribute the total value of his assets among different kinds of assets.

4. He must decide how he will distribute his expenditure among different consumers' goods.

Clearly these decisions are all connected with one another. The size of his income will vary with the amount of work he does, and if he decides to save more, the total value of his assets will be greater, and the sums available for current expenditure will be less, than they would otherwise have been. A fifth kind of decision is sometimes important: the decision to choose one job rather than another. In so far as a worker prefers one job to another, and is prepared to forgo, up to a point, a higher wage in order to take the job he prefers, this kind of decision also should be classed as "private."

Later I shall discuss these decisions at some length. For the moment

I shall confine myself to some general remarks about them. To begin with, I have called them "private" because they all depend upon the tastes of the persons concerned. Different people have different tastes. One man is glad to work longer hours in order to get more pay, while another prefers his leisure; one man is thrifty, and another is a spend-thrift; one loves garlic, and another hates it. There is no accounting for tastes. Unless we know the tastes of a person, it is impossible to predict what he will do when constrained to make the kind of choice under discussion.

I may point out at once that all these choices relate to the appor-tionment of some fixed total among different "uses." Twenty-four hours a day, a given money income, a fixed total value of assets, a definite sum available for expenditure, has to be distributed, and the more of it is devoted to one use the less of it is available for other uses. As time goes on, the size of the total available may change (except for the twenty-four hours a day). The man may get a bigger income, or may decide to save more, or the value of his assets may rise, or conversely. He may then divide the total among different uses in different proportions, even if his tastes remain the same. But at the moment when he makes his decision, the total is fixed. If there were no such limitations, if everybody could have everything he wanted without any effort, there would be no need to make choices, involving the sacrifice of alternatives forgone, and there would be no economic problems. Economic problems arise precisely because people are compelled to choose.

The word "decision" suggests a deliberate choice made after care-fully considering, and rejecting, possible alternative courses. Many economic decisions are made in this way; most people have to watch their shillings, if not their pennies, and cannot afford to be careless. But some decisions are made impulsively, on the spur of the moment, and others would perhaps not be called "decisions" in ordinary speech, for they are the result of habits formed in the past: people may just go on doing what they have done before, until something happens to make them consciously ask themselves whether they would not prefer to do something different. Nevertheless all such acts of choosing, whether deliberate or impulsive or the result of habit, can be treated as "decisions," for we are trying to explain how the economic system works and are therefore interested in the results of these acts of choos-ing, and the results are the same however much or little deliberation took place before they were made.

I turn now to "business" decisions. These are made by the person or committee controlling the policy of a firm. I shall use the term *entrepreneur* to stand for such a person or committee. The entrepreneur must decide what his firm shall produce, how large its output shall be, what methods of production shall be used, and where its various establishments shall be located. Later I shall discuss such decisions at length. For the moment we may merely note that, provided we make the reasonable assumption that the entrepreneur wishes to get as big an income as possible for himself (supposing him to have already made his "private" decision as to how much time he will devote to his business rather than to his leisure), these decisions are not questions of taste. On the contrary, if we know the different alternatives that confront an entrepreneur, we can often predict exactly which course he will adopt, for often one course will clearly give him a bigger income for himself than any other. The main reason why we cannot always predict what he will do is that he may sometimes give considerable weight to his belief that various prices will change in one way rather than another, and we cannot say *a priori* whether he will take an optimistic or a pessimistic view.

The great problem for a community, regarded as an economic organization, is what to produce. Its members want consumers' goods, but it is quite impossible to provide everybody with as many consumers' goods, that is with as high a standard of living, as he would like. If all people were like Jains—members of an Indian sect who try to subdue and extinguish their physical desires—it might be done. If consumers' goods descended frequently and in abundance from the heavens, it might be done. As things are, it cannot be done. There are not enough consumers' goods to satisfy wants at all fully—only the fortunate few are rich enough to have practically as high a standard of living as they wish. Why are there not enough consumers' goods? All goods, except gifts of Nature, are produced. In order to produce them we need such things as land and labour and machinery. Economists call such things means of production or factors of production. Consumers' goods are scarce, relatively to the desire for them, because means of production are scarce. Man's energy is limited, and to multiply the people would also multiply the need; and there is not an unlimited amount of good land and natural resources or of plant and equipment. Hence total output is limited.

But a community must somehow decide how its available means of production shall be used. For many of them are capable of alternative uses. Much land can grow any one of several crops, or can be used for pasture for different kinds of animals, or can serve as a golf course or a park or a building site. Much labour can be used for any one of a number of different tasks, and many buildings and machines can serve any one of several purposes. It is clear that if more land is used for growing wheat, less is available for other uses, if more labour is used in making armaments, less is available for other industries, and so on. Thus a community in deciding how means of production shall be used is deciding what assortment of goods shall be produced out of the infinite number of alternative assortments that could be produced from the means of production available. That is, it is deciding which wants shall be satisfied at the expense of leaving others unsatisfied.

7. John Maynard Keynes

The late Lord Keynes was one of our great men. As a thinker, scholar, and writer, as an administrator and counsellor of the Government, as a patron of the arts, he was outstanding. He has made a deep impression on economic thought; some of his followers would claim that he has revolutionized it.

His main work is *General Theory of Employment, Interest and Money*, published in 1936. In the language now fashionable among economists, it is mainly a book on *macro-economics*, whereas Alfred Marshall's *Principles of Economics*, published in 1890 and generally accepted as the leading English work on economics, is concerned mainly with *micro-economics*. Macro-economics deals with aggregates such as total output, total expenditure on consumers' goods and on investment, the average level of prices, wages, and interest rates, and how these aggregates affect one another and act on the economic system as a whole. Micro-economics deals more with the Theory of Value and discusses the reasons for differences in prices, wage rates, and so forth. Clearly a comprehensive view must cover both macro-economics and micro-economics; it may be claimed that the former was not sufficiently considered before Keynes.

Our preceding section pointed out that if the community wants more of this, it must have less of that. But if there is heavy unemployment of labour and resources, this is not true. We can have both more guns and more butter if we can set the unemployed to work.

One of the most important lessons that economics can teach is to distinguish between situations when we can have more of something without giving up anything else and situations when we have to weigh the gain from more of X against the consequent loss from less of Y. Unfortunately, the latter type of situation is by far the more frequent.

An outstanding example of the former is the achievement of the United States during the war, when the output available to civilians was maintained at above pre-war levels despite the gigantic war effort. This was done partly by working longer hours and by bringing in women and retired workers, but it was partly due also to the absorption into employment of several million workers who were formerly unemployed.

A small-scale illustration, based on fact, may be of interest. In a certain country there was a mill producing coconut oil from copra. The price of coconut oil was fixed by the Government. The mill was paying a certain price for copra, but was getting relatively little copra. The coconut growers preferred to pound their nuts into a crude type of coconut oil, which they could do very cheaply, and to use the residue for feeding to pigs. It was too oily and made the pigs too fat and their flesh rather rancid, but the growers preferred to do this rather than to make copra at the price offered. So the mill was working far below capacity and making losses. Then the mill was induced to offer a substantially higher price for copra. The copra came pouring in, and the mill made a profit, although the price of its coconut oil remained fixed at the old level. The copra cake, a by-product of the coconut oil, was mixed with other things to provide a better diet for the pigs. So the people were better off because they had a better type, literally a more refined type, of coconut oil, and better pork; the coconut growers were better off because they got more for their copra; the mill was better off because it made a profit. And the secret was simply that there had been a lot of idle capacity in the mill which was now brought into use.

The scope for increasing output by using labour and resources at present unemployed or under-employed is usually, as I shall argue later, very limited. At present, for example, we have little unemployment or idle capacity in Great Britain. Nevertheless we should always bear this possibility in mind. I shall discuss some of Keynes's views at the appropriate places, and meanwhile we may remind ourselves of this general point by defining economics—not that a formal definition matters much—as *the study of the factors affecting employment and standards of living.* Before Keynes, I for one should have left out the word "employment."

8. The Plan of this Book

The following chapter discusses the aims of economic policy: full employment, higher standards of living, improved working conditions, and a certain measure of economic equality and social security. As we shall see, these aims are to some extent incompatible with one another, and some measures which help one of them may hinder another of them. Nevertheless, I think that most people regard each of these aims, taken by itself, as desirable, and would agree that together they cover the main objectives at which economic policy should aim. To put the point the other way round, they think of unemployment, poverty, bad working conditions, and too much inequality and insecurity, as the major economic evils.

Our task, therefore, is to explain what are the influences affecting the amount of unemployment, the levels of standards of living and working conditions, and the extent of inequality and insecurity; and how public policy can help to shape the economic world nearer to man's desire, or, at any rate, nearer to the wishes of the majority.

The most important of the basic economic platitudes is that

standards of living depend on output. You cannot share out more than there is to share. The more is produced, the more there is to share, and the less is produced, the less there is to share. Improvements in productivity, in the amount produced per man-hour, make possible either higher standards of living or better working conditions (especially shorter hours of work) or some of each; to that extent, standards of living and working conditions can be grouped together, both depending on productivity. I shall have a good deal to say, therefore, about output or production.

Part I is introductory. In addition to the present chapter and to the following chapter on the aims of economic policy, it contains two more preliminary or "background" chapters. Chapter III is about the framework of social institutions. It discusses the fundamental economic institutions of a free society, namely private property, freedom of enterprise, and freedom of choice for consumers; and it considers the part played by the Government in controlling and regulating economic activity in a free society. Chapter IV, on the national income, gives a broad general view, call it a macro-economic view if you like, of such an economy. It shows how the aggregate output is continually being shared out among individuals, and appearing as individual incomes, and how it is used, most goods being consumed and some being added to assets.

Part II discusses some very important factors affecting the amount produced per worker. These factors exert their influence however the community is organized. They are equally relevant to Russia or the United States or a South Sea island. But as our chief interest is in Great Britain, I shall draw my illustrations mainly from this country.

But in addition we must study the effects of a more or less freely-working price system upon what is produced, and by what methods, and in what places. We must see how the price system makes the whole machinery of production respond to changes in conditions, continually adjust itself to new situations. This is a part of the story which does not apply, or applies only to a very limited extent, to a country where nearly all economic life is planned and directed from the centre, or to a primitive community which makes little use of money and prices. Part IV discusses the working of the price system, its merits and its defects, and how it affects output. The way is paved for Part IV by Part III, which explains how prices are formed by the play or the forces which can be grouped under the twin heads of demand and supply.

All this discussion of output would flow more smoothly, as a piece of logical exposition, if we could consider a *closed economy*—an isolated self-sufficient country without any foreign trade. Everything which such a community consumes it must itself produce, for there is no outside source from which it can come. In the same way, everything which it produces must be either consumed by its own population or added to the assets within its borders. This is true of the world as a whole but not of any one country, and certainly not of Great Britain. A considerable part of British output is for export, and much of what we consume is imported. Our population of 50 million could not maintain anything like their present standards of living if they had to forgo the advantages of foreign trade and to restrict their consumption to what they themselves produced.

The large part which international trade plays in our economy does not in any way invalidate our general conclusions about the importance of output. Exports are needed to pay for imports, and exports must be produced. But international trade, including questions of foreign investment and of external aid given to Great Britain (for example, by the United States) or by Great Britain (for example, to her Colonies), is a subject that calls for separate discussion. Clearly we are better off than before if, output remaining the same, our export prices rise or our import prices fall. The quantitative importance of international trade varies with the proportion of a country's output that is exported. In the United States the proportion is low, and American writers do not usually discuss this subject very fully: "5 per cent of the output, 5 per cent of the space," as one American writer on economics told me. In Great Britain, international trade is more important, and I discuss it at some length in Part VII.

Part V deals with the subject of economic inequality. It discusses the distribution of the national income among individuals, with special reference to wages, interest, and profits. It also supplements our discussions of the price system. For while earnings and property incomes are clearly incomes to their recipients, wage rates and rates of interest are "prices," parts of the price system, and play a major part in the working of the economy.

Part VI is on Money and Banking. I have already stressed the vital part played by the use of money and of prices expressed in money. Part VI discusses this subject in some detail. It explains also the factors affecting the value, or purchasing power, of money. This is a question of especial importance to the millions of pensioners, "small savers," and workers on fixed salaries, who suffer when the cost of living rises and their money buys less. For them, social security means first and foremost maintaining the value of the pound sterling in terms of what it will buy.

We seem to have left unemployment rather on the side-lines instead of placing it, as the followers of Keynes would place it, in the very centre of the picture. But it is never forgotten; whenever it is relevant I refer to it; and Chapter XXIII discusses it at length.

CHAPTER II

THE AIMS OF ECONOMIC POLICY

THE most important aims of public policy, in my view, are the maintenance of liberty and of peace. We must safeguard our civilization and its ideals of personal freedom—freedom of thought, speech, and religion—from external aggression and if possible we must achieve this aim without the horrors, misery, and devastation of war. Another major aim is to maintain law and order and to see that justice is done to all. These aims lie outside the field of economics, although a question such as how to provide for expenditure on Defence or Police is an economic question.

Within the field of economics, the broad objective that most people desire is freedom from want. The aims discussed below are all part of this objective, except for the aim of better working conditions, which relates to people as producers and not as consumers.

1. FULL EMPLOYMENT

"What if I should lose my job?" That is the dominant fear, so far as their economic lives are concerned, of the great majority of employed workers. And they have reason for it. There was virtually no unemployment during the war, and since the war jobs have been easy to find, but the memory of the years between the wars is still clear and strong in the minds of the older generation. During the nineteen-twenties the number of unemployed in Great Britain averaged a million; in the Great Depression of 1930 to 1932 it rose to a peak of nearly three million; and for the rest of the decade it averaged about one and a half million.

The chance of becoming unemployed, even in the period of heavy unemployment between the wars, was only about one in ten, taking one year with another. It was considerably higher in the exporting districts, where unemployment was concentrated, but it was lower in the rest of Great Britain. But most workers are not reassured by such calculations. The danger may be small, but it is always there; if another general world depression, like that which began in the autumn of 1929, should come upon us, the danger would become much greater; and each says to himself, "It may be my turn next." If the breadwinner is out of work for any length of time, the standard of living of his family may be drastically lowered, their plans upset, their hopes destroyed. True, there is unemployment insurance and, in the last resort, national assistance. But the income from these sources is less, for the higher-paid workers much less, than what the bread-winner, or bread-winners, used to earn. Moreover, a worker likes to feel that he is playing his part in the community; to be "on the dole" for long hurts his pride and saps his morale. It is no wonder, then, that "full employment" has stepped out of the pages of the economic text-books to become one of the most powerful political slogans of our time.

A certain amount of unemployment, however, is inevitable. On any given day some workers, such as builders and fishermen, will not be working because the weather is too bad; some will be at home through sickness; some, whose work is of a seasonal or intermittent nature, will be temporarily unemployed; some will have lost or left one job but will soon find another. This last point is very important; I shall return to it shortly.

The foregoing list of reasons is not complete, but it will suffice to show that "full employment" does not mean a complete absence of unemployment. For example, in the prosperous years just before the Great Depression, the United States had, in any realistic sense, full employment—but she had at the same time nearly two million out of work. It is generally accepted that for Great Britain it would be con-sistent with full employment to have over half a million out of work. Provided that the unemployed are a changing army, no large number being out of work for a prolonged period, and provided that those who are out of work can be tided over by unemployment benefits, this more or less temporary unemployment does no serious harm. It is unem-ployment over and above this minimum which we should try to prevent, and especially the heavy unemployment due to general depressions of trade.

One of the basic platitudes of economics is that economic progress, and therefore improvements in standards of living, cannot take place unless the economic system is flexible. If everybody insists on doing exactly the same job, in the same way, in the same place, for ever and ever, there can be no progress, no improvement, but only stagnation.[1] In Great Britain, at the moment of writing, this seems to be the mood of many workers. They want to be guaranteed their present jobs; they are reluctant either to move their homes to another place or to change their present occupations. If the Government were to adopt this interpretation of "full employment," and were to try to avoid any changes, the result would be worse than stagnation. For Great Britain relies heavily on foreign trade to provide her with food and with raw materials for her industries. She pays by her exports. Con-ditions are constantly changing. Her customers want rather different

---

[1] Except for the gradual improvement which may come about by new entrants (mostly boys and girls leaving school) going where they are most needed.

things this year from what they wanted last year, and if the sales of British exports are to be maintained, their wishes must be met; her rivals adopt improved methods of production, and if Great Britain is to keep well in the picture, she must do the same. Otherwise her exports will fall off, she may not be able to pay for the raw materials she needs, and a policy of trying to maintain full employment by maintaining the *status quo* may result in the very evil that it strives to avoid —heavy unemployment, especially in the export industries.

For the home market, too, constant adaptation to changing conditions is desirable. The tastes of consumers change: why should they not have what they want now instead of what they had last year? Technical progress shows us improved methods of production; why not obtain a greater output by adopting them, even at the cost of some unemployment?

If, therefore, we want economic progress, a certain amount of unemployment is inevitable. At any given time, some workers will have lost or left their old jobs but will soon find new ones where they can be of more service to the community.

The loss of output due to unemployment that is avoidable is relatively small. Since the war, most countries have had fairly full employment—some contend, for the reasons just given, that in Great Britain there has been over-full employment, because there has been too little flexibility—and I shall therefore look at the period between the wars, including the Great Depression.

We must remember that some workers are not employees; they are working on their own account or are employers. Most countries are not very industrialized. The majority of their workers are engaged in agriculture, and the smallholding or family farm is predominant. These workers did not become unemployed during the Great Depression. The world output of agricultural products did not fall, whereas the world output of industrial products fell by 30 per cent. The farmers and peasants suffered heavy reductions in their incomes, because the prices of their products fell, in some important instances by more than half, but for the most part they kept on working. They were their own employers, and they could find no better jobs to move to; they just had to put up with cuts in their incomes of a size which organized industrial workers would not dream of accepting. Hence we must measure the loss of output not with reference to the total of employed wage-earners and salary-earners, but with reference to the total working population.

In Great Britain unemployment was heavier than in most countries between the wars. Yet if we take avoidable unemployment as anything above the low figure of half a million, the average amount of avoidable unemployment between 1920 and 1939 was only about 800,000 a year. which is 4 per cent on her working population of about twenty million. The actual loss may have been less, for on the whole the unemployed may have been somewhat less efficient than those who kept their jobs or found new ones, and the under-employment of resources such as factories and mines may have been less than the under-employment of labour. But let us call it 4 per cent.

This is a significant loss, and the suffering and anxiety to which it gives rise cannot be measured. We should certainly try to avoid it. But the loss to output is not catastrophic. Compare it with the gain from technical progress, combined with the growth of plant and equipment and other "capital." Science and invention continually give us new and better methods of production and new and better products. The consequent gain in output is more marked in industries such as manufacturing than in "service" industries such as the distributive trades. But on the average it amounts to between 2 and 3 per cent a year in Great Britain. And this gain is cumulative. The average British worker is producing well over 50 per cent more per man-hour than he was just after the first world war. This far out-weighs the 4 per cent loss due to preventible unemployment. Keynes and his followers were greatly influenced, I think, by the heavy and prolonged unemployment in the United States from the autumn of 1929, when the Great Depression began, until the outbreak of the world war. Throughout this period, unemployment in the United States averaged over ten million, seldom falling below eight million and in the worst years (1931–33) rising to more than twelve million. But such heavy and prolonged unemployment has no parallel in history. Nor, despite the gloomy forecasts of some economists, has it recurred. In such a situation, the central problem of economics—how best to distribute labour and other resources among alternative uses—apparently disappears, for it is possible, by setting unemployed labour and other resources to work, to have more of some things without giving up anything else. We are in a world of slump, expounding the economics of slump.

The present book does not follow these lines. I assume that, thanks partly to the contributions to economic thought made by Keynes and his followers, heavy and prolonged general depressions of trade can and will be avoided in the future. I therefore assume moderately full employment during most of the book; but Chapter XXIII is devoted to the problem of preventing general depressions and avoiding heavy unemployment.

Some writers, influenced by the Great Depression, used to argue that heavy unemployment was inevitable under "capitalism," that is to say, under a free-enterprise system as distinct from a completely planned economy, such as that of Soviet Russia. I repeat, there is no proof that this view is right, and the post-war facts are against it. But suppose it were true. We might still prefer the greater liberty of a free economy, even at the cost of occasional slumps.

The demand for full employment is sometimes interpreted to mean that the Government should provide jobs for all who want them. But the danger is that if the numbers applying became large—as they might do if the wages and working conditions were good—the Government would have to embark on projects with a value well below their cost. This means that it would be employing workers, in practice largely on pick-and-shovel work, who had been attracted to the Government from other occupations where their services were more valuable to the community. There is also the further point that workers often do not exert themselves as much on such "relief work" as when they are working under the supervision of a private employer, with the risk of losing their jobs if they are too inefficient. In my view, the best course is for the Government to create conditions under which most workers can find jobs in the normal way, and to include in public works programmes only those projects that are really worth while. It may well, however, have a large and flexible programme (and in this context local government and other public authorities are included) of public works really worth undertaking, and it may accelerate this programme when unemployment increases.[1]

I conclude therefore that "full employment" does not mean a complete absence of unemployment, and that economic progress will be retarded if it is interpreted to mean "no change" or "guaranteed jobs for all." Public policy should aim at creating or maintaining conditions under which a high and fairly stable level of employment can be achieved. It should aim in particular at preventing heavy and prolonged general depressions of trade.

2. HIGHER STANDARDS OF LIVING

The man in the street and his wife want a better and more varied diet, better clothes and more of them, better housing, a better education for their children, more opportunities to travel and to enjoy themselves; in general, more of the necessities, comforts, amenities, and pleasures of life. The phrase which covers all these things is *standard of living*. They want a higher standard of living.

And the general aim of economic policy is to maintain and improve the standards of living of the people. This general aim, of course, covers a large number of more specific aims, such as improving standards of nutrition (especially, perhaps, for children) and of housing, ensuring that adequate health services are available for all, providing public parks and playgrounds, and so forth. At times, standards of living must be sacrificed to some extent in order to provide better for

[1] On all this, however, see Chapter XXIII.

Defence, and people may differ as to how far this sacrifice should go; it was on this issue that Mr. Bevan and others disagreed with the official Labour Party policy in 1951. Again, people may disagree on how much weight should be given by the Government to different constituents of standards of living: for example, some think that the British Government has been spending too much on health services and other "welfare" measures, and that it would be better to reduce public expenditure on these purposes, reduce taxation, and leave people more money to spend for themselves. But all such disagreements are about the best means of achieving the general aim. There is no dispute about the general aim itself, which is to maintain and improve standards of living.

How this can best be done is what this book is about, and what every general text-book on economics, from the time of Adam Smith and earlier, has been about. Or perhaps I should say rather that economics discusses the various factors affecting standards of living: why, in the words of Edwin Cannan (*Wealth*, 1913), we are all as well off (or as ill off, if that way of putting it be preferred) as we are, and why some of us are better off than others. It is only taking one step further for a writer to express his own conclusions on the general lines which he thinks public policy should follow. But it is an important step, involving the personal judgments of the writer on what aims are desirable and how people would respond to different possible measures of intervention, or non-intervention, by the Government, and how, therefore, the economic system would work under different public policies. It is a step which some economists, from Adam Smith to Keynes, have taken boldly; but others have preferred to confine themselves to describing and analysing the economic system, leaving the reader to draw his own conclusions. At all events, the subject of factors affecting standards of living is practically the same thing as economics. As we shall be concerned with this subject, explaining how the economic system works and what are the forces which determine standards of living, throughout this book, I shall spend the rest of this section in trying to make the meaning of the phrase a little more definite.

Consumers' goods, or *consumer goods*, or *consumption goods*, is a necessary and useful piece of economic jargon. Consumers' goods consist of all the things (except free goods, such as sunshine) that directly satisfy people's needs or give them pleasure. Other goods, that satisfy wants only indirectly, such as factories, machinery, railways, lorries, and raw materials, are called *producers' goods*, or *capital goods*, or *investment goods*. It is the quantity and quality of the consumers' goods which people consume, week by week, which constitutes their standard of living.

Everything that is sold retail, except for goods which people use in their occupations to earn their living, such as the tools of a carpenter or the petrol of a taxi-driver, is a consumers' good. In addition, some consumers' goods are provided by the Government or other public authorities; some, such as education, may be provided free, while others, such as water, may be charged for.

The same good may be either a consumers' good or a producers' good; it depends on how it is used. Coal may be burned in the domestic hearth, in a factory, or in a locomotive engine; a motor-car may be used either for business or for pleasure. Textiles are consumers' goods if they are bought by the woman who makes her own clothes; they are producers' goods if they are bought by the professional tailor or dressmaker. Stocks of consumers' goods in the hands of manufacturers or traders are part of their *capital*; it is only when they are consumed—eaten or worn or used—by the *final consumer* that they enter into the standards of living.

For most purposes, the term "consumers' goods" will suffice, but for some purposes we must distinguish between *goods* and *services*, and also between *durable* and *non-durable* goods. A good is something tangible, like a loaf of bread or a pair of shoes. A service is not tangible; you cannot touch it or photograph it. A service may be rendered by a person, for example by a doctor or a teacher or a domestic servant; or by a durable good, such as a house; or by a combination of the two, such as a taxi-driver and his taxi. You can touch or photograph a surgeon and his instruments, but you are not buying the surgeon or his instruments; you are paying (or the Government is paying for you) for the service of having an operation performed on you, and that service is not tangible. A house is tangible, but it is not the house which enters into your standard of living; it is the service, rendered by the house, of providing shelter and accommodation.

The line between durable and non-durable goods is inevitably an arbitrary line. It is customary to include in durable consumers' goods houses, furniture, refrigerators, wireless and television sets, motor-cars and pleasure boats. But what, for example, of clothes? Some men wear a suit for many years; some women discard a dress after a few months. The question is one on which there is no need to ponder deeply. The practical problem of measuring standards of living, or family expenditure, on a weekly basis can be solved by taking the average weekly expenditure on items such as clothes and kitchen utensils over a long period, of at least a year.

The man in the street may not say, "I want a higher standard of living." He is more likely to say, "I want more money." But he wants more money in order to spend it on raising the standard of living of himself and his family. If he had, say, 10 per cent more money, and the prices of all the things he wanted to buy were 10 per cent higher, he would be no better off; if they were more than 10 per cent higher, he would be worse off. On the other hand, a fall in their prices would improve his standard of living just as much as a corresponding rise in his money income. Most people are well aware of this relation between their money incomes and their *cost of living*, and would agree that what they really want is an increase in their *real income*, which will give them a higher standard of living plus any extra saving which they wish to make. "Real income" means what can be bought with money income.

This leads us to my last point. The point is that in the long run standards of living depend on income, so that income is a more important concept than the more familiar concept of standard of living.

In the short run, the two may diverge. A spendthrift may raise his standard of living for the moment by borrowing in order to live above his income. But unless his income increases, his standard of living will fall when he has to repay the loan plus interest. Conversely, a man may provide for the future by saving, and the return from his investments will swell his future income and enable him to have a higher standard of living than he could have achieved without saving. But while he is saving, his standard of living is lower than it might have been, for he could have spent the money on his current consumption instead of saving it.

The same applies to a nation. A nation can spend less on current consumption in order to make loans and investments abroad, the returns from which will increase its income in future years. Conversely, a nation can sell some of its foreign investments, or borrow from abroad, and spend the proceeds on current consumption. For the time being, its standards of living will be raised, but in the future its income and standards of living will be lower.

Apart from income received from abroad, or paid abroad, in this way, the income of a country depends on its output. A country cannot borrow from itself or lend to itself (although individuals can lend to the Government, or to one another). But a country can increase or decrease its productive assets, thereby making its output greater or less than it otherwise would be. For example, it can raise its future output by devoting more of its labour and resources to increasing its assets and less to providing goods for current consumption. When it has carried out projects such as providing better control against soil erosion or floods, or better drainage and irrigation, or improving its crops by replacing them with higher-yielding varieties, it will reap bigger harvests. When it has built up better means of transport and communication, larger supplies of electricity, more factories and machinery, its output will be larger. But in order to increase its assets it must for the time being consume less than it otherwise could. Conversely, if it neglects the maintenance of such assets, the labour and resources which would have provided for repairs, renewals, and replacements can be used instead to produce more for current consumption. But as time goes on, such assets will become less and less useful, as they wear out, and consequently output will fall. When they become useless, and no replacements for them have been provided, output will fall heavily.

It is true that the final purpose of production is consumption, and that income is wanted in order to maintain and improve standards of living. But the best guide to the long-run standards of living of either a family or a nation is not its current level of consumption, which may be temporarily raised by over-spending or temporarily reduced by saving, but its real income.

3. Better Working Conditions

Most workers spend a large part of their waking lives at work. Hence the conditions under which they have to earn their living are very important to them.

These conditions include hours of work. Practically all workers, except those who are completely wrapped up in their work and have no other interests, would like more leisure. It is true that a life of complete idleness would be dull and boring. It is also true that hobbies and recreations are work for those who have to earn their living by them: gardening is work for the professional gardener, golf for the professional golfer, going to cinemas for the professional film critic. But most of us want some variety in our activities, and leisure is necessary for us to develop and cultivate all those interests which lie outside our work.

In Western countries, there has been a progressive reduction in hours of work, and an increase in paid holidays, since the early nineteenth century. At that time, many workers had to work for twelve hours a day or longer; in Britain, the Act of 1847, which established a ten-hour day for women and young persons (in textile factories only), was hailed as a great advance. Now the average working day is eight hours or less, and before long the Australian practice of a forty-hour five-day working week may become widespread.

In many occupations a worker cannot achieve his maximum output, week in and week out, if he works for very long hours. He suffers from constant fatigue and is less alert; hence he makes more mistakes, there is more spoiled work, and there are more accidents. In most instances, therefore, very long hours were a mistake, due to the ignorance of employers. They would have obtained a bigger weekly output by reducing them from, say, eighty hours a week to seventy or less. In most instances, the ten-hour day probably gave the employer a bigger output besides giving the workers more leisure.

Probably most workers would achieve the maximum weekly output, over a long period, with a working week of between sixty and

seventy hours. For some workers, in occupations demanding close
attention and accuracy or subject to considerable mental strain, the
figure may be below sixty, but it is probably well over fifty. The
question becomes of practical significance only during a period of very
special stress, such as war-time, when the overruling aim is to maximize
output. In normal times, it does not arise. The relevant question is
to what extent workers prefer more leisure to higher earnings.

For nowadays, with a working week usually between forty and
forty-eight hours, either a small increase or a small reduction in hours
of work would lead to a roughly proportionate increase or decrease in
output. When the workers in an industry feel that they are in a
position to get better terms from their employers, they can ask for
higher wages or for shorter hours or for some combination of the two.
If they get shorter hours, then they could have obtained somewhat
higher wages instead.

Apart from increases in money wages which merely keep pace with
the rise in the cost of living, the general pattern over the last hundred
years or so has been as follows. Technical progress and the growth of
capital have tended continuously to increase the hourly output per
worker. The workers, through their trade unions, have consequently
been able to obtain higher wages. The extent to which they have
taken some of this potential gain in the form of increased leisure,
rather than still higher wages, has depended mainly on their own
choice. Conversely, most workers could get higher wages, higher real
wages, tomorrow if they chose to work correspondingly longer hours.
In most industries, an individual worker must conform to the hours
decided by the majority, but the majority can express their wishes
through their trade union; and often the individual can work as much
or as little overtime as he pleases.

Much the same reasoning applies to other working conditions. No
doubt clean, healthy, cheerful surroundings tend to increase the output of the workers. Up to a point, they are therefore a good investment even from the standpoint of a completely selfish employer. But
that point has probably been passed in most British factories and other
places of work. Further improvements, such as free or subsidized
housing provided by the employer, would add to his costs without
appreciably increasing output. They are therefore an alternative to
the higher wages which the workers might have obtained instead. In
so far as there are improvements and amenities which would pay for
themselves by increasing the productivity of the workers, their introduction would be a benefit for all. But this is probably very much
the exception rather than the rule. Further improvements in working
conditions will mostly be at the expense of higher wages.

The reader will note that the question of how far profits can be
"squeezed" further for the benefit of the workers, a question which I

shall discuss later, is not relevant to the points made above. What I have tried to show is that whenever workers can get more they can take this benefit either entirely in the form of higher wages or partly in the form of increased leisure or of other improvements in their working conditions.

Other aspects of working conditions are rather outside the scope of this book, but a few comments may be made. Some kinds of work are dirty and disagreeable. As time goes on and capital increases, it may be possible to perform some of these unpleasant tasks by machinery rather than labour.

The great majority of workers have to take orders from foreman or other "bosses"; the little "bosses" may have bigger "bosses" over them, and so on. This is inevitable if the work is to be done efficiently and according to plan. It takes place in nationalized industries just as in privately-owned works, and in Soviet Russia just as in Great Britain.

It may be useful and desirable, however, to have some kind of works committee for each works of any size, where representatives of the workers and of the employers can meet one another to discuss working conditions, and especially any grievances or suggestions for improvement put forward by the workers.

It is sometimes urged that the general policy of any undertaking should be determined by the workers rather than by the shareholders or other owners of the capital of the undertaking. The argument for this course is that the workers have more at stake than the shareholders. Their livelihood, it is said, is at stake; should the undertaking have to close down, or partly close down, workers will lose their jobs whereas shareholders will lose only their money. But if the Government follows a wise economic policy, the workers will normally find other jobs, whereas nobody will compensate the shareholders for the loss of their capital. Moreover, investors are not likely to sink their capital in an undertaking whose policy is controlled by the workers. The workers expect steady or rising wages, even if the undertaking does badly, but in that event the shareholders get lower dividends or none at all. The general practice, therefore, is for the control of industry to be in the hands of the owners of the capital and not of the workers. Some progressive firms explain their policy to representatives of the workers, and discuss it with them, but the management makes the final decisions.

4. LESS ECONOMIC INEQUALITY

The two chief questions to ask about a person's economic position are: "How much has he?" and "How much does he get?" The answer to the first tells us his capital: the money value of all his possessions. The answer to the second tells us his income: how much he earns, or receives from his property, over a period of time such as a week or a year. There is considerable inequality both of capital and of income; some people have much more than others and some people get much more than others.

Some figures for Great Britain may be cited by way of illustration. Before the war, three-quarters of the adult population had less than £100 capital and the wealthiest one per cent, with over £10,000 each, between them owned over half the total of private capital. Inequality of income is much less marked, especially since the war, than inequality of capital. The top 405,000 persons, with incomes of over £2,000 a year, receive over 8 per cent of the total of all personal incomes before taxation, but income-tax and surtax reduce this percentage to less than $5\frac{1}{2}$.[1] At the bottom of the scale, the lowest wage (with relatively few exceptions) for a man is about £7 to £8 a week and for a woman about £5 a week.

To some extent, inequality of income arises from inequality of capital. But the extent is less than is often supposed. In the first place, little more than a third of all personal incomes are derived from capital. In the second place, only about a fifth of these "unearned" personal incomes go to people with over £2,000 a year before tax. The bulk of the capital is owned by the middle classes, with less than £2,000 a year.

A large proportion of privately-owned capital has been inherited. There are no statistics to show how large this proportion is, but it is probably well over half. Some people object to inheritance, at any rate of more than a very moderate sum by any one person. They think it is all right for a man to enjoy the fruits of capital which he has saved from his own earnings, but they think it is all wrong that a man should be able to live in idleness, as a "functionless property-owner," just because his parents were rich and he came into their money when they died. Others, however, think that it would be wrong to prevent a man from passing on his savings to his children, and point out that this possibility is one of the biggest incentives to people to work hard, thereby increasing the national output. Moreover, the possession of a certain amount of capital gives a person a measure of economic freedom. It will tide him over bad times; it will help him to choose the type of job he likes; it will enable him to speak his mind without the fear that this will make him lose his livelihood because his employers or his customers object to his views. Hence some people urge that one of the finest ideals for a nation is to build up a democracy of small property-owners.

The compromise we have reached in Great Britain is to tax inherited

[1] Their total income (1958) was £1,580 million before tax and £919 million after tax. See Table 22 in Blue Book, *National Income and Expenditure*, 1959.

capital ("estates" of deceased persons) progressively, that is to say, taking a higher proportion from a larger estate. The "death duties" have been increased several times during recent years and at present (1959) an estate of £50,000 pays about a third in taxation, one of £100,000 a half, one of £1,000,000, four-fifths. Furthermore, high income-tax and surtax make it far more difficult nowadays than it was in the past to build up a large fortune either for one's own enjoyment or to pass on to one's children.

I think most people feel that great inequality is an evil. It breeds bitterness and envy, dividing a country into Disraeli's "two nations" —the privileged few and the under-privileged many. All may have a vote, but in fact economic power is in the hands of a small minority of company directors, newspaper proprietors, and others whose wealth has placed them in a position to exercise influence and a substantial measure of control. All may be equal before the law, but in fact the expenses of fighting a lawsuit may place justice beyond the reach of the poor. The rich may be arrogant and snobbish; some of the poor may feel justified, by the glaring contrast in their fortunes, in robbing the rich, and the latter may try to deter them by making even a small theft a hanging offence, as it was in Great Britain until early in the last century.

This type of argument has little application to Great Britain today, but it has applied to most countries in the past, and it still applies to some. It is valid as an abstract argument against great inequality.

Another argument is that the money, the national income, would go further if it were divided less unequally. It would satisfy more urgent needs. The rich man in his castle could well afford to go without a few luxuries in order to relieve the hunger of the poor man at his gate. This is an opinion which, like most opinions, cannot be proved, but it is widely held and appeals to most people as a common-sense statement. What is often not realized, however, is that the "rich" are very few compared with the "poor," and therefore a re-distribution of wealth would not help the poor very much. For example, if we take the rich in Great Britain as people with over £1,000 a year, there are only 2,210,000 of them. Their total income is £3,887 million. Suppose we leave them £1,000 a year each, but no more. The excess is £1,677 million. They already pay £1,002 million in income-tax and surtax. The remainder (£675 million) would not go far if divided among the rest of the population; it would represent only about 5s. a week extra per head.

Lastly, a very important argument against great inequality is that it leads to an enormous waste of potential talent. So far as psychologists and others can judge, innate ability is distributed fairly evenly among the population. There are no grounds for supposing that the innate

¹ Figures from Table 22 in the Blue Book *National Income and Expenditure*, 1959.

capacity of the rich is superior to that of the poor. Yet most of the leaders of a community, in all walks of life, come from the children of the relatively rich, whose parents have been able to give them a good education or to provide the capital to set them up in business. The children of poor parents do not get the same start. They have to begin earning early, to help with the family income, so that most of them cannot go to a secondary school, let alone a university. Only a few exceptional ones can make up enough lost ground to reach the front rank in politics, or the professions, or business. Many whose native talents, if developed, would have placed them in the front rank, or near it, never overcome their initial handicap of poverty, and live and die as undistinguished citizens.

Here again this argument has not much force, although it still has some, when applied to Great Britain today. We have free education, including secondary or technical education, for all, and university scholarships with maintenance for those who show sufficient promise; large companies with "functionless" shareholders do provide opportunities for men and women of ability, but with little capital of their own, to rise to high executive positions; the budding politician can enter Parliament in various ways without an independent income.

The case against great inequality is very strong. On the other hand, I think few people would favour complete equality. They would not agree that the wastrel and the slacker should get as much as the hard and efficient worker. Some would argue that a certain degree of inequality lends colour and variety to life; others have urged that a well-to-do class, with a fair amount of leisure, is necessary for the development of art in all its forms.

Whatever we may think of complete equality as an ideal, it is hardly practicable as a realistic aim. Some correspondence between work done and remuneration received is normally essential as a stimulus to effort. If everybody got the same income whether he worked much or little or not at all, the total amount of work done would fall heavily, the national output would shrink, and equality would be attained at a low level—we should all be poor, very poor, together. I calculated above how much would be available for redistribution if all the excess over £1,000 a year of incomes above that level were taken away. But what would happen the next year? How many would continue to have incomes of above £1,000 a year knowing that every penny above that sum would be taken from them?

Soviet Russia realizes the need for incentives to effort. She pays much higher wages for special skills, and insists on piece-rates whenever possible. Hence she has large differences in individual incomes; her richest fifth takes over 40 per cent of her national income and her lowest fifth less than 8 per cent.

In "capitalist" countries, income from property is necessary in order to encourage people to make the best use of their property and to create real capital (productive assets) through investment.

The practical problem, therefore, is how far to go in reducing inequality at the cost of weakening incentives to work and invest, and thereby reducing output and consequently lowering standards of living. It is a complex question. Some ways of "soaking the rich" reduce incentives less than others, and some ways of helping the poor, such as expenditure on education and public health, tend to increase output more than others. In the last resort, however, it is a question of opinion—a value-judgment. Great Britain has already gone a long way. She taxes "the rich" very heavily. An income of £15,000 a year is reduced to between £4,000 and £6,000, and above £15,000 the taxpayer keeps only 2s. 3d. out of each extra £1. She spends over £2,500 million a year in ways which help mainly "the poor"— education, public health, retirement pensions and other national insurance benefits, public assistance, other social services, and subsidies to housing. How much further she should go, and in what ways, or whether she has already gone too far in some directions, are among the main controversial questions of today in the field of economic policy.

5. Social Security

Most families live in the shadow of economic insecurity. The family income would cease abruptly should the bread-winner die, or lose his job, or fall sick, or meet with an accident. Many parents are worried by the difficulty of providing for their children, and another baby, however welcome in other respects, would impose a severe strain on the household budget. The approach of old age raises serious economic problems for the poor: who will look after them when they are too old to work?

Some "rugged individualists" may say that people ought to make their own provision against such contingencies, by setting aside a sufficient reserve of savings. But the poorer families have little margin from which to save; they need almost all their income to buy current necessities. It is an obligation of the State, admitted by all, to see that none of its citizens starves. The Poor Law of 1832 accepted this obligation, but provided relief in a harsh spirit, in order to deter people from becoming paupers. The able-bodied poor had to live in the workhouse, and outdoor relief to the aged and infirm was kept down to the barest minimum. During the present century, the trend of public opinion has been towards a quite different outlook. Poverty is no longer regarded as a fault for which the poor are to be blamed, but as a social evil which should be abolished. It is the duty of the State to provide a minimum of economic security for all its citizens,

In Great Britain this view has prevailed, and has been put into effect by legislation. We now have what has been labelled the *Welfare State*.

The phrase commonly used for this minimum of economic security is *social security*. There is no clear-cut line, established by general usage, between social security measures and other measures which reduce inequality, such as free hospital treatment, medical advice, and medicine; free education; and subsidies on foodstuffs and on working-class houses. The general practice is perhaps to include under social security measures only schemes for providing money benefits to persons suffering economic hardship. Such schemes include insurance against unemployment and sickness; compensation to workers who have met with accidents in the course of their employment; maternity benefits; family allowances for children; pensions to old people, widows, the blind, and those injured in war; and in the last resort National Assistance.

It will be seen that logically the central idea of social security is to provide a minimum income for the family when its normal sources of income are cut off. (An additional aim is to increase the family income when its needs increase, notably by *family allowances*, paid in Great Britain at the rate of 8s. a week for each child after the first.) Numerous questions of principle arise, of which I shall discuss only four, namely, who should be entitled to benefits, should benefits be paid partly in kind, how high should they be, and who should bear the cost.

It is not practicable for a country to provide social security for all who choose to come to it. A country which did this, on a fairly generous scale, would become the magnet for the poor of all the world, and the cost would be far greater than it could bear. Social security therefore implies restrictions on immigration and possibly a minimum period of residence before an immigrant becomes entitled to anything more than national assistance. But all citizens of the country have an equal claim to social security. A small shopkeeper, or a farmer, or a widow, is just as entitled as a wage-earner to assistance from the community, as a right, when in economic distress. Before 1946 the British system had serious gaps; it was designed primarily for wage-earners. These gaps have now been filled. The National Insurance Act of 1946 provides for "a unified and comprehensive system of social insurance, which will cover practically everyone in Great Britain," whether employed, self-employed, or non-employed.

The argument for paying benefits partly in kind, and not in money, is that the money may be spent unwisely, or on purposes for which it was not intended—for example, family allowances paid in money to the parents may be spent on drink. Further, some things—for example, meals—can be supplied more cheaply on a large scale. On these and other grounds we already have free education, free hospital and medical treatment, free or subsidized meals for school children, and subsidies on working-class housing.

Until 1954 we had also subsidies on bread and certain other food-stuffs, to keep down the cost of living. In order to limit Government expenditure on these food subsidies, food rationing was continued years after it had come to an end in nearly every other country in the world; those who would gladly have paid the world market price to buy more meat or butter or other rationed foodstuffs were not allowed to do so. The amount spent on food subsidies was reduced as time went on, and most of them were abolished altogether in 1954, permitting rationing to end in July of that year. The agricultural subsidies which remain in force are subsidies to farmers rather than to consumers.

The argument for payments in money is that they leave the recipient his independence and his freedom of choice. He can spend the money on what he wants most, and there are wide differences in the needs and wants of different people. To provide goods free is to encourage wastefulness in their use; when Great Britain provided medicines, drugs, dentures, spectacles, and so forth free of charge there was a startling increase in their consumption. Subsidies give rise to a number of problems. There is the problem of determining who will benefit from the subsidy and who will not. For example, the alloca-tion of a limited number of houses at subsidized rents among a much larger number of applicants is bound to cause discontent among the majority whose applications must be refused. If everybody is allowed to share in the benefits, as under the British food subsidies, the rich benefit as much as the poor. Then there is the problem of meeting the cost of the subsidies. There is likely to be public pressure to extend the range of subsidies; if one "essential" is subsidized, why not another? If the prices of subsidized goods should increase, either the amount of money spent on subsidies must increase too, or the prices of the sub-sidized goods must be allowed to rise. Again, once a country has saddled itself with such subsidies, it is difficult to get rid of them. Their abolition would mean a rise in the cost of living, demands for higher wages, and inflation.

To what extent assistance should be given in kind rather than in money is a question of opinion. I think that in Great Britain most people approve of free education and of free hospital and medical treatment, although some consider that the well-to-do should be charged part of the cost. The improvement in the health and physique of children brought about by adequate supplies of milk has been demonstrated so clearly that the case for free or subsidized milk for children is generally admitted. There is much less agreement on free medicine, drugs, dentures, and so forth, as experience suggests that if they are completely free people may ask for much more of them than they really need. There is also a sharp division of opinion on food and housing subsidies; some consider that it would be better to give money payments—for example, increased family allowances—to those who need help, and to abolish any such subsidies, leaving people free to spend their money as they please.

The level of benefits must depend on the national output per head; a rich country can afford higher levels than a poor one. The danger of money benefits approaching the normal height of the family income is that they may lead to loafing and malingering. Some people may not try really hard to get work if they, or their families, receive nearly as much under social security measures when they are idle. The extent of this will vary, of course, between individuals and countries. The mobility of labour, so important for economic progress, may be greatly lessened; people will be reluctant to leave their districts or to change their occupations if they can get nearly as much by staying where they are and remaining unemployed. On the other hand, even the normal income of the poorest families does not properly meet their needs, and the social conscience of many people would not condone benefits much below that level. There is thus a conflict between economic progress, which depends mainly on output and on the adaptation of the labour force to changing conditions and wants, and social security.

Who should bear the cost of social security measures? In Great Britain we have adopted the "insurance" principle. The funds to pay unemployment and sickness benefits, and retirement pensions, are provided by those who run the risk of becoming unemployed, or sick, or retired. But their contributions are supplemented, in the case of employees, by contributions from their employers, and the State also makes a substantial contribution to social security measures.

The British system is perhaps the most practicable and acceptable way of raising the large sums of money which are needed. But it is open to several criticisms.

The principle of insurance is that the greater the risk the greater should be the contribution. This principle is not followed. Both contributions and benefits are at flat rates. Workers such as Government servants who are very unlikely to become unemployed have to pay just as much as workers in industries where the risk of unemployment is high. The robust have to pay as much, to cover the risk of their falling ill, as the sickly. In fact, the British system is not really insurance at all; it is a gigantic system of special taxation for special benefits.

The contributions levied on employers are at the rate of so much per worker per week. For the most part, they do not come ultimately out of the pockets of the employers. They are passed on to the public in the form of higher prices, or they are borne by the workers, who would be able to demand and obtain higher wages if their employers did not have to pay these contributions. Nevertheless they are a tax on employment, and they may actually create unemployment. When times are bad, some employers may not be able to employ as many workers as they could if each worker did not cost them this special tax in addition to his wages.

On the principle of taxing according to ability to pay, the cost of social security measures should be met by those who can best afford to pay them. Under the British system, the worker on £7 or £8 a week has to pay just as much as the worker on £20 a week or more. The few shillings a week [1] are a serious burden to the lower-paid workers. Hence there is a conflict, in Great Britain, between the aim of providing social security and the aim of reducing inequality.

6. A STABLE POUND

Many people rely, in one way or another, on receiving a fixed sum of money or a fixed money income at some time in the future. The chief example is perhaps pensions. Most workers look forward to a pension, or annuity, fixed in terms of money, when they retire. Another important example is life assurance. People pay premiums in order to leave a fixed sum of money to their dependants when they die. The social insurance benefits which we have just been discussing come under this same head. People pay contributions now in order to get fixed money benefits when they become unemployed or fall sick or retire. Other forms of saving are similar in so far as the savers aim at setting aside a fixed sum of money.

If the general level of prices rises, money does not buy as much. The contributors or savers get the full amount of money to which they are entitled, but it is worth less in purchasing power; it does not go as far as they had expected. They have been cheated by the fall in the value of money.

In France, for example, the franc, which was worth about 10d. before the 1914 war, is now worth less than a farthing. Nearly all the purchasing power of the money owned by French families before 1914 has been wiped out by the rise in French prices.[2]

In Great Britain the retail price level is now $2\frac{3}{4}$ times as high as before the last war and over four times as high as before the 1914 war.

Social security means not merely a minimum money income but a minimum real income. It means keeping the purchasing power of the pound fairly stable.

One powerful influence tending to raise prices is the pressure for higher wages. Men of goodwill all sympathize with the desire of workers to improve their conditions. But increased wages leading to

---

[1] 9s. 11d. for men (1959).
[2] A new "heavy" franc, equal to 100 old francs (and therefore 13·80 instead of 1,380 to the £) was introduced in 1960.

THE AIMS OF ECONOMIC POLICY

increased prices do not really help. It is no use to have more money
if the cost of living rises just as much. The solution is greater output
per worker. This would enable higher wages to be paid without a
corresponding increase in prices.

7. Conflicts of Aims

General lines of policy and particular measures adopted by the Government and other public authorities, and the action taken by groups
such as employers' associations or trade unions, may be favourable to
one aim but unfavourable to another. I have already given some
illustrations of this point, but it is a point which needs to be stressed.
We often have to decide which of two desirable aims shall be sacrificed
to the other, or to what extent we shall compromise: how far we can
promote one aim without affecting another too adversely.

One of the biggest clashes is between economic progress and economic security. "Security some men call the suburbs of Hell," said
Daniel de Bosola, but the general view nowadays is quite the contrary.
Most manufacturers and farmers want to be protected against foreign
competition, although cheaper imports would raise the standard of living
of the whole community. Many workers want their present jobs to be
safeguarded, although a larger national output could be obtained if
some of them moved to another district or learned a new occupation.

Yet it is clear that if everybody goes on doing just what he is doing,
in the same place and by the same methods, there can be no economic
progress. The great improvement in British standards of living which
has taken place continuously over the past hundred years and more,
has been made possible only by great changes: constant improvements
in methods, to keep abreast of the march of technical knowledge; the
rise of one new industry after another; movements of workers between
districts and occupations; the expansion of foreign trade. We cannot
stand still. Fifty million people on a small island, we must keep up-
to-date in our methods, we must make the most efficient use of our
manpower and other resources, if we are to maintain, let alone improve,
our present standards of living. We cannot survive without a large
inflow of imports, and we must adapt ourselves to changes in world
conditions and in the demands of our customers in order to sell enough
exports to pay for them.

But what about the textile workers who may lose their jobs because
the world wants less of our textiles and more of, say, our engineering
products? What about the railwaymen who might become unemployed if the roads were allowed to take traffic from the railways
merely because they can carry it more cheaply? What about the
coalminers who have worked all their lives in a particular pit and are
threatened that it may close down because it cannot cover its costs?

What about the farmer who would be badly hit, perhaps ruined, by imports of cheap food?

The argument, based on both theory and experience, that except during a general slump those thrown out of work can soon find employment elsewhere, where they will be of more value to the community, carries little weight with the men who would lose their jobs. The argument that wages must come from the national output and that a larger output will mean higher real wages is no consolation to them. There is a conflict between their immediate interests and the long-run interests of the community as a whole; there is a clash between progress and security, which must somehow be resolved.

Again, there is often a conflict between the aim of increasing output and the aim of reducing inequality. The Welfare State needs a large revenue from taxation. It is entirely in harmony with the aim of reducing inequality that taxation should be *progressive*, taking a larger proportion from those who are better off, and that the proceeds should be spent mainly for the benefit of the poor. Yet a high and progressive rate of income-tax is very likely to discourage effort. Why work harder, to earn an extra £1 a week, when the Government will take a substantial slice of it—ranging from 3s from the (single) £7 a week man to 7s. 9d. from the (married) £15 a week man? On earned incomes of over £2,100 a year, liable to surtax, the levy is greater, rising to a maximum of 17s. 9d. on each extra £1 over £15,000 a year.[1] How far the income-tax is responsible for absenteeism, and for refusals to take better-paid but more strenuous jobs or to work overtime, is a controversial question, but clearly it weights the scales in favour of leisure and against extra effort.

A high and progressive income-tax also checks private investment. It reduces the margins available for private saving; and it also reduces the net yield, especially on investments with a substantial element of risk.[2]

But standards of living depend mainly on the volume of output, and the volume of output depends on the amount of work done and on the amount of capital with which workers are assisted. Innovation and risk-taking blaze the trail of economic progress. There is clearly a danger that heavy taxation, while reducing inequality, may tend to keep down standards of living.

Another conflict may arise when social security measures provide money benefits at levels approaching the normal family income. An unemployed worker has less incentive to move to another district in

[1] The first £140 for a single man and £240 for a married man is exempt. Allowances for dependent children are: £100 for a child under 11, £125 for a child of 11 to 16, and £150 for a child over 16. There are various other allowances (dependants, part of life assurance premiums, etc.). Two-ninths of earned income (up to £4,005) is deducted as earned income relief. Thereafter, the first £60 pays 1s. 9d. in the £, the next £150 pays 4s. 3d. in the £, and the next £150 pays 6s. 3d. in the £. Thereafter the standard rate of 7s. 9d. in the £ is paid. (These are 1959 rates.)

[2] See Chapter XXIX, Section 5.

search of a job when he can draw substantial unemployment benefit by staying where he is.   The more generous the benefits, the greater is the danger that they will reduce mobility and increase unemployment.

Trade unions, wishing to raise the standards of living of their members, press for increases in wages from time to time.   If two or three large unions succeed, others will follow suit in order not to lose their relative positions in the occupational wage-scale.   There will be a "round" of wage increases.   If productivity per worker has increased, or does increase very soon, sufficiently to match the higher wages, the employers may be able to pay them without raising their prices.   But if not, their prices must be increased or there will be unemployment.

A general upward trend in prices, due to wages running ahead of productivity, undermines the security of all on fixed incomes.   It may also create a "balance-of-payments" crisis.   Higher money wages both increase the demand for imports and raise labour costs in the export industries, and it becomes difficult to export enough to pay for the imports we need, both of foodstuffs and other consumers' goods and of materials for our industries.

What can be done?   We value freedom; we cannot deprive the trade unions of their right to demand higher wages and, if need be, to strike for them.   The Government might keep prices from rising by an anti-inflationary monetary policy, but that would create unemployment.   Yet if inflation is allowed to take its course, millions of people on fixed incomes will suffer and our trade may be handicapped because people think that the exchange value of sterling will fall.

I fear that these illustrations may be set out too briefly, but I discuss most of them more fully later in the book.   The point I want to make is that different aims often conflict with one another.   We must often sacrifice, to some extent, one aim to another, or try to find some solution whereby we can promote one aim without affecting another too adversely.

CHAPTER III

THE SOCIAL FRAMEWORK

1. INTRODUCTION

THE unit of government in the modern world is the country, the territorial nation-state. How can a country organize itself to carry out the aims discussed in the preceding chapter?

Some kind of organization there must be. No doubt it is attractive to think of a group of people without any formal government, settling their problems by general discussion, sharing their possessions and possibly their children, and following the maxim of "from each according to his ability, to each according to his need." This would be communism—true communism, quite unlike the system of state ownership and state control which exists in Soviet Russia. But it would work, if it would work at all, only with a small group. A modern country is far too large to be run on these lines.

The problem is how to control the activities of millions of people, how to determine for what purposes the land and other means of production shall be used. The popular view is that the solution should lie somewhere between the two opposite poles of complete *laissez faire* and complete central planning.

There never has been, nor could there be, complete *laissez faire* in a country of any size. A country is not just a collection of individuals, each doing exactly what he likes. It is a community, with a Government which makes and enforces laws, and with social customs and social institutions which considerably restrict the freedom of the individual to do whatever he thinks fit. A small group like the Cocos Islanders (among whom crime is unknown) can live without police, but a country such as ours must have rules—laws against murder and theft, traffic regulations, and so forth—and the means to enforce them. The question is how much or how little the Government should restrict the freedom of the individual for the general good.

Central planning, on the other hand, must be fairly complete in order to be effective. Suppose, for example, that the plan calls for a certain output of coal. If workers are free to take whatever jobs they please, and too few of them are willing to work in the coal-mines, the coal required is not produced. The central planning authority must have power to "direct" labour, in this case to order workers to go to the coal-mines, or the plan will break down.

The debate on whether or not complete central planning is desirable is often confused by considerations which are really irrelevant. For example, many people who love liberty and toleration are revolted by the suppression of freedom in Soviet Russia. The citizen of Soviet Russia cannot listen to foreign broadcasts; the University professor cannot teach the scientific views which he believes to be true, unless the authorities favour them; the newspaper cannot say what it likes. But all this is not inevitably associated with central planning. It is true that any form of dictatorship tends to support itself by such devices: control of all organs of propaganda, and a big force of secret police to nip any possible revolt in the bud. Nevertheless complete central planning is quite possible without any such measures.

Our own system of social organization, in Great Britain, is still fundamentally *capitalism*. Much of this book, and especially Part IV, explains how it works. But here, in this preliminary general survey, I shall point out its chief features—private property, freedom of enterprise, and freedom of choice for consumers. We take these features so much for granted that it seems necessary to draw special attention to them. It will be useful, it will bring out their significance, if I first outline the economic organization of a central-planning community, by way of contrast. This will help us to grasp the two opposite ways of tackling economic problems: the way of making decisions at the centre, and the "capitalist" way of letting individuals, within limits, make their own.

First, however, I should mention one or two institutions which may exist under either system. One of these is the family. This plays a very important part in our social life. If parents did not take care of their children until they were old enough to earn their own livelihood, some other means of providing for children would have to be found. We have already noted that, under capitalism, the desire to provide for one's family after one dies is a powerful incentive to work and saving, and that it is an advantage (although much less of an advantage today than it was in the past) to be born of well-to-do rather than of poor parents. The family exercises a considerable influence on demand— for example, the size of the family affects the type of house or flat which people want—and children to some extent tend to enter the same occupations as their parents; but these and similar details are outside the scope of this book.

Another institution is money, about which I shall have a good deal to say later. I discuss also trade unions. These normally have more power under capitalism than under central planning, for the planners must be able to control and direct labour in order to carry out their plans, and cannot allow themselves to be thwarted by the views of trade unions. Institutions such as the joint-stock company and limited liability belong to capitalism, and are discussed below.

2. CENTRAL PLANNING

Under a system of complete central planning, one person or committee would act as economic dictator, surveying all the labour and other resources of the community and deciding how they should be used and what should be done with their products. Soviet Russia attempts to do this.

The magnitude of such a task is enormous. In order to carry it out, the dictator must make a vast multitude of decisions; and in order to carry it out at all well, he must somehow obtain and digest a very large amount of information. He must decide how each worker and each piece of land are to be employed. He must decide where each works is to be located and what methods of production it must use. He must decide what plants are to get the various materials, fuel, and items of equipment that are produced, how many houses are to be built and where, how many buses and lorries are to be run and along what routes, and a host of similar questions. Clearly no single person or committee could do all this unaided. In practice, the task of suggesting decisions on whole groups of problems would be delegated to various subordinate committees, who in turn would rely largely on the advice of local subcommittees. But it would be very difficult for the dictator (or central planning committee) to co-ordinate successfully the suggestions of the various subordinate committees. For example, each industry might demand so many workers, or so much coal, and there might not be nearly enough workers or coal to give every industry all it requested. In the last resort, therefore, the dictator could not split up his economic problems and delegate the solution of one set of problems to one body and of another set to another body. He himself would be compelled to make the final decisions. Only a superman could avoid making many mistakes; that is to say, taking many decisions which he afterwards regretted or found to be impracticable. And it is very unlikely that the political processes that led to the establishment of such a system would throw up to the top the best executive ability available, let alone supermen. Those who are best at mob oratory and political intrigue are not necessarily those best qualified to plan and control the economic life of a country.

Both the advantages and the disadvantages of such a system are often exaggerated. For example, it is usually claimed as an advantage that it abolishes profit and replaces production for profit by production for use. But if the owners of means of production are bought out by the State, and given interest-bearing Government bonds, they will get nearly the same income as before, and it will be more secure. Under private enterprise there are losses, heavy and numerous losses, as well as profits, and on balance the profit-receivers as a whole get little more, taking one year with another, than if they had invested instead in

Government bonds. Nor is the contrast between "production for profit" and "production for use" necessarily an argument for central planning. Production "for profit" means producing what buyers want, and producing it as efficiently as possible. Production "for use" means in practice producing what the dictator thinks ought to be produced. Many people may not agree; they would prefer something else. But they have no means of saying so, whereas under private enterprise they can buy what they prefer—every shilling they spend is a vote in favour of what they want. The argument that the rich have more votes than the poor can be met, and is met, by measures which reduce inequality of incomes in so far as this can be done without unduly weakening incentives to work and invest.

On the other hand, the argument that under central planning there can be no proper economic calculations, in order to determine which methods of production are most efficient, is not valid. Money can be used, accounts can be kept, the performances of different factories or other production units can be compared with one another, one method can be tried out in one factory and another method in another factory. Nor is it true that adequate incentives cannot be provided. Soviet Russia pays piece-rates, and gives high salaries and various privileges to managers and others in key posts.

It is true that the planning organization as a whole, including all those engaged in obtaining information, would absorb a considerable proportion of the personnel and other resources of the community. On the other hand, in so far as consumers had to take what they were given, there would be no need for persons to be engaged in advertising and otherwise promoting the sale of particular brands; they could be employed in assisting production more directly.

One important advantage of such a system is that it would abolish unemployment. As we shall see later, a major point made by Keynes is that under free enterprise decisions to save and decisions to invest are made by different people and may not coincide; insufficient private investment may lead to large-scale unemployment. There is no such conflict under central planning. Decisions to save and decisions to invest are one and the same decisions, made at the same time by the same person, the economic dictator. Nor will workers be unemployed because they want higher wages than private employers are prepared to pay; they will be ordered to work for whatever the dictator decides they should get. If they must move to their jobs, they will be ordered to move, whereas under private enterprise they can stay where they are and draw unemployment benefit.

A central planning system, however, is inevitably a bureaucratic system, with all its disadvantages. Government officers tend to be unwilling to take decisions to do something new, lest they should be blamed and lose their secure positions if their decisions turn out badly;

they prefer to follow their orders. Hence a central planning system is likely to be rather wooden, to lack flexibility and initiative. There are also the dangers of graft and bribery, and of undue officiousness by some of the civil servants who control the economic lives of the population.

This brief discussion of central planning is, of course, by no means exhaustive or conclusive. Whether or not capitalism is a better system is a matter of opinion. It certainly leaves far more scope for personal freedom and initiative in economic affairs. On the other hand, it may lead, unless properly controlled, to abuses and evils, such as private monopoly and large-scale unemployment. My purpose in outlining a central-planning system was to bring out, by way of contrast, the basic institutions of capitalism, which we tend to take for granted as "natural." But they would not be present, except to a very limited extent, under central planning. They are private property, freedom of enterprise, and freedom of choice by consumers.

3. PRIVATE PROPERTY

If anybody could have whatever he was powerful enough to seize, output would be very limited. A man would hesitate to sow for somebody else to reap, or to build a house which might be taken from him. Hence it is generally agreed that law and order are desirable, rather than the law of the jungle. Moreover, nobody wants to deprive a person of the exclusive right to the use of his purely personal possessions, such as his clothes or his furniture, although many think that the amount owned by any one person should be strictly limited. The real issue is whether means of production, such as land, mines, factories, ships, and railways, should be owned by the State or by private persons.

In Great Britain, the State has "nationalized" certain industries, including the railways and the coal-mines. But over most of the economic field, means of production are still privately owned. The State paid full compensation to the owners of property which it nationalized, and they were free to invest the proceeds elsewhere. Our system is still essentially one of private property.

The institution of private property means that the owner of any kind of property may use it, or may hire it to somebody else, provided he complies with the law of the State, as he pleases. Thus, if a man owns some land, he may turn it into a private park, or build upon it, or use it for growing, say, wheat, or lease it to somebody else, or leave it idle. His choice is restricted, of course, to the realm of what is possible. His land may be too small in area to make a full-size golf course, and it may not get enough sunshine to produce bananas. But within this realm he is free [1] to do whatever he pleases with the land —and to keep or exchange whatever it yields him. The land is his private property.

Under a system of private property, the simplest form of business organization is individual proprietorship, the "one-man concern," owned and controlled by a single person. This was the dominant form in the period of small-scale industry, and it is still predominant in agriculture and in retail trade; in Great Britain there are about 300,000 farmers and 500,000 shopkeepers who are individual proprietors.

We can see the advantage of individual proprietorship. The owner has a direct incentive to take care of his property and to make the best use of it, for it is he who takes all the profit from it—and bears all the losses. Moreover, many people take a positive pride and pleasure in owning their own farm or shop or factory. It certainly gives them independence; an owner is his own boss and can run his business as he pleases and take time off when he wishes.

But in some fields—for example, heavy industry, railways, ocean liners, banking, insurance—a firm must be large to be efficient. It must be so large that few individuals have enough capital to be the sole owner. Therefore such firms are companies, the assets of the company being owned jointly by a number of persons, each of whom has provided a part of the capital and gets a corresponding share of the profits. Another reason for the company form of organization is that there is no close correlation between owning capital and possessing business ability. The device of the company enables men of business talent and managerial ability, but with relatively little capital of their own, to manage businesses on behalf of shareholders who could not manage them so well.

"The magic of property," wrote Arthur Young, "turns sand into gold." He was writing of individual proprietorship in farms, towards the close of the eighteenth century in England. Under the old system, large open fields had been farmed in common by a local group. The enclosure movement resulted in individual farms enclosed by a hedge or fence or stone wall. Each farmer himself reaped all the benefit from the hard work and good farming he put into his land. He was free—at his own risk—to try out new crops and improved methods, whereas before he had been compelled to follow the traditional methods under which land was farmed in common. The result was a great improvement in productivity. More care was given to the land, more efficient work was done, more up-to-date methods were applied.

A company is managed by a Board of Directors elected by the shareholders. A Managing Director controls the day-to-day affairs

---

[1] Subject, in Great Britain, to the approval of various authorities under the legislation controlling the development of land in the interests of town and country planning.

of the company; he may have managers of departments or branches under him. The Managing Director and managers are usually paid salaries. The "magic of property" is not so potent with them as with an individual proprietor. But they may be paid partly in the form of a bonus which varies with the profits of the company. A majority of the shareholders can turn out their directors, if they are not satisfied with them, and appoint new ones. The Managing Director can dismiss a manager if he is not efficient enough. Hence there is some "profit incentive" combined with the desire to keep a well-paid job.

The company form of organization has two advantages which may be mentioned here. In the first place, most companies write "limited" after their name; they are limited liability companies. Limited liability was introduced in Great Britain by an Act of 1855. It means that a shareholder is liable for the debts of the company only up to the value of his shares in it. An individual proprietor, on the other hand, is liable for the debts of the business to the whole extent of his private fortune. The device of limited liability has given a great stimulus to investment in companies.

In the second place, the shares of a public (but not a private) company can be transferred by sale, through the Stock Exchange or otherwise. This is a great advantage to the shareholder. His capital is not permanently tied up. He can sell out his shares if he needs the money for some other purpose or if he thinks he can make a better investment elsewhere.

The company and the individual proprietorship are the two chief forms of business organization (apart from State enterprises). But there are several other forms. For example, there is the partnership. A man with an established business that needs more capital for expansion may take a suitable man, who can provide the extra capital, as his partner. A number of solicitors, or doctors, each specializing in some particular branch of his profession, may enter into partnership. But it would be tedious to discuss all the different forms of business organization in any detail. Their general purpose is to bring together ability and capital in the most suitable way.

The State restricts the rights and powers of private property-owners. The owner of property must not use it in ways harmful to his neighbours or to the community as a whole. For example, he must not deliberately burn down his house or pollute a river or produce noxious fumes; he may be forbidden to manufacture or trade in dangerous drugs, to run a public gambling place, to publish or distribute obscene books or photographs; he may be compelled to slaughter his cattle if they suffer from certain contagious diseases; he must obey laws requiring him to keep his premises in good sanitary condition and to take precautions to safeguard his workers against accident.

The modern tendency is to control more strictly the rights of property-owners. Building may be prohibited in certain areas, for example in the "green belt" around London; as part of town and country planning, factories are forbidden in some places and shops in others; land required for public purposes may be bought (whether the owner wants to sell or not) at a "fair price." Until 1953, in order to try to surmount Great Britain's economic difficulties, the use of materials such as steel was restricted to approved users for approved purposes, and a firm wishing to put up a new works may still be allowed to do so only in certain parts of the country—for example, in South Wales but not near London.

Nevertheless, the basic features of the institution of private property still survive. The owner of property can decide for himself, subject to the laws of the State, what he will do with his property. Hence the great contrast with central planning is that the taking of such decisions is decentralized. They are left to all the millions of property-owners, each using his own judgment and his own knowledge of relevant local facts, under the stimulus of the "profit motive." Under central planning, all means of production are owned by the State, and all such decisions are taken by officials and are subject to approval or otherwise by the central planning committee.

4. Freedom of Enterprise

Freedom of enterprise means that everybody is free to engage in whatever economic activity he pleases. No industry or trade or occupation is barred to him. He can choose for himself whatever line he prefers or in which he thinks he will do best. True, he may not have enough capital to set up in business, and he may lack the ability or training to follow certain occupations. But subject to these limitations, and to the laws imposed by the State in the public interest, he is perfectly free to follow his inclinations and to use his judgment and initiative at his own risk. He can decide for himself what part he will play on the economic stage.

This means that the gates are wide open for experiment and innovation. If somebody thinks that a new type of product will appeal to consumers, he is free to risk his own capital (and to try to persuade others to risk theirs) on the venture. Should he succeed, the public benefits as well as he; should he fail, the loss is his. Similarly with methods of production. Anybody is free to try out a new invention (unless it is patented—I discuss this later) or a new idea. If he can get the same output at less cost (which means by using less labour and other resources), both he and the community benefit; if he is wrong, the loss is his.[1]

---

[1] He must pay the market prices for his factors of production, and the excess of his expenses over his receipts comes out of his own pocket. Nevertheless, the community

Some people claim that consumers would gain, under central planning, by standardization of products. Instead of countless varieties, just a few standard varieties would be produced and, being produced on a large scale, they would be cheap. But under private enterprise it is open to anybody to take the risk, as Henry Ford took the risk, of embarking on large-scale production in the belief that he could sell large quantities at a lower price.

A wage-earner can choose his industry and occupation and employer. If he does not like his job, he has the right to give notice and move to another, or to remain idle. If it is clear that a group of workers can demand and obtain higher wages, they can choose for themselves (or through their trade union) whether they will take their gains entirely in higher wages or partly in shorter hours.

A man who has saved money (whether to provide for his old age or for his children, or just as a general reserve against possible bad times) can invest it exactly as he pleases. The more adventurous can choose risky securities which may yield a large return, or, on the contrary, may fall heavily in value; the cautious may choose Government bonds or keep their money in a bank or under a mattress. The owner of assets is free to sell them whenever he wishes and to do what he likes with the proceeds.

All this may seem perfectly natural and right to the reader brought up in the tradition and atmosphere of freedom of enterprise. Of course, he will say, a person should be allowed to make whatever use he pleases of his own abilities, his own property, his own money. But comprehensive central planning would be impossible under these conditions. The advocates of planning believe that if the whole economy is directed from the centre, the wealth and productivity of the country will increase more than if economic progress is left to the decisions and whims of individuals, each acting as he thinks best, instead of being fitted into a general scheme.

5. Freedom of Choice by Consumers

The third basic feature of capitalism is freedom of choice by consumers. We are free to do as much or as little saving as we please, and we can spend our money as we like. In normal times of peace, we are not rationed and we can give full scope to our tastes and preferences. We are limited only by the size of our incomes.

This is clearly incompatible with complete central planning, under which consumers can have only the goods which the central planning authority decides to produce. For example, under Russia's five-year

also may lose in so far as he diverts factors from other fields where they would have been used in ways of more advantage to the community. On the other hand, the community may gain in so far as he employs workers who would otherwise have remained unemployed.

plans most of her labour and resources have been diverted into developmental projects and heavy industries. Russia embarked upon a gigantic public-works programme designed to increase her future productivity. Consequently, her people had to go short for the time being of housing, clothing, food, and other consumers' goods; it was they who performed the saving and investment as directed by the plan. Within the field of consumers' goods, they could indeed choose freely among those which were unrationed and available, but only those kinds and varieties were available that had been produced in accordance with plans decided upon in advance.

Some people are in favour of consumers being compelled to take what is good for them, instead of being allowed to have what they please. They say that most people are ignorant or foolish, or misled by advertisements. They spend their money unwisely. For example, they get less nutritional value than they should out of their expenditure on food because they buy the wrong kinds of food; or they spend too little on food in order to buy drink or nylon stockings or to go to the cinema.

The same contention is applied to the realm of art. Left to themselves, it is said, most people tend to buy ugly things rather than beautiful ones, and show a poor taste in music, literature, and architecture. They should be made to follow the dictates of persons of good taste—for example, housing plans should be censored by an arts committee, and trashy or vulgar books and films should be forbidden.

Others reply that they would rather eat what they like than what experts say is best for them, that opinions on art change from one generation to another and in no event should be used as an instrument of dictatorship, and that they want to be free to live their own lives. Doubtless the State should help consumers to choose by forbidding advertisers to make false statements, by publishing analyses of the composition and qualities of various branded products, by prohibiting adulterated foodstuffs, by letting the public know the views of expert dieticians, and in similar ways. It should help them to choose wisely, but it should not choose for them.

I shall not discuss this issue further. It is one which arouses strong feelings—witness the fierce debates on Prohibition. My present point is that freedom of choice by consumers is one of the basic institutions of capitalism. The whole system depends on sales; the struggle for profits is a struggle to satisfy as efficiently as possible the wants of the buying public.

6. The Working of the Price Mechanism

The surprising thing about capitalism is that it literally produces the goods—and distributes them. No central plan, everybody doing more or less what he pleases, and yet every morning there is the milk, there is the paper, there are your means of transport, and the shops and restaurants and theatres are ready to supply you with whatever you want if you can pay for it. What is it that makes the wheels go round?

The dominant motive behind all the decisions of businessmen, farmers, and others is the desire to make money. This is sometimes called the profit motive, but it applies to all kinds of producers, including wage-earners. A wage-earner will choose the job which pays him best, taking into account the hours and working conditions, just as a businessman will choose whatever course pays him best.

This does not imply that everybody is selfish. A man's character shows itself in the way he lives and in what he does with his money; a keen businessman may be a great philanthropist. But, other things being equal, it is only common sense to choose the course which pays best, provided that it is honourable and within the law.

People want money in order to satisfy their wants (which may include helping others). Let us now think of them as consumers. Each has his own tastes, his own preferences, and tries to satisfy them as fully as possible from his limited means. If he would rather spend a shilling more a week on one thing and a shilling less on something else, he does so. He therefore tends to distribute his expenditure so that he would not prefer to transfer a little from one line to another. And under capitalism he is free to spend his money as he pleases, to decide for himself (perhaps acting on behalf of his family) what assortment of goods and services he prefers out of the many possible assortments that he could buy with a given sum, at the prices ruling in the market.

How can consumers make their wants known to producers? Simply by spending, by buying what they want most. If all goods were produced to order, it would be quite clear that the consumer calls the tune, determines what goods shall be produced and in what proportions, and therefore decides for what products means of production shall be used. Most goods are not produced to order ; they are ready and waiting for the purchaser. But this comes to much the same thing. All concerned are alert to anticipate the wants of the buying public; that is how they make their living. The whole system depends upon sales. If people buy less of one line, the shops order less of it next time, and less of it is produced; if they buy more of another line, the shops increase their orders, and more of it is produced. If they want something which is not there—for example, a hairdressing saloon or a restaurant in a particular district, a book on a certain subject, a particular type of clothing—it pays somebody (if the potential demand is large enough) to meet their wishes. True, many of the goods produced are not consumers' goods but intermediate products bought by other businesses, yet the same applies to them. If the public demand for canned goods increases, the manufacturers need more cans and therefore more tin-plate; the increased demand for tin-plate (and therefore for tin and steel) has its origin in the anticipated or actual demand of consumers.

If it happens that changes in the demands of the buying public are not anticipated, or met promptly (sometimes they cannot be, because some things take time to produce), what happens? The prices of the goods more in demand go up, for more people want them and so they become relatively more scarce. The prices of the goods less in demand go down, for fewer people want them, and so they become relatively more plentiful. Clearly, then, it pays to produce more of the former and less of the latter. The price mechanism registers the changing demands of consumers, and serves as a guide to producers. The purpose of economic activity is to satisfy people's wants; the dominant motive behind economic activity is the desire for gain; and the two are harmonized by the price system. It pays to produce what people want.

It pays, moreover, to produce in the most efficient way—efficient in the economic sense of keeping the costs of a given output as low as possible by good organization and by using the most suitable methods. The lower the costs of a given output, the greater the net return to the producer.

Changes may occur on the side of supply as well as on the side of demand. A large crop will bring down the price and stimulate consumption; a small crop will do the opposite. Nobody compels consumers to change the amounts they buy, but the rise or fall of prices induces some of them to do so. Again, an invention (when it comes into general use) may reduce costs of production and bring down the price of the product; less labour and resources are now needed to make the product; this good news is passed on to consumers in the form of a lower price for the product. If one producer does not lower his price, another will (in the absence of monopolistic agreements between them) because he can now increase his profit by selling more, even at the reduced price.

In the absence of monopoly—about which I shall have a good deal to say later—the price system is a marvellous mechanism for regulating economic activity. Some labour, some land, some buildings, and some materials can be used for any of several purposes. How shall they be used? The consumers decide. The means of production which can be transferred to other uses will be transferred if, and only if, consumers would prefer them to be transferred. The consumers indicate their preferences by being willing to pay more for their products in the other lines. If it is possible (assuming full employment) to produce X more of one product at the cost of producing Y less of another—by transferring means of production from the latter industry to the former—this will be done if consumers would rather have the extra X and give up the Y; that is, if they are prepared to pay more for the X than they were for the Y. In this way, the price system *is* a system. Prices reflect alternatives. The public can have £1,000 worth more of one thing by giving up £1,000 worth of something else. Do they want this? If they do, it will pay the owners of the means of production to meet their wishes. Some wage-earners will find they can earn more by moving into the former industry, or some landowners will find they can get a higher net return by growing the former product. That is the way the wheels go round. Every producer, including wage-earners, does what pays him best; and it pays him best to use the means of production under his control for whatever purposes consumers will pay most for, relative to the costs of production. Hence, out of the multitude of different assortments of goods and services that could be produced from the labour and other resources available, the tendency is to produce that assortment which the buying public prefers, which satisfies its wants most fully. And this comes about because producers adjust their behaviour to the preferences of consumers, as indicated by the way they spend their money.

7. The State

The State, that is to say central and local governments and other public authorities acting on behalf of the community as a whole, plays a large part in modern economic life. In Great Britain, the State does considerably more today than it did before the war. The coal-mines and the railways have been nationalized; so have the Bank of England, Cable and Wireless, and the electricity and gas industries. The Post Office (including the telephone system), Broadcasting, and Civil Aviation were already nationalized before the war. The State controls a comprehensive nation-wide system of social insurance. Until May, 1954, it rationed certain foodstuffs. It closely controls economic development, in particular the siting of houses and factories, foreign exchange transactions, and the quantities of imports which are permitted.

Whether we should be better off with less State control is a very controversial question which cannot be discussed adequately in a few sentences or paragraphs. At this stage, I shall merely try to set out the main general principles governing State action.

The dominant economic purpose of the community is to satisfy its wants as fully as possible from the labour and other resources available. To quite a considerable extent the economic self-interest of individuals tends to make them act in harmony with this purpose. But this harmony is not always present or complete. It is the economic function of the State to try to make it complete.

It is agreed by all that the State should maintain law and order. People must be prevented from killing or injuring one another, and from stealing or damaging the property of others. Contracts must be enforced; business would be impossible if people could refuse with impunity to provide the goods or services which they had promised to provide or to pay money which they had promised to pay. And in general, although here there is less agreement on exactly what the law should be on various points, the State should prevent people from behaving, or using their own property, in ways that are harmful to others. As the old gentleman said to the youth twirling his cane in the air: "Your freedom ends where my nose begins."

However highly they may value their liberty of action, most people are quite willing to be forced to conform to some general rule which is in the interest of all. A simple illustration is the general rule that traffic should keep on the left. Maybe some individuals would prefer to drive as they please, provided that everybody else had to keep to the left, but clearly that is not possible, and therefore they, too, are prepared to conform to the general rule.

The price system cannot do everything. However smoothly it may work, there will always be some services which cannot or should not be left to private enterprise. Private enterprise provides goods and services which are divisible into units. If a loaf of bread costs 8d. you buy two loaves for 1s. 4d. or three loaves for 2s.; the more you pay, the more you get, and if you pay nothing, you get nothing. So bakeries can be run by private enterprise for profit. But an army, for example, guards the whole area; it affords the same protection to any given citizen whether he has paid much or little or nothing towards the cost of it. The benefit which it provides is *indivisible*; it cannot be divided like bread, into units, each person buying as much or as little of it as he pleases. Hence Defence is provided by the State. It might be paid for by public subscription, but this would be unsatisfactory. Public subscription would probably provide far too little money for armed forces of a size which people thought necessary; each might give little or nothing in the hope that others would give more. The fairest method is to pay out of taxation, levied on some system generally approved as being "fair." The same applies to other services that are generally desired and that yield an indivisible benefit—for example, public health measures to prevent diseases from arising or spreading.

Again, the State provides some services which could be brought into the price system but are better provided free. For example, if cars or lorries were charged each time they used a road this would mean frequent stoppages to pay tolls; it is simpler to have "free" roads and to tax motor vehicles and petrol. When fuller use of a public park or a bridge or a museum would add very little to the costs of maintenance, it is usually better to charge nothing and to let it be used by people as much as they wish.

The State provides education, making it compulsory and free. It is generally thought desirable that children should receive a good general education, and specialized training in the professions and in technical subjects is needed to provide enough experts and technicians. But this form of investment, investment in "human capital" as against investment in physical assets, would not be carried far enough if it were left entirely to private enterprise. Children usually have no means of paying for their own education; their parents are often unable, and sometimes unwilling, to pay the whole cost; and it is not legally possible, nor would it be desirable, for speculators to invest in financing the education of boys or girls, obtaining in return a percentage of their future earnings. Hence education is, in the main, provided and paid for by the State.

Another of the State's major tasks is to prevent monopoly. Monopoly distorts the price system. Output is restricted in order to keep up prices. Hence prices do not properly reflect the alternatives available. If more of a monopolized product could be supplied to consumers at a price of 6d. a unit, and the actual price is kept at 1s., the influence of consumers on economic activity is, to that extent, thwarted. They would like a good deal more of the product at 6d., but not at 1s. Hence output and employment are lower than consumers wish in industries where monopoly prevails. The labour and resources of the community do not satisfy wants as fully as they should, for too few of them are in the monopolized industries and too many in other industries, or unemployed. The remedy is for the State to do away with monopolies and monopolistic practices, itself owning or controlling those monopolies which are inevitable.

I discuss public policy in relation to monopoly, unemployment, and other matters, in later chapters. The above paragraphs are intended only to illustrate how the State endeavours to harness self-interest to the service of the community as a whole, and to supplement the price system, as well as ensuring that it works efficiently.

CHAPTER IV

THE NATIONAL INCOME

1. INTRODUCTION

THE best way to get a general picture of the economic life of a country is to study detailed estimates of its national income. Indeed, economics, with reference to a particular country, could be defined as a study of the factors affecting the size, distribution, and stability of its national income.

The concept of national income has become more prominent during recent years. For example, countries contributed to the United Nations Relief and Rehabilitation Administration on the basis of one per cent of their national income. Every year the British Government publishes detailed estimates of the national income; and similar estimates are published, officially or privately, by most other countries.

The national income of a country could be measured in three different ways if we knew all the relevant facts and figures. These three ways can be illustrated by a simple analogy. Suppose we wanted to know the number of cakes, oranges, and bottles of lemonade supplied to a children's picnic. One way to find out would be to go to the sources of supply. If the goods were supplied by shops, we could ask each shop how much it supplied, and add up the total. Alternatively, we could measure the goods after they had been distributed, putting down the number of cakes, oranges, and bottles of lemonade distributed to every individual child (if all were distributed, and none were lost or held back), and adding up the total. Finally, we could add up the amounts consumed by each child, plus the oranges and so forth that he did not consume on the spot but "saved," taking them home in his pocket. Clearly all three methods should give the same result. If there were only three items—cakes, oranges, and bottles of lemonade —we could show the total for each item. But if there were many thousands of items, as there are in the national income of a country, we should have to add together their money values in order to get a single total. This would mean that in making comparisons with other countries, or other years, we should have to allow for differences in prices in order to get a comparison of real incomes.

The same three methods apply to a country, although of course the national income of a country is merely a statistical aggregate; it is never gathered together in one heap like the food for a picnic;

production, distribution, consumption, and investment are going on more or less continuously all the time, and we arbitrarily select a period, usually a year, and measure the amount of this continuous flow during that period. The "output" method measures it by its sources, when it is produced. The "incomes received" method measures it after it has been distributed and has appeared as incomes in the hands of the recipients. The "consumption plus investment" method measures how it is used, or disposed of, by its recipients; it is either spent by them on consumers' goods and services or it is added to the assets of the country. I shall discuss Saving and Investment later; in the present context, when we measure what has in fact taken place, we can call net additions to assets either Saving or Investment.

All three methods would measure exactly the same aggregate, namely the national income of the country for that particular year, were it not for the fact that payments are made abroad and received from abroad. For the moment, I shall leave this complication on one side.

2. Gross and Net National Product

The output method measures the value of all goods and services produced in the country during the year; the total is called the Gross National Product.

For an isolated country, the national product is identical with the national income. The value of everything produced forms part of somebody's income—whether it be the income of an individual, of a firm, of a Government, or of an institution—and all incomes come 'out of" the national product: there is no other source from which they can come. All the goods and services produced, taken together, make up the total of real incomes. And they are all either consumed within the country or added (if they are capital goods) to the real assets of the country: the national product equals consumption plus investment. Nor is the picture fundamentally altered for most countries (as we shall see in Section 5) when we take account of transactions with the rest of the world.

When we compute the national product, we must remember that four classes of items do not change hands against money. They are: (a) goods consumed by those who produce them, such as farm produce eaten on the farm or fish eaten by the fishermen and their families; (b) services rendered by houses occupied by their owners; (c) "free" Government services, such as defence, health, and education services for which no charge is made; and (d) unpaid personal services, notably those rendered by housewives.

There is not complete agreement among experts as to how these four items should be treated. It is generally agreed that (a) should be included. But some (including myself) think that they should be valued at their prices in the nearest local market (which is what the neighbours of the producers have to pay for them), while others think they should be valued at the net price which the producers could get for them if they sold them. It is generally agreed that (b) should be included, at the current rental value of such houses.

Most experts would include (c), valued at the cost to the Government of supplying these services. But some argue that the benefits of such services, for example of the preservation of law and order or of the maintenance of roads, go largely to industry and trade: that they assist in the production of the national output, and that their value is really included in the value of the output produced by private enterprise.

No doubt if there were no police or no roads provided by public authorities, some private firms would provide their own. But in that event the composition of the national income would be different. For example, private firms might have to charge more for their products in order to cover the extra costs of the police and roads that they provided.

As things are, the community as a whole pays for "free" services by taxation. Public servants are engaged in providing these services, and their salaries and wages form part of the national income as measured by the "incomes received" method. If "free" public services were excluded from the Net National Product, therefore, the two concepts would no longer coincide. I consider that the best course is to treat such "free" services as distinct and separate contributions to output, additional to the output produced by private enterprise, and to value these services at what they cost.

As to (d), unpaid personal services, the general practice is to omit them. If we included them it would be difficult to know where to draw the line: should we, for example, value the services of a man in shaving himself or in valeting himself? But we must be careful, when making comparisons between countries, to allow for any marked differences in the amount of unpaid services rendered by housewives. And a change in social habits in a country—for example, more women entering paid employment and engaging domestic servants to look after their homes and children—would lead to an apparent change in national income much greater than the real change.

Whatever decisions we come to about these four items, we should include them (valued in the same way) in "incomes received" and in "consumption" if we include them in the national product, and we should omit them from "incomes received" and from "consumption" if we omit them from the national product.

No item should be counted more than once. For example, if flour is used to make bread, the value of the flour is included in the value of the bread, and it would be double-counting to include both. There are many items of this kind. A great deal of output is bought by businesses, enters into their costs, and is embodied in their products. The goods or services produced by one firm are bought by others and used by them as materials or, in the case of services, for providing them with the heat, light, power, water, and other services which they need to produce their own output.

One way to avoid double-counting is to show only the *value added* by each business. This is done by deducting from the total value of its output the cost of all items such as materials, fuel, containers, and services that it bought from other businesses, on the ground that these items are shown already in the outputs of those other businesses.

The "value added" by a business is the net contribution made by the business to the national output. Some of it is paid in taxes to the Government, and some is set aside as a reserve against depreciation; the rest all goes in incomes either to the employees of the business or to the owners of the business (who may decide to leave some of it in the business as "undistributed profits").

The total output of the country, measured in the way described, counting nothing more than once, is known as the Gross National Product at market prices.

Part of it represents "indirect" taxes on the goods produced. These are paid to the Government, and hence are not available to be paid out as incomes to the employees or owners of the business. For some purposes, therefore, they are best deducted. The result is known as the Gross National Product at factor prices.

Again, the mere passage of time renders some assets less valuable. At the end of a year, plant and machinery are a year nearer the scrap-heap. This is *depreciation*. If the business is to continue, depreciation must be made good, from time to time, by repairs, renewals, and replacements of assets that have become, or are becoming, worn out. Hence it is usual to set aside a reserve for depreciation. Moreover, there is always the possibility of obsolescence. The present machines, or other assets, may become out of date, and it may be necessary to replace them by newer types, although they are still in good physical condition. The depreciation reserve covers obsolescence as well as physical wear and tear. Finally, some assets may disappear, being destroyed by disasters such as fire and flood. Mines will be the poorer by the minerals extracted from them. This is known as *consumption*, or *depletion*, *of capital* or as *disinvestment*.

For some purposes, depreciation and capital consumption should be deducted from the Gross National Product. The resulting figure is known as the Net National Product (measured either at market prices or, after deducting indirect taxes, at factor prices).

3. Incomes Received

The second method of measuring national income is to add together the incomes of all persons in the country, plus incomes earned by contributions to output but not distributed to individuals: the trading profits of public authorities, the undistributed profits of companies, and any income from property owned by public authorities or by institutions. This method measures the national income after it has been distributed, and appears as incomes received by individuals and others as the value of their contribution to the national product.

Again, we must be careful not to leave anything out. Items such as farm produce consumed on the farm should be included if we include them in our estimate of the national product. Nor should we count any income more than once; for example, the distributed profits of a company appear as incomes received by its shareholders and should not be counted twice.

A person's income should be taken after deducting business expenses, such as the cost of leather to a shoemaker. But only strictly business expenses, which he must incur in order to gain his income, should be deducted. It may well be claimed that a worker must have a certain amount of food to keep up his strength, that in some jobs one must be well dressed, and that some workers have to travel a considerable distance from their home to their work. For this purpose, these outlays must not be treated as business expenses. The whole of the income available to the recipient for spending on food, clothing, travel, and other items for himself or his dependants, for paying his personal taxes and social security contributions, and for saving, should be counted.

Some incomes, which are real enough to their recipients, are *transfer incomes*, and for our present purpose they should be excluded. Suppose that a doctor earns £3,000 a year, and makes his mother an allowance of £300 a year. Her £300 a year is a transfer; it is a gift from her son, and is not paid her in return for any contribution which she makes to the national product. Non-contributory old age pensions are also transfer incomes: a collective gift from the taxpayers to the aged, who make no contribution to output in return for their pensions. An important class of transfer incomes arises because in the past the British Government has raised loans to pay for wars. The interest payments on these loans are a transfer, to which no current output corresponds, from the taxpayers to the holders of these Government securities.

But suppose that the doctor, earning £3,000 a year, pays his gardener £300 a year. This should be included. The doctor produces £3,000 of medical services a year, and the gardener £300 of gardening services a year: total £3,300. We should not be led astray by the fact that money circulates. It is true that the £300 comes out of the

pocket of the doctor, and is part of his £3,000 a year. But it is paid
to the gardener in return for services rendered, just as most of our
incomes are paid away in return for goods supplied or for services
rendered. In the same way, a company may have borrowed money
(for example, by issuing debentures) on which it has to pay interest.
Such payments come out of the value of the output of the company
and should be included; they are not transfer incomes.

It is customary to measure individual incomes without deducting
income-tax or surtax. Yet we include also the incomes of civil servants (who may be paid out of receipts from income-tax). Is this
double-counting? No; for income-tax payers and civil servants alike
earn their full salaries by their contribution to the national output.

The sum total of the incomes of individuals and other bodies,
measured in this way, equals the national product; every income
comes out of the national product and is paid in return for contributions to the national product rendered by the persons themselves or by
their property.

4. Consumption and Investment

The third method of measuring national income is to measure consumption plus investment. *Consumption* is the total amount spent on
consumers' goods and services. Such items as foodstuffs consumed by
their growers, the rental values of owner-occupied houses, and free
board and lodging provided for domestic servants, should be included
if they are included in the "net national product" and "incomes
received" estimates. *Investment* is the value of net additions, including
stocks of goods in the hands of traders, to the physical assets of the
country. In everyday speech a man is said to invest when he buys
existing securities or real estate or other assets from somebody else.
But such a transaction is merely a transfer of ownership; it neither
increases nor diminishes the total assets of the country. Investment as
used here means new investment. It is the value of all additions and
improvements made to real, physical assets in the country during the
year, less any changes in the opposite direction, such as the depletion
of coal reserves. It is measured by the value of all such assets at the
end of the year, minus their value at the beginning of the year. Investment in this sense is net investment. Gross investment includes assets
used to provide repairs, renewals, and replacements to make good
the wastage of depreciation.

We are still assuming that the country is isolated from the rest of
the world. It follows that all the goods and services produced must
be either consumed in the country or added to the physical assets of
the country. In other words, consumption plus investment should
equal Net National Product.

5. Transactions with Other Countries

We must now drop our assumption that the country is isolated.

A country trades with the rest of the world. She produces goods which she does not herself consume (or invest); they are exported. And she consumes (or invests) goods which she has not herself produced; they are imported.

Foreign trade may be of vital importance to a country. Great Britain, for example, imports half her food and much of her raw materials. Without foreign trade it would be impossible for her to maintain her 50 million people at anything like their present standards of living.

A change in the volume of foreign trade may thus be very significant. So may a change in the terms of trade (discussed in Chapter XXXIV); if the export prices of a country rise (relatively to the prices she must pay for her imports), she can purchase more imports than before with a given quantity of exports.

Nevertheless the arithmetic of national income estimates is not directly affected by the exchange of exports for an equal value of imports. The value of the national product still equals the value of consumption plus investment, although some of the goods produced are exported and some of the goods consumed (or invested) are imported.

A discrepancy between national product and national income does arise, however, if a country makes interest payments to the rest of the world. Part of her output is neither consumed at home nor exchanged for imports; it goes away as "unrequited exports" to pay interest on loans borrowed abroad or to pay profits on investments made in the country by foreigners. Her national income (available for distribution) is her national product less such payments made abroad.

Conversely, a country that has lent or invested money abroad receives interest payments (and dividends, etc.) from abroad which make her national income greater than her national product.

For some purposes, account may be taken also of capital transactions with the rest of the world. For example, since the war Great Britain has received loans and other assistance from the United States. She has therefore been able to consume (or invest) a greater value than she produced.

On the other hand, Great Britain has released some of the sterling balances [1] built up in London during the war by India and other countries. These releases, like any repayments of foreign loans, involve unrequited exports to that value.

For most purposes of national income estimation, however, we can ignore such capital transactions, and define national income as

[1] See Chapter XXXVI, Section 3.

national product plus or minus net interest payments (and dividends, etc.) received from or made to the rest of the world.

6. THE NATIONAL ACCOUNTS

For some under-developed countries, the only practicable method of estimating the national income is the output method. We must estimate the national product by valuing the goods and services produced, checking our estimate if possible by estimates of incomes received and of consumption plus investment.

But for the countries where more data are available, the standard practice nowadays is to prepare an estimate of the national income in the form of national accounts. The national accounts combine and consolidate estimates of national product, incomes, and consumption plus investment, and give a comprehensive view of all transactions.

In their simplest form, the national accounts present an account for Households, another for Enterprises, and a third for Government ("the public sector"), together with an account showing Capital Formation (Investment) and one showing transactions with the rest of the world (the Balance of Payments).

The accounts are based on double-entry book-keeping. For every seller there is a buyer. Every transaction, therefore, has two sides to it, and appears as a debit in one account and as a credit in another; the accounts, therefore, must balance.

For example, the account for all Enterprises (businesses), taken together, shows on the debit side their receipts from the goods and services which they have sold to the public or the Government. (Sales from one enterprise to another cancel out and are not recorded; this is a simple method of showing only "value added"). These items reappear on the credit side of the Households Account, showing sums spent by households on purchases from enterprises, and on the credit side of the Government Account, showing purchases by the Government from enterprises.

The items on the credit side of the Enterprises Account show how businesses disposed of their receipts. For example, they paid wages and salaries to their employees and dividends to their shareholders. These items appear on the debit side of the Households Account; they are costs to the enterprises, but incomes to the recipients. Again, enterprises pay taxes to the Government, and these appear on the credit side of the Enterprises Account and on the debit side of the Government Account.

A note on the British national accounts for 1953 is given at the end of this chapter.

This system of estimating and setting out the national income ensures that all items are consistent with one another. On the other hand, if there is an error, it is repeated throughout the Accounts; and on this system it is a little awkward to deal with transactions which do not involve money payments.

7. THE SIGNIFICANCE OF NATIONAL INCOME ESTIMATES

The ostensible purpose of national income estimates is to arrive at a figure showing the total national income. But their value lies mainly in the detailed figures of the various components of national income. It is the details which throw light on the working of the economy. They show the contributions made by the various branches of industry and trade to the national product, how the national income is distributed among different categories of income—such as wages and profits—and the sources and forms of capital formation. We can imagine the streams of expenditure on consumption and investment generating incomes and employment; we can see the part played by the Government in the national economy.

It is true that the figure of national income is a basic and comprehensive figure. The national income is the source from which all wages, salaries, profits, and other incomes must come. It is the source of all expenditure to maintain and improve standards of living, to increase the physical assets of the country, and to provide revenue for the Government. If we had no estimates of national income we should be compelled to rely on less complete and less satisfactory statistics for an indication of the economic position of the country. For example, we should have to rely on such statistics as the revenue of the Government, the amount of foreign trade, the output of certain industries, the wages of certain types of workers. Such statistics, because they are less comprehensive than a national income estimate, might be misleading. For example, one government might tax more heavily, or collect its taxes more efficiently, than another; some countries have a larger proportion of foreign trade (relatively to their total output) than others; figures on particular industries or particular wages might give a false impression of the general trend.

If we had to restrict ourselves to one single figure as a measure of the economic position of a country, the most comprehensive figure would be that of national income. For most purposes of comparison, however, we should allow for differences in population and in price levels; the appropriate figure is that of "real" national income per head of population.

But we are under no compulsion to restrict ourselves to a single figure, and in order to give a more complete picture we should supplement the figure of national income by other data. The most important of these other data are: the amount of unemployment; the extent of inequality of personal incomes; assets and liabilities; the state of health, education, and research; and working conditions.

I have already discussed the first two and also working conditions. I should, perhaps, say a little about the other two.

It is true that assets and liabilities are to some extent reflected in the size of the national income. For example, a fairly developed country is likely to have a bigger output per head than an under-developed country which is only sparsely provided with roads, railways, power stations, irrigation systems, factories, and other assets. Again, a country with substantial foreign investments receives net income from abroad, whereas a country with a large foreign debt has to use part of its output to pay interest to non-residents.

Nevertheless assets and liabilities are important in themselves; they are a partial indication of how well the country is equipped to meet the future. For example, the sterling balances mentioned earlier represent a potential claim on the output of Great Britain which is significant both to the countries which own them, to whom they are assets, and to Great Britain, to whom they are a liability.

The improvement of the health and education of the people, and the development of research, are often at least as fruitful a way of providing for the future as investment in material assets. Output depends on the quality of the people, and on their knowledge, as well as on their environment. Some measure of the former factors is very relevant to an assessment of the economic position of a country.

Other facts also may be relevant; some examples are given in the next section. The general conclusion is that the figure of real national income per head is the best single index of the economic position of a country, but that it should be supplemented by other data in order to provide a more complete picture.

8. COMPARISONS OF NATIONAL INCOMES

Before comparing the national incomes of two countries, we should make sure that they are both estimated in the same way. For example, one estimate may be made at market prices and another at factor prices (by deducting indirect taxes from the market-prices estimate), or one may value foodstuffs consumed by their growers on a different basis from the other. Adjustments may be needed for a true comparison.

For most purposes, we should "divide by the population." For example, in 1958 the national income of India was perhaps £10,000 million, over half that of the United Kingdom. But India had a population of 400 million and the United Kingdom of less than 52 million; national income per head was only £25 for India as against £350 for the United Kingdom.

In order to compare real national incomes per head, allowance must be made for differences in price levels. Even when indirect taxes are deducted from prices, the level of prices in one country may be much higher than in the other. If so, it would be misleading simply to convert one currency into the other at the official rate of exchange between them. The official rate of exchange of an Indian rupee is 1s. 6d. But if a rupee buys twice as much in India as 1s. 6d. buys in the United Kingdom (in fact it does not—this is merely a hypothetical illustration), then the real national income per head of the United Kingdom is not fourteen times that of India (£350 to £25), but only seven times.

In order to compare the economic position of two countries, we must take account not only of their real incomes per head, but also of the supplementary data mentioned in the previous section and of any other relevant differences in conditions.

For example, Italy is a more pleasant country to live in than most because of her fine buildings, art treasures, beautiful scenery, and sunshine. Again, in one country most of the women may be housewives, while in another most of them go out to work. Again, one country may need to spend more than another on such purposes as defence or flood control; and in the tropics, the need for substantial houses, warm clothing, and fuel is less than in cold climates.

Specialization by areas, giving rise to external and internal trade, increases the real income of a country. But the consequent increase in its money income, which is swollen by the costs of transporting and distributing exports and imports, and of trade between town and country or between one district and another, exaggerates the extent to which its real income exceeds that of a country where there is less specialization by area and where most of the population consists of local groups which are largely self-supporting.

The same considerations apply to comparisons of national income per head for the same country between two periods of time. Allowance must be made for changes in price levels: a higher money income may merely reflect inflation. Any particular year may have been abnormal in some respects. For example, it may have been a year of boom or a year of slump. The harvest may have been especially good or especially poor. There may have been disasters such as earthquakes, floods, or civil war. The terms of trade may have been especially favourable (giving a larger real income for the same physical national product) or especially unfavourable. And account should be taken of any changes in other relevant conditions, such as assets and liabilities, working conditions, the health of the people, and the amount of unemployment.

The general conclusion is that too much weight should not be given to comparisons of national income, whether between countries or between the same country at different times. Differences in ways of living may be too great for any close comparison to be made; it is difficult, as we shall see later,[1] to make proper allowance for differences in price levels; and many other data may be relevant to a complete picture.

9. National Income and Public Policy

A number of countries rely heavily on forecasts of their national income, or rather on forecasts of what the various items would be if the Government did nothing to change them, in determining what their economic policy will be. In Great Britain, the Chancellor of the Exchequer frames his policy in the light of such forecasts, some of which are published (usually in March, just before the Budget) in an annual White Paper called *Economic Survey*.

Of course, forecasts may prove wrong. Nevertheless they are necessary. A Government which exercises a good deal of control over the economic life of the country must make up its mind in advance on the extent to which relevant conditions are likely to change, although it should be ready to alter its tactics as soon as the first danger signals indicate that its views were mistaken.

One important question with which post-war Economic Surveys have been concerned is the Balance of Payments.[2] They have said, in effect: "The national income this year looks like being so many million pounds. This means that if people are free to spend as much as they please on imports, so many million pounds will be spent on imports. But that is more than we can pay for with our exports. So we must cut down on our imports, prohibiting or restricting certain items of our imports, and we must try to increase our exports. This applies especially to our trade with the United States and other 'dollar' countries."

In general, forecasts of national income and its components assist the Government to frame its economic policy concerning such matters as employment, inflation, investment, and saving. These subjects are discussed at length later in the book, but at the risk of being unintelligible I will give a few illustrations now.

Suppose it appears that the amount of money likely to be spent will not be sufficient to provide fairly full employment. The Government may decide to borrow in order to expand public expenditure on public works or other purposes. Or it may reduce taxation, leaving people more money to spend; or it may reduce interest rates, thereby encouraging expenditure on Investment.

If, on the other hand, the amount of money likely to be spent is so

[1] Chapter XXXIII, Section 2.
[2] Discussed in Chapter XXXV, and in Part VII generally.

large that it substantially exceeds the value (at present prices) of the
expected supplies of goods, the cost of living will be likely to rise. The
Government may therefore take opposite measures to those named
above, increasing direct taxation, for example, in order to prevent
prices from rising.

Again, it may appear from the forecasts that Investment is likely to
be too small or too large, or not to take the most desirable forms.
Private investment can be stimulated by, for example, tax concessions
or low interest rates, and checked by opposite measures. The Government can control the form of private investment—for example, by
allocating scarce materials such as steel and by permitting new
factories and other buildings only if it approves. And the Government
itself carries out Investment (for example, in the nationalized industries) and can vary the amount and directions of its own Investment.

Again, it may seem likely that there will be too little private saving.
In that event, the Government may budget for a surplus (as the
British Government has done during recent years) in order to supplement private saving by savings made out of tax receipts; and it may
take various measures to encourage private savings and to keep down
private expenditure on consumers' goods: for example, it may impose
purchase taxes on luxuries and semi-luxuries.

I hope these illustrations will suffice to show that estimates and
forecasts of the national income may play a leading part in the formation of economic policy.

NOTE

The National Income of the United Kingdom, 1958

Every year, about August, the British Government publishes a Blue
Book giving estimates of the National Income and Expenditure of the
United Kingdom. The following figures are from the 1959 Blue Book.
It contains sixty tables, of which the first seven together constitute the
national accounts. Their headings are as follows—

1. National income and expenditure.
2. Personal income and expenditure.
3. Corporate income appropriation account.
4. Revenue account of Central Government, including National
   Insurance Funds.
5. Current account of local authorities.
6. Combined capital account of the United Kingdom.
7. Transactions with the rest of the world.

Each table has a left-hand (debits) and a right-hand (credits) side;
in the Blue Book the former is printed above the latter.

All the above tables give estimates for each year from 1948 to 1958, but I shall quote only the 1958 figures.

Six "sectors" of the economy are distinguished, namely (1) persons, (2) companies, (3) public corporations (such as the National Coal Board and the British Transport Commission), (4) the central government, (5) local authorities, and (6) the rest of the world, in so far as it has transactions with the United Kingdom.

The choice of these six sectors has been governed partly by convenience and by the information available. For some purposes, it would be preferable to group all enterprises together in an Enterprises Account. Table 3 does combine companies and public corporations, but the trading income of the central government is shown, for convenience, in Table 4 and that of local authorities in Table 5. It would be very desirable to separate the business accounts of self-employed persons, such as farmers, from their household accounts. But this is not possible, and therefore this group is included under persons in Table 2.

I think that the reader will find it helpful to regard all these tables as recording *flows of money*, although for some items, such as the provision for depreciation made by companies, no money may actually change hands.

For each table the totals of the two sides (receipts and payments) are equal to one another. This result is brought about in Tables 2, 3, 4, and 5 by a surplus on the right-hand (expenditure) side. This surplus is the estimated sum available to provide for depreciation and stock appreciation [1] and for saving.

Every item appearing on one side of a table appears also on the opposite side of another table. Thus the surpluses just mentioned all appear again on the left-hand side of Table 6: "Combined Capital Account." To give another example, taxes on income appear as payments by persons (1735) [2] and corporations (983) on the right-hand sides of Tables 2 and 3 and as revenue to the central government (2718) on the left-hand side of Table 4.

Table 1: "National Income and Expenditure" is a general table covering all sectors. The left-hand side shows three broad streams of expenditure at market prices: on personal consumption (14,925), on goods and services currently purchased by public authorities (3,724) and on gross domestic capital formation (3,566). These three streams of money expenditure generate the "factor incomes"—income from employment, gross trading profits of companies, and so forth—shown on the right-hand side of Table 1.

If these streams of money expenditure become larger or smaller, then so will the money incomes which they generate. As we shall see

[1] Discussed in Chapter XXIX, Section 2.
[2] Figures are in £ million and relate to 1958.

in Chapter XXIII, the stream most likely to fluctuate considerably is gross domestic capital formation, or gross investment. If private investment falls off, because prospects of profit are poor or rates of interest high, or for any other reason, then total money incomes will fall. In a country such as Great Britain, this fall will largely take the form of increased unemployment. When money incomes fall, the stream of expenditure on personal consumption tends to fall too, making incomes fall, and unemployment increase, still further. This happens unless the fall in private investment is offset by an increase in public investment or in current public expenditure.

Keynes pointed out that if people try to save more, this will reduce the stream of expenditure on personal consumption, and will reduce money incomes and create unemployment unless there is an offsetting increase in investment (or in current expenditure by public authorities). This is perfectly true. But the practical problem nowadays is to induce people to save more, in order to provide money for all the "capital formation" (investment) which we need and cannot pay for. [At present, increased saving is likely to be matched by increased investment.]

Expenditure on personal consumption and on private investment comes out of factor incomes. But it is more helpful to regard money expenditure as generating factor incomes than to regard incomes as generating expenditure. For the amount of expenditure depends on other influences as well as on the size of incomes. It is reduced, to a greater or less extent, by the amount taken by the Government in taxation; and it can be increased or reduced by expanding or contracting the volume of bank credit.

I return to Table 1. The three streams of expenditure which I have already mentioned are supplemented by expenditure, by the rest of the world, on British exports and other items (5,135) and are diminished by British expenditure on imports and other payments made abroad (4,607), giving a gross national expenditure at market prices of £22,761 million.

From this total, taxes on expenditure (3,031) are deducted and sub-sidies (400) "added back," showing a gross national expenditure (at "factor cost") or gross national product, of £20,130 million.

This is a "gross" figure of national product because depreciation has not been deducted. It is a "national income" estimate; that is to say, it relates to the incomes of residents of the United Kingdom and not only to output originating within the geographical area of the United Kingdom. For it includes property incomes received from abroad (758) less property incomes paid abroad (489).

The left-hand side of Table 1 is thus a summary of gross national income estimated by the Consumption plus (gross) Investment method. If we deduct the estimate of £1,895 million for capital consumption on all fixed assets (excluding, however, depletion of mineral resources) and ignore stock appreciation (which was slightly negative in 1958) we get a figure for net national income of £18,235 million, equivalent to rather more than £350 per head of population.

The right-hand side of Table 1 shows how the total of £20,130 million was divided into shares in the gross national product: £13,413 million to income from employment, and so forth. It is a summary of gross national income by the "Income Received" method. (Table 2 gives fuller details of personal incomes. They are reproduced in Chapter XXV, Section 2.)

Tables 2, 3, 4, and 5 relate to sectors of the economy. They show on the left-hand sides the income or revenue and on the right-hand sides the expenditure on current consumption (or in Table 3, on dividends and interest paid out) and on gross capital formation, together with some "transfer" items (such as national debt interest (783) paid by the central government, shown in Table 4.)

Table 6 is a combined capital account. The left-hand side (reproduced in Chapter XXVII, Section 4) brings together the "surpluses" available for gross capital formation, amounting (after adjustments) to £4,004 million. The right-hand side shows how these surpluses were used:

	£ million
Gross fixed capital formation at home	3,516
Value of physical increase in stocks and work in progress . .	50
Net investment abroad (including increase in gold and dollar reserves)	438
Total investment .	4,004

Table 7 summarizes transactions with the rest of the world. These transactions are discussed in Chapter XXXV, Section 3.

I reproduce the following three tables (relating to 1958) from the 1959 Blue Book, as likely to be of general interest.

GROSS NATIONAL PRODUCT BY INDUSTRY, 1958

	£ million
Agriculture, forestry and fishing	865
Mining and quarrying	705
Manufacturing	6,992
Building and contracting	1,144
Gas, electricity and water	522
Transport and communication	1,602
Distributive trades	2,446
Insurance, banking and finance (include real estate) .	612
Other services	2,002
Total production and trade	16,890
Public administration and defence	1,232
Public health and educational services . . .	724

GROSS NATIONAL PRODUCT BY INDUSTRY, 1958

	£ million
Ownership of dwellings	750
Domestic services to households	92
Service to private non-profit-making bodies	93
less Stock appreciation	− 20
Residual error	− 60
Gross domestic product at factor cost	19,861
Net income from abroad	269
Gross national product	20,130

CONSUMERS' EXPENDITURE AT MARKET PRICES

1958   £ million

1. Food
   a. Household expenditure

	£ million
Bread and cereals	559
Meat and bacon	1,129
Fish	136
Oils and fats	206
Sugar, preserves and confectionery	419
Dairy products	602
Fruit	282
Potatoes and vegetables	479
Beverages	261
Other manufactured food	114
Total household expenditure	4,187
b. Other personal expenditure	485
Total food	4,672

2. Alcoholic drink

a. Beer	567
b. Wines, spirits, cider, etc.	374
Total alcoholic drink	941

3. Tobacco

a. Cigarettes	903
b. Pipe tobacco, cigars and snuff	128
Total tobacco	1,031

4. Housing

a. Rent, rates and water charges	1,120
b. Maintenance, repairs and improvements by occupiers	254
Total housing	1,374

CONSUMERS' EXPENDITURE AT MARKET PRICES

1958   £ million

5. Fuel and light
   a. Coal 271
   b. Electricity 194
   c. Gas 138
   d. Other 74

    Total fuel and light 677

6. Clothing
   a. Footwear 241
   b. Other clothing
       i. Men's and boys' wear 373
       ii. Women's, girls' and infants' wear . . 769

    Total clothing 1,383

7. Durable goods
   a. Motor cars and motor cycles, new and second-hand 384
   b. Furniture and floor coverings . . . 428
   c. Radio, electrical and other durable goods . 335

    Total durable goods 1,147

8. Other household goods
   a. Household textiles, soft furnishings and hardware 275
   b. Matches, soap and other cleaning materials . 176

    Total other household goods . . . 451

9. Books, newspapers and magazines
   a. Books 55
   b. Newspapers 131
   c. Magazines 47

    Total books, newspapers and magazines . 233

10. Chemists' goods 224
11. Miscellaneous recreational goods . . . 161
12. Other miscellaneous goods . . . 206
13. Running costs of vehicles 342
14. Travel
    a. Railway 134
    b. Other 387

    Total travel 521

15. Communication services
    a. Postal 66
    b. Telephone and telegraph . . . 66

    Total communication services . . 132

16. Entertainments
    a. Cinema 85
    b. Other 108

    Total Entertainments 193

Consumers' Expenditure at Market Prices

1958   £ million

17.	Domestic service	92
18.	Insurance	164
19.	Other services	867
20.	Income in kind not included elsewhere . .	56
21.	*less* Expenditure by foreign tourists, etc. in the United Kingdom	−163
22.	Consumers' expenditure in the United Kingdom	14,704
23.	Consumers' expenditure abroad . . .	221
24.	Total	14,925

Gross Fixed Capital Formation by Type of Asset

1958   £ million

1.	Road goods vehicles	163
2.	Buses and coaches	18
3.	Passenger cars	120
4.	Railway rolling stock	86
5.	Ships	154
6.	Aircraft	36
7.	Plant and machinery	1,311
8.	Dwellings	581
9.	Other new buildings and works . . .	1,012
10.	Legal fees, stamp duties, etc. *less* destruction of buildings	35
11.	Total	3,516

PART II

PRODUCTION

CHAPTER V

THE VOLUME OF PRODUCTION

1. The Significance of the Volume of Production

I CANNOT stress too strongly the great importance of the volume of production, the national output of goods and services. Manna no longer falls from heaven. Everything we eat, drink, wear, enjoy, or use—everything except gifts of nature—comes into existence by being produced. The greater the volume of production, the more there is available for consumption by the community as a whole, and the higher can be the general standard of living. Conversely, it is impossible to share out more than there is to share, to get a quart out of a pint pot. The volume of production sets a maximum upper limit to standards of living. These fundamental platitudes, so obvious and yet so often ignored, are the most important lessons which economics has to teach.

It is true that there are other influences which affect standards of living and that it is possible for standards of living to improve, at any rate temporarily, without any increase in the volume of production per head. But these other influences are of much less quantitative importance, in the long run, than the latter. They may be grouped under the four headings: measures to reduce inequality, investment and disinvestment, the terms of trade, and loans and gifts from or to other countries.

Something can be done to relieve poverty, and to raise the standards of living of the masses at the expense of the relatively rich, by sharing the available goods and services more evenly: by taxing the rich for the benefit of the poor. Such measures do not directly affect the size of the total to be divided (although they may indirectly increase it by improving health and education, or indirectly reduce it by weakening incentives to work and invest), but they do divide it more equally. But, as we have seen already, social reformers have not much to hope from further redistribution of this kind in a country such as Great Britain, which already does a great deal to reduce inequality. The rich are so relatively few in numbers that further measures of redistribution would have little effect in raising the standards of living of the masses.

In the short run, current output can be supplemented from stocks of goods, and workers and materials can be diverted from the production of buildings, machinery, and other capital goods, and employed instead on increasing the output of consumers' goods. This is capital consumption, or disinvestment. But it can raise standards of living only for a short time. It is necessary to maintain working capital, such as stocks of materials and other goods, and fixed capital, such as buildings and machinery, in order to keep up the output of consumers' goods. If capital is not maintained, then after a time there will be a substantial fall in output and, therefore, in standards of living.

The output of a country can be divided into two parts: goods and services consumed at home (H), and goods and services exported (E). The latter exchange against imports (I). Hence the volume of production is $H + E$, but the volume of consumption plus investment is $H + I$. A favourable change in the terms of trade of a country, a unit of her exports exchanging for more imports than before, will give her a larger $H + I$, making possible higher standards of living, for the same volume of production. But the quantitative importance of the terms of trade to a country depends on how large a proportion of her output she exports. Great Britain exports about 20 per cent of her output, so that a given percentage improvement in her terms of trade would increase her $H + I$ by only a fifth of that percentage. The percentage improvement (or worsening) in her terms of trade is usually quite small from one year to another. The biggest movements during recent times have been an improvement of about 20 per cent in 1930–32 (when the prices of her imported foodstuffs and raw materials fell heavily during the Great Depression) and a worsening of about 20 per cent between 1949 and 1951 (when raw material prices rose with rearmament and stock-piling); these movements were exceptional Hence for Great Britain changes in the terms of trade (although they may have a dominant influence, if they are large, in the short run) are of much less importance in the long run than changes in output; they are more significant for countries like Australia and Malaya, which export a larger proportion of their output and whose principal exports (wool from Australia and rubber from Malaya) are subject to wide variations in price.

Finally, a country may borrow or receive gifts from abroad (or conversely). An external loan increases the goods and services available to her for the time being, but it must eventually be repaid, usually with interest. Gifts from other countries do not have to be repaid. But if such gifts are on a large scale, they are usually made only for a short period in order to help the recipient countries to get on their feet again; the leading example during recent times is the gifts made by the United States to Great Britain (under Marshall Aid and, later, Defence Aid) and other countries after the war.

The conclusion is that all these other influences affecting standards of living are less important in the long run, for most countries, than the volume of production per head. The really big differences in standards of living are predominantly due to the latter. For example, standards of living in Great Britain today are two to three times higher than a hundred years ago, and this is mainly because output per head is two to three times higher today than it was then. Again, the main reason why standards of living today are so much higher in Great Britain than in under-developed countries is that output per head is so much higher in Great Britain. Measures to reduce inequality are of great social importance, but they do not increase the total to be divided. We cannot escape the fact that consumption is limited by production; unless output increases, measures of redistribution cannot do much to raise general standards of living.

2. THE MEASUREMENT OF THE VOLUME OF PRODUCTION

The volume of production of a country is the same thing as the size of its national product. It can be measured either gross or net; the latter is the former less deductions for depreciation and capital consumption.

Many thousands of different goods and services are produced. The only way to add them together to form a statistical total is to add their money values, avoiding double-counting. But over a period some prices will have risen and others fallen; on the average, there may have been a significant rise (or fall) in the general level of prices. It is the quantities and qualities of the goods and services, and not their prices, which affect standards of living and the amount of real Investment. In order to make significant comparisons, either over time or between countries, we must somehow eliminate the effect of price changes. We are then said to measure "volume." The "volume" of output is not, of course, its weight in tons or its size in cubic feet. If a country were to produce a million more tons of iron ore and a hundred thousand tons less of textiles, its volume of production would fall (because textiles are worth more than ten times as much, per unit of weight, as iron ore). The volume of production is the value of production measured not at actual prices, but at constant prices.

Suppose, for example, that the year 1950 is selected as the "base" year. All the goods and services produced in subsequent years could be valued not at their current values, but at what their value would have been in 1950. Thus, if a bushel of wheat was 10s. in 1950, every bushel of wheat would always be valued at 10s., and so on. This method would give us for each year the value of the national product at constant prices, in fact at 1950 prices. We could then say by how much the volume of output had risen or fallen—we should have eliminated the effects of price changes. For some purposes—for example, in order to measure changes in the volume of output per worker over

D

a period—it is the volume of production $(H + E)$ which we want to measure. But for most purposes it is more significant to measure the volume of consumption plus investment $(H + I)$. The latter consists of the goods and services available for consumption and investment after exports have been exchanged for imports; it therefore reflects the terms of trade.

The following estimates of the latter for the United Kingdom are of interest in themselves and also show how allowances are made for changes in population and in price levels.

NATIONAL INCOME OF UNITED KINGDOM [1]

(1) Year	(2) National Income £ million	(3) Income per Head £	(4) Price Index (1900 = 100)	(5) Income per Head at 1900 prices £
1870	929	29·8	120·9	24·63
1880	1073	31·1	115·4	26·97
1890	1399	37·3	97·8	38·16
1900	1756	42·7	100·0	42·67
1910	2063	45·9	105·5	43·54
1920	5664	129·6	272·5	47·56
1930	3957	86·2	172·5	49·98
1938	4671	98·3	171·4	57·37

The figures in column (3) are obtained from those in column (2) by dividing by the population. For example, in 1870 the population of the United Kingdom (which then included Southern Ireland) was 31,174,500, and £929 million divided by 31,174,500 is £29·8.

It is not possible to measure the price of every single good or service at a constant figure, as we have not enough data. The same broad result is achieved by using a price index which measures changes in the general level of prices. Column (4) is such an index. It measures the general level of retail prices ("the cost of living"). It is based on 1900 = 100. For example, in 1870 prices were on the average 20·9 per cent higher than they were in 1900. Therefore income per head in 1870 measured at 1900 prices was £29·8 divided by 1·209 = £24·63.

It will be noted that in 1920 (a year of post-war boom) national income per head was at a peak of £129·6. In 1930 (a year of depression) it was only £86·2. But prices were 58 per cent $\left(\dfrac{272\cdot5}{172\cdot5}\right)$ higher in 1920 than they were in 1930. Real income per head

[1] A. R. Prest: "National Income of the United Kingdom," *Economic Journal*, March, 1948.

was higher (£49·98 as against £47·56) by 5 per cent in 1930 than in 1920.

It will be seen that real income per head was about two and a third $\left(\frac{57\cdot37}{24\cdot63}\right)$ times greater in 1938 than in 1870.

Such calculations, however, although arithmetically precise, can never give more than a rough indication of changes in the volume of production or in real income. What we are really trying to measure is the extent to which the output (or income) of one year satisfies wants more fully than the output of another year. It is impossible to measure this accurately. As time goes on, changes take place in the influences affecting the relative demand for different goods, such as the composition of the population by age, sex, and race, their tastes, and the distribution of income among different sections. Consequently some goods may be more in demand, and others less in demand, in one year than in another, quite apart from any change in the general level of prices. Moreover, new goods, and new types and qualities of goods, come into use. One has only to look at an old cinematograph film to see the many changes that have taken place in our clothes, furniture, and motor-cars, and other consumption habits. The more the composition of the output differs between two years, the more difficult it is to make a comparison. Hence, in practice, comparisons between years that are far apart have less significance than between years that are fairly close together. (The same applies to countries. Comparisons between countries with similar consumption habits have more significance than between countries with widely different modes of life.)

In 1958 the national income per head of the United Kingdom was about £353. How can we compare this with the corresponding figure for 1938 which (on the Blue Book's revised estimate of £4,816 million for the national income) was not £98·3 but nearly £102? There is no suitable price index number available; the price index used in the above table for 1900–38 was based on consumption habits in 1900 and was out of date and irrelevant by 1958. The general level of retail prices was about 172 per cent higher in 1958 than in 1938,[1] so that real income per head was about 20 per cent higher. But this estimate is inevitably very rough.

Nevertheless, although accurate measurement is not possible, no reasonable person can doubt that the volume of production per head in Great Britain today is much greater than it was a hundred, or even fifty, years ago, or than it is in most under-developed countries at the present time. And the difficulty of measuring it does not make it any the less important. I turn, therefore, to the question of what determines the volume of production of a country.

[1] Based on calculations by R. G. D. Allen in *The London and Cambridge Economic Service Bulletin*, now published quarterly in *The Times Review of Industry*.

3. What Determines the Volume of Production?

One possible division of the forces determining output is into those forces which are peculiar to our system of social organization, namely, modern capitalism, and those forces which operate in any community, however it may be organized. Economists discuss mainly the former, because it is the former which are especially subject to control through governmental action and public policy. They discuss the theory of value in order to explain the working of the price mechanism, and they go on to consider how the price mechanism should be controlled or supplemented, how monetary policy affects the amount of employment, how foreign trade affects output and employment, and other questions which fall within the scope of public policy.

The forces which operate in any community, whether it be Great Britain or Soviet Russia or a South Sea island or indeed any country at any period of history, are of great importance. They may be divided into three groups.

In the first place, there are influences beyond the control of man. Production may be diminished by earthquakes, floods, or dust storms; favourable weather conditions bring good harvests, and unfavourable ones bad harvests. In this group we may include wars, although they are man-made. War on the modern scale is very harmful to the output of goods and services for peace-time needs. It destroys life and property and it checks normal peace-time investments, including the proper maintenance of capital.

In the second place, output depends on the people and their environment. The more healthy, vigorous, and hard-working, the more intelligent, well-informed, and skilled are the people, the more they will produce, whatever their environment. The more fertile their land, the more abundant their mineral resources, and the more favourable in other ways are their natural surroundings and climate, the more they will produce. The more abundant and efficient are their man-made assets, such as electricity and other power supplies, buildings, machinery, and means of transport and communication, the more they will produce. All these facts are important, but the detailed study of physical and mental qualities, whether innate or acquired, and of the environment, whether natural or man-made, belongs to other sciences and not to economics.

There remain those relations between people and their environment that are valid for any community, however organized. These include specialization, diminishing returns, economies of scale, size of population, investment, and technical progress. They form the subject-matter of the present Part.

4. The Scope for Greater Output

During the thirties, "poverty in the midst of plenty" was a popular catchphrase. It was widely believed that everybody could have a comfortable living if only economic affairs were better organized.

Let us translate this claim into figures. Suppose that enough were produced to give every man, woman, and child as much as £15 a week will buy at the present time. This could hardly be called luxury. Yet it would mean that the volume of output in Great Britain, even if shared equally among the population, would have to be doubled. In the poorer countries of the world, output would have to be far more than doubled. On what possible grounds can such a fantastic claim have been believed?

First and foremost, there was the loss of potential output due to unemployment and under-employment. The loss was real enough, but its extent was grossly exaggerated. Now that the post-war years of full employment have failed to give us any spectacular increase in output, we hear little or nothing about poverty in the midst of plenty.

Next, there was a belief that a large proportion of output was deliberately destroyed. The example always quoted was the destruction of coffee in Brazil. It is true that during the years 1931 to 1934 some two million tons of coffee were destroyed in Brazil. (At first it was thrown into the sea, but it impeded navigation and poisoned the fishes, so it was finally decided to burn it; it would burn only with the aid of kerosene.) It is worth noting that the coffee was destroyed not by private monopolists, but by the State, in what it thought to be the interests of the peasant producers. A considerable amount of agricultural output was destroyed, again by order of the Government acting in the supposed interests of the farmers, during the early years of the "New Deal" in the United States. But the total proportion of world output deliberately destroyed, even during the Great Depression of the early thirties, was less than one per cent; today it is negligible. It is true that monopoly often has harmful effects, but these seldom take the form of actually destroying output. If all harmful monopolistic practices could be abolished, there would be a significant increase in output, but it would come nowhere near transforming poverty into plenty.

Another belief, which is still widely held, is that there are far too many "middlemen" standing between the producer and the consumer. It is true that the farmer often receives for his meat, vegetables, fruit, and other produce less than half the price which the final consumer has to pay. But the intermediaries, who get the rest, do render services in return. They pay for the transport; they pay for the shop assistants who serve the final consumers; they put up the capital to hold stocks; and they take the risk that some of the stocks will go bad or remain unsold. If either producers or consumers think that middlemen are taking too high a toll, they are quite free to set up their own co-operative societies in order to perform these services for themselves. Some producers' co-operative societies, and more consumers' co-operative societies, have been successful, although others have failed. But only a small proportion of total sales are made by co-operative societies. As this possibility of cutting out the middlemen does exist, and as nevertheless most of the marketing is still carried out by middlemen, it seems reasonable to conclude that they are useful and that no significant increase in output could be achieved by eliminating them.

Again, it is often pointed out that a country could produce more if fuller advantage were taken of technical progress by employing more machinery and by modernizing its plant and equipment and its means of transport, providing more electric power, and so forth. Of course any country could produce more if it had more capital, just as you and I could have larger incomes if we had more capital. The only problem is how to acquire more capital. A country can acquire more capital by its own efforts only by saving, that is to say, by accepting lower standards of living for the time being. It is not very helpful to point out that present sacrifices would bring future gains. We all know that, but we may feel that the sacrifices suggested are too heavy to bear.

It may be that some people have been impressed by the rapid expansion of certain industries, such as the motor-car industry, during recent years, and believe that what is possible for one industry is possible for all. Would that this were true! Then indeed the economic problem would disappear. But, unfortunately, output in one industry can expand (in the absence of heavy unemployment) only by drawing labour, materials, and other resources away from other industries. If we want more motor-cars or more armaments, we must go short of other things. There is no magic wand that will make everybody, from the manager downwards, much more efficient; there is no magic lubricating oil that will make wheels turn twice as fast. Some farmers and businessmen are not as good at their jobs as others, but this applies to every type of worker. Anybody who thinks he could double the present output of, say, a factory, with its existing staff of workers and its existing plant and equipment—that is to say, without drawing away resources from other firms, robbing Peter to pay Paul—should go ahead and do it. He will make a fortune—if he succeeds.

It is possible, however, to expand output very considerably for a short period and in exceptional circumstances. Such an expansion took place during the war. Housewives, students, retired persons, and others who would not normally seek employment gave their services to the war effort. Hours of work, including overtime, were substantially increased. Workers gave their utmost, devoting all their energy and zeal to the supreme task of winning the war. There was practically no unemployment. Under these exceptional conditions, with everybody working at full stretch, the gross output of Great Britain expanded, despite the large numbers in the armed forces and despite enemy bombing, by about 20 per cent.

In normal times of peace, however, the most that we can reasonably expect is a steady expansion in the volume of production per head of the order of 2 or 3 per cent a year.

CHAPTER VI

SPECIALIZATION

1. The Significance of Specialization

ADAM SMITH begins his *Inquiry into the Nature and Causes of the Wealth of Nations* with a discussion of the division of labour. He says: "The greatest improvement in the productive powers of labour, and the greater part of the skill, dexterity, and judgment with which it is anywhere directed, or applied, seem to have been the effects of the division of labour." The term "specialization" is perhaps better than "division of labour," for besides the specialization of labour into different occupations we have the specialization of capital into different kinds of machinery and other assets, and the specialization of land into different uses.

A modern community is utterly dependent on specialization. Without it, economic life as we know it today simply could not exist. If each household had to produce everything for itself—to grow its own food, make its own clothes, and provide its own amenities and amusements—we should all have to be peasants, and each family would have a very low standard of living, being restricted in its consumption to the products of its own holding and its own hands.

We have only to count up the enormous number of different workers, areas, and types of plant and equipment that have contributed to the goods and services consumed every day by an average family to realize how completely we depend on other people, on specialization, to satisfy our wants.

Specialization implies exchange. The products of one factory or of one agricultural or mining district may be sold to consumers throughout the country, perhaps throughout the world. It is the exception nowadays for one person to make a complete article. He plays his part in the productive system by tending a machine or driving a lorry or writing figures in a ledger or serving in a shop. In return, he gets money, with which he can draw on the products of the world. He has exchanged his services, through the medium of money, against the things which he buys.

In the modern economic world, therefore, no man can be "an Iland intire of itselfe." He must be "a piece of the continent, a part of the maine." He depends for his livelihood on the community in which he lives and indeed, since most countries are dependent to some extent on foreign trade, on the great society of the whole world. The food which he eats and the clothes which he wears have been produced and brought to him with the assistance of thousands of workers whom he has never seen.

The advantages and disadvantages of specialization, therefore, are those of modern economic life as compared with self-supporting households in a primitive economy. It makes possible the communication of knowledge and ideas through media such as schools, books, films, and broadcasts. It opens up to all the world of art and music. Without specialization, travel would be possible only if each person provided his own means of transport. People living where certain products— for example, tropical fruits—could not be grown would never be able to enjoy them. Large-scale production would be ruled out, for no single person would find it worth while, even if he knew how, to construct the necessary plant and equipment. The specialist who now makes a good living by doing one thing well, but who can do nothing else, would be lost. For example, a saxophone player may enjoy his vocation if he can obtain the necessities and comforts of life by playing it for a few hours a day, but if he could provide himself with nothing but moans from his saxophone he would perish miserably.

On the other hand, too much specialization is deplored by those who dislike the noise, bustle, dirt, and squalor of towns, who consider that the inventions of the internal combustion engine and of radio were disasters, and who prefer the simple life. Again, a specialized occupation, such as screwing a nut in a factory, may be monotonous. (But if the worker is well paid, he can do whatever he wishes in his leisure.) And a big disadvantage of specialization is that the demand for a man's particular services or products is beyond his control; he may become unemployed or may have his income reduced (by a fall in the price of his products) through no fault of his own.

On balance, however, I think that most people are glad to accept the benefits of specialization, despite its drawbacks. And there are still plenty of lonely islands and other primitive places in the world available for those who dislike modern economic life.

I shall discuss separately the specialization of labour, of capital, and of land. But all three are closely interlinked. Most occupations today are derived from the specialization of machinery and equipment, which could not be worked unless there were different types of specialized workers to operate it. And in so far as products are sold some distance afield, there is specialization by areas.

We should not, however, attribute all the increase in productivity which has taken place during recent generations to the development of specialization. Part of it has been due to the continuous increase of technical knowledge, although this itself has been greatly facilitated by specialization in different fields of research. Part of it, again, has been due to the growth of capital (Investment) although this too has been facilitated by the increased output made possible by specialization. In many cases, to create new occupations by splitting up production into more processes requires more capital, in such forms as specialized machines and equipment. Thus specialization and technical progress and the growth of capital combine together to increase output.

2. SPECIALIZATION OF LABOUR

Adam Smith gave an illustration, which has become famous, of the advantages of division of labour. It relates to the trade of pin-making, as it was organized in the latter part of the eighteenth century. He wrote:

"A workman not educated to this business (which the division of labour has rendered a distinct trade), nor acquainted with the use of the machinery employed in it (to the invention of which the same division of labour has probably given occasion), could scarce, perhaps, with his utmost industry, make one pin in a day, and certainly could not make twenty. But in the way in which this business is now carried on, not only the whole work is a peculiar trade, but it is divided into a number of branches, of which the greater part are likewise peculiar trades. One man draws out the wire, another straights it, a third cuts it, a fourth points it, a fifth grinds it at the top for receiving the head; to make the head requires two or three distinct operations; to put it on is a peculiar business, to whiten the pins is another; it is even a trade by itself to put them into the paper; and the important business of making a pin is, in this manner, divided into about eighteen distinct operations, which, in some manufactories, are all performed by distinct hands, though in others the same man will sometimes perform two or three of them. I have seen a small factory of this kind where ten men only were employed, and where some of them consequently performed two or three distinct operations. But though they were very poor, and there-fore but indifferently accommodated with the necessary machinery, they could, when they exerted themselves, make among them about twelve pounds of pins in a day. There are in a pound upwards of four thousand pins of a middling size. Those ten persons, therefore, could make among them upwards of forty-eight thousand pins in a day. Each person, therefore, making a tenth part of forty-eight thousand pins, might be considered as making four thousand eight hundred pins in a day. But if they had all wrought separately and independently, and without any of them having been educated to this peculiar business, they certainly could not each of them have made twenty, perhaps not one pin in a day; that is, certainly not the two hundred and fortieth, perhaps not the four thousand eight hundredth part of what they are at present capable of performing, in consequence of a proper division and combination of their different operations."

Under specialization one man alone may "make" a commodity, such as a pair of shoes or a chair, exchanging units of this commodity for other goods that he wants. Even so, he would probably not produce his own raw materials or tools. In a modern community it is the exception for one person alone to make a commodity.

In a factory, on a railway or ship, or in any other productive unit the workers are usually divided into groups, each performing a different task, as in the above illustration of pin-making. Scores or hundreds of different "occupations" may be found inside the same works. And nearly all goods require the co-operation of a number of different industries to transform the raw materials into the finished product. For example, the transformation of raw cotton into handkerchiefs (in the hands, or pockets, of the consumers) requires the co-operation of the "industries" of cotton-growing, cotton-ginning, cotton-spinning, cotton-weaving, bleaching and finishing, and of the relevant branches of wholesaling and retailing, to say nothing of transportation, building, the manufacture of textile machinery, warehousing, advertising, and so on. This implies that the labour involved is specialized into many different occupations, each performing one or more specialized tasks.

The special aptitudes of different persons for different tasks may be either innate or acquired. Specialization enables differences in natural aptitudes to be utilized. It also enables persons to acquire an aptitude for a particular task by learning it and practising it.

Many people could perform any of several different jobs, could work at any of several occupations. Specialization does not mean that everybody does the work which he can do best. That would be a very foolish arrangement. For example, a doctor may be only an average doctor but a superb typist. Yet he spends his time, quite rightly, as a doctor and not as a typist. Indeed, he may actually employ a typist who cannot type as well as he can. Doctors are scarcer than typists, and the community needs his services as a doctor more than as a typist. He is more use to society as a doctor; therefore, under capitalism, he can earn more as a doctor, and under central planning he would be ordered (if the dictator knew the facts) to serve as a doctor and not as a typist.

In the same way, many relatively well-paid workers may be very good, better than at their present jobs, at such tasks as gardening or carpentering or cooking. They may do some work at these tasks as a hobby in their spare time. But society needs them more where they are, and therefore they can earn more where they are.

The relative need for different types of workers may change from time to time. For example, a man may be normally efficient both as a house-painter and as a lorry-driver. At one time house-painters may be scarcer than lorry-drivers and at such a time this man would be directed, under central planning, to serve as a house-painter; under capitalism he would be able to earn more as a house-painter, and unless he preferred driving a lorry so much that he was willing to forgo his potential higher earnings as a house-painter, he would move into the latter occupation. When lorry-drivers were more needed, the opposite situation would prevail.

The objective, either under central planning or under capitalism, is not to give people the jobs they can do best, but to employ them at the tasks in which they will be most useful to the community.

3. Specialization of Capital

The specialization of capital, "fixed" capital rather than stocks of goods, is displayed in the vast number of different types of man-made assets, each designed for its particular purpose, which we see around us. They range from the great dams which provide irrigation for millions of acres to gadgets such as corkscrews.

Most of them are themselves the fruit of specialization. Men have specialized on inventing and improving them. Skilled workers of many types, especially in the iron and steel, engineering, building, and other constructional industries, are employed in producing them to the correct specifications. And the specialized assets have created many thousands of new occupations—to give only a few examples, all the many occupations connected with railways, ships, aeroplanes, radio, and the film industry.

The development of means of transport and communication has greatly widened the area over which exchange, and therefore speciali-zation, can take place. Nowadays many commodities have a world market. This development has been assisted by discoveries and improvements in refrigeration, canning, and other means of preserving foodstuffs.

Power-driven machinery enables us to perform many feats which would otherwise be quite beyond our powers, and to carry out other operations with a speed and precision not possible by hand. Often the use of machinery means splitting up a task—for example, making a pair of shoes—into a large number of different processes, each process being performed or supervised (for the machinery provides the energy) by a worker who does only that particular job. Thus a large number of "occupations" are often found in association with machinery. As a rule, they do not take long to learn, but here as elsewhere "practice makes perfect." One of the advantages of specialization mentioned by Adam Smith is that no time is lost in changing over from one job to another and "warming up" to the new task. This is certainly true of a man performing one of the scores of operations on a conveyer-belt or tending a machine which works almost automatically; he does the same thing, over and over again, all the time.

Another advantage of specialization mentioned by Adam Smith is that it economizes tools. Only the specialist—for example, the carpenter—need keep a set of special tools; others can call in the specialist when they need him, instead of everybody having to keep a set of tools to do such jobs for himself. Far more important is the fact that specialization makes possible large-scale production, employing plant and equipment which are more efficient but worth while only if the volume of sales is large enough to keep them used near to full capacity. For example, a large shoe factory with elaborate machinery can produce many more shoes than could be produced by the same amount of labour and capital divided among scores of tiny workshops. But if its sales were restricted to a small area, the machinery would be left idle for most of the time, and the people of that small area could have satisfied their wants more fully by putting less capital into simpler shoe machinery and using the rest of their capital for other purposes. Large-scale production is an aspect of specialization; it is possible only because each little district does not try to produce everything for itself.

4. THE LOCATION OF INDUSTRY

Districts, as well as persons, specialize; there is "territorial division of labour." The question of why certain districts specialize in certain products and not in others is the same as the question of why certain products are made in certain districts rather than in others. It is the question of why industries, in a wide sense of the term, are located where they are.

In some cases, the answer is easy and obvious. Mining has to be carried on where the minerals happen to be. Tropical countries are far more suitable than temperate regions for producing tropical products. Fur-covered animals must be hunted (or bred) in a cold climate. Lumbering must be carried on where the forests are, fishing where the fish can be caught; ocean shipping must be based on suitable harbours.

Let us consider agricultural land. In some districts a rotation of crops is desirable to preserve the fertility of the soil, and in others there are advantages in "mixed farming"—it keeps the farmer more fully employed, enabling him to get a bigger income; the manure of his animals can fertilize his crops; and so forth. Apart from these complications, the objective is not to use the land to grow what it will grow best, but to use it in the way in which it will best satisfy the wants of the community. For example, certain land might be capable of producing either record crops of tapioca or rather below average crops of, say, Manila hemp. If Manila hemp is much scarcer than tapioca, and does not require a great deal more labour or fertilizer, that land can best serve the community by growing Manila hemp, and not the tapioca for which it is "best suited." Under a price system, Manila hemp would pay better than tapioca, and would therefore be grown.

Another parallel between land and labour is that the qualities of land may be natural or acquired. Some land is naturally suitable, owing to climate and soil, for certain crops. Other land can be made suitable—for example, by irrigation or fertilizers. Most specialized land today is a blend of natural and acquired advantages.

Some countries specialize on export crops such as cotton, tobacco, sugar, rubber, tea, cocoa, and citrus fruits. They are often urged to "diversify" their agriculture, in order to become more self-supporting in foodstuffs. In some cases this may be good advice. But as a rule land under export crops produces a considerably greater net value than if it were under foodstuffs for local consumption, and the real income of the country is substantially higher than it would be if the land were used to produce a smaller amount of foodstuffs than can be obtained by exporting its present crops and importing foodstuffs in exchange.

The location of manufacturing industries may be influenced by many factors, but often the dominant influence is transport costs. An industry which uses considerably more than a ton of materials to make a ton of output will tend to be located near its materials, provided that its products are fairly easy to transport. A leading example is the iron and steel industry. In order to produce a ton of pig-iron, about two tons of iron ore are needed if the ore has an iron content of 50 per cent, about three tons if it has an iron content of 33 per cent, and so on, in addition to slightly over a ton of coal (in the form of coke). Hence blast furnaces are located on the coal or iron-ore deposits. If the materials are not found close together, the industry tends to be located near the material of which it uses most. In the early days of the modern iron and steel industry, when several tons of coal were needed to produce a ton of pig-iron and the iron-ore had an iron content of 50 per cent or more, transport costs were saved by having the blast furnaces on the coalfields. Today, owing to constant technical improvements, little more than a ton of coal is needed to produce a ton of pig-iron. But in Great Britain and Western Europe the richer iron-ore deposits have been largely exhausted, and most of the iron-ore has an iron content of 33 per cent or less. Hence it pays to have the blast furnaces near the iron-mines, and to transport only a ton of coal to the ore, instead of three tons or more of ore to the coal. This is not the whole story, but it does largely explain why British blast furnaces are concentrated today more in the Midlands, near the ore, whereas they used to be mainly near the coal.

Another example is saw-mills and pulp-mills, which tend to be near the timber, or at a place to which the logs can easily be floated down. Furniture, however, is bulky and therefore expensive to transport;

furniture may therefore be made nearer the towns—that is to say, nearer the market.

Sea transport is much cheaper than land transport. Export industries, especially those using imported materials, tend to be located in or near ports. If a port has certain advantages—for example, if it is near a large market or near certain materials—it may prove a good site for even a "heavy" industry, materials being imported cheaply by sea.

The manufacture of products such as bricks or mineral waters, which are about as heavy as the materials used, is widely distributed; such industries tend to be located near the various towns that are their chief markets. The same applies to products such as bread and ice which must be sold fairly quickly. It may be that a commodity, bricks for example, can be produced more cheaply in A than in B, but if this advantage is outweighed by the cost of transporting it from A to B, it may be produced in B as well as in A.

Some industries, however, consist of a few large plants, each with a big output. Where such a plant happens to be may have been partly a matter of chance; for example, Henry Ford chose Detroit for his motor-car plant because it was his home town. But clearly there cannot be such a plant in or near every town.

Again, there are sometimes advantages in *integration*—that is to say in carrying out a series of processes in the same works. A leading example is the iron and steel industry. There is a saving of fuel if the metal can be passed from one stage to another while it is still hot. Hence the manufacture of steel tends to be carried on where the blast furnaces are.

Yet again, there are sometimes advantages in the *localization* or *concentration* of an industry in one area. The classical example of this is the Lancashire cotton industry. There is a constant supply of skilled labour available; subsidiary industries are close at hand, so that machinery can readily be replaced or repaired; the banks understand cotton and the financing of its importation and manufacture; the transport system is constructed to serve a localized industry; and so on.

A hundred years, or even fifty years, ago a large proportion of manufacturing was carried on, not only in Great Britain but also in other countries, near coal deposits. But the pull of coal has diminished with the wide distribution of electric power and with constant improvements in the efficiency of boilers and other coal-using apparatus. Nowadays many industries, at any rate "light" industries, could be carried on almost anywhere, and their actual location depends on such factors as where suitable labour happened to be available when they were established, or on Government policy, about which more later. One general factor is that a place which is pleasant to live in tends to be preferred to one that is not. If rich deposits of coal and iron were found near the North Pole, they probably would not attract manufacturing industries. The minerals would be shipped to more temperate regions (as in fact iron-ore is shipped from the north of Sweden). The Greater London area exerts a big pull on light industries. London is itself a big market; it is a port; and it is a place where many workers, not to mention Directors and their wives, prefer to live.

Once an industry is established in an area, it tends to stay there, unless something better comes along. For example, the "five towns" in Staffordshire specialize in pottery, but their clay comes largely from Cornwall. In the eighteenth century there was suitable clay in Staffordshire; the industry expanded greatly; Staffordshire clay-beds became quite inadequate to supply its needs, but the skilled workers were now in Staffordshire, and so the industry continued there, importing its clay from Cornwall and elsewhere.

Services obviously tend to be supplied where the consumers are; retail shops, laundries, restaurants, cinemas, and so forth tend to be distributed (apart from the concentration of shops, restaurants, theatres, medical and other specialists, and so forth, in the central parts of the cities) in the same way as the population.

The general principle that labour and other resources should be employed in the ways most useful to the community applies to specialization by districts. If the transport of materials can be reduced by locating an industry near its materials, the resources that would otherwise be needed to transport them can be employed to produce other goods or services. If a district could specialize in any of a number of industries, but is not large enough to specialize in them all, it should specialize in those for which it is relatively best suited—relatively to the needs of the community and to the production possibilities of other districts. If conditions change, the location of industry should adapt itself to the changed conditions, as the British iron and steel industry has been moving to the Midlands and as engineering is expanding relatively to cotton textiles (for which the overseas demand is falling) in Lancashire. These are among the problems which the dictator or central planning committee would have to solve under central planning, and which under capitalism are solved, more or less successfully, through the price system.

5. The Extent of the Market

Adam Smith laid down a very important principle. Division of labour, he said, is limited by the extent of the market. Although this principle has been implied throughout the foregoing discussion, it should be explicitly explained and elaborated.

The size of the market for the products of a particular factory or farm or other productive unit is not measured by the geographical area over which its products are sold, nor even by the population of that area. It is measured by its potential volume of sales. London is a much bigger market than the Sahara Desert. China, despite her "seven hundred million customers" [1] is not a big market for goods such as motor-cars, which only a few of her people can afford. Anything which increases the total real income, or purchasing power, of a country tends to increase its importance as a market.

Historically, markets have expanded largely owing to improvement in transport, which have enlarged the geographical area over which a productive unit can profitably sell its output. The coming of the railways opened up whole continents, and the steamship cheapened ocean travel. After about 1870, foodstuffs and materials from all over the world began to pour into Western Europe in exchange for her manufactured goods. But other influences, such as the growth of populations, rising real incomes, reductions in import duties, and inventions such as refrigeration, also played their part in widening the extent of the market for many products.

Specialization is worth while only if the market—that is to say, the potential demand—for the services of the specialized factors of production is big enough to keep them fairly fully employed. A doctor whose practice was confined to a small village could not specialize exclusively on one branch of his art; he would have to be a general practitioner. Indeed he might have to supplement his earnings as a doctor by doing some other kind of work. The same applies to other specialists, such as tailors or plumbers. Nor is a village a big enough market to support shops specializing exclusively in goods such as jewellery, for which sales would be small and infrequent. A small village often cannot support an hotel, a restaurant, or a cinema. All these are services which must be supplied on the spot. What happens, of course, is that the villagers go to the specialists—for example, in the nearest town—if they need their services, and the specialists are employed sufficiently fully because their market covers the whole area from which customers come to them.

Methods of production which involve the use of specialized fixed capital, and of the vast range of occupations which go with it, would not be worth while unless the market, and therefore the output, were large enough to keep the specialized assets used somewhere near to full capacity. The costs of producing goods and services—that is to say, the resources required to produce a unit of output—are often very much less when such methods are used. But it would clearly be folly to produce pins, or anything else, by such methods if the potential sales were so small that the elaborate plant and machinery would remain idle nearly all the time. A modern tin dredge can mine tin at a fraction of the cost of more primitive methods, but it costs hundreds of thousands of pounds; it is worth while only if the demand for tin is large enough

[1] Estimate for end of 1959, based on her last Census.

to justify the initial expense of the dredge. Suppose the dredge can produce about 1,000 tons a year if used to capacity. The cost per ton is low when it is producing 1,000 tons, but the cost per ton (including the costs of the dredge itself) is very high if it produces only a few score of tons because that is all the market can absorb. Again, the cheapest method of carrying cargo by sea may be to employ ships of a fair size— say, a thousand tons or more. It is the cheapest method, that is to say, provided that there is enough cargo available for such a ship to be fairly fully loaded on each voyage. But if only a few tons per voyage are available, it will clearly be absurd to use a ship of such a size.

It is the potential rather than the actual size of the market which matters. Large-scale methods of production may enable prices to be reduced so much that the demand expands sufficiently to make them worth while. There have been many examples of this, from the mass production of motor-cars to the mass production of "Penguin" books.

A hypothetical example will serve to illustrate the gain from specialization and exchange. Suppose there are two islands, A and B. A is especially suited for producing, say, bananas, and B for producing, say, potatoes. To begin with, suppose that each island is isolated and self-supporting. A could produce annually either 2,000 tons of bananas or 400 tons of potatoes; in fact, she produces 1,000 tons of bananas and 200 tons of potatoes. B could produce annually either 2,000 tons of potatoes or 400 tons of bananas; in fact, she produces 1,000 tons of potatoes and 200 tons of bananas. A would like more potatoes, but they are so difficult to grow in her climate and soil that she produces, and consumes, only 200 tons a year; the same is true of B and bananas. Now suppose that A and B open up trade with one another. A can specialize entirely on bananas, producing 2,000 tons a year, and B can specialize entirely on potatoes, producing 2,000 tons a year. A can then exchange, say, 1,000 tons a year of bananas for 1,000 tons of potatoes from B. A gets 800 tons a year more of potatoes, and B gets 800 tons a year more of bananas—an increase of two-thirds in their real incomes—from the same means of production, merely by specialization and exchange.

This is not the whole story. The gain is not quite as large as that. For men and other resources have to be employed in transporting bananas from A to B, and potatoes from B to A; these resources were not needed for that purpose when the two islands were self-supporting. But if the resources needed for transport are small relatively to those employed in producing the exports—in terms of money, if costs of transport are only a small proportion of the value of the goods transported—the gain is still very large. The more costs of transport can be cheapened, the greater will it be.

This example may seem unrealistic merely because specialization is so widespread and trade does take place between districts and countries. If this were not so, each self-supporting island or district would have to use its resources to produce what its own inhabitants wanted for their own needs. Persia could not specialize on oil or Egypt on cotton or Zanzibar on cloves; their local markets for these commodities are far too small. The possibility of trade, of producing for a world market instead of a local market, enables real incomes to be greatly increased merely by specialization. The process was seen in reverse when the clock was turned back, during the last war, for countries such as the Philippines which were occupied by the Japanese. Confined to what they could produce for themselves, deprived of export markets, the standards of living of these countries fell to very low levels. They learned, "the hard way" as our American friends say, that specialization is limited by the extent of the market.

CHAPTER VII

FACTORS OF PRODUCTION

1. THE ECONOMIC PROBLEM

OF course there are plenty of economic problems, thousands of them, but they all come under the umbrella of the comprehensive generalization that *the* economic problem for any community is to make the best use of its labour and other resources. In economic jargon, the labour and other resources are called *means of production* or *factors of production*.

It is obvious that the volume of output is limited by the amount of factors of production, for it is they which produce the output. In order to produce more milk we need more cows, more grazing land and cattle feed, more milkmaids or milkmen or milking machines, and so forth. In order to produce more houses we need more men and more equipment in the building industry and in the industries producing building materials. The more factors of production we have, the more we can produce.

Under full employment, however, we can increase the factors in one industry only by drawing them away from other industries. We can have more of one thing only by having less of other things. If more land is devoted to pasture, less is available for other purposes such as growing crops. If more workers go into the building trades, there will be that many workers fewer for other industries. If more steel is used in making armaments, there will be less for other purposes.

So the problem for any community is how to use its factors of production, how to deploy them to the best advantage. In general, it is wasteful for workers to be unemployed, and the community will probably aim at fairly full employment. But some other factors, such as poor land, it may be better deliberately to leave unused; this point is discussed later in the present chapter. Most of the factors that are used could be used for any of several different purposes; most workers could be employed (perhaps after a little training) in any of a number of occupations or industries, most land could be used for any of several crops, or for pasture, or as building sites. If a factor can be used for one purpose only, it is said to be *specific* to that purpose. Most fixed capital is specific, but many materials are not; steel or timber, for example, are used in a wide variety of industries. And the services rendered by specific plant and equipment can often be used in any of a number of industries; for example, railways can transport any type of good, power stations can supply electricity to any type of undertaking.

Hence the economic problem is how to allocate factors among different industries in order to produce what the community wants most. We cannot have as much of everything as we want, because factors of production are limited in amount (and because an increased supply of "labour" due to an increase in population would also add to the number of consumers). But at least we can try to produce, out of all the infinite assortments of goods and services which could be produced by the available factors, that particular assortment of goods and services which the community prefers.

The main purpose of this chapter is to set out a few important generalizations, which are true for any community however it is organized, about the effects on output—quantity, not value, of output —when factors are grouped in different ways, combined with one another in different proportions, some factors being transferred from one industry to another. It is these physical relations between different combinations of factors and resulting quantities of output which determine, given the wants of the community, whether anything would be gained by shifting factors about, moving some workers from one industry into another, and so on.

But first we must discuss at some length the meaning of the term *factor of production*.

2. What is a Factor of Production?

It is customary to group all factors of production under the three broad heads of Land, Labour, and Capital. Land includes all types of natural resources. Labour includes all types of workers, from captains of industry to navvies. Capital includes all man-made productive assets, from buildings and machinery to materials and fuel.

Some elements, such as sunshine, cannot be appropriated by man, do not enter directly into costs, and are therefore usually not counted as factors of production. They may have very significant effects. For example, differences in climate are a major cause of specialization and trade between districts and countries. But it is more convenient to consider only the land, which can be bought and sold, and not the climate (although it is the climate which affects its productivity), as a factor of production.

Even so, we are left with a very large number of different types of land, workers, and capital goods. It is all very well to measure land in acres, but an acre is merely a measure of area; some acres are more fertile, or better situated, than others. Similarly with labour. We can count heads, and state the number of "the working population." But even this is by no means absolutely fixed. It depends partly on such circumstances as the ages at which children leave school, the ages at which elderly persons retire, the number of housewives willing to take a paid job, and the number of immigrants or emigrants. The number of persons available as a labour force can be increased considerably in an emergency, such as a war. And even if we know the number of the working population, and it is more or less fixed in the short run, it still includes many different types of workers. "Free" capital can be measured in money, in homogeneous units of £1 or £100. But money as such does not produce anything. It must first be transformed into actual physical assets, and of these there is a very large variety.

For purposes of planning, therefore, or for any practical economic problem, it is of little use to speak of land, labour, and capital. We need much more detailed information. We must group together only similar units, so that one unit is practically a perfect substitute for any other unit in the same group. This gives us a very large number of "factors of production," counting each group as a separate "factor." Not quite as large, however, as one might think at the first blush. For we can group together units that are now doing different things, provided that they are equally capable of doing the same things. Workers who would all be about equally competent at a number of occupations can all be grouped together, although in fact some may be in one occupation and others in another at the present moment. For purposes of planning we must consider what contribution factors of production might make towards output if they were used in different ways, and not merely what they are contributing now.

We should therefore consider factors of production as a large number of groups of fairly homogeneous units. For some purposes of general discussion, land, labour and capital is a convenient phrase. But the line of distinction between land and capital is not clear. It is usually said that land is a gift of nature, while capital is produced by man, and that the supply of land cannot be increased or diminished, whereas the supply of capital can. All these statements can be challenged. The Suez Canal, the railway tunnels through the Alps, the land reclaimed by Holland from the Zuyder Zee, are hardly gifts of nature. What is the "supply" of land? It is the productivity of land, and not its acreage, that affects output; and the productivity of land can be increased by clearing it, draining and irrigating it, and fertilizing it. The "original and indestructible powers of the soil" are somewhat of a myth, as the ravages of soil erosion have shown. For some purposes, therefore, a two-fold classification into Man and his Environment, with a corresponding division of incomes into incomes from work and incomes from property, is more realistic.

I have not yet finished with this question of definition. There is a possible source of confusion that must be pointed out. It may be illustrated by "labour." An employer wants labour services, man-hours of work performed, and not men as such. Under slavery, men are bought and sold, but their price reflects the estimated present value of their future services; it is their services, and not the men as such, which contribute to production. A given number of men may perform more or less work per year. They may work more or fewer hours or—yet another complication—with more or less intensity. Hence the expression "the supply of labour" is ambiguous. It may be measured by the number of workers or by the number of man-hours of service rendered or (in some industries, where payment is by results) by the actual amount of work performed.

In the same way, land and fixed capital may be worked more or less hard. The machinery in a factory may be worked for eight hours a day or, under a two-shift or three-shift system, for sixteen or twenty-four hours, and for anything up to 365 days a year, less the time needed for cleaning and overhauling it. Under-developed countries which are now expanding their education programmes often use school buildings, which are scarce, for two or even three sets of pupils a day.

Are we to think of the factors of production as the actual men, machines, and so forth, or as the services they render? When we consider the relation between input and output, we must think of the latter. Anything that contributes towards output is a factor of production. The finished products of one firm are factors of production in so far as they are used as materials by another. Coal is a product of the coal-mines, but when used as a production good, as in the boiler-room of a factory, it is a factor of production. Pigs are products to the farmer, but factors of production to the sausage-maker. Anything that forms part of the "input," that goes into the productive process at any stage and helps to produce the output, the gross national product, is a factor of production. Materials and fuel do actually and literally go into the productive process. In goes the pig and out come the sausages. But land, and men, and fixed capital do not. It is their services, and not they themselves, that form part of the input.

But when we are looking ahead and planning, or surveying the various production possibilities open to the community, we must think of the former. For they can be used in different ways. They can be more or less fully employed. More workers can be employed in some industries and fewer in others, and the same is true of land or capital. To some extent, they can be specialized to different tasks, although this may involve some cost. For example, men can be trained for different occupations, buildings can be converted to serve different purposes, land can be irrigated or fertilized to make it suitable for different crops. The central economic problem for any community is how to make the best use of its labour and other resources, and for this purpose the community must consider the various alternatives. It must consider what the men and the land and the capital might contribute towards output if they were used in different ways, and not merely what in fact they are contributing now.

3. SUBSTITUTION OF FACTORS

Few economic tasks are performed by one factor alone. Labour as well as land is required to grow wheat, and machinery as well as labour is required to make pins. Nearly every productive unit, whether it be a factory or a farm or a railway or a school, uses a number of different types of workers and equipment and other factors. It combines their services in order to produce its output.

In the short run, it sometimes appears that the proportions between the different factors are fixed and cannot be altered. Thus a plant may be designed to employ a certain number of men—for example, one man to each machine—and it appears obvious that taxi-cabs and drivers must be combined in the proportion of one to one. But the proportions are seldom absolutely fixed even in the short run. More or fewer workers can be employed in supervising; different types of materials or fuel can be used, or the present types can be combined in different proportions; two or even three men may share a taxi-cab and take turns in driving it; more workers can be employed with the same machinery by working two or three shifts a day.

In the long run, the proportions between the factors can usually be varied. Plant or equipment which wears out or is scrapped can be replaced by a different type, embodying more or fewer labour-saving devices. A farmer who expands his output can either acquire more land or buy more agricultural machinery or engage more labour.

As a rule, therefore, one factor can be substituted for another, within limits. Machinery can be substituted for labour, oil for coal, and so forth; although sometimes, as when one textile material is substituted for another, the resulting product is somewhat different.

As factor A is continuously substituted for factor B, more and more of factor A is usually needed to replace a unit of factor B and still yield the same output. This is because A and B are different factors; they are not perfect substitutes for one another. How much A and how much B should be used in any particular process? Under a price system, that will depend on their relative prices. A should be substituted for B so long as less than a shilling's worth of A can replace a shilling's worth of B and still yield the same output. In other words, if a unit of A costs, say, three times as much as a unit of B, A should be substituted for B so long as a unit of A can replace more than three units of B and still yield the same output. In this way, a given output will be produced at the lowest total cost possible, given the prices of the various factors.

For example, the cheaper is scrap-iron relatively to pig-iron, the more of the former and the less of the latter will be used in open-hearth furnaces for making steel. But if more than, say, 70 or 80 per cent of scrap-iron is used, the quality or quantity of the output may suffer. Suppose that $1\frac{1}{2}$ tons of scrap-iron cost the same as 1 ton of pig-iron. Scrap-iron will be substituted for pig-iron up to the point at which using 1 ton less of pig-iron and $1\frac{1}{2}$ tons more of scrap-iron would reduce, rather than increase, the output of the furnace.

Often it is not possible to make such continuous changes in the proportions. There must be either a fairly big change—for example, machinery replacing labour in a particular task, such as loading ships or rolling cigarettes—or none at all. But the above principle still applies.

If the price system is not distorted by monopoly, the relative prices of A and B measure the relative values that they could contribute to output in other industries. There is a kind of continuous auction going on among employers in different industries to obtain the services of particular factors. Each has to pay what the others are prepared to pay, and that depends on the contribution which the factors can make to their output. A builder, for example, may complain that he would like to use more steel, but cannot afford it; steel is too dear for him. This merely means that the available steel is needed more by other firms, who can afford to pay more for it than he can because they can use it in ways that are more valuable to the community. This type of problem continuously confronts an economic dictator or a central planning committee. Should, say, 1,000 workers be transferred from building houses to mining coal? That depends on whether the community needs the extra coal that it would get more than the extra houses that it would otherwise have had. Who is to say what the community needs most? Under central planning it is the planners. Under the price system it is the buying public; every shilling they spend on one commodity is a vote in favour of that commodity (and, therefore, of factors being employed in producing it) rather than some other.

4. Diminishing Returns and the Growth of Population

The English classical economists, notably John Stuart Mill, discussed diminishing returns in the context of the growth of population. They said that the growth of population tended to diminish the average return to labour. More workers would have to be employed in producing food for the growing population. But the total amount of land was fixed. Therefore the output per worker would fall, thereby lowering standards of living, as more labour was combined with a given amount of land.

It was true that, as population increased, some land not formerly used might be brought into cultivation. But this did not affect the argument. The new land would be poorer than the land at present under cultivation, or it would have been cultivated already. It would become worth using only because more intensive cultivation of the better land had diminished the returns per worker: after a point, additional labour would produce as much on the worse land as on the better land. Standards of living would fall owing to diminishing returns to labour upon the given area of better land already cultivated.

In agriculture, therefore, output per worker would tend to fall (although total output would increase) because each worker on the average would be assisted by a smaller amount of land than before. In manufacturing, however, they thought that output per worker would tend to increase. For machinery was taking the place of hand labour, and it seemed probable that, as time went on, each worker on the average would be assisted by more capital than before.

Why, on these assumptions, would not increasing returns in manufacturing (which includes the processing of foodstuffs—for example, the manufacture of flour from wheat and of bread from flour) more than outweigh diminishing returns in agriculture?

Because the great majority of the population were employed, and had to be employed, on the land. Food is the basic need of mankind. When incomes are low, as they were a hundred years ago, they are spent mainly on food. So long as the labour of one man on the land provides food for little more than one family, the bulk of the population must be engaged in agriculture. Only a small proportion of them can be spared for providing for less urgent needs by working in manufacturing and other industries where returns to labour might be increasing. Unless, therefore, the productivity of labour could be increased in agriculture, standards of living were bound to fall as population continued to grow. No inventions and improvements in other industries could avert this long-run tendency.

Hence it is not surprising that the English classical economists strongly advocated a reduction in birth rates in order that standards of living might be maintained and improved instead of being forced down by the pressure of population.

John Stuart Mill published his *Principles of Political Economy* in 1848. At that time there was little indication of the great developments in transport that would enable Great Britain to be fed on wheat from Canada, beef from the Argentine, mutton from Australia, and butter and cheese from New Zealand. Still less could anybody have been expected to foresee what has been called "the industrial revolution in agriculture"—the invention and improvement of machines such as the combine-harvester—for this has produced its most spectacular results in increasing output per worker (in countries where there is enough land, or enough employment available in occupations other than agricultural ones, to permit of fairly large farms) only during recent decades. Again, the progress of engineering has made possible the investment of capital in drainage and irrigation projects which greatly increase the productivity of the land.

In actual fact, the gloomy forebodings of the English classical economists have not been borne out by events. Populations have expanded greatly but, at any rate in the Western world, there has been a marked and continuous increase in the returns to labour, in agriculture as well as in other industries, over the past hundred years.

They did point out, however, that the tendency to diminishing returns might be counteracted for a time by "the progress of knowledge." No doubt they were thinking of the kinds of improvements that had been taking place since about the middle of the eighteenth century—discoveries such as the rotation of crops, improved breeds of cattle, improved varieties of crops, better methods of controlling pests and diseases of plants and animals. But they thought that the tendency to diminishing returns was always present and would prevail in the long run if population continued to grow.

This view is not entirely put out of court by the great economic progress of western countries over the past hundred years. It is relevant at the present time to overpopulated countries with growing populations, such as India. The need to provide food, let alone clothing and health and education services, for a constantly increasing number of children is a severe drain on the resources of a country with a limited amount of cultivable land, unless it has some product, such as oil, which it can export. A considerable amount of capital investment is required merely to maintain present levels of output per head.

But a long-term forecast which has been quite wrong over the last hundred years and which may or may not be true of the next hundred years, or which may apply to some countries and not to others, can hardly be called a "law." A scientific law is a generalization that is universally valid. There is such a Law of Diminishing Returns, which applies to every individual factor of production and not only to labour, whether that factor is employed in agriculture or in any other industry, and whichever country is under consideration.

5. THE LAW OF DIMINISHING RETURNS

The Law of Diminishing Returns relates to the very short run, to the situation that confronts a community at a given moment. It says nothing about what will happen to standards of living in the long run. It considers only the present possibilities of reshuffling factors, of rearranging them in different combinations, as they would have to be reviewed by a central planning committee for the country as a whole or considered by a farmer or any other controller of a business within the narrower sphere of his own farm or other productive unit. Improvements in technical knowledge will take place as time goes on, but at the moment the state of technical knowledge is what it is, and the problem is what to do with the factors available in the light of our present knowledge. When improved techniques are discovered and applied, various combinations of factors will give a greater output than at present, but that is another matter. The Law takes the state of technical knowledge as given.

The Law itself is simple and obvious, although some of its implications are not. It merely points out that while we should expect doubling all the factors to double the total output, if we double only one of them, or only some of them, and not the others, we should expect the total output to increase, but not to double.

There is one proviso, however. In any branch of production, an increase in the scale of output might make it worth while to use specialized machinery or other equipment, with a consequent increase in division of labour among the workers. As a rule, it would need quite a large increase in output to make such a radical change worth while. I discuss these "economies of scale" in the following chapter. The Law assumes that no such radical change in methods of production takes place.

In these circumstances, it needs no elaborate proof to demonstrate that if one factor alone is increased by x per cent, the total output will increase by less than x per cent. There will be diminishing returns to the factor that has increased, because each unit of it will be combined with fewer units than before of the other factors.

In order to bring out certain points, however, I will give a very simplified arithmetical example. Suppose there are only two factors— land and labour—each of uniform quality, engaged in the production of, let us say, wheat. We can assume that each worker is equipped with the same implements, seed, and fertilizer. Instead of assuming a fixed quantity of land I shall speak of men per square mile, for the number of men per square mile can be increased either by increasing the number of men or by decreasing the amount of land, giving us variability both ways and illustrating the point that it is the change in the *proportions* of the factors which matters. I have kept the table short, in order not to complicate the illustration; this makes returns diminish more rapidly than they would in practice, but it does not affect the argument.[1]

---

[1] My figures for most countries would be more realistic if I took a smaller unit of land, say 100 or 200 acres. But in Saskatchewan, where wheat-growing is fully mechanized, "a farm of four and a half sections (2,700 acres) can be worked from seed time to harvest by the farmer, his manager, and two hired men—all expert mechanics as well as good farmers." ("Canada's Wheat Province," *The Times*, 29th April, 1953.)

PRODUCT OF LABOUR (IN UNITS OF WHEAT)
PER SQUARE MILE OF LAND

Number of Men per square mile	Total Output per square mile	Average Product per man	Marginal Product per man
1	50	50	50
2	164	82	114
3	285	95	121
4	400	100	115
5	500	100	100
6	576	96	76
7	630	90	54
8	656	82	26
9	656	73	0
10	640	64	−16

The *average product* per man is the total product divided by the number of men. The highest average product per man, namely 100 units of wheat (a year), is obtained when 4 or 5 men are employed per square mile. If more men per square mile are employed, the average product per man falls; in other words, there are diminishing returns to labour.

The *marginal product* per man is the addition to the total product (per square mile) due to the addition of another man. It reaches its maximum of 121 units of wheat when 3 men are employed per square mile; thereafter it falls.

It will be noted that the table shows increasing returns to labour as the number of men per square mile is increased from 1 to 4. Why is this? Does it not contradict the view that (apart from economies of scale) diminishing returns are inevitable?

The reason is that a square mile is too large an area for 3 men to cope with, if they try to work it all at once. (The reader who does not like these figures can substitute others which he thinks more realistic— some area will be too large for 3 men to handle.) Consequently, 3 men would not try to cope with it; increasing returns due to this reason will never be found in practice. For example, if we accept the figures in the table, 300 men in a new colony with unlimited land at their disposal would cultivate only 60 or 75 square miles at a time. This would give them their maximum possible output of wheat, namely 30,000 units.

This means that increasing returns of this type are to be avoided. They indicate that more could be produced by using less of the other factor (in this example, by using less land). The marginal productivity of the other factor is negative if a greater product can be obtained by using less of it. Thus, if the 300 men cultivated 100 square miles, they would produce only 28,500 units; the additional 25 square miles would reduce their total output by 1,500 units.

This point is brought out again in the last line of the table. When more than 9 men are employed per square mile, the total product falls. More than 9 men (and again the reader can substitute a much larger number if he wishes) impede one another and produce a smaller output; the marginal productivity of labour is negative. This means that there are increasing returns to land. As the amount of land is increased, reducing the number of men per square mile towards 9, the aver age output per square mile increases towards its maximum o 656 units. Clearly not more than 9 men per square mile will be employed.

Hence in practice there would be diminishing returns to both factors. The number of men per square mile would be not less than 4 and not more than 9. How many exactly would it be?

If land were free, the number would be 4, for this would maximize output per man. If labour were free (for example, if farmers could use any number of prisoners of war), the number would be 8 (or 9), for this would maximize output per square mile.

In practice both land and labour are scarce. It would be folly to employ 9 men per square mile. The ninth man would add nothing to the total product; if he were employed instead in some other industry, he could make a positive contribution to output. The eighth man per square mile adds 26 units of wheat per square mile. Could he add something worth more than 26 units of wheat if he were employed instead in some other industry? If so, he is better employed there, and not in wheat-growing. Under a properly working price system, the number of men per square mile will be such that their marginal product is equal in value to the marginal product of that type of labour in other industries.

The same applies to land. It would be folly to allow as much as a square mile to be used in conjunction with 4 or 5 men. For in that event the marginal productivity of land would be zero. (For example, 100 men and 20 square miles produce 10,000 units; 100 men and 25 square miles also produce 10,000 units; the extra 5 square miles add nothing to the total output). The question to be asked is whether some wheat land could make a greater contribution to national output if it were used for some other purpose; if the answer is yes, it should be transferred to that other purpose.

In general terms, and assuming full employment, the *best allocation of factors among industries is achieved when the community places the same value upon the marginal product of a factor in every industry in which that factor is employed*. Otherwise, there would be a gain in moving factors to where their marginal productivity is greater.

The Law of Diminishing Returns may be stated as follows: *As the proportion of one factor in a combination of factors is increased, after a point, first the marginal and then the average product of that factor will diminish.*

This assumes that the state of technical knowledge is given and that there are no "economies of scale."

It is true that output per man has increased considerably in most industries over the past hundred years, or even the past ten years. But this has been due to increased investment (more capital per worker) and to changes in methods due to the growth of technical knowledge and to greater territorial specialization owing to improvements in transport. The Law relates to *a given situation*, to the situation which confronts a farmer or a business man or a planning committee *at any given moment*. It is this which is relevant to the allocation of factors among industries, and to the theory of costs.

6. UNUSED FACTORS

"We should make the fullest possible use of *all* our resources," says the orator, and everyone applauds. Except the economist. He knows that it is nonsense, and so would others, if they thought about it.

What is the use of trying to cultivate jungle or swamp, mountain or desert, if the same number of workers could produce more by concentrating on the more fertile or better situated land? In Australia, for example, most of the interior has a low and unreliable rainfall. The population has grown during the past hundred years from less than half a million to more than ten million, but it has continued to concentrate on the more fertile coastal regions, leaving the interior severely alone except for sparse pastoral cultivation, with sometimes only two or three sheep or cattle per square mile. Are they wrong not to make the "fullest possible use" of the interior? Of course not. Their labour produces more where it is.

Again, suppose that a community has two coal deposits, one of thick seams near the surface and the other of thin seams, deep down and difficult to work. If it concentrates entirely on the better deposit, 1,000 men will suffice to produce a million tons a year. It would take, say, 5,000 men to produce a million tons a year from the worse deposit. Additional men employed on the better deposit would produce several times more coal than if they were employed on the worse deposit. Clearly, it would be sheer waste to work the worse deposit.

In general terms, poor land or poor mineral deposits are worth working only if the marginal productivity of labour employed on them is as great as it is on the better land or deposits. We must take account, however, of the transport and distribution of goods to consumers. It may be better in some cases to work poor land or poor mineral deposits for local consumption than to import the products from elsewhere. This will be so if the extra costs of transport would outweigh the difference in production costs.

The same principle applies to fixed capital. Suppose, for example, that a new type of machine is invented that will perform a certain task more efficiently than the type of machine at present in use for that purpose. The community may attain its ends more fully by applying the invention at once and scrapping all the old-type machines, even if many of them are practically new. Whether this will be so depends on two things.

1. Suppose that a machine of the new type (if it were produced) and a machine of the old type (which has already been produced) would each last for ten years. Can the community satisfy its wants more fully over these ten years by using the less efficient machine, which is already in existence, or by employing co-operating factors, such as labour, to produce a machine of the new type and to operate it? If the latter, then the community may gain by producing the new machine and scrapping the existing one.

2. But this is not all. The community has a limited supply of savings. Some of these savings would be absorbed in producing machines of the new type. A still greater gain might be possible by using its limited savings in other ways and by continuing to work the existing machines. But if this is not so, then clearly the best course is to scrap all existing machines of the old type.

This point is not fully realized by those who deplore what they call "the loss of capital" due to inventions and who wish to restrict, for example, the competition of road transport in order to preserve the capital value of the railways.

A final example of our principle may be drawn from public works to relieve unemployment. It is sometimes urged that any such relief works must increase production since the unemployed will produce something instead of nothing. This may not be true. In order to produce something—say, roads—the unemployed must be combined with other factors such as engineers, supervisors, equipment, and materials. These co-operating factors, including the labour and capital employed in making the equipment and producing the materials, must be drawn from other uses. As a consequence of this reshuffle, the total assortment of goods and services produced may satisfy the wants of the community less fully than the assortment that would have been produced in the absence of relief works. But again I must point out that this is not necessarily conclusive. The community may prefer to maintain the morale and working habits of the unemployed even at this cost. Further, if there is heavy unemployment, relief works may be an effective means of expanding the total monetary demand for goods and services and thus promoting a general revival of economic activity and employment.

NOTE

AVERAGE AND MARGINAL PRODUCT

The marginal product of a factor is the addition to the total product due to the addition of one more unit of the factor. The last column of our table on page 109 shows the marginal product of labour per square mile. Increase the number of men per square mile from, say, three to

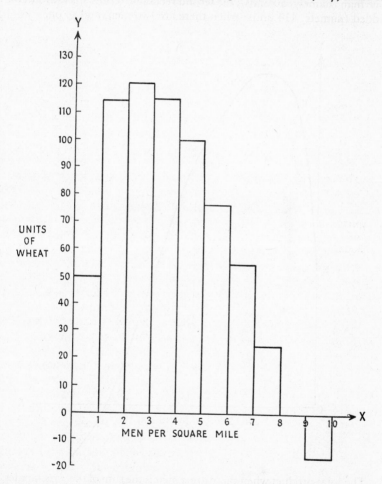

four, and the marginal product of labour (per square mile) falls from 121 units to 115 units. The figure of 115 is obtained by subtracting 285—the output per square mile when there are three men per square mile—from 400—the output per square mile when there are four men per square mile. It is not strictly correct to say that the extra 115 units

F

are "due to the fourth man" since, by definition, the fourth is equal in efficiency to any of the others. The 115 units are the marginal product of labour per square mile when four are employed thereon.

The marginal product of labour per square mile, as shown in the table, is represented diagrammatically on page 113. Reading from left to right, the first rectangle or pillar represents the product when there is one man (namely, 50 units), the second rectangle represents the amount added (namely, 114 units) when there are two men, and so on.

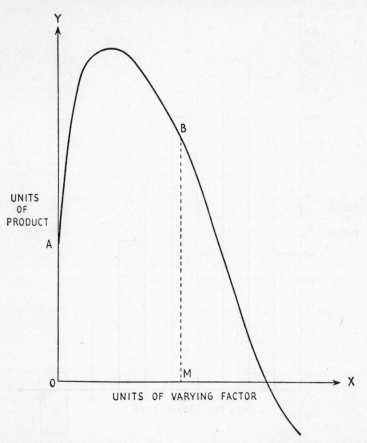

The total product when there are *x* men is the sum of the *x* rectangles, and the marginal product is the *x*th rectangle. If the marginal product is negative, it is represented by a rectangle below *OX*, and the total product is the rectangles above *OX* minus those below *OX*.

The diagram is usually simplified, as above, by joining the tops of the rectangles and showing only the smoothed curve.

The total product of *OM* men is the area *OABM*; their marginal product is *BM*.

The curve of average product per man can be constructed in the same way.

When the average product per man (or other factor) first rises and then falls, as in our example, the corresponding marginal-product curve will rise faster and higher, and will begin to fall sooner and more steeply, cutting the average-product curve at the highest point of the latter:

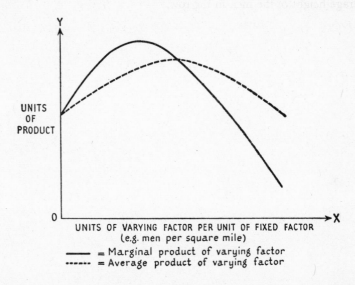

= Marginal product of varying factor
= Average product of varying factor

The total product is the sum of the marginal products. The average product is the total product divided by the number of men. So long as the marginal product (even after it has begun to fall) remains above the average product, it will raise the latter; the average-product curve must be rising. And when the marginal product is below the average product, it will reduce the latter; the average-product curve must be falling. When the marginal product due to one more man being added is the same as the former average product, the latter has ceased rising and has not begun to fall; that is to say, it is at a maximum.

Some readers may be able to convince themselves by working out illustrations in terms of cricket scores. Or we can think of men being arranged in a row. If the first man is 5 ft. tall, the second 5 ft. 2 in., the third 5 ft. 6 in., and the fourth 6 ft., these increases in the "marginal height" will make the "average height" increase, but it will remain below the "marginal height." Thus the average height of these four men will be only 5 ft. 5 in. Now suppose that subsequent men are progressively shorter—say the fifth man is 5 ft. 11¾ in., the sixth 5 ft. 11¼ in., and so on. Clearly for some time the average height in the row will continue to increase. When the average height reaches a maximum, it is neither increasing nor decreasing—for a moment the curve representing it is neither rising nor falling, and must therefore be horizontal. The last addition neither raises nor lowers the previous average, hence it must equal it. Thus, if the average height of our men first rises and then falls, and if at the point when it ceases to rise the next man does not make it begin to fall, his height must equal the average height of the men in the row.

CHAPTER VIII

LARGE-SCALE PRODUCTION

1. INTRODUCTION

THERE is a widespread belief that large-scale production is more efficient than small-scale production. Often this is true. Production on a large scale may make possible more specialization. A large machine, or other unit of plant and equipment, is often more efficient than a smaller one. There are sometimes technical economies in the integration of different processes.

On the other hand, small-scale production is still predominant in some fields and we often find small firms holding their own in competition with giant concerns, and perhaps producing at lower costs.

We should distinguish between the size of the industry, the size of the firm, and the size of the factory, farm, or other "establishment."

Some economies depend solely on the size of the industry. For example, a large industry which is also localized usually benefits from various *external economies*. Other firms will cater for its special needs, providing it with transport and banking services, repairing its machinery, supplying its accessories, purchasing its waste products for processing, and so forth. This will be so whether the industry consists of a few large firms or many small ones. The economies spring from the size of the industry as a whole and its concentration in one area; they have nothing to do with the size of the individual firm or of the individual establishment.

Other economies depend solely on the size of the establishment. These are technical economies springing from the greater efficiency of larger capital goods, such as machines, or from carrying out within the same establishment a number of successive stages in the process of production. The firm which owns the establishment may own only that one, or it may own many others, but these economies depend only on the size of the individual establishment and not on the size of the firm. Nevertheless two or more firms cannot both control the same establishment. Hence in industries where most establishments are large, most firms will be at least correspondingly large. But a single firm can control any number of establishments, large or small.

The advantages of a large firm, as distinct from a large establishment, may lie mainly in the field of monopoly. A large firm may be able to charge higher prices, or to pay less for its materials or other factors, than small firms actively competing with one another. This subject does not properly belong to the present Part, which deals with the influences affecting the volume of output under any system of social organization; private monopoly gains arise only under capitalism, but I mention them in this Chapter for the sake of completeness. Another advantage of a large firm is that it can afford to pay for the full-time services of various experts.

However, both large establishments and large firms may have their disadvantages, as we shall see.

2. ECONOMIES OF SCALE

The present chapter supplements the preceding one. There I explained why we should expect to find diminishing returns to every factor in every industry—at any given moment. But over a period of time we may find exactly the opposite. During the past few generations the returns to labour, and indeed to nearly all factors, have continuously increased, at any rate in the Western world, in almost every field of economic activity. What are the reasons for this paradox?

There are two main reasons. The first is the growth of technical knowledge. We are using new and improved types of machinery and equipment for production and transport, growing new and improved varieties of crops, and in general applying our increased knowledge to exercise a more effective control over our environment and to obtain a greater output per worker. The second reason is that the expansion of an industry may make possible what are known as *economies of scale*.

A large expansion in an industry may lead to the adoption of a different method of production. Quite apart from any increases in technical knowledge, the growth of an industry may make it possible to take fuller advantage of specialization. Men may specialize more upon particular tasks, and machinery may be used which formerly was not worth while. Take printing as an example. When the numbers of men and the amount of capital employed are small, hand printing-presses may be used, although the people concerned know quite well how to construct and operate a linotype machine or a rotary press. Multiply the scale of the industry by ten, and one or more of these large machines may be used, while workers specialize in the various occupations created by the new methods of production. The same applies to the production of newsprint. The cheapest way to produce newsprint is to use a large machine which turns out several tons an hour. Clearly such a machine is not worth using when the total demand is only a few tons a day; it would be idle nearly all the time.

This point is illustrated by many of the small-scale industries in under-developed countries. The people of these countries know quite well that the large-scale methods of the West are more efficient, but they cannot use them because their local demand is too small. What would be the use of installing a modern large-scale chocolate factory in Trinidad (which produces cocoa and sugar) when the local demand would keep it employed for only a few days a year? What would be the point of establishing a continuous-strip mill for making tin-plate in a country such as Burma or Ceylon, when its output exceeds local demand more than a hundredfold? We therefore find that such countries either import the products of industries where large-scale methods give much lower costs of production or else employ more primitive methods, using more labour and less capital, and giving lower returns per worker. Handicrafts, cottage industries, and small-scale factories may be a means of providing employment, and in some cases may yield products superior in craftmanship or design, but in many fields the output per worker is much lower than it would be if modern mechanized methods were used.

Economies of scale mean that the assumption I made in the preceding chapter—namely, that increasing all the factors engaged in an industry by a certain percentage would increase the total output of the industry by exactly same percentage—may not be true. When all the factors are increased by x per cent, the total output may increase, if x is large, by more than x per cent.

The careful reader will note again the ambiguity of the term "factor." To revert to our example of printing, we can say (as most economists do) that the amount of the factor "capital" has increased tenfold, or we can say that one type of capital good—linotype machines—has replaced another type—hand printing-presses.

Economies of scale may be realized when the expansion of an industry takes place by some factors increasing more than others; there is no need for them all to increase by the same percentage. The increase of capital in the Western world during recent generations has been much greater than the growth of population. A large increase in the capital employed in an industry may lead to the adoption of methods which formerly, although known, were not worth while because the proportion of capital available was too small. Thus it might become worth while to construct a water works and to lay pipes for the distribution of water instead of carrying it in buckets. This point also is amply illustrated in under-developed countries. They are nearly all short of capital and therefore cannot use many labour-saving devices which would be worth while if capital were more abundant and therefore cheaper.

A large increase in the scale of an industry may result in a separation of processes and occupations. For instance, instead of one household or one little factory making a finished textile product, such as a shirt or a carpet, some firms may do the spinning, others the weaving, others the dyeing, and so on, and new occupations may be created by the use of new types of specialized machinery and equipment.

A general expansion of industry and trade may bring with it various economies. For example, the growth of factories of various types in an area may benefit them all. The railways and roads can carry their goods more cheaply because the total volume of traffic is larger; the cost of electricity may fall because it can now be produced on a larger scale; it may become easier, in time, for any particular factory to obtain skilled labour or to get its machinery repaired or parts of it replaced.

3. THE CONCEPT OF INDIVISIBILITY

It is worth while asking an apparently silly question, for the answer will bring out the main reason for economies of scale. Why are not large-scale methods used, if they are known, even where the demand is relatively small? Granted that the large machines and other capital goods employed in the big industrial centres could not be used, because they would be idle most of the time, why not use much smaller models of them?

The answer, of course, is that many capital goods must be a certain minimum size in order to do their job and that many are more efficient, up to a point, the bigger they are. In economic language, they are *indivisible*. We cannot divide their dimensions by 2 or 10 or 100 and get miniatures which do a half or a tenth or a hundredth of the work done by those of the normal size.

A minimum size is sometimes necessary for various technical reasons. For example, a plant generating electricity from water power must be fairly large, and a miniature combine-harvester would not work. The minimum size is often related to the size of human beings. For example, a motor-car must be big enough to hold two or more people, and the size of the car determines the size of the conveyer-belt which assembles it.

There are also various technical reasons why larger units are often more efficient, up to a point, than smaller ones. One general point, which applies to boilers, tanks, furnaces, ships, and many other capital goods, is that carrying capacity varies roughly with the cube of the dimensions, whereas the material required to construct the capital good varies roughly with the square of the dimensions. A $2 \times 2 \times 2$ box holds eight times as much as a $1 \times 1 \times 1$ box, but contains only four times as much material. Another general point is that often only a few more men are needed, in some cases only the same number, to operate a bigger unit. Up to a point, a big ship is cheaper to run than a smaller one, for it requires less engine space and less fuel and less crew per unit of carrying capacity. Five blast furnaces of 200 tons capacity are more expensive to construct and require more coke and more labour than one of 1,000 tons.

It is often possible to produce a large unit by assembling a number of parts, just as a house is built of bricks and mortar, tiles, pipes, doors, windows, and other parts. On the other hand, large units sometimes call for large establishments to make them and handle them. For example, if ships are large, shipbuilding yards and ports and docks must also be large.

4. Excess Capacity

It may be worth while to install a fairly large capital good although the demand is not sufficient for it to be used to full capacity. For example, it may be worth while to use a ship of, say, 2,000 tons on a certain route although it is known that the cargo space will seldom be completely filled. It may be worth while to put up a power station large enough to meet a peak demand for electricity although for much of the time the demand may be considerably lower. Under imperfect competition, as we shall see later, a firm may work below full capacity because it maintains fixed selling prices, and at those prices it cannot sell all its potential output.

In these circumstances, there is *excess capacity*: the fixed capital could be worked harder.

Suppose that fixed capital is being worked well below capacity, and that the demand for its products gradually increases. For a time, as more and more labour is employed, the marginal productivity of workers may fall only slightly, or not at all. In other words, there may be constant, or nearly constant, returns to labour. The same may apply to other co-operating factors, such as fuel. But when the fixed capital is being worked nearly to full capacity, the marginal productivity of labour and other factors often begins to fall sharply as still more of them are employed.

There may be excess capacity in the labour force also. For example, much the same number of men may be required to run a power station whether it is producing all it can or only half as much. A change from the latter to the former situation will double the output per worker. But it would be misleading to think of this as increasing returns to labour. In effect, each worker is now assisted by twice as much capital as before, because the station is fully used instead of half used. Where the number of workers needed to operate a plant is more or less fixed, the productivity of additional workers would be nearly zero, for they would add little to the output of the plant.

5. The Size of Establishments

We can measure the size of an establishment by the value of its output, or by the number of workers it employs, or by the value of its fixed capital, such as buildings, plant, and equipment. For some establishments other measures are often used—for example, the acreage of a farm or the tonnage of a ship.

For most purposes, the value of output is the most informative measure. It is usually better to take the value added rather than the gross value, for the latter exaggerates the importance of establishments such as oil refineries which add only a small percentage to the value of the materials which they process.

In some industries, such as iron and steel, motor manufacture, the processing of aluminium, oil-refining, and flour-milling, large-scale establishments predominate. The main reason is that they use large units of plant and equipment which would be less efficient if they were smaller.

In agriculture and retail trade and in a number of manufacturing industries, such as cotton-spinning and weaving, woodworking, and pottery, there is no advantage in very large units of capital goods, and many of the establishments are of medium size or quite small. In such industries a large factory, for example, merely contains more machines of the same size and type; the chief advantage of a larger factory arises from the indivisibility of human beings: a works manager or accountant may be working below capacity in a small factory. In such industries, the size of any particular establishment often depends mainly on the capital available to the firm that owns it.

In some industries large-scale and small-scale methods exist side by side. For example, goods may be transported either by a large railway system or on a lorry. A large gold-mine uses elaborate large-scale machinery, but gold is also won from small deposits and rivers by more primitive methods. The same applies to a number of other minerals.

The size of an industry is limited by the demand for its products. We should not expect to find large factories producing only glass eyes, for the total demand for glass eyes, even at a low price, is relatively small.

The size of an establishment may be limited by local demand, and by transport costs. It is local demand that restricts the size of a village shop, or the size of a ship plying between ports where there is not much cargo available. It is transport costs that make it worth while to set up small establishments, although larger ones some distance away have lower costs of production, to use local materials for making heavy or bulky products such as bricks, cement, and furniture, to supply the local demand.

In countries which produce and consume rice there are usually a number of small rice-mills distributed over the rice-growing districts. A few large mills would have lower costs of production because they would use large-scale machinery and equipment. But the transport costs of sending paddy a long distance to be milled and returned for local consumption in the form of rice outweigh (especially as it takes 160 lb. of paddy to produce 100 lb. of rice) the lower production costs of a large mill.

The same point may apply even when the commodity is not consumed locally, but exported. For example, a large sugar factory is more efficient than a small one. But it takes 7 to 13 tons of cane, depending on the sucrose content, to make a ton of sugar. If there is enough cane in the area to supply a large factory, well and good. But if the cane is grown in a number of scattered areas, it may be better to save transport costs by having a small- or medium-sized factory for each area instead of bringing all the cane to one large central factory.

For this reason we often find relatively small factories processing tea, rubber, and other agricultural products near the places where they are grown.

Establishments that render personal services to consumers, such as restaurants and hairdressing saloons, or whose products, for example bread or ice, must be delivered fairly quickly to consumers, tend to be distributed over space in much the same way as the population. A large bakery or laundry is more efficient than a small one, but is only worth while where the local demand is large enough to keep it employed fairly near to full capacity.

I wrote that the main reason why large-scale establishments predominate in certain industries is that they use large "indivisible" units of plant and equipment. There is sometimes another reason also. There may be technical advantages in integration.

6. Integration

Integration is the carrying-out, within the same establishment, of successive stages in the process of production. The product of one process is the material for the next. For example, cotton yarn is both the product of the spindles and also the material used by the looms which weave the cloth. At any stage, however, other materials also may be used; for example, other textile materials may be combined with cotton yarn to make cloth. Integration may take place either by establishments which make the materials or semi-finished products expanding forward to make the more-finished products also, or by establishments which make the latter expanding backward to make their own materials. Other things being equal, an integrated establishment will be larger, because it carries out a number of processes, than an establishment that specializes on one or two processes only.

The iron and steel industry provides a leading example of integration. A modern integrated steelworks normally has at least two blast furnaces, for at any time one may be under repair and out of operation.

The most efficient size of blast furnace is large, producing at least 800 tons a day of pig-iron. The rest of the plant and equipment has to be adequate to cope with this large output of pig-iron, transforming it (probably in open-hearth furnaces, with the addition of scrap) into steel ingots, transforming the ingots into semi-finished steel products such as blooms and billets and bars, and putting the semi-finished products through a series of further processes to make a whole range of more-finished products, including plates and sheets, wire, rails, and possibly tubes or tin-plate.

It would be physically possible to carry out almost any of these processes in a separate establishment, and this is sometimes done. The coke for the blast furnaces could be produced elsewhere—for example, near the coal-mines. Blast furnaces could be isolated, selling their pig-iron in cold solid slabs (known as "pigs") to steel-makers and foundries elsewhere. An establishment could have only open-hearth furnaces, selling cold steel ingots. An establishment could specialize in producing billets or blooms or bars. Other establishments could specialize on some particular finished product, such as plates, or plates of a certain thickness.

But there are considerable technical advantages in carrying out all these processes within the same works. Fuel is saved by passing the metal from one stage to another while it is still hot; the gases produced by the blast furnaces and coke ovens can be used to provide heat and power for the plant as a whole instead of going to waste; the scrap from the finished products can be fed back into the steel furnaces.

In most industries similar technical advantages of integration do not exist, or are much less marked. There are always some general advantages. The prompt supply of materials for the various processes is assured, and their quality is known, if they are produced in the same establishment; and the costs of transporting them from one establishment to another are saved. These advantages, however, may be outweighed by various disadvantages.

A factory may not use enough of some materials or accessories to produce them in the most efficient way. A separate factory that specializes in such a product may produce it more cheaply, because it can keep the "indivisible" plant and equipment, and the specialized workers, fully employed. We do not find a printing works making its own paper or a rubber factory going a stage further and making motor-car tyres, for paper and tyres are produced more cheaply on a large scale.

Most factories pack their products in containers—boxes or cartons or tins or bottles. Why does not every factory make its own containers? Tins and bottles are produced more cheaply on a large scale, and relatively few factories use enough to make their own. Quite a number make their own boxes. But some do not use enough to keep modern box-making machinery fully employed; it is cheaper for them to buy from a firm that specializes in making boxes.

In the same way, an establishment that does not deliver enough goods to send them, at any rate for long distances, in its own lorry or van will find it cheaper to send them by a firm that specializes in transport. The latter can get full lorry-loads by carrying goods for a number of different establishments, and can therefore carry them more cheaply.

By employing specialized firms in this way, a small establishment can overcome many of the disadvantages of being small. Sometimes a number of small establishments may deliberately co-operate for such a purpose, while remaining separate and independent in other respects. For example, several small farms adjacent to one another may share a combine-harvester which each alone is too small to use to capacity. As a general rule, however, this kind of co-operation is achieved through the price system. The various firms which in effect co-operate with one another by sharing the equipment and services of a firm specializing in, say, making boxes or carrying goods, may not even know one another's names. Each of them goes to the specialized firm because the latter can do the job more cheaply than it could do it for itself.

Another reason why one process may be carried on in a different establishment from a subsequent process is that transport costs are saved by processing the materials where they are grown or mined, whereas the establishment that uses them may be best located elsewhere (for example, near the market or near a source of cheap power). I have made this point already, but it is relevant in the present context also. For example, sago palm (which is bulky) is processed into sago flour where it is grown, but the textile and other factories using sago flour as a material are located far away, in manufacturing countries.

An establishment that specializes in one or two processes can buy its materials wherever they are cheapest; in so far as its plant and equipment can process different types of materials, it can substitute one type for another when their relative prices change; and in some industries it can blend materials in different ways in order to meet the changing tastes of consumers. An integrated establishment is less flexible. A weaving mill can buy whatever types of yarns are relatively cheapest or most suitable, but an integrated factory is tied to the types and qualities of yarns that can be produced by its own spindles. An integrated steelworks is tied to its blast furnaces, which it must try to keep working to capacity; a non-integrated open-hearth steelworks can buy pig-iron wherever it is cheapest and can use a bigger proportion of scrap, and a smaller proportion of pig-iron, whenever it pays to do so.

The general conclusion is that the special advantages of an integrated establishment must be quite marked to make it worth while to forgo the advantages of specialization by a number of separate establishments

7. THE SIZE OF FIRMS

Many firms have only one establishment; the firm and the establishment coincide, and our discussion of the influences determining the size of an establishment applies also to the firm. Some firms, however, own a number of establishments. Restaurants must be near their customers; hence the big catering firms own chains of restaurants as well as factories processing foodstuffs. Some products are processed more cheaply where they are grown; hence a firm such as Unilever owns factories processing vegetable oils in a number of countries and districts producing copra, palm oil, and groundnuts.

The size of a firm is limited by the amount of capital that its owner possesses or can borrow. This puts a considerable brake on the rate of expansion of a firm owned by a man with little capital of his own, however great his ability may be. As time goes on, a firm can expand by "ploughing back" its profits. The greater its own assets, the more it can borrow from the public or the banks. Many of our leaders of industry have built up large firms in this way from small beginnings. Nowadays this is more difficult in Great Britain, for the rate of taxation on incomes and profits is too high to leave much margin for private investment.

When a few large firms dominate an industry they are in a position, by open or tacit agreement among themselves, to fix the prices of their products; and smaller firms may follow suit. I discuss monopoly and imperfect competition in later chapters. My point is that such a firm may not expand its output further, although it could do so, because this would mean reducing its prices and its profits.

A large firm may also be able to use its bargaining power to buy some of its materials or services more cheaply. There is no social advantage in this in so far as it merely gains at the expense of its suppliers. But sometimes it can buy more cheaply because large quantities can be produced or transported more cheaply. For example, a full train-load can be carried more cheaply per ton of freight than a number of half-empty trucks, or a smaller number of trucks than the locomotive could pull. In such a case there is a real saving of effort and resources reflected in the lower prices charged to the large firm.

An owner-manager can personally supervise his establishment until it gets beyond a certain size, or until he acquires other establishments also. He must then employ managers for his various departments or branches, and must incur extra expenses in book-keeping and other means of preventing fraud and of providing him with detailed information about his business.

Owner-managers differ in ability. As time goes on, the most competent tend to expand the size of their firms, whilst the least competent go to the wall. If a man has exceptional business ability it is a waste of his talents for him to be engaged in controlling only a small firm; he is being used below capacity. On the other hand, a man of limited ability can run a firm of small or medium size but will get out of his depth, and make too many mistakes, if his firm becomes much larger. This is an aspect of the law of diminishing returns. As more plant and more other factors are combined with a fixed amount of executive ability, the returns to the other factors tend to diminish.

CHAPTER IX

POPULATION

1. THE SIZE OF POPULATION

MALTHUS published the first edition of his *Essay on the Principle of Population* in 1798. His purpose was to demonstrate, in his own words—

"That the increase of population is necessarily limited by the means of subsistence. That population does invariably increase when the means of subsistence increase and that the superior power of population is repressed, and the actual population kept equal to the means of subsistence, by misery and vice."

Another writer, Robert Wallace, has pointed out that if there were six children to a marriage (a realistic figure for those days, although not for ours), of whom four survived to become fathers and mothers, then the total population would increase in 1,233 years from the original couple to over 412 milliard. As there has never been anything like that number of people in the world—the present 2·9 milliard is the highest so far—it is clear that some checks must have been imposed on the "power of population" to multiply itself. Malthus thought that all these checks, such as famines and plagues, wars and infanticide, resolved themselves into misery or vice.

In his second edition, however, he conceded that another check is possible: prudential (or moral) restraint. By this he did not mean birth control; he meant postponement of marriage and abstinence after marriage.

His views were adopted, as I have already remarked, by later British economists. They believed that there is an inevitable tendency to diminishing returns to labour in agriculture. With every mouth God sends a pair of hands, but the new hands do not produce as much. The tendency to diminishing returns may be overcome for a time by "the progress of civilization," but sooner or later it must prevail. No lasting improvement in the condition of the people would ever be possible, for as soon as a temporary improvement took place, the "power of population" would assert itself and the increase in numbers would drag standards of living down again. A lasting improvement would be possible only if people desired it strongly enough to limit their numbers; in moral restraint lay the hope, the only hope, for mankind. No wonder that economics was called "the gloomy science"!

In fact, the population of Great Britain has increased since Malthus wrote from about 10 million to 50 million, and this expansion has been accompanied by a marked upward trend in standards of living. Similar movements have taken place in most countries of Western Europe and in the New World. Malthus did not foresee the great improvements in transport which enable us to be fed from the vast lands of the new continents, nor did he foresee the extent to which technical progress and the growth of investment would raise output per head.

Nevertheless today many parts of the world, including China, India, Japan, and Southern and Eastern Europe, are overpopulated. Their standards of living are far below those of Western countries and their death rates are high, especially among babies and young children, largely from lack of proper nourishment. Their populations are too large relatively to their resources of land and capital; if their numbers were smaller their output per head would be greater.

The biggest disadvantage of too large a population is that there is too little land per head. In all overpopulated countries the average size of the family farm is very small. In India, for example, it is less than five acres; and the output of cereals is only $1\frac{1}{2}$ tons a man-year as compared with 30 tons in the United States. Less can be produced from a tiny holding than from a fair-sized farm. In overpopulated countries most of the population is engaged in agriculture, and productivity per worker in agriculture is low because each worker has too little land.

Foreign trade enables a country to raise its national income by specializing on exports. No doubt some overpopulated countries might follow the example of Japan and specialize more on exports. But the larger the population, the smaller tends to be the proportion in the export industries. China, India, and Pakistan have between them over 1,100 million people, consuming over 90 million tons of rice a year. What other countries could supply them with more than a small proportion of this great quantity of rice? And what could they export in exchange for it? In practice, they must grow nearly all their rice within their own borders, because their populations are so large; and their exports form only a small proportion of their total output.

How can such countries increase their output per head? It may be that new land could be opened up, or that land at present under cultivation could be made to produce two crops a year instead of one, by irrigation projects and other forms of investment. It may be that many of their peasants are not using the most suitable techniques and could be trained, for example, to use more fertilizers or to grow higher-yielding varieties of crops or to cope more effectively with pests. But this would require an army of competent instructors.

If it were possible to uproot most of the peasants from their tiny holdings and to divide the land into much larger farms, equipped with agricultural machinery, output per head in agriculture would greatly increase; a small proportion of the present number of agricultural workers would produce the same amount of food. But this would mean a complete social upheaval. And employment would have to be found for the peasants who were divorced from their land; they would have to be trained for other occupations and employed in manufacturing or in rendering services of various kinds.

All these measures would require capital. To be on a scale large enough to raise appreciably the present very low standards of living they would require an immense amount of capital. But overpopulated countries are poor, largely because they are overpopulated. They have little margin for saving. Where is all this capital to come from? If their numbers were smaller, this problem—which may well prove insoluble—would not arise. They need so much capital because their populations are so large. In the long run, the most effective way, and perhaps the only way, to maintain and improve their standards of living is for them to reduce their numbers by having fewer babies.

It is possible for a country to be underpopulated. If there is plenty of fairly good land available, or if there are opportunities for a large expansion of exports, a bigger population might result in more specialization and a greater volume of output per head. It may be that some countries, for example Australia or Canada, are in this position today. A denser population gives more scope for economies of scale. It can be supplied more cheaply—that is to say, at the cost of less labour and other resources per unit of output—with transport, electricity, and similar services, and with mass-produced commodities. Moreover, a larger population is likely to contain more inventive talent and more men and women of outstanding ability than a smaller one.

It is not very profitable, however, to speculate on what is the "optimum" size of population for any particular country. A large increase or decrease in its numbers would in practice take a considerable time to achieve. In the meantime, the situation might change. The country might discover oil or other minerals, or technical progress might show it how to make better use of the resources which it already knows it has, or a change in tastes or knowledge (such as the discovery of synthetic substitutes) might affect the demand for its exports. We can feel certain that countries which are clearly overpopulated would have a bigger output per head if their numbers could be reduced, but we cannot say what size would maximize their output per head (given their hours of work) over the next fifty or a hundred years, nor can we be sure whether a country like Australia (with a high proportion of foreign trade) would be well advised to aim at a substantial increase in her numbers.

In any event, this is by no means entirely an economic question.

Some may want a larger population because they wish their nation to play a more important part in world affairs or because they want enough manpower to defend their country against a potentially aggressive neighbour. Others may want a smaller population in order to secure more amenities: a quieter countryside, more parks and playing fields, less traffic congestion.

In Great Britain a Royal Commission on Population was appointed in 1944 and reported in 1950. It set up an Economic Committee which reached the guarded conclusion that "a smaller population would, as such, be on the whole advantageous." But the Commission itself had "no hesitation in concluding that a replacement size of family is desirable in Great Britain at the present time." They reached this conclusion because they feared the effect of declining numbers among Western peoples on "the prestige and influence of the West" and on "the maintenance and extension of Western values, ideas and culture."

2. Migration

The Royal Commission on Population points out (page 7) that the increase in the population of Europe (from about 140 million in 1750 to about 400 million in 1900) helped "to build up the great system of international trade, international investment, and the development of non-European territories which was such an essential part of the economic history of the Victorian age. European countries, needing food and raw materials for their expanding populations, provided the markets without which the rapid development of North America and the other 'new' countries would not have been worth anybody's while. They also provided by overseas migration the manpower needed for the work of development, and by international investment they provided the necessary equipment. Thus they not only built up their own highly-developed industrial system, but also created a new overseas world mainly inhabited by people of European descent, with European social and political systems and imbued with European culture." In 1750 the population of North America, for example, was little over one million. The present population of over 17 million in Canada and 175 million in the United States are nearly all the descendants of immigrants (plus those who are themselves immigrants). The Economic Committee (page 18) point out that "well over 50 million persons migrated from Europe between 1846 and 1932, about 18 million of them from the British Isles; roughly two-thirds went to the United States, the remainder chiefly to the British Dominions and South America. The huge total figure reflects the fact that the annual flow of migration was sustained at a high rate for many decades. It was not, however, until the age of railways that the movement attained large dimensions. Before 1830, the annual migration to the United States was, for most practical purposes, a mere trickle, contributing little to the growth of American numbers, and still less to the relief of the pressure of numbers in Europe. During the next generation the movement underwent a rapid acceleration which gave it an entirely new significance."

The migration of the nineteenth century, from the Old World to the New, was generally accepted as desirable. It relieved the pressure of numbers in Europe and made possible the development of new countries which supplied Europe with foodstuffs and materials in exchange for her manufactures.

Even so, the new countries felt they could not remain indifferent to the racial origins of their immigrants. The United States and all British Dominions limited the immigration of Chinese and Japanese, and after the 1914–18 war they limited immigration from Eastern and Southern Europe; most of their immigrants had been coming from countries such as Italy, Greece, and Poland. These restrictions were imposed on social grounds; the new countries wished to preserve their existing "way of life." Another argument for them is that an over-populated country should learn to limit its own numbers. Otherwise emigration will give it only temporary relief; its natural increase of population will soon fill the gaps. And why should its emigrants, with their habit of having large families, be permitted to carry the seeds of overpopulation to a country that maintains good standards of living largely by exercising moderation in the numbers of its own births?

During recent years there have been large movements of refugees, after the world war and after the partition of India, but there has been much less voluntary migration than during the years before the 1914–18 war.[1] Migration has been limited by restrictions imposed by countries of immigration on racial or national grounds. The populations of most countries in Western Europe are expanding very slowly or not at all. And the development of most "new" countries has reached a stage where it is not certain that further immigration would be to their advantage. In the words of the Economic Committee (page 19), "as the supply of uncleared land available for settlement became exhausted, and as life became increasingly industrial and urbanized, the idea that it might be desirable to limit the actual rate of immigration began to gain ground alike in the United States and in the British Dominions."

Migration has economic effects on the migrants themselves, on the countries they go to, and on the countries they leave.

The migrants themselves may be disappointed. For example, during the 1930s a number of people who had emigrated from Great Britain returned disillusioned. But this was exceptional, due mainly to the Great Depression. As a rule, the migrants themselves are better off.

[1] Some three million, however, have migrated from East to West Germany.

They can produce more and earn more in the countries to which they go; that is why they move.

Immigration affects some groups favourably and others unfavourably. It tends to raise real estate values; owners of land and buildings gain, while those seeking to buy or rent real estate have to pay more. It benefits the employers of the immigrants, including housewives in so far as the immigrants enter domestic service, and consumers of their products; it may affect adversely those groups of workers with whom the immigrants compete. In some countries, immigrants have tended in the past to enter occupations which local workers do not find agreeable (for example, mining in France) or which are relatively badly paid, while the workers already there have moved up in the occupational scale. When this is the general tendency, immigration is seldom opposed by the workers of the country, except when unemployment is heavy.

The country of immigration is likely to benefit if the immigrants open up new land. Again, there may be unused capacity in the supply of services, such as transport or electricity, or of mass-produced articles (newspapers, for example); such undertakings will be able to sell more (to immigrants) without increasing their fixed capital. Again, immigrants may introduce new skills or new products, including better cooking. On the other hand, they must somehow be provided with housing and other capital which could have been used instead for the benefit of the existing population.

The country of emigration will benefit, at least for a time, by the relief from the pressure of numbers. But the emigrants are likely to be younger, and to include more males, than the average of the population. Emigration is likely, therefore, to increase the proportion of dependants, although some of the latter may receive remittances from their relatives who have migrated. It may be, too, that on the whole the emigrants are more able and enterprising than those who remain; they may be just the people whom the country can least afford to lose.

During the decade 1931–39 there was net immigration into Great Britain, averaging 60,000 a year. Since the war, according to the reports of the Oversea Migration Board, there has been a very slight excess of emigration amounting to an annual average (for 1946–57) of just over 40,000 a year. In 1958 there may have been a very slight excess of immigration. The chief country to which emigrants go (109,000 out of 230,000 in 1957) is Canada; the chief country from which they come is the Irish Republic. Nearly 30,000 immigrants came from the British West Indies in 1956, but since then their numbers have been falling.

3. CHANGES IN POPULATION

I shall now leave migration out of account in order to discuss the economic effects of a growing population and of a declining population.

The former will contain a relatively large proportion of children and the latter a relatively large proportion of old people. The demands for different types of goods and services depend partly on the age-composition of the population: for example, a high proportion of children implies a greater demand for education and for bread, while a high proportion of elderly people implies a greater demand for medical services.

A growing population gives more flexibility in making adjustments to meet changes in technique or in demand. Boys and girls can enter the expanding industries and avoid the contracting ones, whereas in a stationary or declining population some industries can expand rapidly only by drawing workers away from other industries. The following figures, in millions, for Great Britain illustrate this point.

	Year 1881	Year 1931
Occupied Population . .	12·7	19·4
Agriculture	1·6	1·2
Metals, Machinery, etc. .	0·9	2·4

The growth of the working population over these fifty years made it easier for expanding industries and occupations, such as "metals, machinery, etc.," to attract more workers. New entrants to the labour market went where they were most needed. Relatively few had to leave declining industries such as agriculture; as workers in them retired or died, they were not replaced in the same numbers by new entrants.

A growing population makes possible a more rapid application of technical progress. New types of plant, machinery, ships, and so forth can come into use side by side with the old. With a stationary or declining population, it may not pay to scrap assets in good technical condition because improved types have been invented; and the latter may come into use only gradually, as the former wear out. (The question of when it pays to scrap is discussed in Chapter XI.)

Again, a growing population stimulates investment; it provides more opportunities for investment, and it reduces the risks. When the demand for goods and services in general is increasing, owing to the growth of population, the demand for any particular good or service is likely to expand, even if it expands less rapidly than was hoped. If there is relative over-investment in one line, the owners of the assets have only to wait a little and the growth of population will raise demand to a remunerative level.

As a growing population is more favourable both to adjustments and to investment, it is likely to be more favourable to employment.

On the other hand, a growing population requires more houses, schools, and capital of all kinds. The resources devoted to providing this capital might have been used, if numbers were stationary or expanding, to raise the standards of living of the existing population.

The opposite conclusions hold good for a declining population. If it contains a large proportion of middle-aged and elderly people, who are reluctant to change their present occupations or to move to another district, it will be less flexible in meeting changed conditions. The application of technical progress may be retarded. Opportunities for home investment will be less attractive and too little investment combined with too little flexibility may make large-scale unemployment more likely.

On the other hand a smaller population means more assets per head, although some existing assets may become less suitable, or out of date, as time goes on.

Moreover, for a country that, like Great Britain, relies to a considerable extent on foreign trade, there is a presumption in favour of smaller numbers. The world demand for her exports will be much the same whether her population grows or declines, but a smaller population will need less imports and will therefore find it easier to sell the smaller volume of exports required to pay for them.

4. THE POPULATION OF THE UNITED KINGDOM

The population of the United Kingdom (including throughout the area which is now Northern Ireland) increased as follows—

Year	Million
1801	11·6
1821	15·5
1841	20·2
1861	24·5
1881	31·0
1901	38·2
1921	44·0
1941	48·2

In June, 1958, it was 51·7 million (England and Wales, 45·1 million; Scotland, 5·2 million; Northern Ireland, 1·4 million).

It will be noted that the rate of growth slowed down considerably after the turn of the century. This decline in the rate of growth is likely to continue. The estimated future population is 54·0 million in 1968, 56·1 million in 1978, 58·0 million in 1988, and 59·7 million in 1998.[1]

There have been great changes in the average size of family, birth rates, death rates, expectation of life, and the age-composition of the population, over the past hundred years or so.

In Victorian times the typical family was large. Of marriages taking

[1] *Annual Abstract of Statistics*, 1959. These estimates assume a continuous fall in death rates, especially for ages under 45 (for which they are assumed to halve) over the next twenty-five years, after which they remain stable; 855,000 births a year over the next five years, 870,000 during the ensuing ten years, rising gradually to 935,000 in 1998; and a net outward migration of 30,000 persons a year.

place around 1860, over 70 per cent had more than three children, the most common numbers being five, six and seven. During the 1930s, only about 20 per cent of marriages had more than three children, and the most common numbers were one and two. In the 1880s there were over a million births a year. Despite the large growth of population, the number of births remained around that level until early 1920s, and in the 1930s it fell to somewhat over 700,000. At that time, the average number of children per family was about 2·2 : 2·5 for manual workers and 1·7 for non-manual workers. During the post-war years there has been an increase in the number of births, which reached 868,000 in 1958, and in the average size of family; it is expected that the number of births will not remain quite so high; nevertheless it is thought that total population will continue to grow, slowly, instead of declining after a time, as was thought probable when the Royal Commission reported.

There has been a great reduction in death rates, which may be expected to continue for at least the next two or three decades. In the 1870s the annual number of deaths exceeded 600,000; today they are slightly lower, although the total population is nearly twice as large. The fall has been especially marked in the deaths of children under one year: 125,000 in the 1870s and only 20,000 today.

At the death rates of over 100 years ago, out of 1,000 girl babies only 696 would survive to the age of 15 and only 323 to the age of 65. The corresponding figures on 1955 death rates were 971 surviving to 15 and 799 to 65.[1] People are living longer than in the past.

The Victorian population was growing and was relatively youthful. In 1891, 45 per cent of the population was under 20 years of age. In 1947 the corresponding percentage was only 28. By 1958 it had risen to 30; the increase in births since 1942 has created problems of providing more teachers and schools for the growing number of children of school age.

As time goes on, the number of old people in our population (especially women, who live longer than men) is bound to increase, for they have already been born. In 1911 there were somewhat over 2 million persons over 65; in 1958 there were 6 million (60 per cent of whom were women); by 1977 their numbers will reach a peak of over 8 million. All pension funds which provide annuities for persons over a certain age, including the National Insurance Funds, will be paying out to considerably more beneficiaries over the next few decades, but the total numbers contributing will increase only slightly. It may well be desirable to encourage elderly people to continue working, postponing their retirement in accordance with their longer expectation of life.

[1] These figures are for England and Wales only. The corresponding figures for boys were 963 and 678. (*U.N. Demographic Year Book*, 1957, Table 26.)

CHAPTER X

CAPITAL

1. THE DEFINITION OF CAPITAL

ONE of the chief factors affecting the volume of output of any community, however it may be organized, is the amount of *capital* that it possesses. The average worker in the United States or Great Britain produces so much more than the average worker in an under-developed country largely because he is assisted by so much more capital. The marked upward trend of output per head in the Western world over the past hundred and fifty years or more has been due largely to technical progress and the expansion of world trade, but another very important factor has been that capital has increased faster than population. How can Great Britain, a small island on the fringe of Western Europe, support fifty million people at one of the highest average standards of living in the world? Partly because of the skill of her technicians and other workers. But we live in the machine age; in many fields the machines do the work and need only competent supervision. The main reason is her plant and machinery, her railways and ships and power stations—in a word, her capital.

Many illustrations could be given of the great extent to which power-driven machinery increases the productivity of labour. I confine myself to one, which will be familiar to all. One driver, with a lorry, can transport, say, three tons of goods for, say, thirty miles in one hour. It would take one hundred and twenty men, each carrying half a hundredweight, to achieve this result with their unaided human efforts, and it would take them ten or perhaps twenty hours instead of one. But the driver needs a lorry, and petrol, and roads—all these are capital.

To the individual, stocks and shares and his bank deposit and other titles to property may all form part of his capital. But not to the community. Such pieces of paper are merely evidences of indebtedness; whatever A is owed by B, B owes to A, and for the community as a whole (apart from debts owed to it by other countries) such debts cancel out. It is "real" capital, physical assets, not pieces of paper, which help to produce a larger volume of output.

What should we include in "capital"; that is to say, in "real" capital? Factories, warehouses, offices, shops, and other buildings used in industry and trade; plant and machinery and equipment;

means of transport and communication. These are sometimes called *fixed capital*. They include publicly-owned property, such as Government buildings. We must not forget *working capital* or *circulating capital*— raw materials, fuel, goods in process of manufacture, stocks held by producers or traders. Working capital is needed just as much as fixed capital in order to carry out the task of providing people with the goods and services they want.

What about land? I discussed this question in Chapter VII, Section 2. Investment in improving the productivity of land is just as important as investment in machinery; and it would puzzle a railway company or a dock company to separate its land from its other physical assets. For some problems, for example problems connected with site values or taxation, we may try to treat land as separate from other assets, but for other purposes we may just as well include it in capital.

What about consumers' goods in the hands of consumers? The argument for excluding them from the concept of capital is presumably that they will make no contribution to output; that they *are* the output, and that the process of production, so far as they are concerned, is completed. But this is not really true. Consider, for example, a dwelling-house. The house goes on contributing to output throughout its life, for as long as it is used. It provides the service of housing; it gives accommodation, shelter, warmth, shade, and all the other amenities of housing. The more houses a community has, the more fully will it be able to satisfy its wants for housing over the future. What matters is the number and size and quality of its houses; they provide just the same housing whether they happen to be owned by a real estate company, which rents them and counts them as its business capital, or whether they happen to be owned by the people who live in them. Why not, therefore, include all houses in the capital of the community? The same reasoning applies to other more or less durable consumers' goods such as motor-cars, yachts, television sets, furniture, refrigerators, even clothes. They all yield their services over the whole of their lives, until they are scrapped. For some purposes, notably in calculating his business expenses, we may have to class a man's motor-car as capital when he uses it for business purposes, but not when he uses it for pleasure, but from the standpoint of the community it is surely much simpler to class all motor-cars as capital. The same argument applies even to stocks of food and other more or less perishable goods. Consumers, like factories and shops, hold stocks of such goods to avoid the trouble of making very frequent purchases of small amounts and as a reserve against possible contingencies. If a country is stock-piling food against the danger of war, stocks held in private homes are as relevant as stocks held in warehouses; what matters is how much food there is in the country as a whole.

We have, then, five categories of "real" capital (as distinct from paper titles, which are capital to an individual or a firm) between which it may be necessary for some purposes to try to distinguish. They are: fixed capital used in industry and trade; circulating capital used in industry and trade; land; durable consumers' goods in the hands of consumers; other consumers' goods in the hands of consumers. I have argued that from the standpoint of the community as a whole there is no need to draw a line, which in border-line cases would be very difficult to draw, between these different categories, and that we can include them all in the national capital or, as it is often called, the *national wealth*. We can include them all because they all contribute, in one way or another, to future output and the future satisfaction of wants.

A house or a machine produced in 1950 formed part of the national output of 1950. From the moment it came into existence, it contributed (except for any periods when it was "unemployed") to current output; if it is still being used, it is still contributing to current output; and at any moment during its life it forms part of the capital of the country. All our present capital (apart from any original gifts of nature) formed part of the output of some former years. It is a heritage from the past. It is output which has not yet been used up, discarded, consumed. The *capital formation* or *investment* or *saving* of a community during any year is its output during that year minus its consumption during that year.

The capital of a community is all its physical assets or possessions measured at a given moment of time. It is a stock, an inventory, a fund, in contrast to output or income, which is a flow over time—so much per week or per month or per year.

It is difficult to make an estimate of national capital or national wealth. On what basis are we to value assets which seldom or never change hands, such as a naval dockyard or the roads of the country or the physical assets of Imperial Chemical Industries? And the same physical assets may become worth much more or much less almost overnight owing to some change, such as a change in the prices of their products, which increases or reduces their probable future earnings.

Nevertheless it is of some interest, provided we bear these warnings in mind, to make the attempt. Where the direct valuation of assets is not possible, they can be valued indirectly, if they are private income-yielding property, by multiplying the net income which they are yielding by a figure representing the number of years' purchase that a buyer might give for them.

Mr. H. Campion, in his book *Public and Private Property in Great Britain*, has made an estimate of the physical assets in Great Britain around 1932–34. Any such estimate should relate to a definite date, but owing to the difficulty of getting data no definite date is given, and each figure is subject to a margin of error.

Private	£ million
Land	620
Farmers' capital	410
Houses and buildings . . .	4,600
Railways	760
Capital of industry, transport, commerce, and finance . .	7,825
Furniture and movable property .	725
	14,940
Public	
Land and buildings	620
Other property	1,480
	2,100

This estimate illustrates the practical difficulty of separating land from capital. The item "farmers' capital" includes land and farm buildings, as well as agricultural machinery and livestock; the item "houses and buildings" (which is largely dwelling-houses) includes the land on which they are built; and the land and buildings of some undertakings (for example, mines and railways) are included under other headings and not under "land" or "houses and buildings."

We should add probably well over £1,000 million for roads and armaments, which Mr. Campion excluded because there was no good method of valuing them.

This gives us a total of over £18 million for physical assets, including land, in Great Britain around 1932–34. The "real" capital in Great Britain is now substantially greater than it was then and the prices of most assets are much higher. The money value today is probably well over £50 milliard.

This guess is confirmed by more recent estimates by Mr. Philip Redfern, published in the *Journal of the Royal Statistical Society* in 1955 (Series A, Volume 118, Part 2). He estimated the net fixed capital at the end of 1953 in certain types of assets in £ milliard at 1948 prices, as follows: Housing 10·2, Other Buildings and Works 7·5, Plant and Machinery 5·1, Vehicles and Ships 1·6.

Since 1932–34, railways and coalmines and other undertakings have been nationalized. Today publicly-owned property may amount to some 20 per cent of the total.

We should take account also of capital owned overseas by the British Government and by residents of Great Britain, and of debts due by Great Britain to other countries. Since the war, she is no longer a leading creditor nation. The best indication available of her present position is that in 1958 her balance of payments showed a credit of £338 million and a debit of £285 million—a net credit of only £53 million—on "interest, profits, and dividends."

2. CAPITAL FORMATION

The amount which a community adds to its capital during a period is known as the amount of its *investment* or *capital formation* during that period.

Any community, however organized, will have some capital; and the more it has, the greater will be the volume of its output. This applies equally to a "capitalist" country, such as Great Britain, and to a "non-capitalist" country, such as Soviet Russia. The distinction between the two types of social organization rests on the ownership and control of capital, and not on the part which it plays in production.

The kernel of Keynes's theory is that decisions to save and decisions to invest are made largely by different people and for different reasons. If people try to save more than is being spent on new investment, there will be a fall in aggregate money spending which is likely to cause unemployment. If people are spending more (with the aid of bank credit) on new investment than the amount of planned saving, there will be a rise in aggregate money spending which is likely to cause inflation.

This disharmony, however, can arise only under capitalism. I therefore reserve it for discussion later. When decisions to save and decisions to invest are one and the same decisions, made by the same people, there can be no such problem. In order, therefore, to bring out some general points, which apply to any community, about the formation and maintenance and consumption of capital, let us consider a small community which takes group decisions.

Suppose they want more fish and they know that if they had more boats they could catch more fish. How can they get more boats?

Of course somebody might give them more boats (for example, under the United States International Co-operation Administration or under the Colombo Plan) or somebody might lend them the money to buy boats, or they might export some of their output and import boats in exchange. But these "solutions" only pass the problem on to somebody else or, by introducing foreign trade, push it one stage further back. So let us suppose they are isolated, on an island.

Isolated, they can get more boats only by building them. Capital formation for them means constructing the capital goods they need. Nobody else can do it for them. Nor will "saving" or "abstinence" or "waiting," as such, give them the boats. If they want the boats they must build them, and that is that.

But what arrangements can they make to build themselves more boats?

If they felt like it, they could simply work longer hours, devoting the extra time to boat-building. This would mean a sacrifice of their leisure. If they did not wish, for the time being, to give up some of their leisure, only three broad courses would be open to them.

The first course would be to store some of the food, clothing, and other consumers' goods which they produce. Suppose that after eleven months they had stored enough to provide them with supplies for a further month. During that month they could all set to work to produce boats instead of consumers' goods.

The second course would be for them all to devote part of each working day to the production of boats. If, for example, they worked twelve hours a day and devoted one of these twelve hours to building boats, they would have as many boats at the end of a year as under the first plan.

The third course would be to arrange for some of their number, say one-twelfth, to work only at boat-building, the others supplying them from day to day with consumers' goods. This plan is the one which corresponds to actual practice. It has the advantage of enabling some men to specialize in the art of boat-building, and it avoids the necessity of keeping large stores of food.

Under any of these courses, the community, for the time being, would produce and consume fewer consumers' goods than before. Labour, and other factors of production, which might have been employed in the direct production of consumers' goods would be employed instead in producing boats. This labour has, as its ultimate object, an increase in the output of fish. It does not achieve this object until a considerable time has elapsed. In the first place, it takes time to build a boat. In the second place, the boat lasts for some time. Thus the fruits of the labour employed in building a boat are the increased supplies of fish obtained, owing to the use of the boat, during the life of the boat. The average length of time between the "input" of this labour and its final "output" may be considerable. Clearly the part played by capital derives its importance from the fact that production takes time. If consumers' goods were all produced instantaneously, without any preliminary work in producing instruments of production, raw materials, and so on, and if no consumption goods were durable, like houses, there would be no possibility of increasing output by adopting methods of production that involve the use of more capital.

In the last resort, all capital may be regarded as the product of labour and land. I include land because at any rate the raw materials—the wood, in the case of a boat—probably require land for their production. Tools, themselves capital, may be used to produce capital goods, but the tools themselves are the product of labour and land. But to increase the amount of capital—in the sense of the stock of goods in existence—requires what is usually called "waiting." It involves a renunciation, for the time being, of consumption. Some people consume less than they could in order that capital may be produced.

The incentive to "wait," in this sense, is that output can be increased by the use of more "capitalistic" or "roundabout" methods of production: that is, of methods involving the use of more capital. Of course, not all roundabout methods are more productive than direct methods, but people choose only those which are. If, for example, the boats built by our imaginary community were to take a year to build and were to last for five years, a considerably greater output of fish might be obtained over those six years by constructing and using the boats than by using the same factors of production to catch fish without the aid of boats.

3. MAINTAINING CAPITAL INTACT

Suppose that the boats of our hypothetical community have a life of five years, after which they are of no use. If our community, having obtained the boats, made no provision for replacing them, at the end of five years they would be back where they began, boatless, and would have to begin the cycle all over again if they still thought that the extra fish were worth the requisite amount of "waiting." But if they wished to maintain a constant output of fish, they would make provision, during these five years, for replacing the boats by new ones immediately they had worn out. Instead of using all the available labour, and other factors, during those five years, to produce consumers' goods, they would employ some in boat-building, so that they would always have the same number of boats in good condition, old ones being replaced by new ones immediately they wore out. This is termed 'maintaining capital intact."

This concept, however, presents difficulties if applied to a period over which there are changes in tastes or technique or external conditions. Suppose that all the members of our community changed their preferences in favour of meat as against fish. In order to maintain their capital intact they would have to divert some factors from the task of replacing boats to the task of increasing the equipment required to produce meat. Suppose, again, that an improvement in knowledge or in external conditions—say, the discovery of new fishing-grounds or an immigration of fish—enabled more fish to be caught per man. Capital could be maintained intact by maintaining a smaller number of boats, yielding the same output of fish as before. In general, capital is maintained intact if—given the co-operating factors—the output of consumers' goods which it helps to produce in any period is regarded by consumers as yielding them equivalent satisfaction to that yielded by the output of the preceding period.

4. CAPITAL CONSUMPTION

Suppose that our community suddenly decided—because, for example, it believed that the end of the world was at hand—to cease bothering about the future. It could considerably raise its standard of living by diverting labour and other factors away from making repairs and renewals and replacements of existing capital, and towards more direct methods of producing consumers' goods. Of course, this higher standard of living could not be maintained for long. Worn-out plant and equipment would not be replaced, buildings would not be kept in good repair, stocks of goods held in reserve would diminish, and the growing shortage of capital would reduce the output of consumers' goods. The community would be constrained to return to more and more primitive methods of production, and, if it persisted in consuming its capital, it would be reduced in the end to an extremely low standard of living. But in the short run it could increase its output of consumers' goods, and therefore its standard of living, by employing more of its factors on the direct production of consumers' goods (with the aid of existing capital, as long as it lasted) instead of maintaining or increasing its capital. This process is known as *capital consumption.* During a war, a country may be constrained to consume some of its capital by diverting factors from such occupations as erecting and repairing buildings to the more urgent task of trying to win the war. It has been estimated that during the last war such "under-maintenance" of capital in Great Britain amounted to some £3 milliard.

Apart from any deliberate decision to consume capital, some assets may be destroyed or damaged by forces such as earthquakes, storms, fires, and floods, or by enemy action during a war. The ordinary operations of mining involve a depletion of capital. The country is the poorer by the minerals that have been taken out of its earth. This is a problem which worries South Africa: what will she do when the gold-mines which provide her with a substantial part of her income have been worked out?

The *net* investment, or capital formation, which took place within the borders of a country over a period, is measured by the value of all the physical assets, including land, within the country at the end of the period, minus their value at the beginning of the period. (If we wish to measure the net investment of the residents of a country, we must include also changes in the amount of their foreign investment or foreign indebtedness.) This measure covers all that has taken place during the period by way of gross capital formation, depreciation, under-maintenance, and consumption (or loss) of capital. But it should be corrected—how, and to what extent, is a problem which economists and accountants are still discussing—if there have been significant changes in the price level of assets over the period.

5. CONCLUSIONS

Before setting out or repeating conclusions about capital I must add some further observations in order to make the framework of the discussion more realistic.

The modern world is much more complex than our imaginary island. Most goods are produced, at any rate in Western countries, by highly capitalistic methods. The great bulk of all the goods existing at any given moment are producers' goods and not consumers' goods. By far the greater part of the productive activity which is going on at any time will not come to final fruition for months or even years. For example, cotton goods are in part the final product of the labour employed in mining the coal to smelt the iron which made the spindles, and so on.

I took as an illustration the building of boats to catch more fish. Of course there are many different consumers' goods; the community must somehow decide how far it wishes to increase the output of some of them rather than of others. In this context "goods" include services, such as housing and education.

The application of more capitalistic methods to the production of fish need not involve a corresponding increase in the output of fish. Factors of production formerly employed in producing fish can be set free for other tasks; less labour and other resources, employed in a more capitalistic way, can produce the same output of fish as before. The same applies, of course, to any other good.

Further, the state of technical knowledge often permits a choice between a whole range of methods of producing any given commodity or service. One method is more capitalistic and more productive than another, a third is still more capitalistic and still more productive, and so on. It is not just a question of boats or no boats, for example; boats may be made more or less durable, or may be equipped with motors.

Another point is that the work of maintaining capital intact includes repairs and replacements of parts. Readers may recall the American story of the wonderful one-hoss shay. It is always some particular part that gives way first, said the owner. I will take care that this does not happen with this shay. Every part will be perfect. And the shay continued in perfect condition, without any repairs, year after year until one fine day it collapsed, every part of it, all at once, and disintegrated into dust. I assumed for simplicity that something like that happened to the boats on our imaginary island. In fact, of course, most capital assets need frequent repairs—the older they get, the more repairs they need, until the question arises (even if no better types have been invented) whether it would not pay to scrap them and replace them by new ones.

F

A modern country specializes on certain goods for export. Hence we cannot measure the amount of its gross capital formation, as we could if it were isolated, by the amount of capital goods which it produces. For example, Great Britain exports engineering products in exchange for food, and the countries which supply the food do the opposite, acquiring capital goods (such as engineering products) in exchange for consumers' goods (such as food). It will be remembered, too, that from the standpoint of the citizens of a country we must take account of their foreign investment or indebtedness as well as of the investment within the borders of the country itself.

I can now set out five conclusions.

The first conclusion is that capital augments the future output of consumers' goods and services, thereby enabling a community to satisfy its wants more fully. This is clear enough for consumers' capital, such as houses and furniture, which contribute directly to the satisfaction of wants. The contribution of capital assets such as machinery is indirect. People want the consumers' goods which the machines (or their products) help to produce, and not the machines for their own sake; but the more of such capital they have, the more consumers' goods they can produce. We should not forget to include stocks of goods in "capital." These stocks are a necessary element in the productive process. They must be carried mainly because of unforeseen contingencies. For example, a manufacturer may receive an unexpected rush order, and therefore carries stocks of his finished product. He may not be able to secure all the raw materials he wants every day, and therefore carries a stock of them. These stocks form part of his capital. Again, production takes time; assets such as houses or ships under construction should not be omitted when making an inventory of the capital of the community at any moment. Nor should what is sometimes called *social capital*, such as schools and hospitals.

The second conclusion is that capital formation involves "waiting" : a sacrifice, by somebody, of consumers' goods that could have been produced instead.

The third conclusion, or rather definition, is that net investment over a period is measured by the value of all assets at the end of the period, less the value of all assets at the beginning of the period.

The qualifications to the second and third conclusions were given earlier.

The fourth conclusion is that somehow or other a community must choose the content of its capital formation. It cannot have all the extra capital it would like. Much of its labour and other resources must be employed in maintaining a flow of consumers' goods to provide certain minimum standards of living and only a part can be spared to construct new assets (or to produce exports to be exchanged for new assets). What forms should its new investment take? Irrigation schemes, electricity projects, new factories, new houses, new schools, new hospitals? It cannot have everything; which shall it choose?

In any country the choice of how much to invest in "social capital" is made mainly by the Government. In other fields the choice is determined largely by the rate of interest; even under central planning, with no private income from property, a notional rate of interest would be needed in order to help the planning authority to decide to which project to give priority. I will discuss this later, when we come to the subject of the rate of interest.

Finally, we should remember that there are other methods of making provision for the future, apart from increasing the stock of capital. Factors of production can be used to increase the productive capacities of human beings, by educating and training them or by improving their health and physique. Further, factors of production can be devoted to promoting the progress of technical knowledge; for example, by means of research. These two methods are alternatives to increasing capital, and they, too, involve "waiting."

CHAPTER XI

TECHNICAL PROGRESS

1. The Industrial Revolution and After

THE past two hundred years, and especially the past two or three generations, have witnessed a striking and quite unprecedented expansion of economic activity. The preceding five chapters have discussed some of the forces behind this expansion: the development of specialization, especially as a result of improvements in transport, which widened the extent of the market and made economies of large-scale production possible; the growth of capital; and the part played by changes in population. One very important force, however, has not yet been explicitly discussed. It is the march of science and invention, and the application of technical progress in engineering, agriculture, and indeed every field of economic activity.

The population of the world has increased from less than 750 million in 1750 to about 1,600 million in 1900, and some 2,900 million today. Great cities have arisen, continents have been opened up by road and rail, power-driven machinery has enormously expanded both the range and the volume of output. Although the growth of capital and of specialization played an essential part in this vast expansion, it was made possible only by the continuous growth of technical knowledge.

Whether an increase in population, without any improvement in standards of living, should be termed economic progress is a matter of opinion. In fact, the growth of population has been accompanied in Western countries by a marked upward trend in standards of living.

It is not possible to measure the extent of this improvement, partly because there are no reliable statistics for the earlier years and partly because there have been such big changes in the kinds of goods and services consumed. But contemporary accounts show plainly that even a hundred years ago many British families, and especially those of farm labourers, lived in great poverty, being at times on the verge of starvation. There is no doubt that the present-day worker enjoys a far higher standard of food, housing, and clothing, and far greater facilities for medical treatment, instruction, travel, and amusement. Since 1880 real wages in Great Britain have at least doubled.

We can measure the fall in death rates. In the first half of the nineteenth century about a quarter of all babies born in Great Britain used to die before they reached the age of five. Today the corresponding proportion is about five per cent, and the expectation of life for all age-groups has been considerably lengthened.

We can measure also the length of the working week. British factory and building workers worked for over sixty hours a week less than a hundred years ago; in 1913 most of them worked for fifty-four hours; today they work for forty-eight or less, the average being about 46 (for all workers) including overtime (48 for men).

A number of important inventions, including the steam-engine and the "spinning jenny," were made and applied to industry during the latter half of the eighteenth century in Great Britain. The modern era of industrialization had its beginnings in this "industrial revolution." It should be noted, however, that technical progress in agriculture was essential for any great expansion of manufacturing and other non-agricultural activities; that industrialization was slow in getting under way and is still most marked in Western countries; and that technical progress and economic development are very live forces today: the industrial revolution is still going on.

Nothing approaching industrialization on the modern scale could have taken place without improvements in the technique of agriculture. The basic need of mankind is food. So long as one man's labour on the land provided food for little more than one family, the great majority of the population had to be engaged in agriculture—as they still are, in most under-developed countries. They could not be spared for other occupations; the most urgent want, the want for a certain minimum amount of food, had to be satisfied first.

In Great Britain, many important improvements in the art of agriculture paved the way for the industrial revolution. The old open-field system was swept away, the rotation of crops was introduced, new methods of breeding and feeding livestock greatly raised output. It is true that the transition of Great Britain from a mainly agricultural to a mainly industrial country did not take place until the railway age provided her with cheap food from overseas. But in the overseas countries themselves continuous improvements in agriculture have enabled one man to produce enough for several families. Only a small proportion of the people of the United States are engaged in farming and nearly half the people of Australia live in the six capital cities. The development of agricultural machinery, which greatly raises output per worker provided there is enough land per worker, has been especially important over the past thirty years; today British agriculture and agriculture in the "new" countries is fairly fully mechanized.

The pace of the industrial revolution was at first very slow. James Watt invented his steam-engine in 1776 and the rotary movement, which enabled machinery of all kinds to be driven by steam, in 1783, but in 1800 there were only 289 steam-engines in the whole of England. Except in the cotton industry, factory production did not become at all general until about 1840 or 1850 in Great Britain, and later still in other countries.

The industrial revolution is often said to have been based on coal and iron. A few figures will show how slow the rate of progress was at first, compared with modern times. The world output of coal rose from a mere 12 million tons in 1800 to 45 million in 1849, 500 million in 1890, and 1,200 million in 1913. But coal is no longer a good indicator; oil and electricity (generated, increasingly, from water power) have partly taken its place. The world output of crude petroleum has increased from 50 million tons in 1913 to about 1,000 million tons today. The world output of electrical energy has quadrupled over the past twenty years and is now about 2,000 milliard kilowatt-hours a year. The world output of pig-iron increased from less than 200,000 tons in 1800 to some 10 million in 1870 and 40 million in 1900. Steel is now a better indicator. Owing to the greater use of scrap as a substitute for pig-iron, the world output of steel began to exceed that of pig-iron soon after 1900 and is today over 300 million tons a year.

Why did industrialization get under way so slowly? In general, because the widespread application of new inventions and other advances in technical knowledge required the movement of workers, mainly towards the coalfields, the training of workers in new skills and new methods, the saving and investment of capital, and the expansion of markets. All this took time.

In a number of countries most workers were bound to the soil, under some form of serfdom, until the nineteenth century was well advanced. In Great Britain they were free to move, but many were reluctant to migrate to the north of England (for the bulk of the population was in the south) and enter the factories. In the early years, Irish immigrants formed a considerable proportion of the factory hands.

Workers had to be trained, especially to make, repair, and use the new machines. The early steam-engines and machines were made largely by hand. They were very defective and were often breaking down. It was not until after about 1825 that important inventions of machine tools began to revolutionize the machine-making industry, enabling accurate and reliable machines to be turned out in large numbers.

Standards of living were so low that there was not much margin for saving. And in most countries there were obstacles, more or less formidable, to the investment of capital. These took the form of laws and regulations imposed in what were thought to be the national interests or, in some instances, in order to provide monopoly profits for the rulers and their friends.

The full utilization of improved technique in one field often had to await improvements in other fields. Decades passed before the power loom enabled the output of cloth to keep pace with the potential increase in yarn production due to improvements in carding and spinning, and still more decades passed before comparable improvements were made in the finishing processes. Moreover, the growth of machinery was partly dependent on the progress of technique in coalmining and in smelting and working iron.

Perhaps the most important obstacle of all was the high cost of transport. In the eighteenth century only quite valuable commodities were worth moving any great distance, especially by land. Improvements were made by Macadam and others in the roads, canals were built, and rivers were made more navigable, but the really big change came with the building of railways. The Stockton and Darlington railway, the first public railway to use steam locomotion and carry passengers, was opened in 1825, but the nineteenth century was half over before Great Britain had a network of railway lines covering most of her area, and in other leading countries this development came still later. The spread of railways, and continuous improvements in the technique of shipbuilding, created a world market towards the close of the nineteenth century.

The growth of trade, and therefore of specialization and large-scale production, was also helped by the general movement towards free trade. Many of the tariffs and tolls which had impeded the movement of goods, and had acted in effect as additional costs of transport, were removed or reduced.

Today there is a great contrast between Western countries, such as Great Britain and the United States, and under-developed countries, such as India and China. The latter have much lower standards of living than the former; their death rates, especially among babies and young children, are high; and their populations are engaged mainly in agriculture. In many ways they resemble Great Britain before the industrial revolution. In order to industrialize themselves they need a great deal of capital, and their workers must be trained. They have the advantages, over pre-industrial Great Britain, of access to the technical knowledge of the West and of a world market. On the other hand, many of them are overpopulated.

Of course, technical progress did not suddenly stop about 1800. On the contrary, it has continued with growing strength. We have harnessed new sources of power: the internal combustion engine, electrical energy, and tomorrow, maybe, the forces in the atom. We have opened up the world with railways, ships, motor vehicles, and aeroplanes; we have provided rapid means of communication by telegraph, telephone, and radio. Scientists, engineers, and others have made countless improvements in every field of economic activity. Large new industries have come into being during the present century, with the development of products such as the motor vehicle, petroleum, rubber, the film, the aeroplane, radio, synthetic fibres, plastics, and synthetic chemicals and drugs.

We should not think of technical progress as applying only to agriculture and manufacturing and transport. Inventions in other spheres are also important. For example, the use of cheques, the device of limited liability, and improvements in cost accounting have all assisted the expansion of industry and trade. Again, the continuous growth of medical knowledge has considerably increased the efficiency of the working population.

Today more persons than ever before, mostly employed by large firms or Governments, are engaged in every type of research. Every year many thousands of inventions are made and applied throughout the various fields of economic activity. Any particular invention, taken by itself, may seem of minor importance, but taken together they continuously transform and improve methods of production or bring new products on to the market. In the late 1920s the United States had a national product so large that it was a main subject of current economic discussion. Today her national product is more than twice as large in volume as it was then, due mainly to technical progress, although partly to the growth of capital. Nearly every year, owing mainly to technical progress, output per worker in Western countries increases by some two per cent or more.

There are many threats to economic progress. A war on the modern scale would be a disaster. Slumps may bring heavy unemployment. Some countries may find it difficult to cope with their growing populations. The tendency for organized groups of workers, including farmers, to demand money incomes increasing at a rate greater than their productivity may give rise to continuous inflation. The forces of economic nationalism may impose increasing barriers to world trade. But there is one powerful force working constantly towards a greater output per head and ever-rising standards of living. It is the march of science and invention; in technical progress lies the economic hope of mankind.

2. Technical Progress and Unemployment

The industrial revolution was largely the substitution of machinery for labour. Tasks which used to be performed by hand, with the aid of simple tools or machines, were performed instead by more elaborate machines. And this process of replacing labour by machinery, or other forms of capital, has continued and is still going on. Agricultural machinery enables a crop to be harvested with far fewer workers. Mechanical devices for loading and unloading ships greatly reduce the number of dock workers needed for each ton of cargo. An excavator can scoop out half a ton of earth at a time and dump it sixty feet away, thus replacing some forty labourers equipped with shovels. Calculating machines and other office machinery enable a much smaller staff of clerks and book-keepers to do the same work as before. We constantly read news items such as this (from the *Economist*, 23rd May, 1953, page 514):

"The Ford Motor Company has just opened in Cleveland what is described as the first automatic factory in the automotive industry, where, it is claimed, electronic devices enable 250 men to turn out twice as many engines as 2,500 men could make in a factory of the older type."

There is clearly a danger that any such change will throw some workers out of employment. In the early years of the nineteenth century in Great Britain, the Luddites rioted and destroyed machinery for this reason, and since then workers in various countries have at times opposed the introduction of labour-saving devices for fear that they would lose their jobs.

Not all inventions, by any means, are labour-saving. Many of them increase the efficiency of plant and equipment, so that less capital is needed for a given output; they are capital-saving inventions. But they too may cause unemployment. For example, improvements in the construction of boilers have reduced the amount of coal required for a boiler; they might have caused unemployment among coal-miners. Again, recent developments in the electrolytic process have enabled tin-plate to be made with only about half the former coating of tin; they might have thrown tin-miners and tin-plate workers out of work. In the same way, higher-yielding varieties of crops or livestock mean that less labour is needed for a given output, and may therefore cause unemployment.

In fact, however, there have been very few instances of severe and prolonged unemployment due to technical progress. The growth of industrialization has been accompanied, on the whole, by a continuous growth in total employment. For example, today the working population of Great Britain is twenty-four million, as compared with perhaps five million in 1800, yet we have very full employment. Some writers argued that the heavy unemployment of the 1930s in the United States was due largely to technical progress. They called it "technological unemployment" and said that it was due to the drying-up of investment opportunities. But since the war the volume of employment in the United States has been greater than ever before. It is obvious that there are plenty of investment opportunities in the United States, let alone in the rest of the world; and nowadays the unemployment of the 1930s is generally attributed to causes other than technical progress.

In some industries technical progress has increased total employment. It has reduced costs and the prices of the products; far more of the products have been demanded than before; employment has increased in the industries themselves. A conspicuous illustration of this is the motor-car industry, which now employs far more workers than it did before the conveyer-belt and mass production brought down the prices of cars. Labour-saving devices have been especially numerous and important in the engineering industries, yet in Great Britain employment in the engineering industries has expanded, and is still expanding, at a faster rate than the total working population. The transport industries have progressively substituted capital for labour, yet today they employ many times more workers than in the days of the stage-coach, the sailing ship, and the canal barge. The lower charges for transport made possible by continuous technical progress have greatly increased the demand for it.

Very often, however, total employment in an industry is reduced, at any rate for a time, by greater mechanization or other technical improvements. Some workers are thrown out of employment for the moment. But there is no fundamental reason why they should not find work elsewhere. It is utterly wrong to suppose that there is only a fixed amount of work to go round, and that if machines do more of it, there is less to be done by labour. Fewer workers are needed, owing to technical progress, for a given output. But the total output required is by no means "given"; on the contrary, it is far greater than is likely to be attained in the foreseeable future, if ever. For the wants of mankind are practically unlimited. Even in a wealthy country, such as the United States, there is much poverty. We could nearly all consume far more than we do; maybe not larger quantities of food, but more expensive kinds of food, more and better clothes, better housing. As real incomes increase, there is a tendency to spend more of them on manufactures and then on services of all kinds, including medical services, education, travel, and sport and amusement. If people spend a smaller total sum on one product, because technical progress has reduced its price or has shown them how to make less of it go further, they will have more money to spend on other products, including the new ones which are constantly appearing on the market.

The problem of avoiding "technological unemployment" is partly a problem of maintaining the total flow of spending, including expenditure on new investment. If a considerable number of workers are dismissed, they will have less to spend, and unless total monetary demand is maintained their reduced spending may start a cumulative increase in unemployment. The problem is also partly one of the mobility of labour. The workers who are thrown out of employment may have to change their occupations, as well as their industries, and perhaps to move to another district, in order to find new jobs. These adjustments will be easier to make when the total population is growing fairly fast than when it is nearly stationary or declining.

Whether technical progress should be rejected because it may be accompanied by unemployment is a matter of opinion. My own view is that we should take the fullest advantage of technical progress, which may double output per head in the course of one or two generations, while making every effort to maintain employment. For a country which relies, as Great Britain does, on international trade, there is virtually no choice. She must keep in the forefront of technical progress or she will not be able to sell her exports. Her unemployment is likely to increase, rather than to diminish, if she fails to adopt improved methods of production.

3. Technical Progress and Obsolescence

Inventions often show how an improved type of machine, or other asset, can perform the same task more efficiently and therefore more cheaply. This reduces the value of existing assets of the old type. They earn less than before because the improved types can produce more cheaply, and the prices of the products therefore tend to fall.

All technical progress causes some loss to somebody. Artificial fertilizers reduced the earnings of the nitrate mines of Chile, nylon adversely affected the silk industry, improvements in road transport tend to reduce the earnings of railways, television hits the cinemas. That is no reason for refusing to adopt improved methods or products. The object of economic activity is not to maintain the incomes of the present owners of assets, even if those owners happen to be Governments, but to satisfy the wants of the people as fully as possible.

The problem for a community is how to make the best use of its labour and other resources. If constructing and using a new type of asset will give a larger output than any alternative course, why not construct it and use it? It may reduce the earnings of some existing assets, as the railways reduced the earnings of canals in Great Britain, but what of it? What the existing assets cost to construct is a "bygone" which does not affect the argument in the least. The problem is entirely a forward-looking problem: given the resources of the community, including the existing assets, what are the most fruitful forms for new investment to take?

Under a system of free enterprise, A will not be deterred from installing and using improved types of machines because he will thereby reduce the income of B, who owns machines of the old type. But B is then faced with the problem of what to do. Should he go on using his present machines as long as they will last? Should he scrap them at once and replace them by the improved types? And a central planning committee, controlling all new investment, is constantly confronted with this type of question.

I have found that students of economics, beginners, are divided in their views. Some are all in favour of scrapping everything that might be considered obsolete. "We must modernize our industries," they say. "We must adopt the most up-to-date and efficient techniques. Just look at the date on that engine! Eighteen eighty something! What is this? A museum? It should have been scrapped long ago. Away with it!" Others are more conservative. "If an asset is working well, surely it would be wasteful to scrap it! Why discard something which is giving good service just because something a little better has been invented? We have not the capital, not by a long chalk, to modernize everything. Why not introduce improved types gradually and still go on using the old, until they wear out?"

There is a precise answer to this type of problem.[1] It is this. An asset should be scrapped and replaced by an improved type provided that two conditions are fulfilled. The first condition is that the total cost of production (excluding interest on the capital invested) with the improved type should be less than the prime cost (the running cost, or operating cost, excluding depreciation and other capital charges) with the existing asset. The second condition is that the rate of return on the capital invested in the improved type should be at least as high as could be obtained by making some alternative investment.

Let us take a simplified example, using "labour" to stand for factors of production of all types. Suppose that the asset is a machine in perfect working condition and that its scrap value is nil. Suppose that it can produce its output (including current repairs but no reserves against depreciation) with 2,000 labour units a year. An improved type is invented which could produce the same output with 1,000 labour units a year. Should it be constructed to replace the present one?

We cannot answer this question without knowing how much the improved type will cost to construct and how much must be set aside as a depreciation reserve to replace it when it is worn out. Suppose it costs 5,000 labour units to construct and that 500 units a year are needed for depreciation.

Our first condition is fulfilled. The total costs of the improved type, 1,500 units a year, are less than the prime costs, 2,000 units a year, of the present asset. In other words, 6,000 labour units could operate and provide for replacement of four new-type machines, whereas the same number of labour units, 6,000, are needed merely to operate three old-type machines. Therefore it appears wasteful to use labour on the latter. It appears better to scrap them and get a third more output from the same labour by constructing and using machines of the improved type.

But this is not conclusive. What about our second condition? Only a limited amount of capital is available for investment. How can it

[1] Compare Chapter VII, Section 6.

best be used? The improved type of machine shows a saving, as compared with present methods, of 500 a year on an outlay of 5,000—a return of 10 per cent on the capital invested. Are there other investments which would yield a return of more than 10 per cent? If so, they should be given preference—the best is the enemy of the good. If not, then our second condition also is fulfilled. The existing machines should be scrapped and replaced forthwith by machines of the improved type.

It seldom happens in practice that an improved type of asset is so much more efficient that it pays to scrap all the old types forthwith and replace them with the new types. Under private enterprise, the course of events may be something like this. Some firms will install some of the new types at once. They will take account of the probability that, owing to increased output (new types and old existing side by side, although maybe under different ownership), the prices of the products may fall. Nevertheless they expect to make at least the current rate of profit on their investment, so they go ahead. The prices of the products do fall. The owners of the old assets receive a lower return than they had expected; nevertheless some return is better than none at all, so they continue in business. But as time goes on, some of the old-type assets will begin to wear out and will cost more for repairs. A point will be reached where they will barely earn enough to cover their prime costs. They will then be scrapped, and if they are replaced, they will be replaced by assets of the improved type. Hence the new invention causes an asset of the old type to be scrapped sooner than it otherwise would have been; it makes it obsolescent and finally obsolete.

A complication is that the improved type may itself be superseded by a still better type. This is a point in favour of changing over gradually. But, of course, if nobody invested in an improved type because something still better might come along next year, there would be little progress; changes would be made only when assets had physically worn out. In practice, this consideration means that reserves are provided against the risk of obsolescence as well as against physical wear-and-tear. An investment is made only if it appears likely to yield enough profit after taking account of the possibilities of further technical progress in that field.

4. Technical Progress and Planning

Is technical progress likely to be greater under free enterprise or under central planning? This is a question on which opinions are divided.

On the one hand, it is argued that Governments are inevitably lacking in imagination, keeping to the well-tried paths rather than venturing into new fields and sponsoring innovations. They are reluctant to take risks which may involve them in losses of public money and lead to adverse criticism; and they are reluctant to adopt inventions which, if successful, would adversely affect established industries, especially if the latter are owned by the State. Under private enterprise, on the contrary, everybody who thinks he has a good idea is free to try it out, risking his own capital or the capital of those who can be persuaded to support him, in the hope of large profits if he succeeds; in this way, new ideas are constantly put to the test and those which are worth while prove themselves and are adopted.

On the other hand, it is argued that under private enterprise the "patent" system may give one firm the exclusive right to use a new invention for a number of years instead of permitting it to come into general use at once, and that monopolies may delay the introduction of improved types of assets in order to avoid having to scrap their present assets before they wear out.

Some applications of technical progress may involve the reorganization of a whole industry or the planned development of a whole area; for example, to carry out a scheme for preventing soil erosion or for providing irrigation and drainage. In such cases, it is argued, the Government must take the initiative, or nothing effective will be done, for in practice a number of different firms or farmers will not be able to reach agreement about how much each shall pay, or how much each shall benefit, although the proposed scheme may be in the common interests of them all.

A good illustration of the need for Government action was provided by the rubber-growing smallholdings of Malaya. Most of the trees on these smallholdings are over thirty years old, and their yields are falling. Improved types of trees would yield three times as much rubber; this difference in yield is so great that it is quite clearly in the interests of the smallholders themselves, Malaya, and the world that the old trees should be replaced by high-yielding ones. But it takes about seven years before a rubber tree begins to yield, and the smallholders were not willing to destroy their present trees and lose the income from them for seven years. This situation cried out for a Government scheme. In 1953 such a scheme came into operation. A levy on all rubber exported provides the funds from which approved replanting is subsidized.

In Great Britain, a good deal of research is sponsored and paid for by the Government. Much of the most valuable research is "basic," not directed towards any specific objective. This may pay handsome dividends, but it is not in the interests of any firm, unless a very large one such as Imperial Chemical Industries, to undertake it. Technical progress in the nationalized industries will depend on the Government; the development of jet-propelled aeroplanes is a recent and notable achievement. There is still scope for privately financed innovations, but the greater the public control over the economy, the greater is the risk that the private investor must take. He may be restricted in his use of certain materials (for example, those imported from "the dollar area"), or constrained to sell in certain markets rather than in others, or prevented from raising further capital for expansion, or confronted with an excess profits tax. The incentives to private investment, and therefore to the private exploitation of new methods and new ideas, are less than they were. The march of technical progress will therefore depend more than in the past on publicly-sponsored research and on public investment.

PART III

DEMAND AND SUPPLY

CHAPTER XII

PRICES AND MARKETS

1. TYPES OF PRICES

THE purpose of this Part is to explain how prices are determined under capitalism. We shall then be better equipped to consider the merits and defects of the price mechanism as a regulator of economic activity, and in what respects Government action to control or supplement the price system may be desirable.

A price is a sum of money paid—not merely asked or offered, but actually paid—in exchange for something.

The prices most familiar to us are the prices of goods sold in shops —retail prices. But most of these goods change hands, some of them several times, before they appear in the shops. Some agricultural products and handicraft goods, such as carpets, made in the home, are sold first to local dealers, who may sell them to larger dealers, and they may go through other middlemen—wholesalers and perhaps exporters and importers—before they reach the shops. Manufacturers, farmers, and others have to buy raw materials, equipment, and other producers' goods, and these goods too may change hands before they reach the factory or other place where they are used. Hence the total value of all transactions in goods is several times the total value of retail sales.

Payments are made for services as well as for goods. These payments are prices, and form part of the price system, although in ordinary speech many of them are not called prices. For example, we call the price we pay for a journey by rail or bus a "fare," and we call the price we pay for the use of a house a "rent."

The prices paid by an employer for labour services—a week's work, for example—are called *wages* or *salaries*. And the price paid for the loan of money is called *interest*. It is expressed as a proportion of the amount lent, and for a period, usually, of one year. The *rate of interest* is 4 per cent when £4 a year is paid for the loan of £100 for one year, and so on.

There are other kinds of prices also, notably the prices of paper titles such as stocks and shares. As these prices do not affect the general analysis of the price system, I shall defer a discussion of them until later.

This leaves us with only two broad categories of prices:
1. The prices of consumers' goods and services.
2. The prices of factors of production.

The first category covers all goods and services which directly satisf
the wants of the final consumers. It includes the rents of dwelling
houses and the wages of domestic servants.

The second category covers all goods and services which contribut
to the output of consumers' goods and services. It includes wages an
salaries (other than those of domestic servants) and interest paid fo
the loan of capital used in production.

The same good or service may fall partly under the first category
and partly under the second. For example, petrol may be used eithe
in a private car or in a lorry or taxi, and electricity is supplied both t
private houses and to factories. Hence the demand for such good
and services comes partly from private consumers and partly from
businesses or public authorities. This does not weaken the fundamenta
distinction between the two categories. On the one hand, we have
goods and services demanded by consumers to satisfy their wants. Or
the other hand, we have goods and services demanded by producer
to form part of their "input." It is the prices of the latter which
constitute the "costs of production" of producers.

2. WHAT IS A COMMODITY?

There are many different *varieties* of wheat, wool, cotton, bread
potatoes, cigarettes, and indeed of almost any commodity one can think
of. Often one variety of a producer's good serves a different purpose
from another variety. For example, the many thousands of varieties
of wheat can be divided into weak wheats and strong wheats. British
wheat is weak wheat, very suitable for biscuits and poultry food but
not ideal for bread—20 to 30 per cent of strong wheat is blended with
weak wheat to make bread for British consumption. Again, specia
types of wheat (hard wheat) are essential for noodles. To take another
example, the many thousands of different varieties of timber can be
divided into softwoods and hardwoods. The former are used for
general building, and very soft woods, such as spruce and pine, are
used for wood-pulp, but hardwoods, such as teak, are used for purposes
such as shipbuilding where special strength and durability are required.

Some consumers prefer one type of a particular consumers' good to
another; non-glutinous rice to glutinous rice, Indian tea to China tea,
Virginian tobacco to Turkish tobacco, or conversely.

Sometimes the different varieties of a commodity are produced in
different districts or in different countries or by different firms. Even
when they are produced in the same place by the same firm, they may
have different costs of production because they contain somewhat
different components or are put through different processes. In short,
each variety is, strictly speaking, a separate commodity for which there
is a distinct demand and often a distinct supply.

Some goods, such as wheat, are physically capable of being divided into *grades* in such a way that all the units in a given grade are practically homogeneous, so that each grade is a commodity in the strict sense. The grading is usually performed by some organization representing the sellers. Careful grading is in the interest of the sellers, as well as of the buyers, for the market is thereby widened. A buyer can confidently purchase goods which he has not seen on the basis of the grade (or other standard description) given to them by the marketing organization, knowing exactly what he will get. Grading also makes possible sales for future delivery even if the goods have not been seen by the buyer, or are not yet in existence.

Some goods, however, cannot be graded or described with sufficient accuracy to be purchased without being seen and examined. Thus buyers of raw wool, or their representatives, inspect each lot of wool before making an offer for it, and buyers of tea taste samples before bidding; wool-buying and tea-tasting are skilled occupations. Such goods are usually sold in lots by auction. At a later stage in their life history it may be possible to grade them. Wool tops can be graded, and tea can be blended so that one package is indistinguishable from another bearing the same brand.

A manufacturer may differentiate a particular product from similar products made by rival firms by attaching to it a *trade-mark* which the law forbids others to use. Many varieties of consumers' goods—motor-cars, toilet requisites, patent medicines, foodstuffs, and so on—are *branded* in this way. As a rule, the maker of a branded article advertises it in order to create a demand for his brand rather than for rival brands. Other varieties of the commodity, whether branded or not, may be very similar to his product, but since he alone can use that particular trade-mark, he has a monopoly of his product.

The same physical thing is logically a different commodity when it is in a different *place*. For example, a steel tube at Corby is a different commodity from the same steel tube at Capetown, and sells for a different price. The difference in price arises from costs of transport, including such items as insurance charges and importers' profits, and from import duties.

In the same way, the same thing is logically a different commodity at one *time* from what it is at another, and may command a different price. The transport of goods over time forms a part of economic activity just as much as their transport over space. Many middlemen, including shopkeepers, carry stocks in order to supply their customers' requirements promptly, and this is a service for which customers are willing to pay: it saves them from the inconvenience of carrying considerable stocks themselves. Two or three centuries ago the grain supply of a region came mainly from the annual local harvest. If nobody had deliberately stored grain to sell it again later, it would have been plentiful and cheap soon after the harvest, but would have become considerably scarcer and dearer in the months just before the next harvest. Speculators rendered a useful service by buying grain soon after the harvest, thus making it less cheap at that time, stocking it, and selling it later, thus making its price less dear towards the close of the harvest year. They made a profit for themselves, for which they rendered a service to consumers by reducing the fluctuations in prices and consumption over the year. Since then, the great improvement in transport facilities has rendered this type of service less important for most commodities. Nowadays hardly a month passes in which wheat is not harvested in some quarter of the globe, ready to be sent wherever it is demanded, so that the danger of famine or serious shortage in any area is slight. The same applies to most commodities; consumers can obtain them at any time from the current output of some region or other, provided that they can afford to pay for them, and world stocks of most commodities are small, as a rule, compared with the annual output (except for "stock-piles" of strategic materials held by the United States and other Governments for defence purposes). Nevertheless, middlemen still render a useful service by holding some stocks to cover the period before the next shipments arrive and to provide a safeguard against an unexpected temporary shortage. Moreover, the bulk of the world output of some goods still takes place at one particular season of the year. A leading example is cotton. Two-fifths of the world's cotton is grown in the United States and is picked in the late summer and early autumn. Hence the bulk of the crop must be "carried" by somebody, if spinners and others are to have a steady supply over the year. The tendency, therefore, is for the price of cotton to rise steadily from one October to the next, the rise being sufficient to make it profitable to hold stocks of cotton. But, of course, the price may rise in fact more or less than this, or may fall, owing to changes in the demand for cotton, or in the expected size of next year's crop, as the year goes on.

3. MARKETS

The price of anything is the sum of money paid for it by a buyer to a seller. The immediate determinants of a price, therefore, are the sums of money which buyers are willing to pay and sellers to accept. The upper limit of a price is the most that the buyer will pay and the lower limit is the least that the seller will take. The actual price will be somewhere not above the former and not below the latter.

In practice, however, the same commodity does not change hands at a number of widely different prices. If this seems to be happening, we usually find when we look more closely that the different prices are paid for different varieties or in different countries or for different delivery dates. The prices paid for the same commodity, in the strict sense of the term "commodity," are usually the same, or very nearly the same. This is because a buyer knows what prices other sellers are offering, and he will not pay more than he need, and sellers know what prices other buyers are paying and will not accept less than they can get. In other words, it is because there are *markets* in which sellers and buyers are brought together.

A market is commonly thought of as a place where commodities are bought and sold. Thus fruit and vegetables are sold wholesale at Covent Garden Market, and meat is sold wholesale at Smithfield Market. But there are markets for things other than commodities in the usual sense. There are real estate markets, foreign exchange markets, labour markets, short-term capital markets, and so on; there may be a market for anything which has a price. And there may be no particular place to which dealings are confined. Buyers and sellers may be scattered over the whole world and instead of actually meeting together in a market place they may deal with one another by telephone, telegram, cable, or letter. Even if dealings are restricted to a particular place, the dealers may consist wholly or in part of brokers or agents acting on instructions from clients far away. Thus agents buy meat at Smithfield on behalf of retail butchers all over England, and brokers on the London Stock Exchange buy and sell securities on instructions from clients all over the world. We must therefore define a market as any area over which buyers and sellers are in such close touch with one another, either directly or through dealers, that the prices obtainable in one part of the market affect the prices paid in other parts.

A market is said to be *perfect* when all the potential sellers and buyers are promptly aware of the prices at which transactions take place and of all the offers made by other sellers and buyers, and when any buyer can purchase from any seller, and conversely. Under such conditions the price of a commodity will tend to be the same (after allowing for costs of transport, and taxes) all over the market. If one seller is prepared to accept less than others, orders will stream towards him until he is sold out or raises his price to that asked by his competitors, or (exceptionally, when he holds a large proportion of the total stocks) until rival sellers are constrained to reduce their prices to the level of his. Conversely, if a seller asks more than his rivals for the same commodity, he will find no purchasers, for although some buyers will be prepared, if necessary, to pay more than the price ruling at the moment, they will not deal with him if they can get the same commodity more cheaply from others.

There is normally a perfect market for commodities which can be graded so that one unit is exactly like another: No. 1 Manitoba Northern wheat or American Middling cotton or No. 1 Ribbed Smoked Sheet rubber. Such commodities can be bought without being seen, either for present or future delivery. If they are below standard, the buyer can reject them or can pay a smaller sum, the difference being assessed by arbitration, as provided for in the contract. There is normally a perfect market for stocks and shares, for each issue is homogeneous; one ordinary share of the Imperial Tobacco Company, for example, is just the same as every other. The same applies to foreign currencies. Again, each tin or package of a particular brand of manufactured goods is the same as every other, or the brand would lose its reputation.

The market is *imperfect* when some buyers or sellers, or both, are not aware of the offers being made by others. This may happen with goods which cannot be standardized, especially when they are bought (for example, at an auction sale) by private consumers rather than professional dealers. A buyer may pay either appreciably more or appreciably less than the market price for, say, second-hand furniture or a painting, because it is difficult to know what the market price is without following closely current transactions in similar goods. The labour market is not very imperfect; for most occupations, trade unions bargain with employers and agree on standard time-rates or piece-rates for particular jobs. The retail market, except for branded goods, is somewhat imperfect. Some shops may constantly sell some non-standardized good, such as a suitcase, for a little more than other shops in the same town are charging. When each price had to be bargained over, as is still a common practice in the East, the retail market was more imperfect than it is today. Today shops have fixed prices, below which they will not sell, and this system enables customers to compare the prices charged by different shops without wasting time in bargaining.

The development of communications during modern times has made markets less imperfect. The prices paid in one centre become known almost at once in other centres, and telegraph and telephone, cable and wireless, enable price differences between different centres to be smoothed out very rapidly. Nowadays many commodities have a world market.

Since the war, however, the United Kingdom and other Governments, for reasons which I shall try to explain later, restricted foreign exchange purchases and imports of commodities, especially from "the dollar area." This resulted in substantial price differences between countries, which cannot legally be smoothed out because Governments will not permit their citizens to buy freely in the cheaper markets. Thus a number of commodities cost more, until recently, in sterling than in dollars.

Within a country, however, the information and advertisements in the general press and in trade journals, the catalogues distributed by large department stores, and the activities of agents and brokers, such as real estate agents and insurance brokers, who bring sellers and buyers together, tend to keep sellers and buyers well informed and to make the markets for most goods and services nearly perfect.

4. Price and Value

A cynic, said Oscar Wilde, knows the price of everything and the value of nothing. He was using "value" in the philosophical sense. In economics, "value" usually means *value in exchange*, and therefore if you know the price of everything you also know the value of everything, for price is merely value expressed in terms of money.

Value in exchange is inevitably relative, since the value of one thing must always be expressed in terms of another; there can be no such thing as "intrinsic" value, in this sense of the term value. The value of X in terms of Y is the amount of Y which can be obtained in exchange for X.

If 1 ton of rubber (R.S.S. No. 1) costs £200 and 1 ton of rice (Siamese No. 1) costs £40, then 1 ton of rubber exchanges (not by direct barter, but by selling the rubber and buying the rice) against five tons of rice. The value of a ton of rubber in terms of rice is five tons; to say the same thing in other words, the value of a ton of rice in terms of rubber is a fifth of a ton.

Values are nearly always expressed in terms of money, as prices, for convenience of calculation, but it is a matter of simple arithmetic to work out the value of any commodity in terms of any other by comparing their prices.

We naturally tend to think of actual prices, absolute prices. Actual prices depend partly on the value of money. There may be a general rise in prices, that is to say, a fall in the value, or purchasing power, of money; or the opposite may happen. Even so, changes in relative prices will be more significant for most purposes than changes in absolute prices. For example, a worker's standard of living depends both upon his money wage and upon the prices of the things which he buys. If his money wage doubles and the prices of the things which he buys all more than double, his standard of living will fall. In the same way, a firm's profits depend both on its money receipts and its money costs. A rise in the selling prices of its products tends to raise its profits, but if at the same time the prices of the materials and other factors of production that it must buy increase still more, its profits will fall.

I will discuss changes in the value of money at a later stage. For the moment, let us suppose that the value of money remains fairly stable, and concentrate upon relative prices—upon the value of one good or service in terms of another.

5. THE RELATIONS BETWEEN PRICES

All prices are related to one another; they form a price system. This section gives a very general account of what these relationships are. For the moment I shall ignore "controls" such as rationing; the reasons why they may be introduced, and their effects, can be discussed later, after we have seen how a freely-working price system would operate.

It will be remembered that there are two main sets of prices: the prices of consumers' goods and the prices of factors of production.

The prices of consumers' goods are all related to one another because consumers' goods all compete with one another for the limited expenditure of consumers. We commonly think of substitutes as being similar, and serving the same purpose. One brand of tea is a fairly close substitute for another brand; beef is a substitute for mutton, and to some extent fish and eggs and cheese are substitutes for meat. But in fact all consumers' goods are potential substitutes for one another, for if consumers spend more on one they have less to spend on others. A man may cut down on his beer and cigarettes in order to pay the higher rent for a better house, or he may do the opposite; a woman may spend less on her lunches in order to buy more clothes; a family may forgo its holiday in order to buy more furniture.

Every shilling, for that matter every halfpenny, spent on a particular consumers' good A is a vote in favour of A and of the continued production of A. It is possible, by some factors of production moving out of one industry and into another, to produce more of one consumers' good and less of another; under full employment, and given the present state of technical knowledge, more A can be produced at the moment only by drawing factors of production away from other industries and thereby producing less B or C or D.

The assortment of goods which is produced depends, apart from uncontrollable influences such as the weather, on the way in which consumers distribute their expenditure: on the votes which they cast for different goods, each shilling carrying the same weight as every other.

If more of A is produced, week by week, than consumers are prepared to buy at the prevailing price, stocks of A will continue to accumulate in the hands of producers until either they produce less A (and more of something else) or the price of A falls.

If less of B is produced, week by week, than consumers want to buy at the prevailing price, then either producers expand their output of B (and reduce their output of something else) or the price of B rises.

If all such tendencies have worked themselves out, and a state of *equilibrium* has been reached—for the moment, until some change takes place in the preferences of consumers or in the relative production possibilities—the following relationships will hold good.

The price of every good will be such that the supply, the amount produced and offered for sale every week, equals the demand, the amount bought every week.

No consumer would prefer to spend rather more than he is spending on some goods and correspondingly less on others. He would not prefer to transfer a shilling (or several shillings) of his expenditure from one good to other goods. This is sometimes expressed by saying that each shilling gives him the same satisfaction or utility at the margin, the same *marginal utility*. And it is sometimes expressed by saying that "marginal utilities are proportional to prices." For example, if butter costs two shillings a pound and sugar one shilling a pound, a person who buys both would not rather have an extra pound of butter and two pounds less of sugar, or an extra two pounds of sugar and one pound less of butter; the marginal utility of pounds of butter is twice as high to him as the marginal utility of pounds of sugar, and that is the ratio of their prices: two to one.

The demand for factors of production is derived from, and reflects, the demand for the consumers' goods which they are used in producing. This is clearly so with raw materials. The demand for wool reflects the demand for clothing and other consumers' goods made wholly or partly of wool; the demand for rubber reflects the demand for rubber tyres and other goods made wholly or partly of rubber.

Many factors of production, however, are used in a number of industries: for example, unskilled labour, clerks, typists, lorry-drivers, fuel and power, buildings and land. When there is a shift in consumers' demands, there may be no change in the total demand for such factors. More of them will be needed in the expanding industries and less in the contracting industries, and there will be some movement of them from the latter to the former.

Some workers can be trained fairly quickly and easily to take on different jobs, now more in demand, where they can earn more. Some other factors of production can also be adapted quickly and easily to different purposes; for example, some land can be made suitable for growing a different crop, which now gives a higher return, or one type of shop can be converted into another type.

Nevertheless a change in consumers' demand may tend to raise the prices of some types of factors relatively to others. For example, an increased demand for wool, which uses a high proportion of land (for growing sheep), will tend to raise the price of land, and an increased demand for armaments will tend to raise the wages of engineering workers.

For producers' goods, the principle that the price will tend to equate supply and demand applies in the same way as for consumers' goods. The same principle applies also to other factors of production. An increased demand for land will tend to raise land values; an increased demand for loans will tend to raise the rate of interest; and conversely. For workers, the situation is more complicated, but if the total flow of money expenditure is maintained, the tendency will be for the wages of any type of worker to be around the level which provides employment for all workers of that type.

We have already seen that, in the absence of monopoly, if a factor is used in several industries it will tend to be distributed among them in such a way that the value of its marginal product is the same in every industry in which it is employed. During a period of change, this will not be the case. The value of its marginal product will be higher in an expanding industry, and it will earn more in that industry than elsewhere. But after enough movement has taken place out of the contracting industries and into the expanding ones, and equilibrium has been reached, no factors will be able to earn more by moving to other industries; the value of their marginal product will be the same in all.

The marginal product of a factor in industry A is so many extra units of commodity A, and as all factors of production are to some extent substitutes for one another, a small increase in the output of A can be obtained, as a rule, either by using a little more of one factor or a little more of another factor. For example, a little more sugar-cane can be produced either by using a little more labour, and getting a higher output per acre by better weeding, or by using a little more land. Suppose that an extra man would yield an increase in output five times as great as an extra acre. Should the cane-farmer employ an extra man or should he add an extra acre, or an extra five acres, to his farm? From his standpoint that will depend on the wages he must pay for an extra man and the rent he must pay for an extra acre. If the former is less than five times the latter, he will take on an extra man; if it is more than five times the latter, he will rent more land. Clearly the wages of such labour, and the rent of such land, will tend to adjust themselves until the equilibrium position is reached when it will not pay any farmer to substitute labour for land or land for labour. In that equilibrium position the wages of such a worker will be exactly five times the rent of an acre of such land. The general rule, therefore, arising from the possibility of substitution between factors, is that the prices of factors will be proportional to the values of their marginal products.

This general rule is often stated in another form, namely, that prices (of products) will be proportional to marginal costs. Suppose that an extra worker would increase the output of sugar-cane by 100 tons a year and an extra acre by 20 tons a year. Suppose that the wages of such workers are £100 a year and the rent of such land is £20 a year. Then the marginal cost of production of cane, the cost of additional output of cane, is £1 a ton, whether output is expanded by employing a little more labour or a little more land or some combination of the two. The rule is that any other product whose marginal cost is £1 a ton will be the same price as sugar-cane; any product whose marginal cost is £2 a ton will be twice the price of sugar-cane, and so on.

The basis for this rule, I repeat, is simply that factors will tend to be employed where they can earn most. If the same factors, or the same collections of factors, can produce a greater value in another industry than where they are, they will tend to move to that other industry, where they can earn more. After such tendencies have worked themselves out, the same factors will produce the same additional value of output in all industries where they are employed. The values of their marginal products, that is to say, will everywhere be the same. Prices will be proportional to marginal costs.

This general rule, however, does not apply where there is monopoly. Moreover, there are difficulties about the concept of *marginal cost*. I discuss these points in Chapter XVIII, Section 5.

A manufacturer often claims that his price is determined for him by his costs of production. My materials cost so much, my labour so much, and so on, he will say; I add a very modest percentage for my profit, and *voilà*, there is my price! On the other hand, he will agree that an increase in the demand for his product, which raises its price, will enable him to pay more for his materials, labour, and other factors, and that a decrease in the demand for his product, which reduces its price, will place him in difficulties—if the prices of some at least of his factors are not reduced he may have to go out of business or to produce something else instead. The fact is that the prices of consumers' goods and factors of production are determined together. They are all part of a system. And the purpose of the system is to shuffle factors about between industries in such a way that consumers get the assortment of consumers' goods—out of all the multitudinous assortment which could be produced—which they most prefer, each shilling they spend counting as one vote.

CHAPTER XIII

DEMAND

1. THE MEANING OF DEMAND

THE demand for anything, at a given price, is the amount of it which will be bought per unit of time at that price. Demand means always demand *at a price*; the term has no significance unless a price is stated or implied. The bare statement that so many thousand motor-cars a year or so many million tons of coal a year are demanded in Great Britain may be intended to mean that for some years the prices of motor-cars and coal have been fairly steady and that every year the volume of sales in Great Britain has been very near the figure named. But such a statement, taken literally, does not make sense. For the volume of sales—that is, the demand—would be different if the prices were different. There is no doubt that if the prices of motor-cars could be reduced enough, twice as many would be sold, and that if their prices went high enough, their sales would be halved. The amount bought of anything will vary, and may vary considerably, with its price; in other words, the demand at one price is usually different from the demand at another price.

Clearly, demand must mean demand per unit of time: per year or per month or per week or per day. For purposes of illustration I shall take the week as the unit, since most workers are paid by the week, and most housewives, therefore, plan their expenditure upon a weekly basis.

Demand, it may be noted, is not the same as desire or need. Doubtless many people who cannot afford a motor-car would like one, and doubtless many children need more milk than they get, but unless desire or need is backed up by ability and willingness to pay, it does not affect the volume of sales. The demand for a thing at a given price is the amount of it which would in fact be bought at that price.

2. DEMAND SCHEDULES

A full account of the demand—that is, of the state of demand or the conditions of demand—for any good in a given market at a given time should state what the (weekly) volume of sales would be at each of a series of prices. Such an account, taking the form of a tabular statement, is known as a *demand schedule*.

The demand for a thing depends upon many influences. Thus the demand for a consumers' good depends upon the numbers of the consuming population, their money incomes, their tastes, and the prices of competing goods, as well as upon the price of the good itself. *A demand schedule is drawn up on the assumption that all these other influences remain unchanged.* It thus attempts to isolate the influence exerted by the price of the good upon the amount of it sold: to show the amount sold as a "function" of the price of the good.

I give below an imaginary demand schedule for a consumers' good —pounds of butter, quarts of milk, tins of sardines, packets of cigarettes, what you will, provided that the good is homogeneous and not subject to rationing or price control, and that we can assume that the market for it is perfect and can ignore transport costs.

I have obviously made up the figures. They are too tidy to be true —demand expanding by exactly one million units (a week) for each fall of 1d. in the price per unit, and the lower half (below a price of 9d.) being a kind of mirror image of the upper half (above a price of 10d.).

The reader may ask: Why not be realistic and take some actual example? In the first place, there isn't an actual example covering the whole range from a price so high that sales are nil to a "price" of zero. Nobody knows or cares, nor is there any satisfactory way of finding out, what sales would be at prices far above or far below the prevailing price: the question is not likely to arise in practice so long as other circumstances (including the size of money incomes) remain the same. In the second place, an actual demand schedule, or part of one, would very likely be non-typical and therefore misleading. For example, the demand for a particular brand of something might well fall off very sharply at a price above the prices of rival brands and expand greatly at a price below the prices of rival brands. The demand schedule given below is too regular to be typical, but in other respects it is typical: more would be bought at a lower price than at a higher price, and total revenue rises to a maximum (àt 10d. or 9d.) and then falls off as sales expand still further. At some price above 18d. a unit there would be no sales, and if the commodity were given away (price zero), some amount greater than 18 million units a week would be "demanded."

Only the first two columns form the demand schedule. They consist of eighteen hypothetical statements, expressed in tabular form. If the price were 18d. a unit, and other circumstances remained unchanged (in economic jargon, the conditions of demand remaining the same as at present), then one million units a week would be bought; and so on for the other seventeen prices shown.

The third column is obtained by multiplying together the figures in the first two columns. It shows the total sum of money which would be spent on the commodity—total consumers' outlay, or total receipts (or total revenue) to the sellers—at each of the prices shown.

Price per Unit d.	Amounts Bought (and Sold) Million Units	Total Revenue Million d.	Marginal Revenue d.
18	1	18	18
17	2	34	16
16	3	48	14
15	4	60	12
14	5	70	10
13	6	78	8
12	7	84	6
11	8	88	4
10	9	90	2
9	10	90	0
8	11	88	−2
7	12	84	−4
6	13	78	−6
5	14	70	−8
4	15	60	−10
3	16	48	−12
2	17	34	−14
1	18	18	−16

The fourth column is obtained by subtracting from each figure in the third column the preceding figure in the third column. For example, at a price of 17d. a unit total revenue would be 34 million pence. At a price of 18d. a unit it would be 18 million pence. Therefore the increase in total revenue, called *marginal revenue*, when sales are two million units a week as compared with total revenue when sales are one million units a week, is 16 million pence on the additional million units or 16 pence a unit. It will be noted that below 9d. a unit, total revenue becomes less at a lower price; therefore marginal revenue is negative.

At any time, there can be only one price in the same market if the market is perfect. Suppose the price is 12d. with 7 million units a week being bought (and therefore sold). Suppose for some reason it rises to, say, 15d., and only 4 million units a week are bought. Or suppose it falls to 10d., and 9 million units a week are bought. That is precisely what the demand schedule tells us would happen. There has been no change whatever in the conditions of demand. The demand for the commodity is such that the amounts named would be bought every week at the prices named. Only if the amount bought at a price were different from that shown in the schedule would there have been a change in the conditions of demand.

3. DEMAND CURVES

The relation between the price and the amount bought can be plotted on a diagram as a *demand curve*. Each of the eighteen statements in the above demand schedule can be represented by a point in a system of rectangular co-ordinates. It is usual to measure the amounts which would be bought (weekly) along the horizontal axis OX and the corresponding prices per unit up the vertical axis OY. The statement that at a price of 18d. a unit one million units a week would be bought

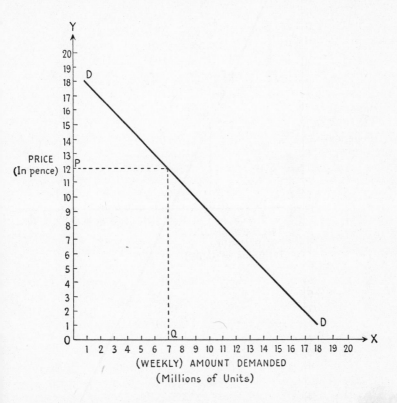

is represented by a point at a height of 18 above OX and at a distance of 1 (million) to the right of OY; and so on. We can assume continuity (for example, that at a price of $17\frac{1}{2}$d. an amount greater than 1 million and less than 2 million units a week would be bought) and join the points together to form a demand curve.

This particular demand curve happens to be a straight line. That is due to the figures which I chose for the demand schedule. A demand curve can be almost any shape—a straight line, or a convex curve, or

G   B.E.

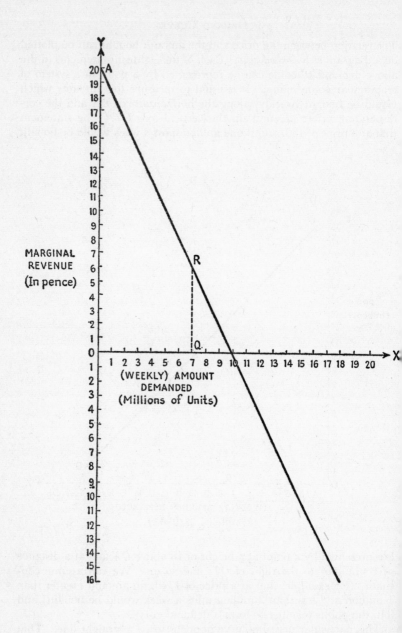

a concave curve, or partly one and partly another. Most actual demand curves are squiggles rather than straight lines. There is no particular shape which is typical. The only feature that is common to nearly all demand curves is that, whatever their shape may be, they always slope downward to the right, indicating that—the conditions of demand remaining the same—more units will be bought at a lower price than at a higher price.

Total revenue, or total consumers' outlay, appears on this type of diagram as a rectangle. At a price OP (e.g. 12d.) an amount OQ (7 million units a week) is demanded, giving a total revenue of $OP \times OQ$ (84 million pence a week).

I turn to the marginal revenue curve. This also can be almost any shape. But when the demand curve is a straight line, sloping downward,[1] the marginal revenue curve also is a straight line and slopes downward twice as steeply as the demand curve. (This is proved in the Note to Chapter XVI.)

I could have shown the marginal revenue curve by graphing the marginal revenue figures of our demand schedule on the same diagram as the demand curve, but I thought it would be simpler to show it separately. It is drawn on the opposite page.

One point that will be noticed at once is that part of this curve is below the horizontal axis OX. This is because marginal revenue for those outputs is negative, as the demand schedule shows. This is quite a usual feature of marginal revenue curves—when sales exceed a certain amount, a further expansion in the amount sold (conditions of demand remaining the same) causes total revenue to fall.

The total revenue from sales of OQ appears on this type of diagram as the area $ARQO$ "under" the marginal revenue curve. This is because the total revenue is the sum of the marginal revenues. For example, the total revenue on sales of 7 million units a week is

$$18 + 16 + 14 + 12 + 10 + 8 + 6 = 84$$

million pence.

A third way of showing on a diagram the figures in a demand schedule is to show the total revenue for each output. The horizontal axis OX remains as in the other two diagrams, showing the weekly amount demanded and therefore sold. The vertical axis OY, however, needs a different scale, for it measures total receipts, which in our example rise to a maximum of 90 million pence a week.

It is fairly typical for such a curve to rise to a maximum and then to fall.

---

[1] When the demand curve is horizontal, the marginal revenue curve coincides with it. This is the case, as we shall see in Chapter XV, for a firm under perfect competition.

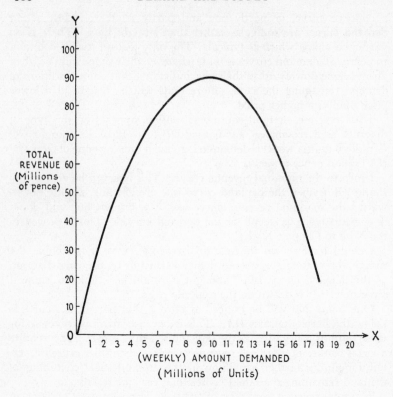

(WEEKLY) AMOUNT DEMANDED
(Millions of Units)

4. The Difficulty of Estimating Actual Demand Schedules

It is easy to make up an imaginary demand schedule, but it is by no means easy to make a good estimate of the actual demand schedule for a particular commodity (or service).

At any given time there is only one price ruling in the market for any particular commodity, and all we know, directly and with certainty, is how many units are in fact being bought, week by week, at that price. What we have to estimate is how many units would be bought, week by week, if the price were different; and we have to make such an estimate for each one of a whole range of possible prices.

Statistics of what happened in the past provide some guidance, but they need very careful interpretation. It by no means follows that if so many units a week were bought at such and such a price at some period in the past, the same number would be bought at that price, week by week, at the present time. Other conditions may not have been the same then as they are now. The general level of prices and incomes may have been higher, or lower; the general state of trade may have been more prosperous, or more depressed. For most commodities, a higher price will prevail for the same volume of sales when incomes and other prices are high than when they are low, and there is often both a greater volume of sales and a higher price during a period of good trade than during a period of depression. Moreover, the size of the consuming population, their tastes, and the prices of other commodities and especially of close substitutes, may have been different then from what they are now. We must make full allowance for all such differences if we use data on how much was sold week by week at a particular price in some previous period to throw light on the actual demand schedule for the commodity at the present time.

One way to estimate an actual demand schedule would be to question a number of buyers. "How much would you buy, week by week, if the price were ten per cent higher than it is now? If it were twenty per cent higher? If it were ten per cent lower? If it were twenty per cent lower?" And so on. Many of those asked would find it hard to say how much they would buy if the price were very much above or very much below its present level. But as a very large change in price is unlikely if other conditions remain the same, it is only that part of the demand schedule around the neighbourhood of the prevailing price that is of practical significance for most commodities.

Another way, and perhaps the best of all, is to ask a few persons of intelligence and good judgment who are in close touch with actual and potential buyers of the commodity, and who are aware of the alternative types of expenditure open to them, to make a guess at the actual demand schedule. (This is the type of service provided, for a fee, by firms specializing in *market research*.)

Every seller who is in a monopolistic position, in that he can fix his own prices, is faced with this problem. The seller may be some cartel or other association of the producers of a particular raw material or of some other commodity or group of commodities, or a public authority supplying transport or electricity or other services, or the manufacturer of a branded article, such as a particular make of motor-car or a particular brand of toothpaste, or merely the proprietor of a local restaurant or cinema. The question he must ask himself is: How much would my sales fall off if I raised my prices by so much? How much would they expand if I lowered my prices by so much? It is true that such a seller must often take account of other matters also. In particular, he must estimate what his rivals would do in response to any action which he might take; for example, if he lowered his prices, they might lower theirs, or they might increase their expenditure on advertising their products. But the chief factor which he has to take into account is the present demand schedule for his particular good or service.

A Chancellor of the Exchequer, in search of revenue, has to form some estimate of the relevant part of the demand schedule for a commodity which he is proposing to tax, or to tax more heavily. It may well be that the greater the tax, the greater the revenue. But it may be that (as happened with sparkling wines in Great Britain in the 1930s) a higher tax produces a smaller revenue. This will happen if there is a large fall in sales when the price goes up in consequence of the higher tax.

How will a group of farmers fare if they have an unusually good harvest or an unusually poor one? That depends on the demand schedule for their product. The community as a whole benefits by a larger harvest. The farmers may or may not. It may be that the price per unit falls so much that they receive less money for a big crop than for a small one. What happens to farmers' incomes will affect the demand of farmers for goods and services and, in particular, for goods such as agricultural machinery.

In these days of public planning, Governments look ahead and estimate what is likely to happen next year. One of the factors they must take into account, although by no means the only one, is the state of demand for goods and services whose prices are likely to change. For example, what will happen to the export sales of British motor-cars if their prices rise by about ten per cent?

My task, however, is not to estimate the actual demand schedule, at the moment of writing, for any particular commodity, but to give a general account of how prices are formed. For that purpose we need a clear idea of the nature of a demand schedule as a series of hypothetical statements, showing the amount which would be bought week by week at any given price, provided that the other influences governing demand remain unchanged. If these other influences change, the old demand schedule ceases to be valid and must be replaced by a new one which gives a true picture of the state of demand that now prevails in the market.

5. Why Most Demand Curves Slope Downward

Most demand curves slope downward to the right throughout their length, although the slope may be much steeper in some parts than in others. This means that, unless something happens to change the present state of demand, more units will be bought at any given price than at any higher price. Any rise in price will reduce the volume of sales, and any fall in price will expand the volume of sales. Why is this?

The total weekly sales of a consumers' good are made up of numerous sales of different amounts to different consumers. Some consumers might buy exactly the same amount every week, whatever the price. But others would not. At a higher price, some would buy less than before, and some might give up consuming the commodity and buy none at all of it. In order to explain why total sales would be greater at a lower price we must consider the behaviour of an individual consumer.

I assume that a consumer has a fixed weekly sum of money to spend. (If money incomes changed, the state of demand would change.) He, or more probably she, must somehow decide in what way to spend this weekly sum. The more money he spends on butter, the less is available for other goods. Hence his expenditure on butter can be said to reflect his *scale of preferences* as between butter and other goods.

If we knew a person's scale of preferences as between different consumers' goods, we could predict exactly how he would distribute a given weekly expenditure among different goods, provided that we knew the price of each good. His scale of preferences is the quantitative expression of his tastes.

The reader probably feels that the assumption that every consumer has a definite scale of preferences is not realistic. Let us consider some possible objections which may be urged against it.

It may be said that a consumer's purchases will vary with all kinds of circumstances, such as the climate or his state of health or the extent to which different goods are advertised. This is true. But we are regarding such a change as a change in his "tastes." If the tastes of consumers change, the old demand schedule no longer applies. We are considering why a *given* demand schedule takes the form that it does.

It may be said that even if a man's tastes remain unchanged he will not order a dinner exactly similar to the one he had yesterday. All this means is that we must consider a period sufficiently long to enable him to satisfy his desire for variety in such matters as diet.

It may be said that part of his weekly expenditure will already be earmarked owing to decisions he has made in the past. For example, he may have contracted to pay a certain weekly sum as the rent of his house. But he is free to spend the rest of his money as he pleases, and if, owing to changes in other prices, he wishes to move into a more expensive or less expensive house, the matter can often be arranged; at the worst, he must wait until his lease expires.

It may be said that some persons buy on behalf of others. Thus housewives buy food for their families, parents buy clothes and other goods for their children, and people buy some goods to give them as presents to others. But this does not in the least affect our argument. In order to explain the formation of prices we do not need to delve into the motives of purchasers. We need know only how they will distribute their expenditure when confronted with any given set of prices.

It may be said that few persons are aware of more than a portion of their scale of preferences. It is improbable, for example, that many housewives have reflected upon how much butter they would buy per week if its price fell to 1d. per lb. or rose to £1 a lb., for there is no need to consider possibilities unlikely to arise. But I must point out that our assumption is that a purchaser acts *as if* he had a definite scale of preferences. It is just conceivable that a person might not be consciously aware of his tastes. Nevertheless, we could construct the relevant part of his scale of preferences by observing his actions.

The above objections to our assumption, therefore, carry little or no weight. If it could be proved that most people act irrationally, in that they spend carelessly and impulsively, following no kind of plan or scheme, whether conscious or unconscious, this would be a valid objection to our assumption. But in fact most people do not behave like this. They cannot afford to do so. Their money incomes are so limited, relatively to their desires, that they are constrained to weigh alternatives and to think before they spend in order "to make the money go as far as possible."

Let us therefore consider a typical "rational" consumer, planning his expenditure. Suppose that he, or she, is careful enough to think about the pennies as well as the shillings. Given the prices ruling in the market, his problem is to distribute his expenditure among different goods in such a way as "to get the most out of it" from the standpoint of his own scale of preferences. He will try to purchase that assortment of goods which he most prefers, out of all the possible assortments which he could buy with the same money. If he succeeds, he will have arranged his expenditure in such a way that he would not willingly spend a penny more on one good and a penny less on another.

Another way of expressing this is to say that he tries to get as much *utility* as possible from his weekly expenditure. The word "utility" has no moral significance. It may be that he would obtain more nourishment from his expenditure on food if he bought more of some foodstuffs and less of others; it may be that he would be more healthy if he spent more on food or exercise and less on clothes or amusements; it may be that he would be more efficient if he spent less on alcohol. But in order to understand the world as it is, we must study how people in fact behave and not how we think they ought to behave. To say that one assortment of goods gives him more utility than another means nothing more or less than that he prefers the former assortment to the latter.

I must now introduce the important conception of the margin. If our consumer distributes the limited amount of money that he has to spend in the way he most prefers, the marginal utility to him of a pennyworth of any good that he buys will equal the marginal utility to him of a pennyworth of any other good that he buys. If we take a penny as our unit, and he spends 1s. a week on butter, the marginal utility to him of a pennyworth of butter is the addition made to his total utility by consuming 12 pennyworth of butter a week instead of 11 pennyworth. We can say, speaking loosely, that it is the extra utility yielded by the last penny per week that he spends on butter: this statement is a little loose in that any pennyworth of butter is indistinguishable from any other pennyworth. If he could get more utility by spending a penny less a week on butter (which could, of course, be done by purchasing butter at slightly less frequent intervals) and a penny more on, say, tea, he has not solved his problem correctly, and, realizing this, he will tend to spend more on tea and less on butter. If he does maximize his utility, he will not wish to transfer a penny per week from any one good to any other. For him, that is, the marginal utility of all the goods that he buys (taking a pennyworth as the unit) will be equal.

Now we must consider the so-called "Law" of Diminishing Marginal Utility. This is a generalization arrived at by introspection and by observing how people behave. It states that if a consumer, with given tastes, increases his (weekly) consumption of one commodity only, the marginal utility to him of that commodity will fall relatively to the marginal utility of other commodities. And this will be still more marked if, in order to increase his consumption of that commodity, he reduces his consumption of other commodities, for this will make their marginal utility to him rise relatively to that of the commodity in question. I state the Law in this lengthy way to avoid implying that absolute utility can be measured. The utility yielded by one good is always relative to the utilities yielded by other goods. A consumer can and does compare utilities—that is, the utilities of different goods to himself—although there is no way of measuring absolute utility.

In so far as most persons' scales of preferences do conform to this Law, we have an explanation of why most demand curves slope downward. A given consumer, let us say, has equated the marginal utility of butter with that of the other goods that he buys. As things are, he will not buy more butter per week, for in order to so so he would have to spend less on something else, and he values the something else that he would have to give up more highly than the extra butter that he would acquire. But if the price of butter falls, the situation is altered. He can now get more butter for each penny than before. He will therefore increase the amount of butter that he buys, thus reducing its marginal utility to him, until the marginal utility to him of the new enlarged "pennyworth" of butter is the same as that of a pennyworth of anything else. Thus a fall in the price of a commodity will usually cause more of it to be sold. Whether the total consumers' outlay on the commodity will be greater or less than before is another matter.

It must be remembered that marginal, and not total, utility varies with relative prices. Suppose, for example, that a consumer spends 1s. per week upon bread and 1s. per week upon periodicals. This does not mean that the total utility which he derives from the periodicals is equal to the total utility which he derives from the bread. If he had to choose, he might prefer, say, half the bread to all the periodicals. But the last penny that he spends on periodicals yields him as much extra utility as the last penny that he spends on bread; if it were not so, he would spend more on bread and less on periodicals until each yielded him the same marginal utility. This concept of the margin helps to explain what has sometimes been called "the paradox of value." Bread, for example, is said to be more "useful" than jewellery: why, then, is it so much cheaper? We must look at the margin. A purchaser of jewellery may be spending so much already on food, dress, and other things, that he—or she—would rather spend, say, £10 a year on jewellery than use some of that £10 to buy additional food, dress, and so on. If he had to decide between going completely without food and going completely without jewellery, he would doubtless choose the latter. But this is not the kind of choice which in fact presents itself. People have to choose between a little more of this and a little less of that, or a little more of that and a little less of this. They tend to equate marginal, and not total, utilities.

The unit of a commodity, in this connection, must always be the amount which can be bought for a given unit of money, such as a penny. To say that a consumer equalizes the marginal utility to him of bread and of milk does not mean that the last loaf of bread per week yields him the same additional utility as the last pint of milk per week. A loaf and a pint are arbitrary physical units. To make a comparison, we must measure in terms of the limited "resource" to be distributed among different uses; in this case the limited resource is money, the different uses are different goods, and the appropriate unit is the pennyworth.

Alternatively, we can take the physical units, say a pound of sugar at 1s., a pint of milk at 8d., and an egg at 4d., and we can say that at the margin the utility of an additional pound of sugar is equal to that of one and a half additional pints of milk or three additional eggs. This gives us the rule that *marginal utilities are proportional to prices* (in this example, 3 : 2 : 1).

Since utility cannot be measured—there are no units in which to measure it—some economists prefer not to use the word at all. Instead of "marginal utilities" they speak of "marginal rates of substitution" between commodities. But it comes to the same thing.

The prices ruling on the market are the same for all consumers. Each consumer adjusts his purchases according to his own scale of preferences. The differences in the tastes of different consumers show themselves, therefore, not in the payment of different prices per unit, but in the purchase of different amounts.

6. ELASTICITY OF DEMAND

The concept of *elasticity of demand* relates to the extent to which the volume of sales will expand in response to a small fall in price.

I have just tried to show that as a rule more units will be bought at a lower price. But will more money be spent on the commodity? Will the total outlay of consumers on the commodity, which of course is the same thing as the total receipts or total revenue of the sellers, be greater or less at the lower price?

In our imaginary demand schedule, total consumers' outlay increases —marginal revenue is positive—with each fall in price down to a price of 10d. a unit. Total consumers' outlay is the same at 9d. as at 10d., namely 90 million pence a week: marginal revenue at a price of 9d. is nil. With each fall in price below 9d., total consumers' outlay diminishes—marginal revenue is negative.

This can be expressed by saying that above 10d. elasticity of demand is greater than unity, between 10d. and 9d. it is equal to unity, and below 9d. it is less than unity.

A more exact measure of elasticity of demand, discussed in a Note at the end of this chapter, is the percentage increase in the amount bought divided by the small percentage fall in price.

Not all demand schedules are as regular as our imaginary one. Some may be relatively elastic over one range, then relatively inelastic, then relatively elastic again, and so on. But the general rule is that elasticity of demand will be greater than unity at high prices and will sooner or later become less than unity at low prices. A fall in price from 18d. to 17d. requires an expansion in the volume of sales of only one-seventeenth to keep total outlay the same, but a fall in price from 2d. to 1d. requires the volume of sales to double. Consumers will not be prepared to expand their purchases by larger and larger percentages indefinitely. Sooner or later they will use some of the money which they had formerly spent on that commodity to buy something else instead; they will buy more units of that commodity than before, but their total outlay on it will be less.

The elasticity of demand for anything is usually different at different points on the demand schedule. Around one price, demand may be very elastic and around another price, very inelastic. It is incorrect, therefore, to speak of the demand for a commodity as being *elastic* (or *inelastic*). What is usually meant is that in the neighbourhood of the prevailing price a fall in price would cause total outlay to increase (or diminish), and a rise in price would do the opposite.

Given the numbers and incomes and tastes of consumers, the

elasticity of demand for a commodity in the neighbourhood of a particular price depends upon the possibilities (as conceived by consumers) of *substituting* it for other commodities, or conversely. The
demand for salt is probably rather inelastic, as there is no good substitute for salt; that is to say, nearly as much salt would be bought if
the price were somewhat higher, and little more if the price were somewhat lower. But it is not always true that the demand for necessaries
is inelastic and for luxuries elastic. The demand for cod depends
largely on the price of herrings and other fish; the amount of cod
bought is likely to vary greatly if the price of cod changes but the
prices of other fish do not. The demand for orchids or diamonds, on
the other hand, may be very inelastic over a certain range if buyers
do not regard other flowers or jewels as close substitutes. The demand
for cigarettes in general may be rather inelastic, around prevailing
prices, but the demand for any particular brand is probably very
elastic. That is to say, on the usual assumption that other prices,
including the prices of rival brands, do not change, a rise in the price
of one brand is likely to cause a large fall in sales, and a fall in its
price to cause a large expansion of sales, because buyers regard other
brands as close substitutes.

A further point is that many commodities are capable of a variety
of uses. Thus the demand for coal is the sum of the demands of blast
furnaces, railways, ships, gas-works, power plants, factories, homes,
and so on. A fall in the price of such a commodity may cause a large
expansion in the amount demanded for some particular use. To
revert to butter, over a certain range a fall in its price might considerably expand the demand for butter for cooking purposes. This, however, would take place at the expense of such fats as lard and margarine: cases of this kind form no exception to our generalization that
elasticity of demand depends upon the possibilities of substitution.

NOTE

THE MEASUREMENT OF ELASTICITY OF DEMAND

The elasticity of demand at any price can be measured by the percentage increase in the amount demanded which would result from a
fall of 1 per cent in that price; or, more generally, by the percentage
increase in the amount demanded divided by the (small) percentage
fall in the price.[1] For example, if a fall of 1 per cent in price expands
sales from 1,000 to 1,020, or from 2,000 to 2,040 per unit of time, the
elasticity of demand at that price is 2; if a fall of 2 per cent in price
expands sales from 1,000 to 1,010, the elasticity of demand at that
price is $\frac{1}{2}$; if a fall of $\frac{1}{2}$ per cent in price expands sales from 50 to 55,
the elasticity of demand at that price is 20.

[1] We owe this concept to Marshall (*Principles of Economics*, p. 102).

The result obtained by applying this method may be different from that obtained by noting the change in total consumers' outlay. Suppose that a fall in price of 10 per cent (from 100 to 90) causes sales to expand by 10 per cent (from 100 to 110). Elasticity of demand, measured by the above method, is exactly 1. But total outlay has fallen (from $100 \times 100 = 10,000$ to $90 \times 110 = 9,900$). The divergence arises because the notion relates strictly to elasticity *at a point* and not over a finite range of price.[1] (The two measures would correspond, over a finite range of price, if the percentage fall in price were measured on the basis of the lower price. For example, if we call a fall in price from 100 to 90 a fall of one-ninth, then an expansion in sales of one-ninth will make total outlay exactly the same at a price of 100 as at a price of 90; and if we call a fall in price from 2d. to 1d. a fall of 100 per cent, an expansion of sales of 100 per cent will exactly maintain total outlay.)

In order to show[2] how the elasticity of a demand curve at a point P can be measured, let us take another point P', on the same demand curve, just below P, and join the two points by a straight line which cuts the Y axis in t and the X axis in T.

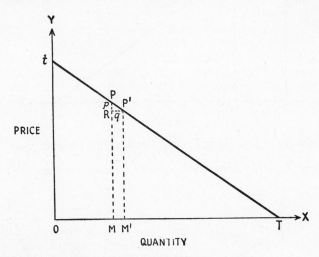

At a price of MP the amount demanded is OM.

At a price of $M'P'$ the amount demanded is OM'.

Call PR, the fall in price, p.

Call RP', the increase in sales, q.

[1] On this whole subject see "The Diagrammatical Representation of Elasticity of Demand," by A. P. Lerner, in *The Review of Economic Studies*, Vol. I, No. 1. He shows how this divergence can be avoided by an appropriate measure of "arc elasticity" (over a finite range of price).

[2] Adapting the proof given by Marshall in his Mathematical Appendix.

The elasticity of demand is the proportionate increase in the amount demanded, $\frac{q}{OM}$, divided by the proportionate fall in price, $\frac{p}{PM}$.

$$\frac{q}{OM} \div \frac{p}{PM} = \frac{q}{OM} \times \frac{PM}{p} = \frac{q}{p} \times \frac{PM}{OM}.$$

The little triangle PRP' is similar to the large triangle PMT.

Hence $\frac{q}{p} = \frac{MT}{PM}$.   Hence $\frac{q}{p} \times \frac{PM}{OM} = \frac{MT}{PM} \times \frac{PM}{OM} = \frac{MT}{OM}$.

When the distance between P and P' is diminished indefinitely, the two points coincide and Tt becomes the tangent to the demand curve at P.

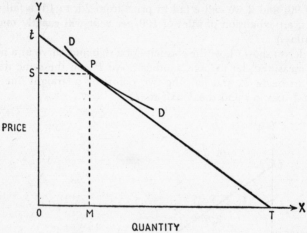

The elasticity of demand at $P = \frac{MT}{OM}$, which is the same as $\frac{OS}{St}$ or $\frac{TP}{Pt}$.

Thus any straight-line demand curve tT, cutting the Y axis in t and

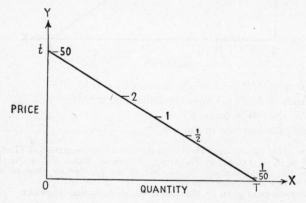

the X axis in T, will vary in elasticity (however steep or gentle its slope) from infinity at t down to zero at T. One-third of the way down its elasticity will be 2; half-way down it will be 1; two-thirds of the way down it will be $\frac{1}{2}$; and so on.

Parallel demand curves will have different elasticities at the same price; for example—

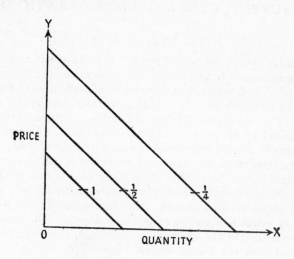

If the elasticity of demand is equal to unity at any price, so that total consumers' outlay is always the same, the demand curve will be a rectangular hyperbola, such as any of the curves below.

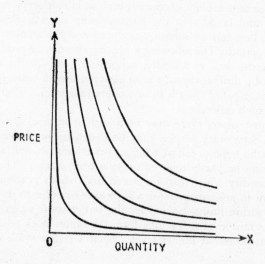

CHAPTER XIV

SUPPLY: GENERAL CONSIDERATIONS

1. THE MEANING OF SUPPLY

IN ordinary speech the term "supply" may have any of several different meanings. It may mean the total stock in existence. The term is often used in this sense when the total stock cannot be increased, or can be increased by only a small percentage, during the next year or two. Thus the supply of Cézanne pictures may mean all the pictures ever painted by Cézanne and known still to be in existence, and the world supply of gold may mean the total amount of gold which has been extracted from the mines and rivers and is still in existence, for the annual output forms only about 3 per cent of that total. Again, the supply of anything which is currently produced may mean the normal output per unit of time. Thus it may be said that the world's supply of wheat is over 200 million tons a year. The term is more likely to be used in this sense if stocks are small, as are stocks of wheat, compared with the annual output. But supply may mean also *the amount offered for sale per unit of time*. This is the meaning that is of most use in economic analysis and that economists therefore adopt.

The general supply-and-demand explanation of how prices are formed applies both to goods and services that are currently produced and to those that are not produced, such as labour services, and loans of money, and land. For the former group there is clearly a close connection between the amount produced and the amount offered for sale over a period. The following three chapters discuss production, and costs of production, as affecting supply. I now ask the question of how and why differences may arise between the amounts *produced* and the amounts *supplied* (that is to say, offered for sale). There are three sources of such differences.

In the first place, there may be additions to stocks, or sales from stocks. A temporary surplus may be stored by producers or dealers or others who hope to sell at a higher price later on, and a temporary shortage may be partly relieved by sales from stocks. The producers of a commodity which can be stored and which is subject to wide fluctuations in price may create a *buffer stock* in order to try to stabilize the price within limits, buying for the buffer stock when the price is below a certain level and selling from the buffer stock when the price is above a somewhat higher level. Such a buffer stock was created

for tin in 1956, but there are few other instances. It is difficult for producers and consumers to agree on fair price limits; financing the buffer
stock may be expensive; and it is difficult to hold a "floor" price by
continuing to buy for the buffer stock when output is considerably
above the amount demanded, and remains so, or to hold a "ceiling"
price when demand is considerably above current output.[1] Again,
Governments may hold strategic stocks as a precautionary measure
against a possible shortage due to war. Purchases by the United
States Government for its strategic stock-pile were a main factor in
the price rises of certain metals and other materials during 1950 and
1951. But as a rule, if present prices have been prevailing for some
time and are not expected to change, any significant alteration in the
volume of stocks is unlikely. In the long run, output and supply
will not diverge from one another appreciably owing to changes in
stocks.

In the second place, output will exceed sales by the amounts which
producers consume of their own products. These amounts are large
enough to be significant mainly for foodstuffs such as rice and vegetables and eggs and fish produced by small farmers and others, largely
for their own needs. Whether an individual producer will consume
more or less of his own products when their prices are high depends
on what they are. We can think of producers as having a demand
for their own products. People tend to consume more of some commodities and less of others when their incomes go up. They tend to
consume more luxuries and semi-luxuries and less of the cheapest
foodstuffs, which give them more nourishment for their money but
which they do not find so appetizing. Butter is in the former category.
Dairy farmers and their families are themselves consumers, or potential
consumers, of butter. When the price of butter is low, their incomes
will be low, and they may decide to sell nearly all their butter for
cash and to consume cheaper fats, such as margarine, at their own
table. When the price of butter is high, and they expect it to remain
high, they may feel that they can afford to consume more of their own
butter instead of selling it. (Nevertheless the total supply of butter
may be greater at a higher price because the higher price stimulates
an expansion of dairy-farming: more factors of production enter the
industry.) Other commodities (for example, tapioca) fall into the
latter category, and most growers may decide to sell more of them
when their prices are high, themselves switching partly to other foodstuffs (such as rice or wheat flour).

In the third place, products such as fresh fruit and vegetables and
fish are perishable. Part of the output of such products may be damaged in transit or handling, or may go bad, before it can be sold retail.
In some countries the loss on goods such as tomatoes, which are easily

[1] See Chapter XIX, Section 5.

squashed, is as high as 20 per cent. In the tropics, even commodities such as wheat flour and condensed milk will not store for long.

Despite these three points, there is a close correspondence for most products and a rough correspondence for others, over a period, between variations in output and variations in supply. The reader should bear these points in mind if he is making a forecast of the future supply of some particular commodity, but for our present purpose of giving a general account of how prices are formed we can treat the supply of goods that are currently produced as equivalent to their output just as we treated demand as equivalent to consumption.

2. OPPORTUNITY-COST

We have just seen that demand can be explained by the scales of preferences of consumers with given incomes and that marginal utilities will be proportional to prices. Is there some similar comprehensive generalization that can be made about supply?

There is such a generalization, but it is by no means universally true. It would be true under perfect competition, which is discussed in the following chapter, but it is not necessarily true under monopoly or imperfect competition, which are discussed in the two subsequent chapters. The generalization is that *prices tend to reflect opportunity-costs*.

When we discussed demand, we saw that each consumer considers the possibility of substituting a little more of one good for something else which he might give up, until he arrives at an assortment of purchases that he prefers to any other assortment which he could buy with the same money. The notion of opportunity-cost is a corresponding notion about supply. It relates to the possible substitution of alternatives in the assortment of goods and services produced.

If there is full employment, then more of some commodities can be produced only at the cost of producing less of others. If it would be possible, by reshuffling factors of production among industries, to produce an extra amount X of one commodity at the cost of producing a smaller amount Y of another, then the opportunity-cost of Y is X.

If consumers prefer X to Y, they will pay more for X than for Y. Firms in the X industry will find it profitable to expand their output and new firms may enter that industry, whereas the Y industry will tend to contract. The X industry will offer more employment opportunities for workers and other factors than the Y industry, and factors of production will tend to move out of the latter and into the former. This movement of factors will continue until equilibrium is reached, and this will happen when no factors can produce a greater value by moving into some other field—in other words, when prices reflect opportunity-costs.

The opportunity-cost of anything is the next-best alternative that could be produced instead by the same factors or by an equivalent group of factors, costing the same amount of money. I add this qualification for the sake of realism. If a farmer is producing wheat, the opportunity-cost of the wheat may be the barley or sugar-beet or potatoes which he could grow instead. He may be able to use the same land, the same workers, the same machines, the same fertilizers, for the alternative crop, but there are likely to be some differences—for example, he will need a different type of seed. An engineering firm may change over from one type of product to another without any changes in its plant and equipment or in its workers, but it may need, for example, somewhat different materials. An expansion of one industry—say, engineering—combined with the contraction of another —say, cotton textiles—will be more complicated. A number of factors will be common to both industries, and easy to transfer. For example, the railways can easily carry more engineering products and fewer cotton textiles. More electric power or coal can be supplied to the one industry and less to the other. Relatively unskilled workers, or workers such as clerks and lorry-drivers, can be employed in either industry. But different materials will be needed—less cotton and more steel—and perhaps a different type of technician, and perhaps some extra special equipment, in order to produce more of a quite different product.

Nevertheless the reasoning remains valid. Workers and other factors of production will tend to be employed where their services are most valuable. This tendency may be frustrated or checked by monopoly and other obstacles, but it will operate to make prices reflect opportunity-costs. To take a simple example, if the same collection of factors could build either twenty houses or a school, the price of the school will tend to be twenty times the price of each of the houses.

The money cost of producing a little more of a product is known as its *marginal cost of production*. If the same, or an equivalent, collection of factors could produce either X or Y, then the costs of production of X and Y are the same: they are made up of the prices paid to the factors used in producing them. We thus come back to the rule, which we noted in Chapter XII, Section 5, that prices will tend to be proportional to marginal costs. But I must repeat that this rule may not apply where there is imperfect competition, as we shall see.

3. Supply Schedules

Suppose that the price of the commodity—say, butter—to which our demand schedule relates is 12d. a unit and that 7 million units a week are offered for sale, and bought. If the price were to settle at 13d., instead of 12d., a unit, it may be that some larger number of units, perhaps 7½ million, would be offered for sale each week. If, on the other hand, the price were to settle at 11d., perhaps only 6½ million units a week would be offered for sale.

In the short run, and in the absence of excess capacity, it is probable that more would be supplied only if the price were higher. For, owing to diminishing returns, the marginal products of the workers and other factors would fall as more of them were employed on the same farms or mines or in the same plants, and therefore marginal costs would rise.

Thus a portion of the supply schedule for butter might read as follows, although no doubt in practice it would not be so regular as in this made-up example—

At a price of 14d. a unit, 8 million units a week would be offered for sale
„   „   „ 13d.   „ 7½ „   „   „   „   „   „   „   „   „
„   „   „ 12d.   „ 7   „   „   „   „   „   „   „   „   „
„   „   „ 11d.   „ 6½ „   „   „   „   ·,   „   „   „   „
„   „   „ 10d.   „ 6   „   „   „   „   „   „   „   „   „

If we look at this schedule side by side with the demand schedule, it is clear that the only possible equilibrium price is 1s. a unit. At this price, the same amount will be supplied as is demanded (namely, 7 million units a week). At a higher price, supply would exceed demand and stocks would pile up. At a lower price, there would be unsatisfied buyers able and willing to pay more rather than to go without their butter.

A supply schedule can be depicted graphically as a supply curve, sloping upwards to the right. The equilibrium price will be where the two curves cut one another, the price at which the amount offered for sale equals the amount bought. The elasticity of supply is measured by the percentage increase in the amount supplied divided by the (small) percentage increase in the price that induces that extra amount to be offered for sale.

At this stage, however, I must point out a number of difficulties in the concept of a supply schedule. I have already assumed away one difficulty by supposing that the supply of a good which is currently produced may be taken as equivalent to its output. But there are several others.

The most formidable springs from monopoly and imperfect competition. Many sellers can fix their own prices and at these prices they are prepared to sell as much or as little as the public cares to buy, although they may try to increase their sales by advertising. This may seem to make nonsense of the whole concept of a supply schedule. However, as I shall try to show in Chapters XVI and XVII, the prices fixed are not entirely arbitrary and may alter from time to time; the amounts supplied do in fact bear some relation to costs of production.

How long a period of time is supposed to elapse between a change in price and a corresponding change in the amount supplied? A large expansion in the output of an industry may take a considerable time. More workers have to be attracted and trained; fixed capital, such as plant and equipment and livestock, has to be increased. The longer the period, the more complete will be the adjustment to either a rise or a fall in the price of the product. The short-run supply curve may look very different from the long-run supply curves; usually it will be much steeper. This question is discussed below under the heading of "The Element of Time."

What assumptions do we make, when drawing up a supply schedule, about what happens to other prices? I think we must assume that the general levels of wage-rates, interest-rates, prices of equipment and materials, all remain unchanged. But it would be unrealistic not to take account of changes in prices that are a *direct consequence* of the expansion or contraction of the industry which we are considering. For example, a large expansion or contraction in the cotton textile industry is likely to affect the price of cotton, although here again the short-run effect may be different from the long-run effect. I discuss such changes below under the heading of "External Economies and Diseconomies."

A good deal of production is in fact joint production. It is quite exceptional for a firm to produce only one commodity. Changes in the output of one commodity may affect the output and the costs of production of other commodities which are produced in conjunction with it. I have taken butter an an example. A great deal more butter could be produced very quickly by selling less milk as liquid milk or by making more butter and less cheese and other milk products. I discuss this question below under the heading of "Joint Supply."

Again, the output of some commodities depends partly on external influences. This applies especially to agricultural products. The weather plays a large part in their yield, especially in districts subject to drought and extreme cold, and especially for tree crops. It is true that the probable variation, from one year to another, in the yield of any product will be greater for any particular farm than for the country as a whole, and least of all for the world, because the good yields of some farms or districts will offset the poor yields of others. Nevertheless an unusually good or bad harvest may upset all calculations. When such a change takes place, the existing supply schedule no longer applies and must be replaced, at least for the time being, by a new one.

All these difficulties arise because the real world, which we are trying to explain, is complex. It is difficult to make valid generalizations about it. Every commodity or service has its own special features.

If we wish to study one particular commodity and to make a realistic appraisal of its conditions of supply, we have to learn the relevant facts. But the general training given by a study of economics is a valuable foundation for this type of research. The concept of a supply schedule does help us to understand how prices are formed, and how the price system works, in spite of the various difficulties which I have just set out.

4. THE ELEMENT OF TIME

Suppose that there is an increase in the demand for some product. The old demand curve DD is replaced by a new demand curve D_1D_1 to the right of the old one. How will the supply adjust itself to this change?

That depends on what the product is. It is easy to produce more of one commodity and less of another if both are made by the same firms with the same fixed capital and the same labour. It is easy, for example, to produce more steel bars and fewer steel plates, more cloth of one design and less of another, more butter and less cheese. Let us suppose, however, that there is a general increase in the demand for all types of steel products, or cloth, or dairy products, so that easy adjustments of this kind are ruled out.

There is often a certain amount of excess capacity, especially for manufactured goods. Let us suppose, however, that the increase in demand is a large increase and cannot be met merely by working existing plant and equipment a little harder. In that event the prices of the products will be forced up, as steel prices were forced up in 1951, in order to restrict the amount demanded to the amount which can be produced.

The *short period* is a period of time too short to permit of any substantial increase in the specialized fixed capital of an industry or in the numbers of specialized workers, who take some time to train, attached to that industry. In the short period, therefore, a large increase in output is not physically possible. Some increase, however, can be obtained. There is a fixed amount of plant, but more workers can be employed on it. There is a fixed number of dairy cattle, but they can be fed better in order to increase their yield of milk. Clearly such increases will diminish the marginal products of the workers (or of whatever factors are increased) owing to diminishing returns, and marginal costs will rise. Hence the short-run supply curve will slope upward even if wage rates and other factor prices do not change. But in practice an expanding industry may have to pay somewhat higher wages (or, what comes to the same thing, pay standard time-rates to workers of less than normal efficiency) in order to attract more labour, and possibly higher prices for some of its other factors, such as materials or fertilizers. This will make marginal costs increase still more; the short-run supply curve may slope upward quite steeply.

The *long period* is a period long enough to permit full adjustment to be made, long enough to allow all the additional fixed capital that may be needed to be produced and installed, long enough to permit all the additional skilled workers who may be needed to be trained and attracted to the industry.

If other circumstances, such as the general level of incomes and prices, remain the same, there is no obvious reason why the output of a particular product should not eventually become twice as great, or twenty times as great, as at present and still be supplied at the present price.

It is true that the industry will need more workers and other factors of production. But other industries will need less. If incomes are the same, a larger expenditure on this product implies a correspondingly smaller expenditure on other products. Once equilibrium has been reached, this industry need pay no more than any other for the same factors. It may have paid more for some factors when it was expanding, but it is no longer expanding; it has increased its *capacity* and is providing a larger, but steady, volume of output.

There is no reason why marginal products should be smaller than now, for enough time has elapsed to install all the extra fixed capital needed to re-establish the old proportions between the various factors.

However, there are exceptions. The industry may need a special type of factor which is physically limited in amount. For example, only a certain amount of land is suitable for growing cocoa. A large permanent increase in the demand for cocoa may permanently raise its price because more of such land cannot be produced. The same applies to some minerals (for example, tin) of which the deposits are limited. On the other hand, a very large expansion of output may make possible the use of "indivisible" plant, as it did for motor-cars (the indivisible element being the conveyer system) and thus lead to a reduction in costs and prices.

The following diagram shows two short-run supply curves and a long-run supply curve.

The first position is that OQ is both supplied and demanded at a price of P. Demand increases from DD to D_1D_1. The short-run supply curve is S_s. In the short run, output expands to OQ_1, and the price rises to P_1. (This has the effect of keeping down the amount demanded to the amount that can be supplied, namely OQ_1.) In the long run, a new equilibrium position will be reached, with output much greater (OQ_2) and price (P_2) only a little higher than P.

If this new equilibrium position were reached, there would be a short-run supply curve (S'_s) passing through P_2 and sloping upwards fairly steeply, like S_s.

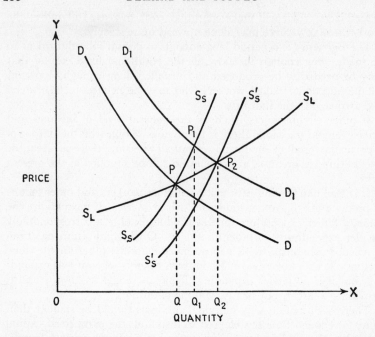

The long-run supply curve $S_L S_L$ joins together all the equilibrium points, such as P and P_2. For any equilibrium position such as P or P_2 there is a corresponding short-run supply curve.

The conception of equilibrium, and of a long-run supply curve, is useful. But in practice equilibrium is seldom or never reached. The long period may be very long. It varies considerably between industries. It may take only a year or so to put up new factories and plants or to grow a different type of crop. But a large integrated steelworks, for example, may take several years to build. Most tree crops, coffee and cocoa and citrus, and palm oil and coconuts and rubber, take five to seven years before the new trees begin to yield. Trees used for timber, especially hardwoods, may take much longer. It is very likely that during such an interval changes may take place in the conditions of supply; for example, there may be a general increase in wage rates, or there may be technical progress. The present short-period supply curves and the present long-period supply curves are no longer valid; they must be replaced by new ones. Equilibrium is a goal towards which movement is always taking place, but it is a goal which is constantly changing.

But suppose the conditions of supply remain the same. Then between the present equilibrium position at P and the new equilibrium position at P_2 there is a kind of no-man's land. As time goes on, fixed

capital will gradually increase, and more skilled workers will gradually
be trained. Capacity will expand. Output will increase towards OQ_2;
the price will fall from P_1 towards P_2. This is the usual situation; some
industries are expanding and some contracting; equilibrium has not
yet been attained. And, if I may venture a personal opinion, I hope
it never will be. For equilibrium means that nobody has any incentive to do anything different from what he is doing. It means
stagnation.

When an industry contracts, the "long period" may be quite different from when it expands. If the fixed capital, or enough of it, can
easily be converted to some other purpose which is now more profitable, if some of the skilled workers can find jobs elsewhere at which
they can now earn more, the transition may be quite rapid. For
example, if there were a fall in the demand for dairy products, some
of the cows could be slaughtered and sold for meat. But if the fixed
capital is specific, of little use for any other purpose, it may continue
to be used so long as it yields any return at all. Indeed, for a time
some fixed capital may be worked, in order to keep the business going
in the hope that demand will revive, even if prime costs are not
covered. In such circumstances, adjustment may take place only
slowly, as existing fixed capital wears out and is not replaced. In the
language of diagrams, the short-run supply curve may slope steeply
below P as well as above P; in the short run the fall in price may well
be greater, and the contraction of output may be much smaller, than
in the long run.

5. PRICE WITH A FIXED STOCK

I have been treating supply as equivalent to output. Let us consider
some instances where the quantity available is more or less fixed.

The stock of some things cannot be increased. Thus there may be
exactly a thousand copies in existence of the first edition of a particular
book. More copies could be printed, but they would not be genuine
first editions. The stock of some things is unlikely to be increased, and
can be assumed to be fixed. Thus there may be exactly one hundred
thousand ordinary shares of a particular company and, unless the company decides to increase its ordinary share capital, no more shares will
be issued. Again, some things which are currently produced are very
durable, like houses, and—especially if they take a considerable time
to produce—current output may form only a small proportion of the
existing stock. In so far as the existing stock cannot be appreciably
increased in the near future, it can be assumed to be practically fixed
for the time being.

Dealers or speculators may buy such things in the hope of selling
them subsequently at a profit, but ultimately the demand for them

comes from people who want to possess them or to use them. Thus the demand for houses comes, ultimately, from those who want to live in them. If the state of demand does not change, speculators for a time may buy and sell to one another, but there will be no profits for speculators as a whole, and after a time it will probably be realized that demand is not likely to increase, and this will make speculation die down. I shall therefore consider only the ultimate, and not the speculative, demand.

The problem is to explain what determines the price per unit of a fixed stock if demand remains unchanged. Of course, if the different units are not homogeneous, they may have different prices. One house may sell or rent for less than another which is larger or more attractive or better situated; the two houses are really different commodities. But if different houses are fairly close substitutes, so that their prices tend to rise and fall together, our explanation will apply to what may be termed "the general level" of house prices. I shall take as an illustration the thousand copies of the first edition of a particular book, assuming that any copy is indistinguishable from any other and that the market is practically perfect.

Under these conditions there will be only one price for a copy of this first edition. But after a time no transactions will take place. Everybody who would be prepared to sell at that price will already have sold; everybody who would be prepared to buy at that price will already have bought; and, by hypothesis, the state of demand remains unchanged. The price would thus be the price which any possessor of a copy could get if he chose to sell it.

Every owner of a copy is a potential seller, but there is a price below which he will not sell. This price may be called his *reserve price*. If his reserve price were £100, and his copy were put up to auction and the highest bid was £99, he himself would bid £99 10s. rather than part with his copy. Of course, different owners have different reserve prices, and if a man owns several copies he might be prepared to sell one copy more cheaply than the second, and so on.

Now let us go back to the time when transactions in copies were taking place, before the price settled down. Each owner of a copy at that time had his reserve price. Assuming that he would have been prepared to sell at his reserve price, we could construct a supply schedule from these reserve prices. Suppose that the highest reserve price is that of A—say, £200; that the next highest is that of B—say, £190; that the next highest is that of C, who wants at least £185; and so on. Suppose that the lowest price is that of Z, who wants only £50; the next lowest is that of Y, who wants only £55; and so on. The supply schedule would show that at a price of £50 one copy (that of Z) would be offered for sale, at a price of £55 two copies (those of Z and Y), and so on, concluding by stating that at £185, 998 copies, at

£190, 999 copies, and at £200, the whole thousand copies would be offered for sale.

Against this supply schedule we could set a demand schedule made up of the demands of all those who do not possess copies or who wish to buy additional copies. The equilibrium price could be shown on a diagram as the point at which the supply curve cuts the demand curve.

Another way of discovering the equilibrium price would be to lump together the reserve prices of the various owners and the demand prices of the would-be purchasers to form a combined demand schedule. For the reserve price of a potential seller (or, more strictly, a fraction below it) can be regarded as the price at which he "demands" his own copy.

Suppose, for example, that the would-be buyer with the highest demand price is A', who would give £200, the next highest demand

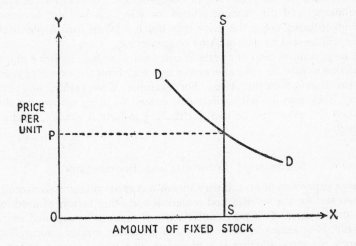

price is that of B', who would give £198, and the next highest is that of C', who would give £190. The combined demand schedule would begin by saying that at a price of £200 two copies would be demanded (one by A and one by A'), at a price of £198 three copies (by A, A', and B'), and at a price of £190 five copies (by A, A', B', C', and B). But there is no reason why any of these should pay such a high price, for there are plenty of sellers willing to sell for less. If the market is perfect, the price will settle down at the level just low enough to enable all the thousand copies to find permanent homes. This is shown in the above diagram. The vertical line SS represents the fixed stock of a thousand copies. The curve DD represents the combined demand schedule. The price, OP, will be that at which DD cuts SS. It is obvious that if the fixed stock were smaller, the equilibrium price would be higher, and that if the fixed stock were greater, the equilibrium price would be lower. Given the state of demand, the price will depend on the size of the fixed stock—diagrammatically, that is, on the distance from OY of the vertical line SS.

Similar reasoning may apply to a local market for fresh fruit or fish which will go bad if kept till tomorrow. If the whole amount must be sold today, the price will depend on the size of that amount and on the demand. Sellers might begin by asking yesterday's prices. But if their stocks were selling slowly, they would ask less in order to get rid of them, and if sales were brisk, they might feel that they could ask more.

In fact, however, large variations in price (except for higher prices at the beginning and end of the season for a particular fruit or vegetable) are unlikely from one day to another. If there is a large catch of fish, more will be preserved in "deep-freezes," or sold for canning or smoking, and the amount offered for sale fresh will not be great enough to bring down the price very much. When fruit is plentiful, more will be sold for jam-making or preserving.

A large annual crop of anything will tend to reduce its price and a small one to raise it. But alternative uses may limit the extent of year-to-year fluctuations in price. For example, if vegetables are very cheap, they may be fed to livestock instead of being thrown on the market, and grain can be used for making industrial alcohol, or even for fuel.

6. External Economies and Diseconomies

A large expansion of an industry means a corresponding expansion in its demand for the services and materials and other factors of production that it uses. This may enable some of them to be supplied more cheaply. For example, the total cost of providing market information is much the same whether it is provided for a large industry or for a small one, so that the cost per unit of output falls as the industry grows. Again, the special equipment needed by the industry may be cheaper to produce if it is produced on a large scale. Some firm (either inside or outside the industry) may buy the "waste" of the industry and process it into various products when there is enough of it to make it worth while to set up plants for this purpose.

Such economies are known as *external economies* because they are external to any particular firm in the industry. Each firm may assume that it will have to pay current prices for its factors if it expands its output. But in fact, if a number of firms expand, and new firms come in, some costs may fall (or, as with the utilization of waste, receipts may increase) owing to the growth of the industry as a whole.

All such economies are economies of large-scale production and therefore, as explained in Chapter VIII, Section 3, they arise from indivisibility. They are external to the industry, but they are internal to the firms that make the equipment, provide the information, utilize the waste, and supply any other services which are cheaper because the demand for them is greater.

On the other hand, there may be *external diseconomies*. For example, the growth of an industry may permanently raise, rather than lower, the prices of some of its materials. The growth of the chocolate industry may raise the price of cocoa and the growth of the canning industry may raise the price of tin. In the short run, the growth of an industry may raise the wages of skilled workers who take some time to train.

The contraction of an industry may have the opposite effects. But firms that have set up specialized fixed capital in order to supply the needs of a particular industry will probably go on doing so until their fixed capital wears out. If the industry is localized, its growth may have led to improved transport facilities (an external economy); the roads and the railways will remain although the industry provides them with less traffic than before.

7. JOINT SUPPLY

Two or more different goods are often produced together. Thus wool and mutton are joint products of sheep, and beef and hides are joint products of oxen. The less valuable product of a process is often termed a *by-product*. Thus the main product of a coke-oven is metallurgical coke; the coke-oven gas which is also produced is regarded as a by-product. On the other hand, the main product of a gas-works is gas, and the gas-coke which is also produced is regarded as a by-product. Many chemical and other processes yield a whole range of by-products, although further separate treatment is often needed to turn a by-product into a form suitable for use or sale. All the by-products, taken together, may be nearly as valuable as the main product. For example, the combined value of the by-products of the Chicago stock-yards approaches the value of the meat.

It is usually possible to change the proportions in which the different goods are produced, although this sometimes involves changing the type of equipment used, or the type of animal that is bred, and may therefore take some time. For example, before the development of cold storage, sheep were bred in New Zealand mainly for their wool. When it became possible to export mutton, the price of New Zealand mutton rose relatively to the price of wool, and cross-bred sheep, yielding more mutton but less wool, and wool of a poorer quality, were largely substituted for merinos.

In a few instances the proportions cannot be varied. For example, the cotton plant yields about 2 lb. of cotton-seed for every 1 lb. of cotton lint (raw cotton). This means that the "unit" produced by the cotton-grower must be regarded as 1 lb. of lint plus 2 lb. of seed. (In practice, he may attribute all his costs to cotton and add the receipts from cotton-seed to his receipts from cotton.) But the demand for cotton lint is quite separate from the demand for cotton-seed. Each has its own uses and its own demand schedule. Thus, if an increased demand for cotton causes more cotton to be grown, it will inevitably cause twice as much extra cotton-seed to be produced, and if the state of demand for cotton-seed remains the same, its price will fall. Supply can adopt itself to demand only within the limits imposed by Nature.

An important instance of fixed proportions is the outward and homeward journeys of a railway wagon or a lorry or a ship which goes from A to B and then must return to A. Here the unit is the round trip. The demand may be much greater in one direction; if so, the tendency will be to charge lower rates for the other half of the round trip in order to sell space which would otherwise be empty.

Many farms produce a number of different products, and do not specialize entirely on one, such as wheat, or on joint products in the strictest sense, such as wool and mutton. Bacon and butter go together in Denmark; the skim-milk is fed to pigs. The dung of grazing animals may fertilize the fields where potatoes are to be planted. The tops of sugar-beet can be fed to cattle. Corn crops, which take nitrogen from the soil, can be followed by leguminous plants, which put it back. Root crops and cereal crops use labour at different times of the year.

The economy of a mixed farm may rest, therefore, on a certain combination or rotation of products. It is possible to vary its output, producing more of a product that has risen in price. But the farmer has to take into account not only the direct costs of producing more of that product but also any indirect effects, favourable or unfavourable, upon the costs or outputs of other products which he produces also.

A somewhat similar problem may face a large department store. One of its departments, for example, the restaurant or the library or the hairdressing saloon, may be working at a loss. But it may attract so many customers to the store that it is worth while to go on running it at a loss.

These illustrations show once again how difficult it is to make generalizations that cover all the complexities of the real world. But that is the task of economics; we must cope with it as best we can.

CHAPTER XV

SUPPLY UNDER PERFECT COMPETITION

1. The Assumptions of Perfect Competition

IN order to draw clear-cut conclusions we must make clear-cut assumptions. We can show what would happen under those assumptions: they provide us with a model. When we tackle some actual problem, we can see in what ways the facts differ from the assumptions of our model and lead to conclusions different from those provided by the model.

One important model is perfect competition. This is a state of affairs that is often approached, more or less closely, in agriculture and in some other fields of economic activity.

There are many firms. The output of each firm is so small in relation to the total output of the industry that it considers, and with reason, that variations in its own output will have no effect on the price of its product. In the language of diagrams, the demand curve for that product—wheat, for example—may slope downwards quite steeply. But each firm—each individual wheat-farmer—can produce and supply more wheat without any effect on the market price of wheat; a few hundred bushels more or less will make no difference to a world output of over 200 million tons. For each individual firm, therefore, the demand for its output is infinitely elastic. It is represented on a diagram by a horizontal line at the height of the ruling market price, indicating that the firm can sell as much or as little as it pleases without affecting that price, which is something quite outside its control.

In such circumstances, there is of course no point in advertising by any individual firm (although they might all agree to contribute to co-operative advertising to promote the sales and keep up the price of the product), and if an individual firm does advertise, then it is not working under conditions of perfect competition.

A similar assumption is that a firm can employ as many or as few factors of production as it pleases without affecting their prices. This assumption may appear less realistic. If there is full employment, a firm may have to offer some extra inducement to attract more workers. However, if changes in the demand for different products lead to a fairly large and frequent turnover in the labour market, it may be true that any one firm could engage additional workers, at present wage rates, without much difficulty. Anyway, that is what perfect competition assumes.

The market for the product is supposed to be perfect. This is usually true of commodities that can be graded and that are sold in substantial amounts every day.

Another assumption, also realistic for a great deal of economic activity, is that new firms are quite free to enter the industry. This assumption becomes relevant when we consider what happens over a period of time long enough for new fixed capital to be produced or for land to be adapted to different purposes.

In fact, most firms produce several products, and this helps them to adapt their output to changes in demand. But it is usual to simplify the discussion by supposing that each firm produces only one product.

2. Fixed Costs and Variable Costs

The *fixed costs* of a firm are those costs that do not vary with the size of its output. They are the same—so many pounds sterling a year— whether its output is large or small. For example, the money which a firm sets aside to form a reserve for depreciation on its fixed capital is a fixed cost. It is true that the buildings, plants, and machinery may wear out a little sooner if they are worked harder (in order to produce a greater output), but such small differences in the probable life of the assets are usually neglected; moreover, the depreciation reserve is usually planned to cover obsolescence as well as physical wearing-out. Another fixed cost is the salary of the manager, and indeed the whole of the salaries of the managerial and office staff, provided that the same staff could cope with a larger output and that none of them would be dismissed if output were smaller.

The *variable costs* of a firm are those costs that do vary with the size of its output. They consist mainly of wages and of payments for materials. In order to produce more, a firm must take on more workers and buy more materials; its total wages-bill and its total outlay on materials will vary with the size of its output.

This distinction between fixed costs and variable costs is a short-period distinction. In the long run, machinery and other fixed capital wears out or is scrapped. It can be replaced by whatever amount and type of fixed capital the firm considers appropriate for the size and type of output that it now plans to produce. The new fixed capital can be adapted to different methods of production; for example, it may embody more labour-saving devices. Or it can be designed to produce quite a different product; the firm can leave its present industry and enter a new one. In the long run, therefore, there are no fixed costs; all costs are variable costs.

Even for the short period, the line of demarcation between fixed costs and variable costs is not always very clear. Some parts of fixed capital need frequent renewal, depending on how hard they are worked. For example, the linings of coke-ovens have to be replaced every few days, the knives of rice-hullers every few weeks, the tyres of lorries every few months; all these are variable costs. But what of parts that last for, say, about two years? Clearly the line must be drawn somewhat arbitrarily. Again, in practice a large increase in output may involve paying a bonus to the manager or taking on one or two extra clerks in the office or perhaps employing another foreman in the works. Nevertheless the distinction between fixed costs and variable costs is useful for short-period analysis, and can usually be applied if the changes in output are not large.

3. MARGINAL COST

The marginal cost of a firm is the addition to its total costs that must be made in order to increase its output, per period of time, by one unit. This may strike the reader as a silly concept. What farmer does or can plan to produce a single extra bushel of wheat, what manufacturer to produce a single extra yard of cloth, what mine to produce a single extra ton of coal? But for this purpose we can define a unit as whatever quantity is appropriate. We can take as a unit whatever minimum amount does enter into the calculations of the firm. For example, the unit of wheat can be taken as ten bushels, or a hundred bushels; and so on. Defined in this way, the extra cost of an additional unit makes sense.

The fixed costs are fixed and therefore do not affect marginal cost. Marginal cost is the addition to total variable costs needed to produce an extra unit.

It is true that some firms do not know exactly how much extra output will result from an extra input. Farming, especially, is something of a gamble. The farmer may have a good harvest or he may have a bad one. But he has to make a guess at how much extra output he will get from employing so many extra workers, or from using so much more fertilizer or so much more cattle-feed. If his guess is too conservative, he will deprive himself of profits which he might have made. He will probably, therefore, count on average yields and consider himself lucky if they are higher and unlucky if they are lower.

Under perfect competition, marginal costs increase, and must increase, as the output of the firm expands. It is increasing marginal costs that limit the expansion of any one firm, and keep it small relatively to the industry as a whole.

The reason for increasing marginal costs is diminishing returns. In the short period, the *capacity* of each firm—that is, its amount of land, buildings, plant and machinery, and other fixed capital—is given and

H   B.E.

cannot be altered. As more workers (or other variable factors) are employed in conjunction with this fixed capacity, their marginal products will fall.

Let us go back to the table on page 109. A part of that table reads as follows, for a square mile of wheat-land—

Number of Men	Marginal Product per Man
5	100
6	76
7	54
8	26

Whatever the rate of wages, and whatever the price of wheat, marginal costs are rising because the marginal productivity of labour falls as output expands.

Suppose that agricultural wages are £300 a year. Adding a fifth man adds 100 units of wheat; its marginal cost is £3 a unit. Adding a sixth man adds 76 units of wheat; its marginal cost is nearly £3 19s. a unit. Adding a seventh man adds 54 units of wheat; its marginal cost is just over £5 11s. a unit. Adding an eighth man adds 26 units of wheat; its marginal cost is nearly £11 11s. a unit.

It will pay to employ as many as five men to the square mile only when the price of a "unit" of wheat (ten bushels, for example) is more than £3. It will pay to employ six men only if the price is £3 19s., seven men only if it is over £5 11s., eight men only if it is £11 11s.

This particular example shows discontinuity, large jumps in marginal cost, because one man per square mile is a substantial percentage addition to the labour force. The addition of one man to a labour force of hundreds of thousands would cause only a very slight increase in marginal cost. It is often possible, in effect, to vary a small labour force by a much smaller percentage than in the above example. This becomes obvious when we think of a man-hour rather than a man-year as the unit of labour. More or less overtime can be worked, or a farmer can hire temporary help, at harvest-time for example, for a few weeks during the year. Hence we are more or less justified in showing marginal cost, diagrammatically, as a continuous curve.

Labour is not the only variable factor. Marginal costs do not consist entirely of wages. For example, a farmer may use more or less fertilizer or cattle-feed, or may use more expensive types which are expected to give better results. But the rule of diminishing returns, and therefore of increasing marginal costs, is valid for any variable factor, and therefore for any combination of variable factors; as the capacity (the fixed factors) of the firm is given, an increase of x per cent in the variable factors only will increase the output by less than x per cent.

4. Why Marginal Cost Equals Price

An assumption usually made is that any firm will try to maximize its profits. On that assumption, a firm will expand its output so long as the extra output adds more to its receipts, or revenue, than it adds to its costs. It will expand up to the point at which its marginal revenue equals its marginal costs. Under perfect competition, the marginal revenue for an additional unit of output is the price of that unit; therefore under perfect competition marginal cost will tend to equal price.

Is this a realistic conclusion? To revert to our example, suppose that the price of wheat is £5 a unit. Would the farmer say to himself: "Well, I will employ only five men, because that will keep my marginal costs down to £3 a unit and leave me well on the safe side?" Why should he? A sixth man costs him another £300 a year and gives him another 76 units—that is, another £380 a year. He will not be likely to forgo another £80 in profits.

If the price were £4 a unit, he might hesitate. In that event, the extra 76 units would sell for only £304, adding only £4 to his profits. He might think it would not be worth the risk and trouble of employing a sixth man; after all, the £4 is based on guesswork: he might have a bad crop, or the price of wheat might fall. On the other hand, he might feel that a larger output would improve his own standing in the community or that it was his duty to get the most out of his land. For one reason or another, many firms go bankrupt every year (there are about 2,000 bankruptcies a year in Great Britain), and some of them fail because they over-expanded. I conclude that it is fairly realistic to assume that under perfect competition a firm will expand up to the point at which its marginal costs per unit equal the price per unit of its product.

This is shown in the diagram on p. 212.

The horizontal line shows the price of wheat, or whatever the product may be; it is the demand curve for the wheat of that particular farmer, since he can sell as much as he chooses to produce at that price.

His total receipts are shown by the area $OPSQ$ (the price per unit OP multiplied by the number of units OQ).

His total variable costs are shown by the area $ORSQ$ under the marginal cost curve. This area can be thought of as made up of a number of thin rectangular pillars; [1] the first, next to O, is the additional cost of producing one unit rather than none, the next is the additional cost of producing two units instead of one, and so on.

Hence the shaded area RPS is the sum available for his fixed costs plus his profits. His object is to make the shaded area as large as possible. He will therefore produce right up to OQ units. True, as

[1] As in the first diagram in the Note to Chapter VII.

he approaches OQ the extra cost of each extra unit increases, but so long as its extra cost is less than its price it is worth producing. Beyond OQ, however, the extra cost of an extra unit exceeds its price and therefore he would be increasing his costs more than his receipts if he produced more than OQ units. In other words, he will produce that output at which his marginal cost of production (SQ) is equal to the price (OP) of his product.

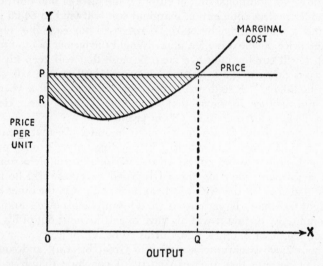

The same reasoning applies to every firm in the industry. All will have exactly the same marginal cost because all will plan their output to make marginal cost equal to price, and the price is the same for all.

Firms may differ widely in other respects. Some may produce a much larger output than others; the main reason for this will be that they have much more capacity—for example, much larger farms. Some may use different methods from others; those who use more machinery, for example, will have a higher proportion of fixed costs and a lower proportion of variable costs. But all will have increasing marginal costs; and all will tend to produce whatever output (given their capacity) will make their marginal costs equal to the price of their product.

5. THE SHORT-PERIOD SUPPLY CURVE

We can now explain how the short-period supply curve is obtained. From the marginal-cost curve of each firm find what output it would supply at a price P_1. The sum of all these outputs is the total output which the industry would supply at the price P_1. Then follow the same procedure for other prices—P_2, P_3, and so forth.

The resulting short-period supply curve may need to be corrected, however, for any external economies or diseconomies that would come about in the short period owing to the expansion or contraction of the industry as a whole. For example, if the materials used by the industry are themselves produced under perfect competition, or at any rate under conditions of increasing marginal cost, a substantial expansion of the industry will tend to raise their prices and thereby to make the short-period supply curve of the industry slope upwards more steeply.

6. The Long Period

In the long run, the output of an industry depends on the number of firms in the industry and on the capacity of each firm. In equilibrium, the rate of profit on the capital employed will be the same as in other industries. If it is higher, new firms will tend to enter the industry and existing firms to expand their capacity. If it is lower, some firms will tend to leave the industry or to reduce their capacity.

The period of time needed to expand capacity depends on the nature of that capacity. New plant and machinery may take only a few months, or only a year or two, to construct and install, but it takes seven years before a newly-planted rubber tree begins to yield.

The period of time needed to contract capacity depends partly on how much of the existing capacity is approaching the end of its life. Plant that has worn out is not likely to be replaced if the money that would be needed to buy new plant of the same type could earn more in some other form of investment. But plant (and other fixed capital) that is still in good working condition will continue to be used so long as it brings in a return greater than could be obtained by selling it for scrap and investing the proceeds.

How many firms leave the industry, either going bankrupt or switching over to some other product, is of little relevance to the contraction of *capacity*. A firm that is inefficiently managed may go bankrupt, but if its plant is fairly new, it may be sold to somebody else and continue to be used in the industry. On the other hand, a firm that continues in the industry may scrap some of its fixed capital (which is old, and costing too much in repairs) or may be able to convert some of it to other uses.

In addition to changes in capacity, an expanding industry will employ more workers and other variable factors, while a contracting industry will employ fewer, as time goes on.

Equilibrium will be reached again—that is to say, there will be no longer any incentive to expand or to contract—when new investment in that industry would yield the same rate of return (after allowing for any special risks) as new investment in any other industry.

CHAPTER XVI

SUPPLY UNDER MONOPOLY

1. The Foundations of Monopoly Power

A MONOPOLIST is, literally, a sole seller. If we interpret the term "commodity" in the strict and narrow sense, we see monopolies all round us. Mr. Blank is the sole proprietor of Blank's tea, and the Grand Hotel is the only hotel of that name in the town. Every manufacturer of a branded article and every owner of an establishment such as a shop or a cinema or a restaurant is, strictly, a monopolist; the proof is that he can fix what prices he pleases. But they are not commonly thought of as monopolists, for their degree of monopoly power is very limited. They have to meet the competition of very close substitutes; Mr. Blank has to meet the competition of other more or less similar brands of tea, and the Grand Hotel has to meet the competition of other hotels.

A monopolist in the popular sense controls the supply of some commodity or service for which there is no very close substitute. He may not control the whole supply, but he controls enough of it to dominate the market and to determine the price. He may be a single large firm, or a group of firms combined together in a cartel, or he may be a Government or some other public authority. His monopoly may be world-wide, like that of the International Nickel Corporation of Canada, or nation-wide, like that of the British Milk Marketing Board, or local, like that of London Transport. The present chapter discusses this type of monopoly.

Even this type of monopoly has to face competition from possible substitutes. Nickel has to compete with other metals; the Milk Marketing Board has to compete with imported canned milk and other imported dairy products; London Transport has to compete with taxis and with private cars and cycles. In the last resort, all commodities and services are rivals in their claims on the limited purse of the consumer. That is why there is no such thing as an absolute monopolist.

In other words, every monopolist is limited by the demand for his product. Despite all his efforts (for example, by advertising) to increase his sales, he cannot force people to buy. Supply and demand have been likened to the two blades of a pair of scissors; he can control the former but not the latter. The demand schedule for his product as for any other, will reflect the substitutes, the various alternatives, available to consumers; and the more he charges the less he will sell.

> The fortunate monopolist
> Can fix what price he chooses,
> But if he cannot sell enough
> He doesn't gain; he loses.

Monopoly power is based entirely on control over supply. The monopolist can keep up the price only by restricting the output. How does he manage to keep out competitors and to remain the sole producer, or at any rate the dominant producer?

He may own all the deposits of some mineral; if there are no other deposits, he can have no direct competitors. Thus the International Nickel Corporation of Canada owns most of the known deposits of nickel in the world, and the Molybdenum Corporation of the U.S.A. most of the molybdenum deposits. A firm that owns the only deposit in a district of coal, or building stone, or some other mineral, has a local monopoly, but the price it can get is limited by the possibility of transporting similar minerals from elsewhere.

Some crops require special conditions of climate and soil, found only in one or two limited areas. The various wine-growing districts of France are examples of such areas. Turkish tobacco grows only in Greece, Turkey, and Bulgaria; cinchona bark (used for quinine) comes mainly from Indonesia; Manila hemp mainly from the Philippines; and a number of other examples could be given. Such circumstances may give rise to monopoly. If there are many separate producers, their Governments may restrict the supply, in order to maintain the price. For example, the Government may restrict the acreage on which the crop may be grown or, if it is mainly exported, may impose special export duties on it.

Some products, especially in the chemical industries, are manufactured by a secret process known only to one firm or to a small group of firms who combine together.

A monopoly may be based on the possession of an exclusive legal privilege. Thus most Governments, in order to encourage invention, grant patent rights which give their possessors the monopoly, for a term of years, of using a new process or invention that they have discovered or that they have purchased from the inventor. Or the State may simply confer a legal monopoly in some field upon itself, as the French Government has given itself the monopoly of tobacco manufacture in France, or upon some public authority such as the British Broadcasting Corporation, or upon existing producers: for example, hop-growers in Great Britain are protected by law from the entry of new capacity into their industry.

As a rule, a monopoly based on legal privileges will have a monopoly only in its home market. Even there, it may be subject to competition from imports. But its Government may strengthen its position by tax-ing or even prohibiting such imports.

Another circumstance which may give rise to monopoly is that the most profitable method of production may require expensive and specialized plant. Hence the number of firms will be relatively small, and this will make it easier for them to combine in some type of cartel in order to exercise a monopolistic control over the supply of their products. This is the case, for example, in the heavy branches of the iron and steel industry.

The same circumstances may deter new firms, in the short run, from entering the industry. They will hesitate before investing a large amount of capital in highly specific plant. Existing firms may be making good profits, but the entry of another firm might increase total capacity so much that the profits of all would be reduced below the normal level—just as one shop in a small village may do well whereas two would both do badly. Moreover, a new firm will need to feel confident of making good profits in the more distant as well as in the immediate future before it decides to enter the industry and to invest in fixed capital which will last a long time.

Nevertheless a period of considerable prosperity is likely to tempt new firms to enter. Since industries of this type, apart from public utilities, are mainly constructional industries, the demand for their products fluctuates considerably as between trade booms and trade depressions. New firms tend to enter during a boom, and when a depression comes, the industry finds itself with an enlarged capacity but facing a diminished demand. Hence such industries tend to make monopoly profits in times of boom but to fare badly in times of depression.

"Public utilities" tend to be local monopolies. I discuss them in Section 5 of this chapter.

The extent to which a trade union may raise or maintain the wages of its members by monopolistic action is discussed in Chapter XXVI.

The foregoing summary covers most of the circumstances that give rise to monopolies in the popular sense of the term.

2. MONOPOLY PRICE

Let us consider a monopolist who is the sole producer of a commodity and who wishes to maximize his profits. These two assumptions enable us to draw clear-cut conclusions. They may not be true. A monopoly may have some competitors who are already established, although they produce only a small proportion of the total output. A monopoly which is run by a Government or by some other public authority will usually act in what it deems to be the best interests of the community instead of trying to maximize its own profits, and even a private monopolist often refrains from exploiting his monopoly power to the full lest by so doing he should arouse public protests and be brought under Government control. Nevertheless I make these two assumptions in order to provide a simple model about which we can make statements that are definite and not vague.

The monopolist can fix whatever price he pleases or can sell whatever (weekly) amount he pleases; but he cannot sell as much as he likes at whatever price he likes. The amount that he can sell at any given price depends upon the conditions of demand for his product. Hence it is a matter of indifference whether we ask what price he will find most profitable or what output he will find most profitable; his volume of sales at whatever price he fixes, or the price at which he can sell whatever output he decides to produce, are determined for him by the conditions of demand.

His most profitable output will be that output at which his marginal costs and his marginal revenue are equal to one another. The rest of this section is merely an expansion of that statement.

It is very rare for a monopolist to have no costs, but it is helpful to begin by considering such a case. He may have cornered the stock of some commodity or he may own the only spring of water in a district, selling the water to customers who fill their own buckets, or he may own the only bridge across a river, and charge a toll. In such a case, all his receipts will be profits and he will aim at maximizing his total receipts. After a point, further increases in his volume of sales, implying a lower price per unit, must *diminish* his total receipts. If consumers spend more money upon his commodity, they have less to spend upon other things, so that there must be some (weekly) sum of money which is the utmost that he can obtain from consumers. A typical curve showing how total receipts vary with output (or sales) will rise to a maximum and then decline. Before this maximum is reached, the elasticity of demand is greater than unity; after it is reached, it is less than unity; and around the maximum it is equal to unity (for since the curve is neither rising nor falling it must be horizontal). The marginal costs of the monopolist are zero, and therefore his most profitable output is that at which his marginal revenue is also zero—a slight increase in his output neither increasing nor diminishing his total receipts, since they are at a maximum.

Suppose now that a monopolist has costs. His *marginal* costs may be rising or falling or constant, but it is certain that his *total* costs will be greater for any given output than for any smaller output. This means that his marginal costs will always be positive, and therefore his most profitable output will be one at which his marginal revenue is positive: it must therefore be smaller than it would be if he had no costs, since in that case, as we have seen, his marginal revenue would be zero. (Hence, if he maximizes his profits, he will charge a price at which

H 2   B.E.

the elasticity of demand for his product is greater than unity.) And even if his marginal costs are falling, there must be some point beyond which his marginal revenue would be less than his marginal costs, and beyond which, therefore, it would not pay him to expand his output.

The following table, in which the figures are of course hypothetical, shows part of the cost schedule of a monopolist and the corresponding part of the demand schedule for his product. I suppose that he would vary his output by 1,000 units at a time and that his marginal costs are constant at 16,000 shillings per 1,000 units. (The table assumes that depreciation charges, managerial and office expenses, advertising, and other fixed costs amount to 300,000s. a week; variable costs are 16s. a unit.) His profits are maximized at a (weekly) output of 14,000 units, since at this output his marginal costs and his marginal receipts are as nearly equal as possible. If he increased his output to 15,000 units, he would increase his total costs by 16,000s. and his total receipts by only 13,000s., thereby reducing his profits. If he reduced his output to 13,000 units, he would reduce his total costs by 16,000s. and his total receipts by 17,000s., so that this course also would diminish his profits.

Output per Week	Price per Unit s.	Total Revenue s.	Marginal Revenue s.	Total Costs s.	Marginal Costs s.	Profits s.
10,000	50	500,000	—	460,000	—	40,000
11,000	48	528,000	28,000	476,000	16,000	52,000
12,000	47	564,000	36,000	492,000	16,000	72,000
13,000	45	585,000	21,000	508,000	16,000	77,000
14,000	43	602,000	17,000	524,000	16,000	78,000
15,000	41	615,000	13,000	540,000	16,000	75,000
16,000	39	624,000	9,000	556,000	16,000	68,000
17,000	37	629,000	5,000	572,000	16,000	57,000
18,000	35	630,000	1,000	588,000	16,000	42,000
19,000	33	627,000	−3,000	604,000	16,000	23,000

The diagram below shows the situation. Quantities of output are measured along the horizontal axis and total receipts and total costs up the vertical axis. The curve labelled *TR* shows the total receipts obtained from the corresponding quantity of output. It rises to a maximum at *M* and then declines. That labelled *TC* shows the total cost of each amount of output. We make it begin above *O* because we assume a certain fixed charge for equipment. It has a constant slope, showing constant marginal costs. If marginal costs were falling, it would tend to flatten from left to right, and if they were rising, it would tend to do the opposite. The object of the monopolist is to maximize the difference *AB* between his total receipts *AQ* and his total costs *BQ*. He achieves this object by producing (and selling)

that amount OQ at which his marginal receipts and his marginal
costs are equal: at which, that is to say, the slope of TR is the same as
the slope of TC (TR near the point A being parallel to TC near the
point B).

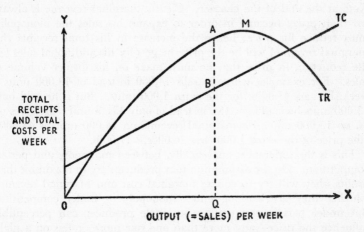

The price per unit is not shown directly. The price per unit of any
output OQ is the total receipts QA divided by the output OQ.

An alternative diagram is given below. The most profitable output
is OQ, for at this output marginal revenue and marginal costs are
equal.

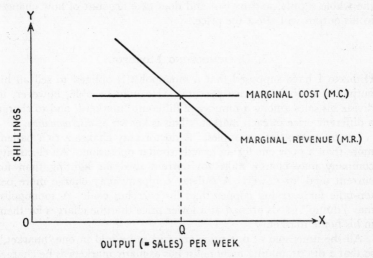

Of course marginal revenue may not be a straight line, but it will
be falling. Nor need marginal costs be constant; they may be increasing

(in which case MC would slope upward) or, in exceptional cases, they may be falling; but sooner or later marginal costs will exceed marginal revenue (MC cutting MR "from below").

The relation between marginal revenue and price is explained in a Note at the end of the chapter. Clearly marginal revenue is always *less* than price, because in order to expand his sales the monopolist must reduce his price; hence the increase in his total receipts (his marginal revenue) will be the price he gets for his additional sales less the reduction in price that he must make on his former volume of sales. For example, when he sells 14,000 instead of 13,000 units a week, he gets 43,000s. for the extra 1,000 units. But if he sold only 13,000 units he could get 45s. instead of only 43s. a unit. He gives up 2s. on 13,000 units; his marginal revenue on 14,000 units is 43,000s. (the price of the extra 1,000) less 26,000s. = 17,000s.

This is the difference, analytically, between monopoly and perfect competition. On the assumption that producers try to maximize their profits, they will try to equate marginal cost and marginal revenue, whether they are working under monopoly or under competition. But under perfect competition no single producer can perceptibly influence the price—any more than one star more or less on a night of stars, one grain of sand more or less in a heap of sand, one hair more or less on most heads, makes any perceptible difference. Hence each producer accepts the ruling price as a market fact which he is powerless to alter. For him, marginal revenue is the same as price. But for the monopolist, marginal revenue is less than price, for he can control the whole supply, and he can and does take account of how changes in his output will affect the price.

3. Discriminating Monopoly

Hitherto I have supposed that a monopolist is obliged to sell all his output at a uniform price per unit. He may be able, however, to divide his sales among a number of different "markets" and to charge a different price in each market. This is known as *discrimination*.

Let me give a few examples. A doctor may charge a rich patient more than a poor one for an exactly similar operation. An electricity company may charge more for current used for lighting than for current used for power. A railway company may charge more per ton-mile for carrying copper than for carrying coal. A monopolist may "dump" goods abroad at a lower price than he charges for them in his home market.

All the units sold at one price are said to be sold in one "market," so that a discriminating monopolist has as many markets as he charges different prices. The same person may of course purchase from the monopolist in two or more different markets, as when a man sends two or more different commodities, charged at different rates per ton-mile, by the same railway.

Discriminating monopoly is possible only if the goods or services sold in the cheaper market (that is, at a lower price) cannot readily be transferred to the dearer market. Thus it would hardly be possible for a firm to charge higher prices to well-dressed customers. For well-dressed persons would then either dress badly in order to make purchases or send their badly-dressed servants or friends to buy on their behalf. (Some Hollywood stars employ "shoppers" for this reason.) But a man cannot readily disguise his identity when he visits a doctor; copper cannot be transformed into coal while it travels by rail; the use of separate meters prevents electric current charged as power from being used for lighting; and the price of goods sold abroad can be lower than the home price by the cost of transport both ways—if the difference is greater, foreign buyers can make a profit by reselling, at a price just below the home price, in the home market.

If a monopolist can divide his sales among a number of markets, between which the conditions of demand are different, he will make greater profits by charging a different price in each market. He will maximize his profits by charging such prices that *his marginal costs (for his total output) are equal to the marginal revenue in each separate market*. For if he does this, he will gain neither by increasing nor by decreasing his output nor yet by transferring some sales from one market to another.

A simple illustration may be useful. Suppose that a monopolist has the same cost schedule as that shown in our table, and can vary his output by 1,000 units at a time, his marginal costs (for a further 1,000 units) being always 16,000s. Suppose that he has two markets. In one, the demand schedule is as shown in our table. In this market, therefore, he will sell 14,000 units at a price of 43s. per unit, his marginal revenue (from the fourteenth thousand) being 17,000s. In the other market, suppose that the relevant part of the demand schedule is as follows—

Quantity	Price per Unit s.	Total Revenue s.	Marginal Revenue s.
1,000	40	40,000	—
2,000	30	60,000	20,000
3,000	26	78,000	18,000
4,000	21	84,000	6,000

In this market he will charge 26s., his marginal revenue (from the third thousand) being 18,000s. His total output, therefore, will be 17,000 and his total profits 602,000 + 78,000 − 572,000 = 108,000s.—

these being the maximum total profits which he can obtain under the given conditions.[1]

It should be noted that discrimination is profitable only if elasticity of demand is different in the various markets. There are doubtless many monopolists who could discriminate if they chose but who, because this condition is absent, do not find this course profitable.

As between two (or more) markets, the most profitable price will be lower in the market where the elasticity of demand is greater. The elasticity of demand for a commodity at any given price depends on how far fairly close substitutes are available at that price. A similar commodity from another country is a very close substitute. Hence the dumping price at which a commodity is sold in the world market will be lower than the price in the home market, especially if the home market is protected by import duties. The elasticity of demand for a producers' good will reflect the elasticity of demand for the product which it is used in making. For example, the demand for "manufacturing" milk is fairly elastic, since products such as chocolate and cheese have to compete with imports. Hence the Milk Marketing Board can charge a much higher price for milk sold for consumption as liquid milk than for the rest of the milk, which they sell to manufacturers. In the same way, a much lower price is usually charged for electricity used in industry than for electricity used in the home.

The possibility of expanding output by dumping on a foreign market will raise the home price if marginal costs are rising, lower it if they are falling, and leave it unchanged if (as in the above example) they are constant.

4. MONOPOLY BUYING

A further complication is that a firm may be a monopolistic buyer of a certain factor, such as a particular type of labour. That will depend on whether or not units of that factor can readily be sold to other firms instead. A firm may have a complete monopoly of its product and yet no monopoly at all in the purchase of its factors, for which it has to compete with other firms and to accept the market prices. On the other hand, a firm may be the main source of employment in a district and may therefore have some monopoly power over the wages it pays, although it sells its products in competition with other firms and must accept the market prices for them.

Just as its marginal revenue is below its selling price for a firm with

[1] I hope that my examples are not misleading. On the figures, marginal revenue (17,000s. in the first market and 18,000s. in the second) exceeds marginal cost (16,000s.). That is because I assume that he varies his output by 1,000 units at a time. If he varied his output by 1 unit at a time, his marginal cost would be 16s. and marginal revenue in each market would also be exactly 16s. Profits are maximized when marginal revenue equals marginal cost.

a monopoly of its products, so is its marginal cost above the price of the factor for a firm with a monopoly in the purchase of that factor. Suppose that such a firm employs 5,000 workers at £10 a week, but would have to pay £11 a week to attract an additional 1,000. If it did so, it would have to pay £11 a week to its present workers also, in order to prevent discontent and to maintain good employer-employee relations. The marginal cost to the firm of another 1,000 workers would not be merely their wages, namely £11,000 a week. It would include also the extra £1 a week to its present 5,000 workers, making £16,000 a week in all.

The consequence is that a firm with some monopoly power in the purchase of its factors will restrict its output to less than it would produce under competition. For it will include in its marginal cost any consequent increase in the prices it must pay for all its units of a factor when it employs additional units. Its marginal costs will therefore rise more steeply than if the market prices of the factors were outside its control; and in so far as it equates its marginal cost with its marginal revenue, it will produce correspondingly less.

5. PUBLIC UTILITIES

Public utilities include undertakings providing water, electricity, gas, telephone and telegraph services, and rail transport. They are called public utilities not because they provide for essential needs—bread is more essential than telephone calls—but because they tend to be local monopolies.

They require a relatively large amount of specialized plant and equipment. Hence their fixed costs are large. They are usually greater, and sometimes much greater, than their variable costs. This is a feature, tending to deter new investors and therefore making for monopoly, which they share with other industries, such as the iron and steel industry. But in addition their market is restricted, like that of a village cinema. It is restricted to the district covered by the rails, cables, pipes, or wires, which form a large part of their fixed capital. A steel plant can sell its products anywhere; potentially, it has a world market, for its products are commodities that can be transported. But a railway can provide transport only between the points through which it passes; a power station can supply electricity only to the customers reached by its cables and wires. Once a public utility is established in a district, it can meet an expansion of local demand, by sending out more tentacles from its main cables, more cheaply than a new-comer, who would have to duplicate the cables, pipes, or wires of the established undertaking (or, in the case of a railway, to build a parallel permanent way). Hence new-comers are deterred; the existing public utility may be making monopoly profits, but if another undertaking entered the same field, supplying the same area, both might make losses. That is why public utilities tend to be local monopolies.

Another feature of public utilities is that they can and do charge discriminatory prices. Railways usually charge more per ton-mile for valuable goods than for heavy goods such as coal or ore. (The demand for transport for the latter is more elastic because transport costs form a higher percentage of their value.) An electricity company often charges the same consumer more per unit, sometimes much more, for current used for lighting than for current used for heating or power. (The demand for electricity for the latter uses is much more elastic, as coal can be used as a substitute.) This discrimination is possible because public utilities provide services that cannot easily be transferred from one customer to another, or from one use to another. Textiles cannot be disguised as coal in order to get the benefit of the lower railway charges on coal; electricity supplied as power cannot be used for light without altering the "points" or tampering with the separate meters, both legal offences; the ordinary person cannot send cables at reduced Press rates.

Since public utilities tend to be monopolies, and discriminating monopolies at that, they are usually either owned and operated by some public authority, as in Great Britain, or closely controlled by the State. In the latter event, the course sometimes adopted is to limit their profits to a certain percentage on their capital. A better plan is to fix their charges at levels that will give them a moderate profit if they show moderate efficiency, but will still leave them with a sufficient incentive to reduce their costs or expand their output and thereby increase their profits.

A public utility is often worked below full capacity. One reason for this is that if the service is to be provided at all for a particular district, fixed capital must be provided capable of supplying more than the existing demand. For example, it may be worth while to build a railway line between two points although only a few trains a day will be required. Yet, once the permanent way is there, it could probably cope with considerably more trains. Again, it may be cheaper to produce a given output—of, say, electricity—from a large plant working below capacity than from a smaller plant.

Another reason for excess capacity in public utilities is that demand fluctuates over time. Unless the product can be stored (as with gas) a plant large enough to cater for the "peak" demand must have excess capacity when the demand is below this level.

Once the plant and equipment have been set up, it may be possible by means of advertising and other propaganda to raise the demand during relatively slack periods up towards the peak level and to reduce the peak level if that strains the capacity of the plant and raises marginal costs sharply. The method of charging may help to achieve this aim. Thus railways may charge cheap fares during the intervals between the rush hours, and telephone calls may be cheaper at night. If a peak occurs for electricity at certain hours, a much higher rate per unit could be charged for current consumed during those periods.

Variable costs are unlikely to be rising if the plant and equipment are worked below full capacity. Hence a price per unit equal to marginal cost would fail to cover the fixed costs; in other words it would cover only a part, perhaps well below half, of the total costs of the undertaking. What should be done? One course would be to charge a price per unit equal to average total cost. This would usually be much higher than marginal cost. But it is in the social interest to meet the potential demand of consumers who are prepared to pay prices for extra units which cover the extra cost of supplying those units.

A possible solution is the *two-part tariff*. In Great Britain this now applies to electricity and telephone service and is employed by a growing number of gas undertakings. The consumer has to pay two charges. The first is a fixed charge, usually per quarter, such as the rental charged for a telephone. This charge does not vary with his consumption. It must be paid whether he consumes much, little, or none of the service in question. All the fixed charges, taken together, would about cover the fixed costs of the undertaking. The second is a charge per unit of service consumed. This covers marginal costs.

This method of charging, where practicable, seems to be the best from a social standpoint. For water, the variable charge is often nil. The marginal cost of supplying water, once all the fixed capital, including pipes, is installed, may be quite low, and it may be thought desirable in the interest of hygiene to encourage people to use water freely. In the same way, the increased use of a bridge may increase costs by very little. It may therefore be wise to pay for the bridge out of taxation (levied partly on the owners of neighbouring land whose value is raised by the construction of the bridge) and to permit people to use it freely instead of paying a toll.

6. Cartels in Manufacturing Industries

The leading firms in an industry may combine together, sinking their individual identities, or one firm may absorb the others. The firm which finally emerges as the result of these amalgamations is called a *trust* in the United States.

But it is also possible for the leading firms in an industry to combine together, retaining their separate identities, and uniting only for the purpose of pursuing a common monopolistic policy in their joint interests. Such a combination of firms is usually known as a *cartel*.

A cartel may be international. A well-known example is the

Shipping Conferences, at which the liner companies of different countries agree on what rates they will charge for freight and passenger fares. (They try to keep their customers by giving them *deferred rebates*. If a customer ships all his goods in Conference ships over a period of, say, six months and continues to do so during the next period, he is given a rebate of, say, 10 per cent on the freight charges which he paid during the first period.) Before the war, there were international cartels in a number of fields, including iron and steel and the chemical industries. In 1952 the United States alleged that there was an international cartel for petroleum products.

The larger the number of firms, the more difficult it is for them to reach agreement. Partly for this reason, and partly because most countries protect their own manufacturers to some extent by import duties or other restrictions on competing imports, most cartels are national. Before the war, cartels were especially common in Germany, and in 1923 they were encouraged by special legislation: a Cartel Court was set up which enforced agreements among the members of a cartel unless they were deemed to be against the public interest.

If a cartel agrees merely on a list of minimum prices for its various products, it is unlikely to last very long. Some firms will receive too few orders and will be tempted to expand their sales by charging a lower price, either covertly, through such devices as secret rebates, or openly, by breaking away from the cartel. Hence a cartel may agree on what proportion of the total sales each firm will get, and may set up a central selling agency, which receives all orders and all payments. Moreover, in order to avoid large unsold stocks (which would lead buyers to believe that prices must fall, and therefore to restrict their purchases) each firm may be given a "quota" of output which it must not exceed.

Even when existing producers, considered as a group, can make considerably greater profits by combining to restrict their output, negotiations to create a cartel may well break down. The divergent claims of different firms must be reconciled. Firms which have produced a relatively large share of the total output in the past will demand the same share in the future. Firms which are expanding—owing, for example, to an unusually efficient management—will demand a larger share than they obtained in the past. Firms with a greater "capacity" for producing, as measured by the size of their fixed assets, such as plant, will demand a correspondingly greater share. As a rule, it will be possible to reconcile conflicting claims and to create a cartel based on voluntary agreement only when the number of firms in the industry is fairly small. This is likely to be the case if there are technical advantages in large plants, as in the iron and steel industry, or if the supply of some essential raw material is confined to a few localities, as with potash, or if secret processes are used, as with dyestuffs and other chemical products. If the number of producers is large, it will be very difficult to organize them for monopolistic action unless some measure of governmental compulsion is employed.

The successful maintenance of a cartel, once it is formed, is threatened both from within and from without. Conditions will change as time goes on, and will make it difficult for the cartel to retain the adherence or "loyalty" of some of its members. Some firms will find that consumers demand more of their particular products than before and will resent having to pass on orders (in excess of their quota) to be executed by other members of the cartel. Again, some firms will outstrip others in taking advantage of the progress of technical knowledge, and will conclude that they have more to gain by expanding their sales at lower prices than by continuing their membership of the cartel. If the demand for the products of the industry falls considerably, the proportion of "unused capacity" will increase, and this will strengthen the desire of some firms to break away and make fuller use of their plants, thus increasing their receipts, by selling at lower prices. Hence cartels which do not rest on Government support tend to break up after a relatively short time and to be revived only if there is a readjustment of quotas among the previous members. Such a reorganization, to be successful, must include also important "outsiders" who arose or expanded during the life of the scheme. This brings us to the second point: the danger from without.

Producers outside the cartel are in a fortunate position. They can take advantage of the monopoly prices due to restriction of output by the cartel, whilst they themselves can produce as much as they please. The greater the success of the cartel in raising prices, or in maintaining them despite falling costs, the greater is the inducement to new firms to enter the industry and to existing "outside" producers to expand their output. But as such outside output increases, the cartel has to restrict its own output correspondingly more in order to maintain the prevailing prices (unless demand also happens to increase), and after a point the burden will become too heavy for it to bear. Either it will break up or there will be a reorganization, and most of the outside producers (faced with the alternative of a collapse of prices) will join the cartel in order that it may survive.

Thus a cartel can succeed in maintaining prices, for any considerable period, only if it can both maintain loyalty among its members and prevent any marked expansion of outside production.

7. COMMODITY CONTROL SCHEMES

The Great Depression of 1929-32 brought about a heavy fall in the prices of most agricultural products. For example, wheat fell from over a dollar in 1929 to 39 cents in 1933, and rubber fell over the same period from about eightpence a pound to twopence a pound. Most farmers suffered great hardship. This was the background to the various national measures taken by a number of countries to help their farmers during the early 1930s, and to the international measures, the commodity control schemes, of that period.

Most agricultural commodities are produced by large numbers of farmers under conditions approaching perfect competition. In Great Britain, most of the work is done by hired labour and minimum wages are fixed by law. But Great Britain is exceptional in both respects. In many countries the family farm or smallholding is the rule. The farmer and his family do most or all of the work. Even when times are bad, the farmer is usually very reluctant to abandon his farm. He may own it, and naturally will not want to sell it for a trifle or to hand it over to his creditors; he may like being his own employer; he may like farming; he may not be able to get another job which seems worth taking. Hence most farmers carry on, working as hard as before, or perhaps harder, despite a large fall in the prices of their products. The land is there to be worked; in the case of tree crops, the fruits or nuts or latex are there for the picking or tapping; there are no heavy current expenses, as in manufacturing, for materials or for renewals and repairs to machinery; and even when a large part of the labour is hired, as on plantations and large specialized farms, workers are often unable or unwilling to find different jobs and will accept a substantial cut in their pay when times are bad.

Hence during the Great Depression of 1929 to 1932 world agricultural output hardly declined at all despite the very heavy fall in prices. The output of manufactured products fell by more than a third, although—largely for that reason—their prices fell less than those of farm products.

Although most of my illustrations will be drawn from the thirties, I want to make this discussion general. There were commodity control schemes before 1929, and there will be again.[1] The Havana Charter, drawn up after the war for an International Trade Organization which was never born, is accepted in principle by a number of countries, including the United Kingdom; it expressly provides for such schemes in order to relieve producers of a "burdensome surplus" which is causing unemployment and distress. Moreover, a number of countries still give special assistance to their farmers.

I shall defer, however, a discussion of whether such measures are

[1] At present (January, 1960) there are international agreements, covering both exporting and importing countries, on wheat, sugar, and tin. The wheat agreement is a multilateral contract scheme, with no provision for restrictions on output. The sugar and tin agreements provide for variable export quotas, and there is a buffer stock for tin. Under the tin agreement, there were heavy reductions in output in 1958–9 to maintain prices despite unforeseen exports from Soviet Russia in 1957–1958.

desirable. The present Section concentrates on the mechanics of them; on how they work.

The producers of an agricultural commodity cannot form a voluntary cartel, for their numbers usually run into many thousands or even into millions. The same applies to most minerals. In order to have any chance of success, a plan for controlling the price of such a commodity must be sponsored and enforced by one or more Governments.

A Government can, if it wishes, guarantee minimum prices to its own farmers. This can be done quite easily if they do not produce enough to meet the home demand at those prices. Imports can be restricted to the amounts needed to meet the rest of the home demand. The burden falls on the home consumers, who have to pay more than the world price in order that their farmers may get more. Some burden falls also on foreign producers, for restrictions on imports tend to drive down the world price still further.

But the Government will be involved in some expense if the guaranteed prices stimulate home output so much that more is produced than can be sold at home. This happened in France with wheat. During the thirties France guaranteed her farmers a minimum price for wheat, as for certain other products; a number of countries, especially in Western Europe, did the same. The output of wheat in France expanded greatly and the French Government had to export wheat for considerably less than it had paid for it.

If the commodity for which a minimum price is guaranteed is one of which considerable quantities are normally exported, the problem is more difficult. The guaranteed price can be maintained in the home market, by restricting imports, but what of the surplus? The Government must either store it or export it at a loss—dump it.[1]

An alternative is to charge home consumers enough to cover the loss on exports. This has been done by a number of countries. For example, it was done for coal in Great Britain under the Act of 1930. Quotas for home sales were fixed for each mine, and minimum prices were fixed; the rest of the coal was sold abroad at lower prices. In Australia the home consumers paid much more for their local sugar than the price at which it was exported; at one time, during the thirties, they were paying £24 a ton when the export price was £10 a ton.

The Australian scheme for butter, during the thirties, illustrates one method of doing this. The price paid by Australian consumers was about 1s. 3d. a pound, the export price about 10d. a pound; about two-fifths of the output was exported. Each producer paid a levy of 2d. a pound into a pool, out of which exports were subsidized by 5d. a pound; each producer, whether he sold at home or exported, therefore,

---

[1] Or give it away, as the United States gave 700,000 to 1,000,000 tons of wheat to Pakistan (and made loans to India and Pakistan to enable them to buy her wheat) in 1953.

received 1s. 1d. a lb. net. Although Australia is a butter-exporting country, a tariff of 6d. a pound on imported butter had to be imposed to keep out butter from New Zealand and elsewhere.

But sooner or later Governments have to accept the basic platitudes of supply and demand. The way to raise the price of a commodity is to restrict its output. From the start (1933) the various measures taken by the United States to raise prices for her farmers were, and still are, accompanied by measures to restrict output.[1] The output of coal in Great Britain was restricted by quotas in the 1930s. (Restrictions were of course removed during the war and have not been reimposed, although demand is now much less than it was during the coal shortage of the immediate post-war years, and stocks are piling up.)

But if one country alone, a leading exporter of the commodity, restricts its output and thereby raises the world price, other countries will tend to produce more. This has happened again and again. Malaya and other British territories restricted their output of rubber from 1922 onwards. This succeeded in raising the price of rubber, but the consequent increase in output in the Dutch East Indies and elsewhere forced the abandonment of the scheme in 1928—and was largely responsible for the very low price of rubber during and after 1930. The United States restricted her output of cotton in the early 1930s, and still does. She used to produce well over half the cotton of the world; expansion of output elsewhere has reduced her share to some 40 per cent. During the 1920s Brazil produced over 60 per cent of the world's coffee; she restricted her output and now she produces only about 45 per cent.

The obvious course is for the chief exporting countries to combine together in a commodity control scheme to restrict output and thereby raise prices. This avoids throwing the whole burden of restrictions on one country (who may not be willing to bear it) and is more effective than restriction of output by one country only. During the Great Depression, various Governments combined to carry out such control schemes for rubber, tin, tea, sugar, and other commodities.

The scope for benefiting producers by such a scheme may be very great. Suppose the commodity is selling at a price at which the demand for it is well below unity: very inelastic. A reduction in output will increase total receipts very substantially. At the same time, it will reduce total costs and also, if the commodity is produced under conditions of increasing costs, it will reduce average costs per unit. This is shown in the following diagram.

[1] The United States Government guarantees maximum prices for various farm products. If it consequently accumulates too heavy stocks of a commodity, it may ask the farmers to reduce the acreage which they plant with that commodity. (A two-thirds majority of the farmers affected is required.) If they do not agree, it may drastically lower the minimum guaranteed price. It now (1959) holds large stocks of wheat and other farm products, and acreages are being reduced.

At present, output is OQ and price OP because the supply curve OS (the combined marginal cost curve of the industry, which is working under perfect competition) cuts the demand curve DD at A (and $OP = QA$). At this price the elasticity of demand is well below unity. The total sum available for fixed costs and profits (if any) is represented by the area OPA. This may not cover the fixed costs; the industry as a whole may be working at a loss.

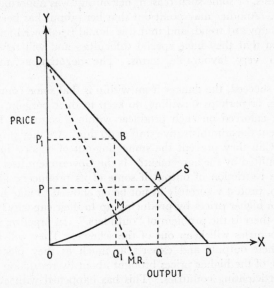

The dotted line is the marginal revenue curve, which cuts the supply (or marginal cost) curve for the industry at M. If output were restricted to OQ_1, the price would be raised to OP_1, and the sum available for fixed charges plus profits would be maximized. It would be represented by OP_1BM, which is much greater than OPA.

No doubt a scheme sponsored by Governments, and subject to criticism by the Governments of the chief consuming countries, would not attempt to raise prices to the levels that maximized monopoly profits. It would probably aim, in the phrase which has become dear to the advocates of such schemes, at prices "fair to both producers and consumers." But the above diagram does show the extent to which producers might gain (even if in fact they are allowed to take only part of this potential gain) if they could be combined together to act as if they were a single monopolist.

But they have to face the same difficulties, despite the powerful advantage of Government enforcement, as an industrial cartel: the difficulty of securing agreement, the danger from within, and the danger from without.

Agreement has to be reached on the extent to which each participating country shall reduce its output, and this may prove impossible. The usual procedure is to fix a quota for the output, or at any rate the exports, of each country based on its past performance during some previous period; for example, 80 per cent or 70 per cent of its output during the preceding year, or the preceding three years. One country may claim that the period chosen as a basis is unfair to her; owing to bad harvests, or some such reason, her output was abnormally low at that time. Another may point out that her output has been showing a marked upward trend, and that this should be allowed for. Others may claim that they have special difficulties and will refuse to join unless on very favourable terms. The negotiations may break down.

If they succeed, the danger from within is that some countries may be unable, or perhaps unwilling, to keep to their bargain. A quota has to be enforced on each producer within a country. Has every Government the administrative staff to do this? Are they proof against bribery? Can they prevent the smuggling-out of exports in excess of those permitted by the agreement? Is the Government itself prepared to enforce restriction of output if some of its producers, after prices have risen, protest vigorously at not being allowed to take full advantage of the higher prices by producing up to their capacity?

Finally there is the problem of "outsiders." In practice, some producing countries will keep out of the scheme. They will be free to expand their outputs and exports as much as they please, taking advantage of the higher prices brought about by restriction of output in the participating countries. This has happened with every commodity control scheme, throwing a still greater burden of restriction on the member countries. For example, the 1931 sugar scheme was abandoned in 1935, by which time the output of "outsiders" had increased from 50 per cent to 70 per cent of the world total.

The conclusion is that even if agreement can be reached on a commodity control scheme, the scheme is likely to break down sooner or later.

I cannot refrain from adding two comments about such schemes.

In the first place, in practice they nearly always protect the less efficient producers, who would otherwise have been forced out of the industry, and hold back the expansion of the more efficient producers. This is the consequence of quotas based on past performance. Moreover, the countries, and the individual producers within a country, who are most likely to receive especially favourable treatment are those who are in special difficulty because their costs of production are higher than those of other producers. The *World Economic Survey* for 1934–35 (pages 96–7) observed: "It is a curious fact that the method most generally adopted to restore a semblance of order in the markets for basic foodstuffs and raw materials has been to reduce output in the most efficient and least expensive areas of production."

In the second place, although such a scheme may be of great benefit to producers in the short run, especially if the demand at the prevailing price is relatively i nelastic, its long-term effects may be less favourable to them. An increase in the price of their product, especially a large increase, stimulates not only its output elsewhere, but also the search for synthetic or other substitutes for it, and the improvement of existing substitutes. A low price for a commodity is a hardship to producers, but it does have a strong influence in expanding the demand for that commodity and in developing new uses for it, while a high price has the opposite effects.

8. The Extent of Monopoly

There is less private monopoly, in the popular sense of the term, than is often supposed. In most Western countries it is forbidden by law although, somewhat paradoxically, the exclusive use of patents is permitted. The United States has had an Anti-Trust Act since 1890 and has broken up large monopolies, or alleged monopolies, from the Standard Oil Company to the big film combines. In Great Britain the common law prohibits *restraint of trade* and there is a permanent Commission to investigate monopolistic practices. Some firms which are commonly supposed to be monopolies because they are the leading firms in the industry do not in fact have any monopoly power and maintain their position through sheer efficiency.

Nevertheless, despite legal prohibition, there are some firms or combinations of firms that are in effect monopolies. But they seldom charge prices high enough to maximize their profits. They fear that this would stimulate the search for new substitutes for their products, or for improvements in existing substitutes; that it might lead to public protests, and perhaps to a boycott, by consumers; and that it might lead the Government to investigate and to put a stop to their monopolistic practices, and perhaps to control their prices or even to nationalize them.

When a Government owns or controls a monopoly, such as a public utility, it does not usually aim at maximizing profits, and the same applies to schemes such as commodity control schemes which are sponsored by Governments.

This does not mean that economic analysis based on the assumption that a monopolist will maximize his profits, by equating his marginal cost and his marginal revenue, is useless. It is somewhat unrealistic. But it does show how a monopolist, or a group of producers acting monopolistically, can gain—at the expense of consumers—by restricting their output. The brief analysis of discriminating monopoly which

I have given (supplemented in the following Note) does explain when it may be both possible and profitable to charge different prices for the same product. It explains why public utilities charge discriminating prices, why the Milk Marketing Board charges so much less for "manufacturing milk" than for milk for liquid consumption, why some countries, guaranteeing minimum prices to their producers, dump their surplus on the world market.

I consider the effects of monopoly later, as part of a general survey of the advantages and defects of capitalism. The present chapter has discussed monopoly in the ordinary sense of the term. There is less of it, at any rate of private monopoly, than is often supposed. But there is a great deal of monopolistic or imperfect competition; many producers can fix their own prices. That is the subject of the following chapter.

NOTE

DISCRIMINATING MONOPOLY

1. When the demand curve is a straight line, the marginal revenue curve will be a straight line also and will bisect a perpendicular from any point on the Y axis to the demand curve.

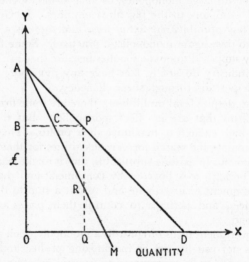

The demand curve is AD and the marginal revenue curve is AM. An output of OQ is sold at a price QP. Total revenue (or consumers' outlay) is measured by the rectangle $BPQO$ (price $QP \times$ quantity sold OQ). It is also measured by the area $ARQO$ "under" the marginal revenue curve (for AM shows the additions made to total revenue by successive units of output).

Therefore these two areas are equal to one another. Subtracting the area $BCRQO$, which is common to both, the triangles ABC and CPR are equal in area and as $\angle B = \angle P =$ a right angle, and the opposite angles at C are equal, the triangles are equal in all respects.

Therefore $\qquad\qquad\qquad\qquad BC = CP.$

(If the demand curve is not a straight line we can find the marginal revenue QR corresponding to any price P by drawing a tangent AD to the demand curve at P and proceeding as above.)

2. The elasticity of the demand curve at P is $\dfrac{OB}{BA}$ (as we showed in our note on page 188).

$$OB = QP = \text{price}.$$
$$BA = PR \text{ (see above)} = QP \text{ minus } QR$$
$$= \text{price } \textit{minus} \text{ marginal revenue}.$$

Therefore elasticity of demand (e)

$$= \frac{\text{price}}{\text{price} - \text{marginal revenue}}$$

or $\qquad\qquad \text{price} = \text{marginal revenue} \times \dfrac{e}{e-1},$

or $\qquad \text{marginal revenue} = \text{price} \times \dfrac{e-1}{e}.$

Thus, for example, if price is 6d. and elasticity of demand is 2, marginal revenue will be 3d. $\left(\text{6d.} \times \dfrac{2-1}{2}\right).$

3. Suppose that a monopolist can discriminate between two markets, and wishes to maximize his profits.

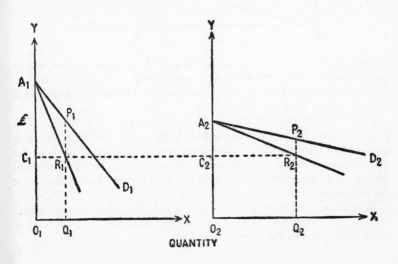

QUANTITY

We saw (p. 221) that he must equate his marginal cost (for his total output) with his marginal revenue in each market.

He will sell O_1Q_1 at a price of Q_1P_1 in the first market and O_2Q_2 at a price of Q_2P_2 in the second market. His marginal cost for his whole output $(O_1Q_1 + O_2Q_2)$ is O_1C_1 $(= O_2C_2)$ and this equals his marginal revenue (Q_1R_1) in the first market and also (Q_2R_2) in the second market.

The price in the first market is higher than in the second because the elasticity of demand is less in the first market than in the second.

4. How can we find the output OQ $(O_1Q_1 + O_2Q_2)$ at which these conditions will be fulfilled if the marginal cost curve is not horizontal, but rising? By drawing the marginal cost curve and seeing where it cuts AR. AR is obtained by "adding together" the two marginal

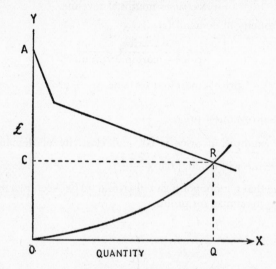

revenue curves. At a marginal revenue of so much, how great would be total sales? The answer to such questions gives the curve AR.

With an output OQ, the marginal cost OC will equal the marginal revenue QR in each market.

In the above diagram the marginal cost curve OR is rising. The output OQ is greater than the output O_1Q_1 which would be the most profitable if only the first market were available. Hence sales to the second market means that the marginal cost (and hence the marginal revenue, and the price) is higher in the first market than if that were the only one.

If, however, the marginal cost curve were falling the opposite would be true. ("Dumping" may make possible economies of scale and so reduce the price in the home market.)

CHAPTER XVII

SUPPLY UNDER IMPERFECT COMPETITION

1. Why Competition is often Imperfect

THERE are two reasons why competition may be imperfect. The number of firms in the industry may be relatively small, and the commodity or service may not be homogeneous.

A small number of firms may compete vigorously with one another. For example, there may be only a few building contractors in a town but each may submit an independent tender for a job, without consulting the others, and keeping the price he quotes as low as he can. But when the number of firms is small each must consider how his rivals would respond to a change in his own policy; for example, if he should cut his prices, they might cut theirs. A few firms may well come to some arrangement to live and let live by following a common policy; the arrangement may be written (unless this is forbidden by law) or oral, or it may be merely the recognized "custom of the trade," which they all follow.

Most of the commodity markets of the world are more or less perfect. Commodities such as wool and tea, which cannot be divided into homogeneous grades, are sold by public auction. But in the field of manufactures each firm can often *differentiate* its products in some way, for example by a trade-mark or a brand, from those of its rivals; and thus each firm may have its own circle of customers. The same applies to many services, such as retailing, entertainment, hotels and restaurants, and professional and technical services; the customer knows from whom he is buying and may for some reason prefer one supplier to another.

I should perhaps add a third reason: transport costs. It is transport costs or, more generally, the existence of space and therefore of different districts, which may give a few firms in a district something approaching a local monopoly, although there may be many such firms in the country as a whole. For example, a local brick-works is to some extent protected from the competition of brick-works elsewhere, for transport costs form a substantial proportion of the selling price of bricks; local hotels are to some extent protected from the competition of hotels elsewhere because visitors may want to stay in that particular district, in order to visit friends or relatives or to do business or to enjoy the scenery or other local attractions; local restaurants and cinemas are to some extent protected because their customers would have to spend time and money in going to a restaurant or cinema in another district.

Clearly there is a great deal of imperfect competition. It does not amount to full-blown monopoly if there are no barriers which prevent newcomers from entering the industry. But it does mean that firms do not accept the market prices for their products as something over which they have no control; they fix their own.

2. Prices under Imperfect Competition

How do they determine what prices to charge? This is a question on which it is difficult to generalize, partly because we have not enough facts and partly because the practice may differ somewhat from one industry to another.

It is fairly certain, however, that most firms working under imperfect competition do *not* equate their marginal costs and their marginal revenue in order to maximize their profits.

In the first place, it would puzzle such a firm to say what its marginal revenue would be if it were to charge a different price. For its volume of sales at the new price would depend largely on what its rivals did. If it raised its price, and they did not raise theirs, it would probably lose some, but not all, of its customers to them; it is difficult to tell in advance how many of its own circle of customers would remain loyal to it. Conversely, if it reduced its price, and they did not reduce theirs, it would probably attract some of their customers, but it is difficult to say how many. If its rivals responded by reducing their own prices or by increasing their advertising or improving the quality of their products without altering their prices, it is again difficult to say what would happen to its sales.

In the second place, even if a firm could make a good guess at the price which would maximize its profits, it might well deem it wise, in its long-run interest, to charge a price substantially lower. For a high price, giving a high rate of return on its capital, would certainly tend to attract new-comers to the industry and after a time the firm would be worse off, because it would have to share the market with more rivals, than if it had followed a less grasping policy.

In the third place, we know that many such prices are kept relatively stable for fairly long periods, despite changes in costs or in demand. The manufacturer of a branded good often considers it good policy to maintain its price, both wholesale and retail; the public becomes accustomed to this price, and the manufacturer fears that to change it in either direction might cause a loss of goodwill. The same applies to professional fees, hotel tariffs, laundry charges, and a host of other prices. They are, of course, changed from time to time, but usually only if there is a marked change in costs which leads all or most firms in the industry to take similar action; for example, there may be a general increase in the prices of cinema seats following an increase in the tax on them, or there may be a general rise in the prices of newspapers and periodicals following a marked rise in the cost of newsprint.

The best general explanation of how prices are fixed under imperfect competition still seems to be that given by Marshall. The current "code of trade morality" prevents a firm from selling at prices only a little above marginal costs. "Each man fears to spoil his chance of getting a better price later on from his own customers; or, if he produces for a large and open market, he is more or less in fear of incurring the resentment of other producers, should he sell needlessly at a price that spoils the common market for all." [1] The rate of profit on the turnover—the percentage "profit margin" added to average variable cost in order to arrive at the price—varies widely between industries "because it depends on the length of time and the amount of work required for the turnover." [2] For example, a shipbuilder would have to add a much higher percentage than a manufacturer of handkerchiefs. "As a matter of fact there is in each trade and every branch of each trade a more or less definite rate of profits on the turnover which is regarded as a 'fair' or normal rate." [3] This is determined, assuming no great change in conditions, by the traditions of the trade. "Such traditions are the outcome of much experience tending to show that, if that rate is charged, a proper allowance will be made for all the costs (supplementary as well as prime) incurred for that particular purpose, and in addition the normal rate of profits per annum in that class of business will be afforded. If they charge a price which gives much less than this rate of profit on the turnover they can hardly prosper; and if they charge much more they are in danger of losing their custom, since others can afford to undersell them." [4]

Although firms often do not spoil the market by cutting prices against one another, they nevertheless usually compete quite vigorously in quality and style, and in the inducements, such as free delivery and giving credit, that they offer to their customers.

Profit margins are sometimes reduced. "These rates," says Marshall, "are always changing in consequence of changes in the methods of trade; which are generally begun by individuals who desire to do a larger trade at a lower rate of profit on the turnover than has been customary, but at a larger rate of profit per annum on their capital." [5] Mr. Henry Ford comes along and revolutionizes the methods of producing motor-cars. He makes himself a millionaire by charging a

[1] *Principles of Economics*, 8th Edition, p. 374.   [2] ibid., p. 615
[3] ibid., p. 617.   [4] ibid., p. 617.   [5] ibid., p. 617.

relatively small profit margin on each car and selling enormous numbers at relatively low prices—made possible by mass-production coupled with a very elastic demand. The changes in "methods of trade" are seldom as spectacular as his. But the man who opens a cafeteria, the road-haulier who charges low rates for return loads, the taxi-driver who collects five passengers all going to the same football match, the author who fixes a low price for his text-book, are all, each in his own humble way, doing the same kind of thing.

3. Manufacturing

Manufacturing is carried on, very largely, under conditions of imperfect competition. A manufacturer can usually fix his own prices, but he tends to fix them at about the same level as the prices of similar products made by his rivals. The price of a manufactured good tends to equal the average variable cost of producing it plus a profit margin which normally covers fixed costs and gives a normal rate of return on capital to most of the firms in the industry. Normally, therefore, the price is neither so high that it attracts new firms nor so low that it forces existing firms out of business. The most efficient firms, however, will make a rather higher return on their capital, and the least efficient a rather lower return, than the others.

If firms refrain from price-cutting, as they often do, there may be a good deal of excess capacity in the industry. The profit margin may be relatively high and yet yield only a normal return on the capital, for some of the fixed capital will be idle or at least not fully used. Under these conditions, average variable costs, and therefore marginal costs, are likely to be more or less constant. A firm could expand its output with its present plant and equipment; its extra costs would be mainly for materials and perhaps for a little more labour. Obviously a price equal to marginal cost would not cover its fixed costs, let alone give it a profit; the price must be substantially higher than marginal cost if the industry is to survive.

A substantial expansion of output, however, may lead to increasing marginal costs. Firms may have to engage less efficient workers at standard rates or to pay higher rates for overtime. A large increase in demand may find the industry unable to cope with it until capacity has been increased by the expansion of existing firms and the entry of new ones. If the policy is followed of keeping prices fairly stable, the consequence may be a marked lengthening of delivery dates. In the British engineering industries during the rearmament of 1950–52, delivery dates for new orders were often years ahead.

Manufacturers usually like to keep their prices stable, especially for branded goods sold to the public. But prices will have to be changed, sooner or later, in response to a marked change in the prices of the factors of production. In some industries, there are one or more large firms that exercise price leadership; in such circumstances, they revise their prices and most of the other firms follow suit.

During periods of bad trade, prices may be maintained, but deliveries will be prompter, and there may be improvements in quality. If a period of bad trade is prolonged, some firms, desperate for cash, may give secret rebates or openly cut their prices.

Having fixed his prices, a manufacturer is prepared to supply (sooner or later) as much as is demanded at those prices. But he tries to expand his sales by competing with his rivals in everything but price—for example in quality, style, and speed of delivery. One way in which he may try to expand his sales is by advertising. Much has been written about this subject, which I discuss later. Here I wish merely to point out that it is only in a few lines, such as patent medicines, that advertising forms a large part of the costs. Most manufacturers make producers' goods and sell to other manufacturers or to farmers or builders or service industries, and not to the public. Such a manufacturer does tend to have his own circle of customers, but he does not retain them by advertising. They have learned by experience that they can rely on his products and his performance; and it is often difficult for a new-comer or even for an established rival to break through his goodwill and tempt some of his customers away.

Over a long period, the prices of equipment and materials and the wages of workers may rise owing to a general fall in the value of money. On the other hand, technical progress is very marked in manufacturing, and therefore output per worker is likely to increase, as it has done in the past. Apart from these two opposing forces, there is no obvious reason why costs should change in the long period, even if there is a large expansion of output. In the short period, a large expansion of output would lead to diminishing returns because more workers would be employed on the same plants. But in the long period, capacity could be increased to maintain the old proportions between fixed capital and labour.

The long-run outlook is therefore different in manufacturing and in agriculture. A large expansion of agricultural output would mean working land more intensively or resorting to worse land. This would tend to raise the prices of agricultural products. Although the latter include materials used by factories, we can draw the tentative conclusion that if the population of the world continues to grow, and if technical progress is not more marked in agriculture than in manufacturing, the prices of agricultural products are likely to rise relatively to those of manufactured products. The prices of minerals will tend to rise, as present deposits become depleted or less easy to work, unless equally suitable deposits are discovered to take their place.

I

4. RETAIL TRADE

The "retail mark-up," the profit margin which a retailer adds to the price that he pays for a good, varies for different goods according to the length of time an average article remains in stock, and according to the risk that stock will deteriorate either physically or in appeal to customers. Thus the British Census of Distribution shows that in 1950 the average gross margin on sales was only 9·2 per cent on tobacco (cigarettes, etc.), where turnover is rapid, and only 14·7 per cent on groceries, as against 33·3 per cent on jewellery and 36 per cent on furs, where the rate of turnover is very slow although the average value of an article is high. For florists it was 36 per cent, and in women's millinery it was 32·5 per cent.

Some shops, especially in the large towns, provide facilities and services such as delivery, credit accounts, and rest rooms. But the customer who wants to buy cheaply can usually do so from "cash and carry" shops or supermarkets, where the mark-up tends to be lower.

The mark-up is reduced, especially for goods which the shop has had in stock for some time, at "sales." In some lines, a considerable proportion of total purchases is made at sale prices.

The retail prices of branded goods, which are usually nationally advertised, are often fixed by the manufacturer. Most shops sell such goods—cigarettes, patent medicines, toilet preparations, branded groceries in packages or tins or bottles—at the prices so fixed. They cannot charge more or customers would go elsewhere. What if they want to charge less and thereby expand their sales? The manufacturers usually object, and withhold supplies from shops which cut the prices of such goods. This question of resale price maintenance is very controversial. I return to it in Chapter XXII.

There are so many shops—over 500,000 in Great Britain today—that most shopkeepers do not make much of an income. Many small shopkeepers probably make less than a senior assistant in a department store.

Why are there so many shops? A man with a little capital who likes to be his own boss finds it easy to set up a shop. Premises can be rented. Stock can be bought on credit. The capital required has not to be tied up in durable and specific plant; it consists mainly of stock-in-trade which, at the worst, can usually be disposed of without great loss. The consequence, it is often argued, is too many shops. Certainly many shops have excess capacity—far more customers could be served by the same staff.

For more shops do not mean lower prices. An increase in the supply of retailing capacity is unlikely to reduce profit margins; it may even raise them. Competition is imperfect. "A retail dealer," says Marshall,[1] "when once he has established a good connection, has always

[1] Article on "Retail Prices," published in *Memorials of Alfred Marshall*, p. 353.

had a partial or limited local monopoly." As a rule, a shop has its own circle of customers, who remain fairly "loyal" to it. It may be conveniently situated for them; it may grant them credit; it may be a centre for local gossip. They may rely on its reputation for goods whose technical qualities, such as durability, they must take on trust. They may take the risk of being charged more than they would have to pay at some other shop, in order to save themselves the time and trouble of seeking out the best bargains. This tendency is clearly strengthened by the growing extent to which goods are "branded" and sold everywhere at prices fixed and maintained by the manufacturers.

The considerations which, as a rule, prevent new shops from cutting prices may be shown by a hypothetical example. Suppose that there is a small grocery and provisions shop at each end of a long street, and that a man starts a similar shop in the middle of the street. He can count on some customers from people who live nearer to him than to his rivals. Will it pay him to cut his prices? On some lines he cannot do this without soon being deprived of further supplies by the manufacturers. If he cuts prices on other lines, most of the customers of the other two shops will remain loyal to them; he will attract away only some of them. Moreover, he will risk forcing the other shops to follow suit and to cut their prices also; if this happens, all three will be in a worse position than if he had followed a policy of "live and let live." Hence he will be very likely to accept current prices and profit margins. The consequence, therefore, of his entry into the trade will be more "excess capacity." Three shops will now be sharing the work formerly done by two.

It does not follow, however, that profit margins in retailing are never reduced. Nearly half of all retail sales are made by department stores, multiple shops, and co-operative societies. These shops are strong enough to follow their own policy; they can introduce new lines in competition with nationally-advertised brands, and they can reduce prices when changes in demand or in costs appear to them to call for such reductions.

5. Conclusions

There is a great deal of imperfect competition in manufacturing, retail trade, and the supply of various services. It is difficult to generalize about price policy under imperfect competition, but we can be fairly sure that most firms do not attempt to maximize their immediate profits by equating marginal cost and marginal revenue. The tendency is often to accept the prevailing prices in the industry, and these tend to be fixed at levels that give the average firm a margin over its variable costs sufficient to cover its fixed costs and to earn a normal rate of return on its capital. Such a margin is necessary because there is normally a fair amount of excess capacity in such a firm, and therefore its marginal costs tend to be constant, and a price well above marginal cost is necessary if the industry is to survive. There is competition, however—in quality, style, and performance, if not in price. An expansion of demand will bring about an expansion of output, and a reduction in the prices of factors of production will probably lead to a reduction in the prices of the products. If there are no obstacles to the entry of new firms into the industry, a new-comer may reduce the accepted profit margins by introducing new methods or a new policy in order to get a bigger turnover by taking a smaller profit on each unit.

The purpose of the present Part is only to show how prices are formed. I discuss the social consequences of imperfect competition, especially whether excess capacity and competitive advertising are wasteful, in Chapter XXII.

CHAPTER XVIII

DEMAND, SUPPLY, AND PRICE

1. THE ADJUSTMENT OF SUPPLY TO DEMAND

WE have seen that at any time there is a short-period supply schedule for any commodity that is currently produced. How much more can be supplied, and at what price, depends largely on the capacity of the industry. It may take a long time for an industry to increase or reduce its capacity sufficiently to adapt itself fully to changes in demand. The long-period supply schedule shows how much would be supplied at any given price if enough time were to elapse for full adjustment to be made. In other words, each statement in a long-period supply schedule relates to a situation in which equilibrium has been attained.

In fact, equilibrium never is attained. Before full adjustment can be made to one set of changes, other changes take place in the conditions of demand and supply. Equilibrium is an ever-changing goal. Nevertheless the concept of equilibrium is useful, and I shall return to it.

Under perfect competition, price will tend to equal marginal cost for every firm in the industry; and the short-period supply schedule of the commodity is obtained by discovering how much each firm would produce at such-and-such a marginal cost, and adding the amounts together. If the industry is making more than normal profits, it will tend to expand, and if it is making less than normal profits, it will tend to contract.

Under imperfect competition, including monopoly, the notion of a supply schedule may seem out of place. For a firm may fix its own price and stand ready to supply as much or as little (within limits) as the market will take at that price. Formally, however, we can treat this as a supply schedule; in a diagram it would appear as a horizontal supply curve at the level of the price which the seller fixes.

But whether or not we speak of supply schedules under imperfect competition is of no importance for our main purpose, which is to discuss how the price system works. Imperfect competition, and especially monopoly, may have serious defects from the standpoint of making the best use of the resources of the community; this question is discussed in Chapter XXII. But under imperfect competition, the response to changes in demand is usually as adequate as under perfect competition, and often it is more prompt.

Under perfect competition, a change in price is needed to bring about the required response to a change in demand. Demand increases, price rises, more is produced. Or demand decreases, price falls, and less is produced. Under imperfect competition, such price changes are not necessary, in so far as each firm stands ready to supply more or less in response to increases or decreases in demand. We can imagine freak cases of queerly-shaped demand curves where a monopolist would maximize his profits by reducing his output (and considerably raising his price) in response to an increase in demand, but in practice this hardly ever happens. If demand increases, more will be produced, and if demand decreases, less will be produced, under imperfect competition just as under perfect competition.

Under perfect competition, a change in the conditions of supply which raises or reduces marginal cost will be reflected in a rise or fall in price; the former supply schedule will be replaced by a new one. Under imperfect competition, some firms may be reluctant to alter their prices, despite a moderate rise or fall in their costs; their supply schedules may remain unchanged. But if the change in costs is substantial, it will tend to be reflected sooner or later in an increase or reduction in the price.

If profits are above normal, capacity will tend to be increased, provided—an important proviso—that new firms are free to enter the industry; and if profits are below normal, capacity will tend to be reduced.

In short, whether competition is perfect or imperfect, supply will tend to adjust itself to changes in demand. This applies equally to factors of production, such as raw materials and equipment, which are themselves currently produced. We have not yet discussed, however, the supply of factors of production such as labour services, loans of money, and land, which are not produced. These questions are deferred until Part V, and this leaves us with a gap. We do know, however, that if we can take the total supply of such a factor as given, it will tend to be distributed among different uses in such a way that its net earnings are the same in every use (except in so far as lower earnings are compensated by other advantages). In fact, we can define equilibrium as a state of affairs in which nobody would have any incentive to do anything different by transferring his own services or his property to some other industry or occupation.

> When no factor sees a gain
> Now or in the days to come
> By moving to another line,
> Then there's equilibrium.

2. CHANGES IN DEMAND

The consequences of any important economic change are not likely to be confined to the one or two commodities immediately and directly affected. But for our present purpose we can ignore such repercussions and consider "one thing at a time."

Suppose, then, that a change takes place in the conditions of demand. The present demand schedule is no longer valid; it is replaced by a new one. If the new one shows that more will be bought than before at any given price, the change is an increase in demand. The consequence will be to raise the price (unless the price remains fixed, under imperfect competition) and to expand the amount supplied.

In the example I have used, the relevant parts of the demand schedule and of the short-period supply schedule are as follows—

Price per unit d.	Demand (million units per week)	Supply (million units per week)
14	5	8
13	6	$7\frac{1}{2}$
12	7	7
11	8	$6\frac{1}{2}$
10	9	6

The price settles at 12d. a unit, for at that price the amount demanded and the amount supplied, week by week, are the same, namely seven million units.

Suppose that demand increases. The relevant part of the new demand schedule may be as follows—

Price per unit d.	Demand (million units per week)
16	6
15	7
14	8
13	9
12	10

A price of 15d. a unit would be needed to restrict demand to the present seven million units a week. But the price will not settle at 15d., for at that price more than eight million units would be supplied week by week, and supply would exceed demand. At a price of 14d. a unit, eight million units a week would be demanded, and the same amount would be supplied (for the supply schedule has not changed); the new price will be 14d. a unit.

Diagrammatically, the old demand curve DD is replaced by D_1D_1. The supply curve SS remains the same. Price rises from P to P_1, and output expands from OQ to OQ_1.

Similarly with a decrease in demand. DD is replaced by a new demand curve to the left of DD; SS remains the same; price falls and output contracts.

By convention the words "increase" and "decrease" are restricted to the causal change, in this case the change in demand. The conditions of supply do not change; more or less is supplied in response to a change in demand, but the supply schedule remains the same. The supply schedule has indicated all along that if the price were 14d., eight million units a week would be supplied. Now that the price is in fact 14d. (owing to the increase in demand) eight million units a week are in fact supplied. There has been no change whatsoever in the conditions of supply.

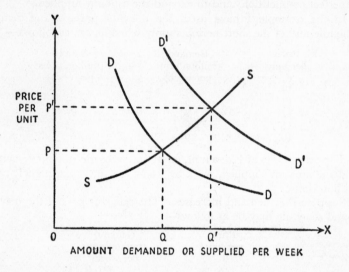

AMOUNT DEMANDED OR SUPPLIED PER WEEK

Changes in demand may take place for a hundred and one reasons. They may be due to changes in the size or age-composition of the population. For example, in Australia the demand for housing has substantially increased owing to the post-war immigration, while in Great Britain the demand for such things as bread and perambulators is less than a generation ago, when there were more children.

They may be due to changes in incomes. A general rise in money incomes, without a corresponding rise in output, is likely to raise costs of production and prices to about the same extent. But a rise in real incomes tends to alter the distribution of expenditure; in general, a smaller proportion than before will be spent on food and a bigger proportion on what used to be regarded as luxuries or semi-luxuries. A change in the distribution of wealth in favour of the poorest sections has a similar effect on their demands, while heavy taxation of the well-to-do reduces their demand for large houses, domestic servants, and other luxuries.

Nowadays over a third of the British national income passes through the hands of the Government, and the expenditure of the Government is a very important factor; during recent years the expansion of the health services, for example, has increased the demand for doctors, dentists, nurses, medicines, and dentures.

Technical progress of course affects costs, but it affects demand also. The coming of the motor-car reduced the demand for horses and oats; artificial silk and nylon reduced the demand for natural silk. The use of rubber powder for road surfaces tends to increase the demand for rubber. Developments in the science of nutrition tend to increase the demand for certain foodstuffs—for example, for those rich in vitamins.

In general, both prices and the volume of sales are greater for most goods in times of good trade than in times of bad trade. This is especially marked for capital goods and for durable consumers' goods, such as refrigerators and radios, the demand for which tends to fall during periods of depression.

Sometimes *expectations* are important. For example, the Korean war led to a rush of public and private stock-piling, sending up the prices of a number of raw materials. If people think that prices are rising, they speed up their purchases; if they think prices are falling, they tend to hold off buying.

Often a change in demand is simply a question of a change in tastes, which may have been assisted by advertising. More is spent today on beauty preparations and cigarettes, and less on hats, than a generation ago.

If incomes and tastes and knowledge are given, as they are at any moment of time, the demand for any particular commodity depends mainly on the prices of other commodities that might be bought instead.

3. Changes in Supply

An increase in supply means that at any given price more than before will be offered for sale. If the demand schedule remains the same, the price will fall, and more will be bought week by week than before. To revert to our example—

Price per unit d.	Demand (million units per week)	Supply (1) (million units per week)	Supply (2) (million units per week)
14	5	8	13
13	6	$7\frac{1}{2}$	12
12	7	7	11
11	8	$6\frac{1}{2}$	10
10	9	6	9

An increase in supply, perhaps due to technical progress which reduces costs of production, makes the new supply schedule (2) replace the old supply schedule (1). The price falls from 12d. to 10d., and the amount bought expands from seven million units a week to nine million. It should be noted that no change whatever has taken place in the

I 2   B.E.

conditions of demand; the demand curve remains the same, but the supply curve shifts to the right.

Conversely, a decrease in supply, due for example to a rise in the price of one or more of the factors used in producing the commodity, will lead to a higher price and a reduced volume of sales.

The same change may affect both demand and supply. For example, a general rise in money wages will raise costs, but at the same time will increase demand by giving the wage-earners more spending-power. If there is full employment, both before and after the rise in wages, the amounts bought and sold may alter little, but prices will rise.

As time goes on, there may be changes both in the conditions of demand and in the conditions of supply for a commodity or service. For example, between 1931 and 1951 the number of women domestic servants in Great Britain nearly halved. The demand for them fell off owing to heavier taxation of the well-to-do. At the same time, the supply of domestic servants fell off because the remuneration of women in alternative occupations became more attractive. The supply of domestic servants decreased more than the demand for them decreased, and their wages and conditions of service improved.

The demand for rubber, to take another example, is likely to increase quite considerably in the future, with the continued growth in the numbers of motor vehicles and the development of new uses for rubber. Nevertheless the price of rubber may fall. The newer trees give three times the yield of the old, and there is constant technical progress in the manufacture of synthetic rubber. Hence the increase in supply may be greater than the increase in demand.

4. THEORIES OF VALUE

Is there some general explanation of the relations between prices, or, in other words, some general theory of value, which is more fundamental than "supply and demand"? Obviously, fluctuations in market prices are due to changes in supply or demand, but is there not some deeper explanation of the relations between the "normal prices" which these temporary fluctuations disturb? To put the same question in another way, suppose that no further changes were to take place. Equilibrium would eventually come about. The price of every commodity would settle down at such a level that the supply of it, week by week, would equal the demand for it; and no factor of production would be able to earn more by moving into a different industry or occupation. Yet a ton of cotton, for example, would be worth far more than a ton of coal. Why?

Ricardo (1817) said that commodities exchange against one another according to the relative quantities of labour embodied in them. (This is very different from saying, as Marx said, that all value is created by labour and that rent, interest, and profits represent exploitation of the workers.) Rent does not enter into price. The price of an agricultural product is determined by its cost of production on land that is only just worth working and that therefore yields no rent; rent is a surplus which accrues to the better land. Capital as well as labour is employed in production. But capital goods are themselves produced by labour, and the proportion of interest to labour costs may be assumed to be much the same in one industry as in another. Hence if one commodity embodies, say, twice as much labour as another, it will be twice as valuable.

I will give only one criticism of this theory. How do we measure the quantity of labour? A Corot can dash off in a few hours a picture which will sell for much more than a picture that has taken a mediocre artist several months to produce. A working jeweller can earn two or three times as much in an hour as an unskilled worker. Why? Simply because the products of a Corot or a working jeweller are more valuable. But this introduces another determinant—namely, demand. It is values that have to be explained, and if we measure labour by the value that it produces we are reasoning in a circle.

Another theory is that value is determined by cost of production. It is true, as we have seen, that under perfect competition the price of a product will tend to *equal* its marginal cost of production. But marginal cost of production does not *determine* price. What happens is that firms expand their output up to the level at which their marginal cost equals the price. If demand increases, the price rises; output expands, and marginal cost rises. In other words, marginal cost depends partly on demand. Under imperfect competition, a firm may fix its prices on the basis of its costs. But how large a profit margin it adds will depend on various factors. One of these factors is the state of demand; it will not fix a price that is so high that its volume of sales is too small to cover its total costs. We cannot get away from the influence of demand.

Moreover, cost of production is made up of the prices of the various factors of production employed in producing the commodity. What determines the price of such a factor? If most units of that factor are employed in other industries, its price will depend on what it can earn elsewhere. If most units of it are employed in that industry, its price will depend largely on the prices of its products. For example, when the price of wool soared after the war, so did the wages of sheep-shearers; when the price of wool came down in 1951–52, so did the wages of sheep-shearers. Clearly the demand for wool partly governs its cost of production.

Jevons (1870) and others approached the problem from the side of demand. It is demand—marginal utility—that determines value.

Prices are proportional to marginal utilities. This view has the advantage that it accounts for the values of commodities that are not currently produced, such as paintings by old masters, as well as for the values of current output. But we cannot ignore supply. If for any reason (for example, technical progress) there is an increase in supply, price will tend to fall, and the marginal utility of a unit will fall correspondingly, for consumption will expand.

The fact is that there is no single fundamental explanation of value. On the one hand, we have the wants of consumers and the existing distribution of wealth; each shilling carries the same weight as every other, whether it is spent by a rich man or by a poor man. On the other hand, we have the difficulties to be overcome in satisfying those wants. Means of production are limited in amount, and many of them can be used either for one purpose or for another. Equilibrium is reached when prices are such that the supply of every commodity equals the demand for it, and no factors of production have any incentive to move into another industry or occupation.

It is true that the prices of products are related to the prices of the factors of production employed in producing them. But it is also true that the prices of those factors depend on the value of their products, both in the industry under consideration and in other industries. The prices of products in one industry are affected by the prices of possible substitutes produced by other industries. Everything depends on everything else. The price system *is* a system; all prices are mutually dependent on one another.

By concentrating on one commodity at a time, we can use the apparatus of supply and demand to point out the main forces at work. And we can lay down two general principles.

The first is that marginal utilities are proportional to prices. This is always true, whether or not the general situation is one of equilibrium. But it is nothing more than a statement that consumers spend their incomes in the ways which they prefer.

The second general principle is that prices tend to reflect opportunity-costs. This covers all prices, and not only the prices of produced commodities. For example, a wage reflects the alternative of what the wage-earner could earn (or, more widely, of the net advantages he would get) by working in another industry or occupation; and the alternative to more work and, therefore, a larger income is more leisure. Again, the opportunity-cost of receiving interest by lending money is either keeping the money "liquid" or spending it on present consumption.

But in a situation of disequilibrium, prices do not fully reflect opportunity-costs, and therefore factors of production tend to move to where they can get a better return. And even in equilibrium the principle applies only where competition is more or less perfect. Under imperfect competition, prices are often fixed well above marginal costs. The time has come for us to consider how far this practice really conflicts with the opportunity-cost principle.

5. PRICE AND MARGINAL COST

We have seen that under perfect competition prices tend to equal marginal costs, but that under imperfect competition prices are often fixed well above marginal costs.

Does this imply a wasteful distribution among industries of labour and other resources? At the first blush, it may seem so. For example, the same labour may have a marginal product which is twice as valuable in one industry as another. Surely labour, and other resources, should move from the latter industry to the former? And surely this type of movement—out of "perfect competition" industries and into "imperfect competition" industries—should continue until the values of marginal products are everywhere the same? This would be achieved if prices were everywhere equal to marginal costs. This would mean large reductions in prices in some industries under imperfect competition; the lower prices would expand the demand, and output in those industries would increase.

But would it? An extra passenger or an extra parcel of goods can usually be squeezed into a train at no extra cost. The marginal cost is nil; therefore, if prices are fixed equal to marginal costs, passengers and goods would be carried free. The railways would get no revenue. How could they survive?

The problem still remains if we take a different unit, for example the cost of running an extra train, to measure marginal cost. Prices equal to marginal costs would not cover the fixed costs, let alone provide a profit.

The reason for this difference between perfect competition and imperfect competition is that under the former, marginal cost is increasing, and therefore marginal cost exceeds average variable cost sufficiently to cover the fixed costs and yield a normal profit, whereas under the latter, marginal cost is often constant, and equal to average variable cost, so that a price equal to marginal cost yields no margin to provide for fixed costs and profits.

The view that prices should always equal marginal costs rests on the premise that consumers should have what they value more highly, provided that it can be produced by the same factors of production. But consumers do not want cheaper rail transport today and none tomorrow. They want prices which permit the industry to survive and to maintain its output.

It has been suggested that this should be achieved, and prices nevertheless fixed equal to marginal costs, by Government subsidies to "imperfect competition" industries, or by the Government taking them over and running them at a loss. But why should the taxpayers pay for consumers of such goods and services to consume more of them, at prices which do not cover the total cost of producing them? To my mind, this suggestion is fantastic.

But we can still apply the opportunity-cost principle. We can apply it to the *distribution of capital* between industries. If capital in certain industries is yielding more than in others, then more capital should flow into the former industries. If this inflow is prevented by monopolistic barriers, this is against the public interest. The tendency should be for industries making more than normal profits to expand, and for those making less than normal profits to contract. For this is the way to conform to the premise that consumers should get the goods which they value more highly, and should go on getting them.

6. THE LAWS OF SUPPLY AND DEMAND

A change in price does not come about by itself. It comes about because some sellers are prepared to accept less or some buyers to pay more. It is the result of a change in conditions that affects the supply schedule or the demand schedule, or both.

If the change affects only the demand, the normal sequence will be an increase in demand, leading to a rise in price which induces an expansion of supply or, in the opposite case, a decrease in demand, leading to a fall in price which induces a contraction of supply. If the change affects only the supply, the normal sequence will be an increase in supply, leading to a fall in price which induces an expansion of demand or, in the opposite case, a decrease in supply, leading to a rise in price which induces a contraction of demand.

The distinction between *increases and decreases*, on the one hand, and *expansions and contractions*, on the other hand, is a useful aid to clear thinking. Increases and decreases are changes in conditions that initiate the sequence of changes; expansions and contractions are merely the responses.

People sometimes speak as if a price could never permanently change. They say, for example: "An invention may reduce costs, increase supply, and lower price for the time being. But demand will increase, owing to the lower price, and this will send the price back to its original level." This of course is quite wrong. The demand curve remains the same. Demand does *not* "increase" but is "expanded," more being bought simply because the price is lower. There is, however, a new supply curve, which is lower than the original one, and hence the new equilibrium price will be below the original price.

I give below four "laws" of supply and demand. But it should be remembered that these laws, like all economic laws, are only generalizations about tendencies. There are often exceptions to law 3; under imperfect competition, many producers can and do increase their output of a particular good, when the demand for it increases, without raising its price, and may maintain its price for a time although demand and sales have fallen off.

1. Price tends to equate the amount that sellers are prepared to offer for sale and the amount that buyers wish to buy.

2. Usually a larger quantity of a commodity will be demanded at a lower price than at a higher price; and a larger quantity will be offered for sale at a higher price than at a lower price.

3. An increase in demand tends to raise the price and to expand the supply; a decrease in demand tends to lower the price and to contract the supply.

4. An increase in supply tends to lower the price and to expand the demand; a decrease in supply tends to raise the price and to contract the demand.

The "supply and demand" approach is to some extent incomplete, because it concentrates on one commodity at a time instead of looking at the whole picture. I discuss the alternative approach of "indifference curves" in an Appendix to this Part.

CHAPTER XIX

SOME APPLICATIONS OF DEMAND AND SUPPLY

1. Price-Fixing

Suppose that a Government tries to keep down the cost of living by fixing maximum retail prices for certain commodities. We can keep to our example of butter. The supply of butter and the demand for it are as shown in our schedules. The equilibrium price is 1s. a unit (and if the reader thinks 1s. a pound too low nowadays, he can call a "unit" half a pound or a quarter of a pound), and at that price supply equals demand at seven million units a week. The Government now fixes a maximum price of 6d. a unit. What will happen?

If the prices of alternative products—milk, cheese, livestock, crops —are not also fixed at correspondingly low levels, farmers will switch over to them. Little or no butter will come on to the market.

This is not what the Government wants. It wants the output of butter to be maintained. What measures can it take to ensure that as much butter as before is produced, despite the lower price?

It has three broad alternatives: compulsion, or fixing all prices, or a subsidy.

A dictatorship could simply order each farmer to produce as much butter as before. Those who did not could be shot "pour encourager les autres" or drafted into forced-labour camps. If dairy-farmers employed paid labour, their workers could be ordered to remain where they were, despite cuts in their wages. This "solution" would penalize farmers and their workers for the benefit of consumers of butter.

The second solution would be to extend price control. Clearly the prices of milk, cheese, and other dairy products would have to be reduced also, or farmers would produce them instead of butter. But if the prices of all dairy products are reduced, the prices of all farm products must be reduced, or farmers—unless they are compelled to remain in dairy-farming—will switch over to livestock or to crops.

In order not to penalize farmers, their costs also would have to be reduced. As this would mean reducing the prices of manufactures such as agricultural machinery and fertilizers, the prices of all manufactures would have to be reduced in order to maintain the output of those manufactures needed by farmers.

The costs of farmers include the wages of farm workers. They would have to be reduced. This means that the wages of all workers would have to be reduced in order to prevent—without compulsion—a transfer of farm workers to other occupations.

Thus the Government would have to fix all prices, including the prices of factors of production. For all prices are related to one another and affect one another. If the Government should leave any gaps, capital and labour would move into the uncontrolled industries, where they could now earn more.

The third solution is the simplest. Pay the producers (or importers) of butter a subsidy, so that their total receipts are the same as before. Fix the margins added to the farm price (or the butter-factory price) by wholesalers and retailers, so that they are the same as before, with the retail price at 6d. a unit. This solution avoids the need for a host of price-fixing committees, to see that "fair" prices are fixed, and are changed from time to time when relevant conditions change, and for an army of officials to see that maximum prices are not exceeded and to prevent "black market" transactions.

Such a subsidy is paid to the producers of butter, but all the benefit of it goes to the consumers of butter. They can buy butter for 6d. a unit instead of 1s.

But they cannot all buy as much butter as they want at 6d. a unit. At 6d. a unit, 13 million units a week are demanded but only 7 million are supplied. Who decides who are going to be the lucky purchasers? Will it be left to the favouritism of shopkeepers, keeping butter "under the counter"? Many of the unsatisfied would-be purchasers would pay not merely 1s. a unit, but considerably more in order to get some butter. Will a "black market" in butter develop, those who can manage to buy substantial quantities reselling (illegally) at some price well over 6d. a unit? The obvious answer is rationing.

2. RATIONING

Rationing seems to be a "fair" way of sharing out limited supplies of essential commodities; each gets the same amount, at a fixed price. In a besieged city, the rationing of limited stocks of food and drink may be inevitable; and it may be necessary in war-time.

In Great Britain, rationing was continued after the war (although the scope of it was gradually relaxed) because it was thought necessary to restrict imports. The prices of imports such as meat and bacon and butter would have risen considerably, in order to restrict demand to the supply available from restricted imports plus home production, if they had not been subsidized. In fact, they were subsidized, and the limited supplies were rationed.

One motive for rationing was to reduce the effects of inequality of wealth. The richer sections of the community could not take full advantage of their greater wealth; within the field of rationed commodities, they could buy no more than anybody else. As restrictions were relaxed, however, this aspect of the matter became less significant; those who could afford it could supplement their rations by eating at restaurants or by buying those foodstuffs that were no longer rationed.

The disadvantage of rationing is that it restricts freedom of choice; it makes no allowance for differences in tastes and incomes. Some people who now got a butter ration may never have bought any butter before; they may have preferred to buy cheaper fats, such as margarine, or to spend their money on something quite different. And some people may have found themselves restricted by rationing to only a part, perhaps less than half, of the amount they bought before.

It is clearly a disadvantage to be allowed to buy only limited quantities of certain commodities. Many consumers would prefer to pay somewhat higher prices and to buy whatever they wanted.[1]

Under rationing, Mrs. A would rather have more butter and less bacon; Mrs. B would rather have more bacon and less butter. Can they get together and swap some of their rations? If the Government permits all such transactions, a market in ration coupons will develop, where people can sell coupons for goods of which they do not want to buy their full rations and can buy coupons for goods of which they want to buy more than their rations. But this would drive a coach-and-four through the principle of "equal shares." The Government is almost certain to forbid it, and to make it an offence even for Mrs. A to swap her bacon for Mrs. B's butter over the garden fence.

Nevertheless a number of Governments during the war introduced a "points" system for rationed commodities. Under such a system, every ration-card holder is entitled to buy so many "points" of rationed commodities each month, taking whatever he pleases, each commodity being given a value of so many points per unit. If the demand for one commodity exceeds the supply, its points value (but not necessarily its price) is raised; if stocks of another remain unsold, its points value is reduced. This system introduces some flexibility. It is half-way back to a system of prices, which allows each consumer to buy exactly what he wants—up to the limit of what he can spend.

Why not go the whole way, in peace-time, and do away with subsidies and rationing? Imports can still be restricted, if they must be, but prices can be allowed to find their own levels. The poorer sections may suffer hardship from high prices. But the extra taxation needed to pay for subsidies might be spent to better advantage in helping directly those who most need help, by such devices as increased family allowances. Under the subsidy-plus-rationing system the help is diffused; all consumers of rationed commodities, rich and poor alike, get

[1]This point is made, in terms of indifference curves, in Section 5 of the Appendix to this Part.

the same benefit from their reduced prices.   Freedom of choice is
restricted, and the administrative expenses of running a rationing
system and trying to prevent "black market" transactions are quite
considerable.   There seems, to my mind, to be a good case for letting
the price system do its work and for relying on more direct and effective measures to relieve hardship.

3. Taxes on Commodities

In a modern community the operations of public finance are very
important.   They affect the volume of employment, the general level
of prices, the composition of the national output, and the distribution
of wealth.   The combined effects of taxation and public expenditure
are likely to change all supply schedules (by altering the relative
prices of the various factors of production) and all demand schedules.
But we can concentrate on the effects of a tax on one commodity by
supposing that everything else, including public expenditure, remains
unchanged.

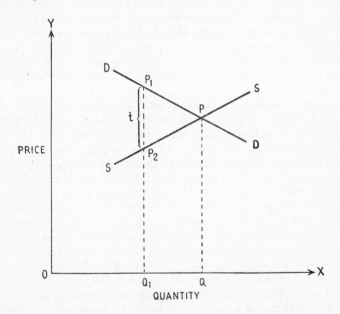

Suppose, then, that a tax t of so many pence per unit is imposed on
the production of a commodity.   Suppose that, before the tax, demand
and supply were equal at a price P with an amount OQ produced and
bought each week.   Suppose, further, that the conditions of demand
and supply remain the same after the tax as they were before it.

We can consider first a commodity produced under perfect competition.

The short-period effect of the tax will be to raise the price to consumers to P_1 and to reduce the net price received by producers to P_2, equal to P_1 less t. The amount produced and bought each week will be reduced to OQ_1; this is the amount that the supply schedule shows will be produced at P_2 and that the demand schedule shows will be bought at P_1.

The new price P_1 will exceed the former price P by less than the tax t. This is because the supply curve slopes upward. Owing to diminishing returns, the marginal cost and, therefore, the supply price are less for OQ_1 than for OQ.

The amount by which P_1 exceeds P will depend on the slopes of the two curves. If the demand curve is very inelastic (nearly vertical) or if the supply curve is very elastic (nearly horizontal), the price will rise by nearly the full amount of the tax; in the opposite circumstances, the price will rise very little. If the two elasticities are equal to one another, the price will rise by half the amount of the tax.

It makes no difference whether the tax is a purchase-tax levied on the buyers, who pay P_2 plus the tax, or an excise duty levied on the producers, who receive P_1 less the tax which they pay to the Government. I have assumed a *specific* tax of so many pence a unit. The same reasoning applies to an *ad valorem* tax. Suppose the latter is 10 per cent of the supply price. We merely have to find a supply price P_2 at which the same quantity will be supplied as is demanded at P_2 plus 10 per cent $(=P_1)$.

Let us now consider a monopolist who maximizes his profits. It makes no difference whether we regard the tax t as an addition to his marginal costs or as a deduction from his marginal revenue. He will reduce his output from OQ to OQ_1 and raise his price from P to P_1.

In the following diagram his marginal costs are shown as constant and the demand curve as a straight line. In this special case, P_1 will exceed P by exactly half the tax t.[1] The reduction in his output, and therefore the increase in his price, will be less if his marginal costs are increasing, and greater if they are decreasing, than if they are constant.

It is often said that the best way to tax a monopolist is to tax him a lump sum, or a percentage of his profits. The argument is that such a tax will not lead to a reduction in his output. Whatever output maximized his profits before will still maximize his profits less £x or less y per cent. But if it is possible to single out a monopolist and to impose a special tax on him, it would surely be better still to control his prices or, if practicable, to remove the foundations of his monopoly power.

In practice, however, a monopolist seldom charges a price high enough to maximize his profits. He may therefore add the full amount of a tax to his price, if he can do so without arousing public hostility;

[1] See Note to Chapter XVI.

and this may pay him better (although he will still be worse off, because his sales will fall) than raising his price by less than the tax.

The same applies to imperfect competition in general. The normal response of producers is to "pass on" the tax to consumers by adding it to their selling price. They may discover after a time that their

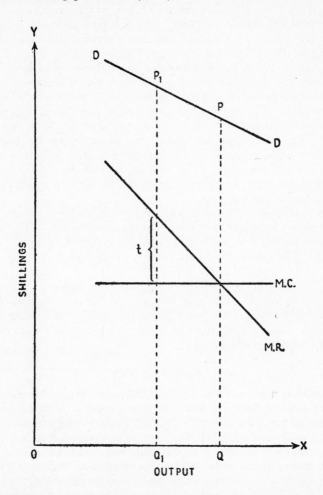

sales fall off so much that their best course is to reduce their prices somewhat, but to begin with they are likely to add on the full amount of the tax.

It is sometimes said that if the price rises by the full amount of the tax, the incidence of the tax is wholly on the buyers; if it rises by half the amount of the tax, the incidence is shared equally between sellers

and buyers, and so on. This is misleading. Even if the price rises by
the full amount of the tax, the sellers are worse off because their sales
are smaller; they have more excess capacity.

As time goes on, fixed capital in a taxed industry will not be replaced
when it wears out. Eventually the capacity of the industry will be
reduced until it again yields the normal rate of return on capital, and
new capital will again flow into it. This is what is meant by the statement that "an old tax is no tax." But this statement also is misleading.
So long as the tax remains, investment in the industry is less than it
otherwise would be, and the prices of its products are higher. Both
producers and consumers would gain if the tax were removed.

During the period of transition, while capacity is being reduced, the
burden of the tax will fall on those factors of production that cannot
move into other industries and earn as much, or nearly as much, as
before. Relatively unskilled workers, for example, are not likely to
have their wages reduced, for they can move to other industries where
wages are still the same. The bulk of the burden will fall on the
owners of plant and equipment, or on skilled workers, specialized to
that particular industry.

The burden on the consumers of a taxed commodity is greater than
the revenue which the Government obtains from the tax. This can be
seen most clearly if we think of a man who stops consuming the commodity. The Government gets nothing at all from him. But he is
worse off, for he would prefer to go on buying it (at its former, untaxed,
price) than to consume whatever he now buys instead. The same
reasoning applies to everybody who reduces his consumption of the
commodity because of the tax.[1] From this standpoint it is better, if
only a few commodities are to be taxed, to select those for which the
demand is relatively inelastic.

4. IMPORT QUOTAS

International trade tends to equalize prices between countries. The
price of wool in Australia would be much lower if Australia had to
consume all the wool she produced and could not export any. The
price of wool in the United Kingdom would be much higher if we
could consume only what we produced, and could not import any.
Under international trade, wool is exported from Australia to the
United Kingdom. If there are no restrictions on this trade, the price
of wool in the United Kingdom will exceed its price in Australia only
by the amount of transport costs and import duties (if any). For the
Australian producer can sell either for local consumption or for export,
whichever pays him best. (In practice both overseas and Australian
buyers attend the wool auction sales.)

[1] This point is made, in terms of indifference curves, in Section 6 of the Appendix
to this Part.

In order to simplify the wording, let us take the United Kingdom to be the sole importing country and let us take Australia to represent all exporting countries. Let us also ignore transport costs and import duties.

Then the price of wool will be the same in the United Kingdom as in Australia. This equality will be brought about by the export of a certain quantity from Australia to the United Kingdom.

The following diagram shows the conditions of demand and supply for wool in each country. If there were no international trade, the price would be P_1 in the United Kingdom and P_2 in Australia. Under international trade, an amount EE ($=II$) is exported from Australia (and imported into the United Kingdom) per unit of time, and the price in both countries is P.

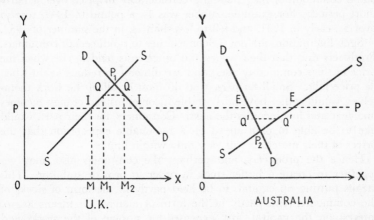

U.K.   AUSTRALIA

Now suppose that the United Kingdom imposes an import quota on wool, restricting the amount of wool she imports (per unit of time) to QQ ($=Q'Q'$). The effect will be to raise the price of wool to Q in the United Kingdom and to reduce it to Q' in Australia.

At the price P, the output in the United Kingdom was OM. At the higher price Q it expands to OM_1. At the price Q, the amount demanded in the United Kingdom is OM_2, which equals the supply, OM_1 plus QQ.

The extent to which Q exceeds P will depend on the size of the quota and on the elasticities of supply and demand in the United Kingdom. The larger the quota, the more elastic the British supply, and the more elastic the British demand, the less will be the rise in price from P to Q. The extent to which Q', the new Australian price, is below P will depend on the size of the quota and on the elasticities of supply and demand in Australia. The larger the quota, the more elastic the Australian supply, and the more elastic the Australian demand, the less will be the fall in price from P to Q'.

It is interesting to note the differences between an import quota and an import duty. An import duty of QQ' per unit of wool would equally restrict imports to QQ, raise the price in the United Kingdom to Q, and reduce the price in Australia to Q'. But whereas the difference in price, QQ', goes to the United Kingdom Government under an import duty, it is divided between importers and exporters under an import quota. And whereas under an import quota the amount of imports is rigidly fixed, under an import duty it may vary: for example, if costs of production in Australia are reduced, the quantity imported will increase.

5. BUFFER STOCKS

Some commodities may fluctuate considerably in price over a fairly short period. For example, rubber was 1s. a pound in 1949, rose to over 5s. early in 1951, and fell to less than 2s. in the summer of 1952.

Such fluctuations are not welcome either to producers or consumers. Producers find that their wages and other costs tend to rise when the price of their commodity rises, and are difficult to reduce again when its price falls. Small farmers, who do most or all of the work themselves, would rather have fairly stable incomes instead of high incomes one year and low incomes the next. Consumers, for their part, would like to be able to plan ahead on a reasonable expectation that the prices of their materials will vary only within limits.

Hence the producers, and perhaps the consumers also, may get together to create a buffer stock in order to provide stability. This means putting up capital, to be held partly in the form of stocks of the commodity and partly in the form of money. It means loss of interest on the capital, and expenses for storage of the stocks and administration of the scheme. If the scheme is later abandoned, there will be losses if the stocks have to be sold for less than they cost.

Suppose that a buffer stock is proposed for rubber. The resources needed may be a stock of rubber equal to perhaps three months' world consumption (say, 500,000 tons), and an equivalent amount (say, £100 million) in cash. The first difficulty will be to agree on which Governments are to provide this capital, and in what proportions.

The next difficulty will be to agree on "fair" price limits. Producing countries are likely to press for higher prices than consuming countries are willing to accept.

Suppose, however, that these difficulties are solved, and that it is decided to stabilize the price of rubber between 1s. 9d. and 2s. 3d. a pound. When the price of rubber falls towards 1s. 9d., the buffer stock buys rubber to keep up its price. When the price rises towards 2s. 3d., the buffer stock sells rubber to keep down its price.

This will work all right so long as fluctuations are first in one direction and then in another. When prices are falling, the buffer stock buys rubber, and holds more rubber and less cash. When subsequently prices are rising, the buffer stock sells rubber and changes some of its rubber back into cash.

But suppose there is a prolonged movement in one direction. Suppose there is a continued increase in demand. If there were no buffer stock, the price would be, say, 3s. a pound. The buffer stock can go on selling rubber at 2s. 3d. a pound so long as its stock of rubber lasts. What will happen when all its rubber has gone? The producers will be unlikely to go on providing it with more rubber to resell at 2s. 3d. when they know that they could sell their rubber for 3s. Indeed, well before the rubber in the buffer stock is all sold, they are likely to revise the "ceiling" price to, say, 3s. 6d.

Or suppose that there is a reduction in costs. At 1s. 9d., supply exceeds demand. The buffer stock has to go on buying more and more rubber in order to maintain the "floor" price of 1s. 9d. What will happen when all its cash has gone, and it is holding all its assets in the form of rubber? Will either the producers or the consumers be willing to provide the buffer stock with more cash, in order to acquire an ever-increasing stock of rubber which they may never be able to sell except at a loss? It is more likely that the scheme will be abandoned or that the "floor" price will be reduced.

The conclusion is that a buffer stock can only smooth out temporary fluctuations. It cannot permanently keep the price either well above or well below the price at which supply would equal demand in the absence of a buffer stock.

An exact parallel to a buffer stock was the *Exchange Equalization Fund* operated by the British Government during the 1930s. The exchange value of sterling was free to fluctuate. But the Fund, with resources partly in gold and foreign exchange and partly in sterling, intervened in the foreign exchange market and bought sterling when its exchange value seemed to be going too low, and sold sterling when its exchange value seemed to be going too high. In fact, the Fund on balance sold sterling and acquired more gold and foreign exchange than it began with. But if the tendency had been for the exchange value of sterling to fall, the Fund would have been unable to prevent such a fall once its assets of gold and foreign exchange had been spent.

INDIFFERENCE CURVES

1. The Nature of Indifference Curves

If there are only two goods between which a consumer can choose, his scale of preferences can be represented on a two-dimensional diagram by a series of indifference curves.

Let us suppose that a number of soldiers are stationed in an out-of-the-way place and that each receives a fixed weekly ration of, say, 10 tots of rum and 50 cigarettes. Each soldier is free to "swap" rum for cigarettes, or cigarettes for rum, with his comrades, but these are the only two goods that enter into the circle of exchange. If the tastes of the various soldiers are not exactly the same, and some have a stronger preference than others for cigarettes as against rum, a market will be established among the soldiers in which rum will be exchanged against cigarettes.

Let us consider the tastes of a soldier whom we will call A. He may like both rum and cigarettes. He would welcome an increased ration of either or both. Nevertheless he has a scale of preferences upon which he will act when he swaps rum for cigarettes, or cigarettes for rum, with his fellows. And it is possible to state his scale of preferences in exact quantitative terms and to represent it on a diagram.

He gets, like the others, 10 tots of rum and 50 cigarettes per week. Suppose we ask him how many extra cigarettes he would require, each week, to induce him to give up one of his tots of rum. Upon reflection, he might decide that he would do this for 5 extra cigarettes but not for 3, while if he were offered 4 extra cigarettes, he would be undecided. This means that to him the combination of 10 tots of rum plus 50 cigarettes is equivalent to the combination of 9 tots plus 54 cigarettes. He is indifferent as between these two combinations. He does not prefer one of them to the other. In the same way, there are many combinations of rum and cigarettes which he will regard as equivalent to these two. For example, he may require a shade more than 10 extra cigarettes in order to give up 2 tots of rum. We thus get another combination—8 tots of rum and 60 cigarettes—which the soldier himself values neither more nor less highly than either of the other two. We can set out some of these combinations in a little table.

13 tots of rum and 44 cigarettes
12   ,,   ,,   45   ,,
11   ,,   ,,   47   ,,
10   ,,   ,,   50   ,,
9   ,,   ,,   54   ,,
8   ,,   ,,   60   ,,
7   ,,   ,,   70   ,,

Such a table represents a part of his "scale of preferences" between rum and cigarettes. We do not inquire into the reasons for his preferences; we accept them as data.

We can show each of the combinations in this table as a point on a diagram, measuring, say, cigarettes along the horizontal axis OX and rum up the vertical axis OY. If we join these points (thus assuming continuity), we obtain a portion of what is called an "indifference curve." This is shown in Fig. 1 on page 268.

The indifference curve slopes downward to the right. This is because an increase in one good not accompanied by a decrease in the other good would give the individual a combination which he preferred to the previous one.

The indifference curve is "convex to the origin." This reflects the fact that the more rum the soldier gives up in exchange for cigarettes, the greater will be the number of additional cigarettes required to induce him to give up yet another tot of rum, and conversely. A scale of preferences usually follows this rule, which is commonly known a the Law of Diminishing Marginal Utility. The marginal utility of one good falls, relatively to that of another, for any given individual, when his supplies of the former good increase while his supplies of the latter remain the same or, as in our example, diminish.

So far we have considered only one indifference curve of soldier A: that containing the combination 10 tots of rum plus 50 cigarettes. If the soldier is sufficiently aware of his own tastes to give correct answers to a number of further questions, we can learn a great deal more about his scale of preferences. For example, we can begin with the combination of 11 tots of rum and 55 cigarettes. It is certain that he prefers this combination to 10 tots of rum plus 50 cigarettes. Suppose that he possessed the former combination. He might be able to say, upon reflection, how many additional cigarettes he would require to compensate him for giving up one of his 11 tots of rum, how many for giving up 2 tots, and so on. In this way we could obtain another indifference curve. This new curve would lie farther from the point O on our diagram than the first curve. Every point on this new curve would represent a combination of rum and cigarettes which the soldier himself valued neither more nor less highly than the combination of 11 tots of rum plus 55 cigarettes, which is represented by a point lying on this new curve. But we know that he prefers 11 tots of rum and

55 cigarettes to 10 tots of rum and 50 cigarettes. Therefore he prefers any combination lying on the new curve to any combination lying on the old one.

In this way we could get a large number of indifference curves and *the resulting "indifference map" would record our soldier's scale of preferences as between rum and cigarettes.* The indifference curves are thus a kind of photograph of the soldier's tastes. Or they may be likened to contour lines. Each curve represents, so to speak, a greater height

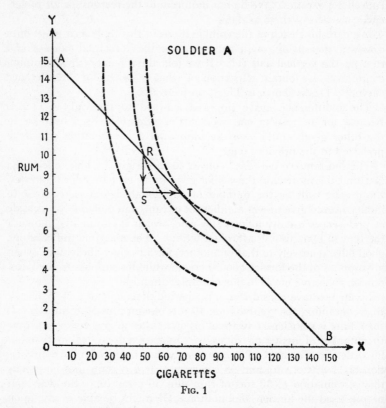

Fig. 1

than the curve to its left or below it. The object of the individual will be to reach the greatest height possible for him under the limitations of his fixed income and of the rate of exchange between the two goods in the market. He will try, that is, to reach the position he most prefers out of all the positions open to him.

Suppose, for example, that the rate of exchange established in the market is one tot of rum against 10 cigarettes. Soldier *A* would clearly gain by exchanging 2 tots of his rum against cigarettes. This would give him 8 tots of rum and 70 cigarettes. But, by hypothesis, he would just as soon have 8 tots of rum and 60 cigarettes as the 10 tots of rum and 50 cigarettes with which he begins. Eight tots of rum and 70 cigarettes, therefore, represents a preferred position to him. He is on *another* indifference curve, one which he prefers to the one on which he started.

The "map" of his indifference curves enables us to read off exactly what he would do at any given rate of exchange. Suppose the rate established in the market is one tot of rum against 10 cigarettes. Then if a soldier, with a ration of 10 tots of rum and 50 cigarettes, exchanged all his cigarettes for rum, he would have 15 tots of rum, and if he exchanged all his rum for cigarettes, he would have 150 cigarettes. This is represented on the diagram by the straight line AB, joining the point on the vertical axis which represents 15 tots of rum to the point on the horizontal axis which represents 150 cigarettes. The initial ration of 10 tots of rum plus 50 cigarettes is represented by the point R, which of course must lie on the straight line.

Given this rate of exchange, a soldier is able to move to any point which he chooses on the line AB. For he begins at the point R, and any exchange which he makes must take him to some other point on AB. What will he do? We know that if he can move from one indifference curve to another which lies farther from O he will do so, because he will prefer any combination on the latter curve to any combination on the former. Therefore he must move to that point on the line AB at which AB is tangential to one of his indifference curves. In Fig. 1, soldier A will move from the point R to the point T. T represents the position which he most prefers out of all those open to him; this is shown by his "indifference map," for T lies on an indifference curve which is farther from O than any other indifference curve to which he can move. He moves from R to T by giving up RS of rum in exchange for ST of cigarettes. ST must represent ten times as many cigarettes as the number of tots of rum represented by RS, since the triangles AOB and RST are similar.

Let us now briefly consider the preferences of another soldier, whom we may call B, who has a stronger preference than A for rum as against cigarettes. The relevant portion of his indifference curve containing the combination 10 tots of rum plus 50 cigarettes, may be as follows—

13 tots of rum and 15 cigarettes
12 ,, ,, 23 ,,
11 ,, ,, 33 ,,
10 ,, ,, 50 ,,
9 ,, ,, 70 ,,
8 ,, ,, 100 ,,
7 ,, ,, 150 ,,

At a rate of exchange of one tot of rum against 10 cigarettes, this soldier would clearly gain by exchanging 20 cigarettes against rum.

This would give him 12 tots of rum and 30 cigarettes. But by hypothesis he would just as soon have 12 tots of rum and 23 cigarettes as the 10 tots and 50 cigarettes with which he begins. Twelve tots of rum and 30 cigarettes, therefore, represent a preferred position to him. He is on *another* indifference curve, one which he prefers to the one on which he started.

The scale of preferences of soldier *B* is shown in Fig. 2. He will move from the point *R* to the point *M*, giving up *RL* cigarettes in exchange for *LM* rum.

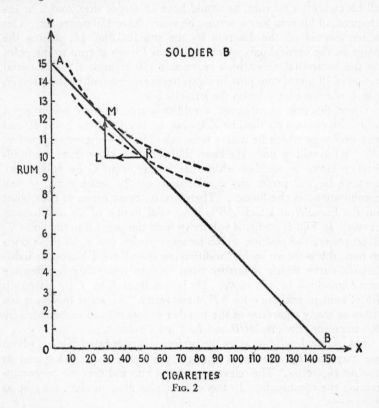

Fig. 2

It will be noted that two soldiers can both gain by exchanging with one another. The contention that exchange is "barren," because the value obtained is only equal to the value given up, is quite false. Both parties gain, each moving to a position which he prefers, because their tastes—their scales of preference—are different. And clearly two people could gain by exchanging, even if their tastes were the same, if in the first place one possessed a different assortment of goods from the other.

2. Exchange with only Two Goods

If our soldiers constitute a perfect competitive market, in the sense that each is aware of all the bargains that are struck and of all the offers which each of his comrades makes, there will be only one rate of exchange between rum and cigarettes. This can be proved by showing that two rates are impossible. Suppose that soldier A were exchanging rum for cigarettes with soldier B at a rate of 1 tot of rum for 15 cigarettes, and that soldier C were exchanging rum for cigarettes with soldier D at a rate of 1 tot of rum for 5 cigarettes. Clearly it would pay B and C to get together at some intermediate rate—say, at a rate of 1 tot of rum against 10 cigarettes. In this way B would get 50 per cent more rum for his cigarettes and C would give only half as much rum as before for any given number of cigarettes. Since the market is perfect, every soldier knows what is going on, and therefore two different rates cannot exist.

It may take some time to find the equilibrium rate, but if each soldier's tastes remain the same, the same kind of situation keeps repeating itself week after week, and before long a rate of exchange will be found which will be permanent. It will be the "equilibrium" rate, because at that rate every soldier who wants to swap rum for cigarettes can swap as much as he wishes and every soldier who wants to swap cigarettes for rum can swap as much as he wishes.

In practice, the equilibrium rate would be found by trial and error. But if we knew the scale of preferences of each soldier, and the quantity of rum and cigarettes received each week by each soldier, we could easily discover what it would be. For we should know what each soldier would want to do at any given price and we should find that at one price alone the amount of rum that would be offered (by soldiers wanting cigarettes in exchange) would be the same as the amount of rum demanded (by soldiers offering cigarettes in exchange).

For example, if the "price" of a tot of rum were 20 cigarettes, some soldiers would wish to give up rum, obtaining cigarettes in exchange. We could add together the amounts of rum that each of these soldiers would wish to give up. This would give us the total "supply" of rum that would be offered in exchange at this price. (Looking at the matter from the other side, this number of tots multiplied by 20 would be the number of cigarettes demanded at this "price.") Some soldiers, on the other hand, would wish to give up cigarettes in exchange for rum. The total amount of rum that these soldiers, taken together, would wish to acquire at this price would give us the demand for rum (and therefore the supply of cigarettes) at this price. The price at which the amount of rum supplied would be the same as the amount demanded (implying, of course, that the amount of cigarettes demanded would be the same as the amount supplied) would be the equilibrium price.

Suppose we found that the equilibrium price would be 10 cigarettes for 1 tot of rum. No other price could be maintained for any length of time. If for a time the price ruling were, say, 9 cigarettes per tot, more cigarettes would be offered against rum than would be accepted. Some soldiers anxious to exchange cigarettes for rum would be unable to do so. Some of these soldiers would rather give 10 cigarettes or even 11 or 12 or more cigarettes for a tot of rum than restrict themselves to the 10 tots in their ration. They would therefore offer a higher "price." They would offer more than 9 cigarettes per tot of rum in order to make sure of getting some extra rum. This would drive up the market "price" until it settled at a level at which everyone who wanted to exchange would be able to exchange as much as he wished—at a level, that is, at which supply would equal demand.

3. CHANGES IN DATA

Once the equilibrium rate of exchange between rum and cigarettes has been established, it will continue indefinitely unless some change takes place in the data. Let us consider in what ways the data may change and how each type of change may cause the rate of exchange to alter.

1. The ration may be increased or decreased, without changing the proportion of rum and cigarettes. For example, each soldier may be given 20 tots of rum and 100 cigarettes, or 5 tots of rum and 25 cigarettes, or 11 tots of rum and 55 cigarettes. It may be thought that a change of this kind would leave the rate of exchange unaltered. But this is very unlikely. For although the tastes of each soldier remain the same as before, it is unlikely that he will be prepared to give up exactly the same number of cigarettes to get an additional amount of rum, or conversely, now that the size of his ration is altered. Suppose that the ration is doubled. It may happen, for example, that each soldier would now be prepared to give up more cigarettes than before in order to have an additional tot of rum. A soldier who would not previously have given up more than, say, 12 cigarettes (thus reducing his cigarettes to 38) in order to get an additional tot (thus increasing his tots to 11) may now be prepared to give up, say, 15 cigarettes (thus reducing his cigarettes to 85) in order to get an additional tot (thus increasing his tots to 21); a soldier who would not previously have given up more than, say, 3 cigarettes to get an additional tot may now be prepared to give up, say, 5; and so on. Under such conditions, rum would still be exchanged against cigarettes, since different soldiers would continue to have different scales of preferences, just as before, but in the new equilibrium the value of a tot of rum in terms of cigarettes would be higher than in the old.

2. The proportion of rum to cigarettes in the weekly ration may be

changed. Suppose, for example, that the ration becomes 10 tots of rum and 60 cigarettes. This will cause the value of cigarettes in terms of rum to fall. For every soldier will now be prepared to give more cigarettes than before to get additional rum; or, to put it the other way round, will require more cigarettes than before to compensate him for the loss of a given amount of rum. Hence the supply of rum offered in exchange for cigarettes, at the old rate, will now be insufficient to meet the demand, and competition among soldiers anxious to exchange cigarettes against rum will drive up its price. But if the quantity of both rum and cigarettes comprised in the ration is increased or decreased, and at the same time the proportion of rum to cigarettes is changed, we cannot be certain *a priori* how the rate of exchange will be affected. The change in the proportion will tend to increase the value of the good whose proportion has fallen. The change in the size of the ration may reinforce this tendency, but, on the other hand, it may weaken it or even outweigh it.

3. The distribution of the total weekly amount of rum and cigarettes among the soldiers may be changed. Instead of each soldier receiving the same ration as every other, some may be given larger rations than others. This would clearly give more weight than before to the tastes of those who now receive increased rations. If, for example, most of them have a stronger preference for cigarettes, as against rum, than the rest of the soldiers, this will tend to raise the value of cigarettes in terms of rum.

4. The personnel of the soldiers might change: for example, one regiment might be replaced by another. This would give us a new set of "indifference maps" and it would be merely a coincidence if this did not cause an alteration in the rate of exchange.

5. There might be a general change in tastes, in favour of either rum or cigarettes. For example, all the soldiers might be more or less influenced by propaganda against alcohol, and this of course would lower the value of rum in terms of cigarettes.

Whatever change, or combination of changes, took place in the data, we could always determine the new equilibrium rate of exchange if we knew the rations received by each soldier and the scale of preferences of each soldier. It might, of course, take some time for the soldiers themselves to discover it. If the data were changing frequently, an equilibrium might never be attained. Nevertheless, at any moment the rate of exchange in the market would be tending towards the rate that would maintain equilibrium under the prevailing conditions.

4. EXPENDITURE CURVES AND DEMAND CURVES

A set of indifference curves, representing the scale of preferences of a given individual between two goods, will of course remain valid

K   B.E.

provided that his tastes do not change. His income may change, or the rate of exchange between the two goods may alter, without causing any change in the indifference curves, for these portray his personal scale of preferences, and nothing else.

If we have a diagram showing the indifference curves of an individual, it is easy to show how he would respond to changes in his income. For this purpose it is convenient to suppose that he receives his income entirely in one commodity and then exchanges some units

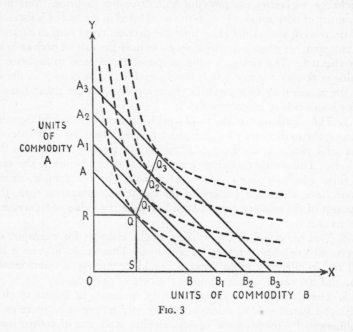

Fig. 3

of that commodity against some units of the other. In Fig. 3 units of commodity A are measured up the vertical axis OY and units of commodity B are measured along the horizontal axis OX. Our individual periodically receives an income of OA units of commodity A. The market rate of exchange between A and B is represented by the slope of the line AB. The combination of A and B that he most prefers out of all those open to him is represented by the point Q. He will therefore exchange AR of A against RQ of B, consuming OR of A and OS ($=RQ$) of B. If his income increases to OA_1, the combination he most prefers out of all those open to him is represented by Q_1, and so on. (The rate of exchange between A and B by hypothesis remains the same, so that A_1B_1 is parallel to AB.) If we join together the various Q's we obtain (part of) what may be termed his "expenditure curve." This shows how he would divide any given income between the two goods A and B, provided that his scale of preferences (represented by the indifference curves) and the market rate of exchange between A and B (represented by the slope of the line AB) remained unchanged.

Similarly we can show how he would divide a given income OA between A and B at each of a series of prices. A rise in the price of B, in terms of A, is shown by a steeper slope of AB. Since his income is fixed in terms of A, at OA, a rise in the price of B will place him in a

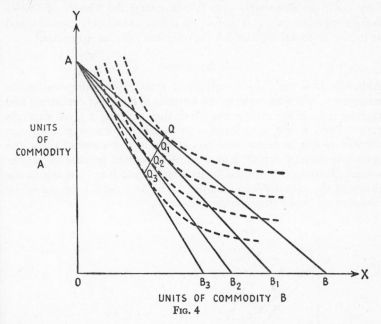

Fig. 4

worse position than before. In Fig. 4, when the rate of exchange is AB the combination that he most prefers out of all those open to him is represented by Q, when it is AB_1 it is represented by Q_1, and so on. By joining the various Q's we obtain (a part of) what may be termed his "demand curve." This shows how he would distribute his fixed income of OA between A and B at each of a series of prices.

Indifference curves can be used to portray a person's scale of preferences between any two alternatives, provided there are only two. Thus they can portray his scale of preferences as between income and leisure, showing how he would divide his twenty-four hours each day between leisure and remunerated work at any given rate of pay per hour. Again, they can be used to show his scale of preferences between present and future consumption, between liquid assets and income-yielding assets, and so on. For any scale of preferences relates to the disposal of some given total among different uses. When there are only two uses, it can be depicted by a series of indifference curves on a two-dimensional diagram. Often there are more than two uses—for example, there are usually more than two goods available to a consumer. In such cases a scale of preferences cannot be represented on a diagram, for we should need as many dimensions as there are "alternatives." Nevertheless, the study, with the aid of indifference curves, of cases where there are only two alternatives will be found very useful by those who wish to understand the Theory of Choice and its implications. It is useful, but it is not absolutely essential, and as it may be found difficult I have relegated it to an Appendix.[1]

5. RATIONING

Although it is the fairest method of reducing consumption in an emergency, rationing restricts the freedom of choice of consumers and thereby reduces the satisfaction which they get from a given expenditure. Even if the actual prices of rationed commodities are not allowed to rise, a person who would like to buy more of them and cannot is thereby forced into a worse economic position as a consumer. Rationing is similar in its effects upon him to a rise in the prices of the rationed commodities. This can readily be shown by means of an "indifference curve" diagram.

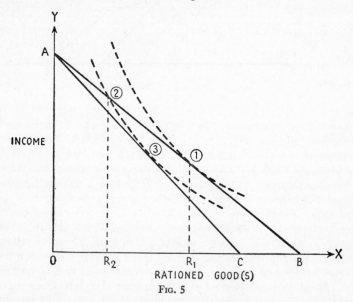

Fig. 5

---

[1] For a fuller account, see Hicks, J. R., and Allen, R. G. D.: "A Reconsideration of the Theory of Value" in *Economica*, N.S., Vol. I.

In the absence of rationing, a consumer with a spendable income OA could apportion this income between a commodity (or a group of commodities), subsequently rationed, and other uses as he chose. He could choose any position on the price-line AB. (If he spent his whole income on the commodity he would be able to buy OB of it.) In fact, he would choose the position (1), where AB is tangential to one of his indifference curves. He would purchase OR_1 of the commodity. Suppose now that rationing is introduced. The price of the rationed commodity (or group of commodities) remains the same, but he can buy only OR_2 of it. His position is now (2). This is on a lower indifference curve than (1). It is on the same indifference curve as (3). But he would have moved to (3), in the absence of rationing, only if the price of the rationed commodity had risen from $\dfrac{OA}{OB}$ to $\dfrac{OA}{OC}$.

Hence the rationing to an amount OR_2 reduces his satisfaction from his income OA, although prices remain the same, as much as the above rise in the price of the rationed commodity would have reduced it in the absence of rationing.

6. The Excess Burden of Indirect Taxation

Suppose that a tax is imposed on cigarettes. We can consider a typical consumer, and draw some of his indifference curves between money income (per week), to be spent on goods of all kinds, and cigarettes (per week). The diagram (Fig. 6) measures his income up to the Y axis and his cigarettes along the X axis, starting from $O = $ Zero.

His total money income is OA. Before the tax, the price of cigarettes is $\dfrac{OA}{OB}$. He can vary his combination of income and cigarettes only by moving along the line AB. All the combinations of income and cigarettes open to him lie on that line. But he wants to get on as high an indifference curve as possible. He therefore will choose that combination represented by the point at which one of his indifference curves just touches AB. That point is P_1.

Now suppose that a tax is imposed on cigarettes which doubles their price. Half the money he spends on cigarettes is received by the Treasury as tax revenue.

The change in the alternatives confronting him is shown by the change from AB to AB_1. It is now only along AB_1 that he can move. The best position open to him is P_3. He reduces his purchases of cigarettes from OC_1 to OC_3 cigarettes, giving up AD money for them. The Treasury gets half AD—namely, AT—as tax.

If instead of taxing cigarettes the Government had taken AT from him in money, the price of cigarettes would have been the same as before. He would have been able to move to any point on TT_1

(parallel to *AB*), and he would have moved to P_2, buying OC_2 cigarettes. Obviously he prefers P_2 to P_3; it is on a higher indifference curve. Hence he loses, over and above the sum AT which he pays in tax, by the rise in the price of cigarettes due to the tax on them.

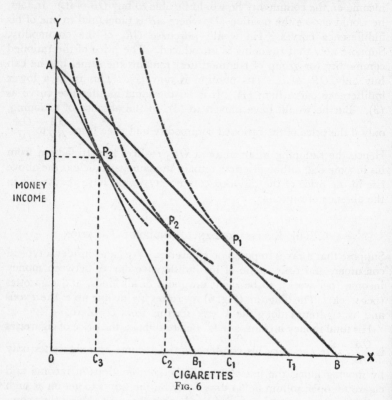

FIG. 6

It will be noted that this loss varies with the elasticity of demand for the taxed commodity. If a person's demand is quite inelastic, so that he buys the same amount as before despite the rise in price, he suffers no such loss; the effect on him is just the same as if the Government had taken the tax from him in money, leaving prices unchanged.

PART IV

THE WORKING OF THE PRICE SYSTEM UNDER CAPITALISM

CHAPTER XX

THE ROLE OF THE ENTREPRENEUR

1. Introduction

This Part discusses the working of the price system under capitalism. Such a discussion cannot avoid raising the question of whether capitalism is the best system of social organization. Would complete central planning, as in Soviet Russia, be better? Or, supposing we reject that alternative, how much control should be exercised by the State? Nobody advocates complete *laissez faire*; it has never existed, and could not exist, in a modern community. The Government must play quite a large part in economic life. But how large? About as large as in Great Britain today? Or larger? Or smaller, as in Great Britain before the war or in the United States today?

These are important and controversial questions. The answers to them are matters of opinion; people of equal intelligence and knowledge may find themselves in opposite camps. In an introductory book such as this, confined mainly to exposition and analysis, I cannot possibly provide enough material for the reader to form a final judgment on them. But I can and will point out and discuss the chief merits of capitalism, of a free-enterprise system, which are stressed by its advocates, and the chief defects which are stressed by its opponents, and I shall try to clear up a few misconceptions.

I cannot, however, discuss everything at once. The two main defects of capitalism are that it may give rise to mass unemployment and to monopoly or milder forms of imperfect competition. Each of these subjects gets a chapter to itself; and other defects, real or alleged, are also discussed in this Part, mostly in Chapter XXIV.

That being so, the present chapter assumes conditions approaching perfect competition and full employment. These assumptions are favourable to capitalism; they place the working of the price system in a rather rosy light. Perfect competition means that costs do reflect alternatives forgone; full employment means that labour and other resources saved on one task are set free for other tasks. It is in the interests of the community, therefore, that firms should try to maximize their profits by producing any given output as cheaply as possible, and by producing whatever pays them best.

This was the thesis of Adam Smith. "It is only for the sake of profit," he wrote "that any man employs a capital in the support of industry; and he will always, therefore, endeavour to employ it in the support of that industry of which the produce is likely to be of the greatest value." Hence "every individual necessarily labours to render the annual revenue of the society as great as he can. . . . He intends only his own gain, and he is in this, as in many other cases, led by an invisible hand to promote an end which was no part of his intention." [1]

Of course there is no "invisible hand." But there is the price system. And the price system does not work in a void. It works within a framework of laws and institutions provided by the community to harmonize the desire for private gain and the interests of society. It is unrealistic to condemn the profit motive because it leads businessmen to defraud their customers or to sell dangerous drugs or adulterated foodstuffs or to pollute rivers with the wastes of their factories; abuses of this kind are forbidden by law, although sometimes, as when the best site for a factory is among beautiful natural surroundings which the factory might spoil, it is a nice question where to draw the line.

I want to keep this book an objective introduction to economics, but as these controversial questions cannot be avoided, I must repeat that the present chapter is favourable to capitalism. In a sense, it presents the case, or part of the case, for capitalism, because by assuming perfect competition and full employment it assumes away two major defects—monopoly and unemployment. This is because we must proceed by stages; monopoly and unemployment are discussed later.

2. ENTREPRENEURS AND FIRMS

We have seen that nearly all commodities are produced by a number of different factors working in combination. This means that some persons must perform the task of combining different factors together, must decide in what proportions they shall be combined, what they will produce, and where, and by what methods.

Economists usually call these persons *entrepreneurs*. There is no really suitable English word for them. "Enterpriser" sounds too dashing, and "undertaker" a little sinister. Hitherto I have used the word "businessman," but this suggests somebody with a white collar and an office, whereas we need a word that covers also the man who runs his own farm or shop or lorry or fishing-boat.

In so far as economic activity is directed by private enterprise, the taking of decisions is decentralized. They are made by the entrepreneurs. In a country as large as Great Britain, there are millions of entrepreneurs. They are constantly taking decisions. Some are big decisions—for example, a decision to build a new plant or open a new branch, or a decision to switch over from making one product to

[1] *Wealth of Nations*, Book IV, Chapter II (Vol. I, p. 421, in Cannan's edition).

making another. Most of them are small decisions—to produce a little more of one product rather than another, to use this material rather than that, to take on a few more workers, to change the layout of a factory slightly, or to make some alterations in the office routine. It is the sum-total of these innumerable decisions that determines the constantly changing pattern of economic activity.

The entrepreneur also bears the risks. He pays fixed prices, market prices, for the factors that he buys or hires. He normally pays his workers fixed wages, whether his business does well or badly; he has to pay them the market rate, in order to retain them. They take the risk that if he fails they will lose their jobs; but, under full employment, they can find jobs elsewhere, whereas if he loses his capital it is gone for ever. In the same way, he pays a fixed rate of interest to his bank for money lent to him as working capital; and if he rents land or buildings or machinery, he pays a fixed rental. He receives for his products whatever they will fetch in the market. If his receipts exceed his costs he makes a profit, large or small; if they do not, he makes a loss. His income, his profit, fluctuates; if his costs go down or his receipts go up he does better, and in the opposite event he does worse.

Nowadays these two functions of the entrepreneur are often divorced from one another; the shareholders of a company take the risks whereas the directors and managers take the decisions. I will return to this point in a moment.

A group of workers could act as entrepreneurs, borrowing the capital to run their own business. They would be their own bosses. Nobody would pay them wages. They would divide among themselves the receipts of the business less all the various expenses. They would take the decisions, and they would bear the risks.

But the amount of capital needed to run many businesses is too large for a group of workers, still less for a single worker, to borrow. Even for a small business, people usually want some kind of security before they will lend money to it. It is difficult, therefore, for a group of workers to start a business unless they have enough savings of their own. Only if they have saved enough to buy plant and machinery, or other assets, are they likely to be able to borrow, pledging their assets as security for the loan.

No doubt a few successful businessmen, including some millionaires, began life as newsboys or in some other low-paid occupation. But it is very difficult for most wage-earners to save enough to set themselves up in business, as entrepreneurs. Those who can, and do, tend to enter one or two fields, such as retail trade, where the initial capital needed is not large; these fields tend to become overcrowded and to yield relatively low incomes. In general, this need to have capital, to start with, restricts the number of entrepreneurs. The son of well-to-do parents, who can provide him with the capital to set up in business on his own or to buy a partnership is an existing business, is lucky. Others may have more business ability than he, but lack the capital to get started.

The entrepreneur, therefore, is usually the owner of capital. His *firm* is the collection of factors—land, buildings, plant and equipment, workers, materials, and so on—that he controls. A firm is a separate planning unit, and it is the entrepreneur who does the planning. In economic jargon, Farmer Giles and his farm, John Smith and his fishing-boat, are firms.

This is all very well for a one-man business, or a partnership, or even for a company in which the managing director owns most of the capital. But what about a company with a number of shareholders, each owning only a small percentage of the total capital of the company?

Here the two functions of the entrepreneur are largely divorced from one another. It is the shareholders who bear the risks. It is they who get a fluctuating income, sharing between them the profits of the company, and it is they who lose their capital if the company fails. Legally, they have the ultimate control. If they are not satisfied with their directors, they can dismiss them and appoint new ones. But in practice most of the shareholders do not know one another, and many of them may not follow the affairs of the company closely enough to come to the conclusion that they should change its management. As a rule, the great majority of shareholders do not attend the meetings of their company. It is very unusual, therefore, for a majority of the shareholders to agree that their directors should be changed, and to exercise their legal rights by changing them. They remain "passive." The broad decisions on policy are taken by the directors and the day-to-day decisions by managers and sub-managers.

The situation is still more complicated in a giant concern such as Unilever or Imperial Chemical Industries or the Co-operative Wholesale Society. The managements of the various subsidiary companies are usually given a good deal of discretion. The same applies to the managements of the branches or departments of most large companies. It is difficult to say whether a subsidiary company or a branch or a department should be considered as a separate "firm."

But all this does not affect our fundamental argument. It may be difficult for an outsider to say exactly how particular decisions are arrived at. But it remains true that the taking of decisions is decentralized. Moreover, as I have pointed out earlier, they tend to be taken by those most suited to take them, for the man of good business and executive ability but lacking capital can work his way up to a responsible position in a company, and can thus play a part in determining how the shareholders' money is spent.

And the profit motive remains. Occasionally there may be a conflict of interest between directors and shareholders. For example, directors loving power may seek to expand the activities of the company more than is profitable. But on the whole there is a fairly close harmony of interests. The directors are themselves shareholders, and therefore want the company to do well. The various managers and sub-managers may get a bonus that varies with the profits of the company. In any event, they know that if the company prospers, they are more likely to get an increase in their salaries, and that if it does badly, they may lose their jobs; and they may be dismissed if their work is not satisfactory. Hence those decisions are taken which offer the best prospects of profit, even when they are taken by directors owning only a small part of the total capital or by managers owning none.

3. The Controlling Power of Demand

The decisions of entrepreneurs on what to produce are based on their estimates of present demand and their forecasts of future demand. It pays to produce what the public wants; not what some government official thinks consumers should have, but what the consumers themselves are prepared to buy.

It is true that many firms grow or make producers' goods, which they sell to other firms and not to the public. But the demand for wool, for example, depends ultimately on the demand of the public for woollen clothing, woollen blankets, and other consumers' goods containing wool. The demand for steel plates, to take a rather more complicated example, comes in the first instance partly from shipbuilding firms. But the demand for ships, and therefore for steel plates, reflects the demand of the public for goods transported by ship, or for goods embodying materials and components transported by ship, and for passenger transport by ship. Always at the end of the chain is the final consumer, and it is his preferences which determine, through the price system and the profit motive, what goods and services are produced, and in what proportions.

When an entrepreneur is deciding which industry to enter, he may give some weight to his personal preferences. He may be a pacifist who wishes to avoid producing anything connected with armaments; he may disapprove of drink and will therefore have nothing to do with brewing or distilling; he may be so fond of animals that he could not contemplate becoming a butcher; and so on. But if the prospects of profit in any field are better than elsewhere, there are usually enough entrepreneurs willing to enter it. The personal preferences of some individuals do not affect the composition of the national output; and we can treat the decisions of entrepreneurs as entirely business decisions and not private decisions.

Some entrepreneurs, who will be managing their own business, have special knowledge of the technical and marketing problems of some particular industry, and will tend to enter that. But most entrepreneurs could equally well enter any one of several different industries; and a large firm can and does employ salaried experts to deal with technical matters. The general tendency, therefore, is for entrepreneurs to enter those industries which offer the best prospects of profit. This depends on the expected volume of sales. The output of those goods and services for which the demand is increasing will expand, and the output of those for which the demand is falling will contract.

The field of choice of the new entrepreneur is not confined to established products: if he can think of something new, which will sell well, at a price above its cost, he may make exceptionally high profits—until other entrepreneurs follow suit. Something new may be an entirely new type of product—plastics and television are fairly recent examples—or a new variety of an existing product, such as a new design for a motor-car or a refrigerator or an armchair. There is a constant search for such *innovations*, both by existing firms and by potential entrepreneurs, for success may mean a fortune. But success depends on pleasing the public, on meeting a demand at present latent because there is no such good available on the market.

Apart from innovations, potential entrepreneurs are always on the look-out for gaps which they could profitably fill. There may be a local demand, unsatisfied or inadequately satisfied, for a restaurant, an hotel, a cinema, a local newspaper, a bus service, a petrol station, a hairdressing saloon, to give only a few illustration. Established firms are equally on the look-out for good opportunities to set up new branches.

In the same way, existing firms are always watching the sales of their various products, or of their different varieties of the same product. If sales or orders are increasing for one line and falling off for another, it will clearly pay them to produce more of the former and less of the latter.

If it pays to produce something, this means that consumers will spend their money on that rather than on some alternative which could have been produced instead at the same cost, which means with an equivalent amount of labour and other factors of production. The desire of the entrepreneur to make profits is thus in complete harmony with the general objective of using labour and other resources to produce that assortment of goods and services, out of all the many possible assortments, which consumers most prefer. It pays to use resources as consumers wish them to be used; it pays to produce what people will buy.

We have, in Great Britain, literally millions of entrepreneurs all guided by the controlling power of demand. The entrepreneur serving the local market studies on the spot the many influences affecting the local demand, and can decide from first-hand knowledge in what directions to expand or contract. The entrepreneur serving a wider market is guided in some instances by his own market research or by trade journals, but always, in the last resort, by the relative prices which he gets for his various products; it is through the price mechanism that consumers indicate their preferences to producers. This great body of entrepreneurs is an unpaid army, all the time collecting information and taking decisions. Nobody pays them, but their profits depend on whether or not they correctly judge and anticipate demand. If they succeed they make good profits. If they fail they make losses, but it is their own capital that they lose, and nobody compensates them. They are out for profit and they take the risks. This is what is meant by decentralization under private enterprise, in contrast to complete central planning. The advocates of private enterprise claim that the system is more flexible, more responsive to changes in demand, more prompt to anticipate new or latent demands by introducing innovations, than a system of complete State control.

Once again, however, I remind the reader that demand implies ability and willingness to pay. It is not the same thing as need. It is based on the existing distribution of wealth; each shilling, whether it is paid by a rich man or by a poor man, carries the same weight as every other.

This, however, is not an argument against the price system or against production for profit; it is an argument against too much inequality of wealth. The price system, working through the profit motive, is impartial and impersonal; it is a mechanism that responds to the forces acting on it. If the distribution of wealth is considered too uneven, it can be made less uneven, as it has been in Great Britain, by taxing the richer for the benefit of the poorer. More of the shillings will then come from the poorer (or from the Government, acting on behalf of the poorer, to provide them with health services, education, and other benefits) and fewer from the richer; the price system will continue to respond to whatever the demand may be, from whatever sources it may come.

But the price system *is* a system. Different prices are all interrelated. The distribution of wealth, and therefore the relative demands of different people and the composition of the total demand, can be changed without affecting the smooth working of the price mechanism. But if the mechanism itself is interfered with, some prices being fixed lower than they would otherwise be, it may be thrown out of gear, as we saw in the preceding chapter.

4. COSTS AS ALTERNATIVES FORGONE

Entrepreneurs must consider their costs as well as their receipts; their profits are the excess of their receipts over their costs. Their receipts obviously depend on demand. So do their costs, although this is less obvious.

The cost of producing anything is made up of the payments to the various factors employed in producing it. What those factors have to be paid depends on what they can earn elsewhere. Under perfect competition, their prices equal the values of their marginal products in other industries. Hence it will pay an entrepreneur to employ labour and other resources only if they can produce something more valuable, or at least equally valuable, compared with what they could produce elsewhere. The value of what they produce for him must exceed (except right at the margin) their costs, and their costs reflect the value of the addition which they could make to output in other fields. In other words, their costs reflect the alternatives forgone by using them for this particular task instead of for some other. Consumers must value more highly what they produce here than what they could produce elsewhere, or it will not pay to employ them here.

Entrepreneurs are constantly searching for ways of reducing their costs per unit of output, and thereby increasing their profits.

Take one of the first questions that faces an entrepreneur about to set up a new firm: the question of location. In many cases, his decision will depend largely on transport costs. He will have to pay for the transport of materials to his works and for the transport of his products to their markets. Other things being equal, he will choose that site at which his transport costs are lowest. This means that fewer workers or lorries or other factors of production will be needed to transport his materials and products; some factors of production, which would be employed in transporting them had he chosen a less suitable site, are left free for other uses.

The royal road to higher standards of living is to get a bigger output from the same resources. This can be done, for example, by introducing higher-yielding varieties of crops and animals, or by improving the layout of the factory or simplifying office procedure. It pays the entrepreneur to make such changes, for he will thereby increase his profits.

Some changes of this type, however, involve additional costs. For example, a greater use of fertilizer may increase yields. But will it increase them enough to make it worth while? In other words, could the labour and other resources employed in making the extra fertilizer, and transporting it, be used to produce something still more valuable than the addition to the crops? This is the type of question which entrepreneurs are continually solving; on such questions their own interests and those of the community are identical, the identity being achieved by the price system.

Take again the question of substitution between factors. For example, fuel costs in steel-making can be reduced by modern methods of combustion control and heat control and by the use of oxygen. These devices, however, cost money. Do they save more in fuel than they cost? If so, they are worth introducing; and it benefits both the steel-makers and the community to introduce them.

It pays an entrepreneur to introduce labour-saving devices (which substitute capital for labour) if they reduce his costs per unit of output. In that event, they benefit the community as a whole, for less labour and other resources than before will now be required to produce a given output. The labour that is saved is available to increase output in other fields; or some of it may be used to expand the output of the firms which introduce these devices.

The layman is usually inclined to think that firms with old and out-of-date plant and equipment should scrap it and replace it by new. The entrepreneur knows that if he does so, his variable costs (his direct costs of operation) will be reduced. But he knows also that there is life in the old plant yet. It is still doing its job, after a fashion; it is still yielding him a profit. Should he discard it? Only if by so doing he can meet the capital charges on the new plant and still reduce his costs below their present level. And his decision, inspired solely by calculations of profit, is in harmony with the interests of the community. Capital is scarce, and new investment should take this particular form only if it yields at least as much as in other alternative uses.

It may be that some individual firms will be worse off, at least for a time, as the result of improved methods of production. Those who introduce them first are likely to do well, but as more and more firms follow suit, the selling prices of the products will tend to go on falling as the output of the industry expands. This fall in selling prices may reduce profits, despite the reduction in costs. Whether it does so or not depends on the elasticity of demand for the products; the sales of some products can be expanded greatly by a relatively small fall in price, but for others the demand is relatively inelastic.

Nevertheless any particular firm will be compelled to adopt the more efficient methods, if they reduce its costs; a firm that clings to the old-fashioned methods will be still worse off. And this is entirely in the interests of the community as a whole. As time goes on, less capital will be attracted to an industry where profits have fallen, until eventually the rate of profit recovers to normal. The relatively large fall in the prices of its products means that consumers do not want so much more of them; they prefer more of something else. But they do want whatever quantity of those products is produced to be produced in the most efficient, and therefore the cheapest, way; and this result is achieved through the price mechanism.

There may well be discrepancies, perhaps very large discrepancies, between the results of the search for profits and the interests of the community. But these discrepancies nearly always arise from monopoly,

in the sale of products or in the purchase of factors, or from unemployment. Under conditions approaching perfect competition and
full employment, the harmony between the interests of profit-seeking
entrepreneurs and of consumers is almost complete. It pays to produce
what the public wants; and it pays to produce it in the most efficient
way.

CHAPTER XXI

THE MOBILITY OF FACTORS OF PRODUCTION

1. THE MEANING OF MOBILITY

AT any moment a community has a certain quantity of factors of production. In the first place, it has a working population. This does not consist only of wage-earners. It includes also farmers, shopkeepers, workers in the professions, housewives, and indeed all whose activities contribute directly or indirectly towards the production of goods and services. In the second place, it has natural resources, including improvements of all kinds (such as roads, tunnels, and dams) made by man. In the third place, it has capital, consisting of goods of all kinds, ranging in durability from buildings to quickly perishable goods such as fish. It will be remembered that there are very many different kinds of factors of production and that we group them under these three headings of Labour, Land, and Capital merely for convenience of exposition. It makes little difference whether we regard, say, a canal or a bridge, as falling under Land or as falling under Capital, or indeed whether or not we include all Land under Capital. The important thing is to realize how the possible output of consumers' goods and services is limited by the quantity and nature of the factors of production available.

It is true that a given quantity of factors of production may render more or fewer services. Thus a given population may perform more or less work. Some people capable of working may choose to live a life of leisure, enjoying incomes received from their ownership of property, and workers may take longer or shorter holidays, or work more or fewer hours per week. But this point is not relevant to our present problem.

Our present problem is to consider how far factors of production are capable of alternative uses. A factor capable of only one use, such as a machine for making newsprint, is said to be completely *specific*. If every factor were completely specific, a community would have little scope for choice as to what assortment of goods and services it would produce. It could indeed decide which factors were not worth utilizing, and to what extent particular factors should be worked, but that would be all. Unless it could acquire new and different factors, there would be no possibility of variation—the same factors would always produce the same products. In fact, of course, this is not the case. Many factors are capable of alternative uses, and thus a given quantity of factors can produce any one of a large number of different assortments of goods and services. Moreover, some existing factors can be converted into, or replaced by, different ones, and this increases still further the range within which the composition of the total output can be altered.

It will be remembered that in modern communities the structure of production is complex. The production of a finished commodity may involve many stages and processes, in the course of which many different kinds of factors are used. Hence we can distinguish two ways in which a given factor of production may make a different contribution to the final output. In the first place, it may continue to render exactly the same kind of services as before, but these may be utilized in a different way. For example, a typist may move from one "industry" to another without changing the nature of her work, and a blast furnace may continue to produce pig-iron, but more of the pig-iron may become, say, bars and less, say, plates than before. In the second place, a factor may change the nature of the services which it renders. For example, a typist may become a shop assistant. We might then say that, whilst remaining the same person, she has become a different factor of production, and we may regard any "costs of conversion," such as the cost of training her for her new job, as an investment of capital.

I have used the term "mobility," rather than "specificity," partly because it includes the notion of geographical mobility. Changes in economic conditions may make it desirable for some factors to move from one place to another. Thus we can speak of mobility between industries, between occupations, and between places. As we have just seen, a factor may move from one *industry* to another without changing its occupation, and it may do so without having to move to a different place. A movement between *occupations* need not involve a movement between industries or places: for example, our typist may have been typing for the shopkeeper in whose shop she now acts as a saleswoman. Similarly, a movement between *places* need not involve a change either of industry or of occupation. Any one type of mobility may be accompanied by either, or both, or neither, of the other two types.

The price system provides incentives to entrepreneurs to change the composition of the national output in response to changes in the tastes of consumers and in the state of technical knowledge. It provides incentives to workers, including boys and girls choosing their first jobs, to enter those fields that offer them the best prospects of remuneration and employment. It provides incentives to investors to direct their capital towards expanding industries rather than contracting ones.

But how far are these incentives effective? How flexible is the apparatus of production? How readily can it adapt itself to meet changes in demand or to take advantage of technical progress or to adjust itself to other changes in the conditions of supply? Can the composition of the national output be radically changed within a short period? How long does it take to alter methods of production or to create new industries?

The answer to these questions depends partly on how far entrepreneurs, investors, and workers correctly forecast future trends. It depends partly on public policy, which may either encourage or discourage mobility. But it depends partly on the physical possibilities of moving factors of production about, between industries and occupations and places, and on the extent to which workers are willing to move. This chapter discusses these questions. Mobility is greater in some countries and periods than in others; I shall take my illustrations mainly from Great Britain during recent years.

2. The Mobility of Labour

The British Census distinguishes about 35,000 different occupations. Some of these, such as interior decorating or dress designing or tea-tasting, require a natural aptitude possessed, in a high degree, by relatively few. Others, such as the professions or printing, require a considerable period of training or apprenticeship, in addition to sufficient natural aptitude. Any occupation, even a so-called "unskilled job" such as pick-and-shovel work, requires certain capacities; and a beginner can usually improve, perhaps quite considerably, with practice.

Nevertheless, almost any worker who is proficient at his own job could become fairly proficient at occupations demanding similar qualities, and there is usually quite a wide range of such occupations. Thus a man who is fairly efficient at tending one kind of machine could usually learn to tend other kinds of machines, a man doing work requiring mainly physical strength could usually do other jobs of a similar kind, a good administrator would be equally efficient in most industries, and so on. And most occupations can be learnt in a fairly short time. Thus it is roughly true to say that occupations can be divided into groups. A worker can move fairly easily from one occupation to another within his group, but may have difficulty in becoming proficient at an occupation in another group, demanding different qualities.

Clearly it is a simple matter for a worker to change his industry, provided that he continues to do the same kind of work and to live in the same place. And quite a number of occupations, such as those of clerks, typists, salesmen, lorry-drivers, and porters, are common to many different industries.

Movements between places, however, may not be easy. A worker may consider more than the monetary cost of moving to a new district.

He may be reluctant to leave familiar scenes and friends and associations and to begin life again in a strange place. He may be still more
reluctant to move to a different country, especially one with a different
language and different customs.

The monetary cost of learning a new job or moving to a different
place is an investment of capital. This investment may sometimes be
made by the State: by providing free training or by paying the fares
of workers moving to jobs in another district or by subsidizing emigration or immigration. It may be made by some employers, who
consider it worth their while to train workers or to pay their fares.
But usually it must be made by the worker himself. He will not make
it unless he believes that the improvement in his future earnings will
repay him with interest. Some workers may not have the necessary
capital, and others may consider that even the probability of repayment plus, say, 10 or 20 per cent interest, in the form of increased
wages for the rest of their working lives, is not sufficient to compensate
them for the present sacrifice of the capital sum. It may be noted that
a given prospect of increased earnings will be more likely to tempt a
younger worker to move than an older one, not merely because the
latter has become more set in his habits, but also because he has fewer
years of his working life left, over which to recoup himself for his present
investment.

The Government requires entrants to certain occupations, including
most of the professions, to pass some kind of qualifying test, and in some
cases to pay a fee. But there are seldom any other legal obstacles to
the mobility of labour within a country, although in some occupations
the trade unions insist on a fairly long period of apprenticeship before
admitting new entrants to the union. Yet movements of labour do
not always take place on a large enough scale, and sufficiently quickly,
to facilitate a rapid and complete adjustment to changes in economic
conditions.

A leading example of inadequate mobility was that of Great Britain
between the wars. Certain areas, notably South Wales, Glasgow,
Lancashire, and Tyneside, were largely dependent on "staple"
industries (such as coal and cotton) which exported a large proportion
of their output and which had been confronted with a large fall,
especially in foreign markets, in the demand for their products. Wages
in these areas fell below wages for comparable occupations in other
parts of the country. Yet the mobility of labour away from these
districts was inadequate. Their percentage of unemployment was at
least twice as high as in other districts, and they were treated as
"special" or "depressed" areas. (They are now called "development"
areas. But the position has changed. At present (1959) there is fairly
full employment, except in cotton textiles.)

There were various reasons for this inadequate mobility. Probably the chief reason was the natural reluctance of workers to leave the places where they had lived for all their lives, or for many years, and where they had grown accustomed to a certain way of life. The shortage of suitable houses in the more prosperous parts of the country also discouraged movement. The weekly money benefits paid to the unemployed from the unemployment insurance fund, and as public assistance, enabled workers to stay where they were, although they could not find jobs there. A generation earlier they would have been forced to move in order to avoid starvation or the workhouse. Nobody wishes for a moment to revive that unhappy state of affairs; but it must be admitted that our social security schemes do tend to lessen the mobility of labour.

It should not be assumed, however, that there was no movement of labour at all during this period. There was not enough, but there was nevertheless a good deal. Between July, 1923, and July, 1935, the number of insured workers (including those who were unemployed) attached to coal-mining fell from 1,244 thousand to 939 thousand, to cotton from 568 thousand to 442 thousand, and to shipbuilding from 270 thousand to 157 thousand, whilst those attached to the distributive trades rose from 1,254 thousand to 2,007 thousand, to building from 716 thousand to 977 thousand, and to the motor industry from 192 thousand to 286 thousand, whilst numerous other changes also took place between industries and occupations. There was also some movement away from the depressed areas and towards the South. Thus the Census Preliminary Report, 1931 (page xiv) remarks: "It will be observed that the counties north of Cheshire and Yorkshire inclusive have on balance lost as many as 443,000 of their population by migration during the past decennium and that from the central belt Wales has lost 259,000, the Midlands 81,000, and the Eastern region 41,000. . . . In the South-eastern section the net immigration numbers 615,000."

Movements between industries and areas have continued during recent years. For example, today the numbers attached to the cotton industry are down to some 250,000 while those attached to building are up to nearly 1,100,000, and there has been a marked expansion in the numbers attached to the engineering trades. The population of the Midland area has increased since 1931 by over 20 per cent, while that of Wales has remained stationary.

On the whole, the mobility of labour *is* sufficient, in most modern countries, to make possible a very large measure of adjustment in response to changes in economic conditions. It must be remembered that it is quite exceptional for changes in conditions to require more than a quite small percentage of workers to move, in any one year, out of any one occupation or industry or district. Only that small fraction of the total working population which is most able and willing to move need do so; as a rule, complete adjustment could be achieved even if the vast majority of workers continued to live in the same place and to do the same work as before. Further, adjustment may, and often does, take place by means of a kind of "reshuffle." Suppose, for example, that a movement of population is required from the North to the South. This could be brought about by a series of ripples, constituting a general southward trend, some people in the North moving some distance southwards, some people in the North Midlands moving southward, and so on. Similarly with a movement between occupations. Suppose, for example, that the coal industry is contracting and the motor industry expanding. It is possible that very few coal-miners could become proficient workers in the motor industry. In spite of this, a transition might be effected by, let us say, some coal-miners becoming builders' labourers, some builders' labourers lorry-drivers, and some lorry-drivers entering the motor industry. Finally, by far the most important influence facilitating mobility between occupations and industries, although not so much between places, is the change in *personnel* of the working population, which is constantly being diminished by deaths and retirements and increased by the flow of boys and girls entering the labour market from school or college. It is easier to decide to enter, for the first time, one occupation rather than another, than to decide to give up an occupation in which one has acquired knowledge and skill, in order to begin afresh, perhaps at a fairly advanced age, in a new field. Most of the youthful new entrants into the labour market are capable of entering any one of a number of industries and occupations, and they tend to be diverted towards those which consumers would most prefer them to enter, for it is those that offer them the brightest prospects. Here, again, the State is often helpful: children may be given "vocational tests" to discover their natural aptitudes, and parents may be advised by Employment Exchange officials and others, who know the prospects of employment and wages in different fields, into what jobs to place their children.

It may be noted that adjustment between industries and occupations is facilitated by an expanding population, for changes in the proportion of the working population attached to different industries and occupations can be brought about mainly by diverting the stream of new entrants towards those fields that are expanding, without many workers having actually to change over from one line to another. This also can be illustrated from Great Britain. In 1881 the total occupied population was 12,739 thousand, of whom 1,593 were engaged in agriculture. Improvements in transport and in agricultural technique made it cheaper for Great Britain to buy more foodstuffs from abroad instead of producing them herself. Thus in 1931, out of an occupied population of 21,055 thousand, only 1,194 thousand were engaged in agriculture. A change from 1,250 per 10,000 occupied persons to 567 per 10,000 occupied persons involved an absolute diminution of only 399,000 in the number engaged in agriculture, owing to the growth of population. Over this period some industries expanded greatly. For example, the numbers engaged in the manufacture of metals, machinery, etc. increased from 927 thousand to 2,412 thousand, that is from 728 to 1,145 per 10,000 occupied persons. These expansions took place largely by the inflow of new entrants to the labour market. A stationary and, still more, a declining population hampers adjustment, since this must take place mainly by workers leaving one kind of job and moving to another. Great Britain has been handicapped in this respect by the recent slowing-down in her rate of population growth, and this handicap may increase in the future, if her population expands only very slightly from year to year.

3. The Mobility of Land

It will be granted that soil can be shifted, that rivers can be diverted, that minerals, once extracted, can be transported, and so on. But it seems absurd to suggest that land itself can be moved from one place to another.

This is because we measure land by its area. But area, as such, is of less importance than productivity, and the productivity of a particular piece of land can be increased or diminished.

The term "land" has sometimes been restricted to the inherent and indestructible powers of the soil. But there seems little point in adopting this definition. In fact much of what is commonly called land is man-made, and it is impossible to separate "improvements" due to man from the original land. Most land requires a continuous investment of free capital in order to keep it sufficiently free from pests, or sufficiently fertilized or drained, to maintain its productivity; and as a rule additional investment will increase its productivity. The confusion between the two concepts of land is well illustrated by the story of the landowner who stipulated when leasing his land that the tenant should maintain intact the indestructible powers of the soil.

Hence if more free capital than formerly is invested in "improving" the land of one region, and less than formerly in "improving" the land of another region, the productivity of land has been increased in the former region and diminished in the latter.

But although man can do much, by irrigation and other means, to improve the natural resources of a region, he cannot give a tropical climate to land in a temperate zone, or transport minerals without first extracting them; and the uneven distribution of different natural resources over the earth's surface is a very important fact. I discussed its implications when I dealt with the location of industry.

Some land is more or less completely "specific". For instance, much

land in the North of Europe grows only forests, and the soil is not rich
enough to make it worth while to clear the forests in order to grow
crops. Again, much land in the interior of Australia receives a rainfall
so small and unreliable that it is suited only for sparse pastoral cultivation. Most land, however, is capable of a considerable range of
different uses. There is very little land that could not be made to serve
as a site for buildings: witness, for example, the Ford factory which
rests triumphantly on concrete piles above the swamps of Dagenham.
Nearly all "arable" land is capable of growing grass and serving as
pasture, and much of it could support any of several kinds of animals.
Obviously the potential uses of any given piece of land are limited by
its climate and by the nature of its soil, but within these limits most land
is far from being completely specific. But some investment of capital is
usually required in order to convert land from one use to another.
Moreover, a considerable time may have to elapse before the supply
of a given product can be substantially increased: for example, a citrus
tree or a coffee tree takes several years before it begins to yield.

A striking example of a change in the use to which land has been put
is afforded by the transfer from grain-growing to stock-raising in the
United Kingdom between 1874 and 1914. Over this period, the area
under wheat fell from 3·8 to 1·9 million acres and that under barley
from 2·5 to 1·9 million acres, while the area under permanent grass
increased from 23·7 to 27·4 million acres. During recent years the area
under wheat has been just over 2 million acres and that under barley
somewhat larger, while the area under grass (including 17,000 acres
rough grazing) has been over 36 million acres. Under the stimulus of
a subsidy, the area under sugar-beet increased from 4,000 acres in 1913
to 440,000 acres today; over the same period the area under turnips
and swedes has fallen from 1,486,000 to less than 500,000 acres.

4. The Mobility of Capital

Much of the capital of a country consists of buildings and plant. It is
often physically possible to dismantle plant, transport it, and set it up
again in a different place, but the advantages of a change in location
are seldom great enough to outweigh the cost of doing so: and it is
very seldom worth while to move buildings constructed of brick or
stone. Moreover, most of this fixed capital seems to be highly specific.
It was designed for a particular purpose, and as a rule the cost of
adapting it to a different purpose would be too great to make the
investment worth while. There are, of course, exceptions to this.
Thus it is claimed that plant designed for motor-cars or agricultural
machinery can often be converted to the manufacture of armaments.
But most fixed capital either stays where it is and does the kind of work
for which it was designed or is broken up and sold as scrap.

Nevertheless, the mobility of capital is considerably greater than appears at first sight.

The "purpose" for which a building or plant was designed is often wide enough to permit considerable variation in the goods or services produced. Thus a building designed as a factory or a shop or an office will often serve equally well for any one of several kinds of factory or shop or office. Many engineering works are capable of producing a wide range of products and can readily produce more of one kind and less of another. Spindles can often be adapted to spin a finer or coarser yarn or even to use a different kind of material.

Many raw materials and other intermediate products are used by a number of different industries, so that although the plant that produces them may be specific to that use, its products are capable of several different uses. For example, a steelworks may produce only steel, but the steel may be finally transformed into part of a railway track or of a building or a ship or a motor-car or a machine. In the same way the services of transport agencies, such as railways and lorries, can be used for almost any kind of goods, and it is a simple matter to supply more light, heat, and power to some industries and less to others. Thus very considerable changes can take place quickly in the composition of the final output of a country, whilst most of the fixed capital continues to render exactly the same services or to produce exactly the same goods as before.

Finally, as time goes on, capital is consumed and need not be replaced in the same form. For example, an entrepreneur who wishes to keep his capital intact will set aside some of his receipts in order to replace machinery and other equipment when it wears out. The money that he sets aside is free capital and will be used to purchase a different type of machinery or a completely different kind of plant, if he thinks that course more profitable. It is true that most buildings and many plants have a fairly long "life." Even so, the distribution of capital between industries can be changed considerably if the total amount of capital is being increased by new investment (which flows towards those industries where it can be used most profitably) just as the distribution of labour between industries is facilitated by an expanding population. Moreover, "working capital," which consists largely of stocks of intermediate products, and much consumers' capital, has a fairly short life and can readily be replaced by something different after it is consumed.

5. PUBLIC POLICY AND THE MOBILITY OF LABOUR

Public policy may affect the mobility of labour in various ways.

The public provision of technical training, and of vocational guidance for boys and girls leaving school, encourages mobility

between occupations, and therefore, to some extent, between industries and places.

It may be thought desirable, on general grounds, for people to own
their own homes. But this tends to discourage mobility. A man may
be reluctant to sell his own home, or may not find a buyer at a suitable price, and therefore may not be willing to move to another
place.

If the money benefits that a man draws when unemployed are not
much less than the wage he could earn by moving elsewhere, he may
be tempted to stay where he is and hope for the best.

It may be argued that national assistance should not be given to a
man who refuses the offer of a suitable job merely because it is in
another district.

The National Insurance Fund could be drawn upon by the Employment Exchanges to pay the expenses of an unemployed worker who
moves elsewhere to take a job, or even to look for a job. It might be
used also to provide training courses for workers who could then find
work in a different occupation.

An important question is the extent to which the State should
control the location of industry.

An entrepreneur will choose whatever site offers him the best
prospect of profit. But there may be *social costs* which do not enter into
his calculations. Suppose he were to establish himself in a rapidly-
growing district, and to attract labour from elsewhere. This may mean
that more houses, roads, schools, hospitals, electricity stations, cables,
pipes, and wires, and so forth, have to be provided to cope with the
growing population. Should he go to another district, where there is
considerable unemployment, all these facilities may be available,
working below capacity. From the standpoint of the community, it
may be better to induce him to go to the latter district. The community has not so much capital available for investment that it can
afford to duplicate facilities which already exist, and could be more
fully used, elsewhere.

If he goes to the latter district, he brings the jobs to the workers
instead of making the workers move to the jobs. If they have a strong
preference for remaining where they are, his factory is far more of a
boon to them than it would be to a district where there is already full
employment.

Hence a Government should exercise some control over the location
of industry. The British Government does so. Certain areas [1] are
scheduled as "development areas," and the Government offers various

---

[1] These are: the mining and coastal areas of Northumberland and Durham; West
Cumberland; South Wales and Monmouthshire; Wrexham; South Lancashire;
Merseyside; and North-East Lancashire (since March 1953). In Scotland, they are:
the industrial area in and around the Clyde Valley, the Dundee area, and parts of
the Highlands.

inducements to firms to site their establishments in those areas rather than elsewhere.

The Board of Trade may build factories for letting to suitable industries in those areas. These factories are grouped into "trading estates," well provided with roads, electricity and other services.

The Treasury may help by making loans or grants to firms unable to secure finance through normal channels.

A permit is required for new industrial premises, or an extension of existing premises, of over 5,000 square feet in area. Such permits have been granted more freely for the development areas, and some have been refused for congested areas such as Greater London or Birmingham.

As a result of these measures, some 30 per cent of over 300 million square feet of new industrial buildings and extensions (of over 5,000 square feet) completed in Great Britain since the beginning of 1945 were in the development areas, although these have only some 18 per cent of the country's workers in manufacturing industry.

How far the policy of bringing the jobs to the people should be applied depends on the merits of each case. The special advantages of one district, such as nearness to raw materials, may be so great that they outweigh the extra social costs. A mine may be getting worked out, and there may be no other productive resources in the neighbourhood; it may be better to move the whole population as a group than to subsidize the mine, as the National Coal Board has done in some instances, to the extent of £1 or more a ton.[1] The demand for some products (for example, cotton textiles), may seem likely to go on falling; the best course for the Government may be to train some of the workers for other occupations, and to encourage them to move to other industries.

These problems are difficult. A country such as Great Britain cannot afford to ignore changes in world demand and improvements in technique, or to compel firms to incur high costs of production by going to unsuitable locations. A high degree of flexibility is very desirable. On the other hand, full weight should be given to the various social costs which do not enter into the calculations of private enterprise seeking only to maximize its profits.

6. CONCLUSIONS

I have been considering a question of fact—namely, to what extent a modern economic system is flexible. Under capitalism, changes in economic conditions act upon the price mechanism and provide

[1] In 1958 nearly half the 301 million tons mined was produced at a loss. The average loss per ton was highest in Scotland, where it was 14s. 5½d. The Board has been closing some pits working at a loss (36 in 1959) and proposes in future to concentrate upon "the most competitive deep-mined tonnage, increasing output from modernized and reconstructed collieries." (Statement of the Chairman, reported in *The Times*, May 29th, 1959).

incentives to entrepreneurs to produce more of some goods rather than of others. But this means transferring some factors of production to different uses. I have discussed how readily such transferences can take place.

The general conclusion is that they can take place more easily than is often supposed. This is borne out by experience. In most modern countries some industries have waxed and others waned, and quite new industries (such as the motor-car and the radio industry) have sprung up and attained a large size very quickly, with little disturbance to the economic system as a whole. But there are obstacles to mobility and it may take some time to overcome them: in general, the longer the time that has elapsed after a change in conditions, the more complete will be the adaptation.

We have seen that adjustment is facilitated when population and capital are expanding, and that the most difficult transference to effect is often the movement of labour from one district to another. On this last point, it must be remembered that there are often social costs that do not enter into the calculations of the entrepreneur. In Great Britain, these social costs are presumably given full weight in the nationalized industries, while the location of new privately-owned plants is controlled by the issue of licences and in other ways.

Nothing has been said in this chapter about the trade cycle. A general trade depression usually involves a marked fall in the demand for the products of the constructional industries. Large groups of unemployed may be marooned, perhaps for years, in districts specializing in such industries, so that problems of transference become particularly important, and at the same time exceptionally difficult to solve. But we must postpone this subject to Chapter XXIII.

CHAPTER XXII

THE CASE AGAINST MONOPOLY

1. THE EXTENT OF MONOPOLY

BEFORE I discuss the case against monopoly, I must point out that the significance of this case depends on how much monopoly there is and on how monopolies in fact behave. These are questions of fact, on which we might expect to find little room for disagreement. But we do find, on the contrary, a great deal of disagreement.

Public utilities tend to be local monopolies. But in Great Britain every one of the public utilities (except water) is nationalized—gas, electricity, rail transport, postal services, telegraph and telephone, cable and wireless, even broadcasting. They are no longer private monopolies, operating for private profit. They are public monopolies, owned and operated by the State. In some countries, such as the United States, they are still mainly in private hands, but they are closely controlled, and their prices are regulated, by the State.

All the international commodity schemes of the 1930s broke down or lapsed. There are only two international agreements at present in force which may involve restrictions of output: the sugar agreement (1954) and the tin agreement (1956). Paradoxically enough, national restriction of output in agriculture is practised mainly in the United States, the home of the anti-monopoly movement, where the acreage under a particular crop can be restricted by law.

There are indeed large firms, very large firms. But are they monopolies? There was a public inquiry before the war into the affairs of J. and P. Coats, Ltd., who manufactured most of the sewing thread produced in Great Britain. The inquiry showed that Coats had attained and maintained their predominant position through sheer efficiency. There were no obstacles to the entry of other firms into the industry, but other firms simply could not produce and sell as cheaply. Are we to say that Coats were a monopoly merely because they produced the bulk of the output? The same question is relevant for a number of large firms. Unilever is very large. But any firm is quite free to buy vegetable oils and process them into margarine and soap. Is Unilever a monopoly?

The Government does not think so. In Great Britain, as in most countries, monopoly and restrictive practices are illegal if they are against the public interest. Under the British Monopolies and Restrictive Practices Act of 1948, a permanent Commission has been set up, to which the Board of Trade may refer for investigation any suspected case of monopoly or restrictive practices. So far, the only industries dominated by one or more giant firms that have been referred to the Commission are the match industry and the oxygen industry.

Nowadays a firm which does have monopoly power (based on patents, for example) is likely to follow a moderate price policy, in order not to arouse public hostility and to avoid Government intervention in its affairs, rather than to go all out for maximizing its profits. It may well co-operate with the Government in carrying out the policy of the Government in such matters as directing its sales towards certain markets (the dollar area, for example) rather than others, or importing its materials from one source rather than another, or siting its establishments where they will be of the greatest social benefit.

Most large firms try to maintain good relations with their employees and to gain the goodwill of the public by providing amenities for their workers, such as canteens, medical attention, sports grounds, and perhaps housing. Whether or not they have the power to exploit their workers, they often pay a little more than the market rate of wages; they probably do not lose by this policy, for they tend to get the more efficient of the workers available.

It may be argued, therefore, that private monopolies of the type that Karl Marx or the framers of the American Sherman (Anti-Monopoly) Act of 1890 had in mind, firms which ruthlessly exploited consumers and workers in order to maximize their profits, are as dead as the penny-farthing bicycle. One can draw diagrams about them, as an academic exercise, in a text-book of economics, but they have no relevance to the real world of the second half of the twentieth century.

On the other hand, imperfect competition is very widespread. In manufacturing and building, in transport and distribution, it is the rule rather than the exception. Open or tacit price agreements are said to be fairly common. It may therefore be argued that private monopoly is still very important, although it takes the form of price agreements and other restrictive practices rather than of domination by giant firms, each with a monopoly in its own field.

This aspect of the question has now been dealt with in Great Britain by the Restrictive Practices Act of 1956. This Act provided for the public registration of an extensive range of restrictive agreements (excluding, however, those relating to services and labour) and for the establishment of a Restrictive Practices Court to determine whether or not any particular agreement is in the public interest. The fact that this machinery exists, and the adverse decisions of the Court on certain agreements (for example, on the minimum prices agreement of the

Yarn Spinners) have already caused over 100 agreements to be abandoned; but some 2,000 remain to be considered. The Act is certainly tending to make British industry and trade more competitive, although the machinery for enforcing the prohibition of an agreement may need strengthening. The Monopolies Commission, reduced in size, will deal with matters, such as single-firm monopolies, not appropriate for reference to the Court.

One interesting point is that a very important field where monopolistic action and restrictive practices are common is the field of trade union action. Opponents of capitalism tend to favour these aspects of trade union policy, on the ground that they help the workers to get a fairer share of the national income and to protect themselves against unemployment. Whether or not this is so, the case against such practices is precisely the case against monopoly; they restrict output, and they prevent workers from entering occupations where their services would be more valuable.

The present chapter, however, will not discuss trade unions. This subject is deferred to Chapter XXVI.

2. THE CASE FOR MONOPOLY

The late Sir Henry Clay, in an article on "The Campaign against Monopoly and Restrictive Practices" in *Lloyds Bank Review* for April, 1952, has urged that monopoly may sometimes be in the public interest.

Monopolies can often produce on a large scale and therefore more efficiently than a large number of small competing firms. "Some of the industries most criticized for monopolistic tendencies turn out to be the most progressive and successful, both technically and commercially. British cement, highly concentrated and operating before the war a quota system, boasts that its prices are the lowest in the world, and its output per man comes nearer the American achievement than any other industry's. British electric lamp prices, we learn from one of the Monopoly Commission's reports, are lower than in any other country except America and, in spite of the general rise in costs, are below their pre-war prices."

Even more impressive, said Sir Henry Clay, is the record of British industries that adopted monopolistic policies in the thirties. In the cotton industry, "the depression of 1929–32 compelled contraction and reorganization; and the opportunity was then taken to organize also some collective control of prices. Losses were stopped, and a process of technical improvement made possible. Similarly steel, after organizing itself to control output towards the end of the great depression, was enabled to put in hand, and carry through in the short time available before war broke out, an amount of re-equipment and new development

L   B.E.

greater than the preceding generation and a half of unrestricted competitive action had produced. Even coal and shipbuilding by resort to 'restrictive' measures checked the calamitous losses which threatened a permanent closing down of these industries in some areas."

Sir Henry's point was that under competition prices may be driven down to levels that do not fully cover the fixed costs. Receipts may be too low to provide properly for the replacement of plant and equipment when it wears out, let alone for new investment in the industry.

The view that a monopoly exploits relatively poor consumers to swell the profits of wealthy shareholders is not always correct. Monopoly sometimes reduces, rather than increases, the inequality of wealth. Most of the farmers and smallholders taking part in commodity control schemes were poorer than the consumers of their products, and trade unions taking monopolistic action would certainly claim that they are trying to reduce inequality by improving the wages and the conditions of work of their members.

Farmers and workers sometimes defend monopolistic action on their behalf by the argument that it only goes some distance towards compensating them for the monopoly prices they have to pay for many of the manufactures and other goods and services which they buy.

3. MONOPOLY AND CHANGES IN DEMAND AND IN COSTS

It is possible to construct a queerly-shaped demand curve to prove that a monopolist might conceivably increase his profits by producing less when the demand for his products increases. But in practice it will always pay a monopoly to produce more in response to an increase in demand, and less in response to a decrease in demand. So far, so good. To this extent, the price system works as well under monopoly as under competition; in fact, the response under monopoly is likely to be more prompt and more accurate than under competition, for a single seller can make the required adjustments in output, without overshooting the mark, more easily than a number of separate firms each acting independently.

A monopoly often keeps its prices relatively stable, at any rate considerably more stable than the prices of raw materials and other products produced under highly-competitive conditions. This policy, however, may be against the public interest. Suppose there is a general depression. By maintaining its prices a monopoly sells less, and therefore gives less employment, than if it reduced them. If it produces capital goods, it is desirable that their prices should be reduced during a slump in order to stimulate a revival of investment. In general, prices should change when there is a change in costs. If a commodity can be produced with less labour and other resources than before, consumers should get the benefit of such a change, and be encouraged to buy more, by a corresponding reduction in price. The same reasoning would apply to an increase in costs if the commodity were produced under competition, but if a monopoly absorbs a rise in costs by reducing its profits, and does not raise its prices, this may have the effect of making its prices nearer what they would be under competition, and may therefore be a move in the right direction.

4. MONOPOLY AND TECHNICAL PROGRESS

A monopoly can often afford to employ a large research staff to discover improved methods of production, or new products, or new uses for its present products. It may employ also experts on "market research," to collect information on the preferences of consumers and the possibilities of expanding sales either at home or abroad. It might be argued that in such ways a monopoly serves the community better than a number of competing firms, each of which is too small to undertake such tasks.

In fact, some three-quarters of the expenditure on industrial research in Great Britain—£224 million out of £300 million in 1955 [1]—is provided by the Government. In 1955 British manufacturing industry carried out scientific and engineering research costing £183 million (including £80 million on aircraft) of which £127 million was paid by the Government for work done on its behalf. 93,000 full-time workers and 38,000 part-time workers were engaged in this research.

There is no doubt, however, that the research undertaken by private firms on their own behalf and at their own expense was performed mainly by relatively large firms having some degree of monopoly.[2] A number of competing firms can subscribe to a joint association, which carries out research on behalf of the industry as a whole, but although there are quite a number of such co-operative research associations their total expenditure in 1955 was only £5 million.

Although monopolies may play a leading part in research, will they apply the results of research as rapidly as would be done under competition? It is often argued that they may retard the application of new methods and new products, and may patent new inventions mainly to prevent competitors from using them.

[1] These figures, and those which follow, are from a report by the Department of Scientific and Industrial Research: *Estimate of Resources Devoted to Scientific and Engineering Research and Development in British Manufacturing Industry*, 1955 (H.M.S.O. 1959).

[2] Over half the research workers, including most of the graduates, are in establishments employing 1000 or more persons. Fifty-eight companies or groups spent about one-third of the £183 million.

This is a question on which we should not jump to hasty conclusions. It will pay a monopoly, in just the same way as it will pay a firm working under competition, to scrap existing plant and to replace it by plant of an improved type if the total cost of the new method is less than the operating cost of the old and the return on the investment is sufficiently high. It will equally pay a monopoly to introduce a new variety of product if it thereby increases its receipts more than its costs. It is true that a new firm just entering the industry will not have any plant of the old type, so that the problem of whether to scrap its existing plant will not arise; it can begin at once with the most up-to-date plant and can produce the most up-to-date products. But there is a parallel to this in the case of a monopoly that owns most of the plant and equipment in the industry; at any time, some of its plant will be due for replacement and can be replaced by the new type. On the whole, progress is likely to be somewhat more rapid under competition, because an established monopoly, making good profits, is likely to follow a more cautious and conservative policy, but the extent of this should not be exaggerated.

In this connection, it is often alleged that monopolies buy patents in order to prevent rivals from invading their fields with new methods or new products. Here again we must not exaggerate. A report by a House of Commons Committee (Cmd 6789 of 1946) reads: "Rumours of this practice are frequent but, in spite of our endeavours to obtain it, no satisfactory evidence of particular examples has been forthcoming." Most of the examples cited in popular discussion have no basis in fact. For instance, anybody is legally free to produce the famous "ever-lasting" match. The patent for it expired long ago, but as "everlasting" merely means striking some fifty times before it is finished, and as it is cheaper to produce a box of fifty ordinary matches, it would not be a paying investment. Nevertheless it seems probable that the existence of a powerful monopoly in any field, a monopoly prepared to spend large sums in lawsuits against new competitors for alleged infringement of its patents, may scare away possible new-comers who would use new methods.

5. Monopoly and Restriction of Output

By far the most important economic argument against monopoly is that it involves restriction of output. The only way in which a monopoly can use its monopoly power is by controlling the supply—in other words, by restricting its output in order to keep up its prices.

Restriction of output may take three forms. First, goods already produced may be destroyed. Thus, between 1931 and the end of 1934, the Coffee Institute of Brazil destroyed over two million tons of low-grade coffee. These were stocks accumulated from a succession of bumper crops. While they existed and potential buyers knew they existed, the price of coffee was unlikely to rise much. But destruction of stocks is clearly a costly way of restricting supply, and a way that arouses adverse criticism. It is better from the standpoint of the monopolist not to allow excessive stocks to pile up. This was not possible in Brazil, as the output from existing coffee trees, owned by many thousands of peasants, could not be effectively curtailed.

Second, a monopoly may leave some of its productive resources idle. Some rubber trees are not tapped; some land suitable for growing cotton is kept out of cultivation; some plant and equipment is not worked or is worked only part-time. The result is that output is kept down and prices can be kept up without accumulating stocks. The waste is there, but it is a waste of capacity and not so obvious as the destruction of goods already produced.

Third, a monopoly may plan its capacity so that it can be fully used but is not large enough to produce much more than can be sold at the prices fixed. Here there is no visible waste. Full and efficient use is made of all the labour and resources employed in the monopolized industry. Yet there is loss to the community. Here is a field in which more labour and capital could be profitably employed. Consumers want more of these products. If prices were lower they would buy more. Prices could be lower, perhaps much lower, and still yield a normal return on capital. But new firms are somehow prevented from entering this field, and the monopoly itself will not expand because this would reduce its profits.

Hence consumers are thwarted. They do not get the assortment of goods that they would prefer. They would rather have more of the monopolized products (at a lower price) and less of others. Under competition, investment would flow into these fields, where it yields a higher return. More labour and other factors would be employed there, producing a greater output. Under monopoly, this expansion does not take place. New investment is kept out by the barriers protecting the monopoly against competition. The distribution of labour and other factors among industries is not in accordance with the preferences of consumers; it is distorted by monopoly.

This situation assumes full employment. If there is considerable unemployment, the case against monopoly is still stronger. For here are fields which could absorb additional workers and additional materials and additional plant. If these fields were thrown open, unemployment would be reduced and consumers would be able to have more of the monopolized products and perhaps also more instead of less of other things.

When the monopoly is a combination of producers, each producer often gets a quota of output, usually based on past performance. The consequence is often that the more efficient sources of supply produce less, relatively to other sources, than they would produce under competition. For example, before coal-mining was nationalized in Great Britain, the coal-mines were grouped into a compulsory cartel by the 1930 Act, each mine being given about the same share of total output that it produced in 1928. Towards the close of the 1930s, it is certain that considerably fewer miners could have produced the same total output (or alternatively, the same number of miners could have produced a considerably greater output) if more of that total had been produced in districts and mines that had increased their efficiency, relatively to other districts and mines, since 1928. The same thing happened under most of the commodity control schemes of the 1930s.

6. Excess Capacity

A common effect of cartel agreements is to call excess capacity into existence. If the cartel succeeds in providing a high rate of return on capital, firms may be tempted to expand their capacity in order to claim a larger quota when the quota arrangements are next reviewed.

But excess capacity is sometimes inevitable; and it often carries with it advantages which partly offset, and sometimes more than offset, the waste of resources which it seems to involve. Let me give some illustrations.

I have already pointed out that a plant worked below capacity may yet produce that output at a smaller total cost than a smaller plant working at full capacity. This arises from "indivisibility." For one reason or another, the larger plant is more efficient; the next "size" which is practicable to build does not yield the same "economies of scale."

A liner keeps to a time-table and therefore often makes a journey with fewer passengers or less cargo than it could conveniently carry. But potential passengers and shippers know in advance exactly when it will sail, and can make their plans accordingly.

The need to use certain things may occur only during certain times or seasons. It is not wasteful to have street lamps which are lit only at night or harvesting machinery which is idle most of the year. Some things are not used continuously, but it is very convenient to have them available whenever they happen to be required. This applies to various things in the home, such as baths and sewing-machines and household utensils. In the same way, a firm may find it convenient to keep various things available. Some of them may be used comparatively seldom, but when they are needed they may be needed urgently.

The concept of *availability* applies also to shop assistants who are not fully employed all the time. A customer appreciates being served at once, and served courteously and well, instead of having to wait in a queue and then being served in a hurry.

The waste in milk distribution, with several roundsmen to a street, is often criticized. But a consumer can choose the dairy she likes— for milk is not homogeneous; and the time she likes for it to be delivered; and possibly the roundsman she likes.

And so we might go on. Imperfect competition *does* usually mean some waste of resources. That is the central fact. In war-time, labour and other resources are urgently needed for the war effort and should not be used wastefully or below capacity. But in peace-time, consumers may value the convenience and the greater freedom of choice offered to them by "wasteful" methods.

7. COMPETITIVE ADVERTISING

Some advertisements give new and useful information. They tell us of new products, or of what transport services are available, what plays and films different theatres and cinemas are offering, what hotel and housing accommodation is obtainable, and so on. But a good deal of advertising is merely the advertising of different brands. This type of advertising is called *competitive advertising*; it arises only because competition is imperfect; it takes place because different brands compete with one another.

It is often claimed that the resources employed in competitive advertising are wasted. Experts may tell us that there is no substantial difference between different brands. It is therefore argued that the community would benefit if firms charged lower prices instead of spending money on advertising one brand against another.

In some fields the profit margin on widely-advertised goods is high. For example, an American monograph on "Price Behaviour and Business Policy" (published by the Temporary National Economic Committee) said that Bayer Aspirin, sold by retailers at 75 cents an ounce, was identical with acetylsalicylic acid, costing 15 cents an ounce.

Nevertheless, most people would probably object to a complete prohibition of competitive advertising. A consumer often derives extra satisfaction from owning or consuming a widely-advertised product, although a cheaper product might be chemically identical or might give an equally good "performance." Most firms advertising branded goods would probably claim that their particular brands have special features and that they are conveying genuine and useful information in bringing these features to the notice of consumers. And many newspapers and magazines derive most of their revenue from advertising, and are therefore sold more cheaply to readers, who presumably like looking at the advertisements.

What the State should do about advertising is a matter of opinion. It is difficult to draw the line between competitive advertising and

advertising that brings innovations and new opportunities and price
reductions to the notice of a wide public. The State might make false
and misleading statements by advertisers a legal offence. The British
Government requires the ingredients of such things as proprietary
medicines to be plainly stated on the package or bottle and is considering
(1959) providing guidance to consumers, presumably similar to that provided in the United States by the Research Council, which makes an impartial appraisal of the nature and merits of various proprietary articles

8. Resale Price Maintenance

An important and controversial question is whether the enforcement
by manufacturers of fixed resale prices for their products should be
permitted or should be prohibited by law. Resale price maintenance
applies, of course, to branded goods, which are usually nationally
advertised: for example, cigarettes, patent medicines, and toilet
preparations. The 1931 Committee on Restraint of Trade found that
it was common for manufacturers to enforce resale price maintenance
conditions upon wholesalers and retailers by threatening to withhold
supplies from them if they cut prices, and that such threats were carried
out. This Committee concluded that "we do not regard the price
maintenance system as free from disadvantages from the public point
of view, but we are not satisfied that if a change in the law were made
there is any reason to think that the interests of the public would be
better served." However, the Labour Government which went out of
office in 1951 was proposing to bring forward a Bill to make resale price
maintenance illegal.

One might think that the manufacturer would welcome "cut" prices.
He makes bigger sales and gets (from the wholesalers or retailers) the
same price per unit. The customers get the goods fresher. The shops
that "cut" have a bigger turnover and less idle capacity.

But the other shops object. In a provincial town, all the tobacconists,
for example, might get together if a shop sold certain cigarettes at cut
prices, and might threaten the manufacturers that they would not buy
unless steps were taken to cut off supplies to the cut-price shop. As a
rule, the manufacturers fall into line. The 1931 Committee accepted
the argument that if a manufacturer "advertised a particular brand at
a given price and if retailers, for purposes of their own, sold it temporarily at lower prices, the effect on the public would be such as to
destroy the reputation of the brand."

The controversy is mainly between those who wish to protect the
small shopkeeper and those who feel that we have too many shops—
nearly twice as many as the United States per million people—and would
prefer the public to get the goods cheaper even if that would mean
putting some existing shops out of business.

9. NATIONALIZATION

One way for the State to deal with a monopoly is to take it over, to nationalize it. It then becomes a public monopoly instead of a private monopoly.

In Great Britain, the Post Office, telegraph and telephone, and broadcasting, have been under public authorities for a long time, and civil aviation was nationalized before the war. After the war, the Labour Government nationalized the Bank of England, Cable and Wireless, cotton-buying, the coal-mines, the railways, electricity, and gas. It also nationalized most of road transport, but the Conservative Government, which came into power towards the close of 1951, has handed road transport (and also cotton-buying) back to private enterprise. There has been much controversy over the steel industry, which the Labour Government began to nationalize and the Conservative Government is handing back to private enterprise.[1] Altogether, the nationalized industries cover rather less than 20 per cent of economic activity.

One strong motive behind the drive for nationalization was the belief that inequality of wealth would be reduced by doing away with private profit in the nationalized industries. Inequality has indeed been reduced, but by heavy taxation of incomes and profits and on estates changing hands at death, not by nationalization. The former shareholders were paid the full value of their shares in Government stock. They could either keep the stock, getting a lower but more secure income (which some people prefer), or they could sell it and invest in other securities giving a higher but riskier return. They still retained their capital, and their income from ownership.

Some of the workers may have hoped that they would run their own industries after they were nationalized. But in any enterprise, whether State-owned or privately-owned, there must be a chain of command; some must give orders and others must carry them out. The daily routine of the average worker was not any different after nationalization.

When the State takes over only one or two undertakings in an industry, it has to compete with the private firms which remain, and this provides some test of its efficiency. Moreover, the industry is still open to new-comers with new ideas and new methods. But when the State takes over a whole industry, the whole of the field is barred to private enterprise. This places a heavy responsibility on the State: the responsibility of running the industry efficiently and in the public interest.

There may be no good test of efficiency. The nationalized industry may make profits but these may be made merely by passing on higher costs to consumers in the form of higher prices. Conversely, losses

[1] Some three-quarters has been handed back so far (1959).

(such as the loss of £30 million made, 1951 to 1958, by the National Coal Board) are not a conclusive proof of inefficiency.

On general grounds, it is often argued that public management is more bureaucratic and shows less initiative than private enterprise. It has to account to Parliament and is reluctant to take risks which might lead to considerable losses. The flair of an entrepreneur may produce better results than the carefully reasoned memoranda of civil servants. There may be a case, therefore, for controlling a monopolistic industry, as they do in the United States, rather than nationalizing it.

This point, however, should not be exaggerated. A very large enterprise under private management tends also to be somewhat bureaucratic. The Post Office is reasonably well run, and if the Boards of the nationalized industries are staffed with first-class administrators and experts, there seems no obvious reason why they too should not be reasonably efficient. As for initiative, the development of the jet-propelled aeroplane, in which Great Britain leads the world, was carried out in a nationalized industry.

But what is the case for nationalization rather than control? In the fairy stories the young couple get married and live happily ever after, and in the same way some people seem to think that the problems of an industry are solved by the mere act of nationalization. Far from it.

The case for nationalization must be that the State will run the industry in the public interest, in a way that would not be possible under private ownership.

Let us take the railways as an example. A great deal of capital has been invested in the railways. But that was in the past; it is a bygone. Now that there are no shareholders whose claims and expectations must be considered, the State need look only to the future. How can the best use be made of all the resources of the community, including the railways and the roads? It may be that the transport needs of the country can be best served by letting the roads have all the traffic they can get in open competition. There is no longer any need to protect railway shareholders by restricting the amount of road traffic. If goods can be carried more cheaply if more of them go by road, it does not matter if the railways earn a low return on their capital. It is good business for the community to allow the profits of the railways to be reduced if for every £1 they are reduced several pounds are saved to the public in transport charges.

The State thus has a great opportunity with its nationalized industries. Will it run them in the public interest? Will it be able to resist demands for higher wages, to be passed on to consumers in higher prices, if it considers they are not justified? Will it be ready to give new methods a fair trial? Will it refuse to protect a nationalized industry against competition from substitutes despite the demands of the workers that their employment—in that particular industry—should be safeguarded? Or will the defects of private monopoly remain, and perhaps be accentuated, under public ownership? Time will show.

10. MONOPOLY AND PUBLIC POLICY

Monopoly is sometimes inevitable, especially in the field of public utilities. If the State does not take over such monopolies, on what lines should it control them?

One useful device, provided the right man can be found, is to place a Government representative on the Board of Directors. He can try to keep the policy of the undertaking in harmony with the public interest. His advice is likely to be heeded, for if it is ignored, the Government might take over the enterprise or might regulate its activities more closely.

What exactly is in the public interest is a question to be decided in the light of all the circumstances. In general, it is against the public interest for any undertaking to make monopoly profits by charging unduly high prices, which means by restricting its output. But the most efficient firms in any industry make greater profits than the less efficient. If the State were to set an absolute maximum to the profits of such an undertaking, this would weaken its incentives to efficiency and enterprise and might deter it from expanding. The best course might be for the State (perhaps through a Commission) to fix its charges at levels that would give it a normal profit if it were normally efficient but would allow it to earn more by reducing its costs. (This is what the Monopolies Commission recommended in 1953 for the British match industry.)

Some economists favour discriminatory charging on the ground that it makes possible some output that would not otherwise be profitable: receipts from uniform rates would not cover costs. This, however, is a dangerous argument. Given full employment, labour and other resources not employed in that enterprise would be employed elsewhere. There are many projects each one of which might pay under discriminatory charging, but the more of them are carried out, the less likely is any particular one to pay, since people's incomes are limited; and the choice between such projects is bound to be somewhat arbitrary. The simplest course is to charge according to the cost of the service. Lower prices can be charged during off-peak periods, in order to "spread the load," and to large consumers, if they can be supplied at correspondingly lower costs. But as a rule A should not be charged more than B for exactly the same service merely because A can afford to pay more.

Suppose the Government wishes the monopoly to do something

which is in the public interest but which will not cover its cost. For example, suppose it asks a private railway company to construct a branch line for which there is not enough traffic but which is needed for strategic purposes. In my opinion, the Government should subsidize such a project out of general revenue; if it is in the interest of the community as a whole, the community as a whole should pay for it. I think it would be unfair to make one particular section, namely the other customers of the railway, pay the losses on the branch line in the form of higher fares and freight rates on the other lines. One wonders whether this principle is followed in the nationalized industries or whether, for example, consumers of coal have to pay for mines that are subsidized on social grounds, and whether the levy on road hauliers to compensate the railways for traffic lost to the roads was in the public interest.

Monopoly, however, is not always inevitable. How can we get rid of it?

The United States, as long ago as 1890, declared monopoly illegal, and their Government has brought lawsuits against alleged monopolies in order to break them up. This has meant fat fees for the lawyers; cases have dragged on year after year. A more effective and cheaper method of direct attack would be to give a body such as our Monopolies and Restrictive Practices Commission the power to enforce whatever decisions they considered were in the public interest; often such decisions might take the form of controlling the prices charged by the monopoly and removing barriers to the entry of newcomers.

The Restrictive Practices Act of 1956 does give the Court the power to prohibit agreements, such as agreements to maintain prices, which it considers not in the public interest. This may well prove to be a big step forward; although it does not cover the whole field, other sections (for example, single-firm monopolies) can be dealt with by the Monopolies Commission. On the question of resale price maintenance, the Act makes collective enforcement unlawful but (in my view, unwisely) strengthens the hands of any individual manufacturing firm in compelling retailers to maintain the resale prices which it lays down.

Another, and perhaps more powerful, method of attack would be to take away the foundations of monopoly power. A number of monopolies are based on patent rights. The State might abolish patent rights, paying inventors sums of money as rewards for useful inventions, which would at once be made available to all. Alternatively, any holder of a patent might be compelled to make it available at once to anybody who wished to use it, the user paying him a fee (fixed by a Commission) for the privilege. This system, known as "licence of right," exists now, but could be extended.

"The tariff," they used to say in the United States "is the mother of Trusts." Import duties protect national firms against competition from other countries, and thus make it easier for them to combine together in order to charge monopolistic prices. Most other "controls" have a similar effect. If raw materials are allocated, the firms that get the allocations are favoured and are safeguarded against competition from potential new-comers in their field. If licences are refused for certain undertakings, this protects those that are already established. Protection, controls, and monopoly tend to go together. If the first two are deemed necessary on broad grounds of national policy, one consequence is likely to be more monopoly than we should have without them. The best safeguard against monopoly is to keep the gates wide open for new entrants, new methods, and new ideas, and not to use the power of the State to protect established firms against competition.

CHAPTER XXIII

UNEMPLOYMENT AND THE TRADE CYCLE

1. TYPES OF UNEMPLOYMENT

THE mass unemployment which has taken place from time to time under capitalism, and which it is claimed, and rightly claimed, would be abolished by complete central planning, is the unemployment due to general depressions of trade. But even in normal times, for that matter even during periods of boom, there is always some unemployment. This section reviews briefly the various types of unemployment that are not directly connected with the trade cycle.

Every country has some unemployables, whose efficiency is so low that they cannot keep any job for long, and fall back upon public or private charity. But their numbers are relatively small.

Again, some workers, whilst not unemployable, are much below the average in efficiency. They are slow workers; if employed on piece-rates they earn substantially less than their fellows. Their slowness may be due to some physical or mental disability. They can keep jobs at relatively low wages, corresponding to their low productivity. But if a general minimum wage is fixed by law, they will often be out of work, for they will not be worth the minimum wage.

Social security measures, including public assistance, may create some unemployment. Most people, for the sake of their own pride, would rather work than live on public charity. But a minority may be without pride, or may have had their spirit broken by a long spell out of work. If they can get nearly as much in benefits as they could earn by working, they may not make any great effort to find another job, especially if the new job would be in a different district.

A trade union which succeeds in raising the wages of workers in a particular industry, other wages remaining more or less where they were, may thereby reduce employment in that industry. If firms in that industry are making abnormally high profits, the increase in wages may be met merely by reducing profits to the normal rate of return on capital. In that event, no workers need be dismissed. But suppose that profits in that industry are at about the normal level. What will happen?

In the most favourable circumstances, the increased wages will be passed on to consumers in the form of higher prices. But there will be some unemployment, for consumers will buy less—how much less depends on the elasticity of demand for these products.

If circumstances are unfavourable, it may not be possible to pass on the increased wages in the form of higher prices. The industry may be producing mainly for export, or its products may be in close competition with similar imports, and any appreciable rise in its prices might drastically reduce its sales. In these circumstances a number of firms may have to close down. Some may carry on, but as time goes on new investment will avoid this industry, where profits are low or non-existent, and the amount of employment in it will continue to fall. It may be that labour-saving devices that were not worth using when wages were at their old level will be introduced now that wages have increased; and they will reduce employment still further.

Some industries employ "casual labour" which is needed only intermittently. For example, a contracting firm seldom manages to secure a steady stream of contracts, which would enable it to give continuous employment to a fixed number of workers. When it has a lot to do, it takes on extra workers, and when it has less to do it dismisses them. They may soon be able to find work with other contracting firms, but if the total demand for contracting, or even the demand in their district, has fallen off, they may be out of work for some time.

Dockers are in a similar situation. A small port needs a good deal of dock labour when there are several ships to be loaded or unloaded, but when there are no ships, it needs none at all. In some places, this situation is met by drawing on the services of smallholders, fishermen, hawkers, and others (paying them attractive hourly or daily rates) when the demand for dock labour is heavy. In London and some other large ports it is met by keeping a list of dockers and sharing the work among them by employing them in rotation. This means that when the demand is slack a considerable number of dockers will not be working unless they can find some other occupation which they can dovetail with their intermittent employment at the docks.

In some occupations, such as building and fishing, men may be out of work from time to time owing to bad weather. Further, many industries are subject to considerable seasonal fluctuations so that some men attached to them are unemployed during slack times unless they can find temporary jobs elsewhere.

Some economists call the type of unemployment that I have just been discussing *frictional unemployment*. It is temporary unemployment due to temporary changes in demand or in circumstances such as the weather. I turn now to what is sometimes called *structural unemployment*. This is more of a long-term phenomenon.

As time goes on, there is a permanent fall in the demand for certain products. This may be due to a change in tastes; for example, in Great Britain fewer hats are worn than before the war, and only about half as many hats are bought. New substitutes, cheaper to produce or more attractive to consumers, may be discovered; the nitrate mines of Chile were hit hard by synthetic fertilizers, cinchona by drugs such as paludrine, and the natural silk industry by rayon and nylon. An export industry of a particular country may suffer because other countries restrict their imports of its products or because rival exporting countries, through greater efficiency, can undersell them in the world's markets. For example, exports of British cotton textiles have been trending downwards since the first world war. Before 1914, about 7,000 million yards a year were exported. Then India and other countries began to produce more cotton goods for themselves; there was also keener competition from other exporting countries, notably Japan. The export of British cotton textiles fell to 3,700 million yards in 1929 and to 384 million yards in 1958.

Clearly such a downward trend in the demand for the products of an industry means that it can provide less employment than before; the British cotton industry employed 646,000 workers in 1911 and employs only 250,000 today. How far such "structural" changes mean a general increase in unemployment is a question of mobility, of how rapidly workers no longer needed in the contracting industries can find jobs elsewhere.

Another type of structural change is a radical change in the methods of production of an industry, which enables fewer workers to produce the same output. For example, higher-yielding varieties of crops may be planted, or more labour-saving devices may be used. Let us consider the mechanization of an industry.

If mechanization is introduced to take advantage of cost-reducing inventions or of a fall in the rate of interest (and not merely as a counter-measure to higher wages in that particular industry), the prices of the products are likely to fall. If the demand for them is sufficiently elastic, at least as many workers as before may continue to be employed. For example, the mechanization of the motor-car industry over the past thirty or forty years has greatly reduced the number of men required to produce a car, yet employment in the industry has continuously expanded. The arithmetic is simple. If only half as many men as before are needed to produce the same output, sales must double to maintain the present volume of employment; if three-quarters as many men are needed, sales must expand by a third; and so on.

In most cases, however, employment will probably be reduced, at any rate for a time, in the industry that adopts the new methods. Then the question of mobility arises: how rapidly can the workers no longer needed in that industry find other jobs elsewhere?

The view that mechanization must diminish total employment is based on the belief that there is only a fixed amount of work to go round, so that if machines do more of the work, there is less to be done by human beings. This is quite wrong. While so many wants remain unsatisfied, while there is so much scope for raising standards of living, there is plenty of work to be done by both men and machines. The problem is not to make more work, or to spread the work over more workers. On the contrary, the problem is to save work, by enabling each worker to produce more than before and thereby contribute more towards the needs and wants of mankind.

The industrial revolution, which is still going on, is a gigantic process of substituting machinery and other capital goods for labour. Yet continuous mechanization has been accompanied, except during general depressions of trade, by a parallel growth in employment. Today the industries of Great Britain, the United States, and other countries are more fully mechanized than ever before, yet unemployment is very low, much less than before a good deal of this mechanization took place.

The same "fixed amount of employment" fallacy underlies the view that if women enter certain fields of employment they will throw men out of work, and the view that immigrants take away jobs from local workers. The short answer to such views is to look at the figures. More employment by women has been accompanied by more employment for men, and not by any increase in male unemployment; in the same way, more employment by immigrants has not resulted in any increased unemployment of local labour.

What is true, however, is that a sudden and large structural change, such as mechanization, may cause some dislocation and unemployment for a while. The way to keep such disturbances to a minimum is to promote the mobility of labour.

In this section, I have distinguished various types of unemployment. But of course any particular worker may be out of work owing to a combination of reasons. For example, he may be well below the average in efficiency; his industry may be contracting; he may be reluctant to move to another district.

Far more important than all these types of unemployment is the heavy unemployment accompanying general depressions of trade. Moreover, at such periods unemployment due primarily to other reasons tends to be magnified. It is more difficult to get another job when times are bad. It seems futile, when unemployment is widespread, to seek work elsewhere, and mobility is therefore less than during good times.

I turn, therefore, to the alternation of boom and slump, prosperity and depression, which is known as the trade cycle.

2. THE TRADE CYCLE

The trade cycle, or business cycle, is a period of prosperity followed by a period of depression. If we include the two periods of transition, it has four phases. First, there is the upturn, the recovery from a depression. This merges, sooner or later, into the seond phase of prosperity or boom. The third phase is the downturn, a contraction of economic activity leading to the fourth phase, a period of depression or slump.

Some writers have tried to show that in the past a trade cycle has always lasted for about the same length of time (ten years, for example), from trough to trough or peak to peak. They have not succeeded. Statistics for earlier times are not sufficiently full or reliable, and even if they were, it is very doubtful whether they would show anything like the same length of life for every trade cycle. Nor can we make any predictions, based on past experience, about the date of the next world-wide depression. Some economists, looking apprehensively at the high level of economic activity which has prevailed in the United States since 1940, have been predicting it ever since about 1947. It has not come yet (1959), and it may not come for several years; indeed it is quite likely that it may never come, or may be stifled at birth.

Each trade cycle in the past has had special features of its own. The Great Depression of 1929–33 was far more severe, and was accompanied by far heavier unemployment, than ever before. The next depression, partly because we now know better how to deal with it, may be much milder and shorter.

The trade cycle consists of fluctuations in the general level of economic activity. Any particular industry will have its ups and downs, due to changes in supply and demand affecting only its own products, but a general boom or a general slump affects all industries. Unless any special influences affecting the fortunes of a particular industry are very strong, they are likely to be swamped by the more powerful influence of the trade cycle.

The trade cycle is international. Only the central planning countries, Russia and her satellites, are immune, for in them the volume of output depends, as in a prison, on the orders of those in power, and not on the market. A country may depend largely on one product, as Australia on wool or Egypt on cotton, and the prosperity of the country will therefore reflect changes affecting that product. For example, Australia will suffer if she has a drought and consequently a low wool clip. But the general upswings and downswings in demand, which are part of the trade cycle, will affect the prices of such products, and such countries usually share in general booms and depressions just as much as other countries which have a wider range of staple products.

It is because the trade cycle is international that the West keeps such a watchful eye upon the economy of the United States. Although the imports of the United States are equal to only about 5 per cent of her own output, they form an important part of world trade. If the United States should have an internal slump, she would buy less from overseas, and this would spread her depression, as in 1929, to other countries.

In most western countries, the general trend of real income per head has been upwards for several generations, and continues to be upwards. The trade cycle has been superimposed upon this secular upward trend. Thus an unemployed worker in Great Britain during the Great Depression probably had a higher standard of living (on £2 to £3 a week, if he had children, from the "dole") than an unskilled worker (on less than £1 a week) before 1914. In some countries, such as India, the secular trend of real income per head may be slightly downward (owing to overpopulation) and a period of "prosperity" may merely keep standards of living from falling.

The chief characteristic of a depression is unemployment. Because labour and other resources are unemployed, the volume of output and the volume of consumption are lower than during the preceding (and following) period of prosperity.

The volume of transactions is less, and the amount of money spent is less. More money is spent during a boom; possibly more money is brought into existence, but in any event the available money circulates more rapidly than during a depression.

As a rule, therefore, the prices of commodities have risen during periods of boom and have fallen during periods of slump. The United States boom of 1925–29 was an exception. The general level of commodity prices remained stable; this was due largely to the marked increase in output resulting from technical progress and additional real capital. Other prices, however, went up. Wages increased and rents increased. The prices of assets rose very considerably, for their earning power had increased and was expected to increase further; this was reflected in a very marked upward movement in the prices of shares on the Stock Exchange.

The depression of 1929–33 was no exception, however, to the general rule that prices fall during a depression. The prices of agricultural commodities fell most, some to less than half or less than a third of their former levels. This was because small farmers were their own employers and maintained their output; they suffered heavy reductions in income, but they were not unemployed. Manufactured commodities fell less in price, but their output fell by a third, and this meant heavy unemployment among the workers engaged in those industries.

The great evil of the trade cycle is unemployment. The dread of unemployment constantly haunts even those workers who manage to keep their jobs. Yet if we look only at real incomes, wage-earners as a whole suffer less during a depression than is often supposed. For prices fall, and therefore their cost of living falls, while trade unions succeed in preventing any very drastic reductions in wages. Hence those workers, the great majority, who keep their jobs can buy more with their wages (despite the lack of any overtime earnings) than during a period of "prosperity." The total real income (including social security payments) of British workers as a whole was greater (owing mainly to the heavy fall in the prices of imported food) during the Great Depression than it had ever been before.

In terms of income, "prosperity" and "depression" affect mainly profits. During a boom, the general level of profits is high. During a slump, there are losses and bankruptcies, and the general level of profits is low. (The farmer working on his own account receives an income of the nature of profits.)

The industries in which output and employment rise most during a period of expansion and fall most during a depression, are those producing durable goods, such as buildings, plant and equipment, ships, motor-cars, refrigerators, and furniture. The output of materials sold mainly to those industries—for example, iron and steel products, timber, cement, rubber—fluctuates in the same way. The output of consumers' goods also rises in booms and falls in slumps, but to a much smaller extent. Thus in the United States at the bottom of the Great Depression—in the first few months of 1933—their output was only 15 per cent below its 1929 peak, whereas the output of durable goods was only a third of its 1929 peak level.

This is the key to the trade cycle. A boom is a period of relatively heavy investment—because prospects of profits are good. A depression is a period of relatively little investment—because prospects of profits are poor.

3. FLUCTUATIONS IN INVESTMENT

The fluctuations in output and employment which constitute the trade cycle are mainly fluctuations in the investment industries. The investment industries include building and construction, iron and steel, engineering, shipbuilding, and the industries supplying them with raw materials.

Investment was defined in Chapter IV. An individual thinks of himself as investing when he buys stocks or shares or real estate. But this merely transfers the ownership of existing assets. From the standpoint of the community, investment means adding to the physical assets of the community: improving its land (for example, by irrigation projects or by opening up new mines); constructing or improving roads and railways, ports and harbours, and airports; putting up more buildings; adding to its plant and machinery; increasing its stocks of goods.

In a "closed" community (that is to say, in an isolated country which has no economic transactions with other countries, or in the world as a whole), gross investment would correspond closely with the output of the investment industries, including those making durable consumers' goods such as motor-cars, refrigerators, and furniture. But foreign trade upsets this for any particular country. For example, Great Britain exports engineering products. An increase in her output of engineering products does not necessarily mean increased investment in Great Britain. They may be exchanged against imported foodstuffs for her current consumption; the investment would then take place in the countries exporting the foodstuffs and importing the engineering products. This example illustrates the international aspect of the trade cycle: a depression in the food-producing countries would soon be transmitted to Great Britain and other countries exporting capital goods through a decline in the demand for their exports.

Every period of boom has been marked by relatively heavy investment. The building of railways, the development of the gold-field of the Rand, the construction of plant and equipment to supply electric power, are illustrations of new developments involving heavy investment. The British recovery, from 1933 onwards, from the Great Depression was associated with a large expansion in house-building. The boom of 1950–51 was due to the fear that the Korean war would spread; it took the form of rearmament and public and private stockpiling.

Wars are usually periods of full employment, when economic activity is stretched to its utmost. Much investment takes place in constructing the plant and equipment and other assets needed to make armaments of all kinds. From the standpoint of human welfare, a war is a disaster. Labour and resources that might have been used to raise standards of living are employed instead to deal out death and destruction. But from the standpoint of economic analysis, a war is a period of heavy investment, high output, and full employment.

Nowadays there is a good deal of public investment, in peace-time as well as in war-time. Governments and other public authorities carry out various development projects. Governments have rearmament programmes. Where some industries are nationalized, as in Great Britain, the modernization and expansion of those industries is carried out by public authorities.

An increase in public investment may stimulate private investment, especially in under-developed countries ; for example, by providing more basic services such as transport and electric power. Or it may do the opposite; I will return to this point later. The question I will now try to answer is why such marked fluctuations take place in private investment.

The incentive to private investment is the prospect of profit. An entrepreneur constructs, let us say, a factory for making television sets because he expects that he will be able to sell enough television sets at a price that will give him a satisfactory return on his investment. It is the expected amount of spending on the final products that governs the amount that entrepreneurs decide to invest. This is one of the main points emphasized by Keynes. An adequate volume of spending on consumption is essential for full employment.

What about costs? Profits are the excess of receipts over costs. The entrepreneur must anticipate adequate receipts, but he must also expect that his costs per unit will be less than the price per unit. This proposition, however, is not as simple as it appears.

Entrepreneurs often borrow in order to carry out their investment. The interest which they have to pay on their loans is a cost. Other things being equal, a low rate of interest will stimulate investment and a high rate of interest will discourage it. But the influence of the rate of interest on the volume of investment is often far less than that of the expected volume of sales.

Wages are costs. If an entrepreneur is producing for export, he can make a profit, and it will pay him to invest and expand, only if wages are low enough for him to compete successfully in the world's markets. But wages are also income, which the wage-earners spend on buying consumers' goods. In a closed community, a general reduction in wages is not only a reduction in costs. It is also a reduction in total spending, and therefore in total receipts. During a boom there are usually general increases in wages, but the boom continues, at any rate for some time, for the higher wages mean greater receipts—more sales and higher prices—as well as higher costs. In the same way, a general reduction of wages during a depression may not stimulate recovery, for it means a further reduction in total spending.

Why, then, does a boom come to an end? Why does investment fall off instead of continuing indefinitely at a high level?

This is a difficult and controversial question. Once the rot sets in, it is easy to understand how it spreads. If some important firms go bankrupt, or perhaps if they merely make losses without going bankrupt, all entrepreneurs will become more pessimistic and more hesitant about making further investments. If a number of workers are thrown out of employment, the total volume of spending falls, and therefore unemployment spreads; investment that would have yielded an adequate profit under full employment no longer does so. But what starts the rot in the first place? As I have just pointed out, rising wages and therefore rising costs are not a complete explanation, since higher wages imply a larger volume of spending.

One possible explanation is that investment opportunities become exhausted. It is said that in countries such as the United States and Great Britain which, in contrast to under-developed countries, have reached "economic maturity," the amount of investment opportunities is limited: once the economic system has had a good dose of investment it must digest it, like a boa-constrictor, before it can absorb any more. This view was at one time widely accepted as an explanation of why heavy unemployment persisted in the United States throughout the 1930s. Little is heard of it nowadays. The continued maintenance of a high level of investment, and of output and employment, in the United States and Great Britain since the war has robbed it of its plausibility. In my opinion, it is quite wrong. There are almost unlimited opportunities for investment. A large number of industries could be modernized, communications could be improved, many more houses could be built, and so on. Provided that investment does not absorb so much labour and other resources that the output of consumers' goods (or of exports to procure them from abroad) is unduly reduced, a high level of investment could continue indefinitely without running into any shortage of investment opportunities.

It is true, however, that investment opportunities in any particular field may become exhausted for the time being. When a number of entrepreneurs have put up factories to make television sets, there may not be room for any more. If still more are put up, some or all of the entrepreneurs in that industry may make losses.

Over-investment in a particular field is especially likely when the maintenance of the demand for its products depends on a continually increasing demand for the goods which they help to produce. This is known as the *acceleration principle*.

Suppose, for example, that machines to make shoes last about ten years. If the demand for shoes remains constant, so will the demand for these machines. About a tenth of the number in existence will be needed each year for replacements. Now suppose that this year the demand for shoes increases by 10 per cent and that in consequence the stock of machines is increased by 10 per cent. The output of machines this year is double what it has been; it is 20 per cent, instead of 10 per cent, of the existing stock—10 per cent, as usual, for replacements, plus 10 per cent for additional machines. But next year the demand for machines will revert to its old level unless the demand for shoes increases again; in order to support a continuance of this year's output of machines the demand for shoes must increase by a further 10 per cent. If it does not increase, then manufacturers of shoe machines (and of equipment and materials for making shoe machines) who had expected that the demand for their products would remain at a substantially higher level than before will be disappointed and may make losses.

To take another example, suppose that the Government embarks on a rearmament programme and places orders, covering several years, with armament firms. The latter in turn will order new buildings and plant to expand their capacity. But once they have obtained the new buildings and plant, they will not need any more unless the Government increases its programme. The firms that provide the new buildings and plant will have received increased orders which are not renewed.

The acceleration principle, therefore, shows that a lasting increase in the demand for consumers' goods is not sufficient to maintain the increased demand for capital goods to which it gives rise. To achieve this latter object, the demand for the consumers' goods must not merely continue at its new and higher level; it must go on increasing; it must accelerate.

Losses due to over-investment in particular fields usually discourage new investment in other fields also. This is largely because labour is not sufficiently mobile. If the workers unemployed in one industry could be absorbed at once in other industries, the total volume of spending would not fall off, and the total amount of investment could be maintained continuously at a fairly high level despite losses from time to time in particular fields.

Another way in which a boom may come to an end is by developing into a marked and growing inflation, leading to a crisis due to loss of confidence in the currency.

During the recovery from a depression there will be a considerable number of unemployed. As these are gradually absorbed into employment, expansion can take place simultaneously in both the investment industries and the consumption industries. Suppose that full employment is reached with, say, 20 per cent of the labour force in the investment industries. A further expansion of investment would involve transferring workers to the investment industries. For the time being, the output of consumers' goods would fall, and their prices would rise. As more and more labour was transferred to the investment industries, the shortage of consumers' goods would become more and more marked, and their prices would continue to rise. There would be growing inflation.

Under a central planning dictatorship, it is possible to maintain a very high level of investment by depressing standards of living. Consumers are powerless to protest; workers have to accept falling real wages without going on strike. Soviet Russia, during the first two five-year plans, achieved a level of investment equal to perhaps 25 per cent of her national income. She produced power stations, dams, armament factories, and so forth, instead of food, clothing, and houseroom; and millions died of starvation. But in a free society such a state of affairs cannot continue for long. Workers will insist that their wages vary, from day to day, with the cost of living, and people will refuse to lend money except at very high rates of interest, for they realize that when their money is repaid it will buy less. Hence the inflationary boom, which gave large profits to entrepreneurs who borrowed money to produce goods for sale on a rising market, will come to an end. Entrepreneurs, each acting independently, have been trying between them to carry out more investment than the community can stand. The consequent rise in wages and interest rates puts an end to inflationary profits due to selling prices rising faster than costs; there are losses and a drastic fall in investment.

The reader may find this subject quite unfamiliar to him, for there has been no runaway inflation in Great Britain (although there have been several elsewhere, e.g. Hungary 1944, China 1946–9) during recent times. This is because the Government has always checked it in time. In practice, a boom is often brought to an end by Government action. The Government decides to put the brake on, mainly by restricting credit, because it fears that otherwise there will be a serious slump in one or two years time; it prefers a mild recession now.

A third way (apart from such preventive action by the Government) in which a boom may come to an end is by people trying to save more. This is explained in the following section, which discusses the Keynes theory.

4. SAVING AND INVESTMENT: THE KEYNES THEORY

Keynes, assuming for simplicity a closed economy, defines Saving and Investment so that they are necessarily equal to one another. That is to say, if we look back at what has happened during any period, however short, these two aggregates must have been the same for the community as a whole, although for any individual the amount he has saved may be quite different from the amount he has invested. Saving is income less expenditure on consumers' goods; investment is output less output of consumers' goods; and national income is the same thing as national output. Hence saving and investment are merely two different names for the same thing, namely the increase in the physical assets of the community.

But decisions to save and decisions to invest are taken largely by different people and for different reasons. For example, individuals save to provide for their children or for their old age, and the amount which they decide to save out of a given income is fairly stable. Entrepreneurs invest, by ordering capital goods, such as buildings, plant, and machinery, to be constructed, in the hope of making a profit. To a considerable extent, they pay for these capital goods by borrowing from the public or from the banks, and not out of their own savings. The prospects of profit, and therefore the amount of private investment, fluctuate greatly from time to time. How, then, is equality brought about between total saving and total investment?

Not, Keynes points out, through the rate of interest. The amount that individuals (and companies) are able to save depends on the size of their incomes. A man with a low income has little or no margin for saving; the bigger his income, the bigger the proportion of it that he is likely to save. The amount that entrepreneurs decide to invest depends mainly on the expected total volume of spending. Equality between saving and investment is maintained not by changes in the rate of interest, but by changes in the size of the national income.

Here the governing force, in practice, is the amount of investment. If the amount of investment is large enough, there is full employment, the national income is large, and the amount of saving is large—equal, as always, to the amount of investment. If the amount of investment is small, there is unemployment, the national income is small, and so is the amount of saving.

Suppose that investment revives after a period of depression and unemployment. More workers are employed in the investment industries. They spend more than before on consumers' goods. This increases employment in the consumers' goods industries and induces entrepreneurs in those industries to carry bigger stocks of goods and perhaps to order new buildings, plant and equipment, vans and lorries, and other capital goods. Hence the process of recovery is cumulative. As more and more workers are reabsorbed into employment, the total volume of spending continues to increase, and investment continues to grow. The consequent expansion of the national income results in an increase in saving, simultaneous with and equal to the increase in investment that is responsible for the expansion.

Conversely, a falling-off in investment has a similar cumulative effect in reducing employment, total spending, national income, and consequently saving.

A reasonably close correlation between fluctuations in (net) investment and fluctuations in national income is shown by the following estimates [1] for the United States—

	(Net) Investment $000m.	National Income $000m.
1929	11·3	87·6
1930	6·4	76·0
1931	3·0	59·6
1932	−2·2	42·8
1933	−2·2	41·9
1934	0·8	50·1
1935	2·8	57·0
1936	5·7	66·9
1937	6·0	72·6
1938	4·3	66·1
1939	6·9	72·0
1940	9·2	79·8
1941	13·7	99·1

[1] From "National Income, Output and Expenditure of U.S.A., 1929–41," by R. Stone, *Economic Journal*, June–September, 1942.

The *Multiplier* states how many times a change in the amount of investment is magnified by the consequent change in the amount of the national income. For example, if the multiplier is 3, this means that an increase of £1 million in the amount of investment will lead to an increase of £3 million in the national income.

The size of the multiplier reflects the proportion of *additional* income that people spend. If they spend two-thirds, and save one-third, their *marginal propensity to consume* is two-thirds and their *marginal propensity to save* is one-third. It is spending, not saving, that creates employment and income. The recipients of the additional £1 million spend two-thirds of it; the recipients of the £$\frac{2}{3}$ million spend two-thirds of that; and so on. The consequent increase in national income is $1 + \frac{2}{3} + \frac{4}{9} + \frac{8}{27}$ and so on, adding up to 3(£ million). The multiplier is 3 – the reciprocal of the marginal prospensity to save.

The reader may remember that I said there was a third way in which a boom might come to an end: people might try to save more. Suppose that the total volume of spending on consumers' goods is £100 million a week and that people try to save £10 million a week more than before. The immediate effect is that they spend only £90 million a week. Those supplying consumers' goods, and materials for them, will sell less, a tenth less, than they had expected. Some of these firms will make losses and perhaps have to close down. In any event, workers will be dismissed, and consequently the total volume of spending will fall further. This will reduce the amount of investment by reducing the prospects of profit. A cumulative downward movement will set in. The community will not in fact save £10 million a week more. Many people will not be able to save as much as before, because their incomes are lower. The actual amount of saving will be less than before; it will be equal to the (reduced) amount of investment, and this equality will be brought about by the fall in the national income.

This hypothetical example shows that changes in the total volume of spending on consumers' goods may have the same cumulative and magnified effect—either upward or downward—on the size of the national income as changes in the amount of the investment. But in practice it is usually the latter which plays the active and governing role, for private investment tends to fluctuate greatly from time to time, whereas saving habits are fairly stable.

It would be quite wrong to conclude from Keynes's theory that the saver is the enemy of society and that thrift should be discouraged. On the contrary, most countries desperately need more capital in order to increase their output and raise their standards of living, and the only way they can get it without inflation or help from other countries is by increasing their own savings. The right conclusion to draw from Keynes's theory is that it is the duty of the Government to see that an increased willingness to save is matched by an increase in investment, so that people's attempts to save more do not run to waste in unemployment and falling incomes.

What happens if investment increases after full employment has been reached? There is no longer any scope for expanding the national output further by reabsorbing unemployed workers into industry and trade. The money national income increases, but the real national income does not; prices rise; there is inflation.

The increased investment, either by private entrepreneurs or by public authorities, may be financed by an expansion of bank credit. The additional money, not matched by a corresponding increase in output, raises prices. Entrepreneurs have to pay higher wages to attract workers from their present jobs into the new investment projects; the cost of living rises; other workers demand increases in their wages to keep pace with the rise in the cost of living. Saving, as defined by Keynes, must always equal investment. Investment has increased. But the corresponding increase in saving does not come from voluntary saving. It comes from *forced saving*. All those whose incomes are more or less fixed find that they can now buy less, because prices have risen. They are therefore forced to reduce their consumption. This is forced saving, saving forced on the community as a whole at the expense of those on fixed incomes, who do not themselves acquire any extra assets (the extra assets belong to the entrepreneurs), but are compelled to consume less than before. The great danger of a full-employment policy which aims at maintaining the volume of employment by keeping up the volume of spending (on both consumers' goods and investment goods) is that it may easily go too far and result in inflation.

The foregoing brief summary of Keynes's views is far from complete. But enough has been said to show how a central planning dictatorship can avoid the slumps and consequent unemployment to which a free-enterprise society is liable. Under such a dictatorship, the amount of investment is planned from the centre and does not fluctuate with prospects of profit. Decisions to invest and decisions to save are one and the same decisions. For example, a decision to construct a new power-station is at the same time a decision to divert workers and materials to that project and away from industries producing goods and services for current consumption. So long as workers can be ordered to go where the planning authority needs them, so long as consumers (including workers) can be compelled to reduce their consumption to whatever level is necessary to set free the labour and other resources needed for investment, there need be no significant unemployment.

5. PUBLIC POLICY AND UNEMPLOYMENT

Some unemployment arises, as we have seen, from causes not directly associated with general depressions of trade. Unemployment in Great

Britain after the slump of 1921 until the slump of 1929 averaged about a million, and from the upswing of 1933 until the outbreak of war about a million and a half. Most of this was due to structural changes; the demand for staple British exports—coal, iron and steel, heavy engineering products, cotton textiles, ships—had declined. (After the war there was a shortage of coal and capital goods, and these industries (excepting cotton textiles) were short of labour.) The Great Depression of 1929–33 added rather more than a million to the total of unemployed, sending it over $2\frac{1}{2}$ million.

The general remedy which follows from the Keynes analysis, the remedy of increasing the total volume of spending, has not much relevance to unemployment that is due to special causes and not to a general trade depression. The remedy for unemployment due to structural changes is to get workers out of the contracting industries and into the expanding industries. The Government can help by such measures as training unemployed workers for new jobs, giving suitable vocational guidance to children leaving school, organizing the movement of groups to districts where employment is expanding and encouraging the building of houses in those districts. The post-war system of paying family allowances to all parents, whether they are in work or out of work, reduces one obstacle to mobility by widening the difference between what a man can earn by finding a new job and what he receives in benefits if he remains unemployed. If structural unemployment is localized in certain areas, which workers are reluctant to leave, there may be a case for the Government to encourage new establishments to be set up in those areas rather than elsewhere; the British Government, as we noted in Chapter XXI, Section 5, has followed this policy.

I turn to measures to promote recovery from a general slump. The particular measures that will be most effective will depend on the circumstances, for each slump has special features of its own. The broad solution, however, is to increase the total volume of spending. The upswing may be brought about, leading to a cumulative recovery of employment and output, by increased spending either on investment or on consumption, but as a rule it will be investment that most needs stimulating, for investment will have fallen off more than consumption, and most of the unemployed will be attached to the investment industries.

The chief measures which a Government might take to promote spending are:
1. Cheap money.
2. Tax reductions.
3. Public works.
4. Purchases of raw materials.
5. Subsidies to wages.

All these measures imply that the Government deliberately incurs a budget deficit, spending more than it receives in revenue. If it borrows from the public to fill the gap, the assumption is that the lenders would not themselves have spent the money either on consumption or on investment. Hence the transfer of their money balances to the Government makes them active instead of idle. Alternatively, the Government may fill the gap with new money. In any event, there will be an increase in total spending.

1. *Cheap Money*

This means that the Government reduces the rate of interest by increasing the quantity of money. I discuss this subject later, in the chapter on Interest. It is difficult in practice to keep the long-term rate of interest below about $2\frac{1}{2}$ or 3 per cent a year; hence the scope for a "cheap money" policy will depend on how high the rate of interest was before.

A reduction in the rate of interest makes it more profitable for entrepreneurs to borrow in order to invest. But if the trade outlook is considered gloomy, and the expected volume of spending low, even a substantial reduction in interest rates may not lead to much expansion in the amount of investment.

The recovery that began in 1933 in Great Britain was due largely to the boom in house-building, and was stimulated by cheap money. People who want to buy a house on the instalment plan can do so more cheaply when interest rates are low; for example, to buy a £1,000 house over 20 years costs £6 13s. 9d. a month when the rate of interest is 5 per cent, and only £5 6s. 11d. when it is $2\frac{1}{2}$ per cent. (These figures cover both interest and repayment of the principal.)

2. *Tax Reductions*

Generous income-tax allowances on capital expenditure on buildings, plant, and machinery, or on improvements to land—on new investment and not on the mere transfer of existing assets—may stimulate investment.

Social security contributions levied on employers are taxes on employment, and could be temporarily reduced or abolished.

Other taxes that might be temporarily reduced or abolished are those that fall on the lower income groups, for they spend nearly all their incomes. The abolition of social security contributions by employees, or purchase-taxes on household goods, or the raising of exemption limits and allowances on income-tax, would lead to a corresponding increase in spending, whereas a reduction in death duties, for example, might be partly wasted in increased saving.

3. *Public Works*

The public may not respond sufficiently to the stimulus of cheap money or tax reductions. The Government can make sure that increased spending takes place by itself spending on wages and materials to carry out public works such as improvements to roads or harbours or airports, modernization of nationalized industries, new schools or hospitals or satellite towns.

Public works require planning in advance. There should be a "shelf" of suitable projects which can be postponed until depression threatens. It is desirable to carry out the projects as efficiently and cheaply as possible. But even if they prove rather expensive, because some of the workers employed on them are unskilled at those tasks, they will represent a large net gain to the community if they succeed in bringing about a recovery and absorbing unemployed in private enterprise as well as in Government public works, owing to the cumulative increase in total spending.

4. *Purchases of Raw Materials*

During a slump the demand for most raw materials falls. Their prices often fall heavily. The Government could step in and buy considerable quantities of them for storage (thus giving their producers more money to spend), subsequently selling them when recovery is well under way. Such purchases might well be profitable to the Government. Clearly, however, it is desirable that the leading Governments should agree among themselves on the details of such a policy, to be followed by all of them, or should all participate in "buffer stock" schemes for various commodities.

5. *Subsidies to Wages*

The Government might give a subsidy to employers who take on additional workers. The subsidy would be a proportion of the wages paid to the additional workers. It would be reduced, and then withdrawn, as recovery progressed.

The subsidy could apply to all employers or could be restricted to employment in particular fields (for example, in certain investment industries and in improvements to land) approved by the Government. Care would be needed to guard against fraud, especially by small employers who might be tempted to put members of their families on their pay rolls without making any fuller use of their services than they did before, when they were nominally unpaid.

The argument for subsidies to wages is that it aims directly at the target—namely, fuller employment. It aims at increasing employment in private enterprise because workers are likely, it is thought, to render more efficient and more valuable service in private employment, doing their normal jobs, than if they are engaged on tasks such as digging, or moving earth about, in public works projects.

All the remedies for a slump have their difficulties and dangers.

As recovery proceeds, they should be gradually reversed. Interest rates should be raised, tax concessions withdrawn, some public works closed down, some raw materials unloaded from stocks on to the market, subsidies to wages reduced. Such a reversal is not easy, in practice, without checking the recovery and bringing about a recession. This happened in the United States in 1938. Public expenditure had been greatly increased during the slump. By 1937 unemployment, although still over 7 million, had been reduced from the 12 million or more of 1933, national income was rising, and recovery seemed to be well under way. But a reduction in public expenditure led to an increase in unemployment and a fall in national income; the upward trend was restored by increasing public expenditure again in 1939.

If entrepreneurs expect the Government to apply these remedies when a slump comes, they may defer making investments and perhaps dismiss some workers when they think that a slump is likely in the near future, in the hope that they will be able to borrow at lower rates of interest and to get tax concessions and perhaps subsidies on workers re-engaged when it actually comes. Such action will hasten the slump and may bring about a slump which otherwise would not have taken place.

The multiplier applies to *net* additional investment. Increased public investment, for example in public works, may be offset to a greater or less extent by decreased private investment, and the latter may be the consequence of the former. If the policies followed by the Government appear "unsound" to business men, create uncertainty about the profitability of new private investment, and tend to raise costs, the consequence may be that private investment is discouraged. This seems to have happened during the "New Deal" in the United States in the 1930s. The Government incurred large deficits which were used partly in rather odd ways, such as paying farmers to produce less, and it adopted various measures unfavourable to private enterprise, including "payroll taxes" on employers for social security purposes, and higher minimum wages. Consequently private investment fell off.

The creation of new money to finance increased public expenditure may produce inflation long before full employment is attained. For the mobility of labour is imperfect. After a time, shortages of various types of skilled workers, or a general shortage of labour in particular districts, may create "bottle-necks" and hamper further expansion. But the increased volume of spending may raise wages and the prices of raw materials, thus tending to check private investment.

Most countries badly need a substantial increase in the amount of their voluntary saving. This is the only way, in the long run, by which they can increase their capital and thereby their output per worker. Yet, in the topsy-turvy economics of slump, saving must be discouraged because investment is so low. This is very bad propaganda for normal times. How can a national savings campaign be successful if during a slump people are told, quite correctly, that they should spend freely and that their attempts to save will make the slump worse?

This point seems to me so important that I am inclined to think that the Government should not attempt to discourage private saving, even during a severe slump. Instead, it should try to stimulate investment and should offset private saving by public dis-saving through budget deficits.

Clearly the best policy is to prevent slumps altogether, or at least to keep them short and mild, by smoothing out the ups and downs of the trade cycle. The greater the debauch, the worse the headache; the greater the boom, the more severe will be the depression which follows.

It is seldom possible for one country alone, with a free-enterprise economy, to isolate itself from world depressions. If it depends largely on exports, it is at the mercy of world forces. In order to abolish the trade cycle, all the big countries must maintain a high and stable level of employment and avoid substantial reductions in the volume of their imports. Should the United States, for example, have another severe depression, it would spread to the rest of the world via a reduction in her imports. It has been suggested that in such a case the country should pay into a fund a sum equal to the reduction in the total value of her imports, the money to be used to maintain the volume of spending in the countries that export to her.

The way to smooth out the trade cycle is to keep investment at as high a level as possible without permitting general over-investment, which can continue only under inflation. This might be done by direct control. In Great Britain we have the Capital Issues Committee, whose approval is needed before entrepreneurs can borrow any substantial sum from the public by floating a new issue of shares or debentures. We have also had Government control over the allocation of materials such as steel, and licences are needed to put up new establishments. A supplementary or alternative method is to keep the rate of interest high enough to discourage over-investment. This makes a cheap money policy more effective when bad times threaten. Direct control of investment is discriminatory; the Government decides which investments are permitted and which are not. Whether this is an advantage depends on whether politicians and Government officials are more competent than entrepreneurs to decide which types of investment are in the best interests of the community.

There may be a case for stabilizing, within limits, the prices of raw materials by setting up buffer stocks which sell when the price rises above a certain level and buy when it falls below a lower level. The ceiling and floor prices should be fixed realistically, in the light of the probable future supply and demand for the commodity, and should be varied from time to time when conditions change.

Inflation favours borrowers and leads to over-investment. Various measures are needed to prevent inflation: one major measure is to tax sufficiently heavily to drain off excess spending power. The view that the Government budget should be balanced in every single year is not compatible with a policy of smoothing out the trade cycle in order to maintain a high and stable level of employment. But while Government deficits and reductions in taxation are popular, the opposite measures are not. Yet both are needed, the latter in good times and the former in bad times, to reduce the swings of the trade cycle. If the Government has acquired a surplus during good times, confidence in its policy and credit will be maintained when it incurs a budget deficit in bad times. If a boom is damped down by relatively high taxation and interest rates, the subsequent depression will be milder and shorter; indeed it may never come.

It needs firmness on the part of Governments to resist demands for lower taxes when they are building up a surplus, to keep up interest rates although this adds to the charge on the national debt, and to oppose producers who want to take advantage of market conditions to get as high prices as they can for their raw materials. But if Governments are courageous enough to follow these unpopular policies during a boom, they will save the world from a repetition of the Great Depression.

I conclude with a note on international trade. In the long run, a country benefits greatly by international trade. Great Britain, for example, could not maintain her 50 million people at anything like their present standards of living without a large volume of imports, mostly of foodstuffs and raw materials. But during a slump it may appear that the correct policy is, as with saving, a topsy-turvy one. Money spent on imports does not create any employment at home; it is, so to speak, a leak in the multiplier. Would it not be wise, therefore, to restrict imports? They could be restricted in various ways. The total quantity or value imported of each commodity could be limited. Or import duties could be increased. Or the cost of imports could be raised by reducing the exchange value of the national currency.

This policy is often resorted to during a slump. In my view, it is very far from wise. It creates difficulties, as we have noted, in the countries from which the imports come, and thereby tends to intensify the slump throughout the world. It is likely to lead, in practice, to retaliation. "You keep out our goods; we will keep out yours." Retaliation will hit the export industries. The sensible course is just the opposite. The leading countries should get together in a concerted effort to maintain the total flow of world trade and thereby alleviate the slump.

CHAPTER XXIV

THE MERITS AND DEFECTS OF CAPITALISM

1. INTRODUCTION

A CHAPTER on this subject seems called for at the present stage in order to round off the discussion. But anything like a complete appraisal of the merits and defects of capitalism is quite out of the question in a book such as this, which is meant to be merely an introduction to economics. For the issue that confronts us is nothing less than the great controversial issue of our time, which may yet land us in the third world war. It is the so-called "conflict of ideologies," the clash between the ideals and ways of life of the West and those which prevail behind the Iron Curtain.

There would be little purpose in a discussion of whether capitalism is in itself a good system or a bad one. The practical question is whether something better could be put in its place. But when we consider what are the possible alternatives, it is clear that the only practicable alternative is the totalitarian State.

A small community, living on an island or in an isolated district, might conceivably practice a primitive form of communism. If they were few enough in numbers to meet together frequently in order to discuss their problems, they could perhaps dispense with any formal Government. They could own their property in common and could follow the principle of "from each according to his ability, to each according to his need."

But when the community is a modern industrialized community, running into many millions, it cannot possibly solve its problems by group discussions. How can each person know what kind of work he should do, what he should produce, and by what methods? Either there must be a system based on private property and freedom of enterprise, which provides incentives, through the price system, for those goods and services to be produced that people want most, and for them to be produced in the most efficient way, or else the State must give the orders and control all economic activity.

Those who favour the system of Soviet Russia believe that private property in the means of production results inevitably in the exploitation of the masses by the property-owners who make the profits. They believe that the only way to ensure that production is directed in the interests of the community as a whole, and that the product is distributed fairly among those who produce it, is for the State to own all means of production and to direct all economic activity.

Those who favour freedom of enterprise value the rights and liberties of the individual. They want people to be free to express their own opinions and to listen to the opinions of others, free to live their lives in patterns of their own choosing. They feel that life as it is in Soviet Russia or as it is described in George Orwell's *1984* would be quite intolerable.

Although anything like an adequate discussion of these great issues is beyond the scope of this book, I shall try to make a few points which are relevant, although not conclusive. In order to clear the ground I shall assume that it is possible to have a totalitarian State which is not a "police State," that is to say, a State in which everyone is spied upon by his neighbours and colleagues, or even by his children, and in which the unguarded word or the ill-considered action may lead to imprisonment or death. I shall assume that the State may own the means of production and direct economic activity without suppressing individual freedom of thought and speech and worship. On the other hand, I shall assume that under capitalism it is possible to limit the power of property-owners to act in ways contrary to the interests of the community as a whole. These assumptions will enable us to side-step the main ideological issues and to concentrate on some economic aspects of capitalism versus central economic planning.

2. PRODUCTION FOR PROFIT AND PRODUCTION FOR USE

I may as well begin by discussing the assertion that under capitalism production is for profit and not for use. This assertion—it can hardly be called an argument—is often considered by opponents of capitalism to be a conclusive indictment of that system. Taken literally, the antithesis is quite false, for profits are made only by producing or selling what people want to use. But there are several different arguments telescoped or combined into this phrase. I shall try to sort them out and to consider them one by one.

To begin with, profits may be made by cheating or swindling. The law tries to prevent all types of fraud. It is an offence to seek to obtain money on false pretences. For example, it is illegal to try to get the public to buy shares in a company by making false statements in the prospectus. It is illegal to fail to carry out a contract or to supply goods, without proper and agreed compensation to the buyer, that are not up to sample or not in accordance with specifications.

But there are many ways of deluding the public, and the law cannot completely protect people from the consequences of their own ignorance or folly. For example, some advertisements may be misleading. Claims may be made for, say, a patent medicine, which experts consider to be without any foundation whatever. Nevertheless some people may benefit, or may think they benefit, from taking it. What can the Government do in such a case, beyond making the manufacturers state the ingredients on the label? Would it not be an intolerable interference with freedom of choice if the Government banned every commodity of which its experts did not approve?

Those who believe in the totalitarian State give little weight to this point. The welfare of the community as a whole, they say, is far more important than the whims of the individual. If all economic activities were carried on by the State, then the State could produce only those commodities which it deemed of real benefit, "of use." If there were no private enterprise, there would be no private profits, and therefore no opportunity for making profits by fraud of any kind. The totalitarian State is thus, in their view, clearly superior to a system of production for private profit.

This point merges into the wider question whether people should be allowed to have what they want or should be permitted to have only what is good for them. Should the consumption of alcohol be prohibited on the grounds that it reduces efficiency and that the money would be better spent on providing for the needs of the family? Should people be prevented from "wasting" their money on betting and gambling, lotteries and football pools? Should they be induced—for example, by rationing or by taxing some foodstuffs and subsidizing others—to change over to a diet that is better for their health and that gives them more nutrition for the same money? Should the less scrupulous newspapers, ready to print anything that will sell however much it may harm the national interests or cause distress to individuals, be suppressed? Should trashy and vulgar books and periodicals be prohibited? What about cinematograph films, radio and television programmes, plays, that appeal only to the baser passions and desires? Should people of bad taste be allowed to build houses that are eyesores?

This general question is doubtless in the minds of those who point out that under capitalism production is for profit. The producers do not care, most of them, whether what they make is of real benefit or is harmful to the minds or bodies of those who buy; their sole concern is to give the public what it wants, in order that they can make their profits.

One answer to this line of argument is to point out that the views of experts may change radically as time goes on. The dietician of today would not recommend the same diet as he would have recommended twenty years ago, and some would say that what is good for one person may be bad for another. Some doctors favour the consumption of alcohol, or tobacco, or certain drugs, in moderation. Some of our acknowledged masterpieces in the realms of art, literature, and music were condemned by nearly all the critics when they first appeared. Who, then, is to judge and decide what is good for us?

But the more fundamental objection comes from those who believe in the freedom of the individual and in his right to "the pursuit of happiness" wherever he thinks he can find it, provided always that he does not injure his neighbours. If nothing could be produced or consumed without the sanction of the State, we might indeed get rid of a good deal that the better-educated among us consider harmful or vulgar, but we should at the same time make deep inroads into personal liberty. If Mr. Smith enjoys filling in football pool coupons more than eating spinach, why not let him? The more Calvinistic of social reformers would take much of the pleasure and colour out of life, leaving it real and earnest, but drab and grim. The gutter Press is the price we must pay for freedom of speech and independent criticism; some vulgarity is the price we must pay for leaving the door wide open to the development of new forms of creative art.

There is thus a basic conflict of opinion between the authoritarians who want to "improve" (as they think) people's ways of life and those who believe that the individual should have the right to do what he pleases, even if it means (in the opinion of some) going to the devil. This is a fundamental conflict of values, which far transcends the bounds of economic analysis. I mention it only because those who hold the former view consider that production for profit—and only for profit—is one of the great defects or evils of capitalism.

Another general point which is implied in contrasting production for profit with production for use is that under capitalism it may pay to produce luxuries for the rich while the poor go short of bare necessities. This is true. The man with £80 a week exercises ten times the "pull" on the market, is ten times as important in deciding what shall be produced, as the man with £8 a week.

But this is not a defect of the price mechanism. The price mechanism is neutral. It works just as well, in providing for the wants of the buying public, whether incomes are very unequal or nearly equal. The question is how far the State should go, whether under capitalism or under central planning, in reducing inequality at the cost of also reducing incentives. Great Britain has already gone a long way; there is probably less inequality today in Great Britain than in Soviet Russia, although Soviet Russia has abolished incomes from property. The profit motive leads producers to produce what will sell, and this depends on how spending power is distributed among individuals. The more heavily the rich are taxed, the less they have to spend on luxuries or on anything. The more the poor are helped, through the machinery of public finance, the more it will pay to produce what they want. We should not blame the price system for the unequal distribution of wealth, since this can be reduced to whatever extent is thought desirable without impairing in any way the working of the price mechanism. In this context, it is not production for profit that is the villain of the piece; it is the inequality of wealth.

At the same time, it would be overstating the case for capitalism to suggest that inequality can be reduced to any extent desired without thereby reducing the efficiency of capitalism in the sphere of production. The more closely we approach the distributive ideal of "to each according to his needs," the more we are likely to weaken the incentives to work, to invest, to take risks, to make innovations.

Soviet Russia realized, quite early in her story, the need to pay more to the man who works harder and to provide adequate inducements for relatively scarce skills and qualities. Wherever possible, Soviet Russia pays by results; and the inequality of wages and salaries is as marked behind the Iron Curtain as in any other country. But she has no inequality arising from incomes from property, for she has no private incomes from property.[1] Under capitalism, inequality in this sphere also is necessary in order to provide an incentive for private investment; those who succeed may reap large gains while those who fail will lose their capital. If taxation is too high, in order to pay for the Welfare State, incentives to investment and risk-taking are diminished. The investor does well, and the State takes the greater part of his profits. He does badly, and he gets no compensation. Why should he take risks?

I have referred to this question before, and shall do so again. It is one of the most important of our current issues of economic policy. Some economists think that the State should not take more than about 25 per cent of the national income in taxation. This is quite an arbitrary figure; there is no scientific basis for it; but in a modern industrial country it may be quite near the mark. In Great Britain the State takes well over a third of the national income, and many economists think that this is too much. However this may be, the dilemma is inescapable—somehow a balance must be struck between the desire to reduce inequality and the need to preserve both the ability and the willingness of free enterprise to maintain an adequate volume of investment and to continue the search for better methods and new products. In a totalitarian State the dilemma is avoided, for it is the State that imposes saving on the community and that itself carries out the investment.

3. MIDDLEMEN

Another common belief is that in a society organized "for profit" there is a great deal of waste in the distribution of the goods to

---

[1] Except that people are permitted, and most workers are forced (by deductions from their pay) to buy State loans, which bear interest.

consumers. It is thought that selling costs are too high because there are too many middlemen, each taking his toll of profit, standing between the producer and the consumer.

It is true that fewer workers (and other resources) would be needed to distribute goods if the freedom of choice of consumers were restricted. Suppose that some consumers' goods (shoes, for example), were produced only by the State, which confined its output to a few standard patterns. Consumers would either have to buy one of these patterns or to go without shoes. All the effort that now goes in trying to sell one brand of shoes against the competition of other brands would be dispensed with. There would be no travelling salesmen, no competitive advertising, if consumers had to take what they were given.

Again, consider a restaurant or canteen. If every customer were compelled to have the same standard meal, fewer cooks and waiters would be needed, and there would be less waste from food left over, than if everybody were allowed to choose what he pleased from a long menu.

In the same way, if all shops were Government shops, their numbers could be greatly reduced. Customers would find this less convenient. They would have to go further to get to the nearest shop. But fewer workers (and other resources) would be needed in retail trade.

During the war, Great Britain considerably reduced the number of workers (and other resources) engaged in retail trade, at the cost of greater inconvenience to consumers, in order to divert labour and other resources from retail trade into the war effort. A totalitarian State could do the same thing as a permanent policy. It takes less effort to provide standard rations for an army than to provide the same number of private consumers with whatever each one happens to prefer. The question is whether the advantages of freedom of choice, and the greater convenience to consumers, are worth the so-called

Indeed, the issue is even less clear-cut, for I may remind the reader that under capitalism it is possible to achieve some of the economies that could be brought about by totalitarian rationing, and at the same time to permit those who so prefer to pay more for special qualities or special services. If it is considerably cheaper to make a few patterns by mass-production, it will pay a manufacturer to do this and to rely for his sales on the cheaper prices that he can offer. Multiple stores, supermarkets, and other shops can cut prices by restricting their range of qualities, making customers choose the goods from display counters instead of taking up the time of shop assistants, and selling on a "cash and carry" basis. Cafeterias can offer cheaper meals to customers who are prepared to serve themselves.

Criticism is usually directed not so much against the retailers as against the wholesalers and other who come between the producers and the retailers. Yet they usually perform useful functions. They save time and trouble by bringing the producers and the retailers together. Some of them grade commodities. Grading enables consumers better to satisfy their respective tastes, and producers to get higher prices; it can usually be done more cheaply and effectively on a large scale. Alternatively, many different qualities—for example, of tea or tobacco —may be blended by the middlemen in order to get some particularly choice combinations. Again, some middlemen hold stocks, running the risk that they may be stolen or burned or infested or otherwise damaged or that they may fall in price. If retailers can quickly replenish their stocks from the wholesalers, they can keep down the size of the stocks that they hold themselves; and so can the manufacturers.

In performing all such functions, the middleman is a specialist, and here as elsewhere specialization tends to reduce costs rather than to increase them. This general point may be illustrated by considering what a manufacturer would have to do in order to cut out wholesalers and to sell direct to retailers. First, he would have to get to know the retailers, to discover the particular requirements and credit standing of each. Next, he would have to engage salesmen to call on the retailers at intervals to show samples of his goods and to take orders. The wholesaler usually does this. But he sells the goods of a number of different manufacturers, so that *fewer* salesmen are required than if each manufacturer employed his own. Further, the retailer may prefer this system. An ironmonger, tor example, sells a great variety of different articles. He does not want to waste his time in interviewing a stream of salesmen from each different manufacturer of each article. He would rather deal with a wholesaler who can sell him an assortment of different things, produced by different firms, at the same time. Again, a manufacturer in, say, Birmingham, may make goods bought by, say, 200 retailers in London. If he dealt with them direct he would have to send 200 separate parcels. Transport and packing costs will be less if he sends one large parcel to a wholesaler. And the economy does not end there. True, the wholesaler breaks this large parcel up sooner or later into 200 small ones. But he gets also other large parcels of other goods from other manufacturers, so that he can still send a relatively large parcel to each retailer. This saving in transport costs is perhaps the main reason why goods may pass through several hands. On the surface it seems wasteful, but it may be really the cheapest method.

It is true that some manufacturers do have their own shops. They may wish to create the impression that their products are "exclusive" and of special quality. Or they may have suspected that retailers, selling rival goods also, did not "push" their products enough. But as a rule manufacturers, and farmers too, find that it pays them to use middlemen.

It is interesting to recall that in 1930 Soviet Russia decided to abolish her wholesaling institutions. The factories began selling direct to the retail co-operatives. But it proved very expensive for each factory to maintain contact with all its retailers, and for goods to be handled in such small lots. Within two years wholesale institutions were back again and were recognized to be performing a useful socialist function.

No doubt some middlemen (for example, certain "rings" of whole-salers) may be in a monopoly position and charge too much for their services. But as a general rule middlemen do perform useful functions; if they did not, they could not survive. And the length of "the chain of distribution" often keeps down, rather than raises, the prices paid by the final consumers. The only way in which a totalitarian State can achieve large "savings" is by restricting the freedom of choice of consumers.

4. Bureaucracy

The greater the amount of control exercised by the State, the more is the life of the citizen governed by orders and regulations and made subject to the decisions of officials. He may have to apply for per-mission, not always granted, to build a house or a factory, to keep a pig, to engage a domestic servant, to import American nylons, to travel abroad.

Some people deeply resent the growing intervention of the State into their business and their private lives. Others accept it, or even welcome it, as essential in order to direct economic activity in the interests of the community as a whole, and to provide social security for all.

I think it is generally agreed that in a modern community the State should do a good deal. It should provide services such as defence, the maintenance of law and order, and preventive public health measures, which cannot or should not be provided by private enterprises operat-ing for profit. It may provide, many people think it should provide or at least help to pay for, various social services such as education and medical treatment. It should endeavour, notably through its monetary policy and perhaps a flexible public works programme, to maintain a high and stable level of employment. It should prevent or control private monopoly. It must impose and collect taxes in order to pay for all these activities.

There is by no means general agreement, however, on how far the State should go in various directions. The totalitarian State, of course, goes all the way. But how much control should the State exercise under capitalism? How far should the State itself—that is to say, either the central or local governments or some public authority—act as an entrepreneur and operate various industries?

The view which I want to discuss is the view that the State is inevitably less efficient than private enterprise. It is a view, or prejudice, that is widely held. If it were correct, it would follow that the State should restrict its activities to the minimum needed to achieve its objects. Let it pay for education for all, if that is the agreed policy, but let private enterprise build the schools. Let it control public utilities, since they tend to be local monopolies, but do not let it nationalize them and run them as State enterprises. Let it try to control the national economy by general monetary and public-finance measures rather than by a host of detailed regulations over individual activities and over the importation, production and consumption of particular commodities.

One general point in favour of this view is that the more controls there are, the greater is the number of civil servants required to administer them. In Great Britain, for example, the number of civil servants employed (apart from the nationalized industries) by the central and local governments is now over $2\frac{1}{2}$ million.[1] Before the war it was less than 1·4 million. If the State were to exercise less detailed supervision over the national economy, a considerable number of civil servants could be released for private employment.

Another general point, which fortunately does not apply to Great Britain, is that in some countries some of the civil servants are open to bribery. Every new control widens the scope for graft and corruption by creating new opportunities for granting or withholding permits.

The view that civil servants are less efficient than their business colleagues is widely held. But how can it be true? Many of them have been drawn from the same circles, have had the same education and upbringing; it is often a matter of chance whether a particular individual chooses a Government or a business career. Business firms have been glad to attract certain civil servants into their employment and to pay them large salaries. The abilities and qualities of the individual do not change because he is working for the Government rather than for a private enterprise.

If, therefore, the State is in fact less efficient as an entrepreneur, this must arise from the special conditions governing State enterprise and not from an inferior personnel. It is claimed, by opponents of State enterprise, that the State is handicapped (except, of course, under a totalitarian dictatorship) by the need to justify its actions to Parliament and the electorate.

[1] This does not agree with the figure of 1·3 million given on page 11 because some workers employed by the central and local governments are now classed under their field of employment; for example, most Post Office workers are now classed under "Communications."

But in June, 1958, the Central Government employed 1·04 million workers, and local governments 1·60 million. Armed Forces and Women's Services were 0·61 million, and 2·58 million were employed in the nationalized industries, such as railways and coalmining.

Hence, it is said, civil servants, dealing with public money, have to be more cautious than business men. When a State enterprise is an obvious failure, as was the ill-conceived Tanganyka groundnuts scheme, it has to face the full glare of adverse publicity. This need for caution leads to delay; it explains the need for "red tape." It is true that in a large business many decisions must be taken by salaried managers and other employees, who have to justify them, like civil servants, to their superiors. But on the whole private enterprise can act more promptly, and take more risks, than the State.

We must not exaggerate this point. But it may reasonably be doubted whether all the many new industries and other innovations of our present age would have come about, at any rate so fast, if there had been no private enterprise to make experiments and take risks in the hope of profits.

5. CONCLUSIONS

The two great defects of capitalism are monopoly and unemployment. The totalitarian State is, or could be, free from both.

The anti-social aspect of private monopoly is that one group tries to benefit itself by acting contrary to the interests of the community. Either it restricts output directly, or it prevents labour and capital from entering its preserves, where they would render more valuable services than where they are. When all means of production are owned by the State and there is no private capital to make profits, there is no private monopoly. Production can go full steam ahead, unhampered by restrictive practices.

In the same way, there need never be any significant amount of unemployment when all economic activity is directed by the State. The decision to restrict the output of consumers' goods to a certain level in order to employ more labour and other resources in the capital goods industries is both a decision to save and a decision to invest; there can be no discrepancy between the amount of planned saving and the amount of planned investment, for the two coincide: they are one and the same. The trade cycle vanishes; it is a phenomenon peculiar to capitalism. Nor need there be any unemployment due to inadequate mobility of labour when workers can be ordered to move to where they are needed.

A democratic Government is often tempted to favour some large group of voters even when this means acting against the interests of the community as a whole. Thus the Government of the United States, although pledged to outlaw monopoly, guarantees high minimum prices for farm products and will compulsorily restrict the output of any farm product in order to keep up its price, if asked to do so by a majority of the farmers concerned. The British Government continues to restrict road transport in order to maintain employment on the railways. Most democratic Governments are reluctant to make a determined drive against the restrictive practices of trade unions.

The totalitarian State can ride rough-shod over such sectional interests. It may have a facade of elections, but in fact it is a dictatorship that has no need to play for votes or to court popularity with particular groups. The State is supreme and can tolerate no rivals, such as independent trade unions, of any real strength. Whatever the State decides to be in the general interest will be done. Each for all and all for each.

How far the policy of a totalitarian State will be directed with wisdom and foresight in the interests of the community as a whole is another matter. A dictator is not necessarily a good economist, nor is there any guarantee that he will receive good advice and follow it. He is in a position to do great harm as well as great good. His personal prejudices or ambitions may lead to famine or may plunge the country into war.

To some extent, whether a person favours capitalism or totalitarianism depends on his view of what is likely to happen. For example, will capitalism be able to prevent mass unemployment? Some think "yes" and some think "no"; we cannot be certain.

But suppose we knew that under capitalism there would continue to be trade depressions, leading to unemployment of, say, 10 per cent (or 15 or 20 per cent) in one year, on the average, out of every ten. Would this mean that capitalism is a hopeless system and at all costs should be replaced by a totalitarian system that guarantees full employment? This is a question on which different people would make different value-judgments.

In other words, as this example shows, the whole issue is "ideological." To what extent are we prepared to sacrifice democracy and personal freedom in order to get rid of unemployment, private monopoly, and other defects of capitalism? Each will answer the question in his own way.

PART V

THE DISTRIBUTION OF INCOMES

CHAPTER XXV

A GENERAL VIEW OF DISTRIBUTION

1. Differences in Personal Incomes

I have called this Part "The Distribution of Incomes." The word "distribution" does not relate, in the present context, to the processes of transport and marketing through which goods are distributed from producers to consumers. It is the traditional term for the division of the national income among the various groups of wage-earners, property-owners and others.

The question that most interests the general public is probably the inequality of personal incomes. Why do some people have larger incomes than others?

It is convenient to approach this problem by considering separately incomes from property and incomes from work. Incomes from property include rent, interest, and dividends and other profits on capital. Incomes from work include salaries, wages, and other incomes earned by personal exertion. There are some personal incomes which are "mixed," derived partly from property and partly from work: for example, the income of a farmer who both owns and manages his own farm; but this does not affect the general argument. There are also some incomes which are derived neither from property nor from work: for example, non-contributory old-age pensions, which may be regarded as "transfers" or collective gifts from the taxpayers. Again, some incomes, such as the royalties of authors or contributory pensions, may be difficult to classify; they can perhaps be regarded as deferred incomes from work performed in the past. But the great majority of incomes are derived either from ownership or from personal exertion.

The inequality of incomes from property is due mainly to the different amounts of property which different people own. Some own a great deal of property, others a moderate amount, and most very little apart from personal effects, such as furniture, which do not yield a money income.

Some large fortunes have been built up from nothing by their present owners. Men of outstanding business ability, aided perhaps by good luck, have developed giant undertakings from small beginnings.

Most large individual holdings of property, however, have been inherited, or have been built up on the basis of a substantial inheritance.

A person who enjoys an inherited fortune does so through no merit of his own. The case for inheritance is that the possibility of passing on one's wealth, or part of it, to one's family is a powerful incentive to work and save. But the amount that can be passed on is restricted, in Great Britain, by "progressive" taxation on fortunes changing hands at death.

It is beyond the scope of economic analysis to inquire into the origins of individual fortunes. Some may go back, for example, to the dissolution of the monasteries, or to favours bestowed by Charles II. I have discussed the arguments for and against the institution of private property; we must accept the present distribution of private property among individuals as a *datum*. The practical political issue is how far it can be modified by taxation without unduly weakening the incentives to effort and investment. Are our present rates of taxation on profits and other property incomes, and on inheritance, too light or are they too heavy?

It does fall within the scope of economic analysis, however, to consider what forces determine the money income yielded by different types of property: the "rent" on land and other assets which are fixed in amount, and the "quasi-rent" on assets which cannot be considerably increased or diminished in amount until some years have elapsed. The forces determining the rate of interest currently paid on new loans and the expected rate of profit on new investment are also within the field of economic analysis—very much so. I discuss these questions in the present Part.

The inequality of incomes from work arises largely from differences in capacities and skills. Some people have innate qualities of mind or body which enable them to earn more than others. Acquired skill, however, and knowledge, depend on education and training. In the past, as in some countries today, only well-to-do parents could afford to give their children a good education, which would open to them the door of a well-paid career; and the number of scholarships was relatively small. In the same way, only the richer parents could provide their sons with capital to set up in business. Inequality breeds inequality.

The question with which economic analysis is most competent to deal is that of differences in rates of pay between occupations, for different types of labour. This is the main subject dealt with in Chapter XXVI, which is headed "Wages" but is meant to cover all types of income from work.

The theory of Distribution has traditionally confined itself mainly to a study of the price system as affecting the prices of factors of production—land, labour, and capital. This is only part, although a large and important part, of the study of inequality of personal incomes. But the other relevant influences affecting inequality—notably differences in the amount of property held by individuals and differences in innate and acquired abilities—fall outside the scope of economic analysis. Economists can make only broad generalizations about them.

2. The Share of Labour

An interesting question is what proportion of the national income goes to incomes from work and what proportion to incomes from property.

The proportions vary somewhat from year to year. Profits vary more than wages and other incomes. Total profits, and therefore the share going to property, tend to be high in good years and low in years of depression.

Personal income in the United Kingdom in 1958 was distributed as follows:[1]

PERSONAL INCOME (BEFORE TAX): U.K. 1958

	£ million
Income from Employment	
Wages and Salaries	12,090
Pay in cash and kind of the Forces	398
Employers' contributions	
(*a*) National insurance and health	398
(*b*) Other	527
Total income from employment	13,413
Income from Self-Employment	
Professional persons	290
Farmers	439
Other sole-traders and partnerships	1,107
Total income from self-employment	1,836
Other Income	
Rent, dividends, and interest	2,191
National insurance benefits and other current grants from public authorities	1,488
Total Personal Income	18,928

Employers' contributions to the National Insurance Funds and to pension schemes and provident funds for their employees are included in incomes from work, as these contributions are for the benefit of employees.

We do not know how much of the income of a self-employed person, such as a farmer who runs his own farm or a shop-keeper who runs his own shop, should be attributed to personal exertion—his work of management—and how much to profit on the capital which he has

[1] Figures from Blue Book: *National Income and Expenditure* (1959), Table 2.

invested in his business. Personally I doubt whether as much as a quarter of the income of a professional worker such as a doctor or a barrister, or of a small farmer or shop-keeper, represents profit on his capital. However, as no direct statistics are available on this point,[1] let us assume that only half, £918 million, represented income from work. But let us deduct from the other half the various allowances for depreciation (£177 million), leaving £741 million.

It follows that the share of labour in the total of personal incomes was £13,413 million plus £918 million, or over 76 per cent, and that the share of property was £2,191 million plus £741 million, or less than 16 per cent. The remaining 8 per cent consisted of national insurance benefits and other current grants (public assistance etc.) from public authorities.

It may be argued that the undistributed profits of companies (less depreciation) should be included in income from property.[2] These amounted to perhaps £1,800 million (of which over half was paid in taxation); their inclusion would raise the share of property to some 23 per cent.

The year 1958 was not exceptional. The percentage of the national income going to work has been around 75, with minor variations from year to year, for a long time.

In the United States the proportion going to work has averaged about 75 per cent during recent decades. In most under-developed countries also the share of labour averages 70 to 80 per cent.

In Great Britain, as in most western countries, the economic position of the average worker has been improved, not only absolutely but also relatively to that of the average property-owner, during recent times. This relative improvement has been brought about mainly through the machinery of public finance. Special taxes on property, such as death duties and profit taxes, have been considerably increased. Heavier rates of income-tax on large incomes have hit property incomes more than work incomes. Hence the net share, after taxation, of property incomes has been reduced more than the net share of work incomes. Meanwhile, public expenditure has been increasingly on social services, which benefit mainly workers rather than property-owners. At the same time, hours of work have been reduced; workers today enjoy considerably more leisure than in the past.

The question whether property-owners have any right to exact a toll of around 20 per cent of the national income, whether the whole

---

[1] In 1958 the various allowances for depreciation to companies operating in the United Kingdom were £979 million on gross trading profits of £3,002 million. The depreciation allowances to self-employed persons were £177 million. If their gross profits were in the same proportion to their depreciation allowances as those of companies, they were only about £530 million.

[2] I exclude the trading profits of public corporations and of the central government and local authorities, as these accrue to the nation as a whole and not to individuals.

of the national income should not go to labour, is the question I have
already discussed at length, of the merits and defects of a system based
on private property. It is relevant to note that only a part of this
20 per cent is spent on the personal consumption of property-owners.
A large slice is taken by taxation, and another large slice is undistributed profits which are ploughed back into the business or invested
elsewhere. If all private property were confiscated by the State and
(a large assumption!) output did not fall off, as much money as at
present would still be needed for public revenue and for investment
(all of which would have to be made by the State if private property
were abolished). A much smaller percentage than 20 would be
available for redistribution to the workers.

An increase in the amount of private investment would benefit the
workers although it might at the same time increase the share of
property. At present some under-developed countries are very short
of capital. Suppose that foreign investment in such a country were to
increase the national output from 100 to 120 a year. Even if the
foreign investors had to be paid 10 a year, the country would still be
10 per cent better off. Formerly the national income might have been
divided 80 to work and 20 to property. Now property would get 30
(10 to foreign investors), but labour would get 90 instead of 80.

What are the forces determining the percentage shares (before taxation) of work and property? Other things being equal, an increase
in the number of workers tends to reduce real wages per head owing
to the consequent fall in the marginal productivity of labour. But it
may increase the share going to labour as a whole, for the increase in
numbers may outweigh the fall in real wages per head. In the same
way, an increase in capital tends to reduce the rate of return on
capital, but it may increase the share of interest and profits in the
national income. The growth of population tends to raise the absolute
total of rents, but it may not raise the percentage of rent in an
increased national income.

On the demand side, a general increase in the demand for labour,
such as occurred during the war, tends to raise the percentage going
to work, whereas a large increase in the demand for capital—due, for
example, to a widespread desire for more housing—would tend to
reduce it. Under perfect competition, capital-saving inventions
(which raise the marginal productivity of labour relatively to that of
capital) would tend to raise the share of labour, and labour-saving
inventions to lower it. We tend to think that most inventions are
labour-saving, but we must remember that every invention that
improves the efficiency of plant and equipment and other capital
goods is capital-saving: it enables the same amount of capital to make
a bigger contribution to output.

A reduction in rates of interest, which can be brought about, within limits, by monetary policy, tends to reduce the share going to capital.

In Great Britain and the United States, the growth of capital during the present century has been about twice as great as the growth of population, but the share of labour has somewhat increased.

3. THE MARGINAL PRODUCTIVITY THEORY

The marginal productivity theory of distribution explains how the prices of the various factors of production would be determined under conditions of perfect competition and full employment.

Some factors of production (for example, materials such as coal or steel or cotton) are commodities which are used up in the process of production and are bought outright. The theory covers them, but it is used mainly to explain the prices paid for the services of factors of production which are hired by the week or month or year: the levels of wages and rents and rates of interest. It explains also the earnings of fixed assets such as plant and machinery. For this purpose we must divide factors of production into homogeneous groups. The price of every unit in such a group will tend to be the same, even if some are employed in one industry and some in another. Each acre of land of a given grade will command the same rent, for by definition each acre is equal in all respects to every other acre in that grade. They are perfect substitutes for one another, and will therefore tend to have the same price. In the same way, each worker of a particular type will tend to get the same wage, for an equal amount of work, as every other worker in the same group; and similarly with every other type of factor.

The essence of the theory can be stated briefly. The demand for a factor of production is a *derived demand*. The farmer, for example, rents land or employs workers or buys a tractor or fertilizers simply and solely for the contribution that each factor makes to his output and thereby to his receipts. The physical marginal productivity of any factor falls, as we saw in Chapter VII, as more units of it are combined with a given amount of other factors, or as the proportion of that factor is increased. The price of any factor, under perfect competition, will equal the value of its marginal product.

Let us consider a firm. Under perfect competition, it must accept the prevailing prices for both its products and its factors. They are market facts which it is powerless to alter. What it can do and does do is to decide how many units of each factor it will employ.

Suppose that one additional worker of a certain type would add x units a week to the output. If the wages of that worker are less than the price received for x units of product, then it will pay to employ him. By employing him, the firm will increase its profits by the excess of its receipts from *x* more units of its product over the wages of the additional worker. The same reasoning applies to any other factor: for example, it pays a farmer to use more fertilizer so long as the resulting increase in his output brings him in more money than he has to pay for the extra fertilizer.

This gives us the rule that the price of a factor equals (or at any rate closely approaches) the value of its marginal product. For example, suppose that a particular firm can vary the number of workers of a certain type which it employs, and that their physical marginal productivity falls as follows—

Number of Workers	Marginal Product (per week)
9	27
10	24
11	20

The firm would be in equilibrium in any of the following situations: price of product (per unit) 5s., wages (per week) £6 15s., 9 workers employed; price of product 5s., wages £6, 10 workers employed; price of product 5s., wages £5, 11 workers employed; wages £6, price of product $£\frac{6}{27}$ (nearly 4s. 6d.), 9 workers employed; wages £6, price of product 6s., 11 workers employed. If the prices of its products remain the same, a firm will tend to employ more of any factor when its price falls, and less when its price rises. If the prices of its factors remain the same, it will tend to employ more factors when the prices of its products rise, and less when they fall.

An increase in the demand for products requiring a particular type of factor (or requiring it in a higher proportion, relatively to other factors, than in other industries) will tend to raise its price. Thus an increased demand for armaments tends to raise the wages of engineering and steel workers, and the price of steel; an increased demand for houses tends to raise the wages of building labour and the prices of building materials; food subsidies tend to raise land rents.

How much the price of a factor rises in such circumstances depends on how far the supply of it can be increased. If a fairly small increase in wages in a given occupation will quickly attract workers from other occupations, the result will be an increase in the number of workers attached to that occupation (an increased supply of the factor) and only a small increase in their wages. If, on the other hand, the number in that occupation is more or less fixed for the time being (owing, for example, to the length of training required), the rise in wages, due to the competition of the various firms for the limited labour available, may be considerable.

To illustrate this point, let us return to our little table. Suppose the firm is in equilibrium with wages at £6 15s., price of product 5s., and

9 workers employed, with a marginal product of 27 units. Suppose
that the price of the product rises, say, to 7s. If the supply of such
workers is fairly elastic, this firm may increase the number it employs
to 11, and other firms also may employ more of such workers. An
increase in their wages to only £7 (equal to the value of their marginal product, 20 × 7s.) might restore equilibrium. Suppose, on the
other hand, that the supply of such workers to that industry cannot be
increased. Their marginal productivity will remain at 27 units, and
their wages may rise to £9 9s. (27 × 7s.).

When the demand for the products of an industry falls, but the
demand for other products remains the same or increases, those factors
of production that can readily move into other industries and earn as
much there, will not suffer. Only enough of them need move to raise
the physical marginal product of those who remain sufficiently to
compensate for its fall in price per unit. For example, if our firm were
formerly employing 10 workers at £6 a week with a marginal productivity of 24 units, and the price of a unit falls from 5s. to 4s. 6d., a
reduction in the number of workers to 9 will again make the value of
their marginal product (27 × 4s. 6d.) equal to (in fact, slightly higher
than) their wage of £6. If this firm is typical of other firms in the
industry, the total exodus of such workers to other industries would
need to be only 10 per cent for their wages to remain unchanged.
Their physical marginal productivity in other industries would be
somewhat reduced, and this would tend to reduce their wages, but
this tendency would be offset in so far as the demand for the products
of these other industries had increased, consumers having transferred
some of their expenditure from the product of the first industry to these
products.

In general, therefore, changes in the demand for different products,
the demand for some increasing and for others decreasing, will have
little effect on the prices of factors that can readily be employed in
any of a number of industries. For example, if the total demand for
agricultural produce remains the same, land rents are unlikely to
change when the demand for one crop rises and the demand for another
falls, provided that enough land can be transferred from the latter to
the former. Again, the wages of workers who could be employed in
any one of many industries, such as porters and typists and lorry-
drivers, are not likely to be affected by changes in the relative demand
for different products.

The factors that do suffer from a fall in the price of a product are
those that are specific to that industry and cannot be used (unless
they accept much lower earnings) elsewhere. For example, skilled
coal-miners working at the face and earning high wages, would suffer
by a large fall in the demand for coal, and rubber-tappers would suffer
by a fall in the demand for rubber. In most industries, the fixed assets

such as plant and equipment are specific to that industry. A blast furnace or a cotton spindle or a printing press cannot be used for any other purpose (except to be sold as scrap). The owners of such assets therefore receive less, making smaller profits or making losses, until enough time has elapsed for the "capacity" of the industry to be reduced sufficiently to restore profits to their normal level. The earnings of such assets were called by Marshall *quasi-rent*, because in the short run they are "price-determined": they depend on the prices of their products and on the prices of the other factors.

Apart from changes in the demand for products, the demand for different factors may change owing to technical progress. Mechanical looms reduced the wages of handloom workers; calculating and recording machines reduced the demand for clerks. Technical progress which causes factor A to be substituted for factor B will tend to raise the price of A and to reduce the price of B—or, alternatively, to expand the supply of A and contract the supply of B—until their prices are equal to their new marginal productivities.

On the supply side, an increase in the supply of any factor will tend to reduce its price because, in the absence of other changes, its physical marginal productivity will fall in all the industries in which it is employed. For example, a large influx of immigrants tends to reduce local wages and to raise local land values and house rents; an increased amount of free capital available for lending tends to reduce rates of interest; an increase in the number of ships tends to reduce ocean freight charges. Conversely, a reduction in the supply of a factor tends to raise its price.

An increase in the amount of a factor employed in an industry (the demand for the product remaining the same) has a twofold downward influence on its price. In the first place, the physical marginal productivity of that factor falls when it is combined with other factors in a larger proportion than before. In the second place, the absorption of more units of that factor in the industry will probably mean an expansion in the output of the industry and, consequently, a fall in the price of its products. The value of the marginal product of that factor will fall both because the amount of it falls and because the price per unit of it falls.

As time goes on, various changes will take place. New methods of production will be employed, and new industries will arise. The supplies of different factors will alter, and technical progress will change the relative demand for them. The theory of marginal productivity is in no way discredited because the growth of population in western countries has been accompanied by a rise and not a fall in real wages; there has been continuous technical progress, and capital has increased considerably more than population. Nor is it discredited because, for example, the prices of horses and oats and land growing oats remain high despite the coming of the motor vehicle; adjustments were made on the supply side, fewer horses being bred and less oats grown. The theory, like the law of diminishing returns on which it is based, applies to the short run, to the situation as it is at any given moment. When the circumstances change, the conclusions drawn from the former data no longer hold good, but new conclusions drawn from the new data may well be valid.

4. Criticisms of the Marginal Productivity Theory

The theory assumes that the proportions between the factors can be varied. I have argued in Chapter VII that this assumption is more realistic than it may seem at the first blush. It is true, however, that in the short run the proportions in some particular firms may be fixed. For example, one man may be needed for each machine. In such a case, the entrepreneur will consider the man and the machine as one unit, and will relate the (weekly) cost of that unit to its (weekly) marginal product. The theory assumes that the price per unit of a factor will be the same in every industry in which it is employed. This implies that there is sufficient mobility to bring about this result. I have discussed this question in Chapter XXI. It may be that some groups of workers will prefer to remain where they are rather than move to where they can earn more; if so, then to that extent the theory needs to be modified. But the assumption is true for most factors.

The theory assumes that the amount and value of the marginal product of a factor is known to the entrepreneur. This is not always true. For example, a farmer does not know how large his crop will be, for that will depend on the weather and other circumstances, nor does he know what its price per unit will be. But he must nevertheless decide how many units of each factor to employ. We can allow for this by saying that he relates the price of a factor to the *expected* value of its marginal product.

Some goods take a considerable time to produce; an entrepreneur pays his factors for months or perhaps years before his products are made and can be sold. He cannot afford, therefore, to pay them the full value of their marginal product, but only its *discounted* value—the present value of what he will receive when he sells the product.

The theory assumes, subject to these minor corrections, that each factor will be paid the value of its marginal product. Why cannot the employer, who hires the other factors, exploit them by paying them less? The theory assumes that this is not possible because any factor can act as the entrepreneur and hire the other factors. If a landlord thinks that the farmer is paying him too little rent, he can work his land himself, perhaps hiring a manager. If a shop assistant thinks he is being exploited, he can rent a shop, obtaining goods on credit, and set up as a shopkeeper on his own account. If a group of workers think that their wages are too low, they can borrow the capital to set up in business for themselves. Hence no factor can gain merely by acting as the hirer of the others.

This assumption is not true for large-scale establishments. A group of workers would not be able to borrow enough capital to buy, say, an oil refinery or a liner. Their defence against exploitation is not the possibility of turning the tables by becoming the entrepreneurs; it is the competition for their services by the different firms in their industry and in any other industries where they could be employed.

The theory assumes perfect competition. Some critics say that this makes it quite useless as an explanation of the real world, where the general rule is imperfect competition.

They say that the distribution of income between labour and capital depends on the degree of monopoly. It depends on the relation between wages bills and gross profit margins. Suppose, for example, that a firm makes an article with an average cost of £1 a unit, 10s. for labour and 10s. for materials. If it adds a profit margin of 50 per cent, fixing the price at 30s., this means that 10s. goes to labour and 10s. to capital. If it added only, say, 20 per cent, fixing the price at 24s., this would mean a division between labour and capital in the ratio of 10s. to 4s., or 5 to 2.

It should be noted that in this type of calculation the share of capital is taken as including the depreciation reserves set aside to provide for renewals and replacements of fixed assets.

It is quite true that in so far as monopoly power is used to make the share of profits greater than it would otherwise be, this is a fact which any theory of distribution should take into account. What proportion of the 15 per cent or so of the national income of Great Britain that goes to profits (after deducting depreciation) represents monopoly profits, over and above the profit that would be earned under conditions approaching perfect competition, is a matter of opinion. It can be argued that in the nationalized industries monopoly power tends to be used to raise the share of labour: that the public corporations are tempted to yield to pressure for higher wages in those industries, and then to cover the increased labour costs by raising the prices of the products—for example, electricity charges or rail or bus fares.

Another consequence of monopoly is that output in certain fields is less than it would be under perfect competition. In such fields, the demand for all factors is less than it would be if output were not restricted. This adversely affects the relative prices of those factors that are employed in a higher proportion in those fields than elsewhere. For example, monopoly in the chemical industries would keep down the demand for industrial chemists and would tend to depress their earnings. But this effect can be counteracted by adjustments in the supply of different factors. Thus, if fewer men trained as industrial chemists, because their earnings were relatively low, the reduction in their numbers would eventually raise their earnings to the levels prevailing in other professions.

In so far as prices are fixed above marginal costs (which are factor-prices) it is not true that the price of a factor will equal the value of its marginal product; the latter will be higher. But I do not think it follows that we should throw the marginal productivity theory over-board. The law of diminishing returns, on which it is based, relates to the effect on amounts of product of varying the combination of factors, and is just as valid under monopoly as under perfect competition. It is seldom that a firm can fix the prices it pays for its factors; in general, firms have to pay whatever prices are ruling in the market for the labour and materials and other factors that they buy or hire. An increase in the supply of a factor will tend to reduce its price, and a decrease in the supply of it will tend to raise its price, owing to the decrease or increase in its physical marginal productivity when more or fewer units of it are employed; the relative prices of factors will reflect their relative marginal productivities; an increased demand for a product will tend to raise the prices of factors employed in a high proportion, relatively to other factors, in that industry, and a decreased demand for the product will do the opposite; and all this is equally true whether competition is perfect or imperfect.

The theory also assumes full employment. If some units of a factor are hired at a certain price while others remain idle, the latter, it is assumed, will offer their services somewhat more cheaply rather than get nothing at all; and in this way the price of a unit of that factor will be reduced to whatever level will enable all units of it to find employment. This assumption may apply, more or less, to land and capital. But it is manifestly untrue of labour. In some countries minimum wages are fixed by law, and in most western countries the trade unions will usually resist reductions in wages below a certain level.

The general reasoning of the marginal productivity theory still applies. But where there is considerable unemployment, an increased demand for the products of those industries will lead to fuller employment rather than higher wages, and a decreased demand for these products will lead to greater unemployment rather than lower wages.

Whether a general reduction in wages would expand employment, as the theory assumes, is far from certain. In certain circumstances it would; for example, the rapid recovery in Australia from the Great Depression was associated with a general reduction in wages of 26 per cent, imposed by the Commonwealth Arbitration Court. In other circumstances it might not; the consequent reduction in the amount of spending by wage-earners might lead to a further fall in the volume of investment.

The marginal productivity theory is a micro-economic theory and needs to be supplemented by a general theory of output and employment such as that of Keynes. Moreover, some of its assumptions, as we have seen, are incorrect or apply only to part of the economy. Nevertheless I repeat that in my view it is useful as a first approximation, and there is no other general theory of distribution which is superior to it.

5. DIFFERENCES BETWEEN COUNTRIES

The effect of relative supplies of different factors on relative factor prices is well illustrated by differences between countries.

In overpopulated countries wages are low. It is bad luck for a child to be born in such a country—bad luck, that is, so far as his earning power is concerned. For the same capacities and efforts will yield him a considerably lower income than in a country where labour is relatively more scarce. The wages of unskilled labour in India, for example, are only about three shillings a day.

Capital, on the other hand, yields a higher rate of return in such countries, where it is relatively scarce. The total share of capital in the national income may be only 20 per cent or less, but that is because there is so little capital compared with the amount of labour; rates of interest and profit (unless kept down by law, in which case new investment, although badly needed, is discouraged) tend to be high.[1]

Where land is relatively abundant, as in Canada or Australia, rents per acre tend to be low; where it is relatively scarce, as in Great Britain or Japan, they tend to be high.

An apparent exception to the generalization about wages is that in some under-developed countries qualified doctors, engineers, and other professional men earn substantially more than in most western countries. It will be found, however, when the facts are examined, that these apparent exceptions confirm the general rule. In such countries there has been comparatively little university and technical education, and the numbers available for such posts are few relatively to the demand for them. In Japan, where technical education has been widespread, engineers begin at only £15 a month, rising eventually

---

[1] Some economists would not agree with this paragraph. They would argue that the marginal productivity of capital may be higher in a country such as Great Britain, which has more external economies; or that the demand for capital in a poor country is limited by its low real income.

Of course, some investments may not pay. A country may be too small a market for a particular factory; some labour-saving devices may not yield a profit because labour is abundant and cheap. Nevertheless, my own belief is that a well-selected programme of complementary investments would usually give high yields, at any rate in terms of national income.

to perhaps £50 a month; in India, where there is quite a number of universities, most doctors and lawyers earn comparatively low incomes.

On the demand side, a change in the demand for the exports of a country affects especially the factors employed in a large proportion in the export industries. For example, the demand for wool increased greatly after the war; its price rose, at the peak, to over ten times its pre-war levels. This had the effect of raising most money incomes in Australia, which is the chief exporter of wool, but especially the capital values or rental values of sheep stations and the wages earned by sheep-shearers.

CHAPTER XXVI

WAGES

1. INDEPENDENT WORKERS

A WAGE may be defined as a sum of money paid under contract by an employer to a worker in exchange for services rendered. There is no need for us to attempt to distinguish between wages and salaries. But the earnings of independent workers require some consideration.

An independent worker is one who works on his own account and not for an employer. His income is partly profit on his own capital, which he has invested in his own business, and partly earnings from his personal exertion.

Some independent workers—for example, those managing large businesses of their own, or successful barristers or authors—have large incomes. I think the general belief is that independent workers are usually better off than wage-earners. But in fact the majority of independent workers in most countries are small farmers, and where they have only tiny holdings (two to three acres on the average in China, for example) they get lower incomes than even unskilled wage-earners. In Great Britain the average shopkeeper or small tradesman, working on his own account, earns less than most skilled wage-earners.

When we consider differences in earnings between occupations we must take account of independent workers. In most professions, for example, many are working on their own account. The tendency is for the incomes of independent workers to exceed those of comparable employees in the same field only by the profit on their own capital. For example, a doctor or a dentist can either have his own practice or work for the National Health Service; a qualified accountant can either work for a firm or set up on his own; even a shop assistant could usually find the capital to take up hawking, if not to rent a shop.

We must therefore include independent workers in the supply of labour, both in general and in particular occupations, and we must include their incomes, less profit on their own capital, in the share of the national income going to labour.

But there is a very important difference between their incomes and those of paid employees. Their incomes fluctuate more, over time, than those of employees. For they are selling their products or services directly to the market, while the latter are selling their services to an employer who pays an agreed rate which it is difficult to alter

367

frequently. Thus the gains or losses arising from changes in the prices of products accrue to independent workers, who are their own employers, but in the case of paid employees they accrue to the firm which employs them.

It is an important fact that many agricultural commodities are produced largely by farmers who work their own farms. When the prices of these products fall, many farmers respond by maintaining or even increasing their output, hoping that this will pay them better than temporarily leaving their land idle and seeking a different occupation; if unemployment is widespread, there may be no other jobs available for them. Thus the prices of such products may fall heavily. Over the period 1928 to 1932, the prices of many agricultural products fell by 50 per cent or more. The incomes of most farmers were reduced to very low levels. They were their own employers, selling directly to the market, and hence they could not escape the consequences of the decreased demand for their products.

An industry such as coal-mining, in which nearly all the workers are wage-earners, provides a striking contrast. A large decrease in the demand for coal reduces the value-productivity of miners' labour. But the miners claim that they are entitled to a certain minimum standard of living and resist any large cuts in their wages. Hence a number of pits can no longer be worked at a profit, and are closed; the diminution in the supply of coal prevents any great fall in its price; and the marginal value-productivity of coal-mining labour is kept about equal to its wage by a considerable reduction in the amount of labour employed.

Broadly speaking, a marked fall in the demand for, say, wheat cuts down the incomes of wheat-farmers, although they remain "fully employed," whereas a marked fall in the demand for coal causes unemployment among coal-miners. The wages of industrial workers are considerably more stable than the incomes of farmers, but unemployment is mainly an industrial, and not an agricultural, phenomenon.

Is the moral that there is more in the marginal productivity theory than it is fashionable nowadays to suppose, and that unemployment during a depression could be overcome by heavy cuts in wages? The real incomes of wage-earners would fall less than their money incomes, for a general fall in labour costs would bring down the cost of living. But the trade unions know that it is difficult for them to obtain large increases in wages when times are good and they resist reductions when times are bad; in practice, remedies for slumps must probably be sought along the lines proposed by Keynes, even if drastic cuts in wages would maintain full employment among wage-earners in the same way that drastic cuts in incomes maintain full employment among independent workers.

2. The General Level of Wages

What really matters to the worker is not his money wage but what he can buy with it. If his cost of living rises more than his money wage, he is worse off; his real wages have fallen.

Trade unions naturally try to obtain increases in money wages whenever they can. If increases in money wages correspond to increases in the productivity of labour, the cost of living will not rise, for the additional spending power will be matched by an additional output of goods. But if money wages are increased without a corresponding increase in productivity, the cost of living is likely to rise, the increase in labour costs being passed on to consumers. Otherwise there will be unemployment, for most firms cannot afford to employ as many workers as before at a higher wage if the value of their marginal product remains the same.

Suppose that an industry is modernized by the investment of capital, embodying new methods and devices. The average output per worker will considerably increase. Should the workers get a corresponding increase in their wages?

The increase in their (average) productivity is due to the new investment and not to any greater efforts on their part. They will gain, in common with other consumers, in so far as the new methods give them better products or cheaper prices. They will gain, as workers, in so far as increased investment tends to raise the marginal productivity of labour relatively to that of capital. But if they insist on so large an increase in wages that the extra profit on successful innovations is swallowed up, they are wiping out the incentive to investors to take risks: they are killing the goose that lays the golden eggs.

Suppose that an increase in the demand for a certain product raises its price. The value, although not the amount, of the marginal product of labour in that industry is thereby increased. It is reasonable for the workers to demand higher wages, now that the industry can afford to pay more, although the extent to which their wages will be raised is limited if similar workers are readily available from other industries whose products have not risen in price.

But if workers demand higher wages when the prices of their products rise, they should equally be prepared to accept lower wages when the prices of their products fall, although any such fall would be limited if workers could readily find employment in other industries.

In practice, there is usually some increase in wages when product prices rise and some decrease when they fall, but wages remain much more stable than profits; it is usually profits that take most of the gain when prices go up and meet most of the loss when they fall.

The general level of real wages, as distinct from money wages, depends partly on the share of labour in the national income, and it

N   B.E.

may also vary from time to time with changes in the terms of trade. But it is governed predominantly by the volume of output per head. Real wages in western countries have doubled or trebled over the past fifty to a hundred years because output per head has doubled or trebled; they are so much higher than in under-developed countries because output per head is so much higher. The only way to give everyone a bigger slice of cake is to have a larger cake to divide.

3. Differences in Earnings within an Occupation

An occupation, in the ordinary sense of the term, may include several distinct kinds or grades of labour. The general and the private are both in the Army, the brain specialist and the general practitioner are both in the medical profession, the leading lady and the chorus girl are both on the stage. But why are there differences in earnings between workers of the same grade, doing the same kind of job?

They may be in different districts. The differences in money wages may merely equalize real wages, the lower money wages being offset by a lower cost of living. This partly explains why wage rates in country districts are often lower than in cities; the city worker has to pay more, as a rule, for house rent and farm produce and transport. Where there are differences in real wages between districts, they are due to those obstacles to mobility, discussed earlier, which hinder workers from moving to places where they could earn more.

In the same district, one worker may earn more than another during any particular week because he works longer hours; for example, he may work overtime. In some occupations, including the public service, it is usual for employers to pay more to workers who have been with them longer, perhaps giving them an annual increment or "rise" in their pay.

Where payment is by results, the more efficient or energetic worker will earn more. For example, one miner hewing coal at a piece-rate of so much a ton will earn twice as much as another if he hews twice as much coal.

In some fields—for example, for most types of work in the public service and in offices—payment by results is not possible. In other fields it is difficult to test the quality of the work done, and payment by quantitative results might lead to bad workmanship. But a great deal of the work done in manufacturing, mining, and building could be paid by results. Would this be desirable?

There is no doubt in my mind that it would be very desirable. The closer the correspondence between work done and pay received, the greater is the incentive to effort. The hard and efficient worker tends to become discouraged, and to slow down, when he sees his fellow workers getting exactly the same pay packet for less work. Payment by results is not only the fairest method; it is also a powerful stimulus to greater output and thereby to higher real wages. Soviet Russia is well aware of this, and pays by results whenever possible.

In Great Britain, however, some of the trade unions object to payment by results and insist on time-rates. This is due partly to the bad behaviour of certain employers in the past. When they saw that their workers could do much more work under the stimulus of piece-rates they cut the piece-rates, leaving weekly earnings not much higher than before for considerably more work. Hence piece-rates have come to be regarded by some groups of workers as a slave-driving device to get more work out of them for little extra pay. The feeling against piece-rates is due also to the fear that too much output may create unemployment and that it is better to spread out the work and make it last. The fear is sometimes partly justified; where the demand for a particular kind of labour (dock labour, for example) is relatively inelastic, a larger output per worker may mean that fewer workers will be needed. But a greater output per worker tends to increase rather than to decrease the demand for labour, although it may call for some transfers of workers between industries or occupations. Payment by results would not create any general unemployment and it would do a great deal to increase the volume of output. One can understand the reasons why some trade unions oppose it, but the country would benefit greatly if they could be persuaded to change their attitude.

4. Differences in Earnings between Occupations

Some types of workers are employed in a wide range of industries, and their wages are not much affected by the changing fortunes of particular industries. A depressed industry has to pay the market rate to secure, say, typists or lorry-drivers, and a flourishing industry need not pay more.

Where the demand for a particular type of worker is confined to one industry, the demand for such workers is derived from the demand for the products of the industry; I discussed this point in the preceding chapter and will not repeat myself here.

If every worker could readily find employment in whatever occupation he pleased, the *net advantages* of all occupations would tend to be equal. Some might pay lower wages than others, but the difference would merely offset the greater attractiveness of the work or of the conditions under which it was performed or shorter hours of work, longer holidays, and so forth. Workers would distribute themselves among occupations in such a way that net advantages were everywhere the same.

In fact the net advantages of different occupations are by no means equal. Within some groups of occupations, net advantages tend to be equalized. For example, a steward on a passenger liner probably earns more, including his tips and his bed and board while at sea, than he could earn on shore, but against this he has to spend most of his time at sea. But on the whole the more disagreeable kinds of work are among the worst-paid, while work in the best-paid occupations, including the professions and responsible business posts, tends to be relatively interesting and pleasant. The reason is, of course, that it is difficult for most workers to enter the better-paid occupations. This keeps down the numbers, and keeps up the marginal productivity, in such occupations. What are the barriers to entry?

They may be barriers enforced by law or by trade unions. For example, in some occupations the number of learners or apprentices is restricted.

Some kinds of innate ability are scarcer than others relatively to the demand for them. Thus many workers earn comparatively low wages because they lack sufficient intelligence or business ability or mechanical aptitude or artistic flair, and so on, to find employment in better-paid occupations which require one or more of such qualities in a fairly high degree.

But the main reason why more workers do not enter the better-paid occupations is that they lack the necessary capital. Entrance to certain occupations, such as the professions, is granted only to those who have proved by some kind of examination that they have attained at least the minimum standard of efficiency that is legally required. Thus many who may possess sufficient innate ability to enter one of these occupations are legally debarred because they cannot afford to pay for the necessary education and training and to forgo what they could earn, during this period, by spending their time in working for pay instead of in study.

Hence earnings in such occupations usually exceed the earnings of relatively unskilled labour by much more than interest and amortization on the original capital outlay. Suppose, for example, that it takes a youth five years of university and hospital training to become qualified as a doctor. During this time he might have earned perhaps £2,000, and he might have paid perhaps £500 in fees and for books and instruments. The interest on £2,500 at 4 per cent is only £100 a year, and the amortization charge over a working life of, say, thirty years is considerably less. If, therefore, such a capital outlay brought him a return of £200 a year, it would be yielding him as much as most investments. Yet in fact the earnings of doctors usually exceed those of relatively unskilled occupations by much more than £200 a year. And this is mainly because young men and women who could become quite proficient in the medical profession cannot afford to make the initial investment and have no parents or friends who have both the will and the means to make it on their behalf. Hence the child of well-to-do parents begins life with a great advantage—an advantage which has been substantially lessened but not destroyed during recent years by the increases in the scholarship and maintenance grants made by the State and other bodies to enable a limited number of children to continue their studies beyond the time at which they would otherwise have been compelled to enter the labour market.

Again, a man requires capital to set up in business on his own account or to purchase a partnership in an established concern. Hence such fields, except overcrowded ones requiring relatively little capital, such as retail trade, are closed to the children of poor parents unless they can manage to save or borrow enough capital, and it is not easy either to save much out of a small income or to obtain a substantial loan without tangible assets to serve as security for it.

Some jobs are obtained partly through influence, and in others, such as stockbroking or selling expensive cars, a personal knowledge of fairly rich people is an asset; so is the old school tie.

We must therefore conclude that the main reason why the numbers in well-paid occupations are not greater is the inequality of incomes, which means inequality of opportunity.

5. The Earnings of Women

The average woman earns considerably less than the average man.[1] This is partly because in many fields her marginal productivity is less and partly because the great majority of women are concentrated in the worst-paid occupations.

When we speak of "marginal productivity," we mean the difference made to total receipts by employing one "unit" more, or less, of a given factor. In some occupations, such as those requiring consider-able strength, the physical output of a woman is less than that of a man; and such occupations may represent a larger demand for labour than those, such as the care of children, at which women are more efficient than men. In other occupations, such as waiting, workers render personal services to customers. Most customers prefer to be served by men, so that a man increases receipts more than an equally efficient woman. Again, most men do not like working under a woman, so that a man in a position of authority may obtain more work from his male subordinates than an equally capable woman. Finally, most employers believe that men are more reliable than women and less likely to stay away owing to sickness or to refuse to work overtime or to leave them in the lurch by suddenly giving up their jobs. Hence a woman may earn less than a man in the same

[1] In October, 1959, average weekly earnings of manual wage-earners in the United Kingdom were: men (21 and over) 270s. 9d.; women (18 and over) 140s. 4d.

occupation either because her actual output is less or because it is believed to add less, especially in the long run, to the receipts of her firm.

The other reason why women earn less, on the average, than men is that relatively few of them are in the better-paid occupations. This is partly because less is spent in educating girls than in educating boys: parents tend to invest their capital in their sons rather than in their daughters. It is partly because the general public is still rather shy of, for example, a woman solicitor or a woman doctor. Again, employers tend to think that the chief aim of a woman is to get married and leave her job, so that it would be a risky investment to train a woman for a higher-paid post in which she could not be readily replaced. Finally, many trades are closed to women, being held by law or custom (often supported by the views of the organized male workers in the trade) to be "men's jobs." Thus in Great Britain women are kept out of mining (underground), iron and steel, heavy engineering, building, most railway transport, and printing. This may or may not be socially advisable; it certainly restricts the field of employment open to women. The combined result of all these factors is that the great majority of women workers are concentrated in a few occupations where, largely for that reason, wages are low.

6. THE EARNINGS OF GOVERNMENT EMPLOYEES

Apart from their nationalized industries and other trading enterprises, Governments do not produce goods and services for sale on the market. There is no question, therefore, of profits or losses. Unlike a firm, which has to cover its costs in order to survive, a Government can pay whatever wages or salaries it pleases.

If a Government pays higher rates than are necessary, it is wasting the taxpayers' money and making civil servants a privileged class. The rates that are necessary are those which will attract and retain enough workers with the qualifications and abilities that the Government requires. If the rates offered are too low, the Government will be left with a number of vacancies which it cannot fill, or can fill only by accepting candidates who are not properly qualified.

Relatively unskilled workers can be engaged on a temporary basis at market rates. They have no measurable productivity in Government service, but, in so far as the Government pays the same rates as other employers, their wages are related to what their marginal productivity would be in private employment.

It is more difficult to fix appropriate rates of pay for the permanent posts. Some posts have no close parallel in private employment. And it is seldom a question of fixing a single rate for a post. In order to attract young men and women who will make the civil service their career, they must be offered a "time-scale," with annual increments, and prospects of promotion to higher scales above the time-scale which they start on.

There are several differences between a career in the civil service and a career in business or one of the professions. The former offers more security of tenure; an established civil servant is there for life and need have no fear of unemployment. The civil servant gets leave and sick leave privileges, and a pension on retirement. The most senior officers have considerable responsibilities and powers in the administration of public affairs, and some candidates are attracted by the possibility of eventually rising to such a position. On the other hand, a successful business or professional man earns much more than a senior civil servant, and the young man who is above the average in ability and drive can get ahead more quickly either on his own account or as an employee in private enterprise.

Young men and women who are choosing their careers will weigh the prospect of a civil service career against the other possibilities open to them. A Government should offer net advantages that compare sufficiently favourably with those alternatives to attract enough candidates with the various qualifications required, without paying more than is needed.

7. The Economy of High Wages

A few employers may find it worth while to pay time-wages above the market rate for that type of labour. This will enable them to attract and retain the more efficient workers, to skim the cream from the labour market. A man who does, say, 10 per cent more work than the average worker is worth 10 per cent more pay; his employer does not lose, indeed he gains in so far as a smaller staff, and therefore less space and equipment, are needed for the same volume of output. Moreover, such firms will suffer less than others from the difficulties of labour turnover: their workers will be likely to stay with them, and it will not be necessary to be continually training new recruits to replace workers who have left.

If a few people stand on boxes to watch a procession over the heads of the crowd, they can see better. But if everybody stands on a box, their advantage disappears. In the same way, if all employers paid higher wages, none would reap the advantages that I have just mentioned.

In some countries, such as the United States, wages are much higher than in others. But they are higher because output per worker is higher. The high wages are the effect, not the cause, of the greater productivity of labour. Workers produce more because they have more capital to assist them, because the country is not overpopulated, because technical knowledge and skills are greater, because they are better trained or work harder. If employers in a low-wage country were to increase their wages, it is unlikely that this would lead to a greater output. It would not make the workers more skilled nor would it offer them any direct inducement to work harder. A better method would be to train them, or to offer them incentives by some form of payment by results.

8. HOURS OF WORK

The "supply" of labour depends not only on the number of workers, but also on the amount of work done by each worker. In most western countries the hours of work are now between 40 and 48 a week. Any increase or reduction in hours, unless they are very long, as they were in the first half of the nineteenth century, is likely to lead to a roughly corresponding increase or decrease in output.

Leisure is an alternative to earnings. Workers can either work longer hours and earn more money or work shorter hours and enjoy more leisure. Many workers in tropical countries work little more than 20 hours a week. The reasons for this are a matter of controversy. But it is not pleasant to work in moist tropical heat, and we cannot blame workers who avoid this discomfort by working only in the cool of the morning or evening instead of increasing their earnings by working longer hours.

In western countries it may seem that workers (apart from "absenteeism") have no choice; they must conform to the length of the working day, or shift, in the establishment where they are employed. But they can choose, collectively, through their trade unions. They can demand, when conditions are favourable, either higher wages or shorter hours.

Each worker has his own scale of preferences between income and leisure. Suppose that some workers (taxi-drivers with their own taxis, for example) are free to do as much or as little work as they please at the rate of, say, 4s. an hour. One may decide to work only a few hours a day; another may decide to work rather long hours in order to earn more. If a man decides to give himself an eight-hour day, this means that he prefers 32s. a day and sixteen hours for rest and recreation to any other combination open to him, such as 28s. a day and seventeen hours leisure or 36s. a day and fifteen hours leisure. He values his sixteenth hour of leisure more highly than a ninth 4s. a day, but he values his eighth 4s. a day more highly than the extra (seventeenth) hour of leisure which he could obtain by forgoing it.

Suppose now that some change (higher fares, for example) enables him to earn 6s. an hour. Will he work longer or shorter hours than before? It is impossible to say. Some men would do more work, others less, others—perhaps the majority—about the same. An extra hour now brings him in another 6s., instead of 4s. as before; on the other hand, an eight-hour day now gives him 48s. instead of 32s. as before, so that his need for extra income is less than before. We can be fairly certain that he will not reduce his hours of work so much that he still earns only 32s. a week, for that would give him considerably more leisure and only the same income. Nor is he likely to increase his hours so much that he has no spare time in which to enjoy his extra earnings. But we cannot say more.

9. MINIMUM WAGES

In Great Britain, Wages Boards were set up in 1909 to do away with "sweated" labour by fixing minimum wages for industries in which wages seemed unduly low or in which workers were not organized. There are now quite a number of these Boards (now called Wages Councils), and by separate legislation Wages Boards have been established for agriculture and catering.

Suppose that the minimum wage fixed for an industry is well above the old wage. What are likely to be its effects?

The workers who keep their job will be better off. The rise in their wages will enable them (if they so choose) to consume more and better food and other necessaries for efficiency, and may somewhat relieve their financial worries; in consequence their output may increase. But this is rather hypothetical; it is unlikely that they will at once increase their output by anything approaching the increase in their wages.

If the employers have been exploiting their workers and making large profits by paying them less than they could earn elsewhere, the minimum wage will put a stop to this practice. But it is difficult, except in isolated districts, for employers to pay much below market rates. In fact, most employers paying low wages, both in Great Britain and in other countries, are small men not making large profits.

The minimum wage will tend to reduce the amount of employment in the industry. Employers will try to raise their prices to cover their increased labour costs. If they can do this, their sales will fall off—how much will depend on the elasticity of demand for the products. If they cannot raise their prices—owing, for example, to keen competition from similar imports—some firms will have to close down and others to reduce their staffs. Moreover, employers will tend to introduce labour-saving devices (at any rate, as time goes on and their existing plant begins to cost more for repairs) which would not have been worth while at the old rates of wages. If possible, they will also make more use of juvenile workers.

What will happen to the workers who are thrown out of work?

N 2   B.E.

There may be some industries in which wages are not controlled where they can find employment at about what they were earning before. Some of them may become workers on their own account, for there is no lower limit to the incomes of independent workers; for example, they may join relatives who have a small farm, or they may take to hawking. Others may remain unemployed. The real difficulty is that the efficiency of such workers is so low that they cannot earn a good income; and this difficulty cannot be overcome by legal minimum wages.

So far I have considered the results of fixing a minimum wage for only one or a few occupations. It is instructive to consider what would happen if a Government insisted upon a substantial rise in the real wages of every worker. Suppose it were to fix a basic minimum weekly wage for adult males, and a lower one for adult females—say, some 20 per cent above the level previously ruling for unskilled labour —permitting nobody to work for less, and were to raise wage rates in all occupations by about 20 per cent. In order to ensure that "real" wages were raised, it would doubtless make money wages vary with the cost of living, so that if the prices of the food, clothing, housing, and other things bought by workers were to rise, their money wages would rise correspondingly.

This would close three loopholes left open when minimum wages are fixed for only a few occupations. Relatively inefficient workers, not worth the basic wage, would not be permitted to take a worse-paid job elsewhere. There would be little redistribution of labour: workers dismissed would remain unemployed. Further, a rise in prices due to a reduction of output would have much less effect in checking the diminution of profits, for higher prices would mean higher money wages. Finally, the prices of labour-saving machinery and other devices would rise nearly as much as money wages, so that there would be much less scope for checking the fall in profits by altering methods of production. The result might well be a serious check to the accumulation, and investment, of capital; after a time, the total amount of capital in the country, represented by plant, stock-in-trade, and so on, might diminish. A fall in the amount of capital co-operating with labour must mean a fall in the marginal product of labour; in the absence of wage fixing, this would lead to a fall in wages; if real wages are maintained, it will lead to further unemployment.

Such a policy might "squeeze" owners of existing plant and other equipment, but our reasoning suggests that it might cause considerable unemployment—much more, proportionately, than minimum wages in one or two occupations only—and that the number of unemployed might increase as time went on. This would be so if the fall in profits and the increase in taxation (to provide for the unemployed) caused the total capital of the country to diminish. The history of wage regulation in Australia, where it has been practised more extensively than in most countries, shows that the dangers of such a policy are real and have been recognized by wage-fixing authorities. On more than one occasion they have shrunk, despite or because of their desire to promote the welfare of wage-earners, from trying to discover by experiment whether the abyss of cumulative disequilibrium described above was merely a bogy created by economists.

10. TRADE UNIONS AND WAGES

Trade unions play a useful part in safeguarding and promoting the interests of the workers. If workers were completely unorganized, increases in wages, and reductions of hours and other improvements in working conditions, would depend, apart from State action, on employers: on firms, wishing to expand in order to increase their profits, bidding against one another for labour. But a tacit agreement among employers not to spoil the market by raising wages would lead to exploitation; profits would get a larger share of the product than was needed to maintain an adequate flow of investment.

In some countries, representatives of trade unions and of employers are closely consulted by the Government on economic policy. In Holland, for example, the trade unions agreed some years ago to accept a general reduction of 5 per cent in real wages, accompanied by a still greater cut in profits; a round-table conference had convinced them that this course was in the best interests of the country and of the workers as a whole. In Great Britain, the Trade Union Congress and the British Employers Confederation are frequently consulted on public policy. The T.U.C. agreed to a general freezing of wages during 1950–52 in order to check inflation.

The difficulty is that the interests of particular groups of workers clash with those of workers as a whole. Each particular group wants to increase its own wages, although it would like the cost of living to be kept stable, which means that it would like other wage rates to be kept more or less stable. Most workers do not appreciate the desirability of maintaining an adequate flow of investment, and think that there is always plenty of scope for "squeezing" profits further. Hence some groups tend to disregard the advice of their leaders (especially if the latter are "suspect" owing to their close association with the Government) and to start "unofficial" strikes.

If two or three trade unions succeed in obtaining wage increases, other trade unions will be very likely to press for increases in order to maintain the relative position of their workers. Such a "round" of wage increases will raise the cost of living, and the net benefit to workers as a whole will be small. The export industries are danger spots. If a country relies largely on exports which have to be sold at world prices, higher wages in the export industries may lead to unemployment and a smaller volume of exports.

If other wage rates remain fairly stable, and there is no general upward movement, there are limits to the wage increases which any particular trade union can secure for its members. On the demand side, the three influences are the elasticity of demand for the products, the proportion of total costs formed by that type of labour, and the possibility of substituting other factors for it.

If the increased wages are added to prices, the demand for the product may fall considerably, substantially reducing the amount of employment in that industry. This is especially likely if the product competes with imports, the prices of which do not rise. Hence trade unions sometimes support employers in asking for greater restrictions on imports, in order that both profits and wages in the industry may be raised—at the expense of consumers. The less elastic the demand for the product, the better are the prospects of obtaining an increase in wages.

If that type of labour forms a small proportion of the total costs, a rise in its wages will increase the price of the product relatively little. For example, a substantial rise in the wages of plasterers would not add much to the cost of producing houses. Contrast a rise in the wages of coal-miners, which form a large proportion of the total cost of producing coal.

There is, however, always the danger of substitution. A rise in wage rates may induce employers to make some change in their methods of production, or possibly in the nature of their product, which enables them to keep down their costs by employing less of this type of labour. Another possibility is that women might be trained to do that type of work for lower rates than those enforced by the men's union.

There are limits also on the supply side. Clearly a trade union will not have much power unless it includes the majority of workers in that occupation. Employers will not be greatly perturbed if only some of their workers, the members of the union, threaten to strike, provided that they can carry on with the help of the non-unionists who remain, and can replace the strikers by workers drawn from the unemployed or from other jobs. (Hence the importance attached by trade unions to the *closed shop*, employing only union workers, and to their right to *peaceful picketing*, to keep away other workers, when they are on strike.) Even if a union controls all the workers in one district, its power is limited if employers can import workers from other districts or even, possibly, move their establishments to other districts where labour costs are lower. These considerations explain the growth of nation-wide industrial unions, embracing all types of workers in an industry. Such a union can force employers to close down when it calls a strike.

Again, the power of a union depends partly upon its funds. Its main weapon is the strike. If the strikers cannot support themselves and their families, they may be starved into submission; hence the importance of union funds. Public assistance given by the State, as in Great Britain, clearly strengthens the hands of the unions. The strikers (or their families) can fall back on public assistance. Moreover, a union may not be deterred from demanding substantial wage increases by the knowledge that, if it succeeds in getting them, a considerable number of its members will be unemployed. It may reckon that the higher wages of those who keep their jobs, plus unemployment benefits for those who do not, will mean a larger total income for its members, taken as a group. If every union took this line, the result would be either a marked rise in the cost of living or heavy unemployment, but from the standpoint of any one union it may seem to be in its interests to insist on substantial wage increases.

Let us suppose that a trade union does succeed in inducing employers to pay wage rates substantially higher than those prevailing in comparable occupations. Can these relatively high wage rates be maintained?

I say "occupations" rather than "industries" because it would clearly be difficult for an industrial union, covering many types of workers, to maintain the wages of, say, clerks or unskilled workers, appreciably above the wages of similar workers in other industries. The industrial union, with a large and comprehensive membership, is more potent in using the weapon of the strike to obtain a general increase in wages, but it is the "craft" or "occupational" union that is in a better position to raise the wages of its members relatively to those of other workers.

A relatively high wage rate will attract new entrants. Boys leaving school will be drawn to that occupation rather than others. Some workers in other jobs requiring similar capacities and skills will try to transfer into that occupation, especially if this does not involve changing their residence.

But a large influx of new workers would tend to rob existing members of the union of their gains. If the new workers all joined the union, and refused to undercut the new and higher level of wages, there would be a corresponding increase in unemployment, in which the original members of the union would share. If the new-comers were left out of the union or refused to join it, possibly forming a new union of their own, they might well obtain employment by accepting wages higher than they could get in other occupations, but nevertheless lower than those secured by the union, and they would dislodge union members from their jobs.

It follows that a union can maintain wage rates substantially above those of comparable occupations only if it can somehow limit the number of new entrants to its occupation. A union, like any other monopolist, can raise its price only by restricting supply.

The most common method is to insist on a minimum period of apprenticeship for new entrants, and to limit the number of apprentices per journeyman. If the State can be induced to give such rules the sanction of the law, so much the better; otherwise the union must try to enforce them by threatening to strike if they are broken. Another method, practised by some unions in the United States, is to insist on a closed shop, that is on the employment of union members only, and to charge high initiation fees which deter new-comers from joining the union. In Great Britain, some unions try to safeguard their position by insisting on strict lines of demarcation. A particular task must be performed only by one particular type of worker, although another type of worker could in fact carry it out quite well and often more conveniently: for example, he may be on the spot while the other has to be sent for.

Another practice adopted by some trade unions is to go slow in order to spread the work; for example, to limit the number of bricks which a bricklayer lays per day. This is another example of a clash between the interests of a section and those of the community. If all workers followed this policy, deliberately doing less work than they could, the volume of output would be kept down and the cost of living would be forced up.

CHAPTER XXVII

INTEREST

1. DIFFERENCES IN RATES OF INTEREST

INTEREST is the price paid for a loan. If you borrow £100 and promise to pay back £105 at the end of twelve months you are promising to pay a rate of interest of 5 per cent per annum.

At any moment, there are many different rates of interest. One borrower can borrow at a lower rate than another, and the same borrower has to pay a higher rate on one type of loan than on another type.

Differences in the rate which different borrowers have to pay for similar loans are due to differences in their credit standing. The lender parts with his money and receives in return an IOU—it may be called a bond, or a mortgage, or a bill of exchange, or something else, but essentially it is an IOU. Will the borrower be able and willing to keep his promise? Will he make the interest payments on the dates specified? Will he repay the loan when it falls due for repayment? There is always some risk of default. This risk is considered quite negligible on loans to the British Government, and the long-term rate of interest is taken to be the rate at which the British Government could borrow for a long period, as measured by the yield on the market price of long-term British Government securities. For example, if £100 face value $2\frac{1}{2}$ per cent Consols can be bought for £60, this means that the present value of a promise by the British Government to pay £2 10s. a year for ever (for Consols have no redemption date) is £60, equal to a yield of $\frac{100}{60} \times 2\frac{1}{2} = 4\frac{1}{6}$ per cent. The rate of interest which the British Government would have to offer to obtain a long-term loan is $4\frac{1}{6}$ per cent. Most other borrowers, whether Governments or local authorities or companies, would have to offer more. For example, if the 5 per cent bonds of the Government of Ruritania are standing at 80, that Government would have to offer about $6\frac{1}{4}$ per cent. The higher rate that another borrower must offer is mainly a risk premium to cover the risk of default.

Another reason for differences in interest rates is sometimes the security provided by the borrower. Often lenders have the right to seize certain assets belonging to the borrower if he does not pay them the agreed interest, or repay them their loans at the due dates. Thus the holders of *debentures* can often seize the assets of the company, and the holders of mortgages the property that is mortgaged. This right lessens their risks; the more valuable these assets compared with the amount of the loan, the lower will tend to be the risk premium that the borrower has to pay.

Other conditions attached to the loan, such as any premiums or discounts when the loan is repaid, the currency in which it is to be repaid, and the extent to which the interest on it is taxed, may affect the rate of interest that the borrower has to offer. Another factor of some importance is the marketability of the IOU. The lender may wish to sell it to somebody else before it falls due for repayment. If it is a well-known bond, readily saleable on the Stock Exchange, it will carry a lower rate of interest than a security less easily marketable, such as a mortgage or the bond of a small company.

Finally, loans are made for different periods of time. At times of financial crisis, when some firms badly need cash to pay creditors pressing for repayment, or during periods of marked inflation or Stock Exchange speculation, when large gains may be made by using borrowed money, short-term rates are often high. As a rule, however, the more distant the date of repayment, the higher must be the rate of interest. This is because of the risk that the market value of the IOU may fall as time goes on. A lender who makes a loan for a short period is due to receive a definite sum in cash at the end of that period, whereas the holder of a long-term bond who needs cash may have to sell his bond for whatever it will fetch.

If the price of $2\frac{1}{2}$ per cent Consols is 60, giving a yield of $4\frac{1}{6}$ per cent, you might expect that a $2\frac{1}{2}$ per cent British Government bond due for repayment in a year's time would sell for about $98\frac{1}{2}$; the buyer would get $2\frac{1}{2}$ interest plus another $1\frac{1}{2}$ on redemption. In fact, it may sell for rather more; the redemption date is so near that it is virtually a short-term security.

The above discussion partly explains the role of financial institutions such as banks and insurance companies which act as middlemen between lenders and borrowers. A bank may create credit, but in addition it acts as a middleman, like a savings bank. It may pay interest on deposits, which are really loans made to it by depositors. It pays a relatively low rate, or nothing at all (on current accounts), because its credit standing is high and because any depositor can withdraw his money at short notice. But in fact payments-in are likely, over a period, to offset withdrawals. Hence the bank can relend, in relatively large amounts and for relatively long periods, at a higher rate of interest. It adds together, as it were, small amounts of short-term loans in order to provide borrowers with the type of loan they want.

If you look at the list of Stock Exchange prices you will find that most of the securities quoted (at least, most in number, although not in aggregate value) are not fixed-interest securities like Consols, but are shares with a fluctuating yield. A fixed-interest security gives the holder a fixed money return; his return from shares depends on the dividends declared. But as anybody can choose to buy either fixed-interest securities or shares, we should expect the current yield on both to be about the same after allowing for risk; shares are more risky than most bonds. This is more or less the case. At the same time, a firm that borrows money at fixed interest from the banks or the public expects to make a profit by using the loan in its business. Hence a low rate of interest tends to encourage new investment and a high rate of interest to deter it.

2. THE MARGINAL PRODUCTIVITY OF CAPITAL

Why do entrepreneurs borrow? And why are they prepared to pay interest on the money they borrow? The obvious answer is that they hope to use the loans in ways that yield them a profit greater than the interest they pay. If an entrepreneur could borrow as much as he wished at the ruling rate of interest—often he cannot—he would borrow up to the point at which the marginal cost equalled the marginal revenue. The marginal cost at, say, 5 per cent would be £5 a year on each £100 he borrowed. The marginal revenue would be the increase in his receipts from using that money. So long as marginal revenue exceeded marginal cost, he would increase his net profit by borrowing more.

How will an entrepreneur use borrowed money? Some firms normally borrow working capital to pay for raw materials, labour, and other items of current costs. But let us consider a firm which borrows to *expand* its activities. Perhaps it is making more than normal profits. It may be so efficiently managed that expansion would pay; or the demand for the types of products it makes may have increased, raising their prices. Perhaps it wishes to launch out into the production of a new type of good or service in the belief that the potential demand is large enough to make the venture profitable. Perhaps it expects to reduce its costs per unit of output by installing a plant of improved design or of a larger and more efficient size. In any event, the firm expects to make a larger total net profit than it is making now. The need to borrow—or, more accurately, to use more free capital obtained from somewhere—arises from the fact that *production takes time*. Expenditure on production is recovered by receipts from the products only after an interval of time. The farmer must wait until his crop is sold before he can recoup himself for his expenditure in producing it; expenditure on constructing durable assets (including planting and tending trees or building up a herd of livestock) is recovered gradually, from the receipts from the products, over the working life of those assets.

The possibility of paying interest arises from *the greater productivity of methods using more real capital.* A given amount of labour will produce more shoes if some of this labour is first used to make shoe machinery and to build a factory than if all the labour makes shoes by hand. (Output is further increased by specialization; some workers specialize on machine-making, some on building, and so forth.) Farmers who install an irrigation system may get larger yields of crops. A railway may save fuel, thus reducing operating costs, by building a tunnel to avoid having a steep gradient. But such investment pays for itself, with profit, only in the future, sometimes only over a long period.

Of course, not all methods of using more capital (or "roundabout" methods) give a greater output. Only those are used that give the greatest gains over more direct and primitive methods. And many projects that would more than cover their costs if interest were zero cannot be undertaken. The total amount of labour and other resources is limited; the community can spare only a part of them for investment —the rest are needed to provide for current wants. Somehow or other the most promising of the many projects must be selected. That is the function of the rate of interest; it rules out projects which cannot cover the interest charge as well as their other costs. A socialist State, in which there was no private property in means of production, would need to use a notional rate of interest for purposes of calculation in order to decide which projects offered the best prospects, the highest probable return, and should therefore be given priority over others (unless some of the others served purposes such as Defence, for which the question of yields of extra output is not relevant).

Free capital flowing into new investment (as distinct from the purchase of securities or other assets from their present owners) tends to go where its yield is expected to be greatest. If one field offers better prospects than others, new firms will enter this field and firms already in it will expand. In this way, sooner or later the expected rate of profit, or marginal productivity of capital, will be equalized between all the various fields that it can enter freely. For example, if the expected rate of profit in making shoes is high, an increase in shoe factories and thereby in the output of shoes will eventually bring down the price of shoes until the marginal productivity of capital in that field is no higher (after allowing for risks) than elsewhere.

This result may be brought about more quickly by a rise in costs. For example, if house-building offers better prospects of profit than other fields, it may take a long time before additions to the supply of houses substantially reduce rents. But if the *rate* of house-building doubles (adding, say, 4 per cent instead of 2 per cent, as formerly, to the existing stock of houses) wages in the building trades and other building costs may rise until rates of profit are reduced to normal.

It will be remembered, however, that under monopoly the assets owned by the monopolist may yield more than the current rate of profit because free capital seeking investment cannot enter that field.

A further point is that the prospective return from some investments, such as new gold-fields or a new type of business, may be very uncertain. But investors in such fields must and do decide, after weighing the various chances of gain and loss, that on balance the prospects of profit are as attractive there as elsewhere, indeed more attractive to those who like a gamble, risking the loss of some or all of their capital for the chance of an exceptionally high return.

I conclude this section by trying to explain why an increased investment of capital tends to reduce the marginal productivity of capital, so that an increase in the supply of free capital seeking investment tends to bring down the expected rate of profit and the rate of interest.

It is easy to see that as more and more capital is invested in one particular field, output will increase, product prices will fall, and the rate of profit will be reduced. But why should a greater investment of capital, spread over all fields in accordance with the preferences of consumers, reduce the general rate of profit? If it brings down the price of shoes, it will equally bring down the price of ships and sealing wax. Whether or not prices fall will depend on monetary policy. But if they do, the prices of producers goods will fall (for investment will take place in the capital goods industries, too) as well as the prices of consumers' goods.

We have to explain why the *physical* marginal productivity of capital diminishes when the amount of capital increases. At first sight, it may seem that we cannot account for this by invoking the law of diminishing returns. For free capital can be turned into any form, can be used to purchase or hire any type of factor, so that we are not dealing with a case in which the supply of one physical factor of production increases relatively to that of others.

The main explanation is that some factors cannot be increased at all, or can be increased only at an increasing cost. The most suitable sites are limited in number; so is the area of fairly fertile land; so also, since we cannot produce robots or slaves at will, is the total labour force. A greater output of many raw materials can be obtained only by resorting to sources of supply that are less fertile or less accessible or more difficult to work—in other words, only at an increasing cost; and after a point increased fertilization and other improvements to land yield a diminishing return.

The consequence is that an increase in the amount of capital used does in fact involve a change in the proportions of the various physical factors, and the resulting combinations are less productive than they would be if every factor (for example, rich mineral deposits and fertile land) could be increased with equal facility. For this reason, the marginal return on capital at any moment, measured by the rate of profit per £100 invested, would be greater if there were less capital and less if there were more capital.

But as time goes on, the march of science and discovery reveals new ways of using capital—that is, of increasing output by the use of more capitalistic methods of production—and this tends to push up the rate of interest. The influence of this force may be greater or less than the influence of the accumulation of capital, which tends to reduce the rate of interest. In Great Britain and most western countries there has been a large increase in the amount of capital during the past fifty or a hundred years, but new ways of using capital have prevented any permanent fall in the rate of interest.

3. BORROWING BY GOVERNMENTS AND CONSUMERS

The last section discussed the demand for loans from industry and trade. I include nationalized industries under this heading; in so far as they aim at making a profit, they will borrow only if they expect that their additional receipts from the investment will at least cover the interest charges on the loan.

There is also a demand for loans from borrowers who do not aim at making a profit. Government and local authorities are the largest borrowers of this type. They do not have to show a profit; interest charges and repayments can be covered by taxation or by new borrowing.

In war-time, Government borrowing may be very large. During the last war, the British Government borrowed some £16 milliard, nearly half its total expenditure during the seven financial years 1st April, 1939 to 31st March, 1946.

Governments sometimes borrow in peace-time, usually to carry out development programmes. Much of this public investment (for example, on roads or on schools and hospitals) may not yield any money revenue, but its value to the community is deemed to exceed its cost sufficiently to justify the loan.

Loans for non-business purposes are borrowed also by persons and by institutions. A man may borrow in order to buy a house of his own, instead of paying rent. A young couple may borrow to buy furniture or other durable household goods, perhaps by paying for them on the hire-purchase plan. Others may borrow to meet heavy unforeseen expenses, such as the cost of an illness, or to spend more now in anticipation of future increases in their income or assets.

All these demands for loans compete with the demands from industry and trade. Other things being equal, increased demands for loans from any source will tend to raise rates of interest. The rates that non-business borrowers have to pay will depend on the expected marginal productivity of capital in industry and trade. That is why interest rates are high in under-developed countries, where capital is scarce and its marginal productivity high, and why they are higher in times of prosperity than in times of depression.

4. SAVING

The supply of loan capital may come largely from bank credit, of which more later. The other source of supply is saving. Not all savings are lent. Some are invested directly; for example, Governments construct roads and other physical assets, companies plough back their undistributed profits, individuals build houses for themselves. Again, some savings are used to buy "old" securities or are held as cash balances. This section discusses the total supply of saving.

Saving may be performed by Governments (and other public authorities) or by companies (and other firms) or by private persons (and institutions).

The expenditure of a Government may be roughly divided into ordinary expenditure to meet current needs and capital expenditure on developmental and other projects. The division is only a rough one. Even the ordinary expenditure of a Government contains some items, such as new buildings, improvements to roads, and other additions to physical assets, which can strictly be termed investment. It also includes a good deal of expenditure on measures to improve the health and education of the community. Such measures are analogous to investment, for future productivity can be promoted by increasing the efficiency of the population as well as by increasing physical assets. The same applies to public expenditure on promoting research.

On the other hand, the revenue of most Governments includes some taxes, notably death duties, that are probably paid out of capital. The taxpayer sells some of his assets to pay his taxes, and thus cancels out, by this *dis-saving*, a corresponding amount of new saving by the buyers of his assets. In Great Britain, taxes on capital averaged £175 million a year during 1953–58.

The conventional measure of the saving or dis-saving of a Government is its budget surplus or budget deficit. When its revenue (including taxes on capital) exceeds its ordinary expenditure (including some expenditure which is really of a capital nature), the excess is a budget surplus. This surplus is available for public investment; it represents compulsory saving imposed on the community by the Government. Conversely, when the ordinary expenditure exceeds the revenue, the excess is a budget deficit; the Government has to borrow in order to cover it and also to pay for any special capital expenditure.

In the same way, local authorities, taken together, may show either a surplus or a deficit.

A Government may compel employers and employees, and possibly, as in Great Britain, self-employed persons also, to contribute to national insurance funds or provident funds, and these funds also may show either a surplus or a deficit on the year.

The saving of companies is the undistributed profits which remain after providing for depreciation and taxation and for dividends and interest. It tends to be high during a period of rising prices, such as 1950 and 1951, because profits include the amount by which the value of stocks of goods owned by the company at the close of the year exceed the value of stocks owned at the beginning of the year.

Personal savings are total personal savings less the dis-saving of persons who sold some of their assets to meet their current expenditure.

In Great Britain, personal saving plays a less important part than it did before the war. It is being replaced, to a considerable extent, by compulsory saving imposed by the State. This is due partly to higher taxation—in so far as tax revenue is spent on capital purposes it is compulsory saving. It has been estimated that the relatively rich, taken as a whole, do not add enough to their fortunes during their lifetimes to cover the death duties payable on them when they die. The relatively poor have to pay heavy taxes on tobacco and beer, purchase-taxes, and insurance contributions; they have not much margin for saving.

At the same time, the motives for personal saving have been somewhat weakened by the Welfare State. Powerful motives used to be a desire to provide for one's old age, to have a reserve against periods of unemployment or illness, to pay for the education of one's children. The State now compels people to contribute to national insurance schemes which give them pensions on retirement and money benefits when they are unemployed or sick, and provides, out of taxation, free health services and free education, including higher education.

Nevertheless the need for private saving is still great. Much investment is needed, both at home and overseas, in order to increase future output, and it is better that this should be provided by voluntary saving than by still higher taxes, or by inflationary measures, or not at all.

Assuming that investment is adequate to absorb all planned saving, what determines the total volume of saving?

The *social framework* plays an important part. Clearly there is likely to be more saving in a society where thrift is encouraged, where institutions such as savings banks, building societies, and the Stock Exchange provide outlets for savings, and where life and property are secure, than in a more primitive or unsettled society, where property may be seized by the Government or by bandits or destroyed by civil war.

The *rate of interest* might be expected, like any other price, to call forth a greater supply when it is higher than when it is lower. But in fact the rate of interest has little direct effect on the amounts saved by Governments or companies; and the savings of insurance funds depend on the number of pensioners and the amount of unemployment, sickness, and so forth, and not on the rate of interest. Very high rates of interest would no doubt tempt many individuals to forgo more present consumption in order to take advantage of them. And very low rates would induce some elderly people to consume their capital by selling income-yielding assets in order to purchase annuities: for example, a man of 50 with an income from property could treble that income for the rest of his life (and die leaving nothing) if the rate of interest were only 2 per cent. It is fairly certain, therefore, that rather more would be saved—other things being equal—at a higher rate of interest. But not much more—at any rate, not within the range of 3 to 5 per cent which has prevailed in Great Britain for many years. The supply curve of savings probably slopes upward to the right, in the usual way, but very steeply.

It may be noted that the net return obtained by a lender is the interest less the income tax on it. If the standard rate of income tax is 7s. 9d. in the £, £100 lent at 4 per cent yields only £2 9s. net.

Expectations of changes in the value of money affect the volume of saving. If people expect a substantial rise in prices, they are likely to buy durable goods and to save less. If prices rise by, say, 10 per cent during a year, anybody who has lent at less than 10 per cent has really made a loss, for £110 at the end of the year (even if the extra £10 is not taxed) buys only as much as £100 at the beginning of the year. During such periods of inflation, therefore, people are anxious to borrow (in order to buy goods to be sold later on a rising market) and not to lend; and money rates of interest may rise to very high levels. If, on the other hand, the general level of prices is expected to fall, people are likely to hold off buying, in other words to increase their saving (perhaps thereby hastening a slump); and money rates of interest are likely to be low.

The main factor governing the volume of saving is probably *the size of the incomes* out of which the savings are made. The amount of Government saving depends, of course, on the policy followed by the Government. But a larger national income makes it much easier for a Government to budget for a surplus by increasing rates of taxation or imposing new taxes; and even if it does neither, the yields from existing taxes will be higher.

Similarly with companies. When profits are high, larger sums can be placed to reserve. Many companies try to pay fairly steady dividends, putting more to reserve when their profits are high and less (sometimes nothing, indeed sometimes depleting their reserves to pay dividends) when they are low.

Similarly with private persons. Experience suggests that as a rule a person will save a larger amount, and probably a larger proportion, out of a larger income. We should expect this to happen. For a person needs to spend only a certain sum on his own consumption, and therefore a rich man has a bigger margin available for saving than a poor man.

I have taken saving to mean net saving, over and above what is required to maintain existing capital intact. But of course everybody who owns marketable assets is free to sell some of them and consume the proceeds. A company need not set aside from its gross earnings enough money to replace all its assets when they wear out or become obsolete. A Government can borrow more than it spends on capital purposes. In short, Governments and companies and individuals must constantly choose not only whether they will save more or less, but also whether, and to what extent, they will consume their capital. The total amount which, instead of being consumed, is spent in maintaining, as well as in increasing, the total stock of capital may be termed *gross saving*.

The following are estimates [1] of gross saving in the United Kingdom during the last three years—

GROSS SAVING: U.K. (£ million)

	1956	1957	1958
Persons	1,215	1,359	1,341
Companies	1,634	1,764	1,786
Public Corporations	197	175	175
Central Government: . . .			
surplus on revenue account . .	410	611	645
less taxes on capital . . .	-166	-176	-182
transfers to capital accounts . .	111	82	93
Local Authorities	130	163	144
Additions to dividend and interest			
reserves	43	35	36
Additions to tax reserves . . .	202	49	-115
Total	3,776	4,062	3,923

The estimates for "persons" include the gross savings of professional persons, farmers, and other sole-traders and partnerships, as well as of individuals not owning any business. They have been calculated as a residual item, and not directly, and are subject to a large margin of error; nevertheless their increase during recent years (they were well under £300 million a year until 1952, when they jumped to £663 million) is an encouraging sign.

[1] From Blue Book: *National Income and Expenditure* (1959), Table 6.

The National Insurance Funds made savings, and built up reserves, for a number of years. Recently, however, current payments of benefits have somewhat exceeded current contributions. Although rates of contributions were increased in July, 1958, the Funds seem likely to show a growing annual deficit, as the numbers drawing retirement benefits will steadily increase.

The figures given in the table are of gross saving, before deducting depreciation and stock appreciation. The 1959 Blue Book also gives estimates (Table 57) of capital consumption on all fixed assets, at current costs. They are: £1,665 million for 1956, £1,778 million for 1957, and £1,895 million for 1958.[1] It gives also estimates of stock appreciation; this was £150 million for 1956 and £100 million for 1957; in 1958, however, the values of stocks fell by £20 million. It thus appears that net saving is now well over £2,000 million a year, and possibly exceeds 12 per cent of the national income.

5. TYPES OF ASSETS

One reason why it has been difficult to present a clear picture of the forces behind the demand for and the supply of loan capital is that a large part of saving (and of increases in bank credit) does not go into new loans. The amount of investment, of new physical assets created, is of fundamental importance to a community. But the volume of lending is, so to speak, accidental. Whether free capital goes into investment directly or via a loan is relatively unimportant.

Moreover, savings are often used in the first instance to purchase existing securities or other assets; the money may change hands a number of times before it finds its way into new investment.

At this stage, it is convenient to consider the various kinds of assets that a person can acquire with his savings instead of spending the money on consumers' goods for his current consumption. With a Government or a company, the alternative to acquiring such assets would be to leave taxpayers, or to give shareholders, more money, which they could spend or save as they pleased.

I shall simplify by considering only the four main types of assets. They may be called for brevity bonds, shares, bills, and money balances.

Long-term fixed-interest securities may be termed *bonds*. When such securities are first issued, they represent a loan made by the public to the Government or the company that issues them. The rate of interest payable on them is fixed. Suppose it is fixed at 3 per cent on each £100 face value of bonds. A lender parts with £100, which he might

[1] These estimates of capital consumption cover publicly-owned as well as privately owned assets. The statutory allowances for depreciation on the latter are on the whole too low to provide adequately for replacements during periods of rising prices. They have been supplemented, however, by "investment allowances" and "initial allowances" (see p. 413).

have spent instead on his current consumption or used to buy some other type of asset, and gets a piece of paper in return. (In some cases—for example, Consols—his name is inscribed on a register and he has no piece of paper, but that does not affect the argument.) This paper title gives him the right to a fixed income of £3 a year. It would perhaps be more enlightening to call bonds "fixed income" securities rather than "fixed interest" securities. For the rate of interest will change, up or down, as time goes on.

The holder of this paper title can sell it at any time, through the Stock Exchange, to somebody else. But he may not get £100 for it. The value of a right to £3 a year depends on the current rate of interest for that type of security; it will equal £300 divided by the current rate of interest.

The advantage of a bond is that it yields a fixed and certain money income, provided only that the borrower does not default. The drawback is that its market value will fall if the current rate of interest rises.

I turn to *shares*. The owner of an "ordinary" share in a company whose capital is represented by 1,000 such shares, owns one-thousandth of the assets of that company and gets one-thousandth of the profits. He plays little part in the management of the business, but he shares in the risks and in the profits. In these respects he resembles the man who invests his capital in his own business or in, say, houses. I use "shares" as a brief term to cover all real capital yielding profits.

Suppose a man owns a share of face value £100 in a shoe company. In a particular year his income from it, his *dividend*, may be, say, £6. Had he bought a British Government security instead, he would have received only, say, £4. The advantage of holding shares rather than (safe) bonds is that their yield is likely to be greater. But so are the risks. For any of several reasons—changes in tastes, a fall in population, the entry of new rival firms, cheaper imports, taxes on shoes, bad management—the demand for the shoes made by that company may fall. If so, the dividend will be less; perhaps there may be no dividend at all. The value of the share will fall. Its holder will have both a smaller income and less capital.

The rate of profit per annum on capital used in industry and trade is the net yield (after deducting depreciation charges) expressed as a percentage of the current cost of the assets. Their original cost is a matter of history, without any present significance. If a firm buys a machine for £1,000 and, soon after, the cost of similar machines falls to £800, its machine should be valued at once at only £800, and the rate of profit should be calculated on that basis.

Clearly there is a close connection between the rate of profit and the rate of interest. In the absence of risks, the two would be equal. For people have the choice of taking either profits or interest, of holding either shares or bonds. Owing to risks, the rate of profit is on the average somewhat above the rate of interest. But the two tend to move together. An increase in rates of profit will tend to increase the demand for loans from industry and trade, and to raise the rate of interest; and conversely.

Short-term fixed-interest securities may be termed *bills*. A three-months' Treasury Bill for £5,000 is in effect a promise by the British Government to pay £5,000 in three months' time. The rate of interest on bills varies with the credit-standing of the borrower and with the length of time before "maturity"; that is, before they are repaid. As a rule, short-term rates are below long-term rates. Sometimes they are far below. Thus in 1946 a three-months' Treasury Bill sold for nearly £4,994, giving a yield equivalent to only $\frac{1}{2}$ per cent per annum. The main reason why short-term rates are lower, as a rule, than the long-term rate is that the risk of loss from a fall in the market value of the security is much less. Suppose, for example, that a man buys a £100 three-months' bill for £99 10s. At the end of three months he will get £100. If he wants to turn the bill into money after, say, six weeks, a bank will buy it from him (or, to use the technical term, will *discount* it for him). Even if the rate of discount on such a bill has risen from 2 per cent to as much as 16 per cent, he will get £98 for it. But a man who bought Consols at £100 in October, 1946, and sold them in 1958 would have had to sell them at about £50.

Hence the advantage of holding bills is that the risk of capital loss is completely avoided unless they have to be discounted before maturity; and even in that event the capital loss will be small. The drawback is that the rate of interest received is lower than on bonds.

The fourth type of assets is *money*—holdings of cash or of bank deposits. The advantage of holding money is that money alone can be used to pay a money debt. The lender on short term runs only a slight risk of losing any of his money. If he can wait until the loan matures, he will get back the exact sum that he lent. But he does forgo the advantages of holding money. We may perhaps regard a short-term rate as a payment to lenders to compensate them for this sacrifice of "liquidity." If there is a general increase in the desire to become "liquid," short-term rates will rise. This happens to a marked extent during a financial panic. Firms are very anxious to borrow money on short term in order to meet their current money obligations and avoid bankruptcy.

6. THE MONETARY THEORY OF INTEREST

So far, I have been considering the rate of interest as a price, which is paid because the supply of loan capital is scarce in relation to the demand for it and which equates the two. The demand for loan capital, as we have seen, comes from industry and trade, where it is dependent on the marginal productivity of capital, and also from Government and other borrowers. The supply of loan capital comes from savings and also from bank credit. I have said little about the latter, but we know from experience that changes in the volume of bank credit may play a leading part, an expansion of bank credit bringing interest rates down and a contraction forcing them up.

This method of approach has proved rather awkward because only a part of the free capital available (from savings or from increases in bank credit) goes into new loans. But Keynes considered that it should be thrown overboard, and replaced by a purely monetary theory, for more fundamental reasons, which I will give in my own words.

Suppose we wish to explain what forces determine the demand for houses. The supply of newly-built houses, and the demand for them, forms only a fraction of the total supply of and demand for houses. For the total stock of houses in existence is very large compared with the annual addition to that stock. Hence the price of houses may change very substantially over a short period during which no new houses come on to the market; all the transactions in houses may be purchases and sales of houses already in existence, of "old" houses.

The same is true of the total stock of Government securities and other paper titles representing loans borrowed in the past. "Old" securities may change in price quite substantially over a short period during which there is little new lending and borrowing.

The alternative to holding bonds is to hold money. (There are in fact other alternatives, as we saw in the preceding section.) The price of bonds—in other words, the long-term rate of interest—will settle at just that level at which there is no general move either to sell bonds and hold money balances instead or to do the opposite. The advantage of holding bonds is that they yield an income in the form of interest, whereas money balances are idle assets which yield no income. The advantage of holding money balances is that one's money capital is quite safe: £100 in money is always £100 but the market price of bonds may fall. These two advantages are balanced, for the community as a whole, by the rate of interest.

The rate of interest, the price of bonds, can be considered as equating either the supply and demand for bonds or the supply and demand for money balances. It is the latter view which throws more light on the working of the economy.

Let us begin with the demand for money. Most people and firms are constantly receiving money and paying out money. Nevertheless every person or firm holds on the average, taking one day with another, a certain amount of money. What determines the amount of money that, on the average, they wish to hold? In other words, what determines their demand for money balances? Part of the money is held to finance current transactions. People know that they will have to make money payments in the near future. They may also have to meet sudden and unforseen demands for cash. Therefore they hold money balances. Given the habits of the community, we can take these balances, held for convenience, as given.

The amount of money held in excess of the balances needed for these purposes depends on what Keynes calls the *liquidity-preference* of the community, that is, on the extent to which people prefer to hold their assests in the completely "liquid" form of cash, which always keeps its money value and is readily available, rather than in the form of income-yielding securities.

A given state of liquidity-preference, however, does not mean that the community wants to hold so many £million of money balances, whatever the rate of interest. Quite the contrary. The higher the rate of interest—in other words the greater the income forgone by holding money rather than bonds—the less will be the amount of money that the public is willing to hold. For any given state of liquidity-preference, there is a downward-sloping demand curve for money balances, illustrating the fact that the lower the "price," the rate of interest, the larger will be the amount of money which people wish to hold.

I turn to the supply of money. In this context, the supply of money means the total amount of coins, notes, and bank deposits in existence. This amount is determined by the banking system and not by the public. And all the money in existence must be held by someone, just as all the houses or all the securities in existence must be held by someone. The public, however, can and does determine the price at which this money will be held. And this price is the rate of interest.

Suppose, for example, that the supply of money is increased. Why should people hold more money than before? They were already holding as much as they thought it worth while to keep in this non-income-yielding form. As more money comes into their possession they will tend to buy securities with it rather than to hold it. But such a general move to buy securities will send up their price; in other words, it will push down the rate of interest. At a lower rate of interest, liquidity-preference remaining the same, people will hold more money than before. The rate of interest will fall just enough to induce people to hold larger money balances to a sufficient extent to absorb the increased supply of money.

Or there may be a change on the demand side. Suppose, for example, that there is a general increase in liquidity-preference, the amount of money remaining the same. People will want to hold more money. But they cannot, for the total amount of money is fixed. They will all try to sell securities in order to get more money. The prices of securities will fall, in other words the rate of interest will rise, until it reaches a level at which people want to hold only the amount of money in existence, and not more. The increase in their liquidity-preference has led to, and has been met by, a rise in the rate of interest.

Hence the rate of interest equates the supply of money, as determined by the banking system, with the demand for money, as determined by people's habits and their preference for liquidity.[1]

7. Conclusions

There has perhaps been too much controversy among economists about theories of interest. Nearly all economists agree about which factors are important, and what are their effects. It surely does not matter much whether they are explained in terms of the supply and demand for loan capital or in terms of the supply and demand for money balances.

Thus we all know from experience that changes in the amount of money may exert a dominant influence on rates of interest. We can either say that an expansion of bank credit is an increase in the supply of loan capital and therefore reduces interest rates, or we can show, as Keynes does, that interest rates must fall to induce people to hold larger money balances.

If, however, a continued increase in the supply of money leads to inflation and rising prices, rates of interest will rise. People will be reluctant to lend money that will fall in purchasing power by the time it is repaid. They will try to hold their assets neither in the form of money nor in the form of bonds or bills. They will try to hold them in the form of shares: of physical assets, such as land and buildings or paper titles to them.

The monetary theory may seem a more satisfactory explanation of interest, because the flow of new loans is small compared with the total stock of securities. But we must not drop the marginal productivity of capital completely out of the picture. It is the fact that production takes time, and that some methods using more capital are more productive, that both gives rise to a demand for free capital

[1] The "cheap money" policy inaugurated in October, 1945 provided some confirmation of the monetary theory of interest. It aimed at reducing the long-term rate of interest to $2\frac{1}{2}$ per cent, and it did succeed in reducing it to nearly that level, indeed, for a week or so in October, 1946, $2\frac{1}{2}$ per cent Consols actually touched 100 But it must be remembered that other opportunities for lending were greatly restricted by control over new investment (including allocation of scarce materials and restrictions on private building).

Even so, the continuous increase in the amount of money that would have been needed to hold the long-term rate down to $2\frac{1}{2}$ per cent was greater than the Government dared to permit (bank deposits had risen by 12 per cent during the six month April to September, 1946), and in 1947 the policy faded out, the long-term rate gradually rising to its former level of 3 per cent.

from industry and trade and also provides the increased income out of which interest payments can be met. The reason why interest rates are high in poor countries is that they are short of capital and its marginal productivity is high; and this state of affairs cannot be changed merely by increasing the amount of money. In a country such as Great Britain, the monetary forces may appear to swamp the "real" forces. But any marked change, upwards or downwards, in the expected rate of profit (that is, in the marginal productivity of capital) would tend to produce a change in the same direction in rates of interest.

A minor point is that the monetary theory, in my view, explains short-term rather than long-term rates of interest. The alternative to holding money, according to Keynes, is to hold securities, meaning bonds. But Bills also yield interest; and their capital value, provided one can wait a little while until they mature, will not fall. One can sacrifice liquidity and get interest, without risking one's capital, by holding bills. From this standpoint, a deposit at the Post Office Savings Bank offers the same opportunities to a poor man as a Treasury Bill to a rich man.

Liquidity-preference varies violently from time to time, and this is reflected in short-term rates. Why should people sell bonds much below their normal value because for the time being short-term rates are high, or buy them much above their normal value because for the time being short-term rates are low? Hence long-term rates of interest tend to be more stable than short-term rates. As a rule, they are higher: the difference, over a long period, may be regarded as a premium received by holders of bonds for taking the risk that their prices will fall.

CHAPTER XXVIII

RENT AND QUASI-RENT

1. Rent in the Ordinary Sense

In ordinary speech the rent of anything is a periodical payment made for the use of it. Thus the owner of a piece of land may lease it for a term of years to a tenant who contracts to pay him a fixed sum of money each year for the use of it. This fixed sum is known as the rent of the land.

The owner of any durable good may hire it out to somebody, in return for an agreed periodical payment, instead of using it himself. Thus rent may be paid for the use of a house or a machine or a refrigerator, to give only three examples, as well as for the use of land. The agreement may stipulate that the rent shall be calculated in terms of wheat or some other commodity, but as a rule rents are fixed in terms of money.

During the period of the agreement the owner is in a similar position to a person receiving a fixed income as interest. Consider, for example, a landlord who has leased his land to a tenant at a fixed annual rent. He and the tenant have made an agreement and both must abide by it. As time goes on, conditions may change. The net money yield of the land may become higher than was expected when the lease was signed. The landlord could now get a higher rent if he were free to make a fresh bargain. But he is not free to do this: he is bound by the terms of the lease. Conversely, if the net money yield of the land becomes lower than was expected, the tenant must nevertheless continue to pay the rent agreed upon. When the lease is up, the landlord can of course make a new agreement, either with the same tenant or with a new one. If the net money yield of the land is expected to be higher than when the old lease was signed, he can obtain a correspondingly higher rent; if it is expected to be lower, he must accept correspondingly less in order to get a tenant.

Clearly, changes in the net money yield of land and, in general, in the market value of the services rendered, per unit of time, by a durable good will make rents fixed by agreement in the past either higher or lower than the rents obtainable at the moment for the use of similar goods. This raises certain problems, such as those connected with the burden of fixed charges during a depression, which we need not consider here. At any moment the annual rent obtainable for a durable good will tend to equal the expected net annual value of its services.

If similar goods can be readily produced, the rent obtainable will also tend to equal the current rate of profit upon their present cost of production. If it were greater, free capital would enter that field, in order to earn more than the prevailing rate of profit, and the increased supply of such goods would reduce the value of their services. Conversely, if it were less, free capital would avoid that field, goods of that type which wore out would not be replaced, and in time the value of the services of such goods would be raised until it again became worth while to produce them.

The term rent is sometimes used by economists to denote the earnings of more or less specific means of production whose supply cannot be increased or diminished. Rent in this sense is a kind of surplus. Before considering whether all land, or some land, or any other durable good, does in fact yield rent in this sense, I shall illustrate this special meaning by a hypothetical example.

2. RENT AS A SURPLUS

Suppose that a given area of land can produce only wheat and nothing else, and that no other land can produce wheat. Suppose further that this wheat-land is homogeneous, any acre being a perfect substitute for any other. These assumptions, of course, are most unrealistic. I make them in order to illustrate the special meaning of rent as a kind of surplus.

If this land produces wheat without the co-operation of any other factor of production, each acre will produce a given quantity of wheat per year, and its annual earnings will be simply the value of that quantity of wheat. Thus, given the amount of wheat-land, and the amount of wheat produced by it each year, its earnings or "rent" will depend upon the demand for wheat. Since the wheat-land is homogeneous, all of it will be employed (unless it is all owned by a monopolist or unless the owners combine to act monopolistically) so that the amount of wheat forthcoming each year is fixed.

Now suppose that the amount of wheat produced in any year varies with the climate. Favourable climatic conditions result in a bigger crop. Whether the owners of the wheat-land gain or lose by a bigger crop depends upon the elasticity of the demand for wheat. They may gain or they may lose. Consumers of wheat of course gain by a bigger crop, and even if the producers lose, it is reasonable to suppose that the gain to consumers outweighs the loss of producers, since the total supply of goods is increased.

In fact, however, land alone can produce very little. It needs the co-operation of other factors. Let us simplify by supposing that it needs only the co-operation of homogeneous labour. If this labour is employed mainly in other industries, the wage that owners of wheat-land must pay in order to hire it is fixed. The wage they must pay will equal the marginal productivity of that labour in other industries.

How much of this labour will be employed per acre—or per square mile—of wheat-land? The more labour there is employed (up to a certain limit), the greater will be the total output of wheat. But after a point, as more labour is employed on a fixed amount of land, the marginal product of that labour will fall. Thus an owner of wheat-land, regarding both the price of wheat and the wages of labour as fixed for him by the market, will employ whatever amount of labour maximizes his own income or "rent" from his land. This amount of labour will be the amount that makes the fixed wage per man equal to the value of the marginal product of the labour.

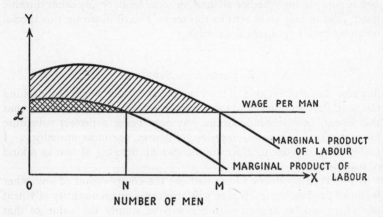

In fact, as more men are employed upon the wheat-land, wages per man will tend to rise owing to the increased demand for labour from the wheat industry. And the price of wheat per bushel will tend to fall, owing to the increased output of wheat. But we can suppose that this has happened in the past, and that for some years both the price of wheat and the wages of labour have been fairly steady. Thus to any single owner of wheat-land the price of wheat and the wages of labour appear to be fixed for him by the market. If the demand for wheat increases, its price will rise, and all owners of wheat-land will employ more labour and increase their output; conversely, if the demand for wheat falls. If the wages of labour fall, owners of wheat-land will employ more labour, and conversely if they rise. In this way the preferences of consumers make themselves felt through the price system.

Thus rent in the economic sense can be defined as a surplus accruing to a specific factor the supply of which is fixed. If the supply of wheat-land were not fixed, some of it would be devoted to other uses when the price of wheat fell and to uses requiring less labour when wages rose, and other land would be put under wheat when the price of wheat rose.

If the fixed supply of wheat-land is not homogeneous, it is easy to understand why better land will earn more per acre than worse land. It will earn more because it can produce more. In the diagram opposite, the more fertile acre employs OM men, and the shaded area represents its rent; the less fertile acre employs ON men, and the cross-shaded area represents its rent.

And it is easy to understand why some wheat-land may be left unused. It will be left unused if the value of the wheat it produces is less than the price which has to be paid to the co-operating factor of

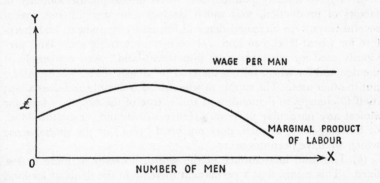

labour. Thus, in the above diagram, the owner of the land would receive less from the sale of its produce than he had to pay in wages, however few or many men he employed.

3. LAND AND RENT

The significance of rent, in the special sense which I have just illustrated, springs from the fact that the supply of a factor which yields rent cannot adapt itself to changes in demand. The supply of such a factor will not diminish, however low its earnings may fall. It has no supply price. If the whole of its earnings, or rent, were taken away (for example, by taxation), the number of units in existence would remain the same. And its supply cannot be increased. A rise in the demand for it will increase its earnings without bringing any additional units into existence, and thereby reducing, towards their former level, the earnings of existing units. Its earnings are a surplus, or rent, and changes in them do not lead to changes in the supply of the factor.

We must now turn to the real world and consider questions of fact. In what sense, if at all, does land yield rent? And do any other factors yield rent?

The "supply" of land, in this connection, may mean (*a*) the supply of land for a particular purpose, such as growing wheat or serving as sites for buildings, or (*b*) the total area of land in the world as a whole, or (*c*) the total area of land in a given country or district. The supply of land for a particular purpose can fairly readily adapt itself to changes in demand. The total land area of the world is more or less fixed, but so is the total number of workers, and neither fact is very significant from our present standpoint. The total area of land in a given district is fixed, and, in so far as land in other districts cannot serve as a good substitute, this may be of considerable significance.

(*a*) I have already pointed out, when discussing the mobility of factors of production, that much land can be used in any one of several ways. An increased demand for, let us say, wheat, and therefore for wheat-land, can and will be met by turning some land previously used for other purposes into wheat-land. And conversely, if the demand for wheat falls, some land previously under wheat will be put to other uses. The supply of wheat-land is flexible and does adapt itself to changes in demand; and this is true of the supply of land for almost any particular purpose. Hence wheat-land, or pasture-land, or building-land, as such, does not yield "rent" in the special sense which we have been discussing.

(*b*) The total land surface of the world, however, is more or less fixed. This means that a permanent increase in the demand for land in general, due for example to the growth of population, would result in a permanent rise in the incomes of landowners, and a permanent decrease would result in a permanent fall in their incomes.

It is true that land can be reclaimed from the sea. Holland has reclaimed many square miles, and Capetown has considerably increased its area in this way during recent years. But it is very unlikely that the land area of the world will be increased by any considerable percentage. The costs of reclaiming land are so high, even in those districts where it can be done most cheaply, that a very large rise in land rents could take place without leading to much new reclamation.

It is also true that the productivity of land can be increased; for example, by the use of fertilizers. Free capital will be invested in this way, in response to an increased demand for the products of land, until the return on such free capital, at the margin, is no higher than the rate of profit elsewhere. But "improvements" to land are not a perfect substitute for land itself. After a point the increased application of fertilizers, or anything else, to a given area of land, yields diminishing returns. If an increased demand for agricultural products makes it profitable to invest more free capital in improving existing land, that very fact indicates that the rent or surplus accruing to the owners of land has increased. In terms of our diagrams, the increased prices of agricultural products have raised the curve showing the marginal productivity, in terms of value, of co-operating factors. The curve showing their physical marginal productivity remains the same, but a rise of, say, 20 per cent in the prices of the products raises the value of any given marginal product by 20 per cent. This increases the surplus accruing to the landowner and makes it worth his while to employ more co-operating factors, thus increasing his surplus still further.

The supply of land as a whole, then, is more or less fixed and does not respond to changes in the demand for land as a whole. Much the same is true of labour. The total number of workers available is more or less fixed. It is not in the least certain that a general rise in wages will increase the number of births and thereby, eventually, the total number of workers. Nor is it at all certain that a general fall in wages will diminish the number of births, although if the fall is sufficiently great it will doubtless eventually reduce numbers by sheer starvation. Neither acres nor workers are homogeneous, so that a general increase in the demand for labour, or for land, may bring into use workers, or acres, not worth employing before. Free capital can be invested in increasing the productivity of either labour or land and in converting one type into another; one can train an unskilled worker to become, say, a plumber, and one can convert some pasture-land into, say, market gardens. The supply of either land or labour *for any particular use* can usually be increased or diminished.

Probably most changes in economic conditions increase the demand for some uses of land and diminish the demand for others. The fact that the total area of land is fixed (whilst always a limiting influence upon output) becomes significant, from our present standpoint, only when there is a permanent change in the demand for land as a whole. And the same is true, within limits, of labour. If we say that the income accruing to land as a whole is of the nature of rent, we must say the same of labour as a whole.

(c) Nevertheless, the geographical location of any particular acre is fixed, and this may be important. Suppose that all the land in a particular district is wheat-land. An increased demand for wheat will mean that land elsewhere is put under wheat. The landowners in that particular district may not get an appreciably larger income than before, because wheat can be grown elsewhere and sold in competition with their wheat.

But it may be that the demand for land in a particular area increases, and that land in another area will not be able to meet this demand. A leading example is the demand for sites in a given district. Thus the growth of London has raised land values in and around London.

The fact that the demand for sites in South Wales has diminished has not prevented (although it may have somewhat checked) the rise in land values in London. Some people and firms may buy land in South Wales instead of in Greater London if the price difference is large enough. But land in South Wales is, for most purposes, a very imperfect substitute for land near London, and sites cannot be transferred from South Wales to London. The supply of sites in London is limited. An increased demand for them raises their value and, therefore, raises rents, even if at the same time land values and land rents are falling in other districts. It is true that people who want to work in London can live some distance out and spend time and money in travelling to and fro. But they will do this only if site rents in London rise so much that they think it worth while to incur these costs.

Another important example arises from the fact that a national government may restrict the import of agricultural products. This raises the prices of agricultural products within that country, and thereby tends to raise the price, and rent, of land as a whole within that country. Land elsewhere is not permitted to compete freely, for obstacles are placed in the way of its products when they try to enter.

The English classical economists laid considerable stress upon rent. That is the main reason why I have devoted a chapter to this subject. For, after all, I am only repeating from a somewhat different standpoint what I have already discussed in connection with the mobility of factors and the significance of specificity. I suspect that the English classical economists were impressed by two facts. Landlords formed a distinct and important social class, and the question whether import duties upon corn should be increased or reduced or abolished was a very live issue at the time when they wrote.

We have still to consider whether there are factors other than land that are fixed in supply, in any significant sense, and that therefore yield rent. There certainly are such factors. The owner of a mineral spring with special and unique properties, or of an historic house which people pay to visit, Danny Kaye, the International Nickel Company (which owns nearly all the nickel in the world), all obtain an income of the nature of rent. And the concept of rent can be extended to include many other incomes, or portions of incomes. It can be extended to the incomes of factors that are durable, so that it takes a considerable time for their supply to diminish if their incomes fall, and that take a fairly long time to produce, so that a rise in their incomes increases their supply only after a considerable interval. I discuss this concept of quasi-rent in the next section. The concept of rent can also be extended to cover the surplus received by any given unit of a factor above its "transfer earnings." I discuss this in the final section.

4. QUASI-RENT

In the long run the earnings of durable goods will tend to equal the current rate of profit upon their current cost of production. If their earnings are greater than this, more of them will be produced, and this will bring down the prices of their products. If their earnings are less than this, they will not be replaced as they wear out—any sums set aside towards replacement being invested in other ways—and this will raise the prices of their products.

But it may take quite a long time for the supply of such a good to adjust itself completely to a change in the demand for its products. If so, the earnings of units of such a good are of the nature of rent and have been termed *quasi-rent*.

Let us consider first a fall in the demand for the products of a particular kind of good. Let us take, for example, a ship. The decreased demand for cargo space reduces the earnings of ships below the equilibrium level, if I may use this term as a brief expression for the current rate of profit on their current cost of production. If it takes a fairly long time to reduce the number of ships sufficiently to raise the earnings of the remaining ones up to the equilibrium level, two conditions must be present. In the first place, ships must have a long life, so that those which wear out or sink or, in general, go out of existence in any year form only a small proportion of the existing stock. The number of motor vehicles, for example, would be reduced by a given percentage sooner than the number of ships because motor vehicles have a shorter life. In the second place, ships must be fairly specific. A fall in the demand for, say, cinemas might not reduce their earnings much if some cinemas could readily be converted into garages, and the demand for garages was increasing. A fall in the demand for one type of ship might be met by converting ships of that type into ships of other types, the demand for which had increased. But if the demand for ships in general falls and there are no other uses to which ships can be turned, the owners of ships are helpless. Their ships must continue to be used as ships, although their earnings may be well below the equilibrium level.

There is, of course, the alternative of withholding the good from use—scrapping it, or laying it up, or closing it down. But it pays to continue using a durable good if the value of its product exceeds the cost of the co-operating factors—that is, more than covers "prime" or "operating" costs.[1] Its owner prefers to earn something, however small, rather than nothing. (I assume that its value as scrap is negligible.) Moreover, there are costs involved in closing down and subsequently restarting such things as blast furnaces and coal-mines. Hence

---

[1] *Prime costs* are variable costs plus those fixed costs (such as office expenses) which must be covered to continue producing.

their owners, hoping that the demand for their products will revive, may continue to work them even if receipts are less than prime costs.

Nevertheless, it should be noted that there is no hard and fast line between "supplementary" and "prime" costs. The division between them depends on the length of the period. Most equipment needs to have some of its parts replaced at fairly frequent intervals, others at less frequent intervals, and so on. This fact may mean that a good (e.g. a machine) is withdrawn from use although its earnings exceed those costs that recur every week. A time may come when a relatively heavy payment for renewals, replacements, or repairs must be made if the good is to continue in use, and its owner may decide to scrap it or leave it idle rather than make this payment. On the other hand, an owner may be led, step by step, to make a series of small payments of this kind, each necessary at the time to keep the good in working order, although over a period the costs incurred add up to more than the gross receipts. This clearly depends on the foresight of owners and on whether they expect conditions to improve in the future.

The owners of durable goods (including land) may have borrowed money at fixed interest upon the security of these goods. A fall in the demand for their products may make it impossible for them both to cover their prime costs and to pay their fixed-interest charges. If this state of affairs seems likely to continue, there will probably be some kind of financial reorganization under which the mortgage-holders or debenture-holders consent to accept less than the fixed money income originally agreed upon.

Let us now consider a rise in the demand for the products of a particular kind of good. If the earnings of such goods remain for a long time above the equilibrium level, two conditions must be present. In the first place, such goods must take a long time to produce or a large increase in their annual output must be possible only at a considerably increased cost. Otherwise the flow of new free capital into that field would soon increase the existing stock until earnings fell again to the equilibrium level. In the second place, it must not be possible for the owners of other goods to increase their earnings by converting them, fairly quickly, into goods of this type. A rubber plantation is a good example of a good whose supply takes time to increase, for rubber trees take six to seven years before they begin to yield.

Ships, to revert to our former example, take time to build. The capacity of existing shipyards is limited and additional skilled workers can be obtained, as a rule, only if wages are raised. And other goods cannot be turned into ships.

As a rule, goods whose supply will not rapidly be diminished in response to a fall in demand are also goods whose supply will not rapidly be increased in response to a rise in demand; although logically we should distinguish between these two classes, in fact they often coincide. The earnings of such durable and specific goods are of the nature of rent. The term quasi-rent is usually confined to the earnings of goods—machines, houses, ships, rubber plantations, and so on—but logically it applies also to the earnings of groups of workers, such as doctors, whose supply cannot rapidly be increased or diminished.

5. TRANSFER EARNINGS

Much land, many workers, and some producers' goods could be employed in any of several industries. The amount of money that any particular unit could earn in its best-paid alternative use is sometimes called its transfer earnings. If the demand for the products of a given industry decreases, that industry will tend to contract. It will contract because the earnings of factors employed in it will tend to fall, inducing some factor-units, including some entrepreneurs, to leave it and go elsewhere. The units which leave will be those whose transfer earnings are now greater than the amount they can expect to earn if they remain in the industry. Conversely, an industry expands by attracting factor-units who can now earn more in that industry than elsewhere.

Suppose, for example, that the industry is wheat-growing. Some land now under wheat could earn just a little less by being used for some other purpose, such as growing barley. Quite a small fall in the earnings of wheat-land, or quite a small rise in the earnings of, say, barley-land, will induce the owners of this land to put it under barley instead of under wheat. Some other land now under wheat could earn, say, 95 or 90 per cent as much elsewhere. A fall of 5 or 10 per cent in the earnings of wheat-land might induce the owners of this land to use it for some other purpose; and so on. At the other extreme there may be some land which is practically useless for anything except growing wheat. It would continue to grow wheat even if its earnings fell to nearly zero. The whole of its earnings, from the standpoint of the wheat-growing industry, are of the nature of rent, for they are not necessary to induce it to remain in the industry. And, in general, the excess of what any unit gets over its transfer earnings is of the nature of rent. Nevertheless, if an industry employs units of a factor with relatively high transfer earnings side by side with other units (which, when employed in that industry, are just as good as the others) whose transfer earnings are very low or zero, these latter suffer no disadvantage from being specific and enjoy an income largely of the nature of rent. For, in general, one unit will earn the same as any other equally efficient unit employed in the same industry, and if a given industry must pay a certain price per unit in order to attract enough units of a given factor away from the alternative employments open to some of them, it must pay that price to specific and non-specific units alike.

The concept of transfer earnings is useful for the light that it throws on the extent to which the costs of an industry may vary with its output. For example, if an industry can expand substantially, at least in the short run, only by drawing upon particular workers and other factor units who are getting considerably higher earnings where they are at present, the industry in question must offer them still more to induce them to move into it. This means that any substantial expansion of its output, at least in the short run, must be accompanied by considerably higher average and marginal costs per unit of product, arising from the increased prices that must be paid to such factor-units, including similar units which were already in that industry.

CHAPTER XXIX

PROFITS

1. WHAT ARE PROFITS?

In ordinary speech we often speak of profit as the gross margin by which the selling price exceeds the buying price or, in the case of a manufactured article, the direct cost of production. Mr. Finn, the fishmonger, buys cod at 2s. a lb. and sells it at 2s. 6d. a lb.; we say that he makes a profit of 6d. a lb., or 25 per cent. The direct cost, in labour and materials, of producing a motor-car is £300; the factory sells it for £450; we say that the profit is £150, or 50 per cent.

These are gross profit margins. Various expenses must be deducted to arrive at the net profit. Mr. Finn may employ assistants, who must be paid wages; he may have to pay rent for his shop; he must buy ice and other items. The factory has to cover capital charges, notably depreciation, and other expenses such as advertising.

The net profit on each transaction tells us nothing about the income of the firm unless we know the turnover, the total value of all transactions over the year. An average net profit of only 1 per cent on each transaction yields an income of £100,000 on an annual turnover of £10 million, whereas an average net profit of 20 per cent on each transaction yields only £20,000 on an annual turnover of only £100,000. (For convenience I take the percentage on the selling price.)

The annual rate of return on the capital employed is quite a different matter from the net profit on each transaction. The relation between the two is that the former equals the latter multiplied by the number of times the capital is turned over in the course of a year. A capital of £1 million turned over ten times (that is, a turnover of £10 million) at an average net profit on turnover of 1 per cent yields an income of £100,000, 10 per cent on the capital employed. A capital of £100,000 turned over only once in two years (that is, an annual turnover of £50,000) at an average net profit on turnover of 20 per cent, yields an income of £10,000, also 10 per cent on the capital employed.

In this chapter I am considering profits as a form of income. I shall therefore say no more about the rate of profit on turnover, but shall concentrate on profits as an annual income on capital employed in industry and trade.

It is impossible to draw a firm line between profits and other forms of income from property. For example, profits are a fluctuating return, in contrast to the fixed income of interest received by the holder of bonds. But the profits of a bank are the interest it receives from the bonds and bills which it buys and from the loans it makes to its customers, less its expenses. The profits of a real estate company which leases its property consist of the rents it receives, less its expenses.

Again, the profits of a company depend on how much money it has borrowed at fixed interest. Two companies may do exactly the same amount of business, on the same terms, but one will show smaller profits than the other because it has to pay interest on debentures or bank loans, whereas the other works entirely on its own capital and therefore has no interest charges to deduct.

These difficulties of computation, however, do not prevent us from treating profits separately, for purposes of analysis. They have some characteristics of their own. A wage is a price paid for a certain amount of work, and interest is a price paid for a loan, but profits are not a price. They are a residual item, a fluctuating return received by owners of capital after all the other claimants have been paid.

2. Profits in the United Kingdom

The following estimates for 1958 are from the Blue Book: *Estimates of National Income and Expenditure* (1959).

	£ million
1. Gross trading profits of companies	3,002
2. Gross trading surpluses of public corporations	341
3. Other corporate income:	
Trading profits earned abroad	295
Non-trading income	783
4. Gross trading income of Central Government	109
5. Gross trading income of Local Authorities	42
6. Gross incomes of self-employed persons	1,836
TOTAL	6,408

How much of this total should be included in profits?

Item 6 is the incomes of professional workers, farmers, shopkeepers, and others running their own businesses. The greater part is income from personal exertion. Perhaps as little as a quarter, and certainly not more than a half, represents profit on the capital employed.

If we wish to include only trading profits and to exclude other income from property, such as interest on securities held as reserves, we must leave out the £783 million of corporate income not derived from trading.

If we wish to measure only private profits, we must exclude the trading surpluses of public corporations and the trading incomes of the central government and local authorities.

It must be remembered that all the figures in the above table are gross figures, before providing for (a) taxation and (b) depreciation.

The Blue Book gives an appropriation account for companies. After paying dividends and interest (£1,162 million), U.K. taxation (£967 million), and other items, they had undistributed profits of £1,706 million.

Out of this £1,706 million, the companies had to provide for depreciation. The statutory provision allowed them was £979 million.

How far are statutory provisions for depreciation adequate? In so far as they are based on the original costs of the assets, they are too low to provide for replacement if the cost of such assets is substantially higher when the time comes to replace them. On the other hand, the British Government may grant initial allowances on investment allowances or both. An *initial allowance* is in effect a depreciation allowance granted in advance when new plant and machinery or other assets are purchased; it is repaid over subsequent years. An *investment allowance* is in effect a permanent remission of taxation on such new assets, equal at present to some 10 per cent of their cost. Whether either or both of these allowances are granted in any particular year, and on what types of assets and to what amount, depends on how far the Chancellor wishes to encourage new investment in that year. In 1958 these allowances accounted for £362 million of the total of £979 million.

During periods of rising prices, profits include *Stock appreciation*. For accounting purposes, the "profit" in any year is current sales, minus current purchases, plus any increase in value of stocks. This last item is a book figure; it cannot be spent or distributed to shareholders until the stocks are sold; and some firms set aside special reserves to cover the higher cost of replacing stocks when they are sold. It is the practice to deduct stock appreciation from estimates of national product, and company and other incomes, on the ground that it is only a book-keeping profit, which will be swallowed up in replacement costs if the prices of stocks remain at their present level.

3. RISK AND UNCERTAINTY

Profits have their origin in uncertainty. Some kinds of uncertainty arise from lack of knowledge about the present facts. For example, capital may be spent in prospecting for minerals in a certain area. It is not known whether the minerals are there, at any rate in deposits worth working. If they are not, capital spent on prospecting will be lost, but if there are rich deposits, it will yield a high return.

Launching a new product on to the market is also rather a gamble. One cannot be sure in advance whether or not it will meet with a favourable reception from buyers. If it does, the capital spent on the plant and equipment to make it, and on advertising it, may yield good profits. If it is a failure, however, most of that capital may be lost.

Even when all the present facts are known, the future is always uncertain. The profits of a business may be affected by almost any kind of unforeseen change: a change in climate, a change in Government at home or abroad, a change in tastes. The progress of knowledge may reveal either new uses for a commodity or new substitutes for it. Who can say what costs and prices will be next month, let alone next year, or five years hence? Clearly anybody who invests free capital in specific physical assets is taking risks. His income will be of the nature of quasi-rent; he will take whatever is left from the receipts after all the costs have been paid.

The risks arise from uncertainty. Some risks can be insured against. For example, an insurance company knows from past experience that each year a certain percentage of damage is likely to be caused by fire to particular kinds of assets. The insurance company can therefore charge an appropriate premium, rather higher than the percentage chance of damage, and in return can compensate any insurer who does suffer damage by fire to his property. Over a period, the premiums paid by those who make no claims, as well as by those who do, will more than cover the payments made to the latter. From the standpoint of the insured, insurance enables him to convert a small risk of a big loss into a definite cost—the insurance premium—and to safeguard himself against the risk. But many risks cannot be insured against, because they are not measurable and their chances of occurrence cannot be calculated, and it is because of them that the return on capital assets is uncertain and liable to fluctuate.

There are losses, as well as profits. When we measure the average rate of profit on capital, we must remember the losses. A million pounds invested in a representative sample of ordinary shares will yield somewhat more, over a fairly long period, than a million pounds invested in "safe" fixed-interest securities. But the difference, which may be regarded as a premium for taking the risk that part or all of the capital will be lost, is considerably less than it appears to be if we look only at the successful companies and forget that the average return covers also those companies which have done badly or gone bankrupt.

4. Variations in Profits

The most important influence affecting the general level of profits is the trade cycle. Profits tend to be high during periods of prosperity, whereas in times of depression a number of firms make losses and have to draw upon their reserves to cover their current costs.

The reason why profits gain more than most incomes during booms and lose more during slumps is that they are largely a residual item.

Other incomes are relatively stable in the short run, and profits are what remain after the other claimants have been paid.

The widest fluctuations in profits, between times of good trade and times of bad trade, take place in the investment industries, including those making durable consumers' goods. The demand for most non-durable goods for current consumption, such as food, drink, tobacco, and newspapers (but not clothing, which is worn longer during bad times) is fairly stable. Profits in those industries seldom fluctuate greatly, and therefore tend to be relatively low. The yield on the shares of well-established companies in such industries is fairly steady, and not much higher than on bonds such as high-class debentures.

A rising price level is often associated with a period of prosperity. But it is quite possible to have rising prices without a boom, as in Indonesia during recent years, or a boom without rising prices, as in the United States during the late 1920s. In any event, a rising price level tends to increase profits. Some firms have paid out costs in the past for products that are only now being completed, and that sell for more than they had expected. Some current costs, such as salaries and wages and interest charges, may not rise as much as selling prices. Conversely, a falling price level tends to reduce profits, possibly turning them into losses. Increases in wage rates that outstrip increases in productivity per worker tend to reduce profits. Rapid technical progress, which increases productivity per worker substantially, is likely to increase profits if the rise in wage rates is only moderate.

Low rates of interest may stimulate investment and tend to raise profits in so far as the cost for interest charges is reduced. But in normal times, with fairly full employment, rates of profit are likely to be lower if interest rates are more or less permanently low than if they are high. For both alike reflect the relative abundance or scarcity of capital. Free capital can either be lent at fixed interest or invested in tangible assets. If the former yields a low return, more free capital is likely to flow into investment, and this will tend to keep down rates of profit.

5. Profits and Taxation

All taxes on a business are included in the costs of the business. A property-tax, such as local rates, is a fixed cost; it does not vary with output. It is therefore a heavier burden when times are bad and output is low. In Great Britain, local rates on buildings used for industry and trade are relatively low, but such property-taxes are substantial in some other countries.

An excise duty, of so much per unit of output or per unit of sales, is a variable cost. In Great Britain we have excise duties (and corresponding import duties) on drink and tobacco and a few minor items. Purchase-taxes are also in this category.

The effect of such a tax is to raise the price to the consumer and thereby to make consumption less than it would otherwise be. As time goes on, less free capital flows into that industry than if there were no tax, until profits in that industry are as high as elsewhere despite the tax.

In Great Britain we have had from time to time, especially during wars, an excess-profits tax. The profits which a firm made in some agreed year are taken as its standard profits. Any profits which it makes over and above this amount (unless they are attributable to new investment) are heavily taxed.

Broadly speaking, this is a bad tax. It penalizes the most efficient firms, whose profits are increasing, and it discourages the search for methods of reducing costs.

In Great Britain, companies deduct income-tax at the standard rate before paying out dividends to their shareholders (the standard rate at present, 1959, is 7s. 9d. in the £). A taxpayer who would pay less than the standard rate (for example, a married man with three children and an earned income of less than £1,200 a year) may claim a rebate. On the other hand, a taxpayer with over £2,100 a year must also pay surtax on his dividends.

The British income-tax, plus surtax, is progressive; that is to say, it takes a larger percentage from a larger income. This is admirable from the standpoint of reducing inequality. But it tends to discourage risk-taking. The more successful an investment proves, the larger the proportion taken in taxation. Some people would prefer, for example, an even chance of £1,000 a year or £5,000 a year to a safe £2,500 a year. But the tax reduces these alternatives to an even chance of £723 or £2,660, as against a safe £1,591; few people would prefer the former.

In the same way, the income-tax, plus surtax, discriminates against the investment industries, which tend to have high profits in good years and low profits or none at all in bad years. More is taken in taxation from an investor whose income has fluctuated greatly over a period of years than from an investor who has had the same total income over that period, but about the same income every year. For example—

			Income	Tax	Income	Tax
Year I	.	.	5,000	2,340	2,000	665
Year II		.	1,000	277	2,000	665
Year III		.	1,000	277	2,000	665
Year IV		.	nil	nil	2,000	665
Year V		.	3,000	1,165	2,000	665
	TOTAL		10,000	4,059	10,000	3,325

Another defect of the British income-tax is that it taxes savings in the year when they are made and subsequently taxes the income which they yield.

One way to overcome these defects would be to impose an annual tax on the capital value of all assets instead of a tax on the income from them.[1]   But this would be a revolutionary change, and perhaps difficult to administer.

[1] See my article "What is the Best Tax-System?", *Economica*, May, 1942.

PART VI

MONEY AND BANKING

MONEY

1. MONEY AS A MEDIUM OF EXCHANGE

THE modern economic world is based on specialization. Few people, except farmers, produce for themselves as much as one-tenth or even one-hundredth of the goods which they consume. Most production takes place for the market. The products are sold and the producers buy what they want with the money. In effect, they exchange their products against others—but through the medium of money. Moreover, the production of most goods, and their distribution to consumers, involve a long chain of processes in which many different factors of production take part.

A community organized on these lines must use money. Any considerable amount of specialization, and therefore of exchange of products, cannot take place unless something is generally accepted as a medium of exchange and a measure of value; in other words, it cannot take place without money.

Exchange without the use of money must take place by barter. The main difficulty of barter is that it requires "a double coincidence of wants": a man must find another who both has what he wants and wants what he has. This is seldom easy even with finished commodities. Thus a story is told—typical of many others—of a traveller in Africa who wished to obtain a boat. The owner of the boat was willing to part with it, but wanted ivory in exchange. The traveller had no ivory. He found a man who had ivory and wanted cloth. He himself had no cloth. But he had wire, and he found yet another man who gave him cloth for his wire, so that he could then exchange the cloth for ivory, and finally exchange the ivory for the boat. Clearly trade under such conditions must be very restricted in scope, and just because it would be so restricted, it is probable that there would be few generally accepted market values, and that a good deal of time might therefore be spent in bargaining. A further point is that some goods (such as boats) cannot be divided into portions without destroying their utility; hence the owner of such a good could not exchange part of it against the goods of one man, part against the goods of another, and so on.

Most exchanges in the modern world are not exchanges of finished commodities. How, for example, would wages be paid under barter? The employer might, where possible, pay his workers by giving them a share of what they had helped to produce, leaving them to barter the wheat, or coal, or yarn, or whatever it might be, as best they could, in order to obtain what they themselves wanted. Clearly this plan could not be followed in the case of workers engaged in supplying transport facilities or other services or in producing indivisible and valuable goods such as buildings. An alternative plan would be for the employer to barter his products for goods that his workers, and shareholders, and suppliers of raw materials, wanted. But this discussion need not be prolonged; its purpose is merely to show that a modern economy could not well continue without the use of money.

Money overcomes the difficulties of barter by serving as a general medium of exchange, or means of payment. Money is something that everybody is prepared to accept in exchange for goods or services. A person will accept money in payment, not because he necessarily wants money for its own sake, but because he knows that other people in turn will accept it from him in return for the goods and services he himself requires.

Hence money can be defined as *a generally acceptable means of payment*. It is something that everybody is willing to accept in payment for goods and services or in settlement of a debt. When this aspect of money is considered, the monetary unit is called a *unit of currency*, because it "runs" from hand to hand. The money of one country is usually not current in other countries, but there are ways, which I discuss in the next Part, of making payments between countries and thus facilitating international trade just as the use of money facilitates trade, and therefore specialization, within a country.

In order to serve as a general medium of exchange, money must be generally acceptable. It is usually legal tender: that is to say, people are compelled by law to accept it in payment. But it need not be legal tender. For example, the chief medium of exchange in parts of Northern Africa has been for many years the "Maria Theresa" dollar, which the London and other Mints continued to provide, in response to the demand for it, bearing the date 1780. This coin has never been legal tender in those areas, and its metallic content has often been worth much less than its face value, yet it has continued by custom to be generally acceptable and the chief medium of exchange. Other examples are the gold sovereign, which is still the chief medium of exchange, for large transactions, in Greece, and the Hong Kong paper dollar which, until the Communist Government prohibited it, was the chief medium of exchange in South China.

On the other hand, a currency that is legal tender may not be generally acceptable. This will be so during a period of runaway inflation, when it is rapidly falling in value and therefore nobody wants to hold it. There are plenty of examples of this. The paper "assignats" issued during the French Revolution did not serve properly as money because nobody wanted them, although the penalty for refusing them was death. Nor did German marks in 1923 or Hungarian pengos in 1944 or Chinese dollars after the war.

When money does properly serve its purpose as a generally acceptable means of payment, it makes possible specialization and exchange on the modern scale; it leads to the establishment of market prices, thus avoiding much waste of time in bargaining; and it can be made divisible: for example, in Great Britain we have shillings and pence as well as pounds.

2. Money as a Measure of Value

When something comes to serve as a generally accepted medium of exchange, it is natural to express values, to make contracts, and to keep accounts in terms of that something. The advantage of this is not merely that everything has a price—that is, a value in terms of money —instead of having a separate value in terms of each of the many commodities against which it might exchange. The use of money as a measure of value immensely facilitates economic calculation. A consumer with a certain money income is confronted with money prices, and these enable him to decide which assortment of goods and services he wants to buy. The changes in the demands of consumers affect prices and thereby induce entrepreneurs to produce more of the goods for which demand has increased and fewer of the goods for which demand has decreased. An entrepreneur knows the market price of each factor of production. He can therefore plan the location of his establishment, the size of his output, and his methods of production, in such a way as to maximize his profits. This means that factors are directed towards those uses in which their products have the greatest value. If, to revert to a simple example, a piece of land yields a greater money return under wheat than under barley, this means not only that its owner will gain more by using it for wheat but also that consumers prefer it to be used for wheat.

Such calculations, however, would be much more difficult and much less accurate if there were no common measure for comparing value and costs. The price mechanism under such conditions would work only roughly and cumbersomely. At present, entrepreneurs take the risk that prices will change to their disadvantage. Under barter, this risk would be much greater owing to the difficulty of calculating and forecasting exchange ratios between the goods they produced and the various goods that their employees and their suppliers demanded in payment. Hence there would be much less division of labour.

The monetary unit for purposes of calculation is called *the unit of account*. Normally the unit of currency and the unit of account are the same, for clearly the use of money as a measure of value springs from its use as a medium of exchange. It is possible, however, for the two units to be different, provided that an exchange ratio between them can be somehow established. Thus in Germany in 1923, when prices were rising very rapidly, contracts were often made in terms of Swiss francs or United States dollars. When the time for payment arrived, the payment was made in marks, the number of marks given being the number required to equal the specified sum of francs or dollars at the rate ruling at the time in the foreign exchange market. The mark remained the unit of currency, but the unit of account was the franc or the dollar.

In the same way, the United States dollar was widely used as a unit of account in China during the inflation under Chiang Kai-Shek, and the United States dollar or the pound sterling in certain European countries, such as Greece and Hungary, since the war.

Some writers say that money fulfils another function, that of serving as *a standard for deferred payments*. Contracts, including loans, are usually made in terms of money. This is because people believe that the value, the purchasing power, of money is not likely to change much during the period of the contract. If they fear that it will, then either they make contracts in terms of something else—for example, in terms of gold or of another currency, such as United States dollars (at the present time)—or they refrain from making long-term contracts. There was not much international lending during the 1930s, largely because foreign investors feared that the values of the currencies of borrowing countries might fall. For example, few British investors bought French Rentes even when they yielded twice as much as Consols. For they feared that sooner or later the exchange value of the French franc would fall—as indeed it did, when the franc was de-valued in September, 1936, and again in June, 1937, and yet again (after a period of gradual depreciation) in May, 1938.

If money is expected to remain fairly stable in value, loans and other long-term contracts involving payment some time in the future will be made to a greater extent than if lenders fear that the value of money will fall. The alternative of using some commodity such as gold as a standard for deferred payments may not be possible—the Government whose currency is distrusted may forbid it—or may not be attractive to the borrower, whose future receipts will be in currency and not in that commodity.

In so far as loans and other long-term contracts promote economic progress, the conclusion that emerges is that it is desirable for money to remain fairly stable in value, or at least for people to expect it to do so. I see no reason, however, for listing as a separate function of money that it serves as a standard for deferred payments, for this is covered by the statement that money serves as a measure of value—for both present and future payments.

Yet another function which is sometimes attributed to money is that of serving as *a store of value*. The Frenchman who has held francs, or their equivalent, since 1914, when they were worth 10d., until today, when they are worth less than a farthing, would greet this pronouncement with a hollow laugh, or groan, which would be echoed in dozens of other countries where money has fallen heavily in value—in some countries far more than in France. Experience suggests that for a store of value gold or jewels or works of art (provided they are chosen wisely) would serve, as a rule, better than money. What is true, as we saw when discussing the monetary theory of interest, is that by definition money is the most liquid of all assets. The money value of securities or physical assets may fall, but a given sum of money is always the same, in money, although its purchasing power may change.

3. Kinds of Money

Many commodities have been used as money in different places and at different periods. Pastoral tribes have used cattle, and some still do; the drawbacks are that cattle are neither divisible nor uniform in size and quality. Some common article of trade, such as tobacco or salt or skins, has often been used, provided that it was not perishable and was easy to handle. Rum (highly liquid but difficult to store, said the wags) was used in the early years of New South Wales. Cigarettes were used, both as a medium of exchange and as a measure of value, in some prisoner-of-war camps during the war and in the black markets of Europe immediately after the war.

Gold and silver have probably been used as money for some five thousand years. They are fairly generally desired for their own sake—although their exchange value would be considerably lower if they were not widely used as money. They are durable and divisible and homogeneous and not too heavy or bulky to serve as a medium of exchange. Moreover, their annual supply from the mines is only a small proportion of the total stock in existence, so that considerable fluctuations in their value, arising from changes in the total supply, are much less likely than in the case of perishable commodities of which the annual supply is greater than the total stock.

At first, gold and silver seem to have exchanged against goods without being coined. This meant that everybody who received gold or silver in payment had to satisfy himself as to the weight and fineness of the metal that he received. Later, the invention of coinage saved him this trouble. A coin is a piece of metal whose weight and fineness are certified by whoever makes the coin. A bank-note convertible into gold is a promise by the bank that issues it to pay on demand, in exchange for the note, a stated weight of gold (usually in the form of a gold coin or gold coins).

Usually, before modern times, the commodity used as money has been generally desired for its own sake. Even so, the fact that it served as money tended to increase its value by increasing the demand for it. This applies to gold today; the greater part of the demand for gold is for monetary purposes, and if the United States and other countries stopped holding gold reserves, the value of gold would fall.

Nowadays most money is paper money, worth as a commodity only the paper on which it is printed. Moreover, it is usually *inconvertible*: that is to say, no Government or bank promises to change it, or "convert" it, into gold or anything else. Yet it serves its purpose very well. Everybody is quite willing to accept it because he knows that he can use it to pay for goods or services or to settle his debts. It seems like a gigantic confidence trick. People part with valuable goods and services in exchange for bits of paper. But nobody is swindled. So long as the paper money remains generally acceptable, anyone who is paid it can always pass it on when he wishes. It is only when too much of it is issued, sending down its value, that people begin to distrust it and may be reluctant to accept it.

The money used for small change is called *token money* when, as is usually the case, its metallic content is worth less, as metal, than the face value of the coin. Normally the Mint which issues such coins makes a profit, known as *seigniorage*. Thus in 1939 a shilling contained less than twopennyworth of metal; it was "a note printed on silver." At times, a rise in the price of silver has made some silver coins worth more as metal than as coins, and they have tended to disappear from circulation, to be melted down and sold as metal. This happened to British silver coins in 1920. The Coinage Act of that year therefore reduced the "fineness" (the proportion of silver to the total weight) from 925 to 500 thousandths. Nowadays British coins are minted from cupro-nickel, not from silver, but the old silver coins still circulate. The copper and nickel in the new coins are worth, as metal, about 6 per cent (at 1959 prices) of the face value of the coins.

4. BANK DEPOSITS AS MONEY

In countries where cheques are widely used, most large payments are made by cheque. In Great Britain over 90 per cent of the total value of all money transactions is settled by cheque, although of course by far the greater number of transactions are relatively small ones, settled by cash.

It seems sensible and realistic, therefore, to call bank deposits money. A cheque is an order on the bank to pay the sum stated from the deposit of the drawer, the person who signs the cheque, to the payee. I pay you a cheque for £10 and when the banks have entered this payment, my deposit has gone down by £10 and yours has gone up by £10. It is the bank deposits which serve as money; the cheques merely tell the banks what to do with their various deposits.

Strictly, cheques can be drawn only on deposits "on current account." But other bank deposits, which earn interest and on which the depositor must give notice if he wishes to withdraw any part of them, are very liquid; in practice a bank would usually honour a cheque drawn, in effect, against such a deposit; and we may therefore count all deposits with cheque-paying banks as money. But we must draw the line there; other very liquid assets, such as Savings Bank deposits or bills of exchange, are not money.

Although the usual practice is to include bank deposits with cash, there is a difference between the two forms of money, a difference which in some contexts is important. Cash is generally acceptable, but we would not usually give value for a cheque from a stranger. During a financial crisis when, in some countries at any rate, there is a risk of bank failures, people may insist on payment in cash and not by cheque. A bank is liable to its depositors to pay cash on demand against their current accounts, and banks must therefore keep a reserve of cash; this means that the monetary authorities, by controlling the amount of cash, can control the volume of bank deposits, as we shall see in the following chapter. But for most purposes we can count bank deposits as money rather than as very close substitute for money.

In October, 1959, the estimated currency circulation of the United Kingdom was £2,439 million, of which £1,981 million was held by the public. It consisted of £185 million coin and £2,254 million notes. (The latter, however, included £120 million Scottish bank notes, of which all but some £7 million had to be backed by Bank of England notes.) The total of net bank deposits (including those held by overseas and foreign, Scottish, and other banks) was well over £8,000 million.

5. THE SIGNIFICANCE OF MONEY

Some economists speak of "the veil of money." It is true that what we really want are goods and services, and that to find out what is really happening we must go behind money prices and look at the changes in the volume of output and in "real" incomes. Money is merely a device for promoting specialization and exchange. It is a very important device. Modern economic life, which is founded on specialization, would not be possible without money. But it is not money that we want; it is what we can buy with the money.

On the other hand, Keynes and others are of course quite right when they insist that in a monetary economy, monetary changes may play a fundamental part in bringing about "real" changes. An increase in the amount of money may lead to fuller employment; if overdone, it may lead to rising prices, which may change the distribution of income between persons and classes and may affect the volume of output—perhaps favourably at first and adversely after a time. A decrease in the amount of money may have the opposite effects.

On the demand side, the fact that money is used may mean that people hold money as a liquid asset. As we have seen, changes in their liquidity-preference or in the amount of money may affect rates of interest.

In so far as the trade cycle arises from a divergence between decisions to save and decisions to invest, it is a monetary phenomenon; it is difficult to conceive of such a divergence in a community which did not use money.

On the one hand, therefore, we must not hastily conclude that a rise in money values always means a real improvement, or conversely that a fall always means a real worsening, of economic conditions. But on the other hand we must bear in mind that monetary changes may have profound effects on the whole economy and that monetary policy may be of great importance.

BANK CREDIT

1. BANK-NOTES

THE purpose of this chapter is to show how banks can create credit. Bank credit is another name for bank deposits subject to cheque; as we have just seen, it forms the greater part of our money. But a good approach to the subject is to show how a bank can put its own notes into circulation, if it is permitted by law to do so.

A bank-note is a promise made by a bank to pay the sum of money stated on the note to the bearer (that is, to anybody who hands the note back to the bank, and asks for payment) on demand. In England, all bank-notes are now issued by the Bank of England; supplemented by coins, they constitute our currency. No other English bank is allowed to issue its own notes. Before the war of 1914, gold coins were in circulation, and a £5 Bank of England note was a promise to pay the bearer five gold sovereigns on demand. Nowadays, the statement on a Bank of England note that the Bank of England "promise to pay the bearer on demand the sum of" £5, or £1 or 10s. means nothing at all.

Some English banks used to have the right to issue their own notes to a limited maximum amount; some Scottish banks still have this right; and in a few countries, such as Canada, notes issued by banks other than the central bank form an important part of the currency.

How would a bank get its notes into circulation? If the currency were gold or silver, the bank might accept deposits of coin for safe-keeping, giving its receipts in return. If such receipts were not made out to the depositor by name, but were in the more convenient form of promises to pay the stated amount of coin to bearer, they would be bank-notes.

If the bank kept coin on its premises to the full value of the receipts, or notes, which it had issued, so that its notes were backed 100 per cent by coin, it would be acting like a safe-deposit company. And in order to cover its expenses it would have to charge its depositors for keeping their coin for them.

But a bank need not, and most banks do not, keep a reserve of 100 per cent against their notes. Day by day, people may present notes and receive the stated amount of coin from the bank in exchange. But day by day other people may deposit coin with the bank, receiving its notes in exchange. Provided that the bank always keeps on its premises a reserve of coin sufficient to meet any excess of payments-out over payments-in, it fulfils its promise to give cash to any holder of its notes who demands cash in exchange.

After a time, its notes will become known. People will be willing to hold them, or to accept them in payment, without rushing to the bank to turn them into cash, for they will have discovered by experience that whenever they do present notes to the bank, they are paid at once in cash. So the notes of the bank will circulate among the public as a means of payment.

Something like this happened to the receipts issued by the London goldsmiths in the seventeenth century for silver deposited with them. The goldsmiths found that they could lend out most of the silver (to the Government, for example) and still have enough to meet all the demands from people presenting their receipts.

Another way in which a bank can put its notes into circulation is by lending them to people who want to borrow money or by using them to buy securities. In this way the bank may derive an income from the interest it receives from its borrowers or upon the securities it has bought. At the same time, it adds to the existing means of payment by providing bank-notes against which it keeps a cash reserve of much less than 100 per cent—say, 20 per cent or 10 per cent; its bank-notes pass from hand to hand among the public, and are in effect money.

Everybody who holds one of its notes, instead of going to the bank and demanding cash from it, is virtually lending that amount, free of interest, to the bank.

Thus bank-notes that are accepted by the public, held by the public, and used as means of payment are an addition (not a net addition because we must deduct the cash reserve held against them) to the supply of money.

In most countries nowadays bank-notes are issued only by the central bank, as in Great Britain, and constitute the currency of the country. But the other banks nevertheless create credit, adding to the supply of money. They do this not by issuing bank-notes, which they are forbidden to do, but by creating or accepting bank deposits subject to cheque to a value much greater than the cash reserves that they hold.

2. The Origin of Bank Deposits

Bank deposits, like bank-notes, can originate in either of two ways. Customers can deposit cash with the bank, or the bank itself can create deposits by making loans or buying securities.

Clearly a bank deposit could originate in the payment of cash, to that amount, by the depositor to the bank. The depositor might feel that his money was in safer keeping with the bank than at his home; and he might find it convenient to make many of his payments by cheque rather than in cash, and to "pay in" cheques he received, letting his bank collect the amounts and add them to the sum standing to his credit, instead of collecting them himself.

It is conceivable that a bank might act like a cloakroom. It might keep a little safe for each customer, and all the cash that he paid in, or that the bank collected on his behalf, might be put in the safe. In this way, people could pay one another by cheque and the corresponding amount of cash could be moved from one safe to another by the bank or banks concerned.

A bank that did this would probably find that it always had a large amount of cash on its premises. All the time, it would be paying cash across the counter to customers who wanted to withdraw some of their deposits, and it would constantly be paying cash, on behalf of its customers, to other banks in favour of whose customers its own customers had drawn cheques. But on the other hand, it would all the time be receiving new deposits of cash across the counter, and from other banks whose customers had drawn cheques in favour of its own customers. The amount of cash in any particular safe might fluctuate considerably from day to day, but when the amount to the credit of some customers was low the amount to the credit of other customers would probably be high, so that day in and day out the total amount of cash in the bank would be large and would not fluctuate very much.

Under these conditions, it is quite likely that it would occur to the banker to lend out the greater part of the cash on his premises. Instead of keeping a separate safe for each customer, he could lump all the cash together, and although he lent out most of it he could still retain enough to enable him to pay on demand (to his customers or, on behalf of his customers, to other banks) all the cash that in fact he would be asked to pay.

A necessary condition for this, it will be noted, is that cash is homogeneous. A depositor who took the number of a pound note that he paid into his bank would have no cause to feel aggrieved if he saw that note in circulation the next day. For his banker would have another pound note ready for him, if he wanted it; and one pound note is as good as another. Another necessary condition is that only a small proportion of the total deposits is likely to be withdrawn in cash at the same time. Suppose the banker decided, on the basis of his past experience, that 10 per cent of his total deposits was an adequate reserve of cash. If— owing, say, to a rumour that the bank was likely to fail—there was a "run on the bank," a large proportion of his depositors demanding repayment in cash, the cash would not be there. The banker might protest that he was perfectly solvent and that, given sufficient time, he could call in his loans, sell his investments, and thus meet his debts, yet his reputation as a banker would be gone, for he would have failed to fulfil his obligation of paying cash on demand.

The banker would receive interest on the loans he made with his depositors' money, and hence he might be able to pay interest (at a lower rate) to his depositors. For a deposit of money with a bank is not like the deposit of an article at a cloakroom: it is really a loan to the bank, and it is generally understood that the bank will relend most of the money.

The money the banks lend will be used by the borrowers to make payments. Suppose, for the moment, that there is only one bank. The people to whom the money is paid may be customers of this bank, and may pay it in again to their credit. In the course of time, the same note or coin might pass and repass several times across the counter of the bank, being deposited by one customer, lent to a borrower, deposited by another customer, and so on. Thus in time the total deposits of the bank might considerably exceed the total amount of cash in the country. This would be quite all right, provided that the bank kept a sufficient reserve of cash to meet all demands for cash which were in fact made upon it. Against its liability to depositors it would hold partly cash and mainly other assets, such as debts due to it by people who had borrowed from it.

In fact, when a bank makes a loan, it does not usually lend actual cash. Instead, it gives the borrower the right to draw cheques upon it, although he has made no corresponding deposit. For example, a bank may grant its depositor A the right to overdraw his account up to the value of £1,000, A agreeing to pay a certain rate of interest on the amount he in fact overdraws. A proceeds to draw cheques, to pay for goods and services he requires (or to pay his creditors, if he has run into debt) and the people who receive his cheques probably pay them in to their own banks, to be added to their deposits. Thus the deposits of these people are increased, and nobody's deposit is reduced, by the grant of the overdraft or loan to A. It is in this way that "loans create deposits." Of course, the same thing happens if the bank, instead of granting a loan to A, purchases securities and pays for them with its own cheque. The seller of the securities "pays in" this cheque and thereby increases his deposit with his own bank, which may or may not be the bank which drew the cheque. Most of the increase in the total deposits of British banks that has taken place during recent decades has come about through the granting of loans or the purchase of securities by banks. The extra deposits have been virtually created by the banks themselves.

3. The Limitations on the Power of Banks to Create Credit

We have just seen that a bank may receive interest simply by permitting customers to overdraw their accounts or by purchasing securities and paying for them with its own cheques, thus increasing the total of bank deposits: that is, "creating credit." This seems a very easy way of making profits. Yet the rate of profits in banking is no higher than in other branches of industry. The banks have expenses—for premises, equipment, and staff—and their power to create credit is limited.

It is limited by their obligation to pay their depositors cash on demand. This means that they dare not let their reserve of cash fall below what they consider a safe level. In Great Britain during recent years the banks have considered that 8 per cent of their deposits is the minimum below which their cash reserves must not fall. Since additional loans or purchases of securities would increase total deposits, they would thereby reduce the banks' reserve of cash (assuming it to be near the minimum, and to remain the same in amount) below this minimum percentage.

In order to expand credit further, therefore, the banks must either increase the absolute amount of their cash reserves or permit them to form a lower percentage of deposits than they previously considered the lowest compatible with safety.

Let us suppose, to begin with, that there is only one bank (with numerous branches) in the country, but that it cannot increase or diminish the total amount of cash in the country, the supply of cash being controlled by the Government. At any moment, all the cash in the country is divided between the bank and the public. The bank cannot permanently increase its holding of cash by forcing the public to hold less. It can temporarily obtain more cash—by selling securities to the public or by requesting some of its customers to repay their loans or overdrafts in cash—but it will be unable to keep this extra cash and use it as a basis for credit expansion. For the public has the whip-hand of the bank in that it can always replenish its holding of cash by withdrawing deposits in cash. Thus, assuming that total deposits exceed the total amount of cash in the country, the public can always hold as much of the total cash as it wishes. If the public's demand for cash remains the same as before, and the total amount of cash in the country is not increased, the bank will be powerless to bring about a permanent increase in its cash reserve.

Suppose that the total cash (notes and coin) in the country is £1,600 million, of which, taking one day with another, a quarter is held by the bank and three-quarters by the public. The bank has £400 million as a cash reserve. Its deposits are, say, £5,000 million. Its ratio of cash to deposits is 8 per cent.

It may appear that the bank could expand credit (in other words, increase its deposits), by a further £1,000 million provided that it was prepared to reduce its ratio of cash to deposits from 8 per cent to $6\frac{2}{3}$ per cent—£400 million cash, as before, against £6,000 million deposits. But in fact an expansion of credit would mean that the public would want to hold more cash, for either prices would rise or there would be fuller employment or there would be some rise in prices together with some increase in employment. The public might now want to hold, for example, £1,400 million cash instead of £1,200 million as before, leaving only £200 million for the bank. £200 million cash against deposits of £6,000 million is a cash ratio of only 3⅓ per cent, not 6⅔.

The bank could expand credit, provided that it was prepared to reduce its ratio of cash to deposits, but it would have to take account of the consequent increase in the amount of cash which the public would want to hold. It might find, for example, that an expansion of £200 million would lead to an increase of £40 million in the amount of cash held by the public. This would leave the bank a cash reserve of £360 million against deposits of £5,200 million—just under 7 per cent. If the bank was not prepared to reduce its cash reserve appreciably below 7 per cent, it could not create more than an extra £200 million of bank credit.[1]

It would seem, therefore, that the total of bank deposits (subject to cheque) depends on three things, namely—

1. The total amount of cash in the country.
2. The amount of cash that the public wishes to hold.
3. The conventional percentage of cash to deposits that the banks maintain as a minimum.

But in most countries there is a fourth factor. The banks themselves hold deposits with the central bank, and regard these deposits as equivalent to cash. The central bank, as we shall see in the following chapter, can make their deposits with it go up or down, thereby bringing about an expansion or contraction of bank credit.

The total amount of cash in the country, plus "bankers' deposits" with the central bank, can be increased only by the monetary authorities—the Government and the central bank.

The public's demand for cash may be diminished by a fall in population or in employment or by a change in monetary habits: for example, groups of wage-earners who had formerly been paid in cash might come to be paid by cheque and to use cheques to make payments they previously made in cash.

The conventional cash ratio depends partly on the extent to which liquid assets, such as money lent at call or short notice or Treasury Bills, are available to the banks. In Great Britain, such assets are amply available, and therefore the cash ratio is low. In countries where few assets of this type are available as a second line of defence

---

[1] These are of course merely illustrative figures. But I have not chosen them altogether at random. The statistics for the past fifty years suggest that in Great Britain the public tends to hold nearly £1 in cash for each £4 it holds in bank deposits. In other words, if the banks increase the volume of credit, the public may wish to increase its holding of cash by nearly one-quarter of the increase in bank deposits.

against heavy cash withdrawals, the cash ratio is higher, perhaps as high as 15 or 20 per cent.

The cash ratio may be affected by general economic conditions. At a time of general prosperity and optimism, the banks may feel that a somewhat lower percentage would be quite safe.

But if none of these factors changes, the total amount of bank credit cannot increase. It can increase only if the total amount of money in the country increases, or if the central bank brings about an expansion in Bankers' Deposits, or if the public holds less cash than before, or if the banks are prepared to reduce their ratio of cash to deposits.

In this section I have supposed, to simplify the argument, that there is only one commercial (cheque-paying) bank. In fact, there are several different banks, but this does not substantially affect the argument. I discuss its implications in the following section.

4. BANK CLEARING

Consider a particular bank—let us say, for example, the Midland Bank. Suppose that it has about one-fifth of the total bank deposits. Every day its customers pay in cheques to their credit, and the chances are that about four-fifths of these cheques will be drawn upon other banks. The Midland Bank could of course collect the cash due to it, on those cheques, from the other banks. But the customers of the other banks will pay in cheques to their credit and presumably the average total value of these cheques will be about four times as great as that of the cheques paid in to the Midland Bank, and the chances are that about one-fifth of them will be drawn on the Midland Bank. Thus the Midland Bank will have to pay the other banks about as much cash as they have to pay to it.

Obviously a convenient arrangement would be for each bank (in any town) to send a clerk to meet clerks from other banks at a central office or *clearing house*. Each bank could then give the Midland Bank the cheques it had received drawn upon the Midland Bank, the Midland could reciprocate, and so on. If at any such clearing the Midland Bank owed, say, the Westminster Bank more than the Westminster Bank owed it, it could pay the difference in cash. Such clearings do take place every day (and in large towns two or three times a day), but the differences are not paid in cash. In England most important banks themselves have deposits with the Bank of England, and settle their differences at the clearing by cheques drawn on the Bank of England. Thus, if the Midland Bank owes the Westminster Bank £50,000 on balance, at any particular clearing, it gives the Westminster Bank a cheque drawn by itself on the Bank of England for £50,000. The Midland Bank's deposit at the Bank of England is reduced, and the Westminster Bank's is increased, by £50,000. The banks consider their deposits with the

Bank of England as equivalent to cash, for they can withdraw them in notes or coins at any time.

Clearly the equilibrium position for any bank is that it neither gains nor loses cash, over a period, at the clearing. If it habitually gains cash, it will expand its loans, so that more cheques will be drawn upon it, until its percentage of cash to deposits falls to whatever it considers the lowest consistent with safety. Conversely, if it habitually loses cash to the other banks, it will be compelled to contract its loans, so that fewer cheques are drawn upon it.

If all the banks decide to expand credit, and keep in step with one another, no bank will lose cash to other banks at the clearing, and the limits to credit expansion will be simply those I discussed in the previous section, on the assumption that there was only one bank.

Suppose that one bank only (say, the Midland Bank) decides to expand credit. It will soon be checked by its loss of cash to the other banks at the clearing. If it expands its loans by £10 million, and has about one-fifth of the total deposits, the chances are that its new borrowers will pay four-fifths of their cheques to people who are customers of other banks, so that the Midland Bank will lose about £8 million cash to other banks at the clearing.

Suppose that the Midland Bank had £1,000 million deposits and £80 million cash (including its deposits with the Bank of England) and that the other banks, taken together, had £320 million cash and £4,000 million deposits. It is prepared to let its reserve ratio fall to about 7 per cent, but the other banks wish to maintain their conventional ratio of 8 per cent.

The Midland Bank cannot expand its loans by £143 million, in the hope that this will leave its cash at £80 million against deposits of £1,143 million—a ratio of 7 per cent. Before it had gone very far along the path of credit expansion, it would be pulled up short by the loss of cash at the clearing.

On the other hand, it would be wrong to conclude that the maximum amount by which it could expand credit is just over £10 million, giving it £72 million cash against £1,010 million deposits—a ratio of 7·13 per cent. For as the other banks acquired more cash, they themselves would expand credit, still keeping to their ratio of 8 per cent. About a fifth of the additional cheques drawn on them would be paid to customers of the Midland Bank ; hence cash to that amount would flow back to the Midland Bank.

By a process of gradual expansion of credit, the latter might reach an equilibrium position with its cash at, say, £75 million and its deposits at £1,070 million, while the cash of the other banks had increased to £325 million and their deposits to nearly £4,063 million. This assumes that the central bank does not intervene, that the total supply of cash remains the same, and that the public does not require any more cash to hold despite an expansion of about £133 million, or 2⅔ per cent, in the total volume of bank credit.

I have illustrated what would happen if one bank alone expanded credit. But in practice, in Great Britain at any rate, all the banks are likely to keep in line with one another. So long as they all keep the same ratio of cash to deposits, they can be treated, in analysing the forces determining the supply of money, as if they were one single bank.

CHAPTER XXXII

THE BANK OF ENGLAND AND THE COMMERCIAL BANKS

1. The Supply of Money

APART from coins and bank-notes issued by banks in Scotland and Northern Ireland (of which all but £4 million must be backed, pound for pound, by Bank of England notes) our money consists of—

1. Bank of England notes, and
2. Bank deposits subject to cheque.

The former may be called cash and the latter bank credit.

Since the banks maintain a more or less constant ratio of 8 per cent cash to deposits, it seems to follow that it is the amount of cash available to the banks that determines the amount of bank credit and that, although 90 per cent (in value) of all payments are made by cheque, it is the amount of cash that governs the total supply of money.

This is broadly true. At the same time, we must remember that the real change which leads to a change in the supply of money may be something outside the monetary and banking system: for example, a series of budget deficits or of wage increases may make it appear essential that the amount of bank credit, and therefore of cash, should be increased.

Theoretically, the Bank of England could control the volume of bank credit simply by varying the amount of its notes in circulation. When it wished the banks to expand credit, it would put more of its notes in circulation—for example, by buying securities and paying cash for them. If prices rose or employment increased, some of these extra notes would be retained by the public. But some would stay with the banks. The banks would then expand credit, by making more loans or buying more securities, to $12\frac{1}{2}$ times the extent of their extra holding of notes, for by so doing they could increase their profits and still maintain their cash reserve of 8 per cent against deposits. Conversely, when the Bank of England wished to contract the volume of bank credit, it would take some of its notes out of circulation—for example, by selling securities for cash. This would leave less cash for the banks, and would therefore compel them to reduce their deposits, by reducing their loans or by selling some of their securities, in order to maintain their cash reserve at 8 per cent.

The Bank of England does in fact control the volume of bank credit in essentially this way. But it increases or decreases the banks' cash by bringing about changes in the amount of their deposits with itself, which they regard as cash, rather than by varying the amount of its notes in circulation. It also employs the weapon of the Bank rate. Moreover, the commercial banks, and the London money market as a whole, accept the leadership of the Bank and do their best to conform to any requests made by the Bank that they should follow a certain policy. For example, they may be asked to restrict certain kinds of loans and encourage others: until recently, loans for speculative purposes and hire-purchase were restricted, and loans for expanding exports were encouraged.

Hence, in order to explain how the supply of money is in fact controlled, I must discuss at some length the chief operations of the commercial banks and the part played by the Bank of England.

2. THE COMMERCIAL BANKS

There are eleven London clearing banks, so-called because they alone are members of the London Clearing House: other banks do their clearing through them. The eleven banks are the "Big Five"—Barclays, Lloyds, the Midland, the National Provincial, and the Westminster—and six others. The latter are Martins Bank, the District Bank, the National Bank (which has many branches in Ireland), Williams Deacon's Bank and Glyn, Mills (both controlled by the Royal Bank of Scotland), and Coutts and Company (controlled by the National Provincial Bank).

In Scotland there are three independent banks—namely, the Bank of Scotland, the Royal Bank of Scotland and the Commercial Bank of Scotland—and three affiliated to English banks—namely, the British Linen Bank (controlled by Barclays Bank), the National Bank of Scotland (controlled by Lloyds Bank), and the Clydesdale and North of Scotland Bank (controlled by the Midland Bank).

Many foreign and Dominion banks have offices in London, but the seventeen I have named, plus two others (in addition to the National Bank) in Northern Ireland, are the only British banks of any size. About five-sixths of their assets and about five-sixths of their 12,000 branches and sub-branches are controlled by the Big Five.

The commercial banks are sometimes called *joint-stock* banks. There is an historical reason for this. When the Bank of England was founded in 1694, it was given a monopoly of joint-stock banking in England. This prevented a few large banks from coming into existence, as they did in Scotland, with branches throughout the country. The banking business of the English provinces was done by a number of scattered and independent "country banks." But after joint-stock banking was permitted in 1833, a number of joint-stock banks were formed. As time went on, they expanded, partly by absorbing private banks, and set up branches, until today, as a result of growth and amalgamations, a few joint-stock banks perform the great bulk of the banking business.

3. The Liabilities of the Commercial Banks

The main items on the liabilities side of a bank's balance sheet are capital paid-up, reserve fund, and deposits ("current, deposit, and other accounts").

At the end of 1959, the combined capital of the London clearing banks was some £163 million and their reserve funds (accumulated out of undistributed profits) some £105 million. These sums belonged to their shareholders. In addition, there were substantial concealed reserves in that their premises were shown at far less than their market value.

The bulk of their resources, however, were deposits, amounting to over £7,400 million,[1] and these of course belonged to the depositors and not to the shareholders.

About two-thirds of their deposits were current accounts, subject to cheque, and repayable in cash on demand. As a rule, no interest is paid on current accounts: the customer enjoys the convenience of being able to make payments by cheque, and to pay into his account cheques he receives, while the bank keeps a record for him of all these transactions.

The other deposits were in effect savings deposits. They can be withdrawn only after seven days' notice and they earn interest. They are not subject to cheque, but as in practice cheques can be drawn against them (the customer arranging, for example, for an overdraft on the security of his deposit), they are usually included in bank credit.

Many institutions other than the commercial banks (for example, the Post Office Savings Bank, the Trustee Savings Banks, the building societies, and some insurance companies) receive deposits and relend or buy securities with their deposits, keeping only a very small cash reserve. They are important channels for savings. But they do not affect the supply of money, for their deposits are not subject to cheque.

4. The Assets of the Commercial Banks

The policy of a British commercial bank is a compromise between three conflicting aims. In the first place, the bank wants to make as much profit as possible for its shareholders. But, in the second place, its funds belong mainly to its depositors. It would not be fair to its

---

[1] This is a gross figure. It includes balances with and cheques in course of collection on other banks and items in transit. Net deposits were some £6,900 million.

depositors, for whom the bank is virtually a trustee, to invest some of their money in risky enterprises without adequate security, even if this course should seem likely to yield high profits. In the third place, it has undertaken to repay its depositors in cash on demand, and it must therefore keep a certain proportion of its assets in cash or in forms that can readily be converted into cash without appreciable loss.

The assets side of a bank's balance sheet shows what use it has made of its funds and reflects its compromise between these three aims of profits, security, and liquidity.

Thus the banks keep a minimum of 8 per cent cash, which of course yields nothing at all, and at least 24 per cent (of their deposits) in loans at short notice and bills discounted, which are "liquid assets" but yield relatively little: during 1946–50 they yielded little more than $\frac{1}{2}$ per cent, whereas long-term securities yielded around 3 per cent and advances around 4 per cent. At present (end–1959) they yield around $3\frac{1}{2}$ per cent, but long-term investments yield over 5 per cent and advances a minimum of $5\frac{1}{2}$ per cent.

Short loans and discounts are known as liquid assets because they can quickly be turned into cash (balances with the Bank) without loss. When the banks call in short loans, the discount houses have to borrow from the Bank to repay them. The banks do not sell their bills; they hold them until they mature. But they can increase their cash by buying fewer Treasury bills to replace those that mature. Investments and advances are less liquid. Securities can readily be sold, but they may have to be sold at a loss; and borrowers are often not in a position to repay advances at short notice. Moreover the sale of securities or the repayment of advances does not increase the cash of the banks but merely reduces their volume of deposits.

The second aim of the banks is security. They invest only in gilt-edged securities, although shares or bonds involving slightly more risk would give higher yields. As far as possible, they buy securities that will mature, and be repaid at their full nominal value, in a few years' time, and they tend to avoid irredeemable securities, such as Consols, which may fall heavily in price. Their advances are backed, where possible, by marketable securities. Although firms often cannot provide such backing, the banks make sure that the standing of the firms, and the value of their assets, provide ample security that the advances can and will be repaid.

The third aim is profits. The bulk of the profits of the banks come from the 60 to 65 per cent of their assets held in the form of investments or advances. Their advances yield them their highest rate of profit, but they are the least liquid of all their assets.

In December, 1959, the combined assets of the London clearing banks (omitting minor items) were distributed as follows—

	£ million	Per cent of Deposits
Coin, Bank-notes, and Balances with the Bank of England .	600	8·1
Money at Call and Short Notice .	560	7·5
Treasury Bills discounted . .	1,218	16·4
Other Bills discounted . .	164	2·2
Treasury Deposit Receipts . .	—	—
Investments	1,720	23·1
Advances to Customers . .	2,795	39·5

These items are listed in order of liquidity. The order of profitability is exactly the reverse.

The picture was considerably different before November, 1951. Liquid assets, including cash, amounted to between 40 and 45 per cent, as against 30 to 34 per cent at present; investments were then about 25 per cent; advances rose from 16 per cent in 1945 to 30 per cent in October, 1951.

The change was part of the new monetary policy. The Government induced the banks to convert some £500 million of their holdings of Treasury bills into a new issue of short-dated securities. The purpose was to curtail the power of the banks to create credit by reducing their liquid assets (which they could turn into cash) to a level they would regard as a minimum, and to check the growth of advances, which had risen by some £450 million during the previous two years.

I now give some brief comments on the various items.

Cash

Nearly two-thirds of this item is till-money: notes and coin held on the premises to meet demands for cash by depositors. The rest (over £220 million in December, 1959) is deposits with the Bank of England—bankers' deposits—which can be withdrawn in cash if more till-money is needed, and which are used to meet payments from one bank to another at the clearing.

The proportion of cash to deposits used to be shown as 10 per cent or more. But this was misleading. Each large bank made up its accounts on a different day and acquired more cash than it normally held in order to show a cash reserve of 10 per cent or over. This futile practice of *window-dressing* was given up at the end of 1946, and the cash reserve now shown, just over 8 per cent of deposits, is the amount normally held.

Money at call and short notice

This consists of loans repayable at call or at very short notice, made almost entirely to the discount market. " The London discount market today consists of twelve major discount houses and some dozen or so other firms which undertake some of the same work."[1] The twelve houses have a combined capital of some £35 million and hold assets (mainly Treasury bills; gilt-edged securities maturing within five years; and commercial bills) which amounted at the end of 1958 to £1,053 million; these were purchased mainly with money borrowed from banks.

The rate of interest charged on money at call and short notice is normally low enough for the discount market to make a profit by buying Treasury bills with it.

Discounts

These are bills of exchange which the banks have bought or, technically, discounted. They become liquid as they mature.

Most of the bills are Treasury bills, which the banks do not buy directly but take over from the discount houses, about half-way through their lives, maturing in one to two months. The volume of commercial bills is now only around £200 million. This is quite small compared with the total of Treasury bills, at present about £6,700 million, of which all but some £2,000 million ("tap" bills, issued to official bodies, such as the Exchange Equalization Account) are put up for tender.

Treasury Deposit Receipts

These were receipts given by the Treasury for loans which the banks were politely ordered to make to it for a period of around six months. They were introduced in 1940 in order to skim off some of the increase in bank deposits created by public expenditure. In 1945 they reached a peak of 38 per cent of deposits. They carried a slightly higher rate of interest than Treasury bills: $\frac{5}{8}$ per cent when the latter were at $\frac{1}{2}$ per cent. They were gradually reduced in volume to 16 per cent of deposits in 1949 and 7 per cent in 1950, and the last of them ran out in February, 1952, since when their issue has been suspended.

Investments

These are gilt-edged securities, readily marketable on the Stock Exchange, but they fall in value if the rate of interest rises. What percentage their fixed income represents on their purchase price depends on when they were bought. A bank that bought, say, 3 per cent stock in 1947 at 100 is getting a return of only 3 per cent; a bank that bought the same stock at, say, 60 in 1958 is getting a return of 5 per cent.

Investments increase during a war, for the Government expects the

---

[1] This sentence, and the figures which follow it, are from the *Report of the Committee on the Working of the Monetary System* (Cmd. 827 of 1959), usually known as the Radcliffe Report, from the name of its Chairman, Lord Radcliffe.

banks to subscribe to war loans. In 1942 they reached a peak of 32 per cent of deposits (as against less than 14 per cent during 1928–30); since the war the percentage remained around 25 until November, 1951, when it rose to 33, as explained earlier.

Advances

Advances are either loans for a fixed period, such as three months, or overdrafts, the customer being permitted to overdraw as he pleases up to an agreed maximum.

Most of the total of advances is lent to firms. In general, British banks aim at providing industry and trade with working capital only, and seldom lend for more than six months. In practice, however, advances are often renewed again and again, and may run on for years. If a borrower is perfectly solvent but would have to reduce his output, or sell stocks of materials at a loss, in order to repay, the bank may agree to renew the advance.

Advances tend to increase during a boom and to fall off during a depression. On the average, they were about 50 per cent of deposits during the 1920s. They fell with the Great Depression and averaged about 40 per cent in the 1930s. During the war they fell further, and in 1945 they were as low as 16 per cent. Since then, the percentage has risen.

Until recently, when it has been rising owing to the removal of restrictions on advances and the mildly expansionist Government policy, it was for several years around 30.

5. THE BANK OF ENGLAND

The Bank of England was nationalized, all its shares being bought by the Government, under the Bank of England Act of 1946. That Act lays down that the Bank shall have a Governor, a Deputy Governor, and sixteen Directors, together forming a Court of Directors. The Treasury can give such directions to the Bank as, after consultation with the Governor, it thinks necessary in the public interest. The Bank can request information from and make recommendations to the other banks; if so empowered by the Treasury it can give directions to any bank.

All this makes no fundamental change. The Bank always acted in close co-operation with the Treasury in the public interest, and the other banks always followed its lead. The Act does rule out, however, the possibility that a strong Governor might disagree with the Treasury and follow an independent line. No doubt the Treasury will be guided by the views of the Bank, but legally the Bank is now the agent of the Treasury, although not part of the Civil Service, and is subordinate to it.

The task of a central bank, in general terms, is to help the Government to carry out its monetary policy by whatever means are most effective. Since the war, a major aim of British policy has been to prevent a deficit in the balance of payments (of which more later), and this has meant in practice restricting imports, especially from the dollar area. These restrictions have been enforced by Foreign Exchange Control; nowadays this forms a large part of the work of the Bank. It also employs a considerable staff in the routine work of managing the long-term National Debt, such as keeping the stock registers and paying dividend warrants. But it still retains the three traditional functions of a central bank, which enable it to control the supply of money. These are to act as—

1. The sole note-issuing authority.
2. The Government's bank.
3. The bankers' bank.

The Note Issue

Any central bank must control the note issue if it is to have full power over monetary policy. It could not command the situation if other banks were free to vary the amount of cash.

The Bank Charter Act of 1844 laid down that every Bank of England note must be backed, pound for pound, by gold, except for a very small *fiduciary* issue, which could be backed by securities. Great Britain was on the gold standard; the Bank had to give gold on demand for its notes, and gold could be exported freely. In September, 1931, Great Britain left the gold standard and Bank of England notes became, and have remained, inconvertible. Nevertheless the notes still had to be backed by gold, although the amount of the fiduciary issue was raised: in 1914 it had been only £18 million, and by 1939 it was £300 million. On the outbreak of war in 1939, the gold reserve of the Bank was taken over by the Government. Since then, the note issue of the Bank has been backed entirely by securities (plus a little coin). The term "fiduciary" is still retained; the whole of the note issue, at present £2,125 million is said to be "fiduciary."

The country has a gold reserve (about £1,000 million, end of 1959) but this does not appear in the accounts of the Bank. Bank of England notes are merely inconvertible pieces of paper, but they are accepted by all and serve their purpose just as well as if they were backed by gold.

The amount of the note issue is fixed by the Government and can readily be increased or decreased if desirable.

The Government Accounts

The Government keeps its accounts with the Bank, paying in its receipts from taxation and other revenue and paying out its various expenditure. Its accounts are shown on the weekly Return of the Bank as Public Deposits. They tend to rise when tax payments are flowing in and to fall when interest payments are made on the public debt.

A rise in Public Deposits means that the Government is drawing in money from the public, who pay by cheque on their own banks, and that Bankers' Deposits therefore tend to fall; the opposite happens when Public Deposits fall. The Treasury usually prevents these fluctuations from disturbing the money market by offsetting them, varying the volume of Treasury bills put on the market in order to maintain Bankers' Deposits at a fairly steady level.

The Government borrows from time to time on short-term from the Bank; these loans are called *Ways and Means Advances*. The Bank acts as the agent for the Government in placing Treasury bills.

Bankers' Deposits

The other banks keep their cash reserves, except for till-money, with the Bank. When Bank *A* has a net payment to make to Bank *B* at the clearing, it pays by cheque drawn on the Bank, and this increases the deposit of Bank *B* at the Bank, and decreases the deposit of Bank *A* at the Bank, by that amount.

As Bankers' Deposits are the base on which the volume of bank credit rests, the Bank can bring about an expansion or contraction of bank credit by making the total of Bankers' Deposits increase or diminish.

The Bank of England Return

The Bank publishes a weekly Return. The latest, as I write, is that for 21st January, 1960. It is given below, with the figures rounded. (Owing to rounding, the Banking Department figures, although all correct, appear not to add up correctly.)

ISSUE DEPARTMENT

	£ million		£ million
Notes Issued		Government Debt	11·0
In Circulation	2,104·3	Other Government Securities	2,110·9
In Banking Department	21·1	Other Securities	0·8
		Coin (other than gold coin)	2·3
		Fiduciary Issue	2,125·0
		Gold Coin and Bullion (at 250s. 8d. an oz. fine)	0·4
	2,125·4		**2,125·4**

BANKING DEPARTMENT

	£ million		£ million
Capital	14·6	Government Securities .	281·1
Rest	3·8	Other Securities	
Public Deposits . . .	13·4	Discounts and Advances .	26·6
Bankers Deposits . .	255·9	Securities . . .	20·8
Other Deposits . . .	62·8	Notes	21·1
		Coin	0·7
	350·4		350·4

It will be seen that the Return, in the words of the Radcliffe Report, takes the "odd form of a combination of two balance sheets." The separate figures for the Issue Department are a survival from the days when additional notes had to be backed by additional gold. Nowadays the gold reserve of the country is held by the Exchange Equalization Account (managed by the Bank, although no figures about it appear in the Return) and additional notes are issued freely as required.

The note issue was £2,125 million. Of this, £21·1 million remained in the Bank as a cash reserve, till-money, held against deposits; the rest was "in circulation"—held by the public and the banks. The note issue was backed almost entirely by British Government Securities, including the Government Debt of £11 million, which is shown separately only for historical reasons.

The Capital and the "Rest"—the reserve fund accumulated out of undistributed profits—are now owned by the Government. The Capital does not change and the "Rest" changes only very slightly.

Public Deposits include Exchequer, Savings Banks, Commissioners of Public Debt, and Dividend Accounts. Bankers Deposits, it will be remembered, are treated by the banks as equivalent to cash. Other Deposits are the deposits of private customers of the Bank, including a number of foreign and Dominion central banks and Governments.

The assets held against these deposits were largely Government Securities. This item covers only direct obligations of the British Government, but it includes Treasury bills bought by the Bank on its own account, and any ways and means advances, as well as long-term securities. Thus it is this item which increases when the Bank pursues an expansionist open-market policy, and buys Treasury bills or other Government securities, and which decreases when the Bank sells securities to reduce the volume of credit.

The item of Other Securities is divided into two. Discounts and Advances comprise Treasury and other bills brought to the Bank for rediscount and advances made by the Bank to the discount houses and private clients. It is this item which increases when the market is "in the Bank"—that is to say, when discount houses and perhaps others are forced to borrow from the Bank because the other banks call in their short loans in order to increase their cash. The other head, Securities, includes such stocks as first-class foreign and Dominion securities, and any commercial bills bought by the Bank on its own initiative.

The ratio between the cash reserve and the deposits is known as the *Proportion*; it is about 6½ per cent in the above Return. It was once an important figure, for when it fell too low the Bank would restrict credit in order to raise it. But nowadays, with an inconvertible note issue which can readily be expanded, the Proportion has little significance.

6. THE BANK RATE

The central bank of a country is "the lender of last resort." When the commerical banks and other finance houses want to borrow short-term loans and cannot borrow enough from one another, the money market as a whole being short of cash, they come in the last resort to the central bank. In most countries the commercial banks themselves go directly to the central bank when they are short of cash, and borrow from it, usually by selling it some of the bills or other IOUs which they are holding. But in Great Britain the convention is that the commercial banks do not borrow directly from the Bank of England. Instead, they call in some of their money lent at call or short notice, and it is the discount houses, and perhaps others, who are forced to go to the Bank in order to get the cash to repay their loans to the commercial banks.

The Bank rate is the minimum official rate at which the Bank of England will lend money on short-term by taking over (the technical term is rediscounting) Treasury bills and other first-class bills. At present (end of January, 1960) the Bank Rate is 5 per cent. It was raised from 4 per cent, as a precautionary measure against renewed inflation, on 21st January, 1960.

When the Bank rate is effective (as it has been since 1951) all the other short-term rates in the London money market behave as if they were linked to it, going up when it is raised and going down when it is reduced.

The commercial banks now pay a maximum of 2 per cent less than Bank rate on their deposits (discount houses paying a trifle more) and charge at least 1 per cent above the Bank rate (with a minimum, at present 5½ per cent) on their advances. At present the rate for money at call and short notice is 3⅜ per cent upwards. The average rate of discount on three-months bills is: Treasury bills, just over 4½ per cent; bank bills, 4⅔ per cent; fine trade bills, 5¼ to 6 per cent. When the Bank rate was 7 per cent, all these rates were considerably higher; for example the rate of discount on Treasury bills rose to 6½ per cent when the Bank rate was first raised to 7 per cent (September, 1957) and was 6 per cent in March, 1958.

All these rates, and also others which I have not mentioned, would go up if the Bank rate were raised (and remained effective) and would go down if it were lowered. When the Bank rate is effective, it governs the price of credit.

The reasons why the Government may wish to raise or reduce rates of interest depend on the aims of its monetary policy. This is a large subject, to which I must return later, but a few remarks seem called for here.

Two leading aims, which may at times come into sharp conflict, are the maintenance of the exchange value of sterling and full employment.

Under the gold standard, the emphasis was on the former, and the Bank rate played an important part. In those days, the Bank rate was raised when gold was tending to flow out of the country; the gold reserve of the Bank had to be maintained if Great Britain was to stay on gold. The immediate effect of higher short-term rates in London was to attract short-term capital from overseas, leading to an inflow of gold.

All this now seems as dead as the dodo. We are no longer on the gold standard. Nor does short-term capital move about freely to the centres where interest rates are highest. It is prevented by exchange control from going to some centres, such as New York. And its owners will not send it to others, despite the lure of high interest rates, because they fear that the currencies of those countries will fall in value or that their Governments will prevent them from subsequently withdrawing it.

But a rise in the Bank rate had also a more fundamental purpose. If gold was leaving the country, this was a sign that we were importing more than we could pay for with our exports, and were meeting the difference in gold; our balance of payments was in deficit. A rise in the Bank rate was intended to bring about a general deflation of money incomes, which would reduce the demand for imports, bring the balance of payments into equilibrium, and stop the drain of gold.

Although we are no longer on gold, we still wish to maintain the exchange value of sterling and to protect our reserves of gold and dollars. Some deflation, some reduction in total spending power, may be needed for this purpose. It was mainly for this reason that the Bank rate was raised towards the close of 1951.

But the amount of employment depends on the total volume of spending. A rise in the Bank rate, bringing with it increases in rates of interest generally and a reduction in the supply of money, means less spending and may cause unemployment. Conversely, a fall in interest rates and an increase in the supply of money may increase employment, although if carried too far it may lead to inflation and higher prices.

Clearly there may be a conflict of aims. I think it is fair to say that from the summer of 1932 onwards, and again during the post-war years until the Conservatives came to power in October, 1951, the dominant aim was fuller employment; and that this aim was pursued even at the risk of a fall in the exchange value of sterling. It was not fully achieved in the 1930s—the number of unemployed averaged 1½ million—but it can be argued that "cheap money" stimulated economic activity, especially in house-building, and that without it unemployment would have been greater. It was fully achieved after the war: possibly too fully, for the increase in the supply of money led to inflation and sterling was devalued (from \$4·03 to \$2·80) in September, 1949. It can be claimed that the rise in the Bank rate towards the close of 1951 was a "disinflationary" measure, correcting the excessive increase in the supply of money which had taken place, and safeguarding the exchange value of sterling without creating any substantial unemployment.[1]

However this may be, it is a fact that from the summer of 1932 until August, 1939, when war was imminent, and again until October, 1951, the Bank rate remained unchanged at 2 per cent. Even at this low level, it was ineffective. Market rates of discount were much lower, and the market seldom had any fear of being forced to borrow from the Bank. During the post-war period, especially, monetary policy took a back seat. The Government used direct physical controls, such as rationing, to achieve its aims, and controlled the volume and direction of investment directly and not through rates of interest, which remained low.

The days, before September, 1931, when a change in the Bank rate was headline news and the City awaited anxiously the decision of the Court on Thursday mornings, seemed gone for ever. Nobody bothered about the Bank rate; it was fixed at 2 per cent, and there it would stay, impotent and unimportant. But since 1951 monetary policy has gradually replaced direct physical controls, and today changes in the Bank rate are again of major importance.

7. Open-Market Operations

I wrote that when the Bank rate is effective other short-term rates of interest behave as if they were linked to it. But there is no legal link. Obviously market rates, for the types of loans made by the Bank, such as rediscounting first-class bills, will be less than the Bank rate, for why should borrowers pay more to the banks or finance houses when they could borrow more cheaply from the Bank? But, subject to this

[1] The 7 per cent Bank rate of September, 1957, to March, 1958, is discussed in Chapter XL.

proviso, there is no necessary connection between the Bank rate and other rates. The latter might conceivably remain unchanged despite a rise or fall in the Bank rate. Why do they in fact follow the Bank rate, rising when it rises and falling when it falls?

It is true, but superficial, to explain this by the fact that the banks and finance houses accept and follow the leadership of the Bank. The underlying reason is that they know that a change in the Bank rate reflects the firm intention of the Government to change the price of credit, and that unless they respond as expected, steps will be taken to make them do so.

The Government can at once support a change in the Bank rate by changing the rate of discount on Treasury bills in the same direction. The Government can vary the volume of Treasury bills that it puts on the market each week and within limits can fix whatever rate of discount it pleases.

It may be, therefore, that a change in the Bank rate becomes effective, parallel changes taking place in other rates, without any alteration in the supply of money. This is what happened when the Bank rate was raised from 2 to 2½ per cent in November, 1951, and again to 4 per cent in March, 1952. Other rates increased too, and although the supply of money was not reduced, the "psychological" effect of the rise in the rate was to cut down the volume of spending.

If necessary, however, the Bank can increase or reduce the supply of money in order to make effective a fall or rise in the Bank rate and to carry out more fully an expansionary or deflationary monetary policy. It increases the supply of money by buying Treasury bills or other Government securities on its own account, paying for them with cheques on itself. These cheques are paid into their accounts at their own banks by the sellers of the securities, and the deposits of the banks with the Bank are thereby increased. The total amount of Bankers' Deposits increases—in other words, the total "balances with the Bank of England" of the banks increases. This enables them to expand bank credit, by making more loans or buying more securities, by 12½ times the amount of the increase in their cash, and still maintain a cash reserve of 8 per cent against their deposits.

Conversely, when the Bank wishes to reduce the supply of money, it sells Treasury bills or other Government securities. The buyers pay with cheques on their own banks, and Bankers' Deposits are thereby reduced.

These operations are known as open-market operations because the Bank employs a broker who buys or sells in the open market. Their effect in expanding or reducing the volume of bank credit is weakened in so far as the public holds more cash when the supply of money is increased (and prices rise or employment increases) and less when the supply of money is reduced (and prices fall or there is less employment). But any such counteracting tendencies can be offset by further expansion or reduction of Bankers' Deposits.

8. BANKING IN OTHER COUNTRIES

Most countries nowadays have a central bank, usually State-owned, which has the sole right of note issue and is the lender of last resort. There are several ways, however, in which most other banking systems differ from the British system.

The volume of Treasury and other bills, and of loans at call or short notice, is greater in London than in most centres. These liquid assets give the British banks a second line of defence, supporting their cash reserves, and enable them to keep a low ratio, 8 per cent, of cash to deposits. In countries with less developed money markets, this ratio has to be higher; in some countries, where few assets of this type or none at all are available, it is 15 or 20 per cent.

The large volume of Treasury bills means that higher short-term interest rates increase the amount of interest which the Government has to pay on the floating debt. The rate of discount on Treasury bills has varied from $\frac{1}{2}$ per cent in the immediate post-war years to over 6 per cent during the period of 7 per cent Bank rate (September, 1957, to March, 1958). On some £3,000 million Treasury bills in non-official hands, the annual charge would be about £180 million at 6 per cent and only £15 million at $\frac{1}{2}$ per cent. It is clearly in the interest of the Treasury to keep short-term rates low, but when greater restrictions on credit are needed, wider considerations prevail.

The intervention of the discount houses between the central bank and the commercial banks is peculiar to Great Britain. In other countries, when the commercial banks need more cash they borrow directly from the central bank, but in Great Britain they call in some of their loans at call and short notice, and it is the discount houses and others, not the commercial banks themselves, who borrow from the Bank of England to replenish the cash of the commercial banks.

The cash reserve of 8 per cent maintained by the British banks is not enforced by law; they could keep a smaller reserve if they wished. In most other countries, the banks are compelled by law to keep a minimum reserve of cash, in the form of balances with the central bank, against their deposits. This minimum is raised when it is desired to restrict credit, and reduced when it is desired to expand credit; changes in the legal minimum therefore serve the same purpose as open-market operations by the central bank, although both methods may be used, reinforcing one another.

In the United States there are twelve Federal Reserve Banks, each acting as a central bank for its district, with a Board of Governors of the Federal Reserve System meeting in Washington. The System is not State-owned, and the views of the Board may conflict with those of the U.S. Treasury, although the latter can usually persuade or compel the Board to follow the policy it favours.

Great Britain, like most countries where banking is well developed, has a few giant banks, each with numerous branches all over the country. If one of the branches makes a loss, the bank is large enough to stand the loss. But a bank that is independent and alone may be ruined by local economic difficulties—a crop failure, for example— which hit its customers.

In the United States, however, there are over 14,000 banks, many of them serving and dependent on a small country area. Branch banking has not been allowed to develop, for fear of creating a banking monopoly. During the years 1921 to 1929 nearly six thousand banks failed, and during 1930 to 1933 nearly nine thousand. The System has since been strengthened (for example, by compelling banks to insure their deposits), but the risks of failure are still much greater than in Great Britain.

CHAPTER XXXIII

THE VALUE OF MONEY

1. Is there a General Level of Prices?

THE value of anything is what can be obtained in exchange for it. The value of money, therefore, is its purchasing power—what it will buy. It is commonly said that the value of money is the reciprocal of "the general level of prices." Over a period, some prices may rise more than others, and some may remain stable or fall, but if the general level of prices has risen, we can equally well express this fact by saying that the value of money has fallen. If the general level of prices has doubled, this means that the value of money has halved: £1 will buy only half as much as before. Conversely, a fall in the general level of prices is the same thing as a rise in the value of money.

But money buys anything and everything that has a price. It buys paper titles, such as Stock Exchange securities, and physical assets, such as land or plant and machinery; it buys the services of labour and other factors of production; it buys commodities at all stages of production, from raw materials to finished products. Is there any sense or purpose in grouping together all these very different items in order to derive from the hotch-potch some measure of changes in the general level of prices—that is to say, in the value of money?

Surely not. This hotch-potch means nothing to anybody. It is the movements of sectional price levels, relatively to one another, that affect the economy as a whole and the fortunes of different groups. Farmers are affected by the relation between the prices of farm products and the prices of the goods and services they buy. To a country which, like Great Britain, must rely largely on international trade, the relation between the prices she gets for her exports and the prices she must pay for her imports is of great importance. To the worker, what matters is the relation between his wages and the prices of the consumers' goods and services which he buys.

During the New York Stock Exchange boom which collapsed in October, 1929, ushering in the Great Depression, the prices of securities rose, on the average, about threefold, but the prices of commodities remained stable, although there was some increase in wage rates. Surely nothing is gained by lumping these facts together in order to strike an average which we call the percentage increase in the general level of prices! Such an average means nothing; it is the divergencies which matter.

I shall therefore write only of sectional price levels, especially the retail price level of consumers' goods and services, often called *the cost of living*. I must point out, however, that if we discard the concept of a general level of prices, we throw overboard at the same time any general explanation (such as the Fisher equation, which I discuss below) of the forces determining the value of money which relates the quantity of money to the general price level of everything against which money exchanges.

2. INDEX-NUMBERS OF PRICES

I turn to the question of how to measure changes over time in sectional price levels or, in other words, changes over time in the value of money in relation to particular groups of items.

Let us consider, as an example, the group consisting of foodstuffs consumed by British working-class households. We all know that every item is dearer than before the war. But some prices have risen more than others. By what percentage have they risen "on the average"? And are they, again "on the average," dearer or cheaper than a year ago?

In order to answer such questions we must decide what commodities to include and in what proportions or, to use the technical term, what *weight* to give to each. These decisions are usually based on the results of inquiries into *family budgets*—into the ways in which families do in fact spend their money.

There is no need to include all the many thousands of different items people buy. Many minor items, covering between them only a small percentage of the total expenditure on food, can be omitted. Unless their prices move very differently from the prices of the items included, leaving them out will make very little difference to the result. Some items, notably of vegetables and fruit, may have to be omitted from month-to-month comparisons because they are available only when they are in season. Again, there are many different brands of tea, for example. We need not include them all. We can take the price of some widely-consumed brand, or the average price of three or four such brands, to represent the price of tea. For we know that the prices of other popular brands will move in the same way, while the price of an expensive tea, such as pure Darjeeling, is not relevant to our inquiry: working-class households cannot afford it. In the same way we can take four or five cuts, such as ribs of beef and loin of lamb, to represent "meat," and two or three of the cheaper fish, such as cod and herring and hake, to represent "fish."

In this way we get a collection of different amounts of different foodstuffs that represents the bulk of the expenditure of a working-class household on food. We can think of this collection as a large "basket of commodities," representing a week's shopping on foodstuffs.

We must then find out the cost of this basketful from time to time, taking care always to get our prices from the same shops or stalls, for some shops or some districts may charge more than others, and making sure that we always take the prices of the same brands or qualities.

Suppose that in June, 1938, it cost £2, in June, 1956, £5, and in June, 1959, £5 10s. This gives us our answer. The price of foodstuffs consumed by an average working-class household rose by 150 per cent between June, 1938, and June, 1956, and by 10 per cent between June, 1956, and June, 1959.

Instead of giving the actual cost of the basket, we could represent its cost at some date, known as the "base" date, by the figure 100, and we could represent its cost at any other date by a figure which bears the same relation to 100 as its cost at that date bears to its cost at the base-date. These figures are known as *index-numbers*. For example, if we were to base our index on June, 1938 = 100, the index-numbers would be 250 for June, 1956, and 275 for June, 1959. It is usual to compile such index-numbers monthly, and it is more convenient for us to make comparisons, when confronted with a long series of monthly figures, if they are all given as index-numbers related to 100 at some base-date.

The base-date should be suitably chosen. If we are interested mainly in comparisons with pre-war prices, a pre-war base-date such as June, 1938, is appropriate. But if we are interested mainly, as most people are, in more recent and current changes, a more recent base-date is more suitable. If we should take June, 1956, for example, as our base-date, the above figures would be rewritten: June, 1938, 40; June, 1956, 100; June, 1959, 110.

There is another, and more usual, way of compiling index-numbers, which leads to just the same results. The price of each commodity included is written as 100 for the base-date. Each commodity is given a weight corresponding to the relative expenditure on it. The index-number for each commodity is then multiplied by its weight, and the sum of all these products, for any month, is then divided by the total of all the weights to give the weighted average.

Suppose, to give a simple example with three commodities only, that the price of bread was 3d. a lb loaf in June, 1938, and 6d. in June, 1959, and that the corresponding prices for sugar were 4d. and 1s. and for bacon 1s. and 4s. a lb. Bread has risen in price by 100 per cent, sugar by 200 per cent, and bacon by 300 per cent. The simple average of these increases is 600 divided by 3, or 200 per cent. But if people spend twice as much on bread as on sugar, and three times as much on sugar as on bacon, we must weight these commodities accordingly (e.g. giving a weight of 6 to bread, 3 to sugar, and 1 to bacon) and this gives us a "weighted average" price increase of only 150 per cent, obtained as follows—

	June, 1938	June, 1959	Weight
Bread . . .	100	200	×6 =1200
Sugar . . .	100	300	×3 = 900
Bacon . . .	100	400	×1 = 400
			10)2500
			250

The Ministry of Labour compiles a monthly index of retail prices, based on information provided by a large-scale inquiry into household expenditures in 1953–54. It measures changes month by month in the average level of prices of commodities and services purchased by the great majority of households in the United Kingdom. In other words, it measures monthly changes in the cost of living of wage-earners and of most small and medium salary earners. The index is divided into ten main groups, of which the weights are as follows—

Food	350
Alcoholic Drink . . .	17
Tobacco	80
Housing	87
Fuel and Light . .	55
Durable Household Goods .	66
Clothing and Footwear . .	106
Transport and Vehicles . .	68
Miscellaneous Goods . .	59
Services	58
	1,000

The index is based on 17 January, 1956 = 100. Its monthly average was 102 for 1956, 106 for 1957, and 109 for 1958 and 1959.

Any such index-number usually gives rise to misunderstanding. It is thought by some that the items included are supposed to provide an adequate standard of living for a family. But this is not so. Whether or not families have an adequate standard of living is quite a different question. The index merely measures changes in retail prices "on the average," the average being weighted to correspond to the actual expenditures of the average family on the various items which are included.

Different families do not all buy the same things, or do not buy them in the same proportions. Contrast, for example, a family with young children and a family without. Suppose they have the same family income. The former will spend more than the latter on such items as bread and milk and children's clothing, and will therefore be able to afford less than the latter for certain other items. Again, the price of meat does not matter to a vegetarian or the price of cigarettes to a non-smoker. The composition and weighting of an index applies only to the average family; for any particular family, the cost of living may have changed either more or less than the index-number shows; indeed it may have risen when the index-number shows a fall, or conversely.

Such differences may be still greater for families with considerably higher (or lower) incomes than those to whom the index relates. For their consumption-patterns will be different. A richer family usually spends a smaller proportion of its income on food; hence if food prices rise more than other prices, the cost of living for such a family rises less than for a manual labourer, and conversely. Again, a richer family tends to buy better qualities than a poor family can afford, and these may change in price by a greater or smaller percentage than the cheaper qualities. A richer family may also spend money on items, such as school fees for the children or wages to servants or petrol for the car, which do not appear at all in the budget of a poor family, and which may change in price either more or less than those which do.

As time goes on, changes take place in consumption-patterns. The British manual worker today has a higher real income than his father had. His family is better fed, consuming more meat and milk and fats, although only about a third of his expenditure goes on food, as compared with a half forty years ago. Tastes have changed: for example, we now consume less beer and spirits but more cigarettes, and women spend more time and money in beauty-parlours but buy fewer hats. Goods which used to be considered luxuries, such as radios and refrigerators, are now bought by manual workers. New commodities, such as nylon textiles, have appeared on the market.

There is no satisfactory way of measuring the change in the cost of living between two dates so far apart that there has been a marked change in consumption habits. If an index exists, based on the earlier period, it is no longer appropriate; it should be scrapped and replaced by a new index which is up to date in the items it covers and the relative weight it gives to each item.

Nor is there any satisfactory way of measuring the difference in the cost of living between two countries with different consumption habits. Tea is cheaper in Great Britain than in France, but wine is cheaper in France; the British workman drinks tea, and the French workman drinks wine.

Somebody who knows all the facts can make a good qualitative judgment on differences in the cost of living between countries, or between different periods in the same country, but measurement is not possible if consumption habits are widely different.

The above remarks have related to index-numbers measuring changes in retail prices or in the cost of living. It is possible to construct index-numbers in the same way to measure the change in any other sectional price level. For example, there are index-numbers showing the weighted average changes in the wholesale prices of different groups of commodities; in the prices of British exports and of British imports; in wage rates; and in the prices of "equity" shares. The same questions arise with any index measuring changes over time. What items should be included? What is a suitable base date? Have the relevant conditions altered so much that the present index is no longer appropriate and should be superseded by a new one?

3. The Effects of Changes in the Value of Money

Although I have suggested that we should discard the notion of a conglomerate all-embracing general level of prices, there are periods when the price of nearly everything is rising and we can speak without ambiguity of a general fall in the value of money. Such periods are usually periods of inflation, which may be defined for the moment as an increase in the supply of money accompanied by a tendency for prices to rise. They are especially likely to occur during a war and the years immediately following. The last war was no exception. The value of money fell in every country, although the fall was much greater in some countries than in others.

There are also periods when the value of money is plainly rising. The Great Depression, from about the autumn of 1929 to 1933, was such a period. Some countries left the gold standard in order to lessen the fall in prices in terms of their own money, but in terms of gold most prices fell by something between one-third and one-half. Some periods of falling prices are periods of deliberate deflation or "disinflation," the monetary authorities reducing the supply of money to reverse an inflation which has gone too far.

What are the consequences of a general fall in the value of money?

All who have incomes or assets fixed in terms of money will lose by the fall in the purchasing power of their money. This covers the whole "rentier" class, such as holders of bonds yielding a fixed income and landlords who have let their land or buildings on long leases, as well as all who receive pensions or other annuities and social security payments. The money value of assets such as savings bank and other deposits, life assurance policies, and debts due to lenders, remains the same, but the money buys less.

Wage-earners suffer a fall in their real incomes unless they can obtain increases in their wages that are prompt enough and large enough to keep pace with the rising cost of living. At first, before wage-earners realize that an inflation is going on, wages are likely to lag well behind prices. It is often especially difficult for salary-earners to get adequate increases in salaries which, by convention, are fixed for long periods.

Entrepreneurs gain, at any rate in the earlier stages. They get higher prices for their products ; and although they probably have to pay correspondingly higher prices for their materials, their fixed charges remain the same, and their labour costs are likely, at first, to rise less than their selling prices.

The gain is especially marked for entrepreneurs who borrow. They use the loans to produce goods that are rising in price. Suppose that prices double during a year. Even if the entrepreneur pays, say, 10 per cent interest, each £100 he borrows produces goods worth £200 at the end of the year, and he pays back only £110. The lender, on the other hand, receives £110, which buys only as much as £55 bought at the beginning of the year.

But the whole of the profits of the entrepreneur are not net profits. If he wishes to keep his real capital intact, he must set aside larger reserves against depreciation, for his plant and other fixed assets will cost more to replace when the time comes. In the same way, he must set aside a reserve to meet the higher prices he will have to pay for replacing his stocks of materials. The official estimate of the U.K. national income shows that £650 million and £750 million of gross profits represented "stock appreciation" in 1950 and 1951 respectively; these were years of rising prices.

The effect of inflation on Government finance is likely to be favourable in the early stages. The revenue from taxes on commodities will increase if the taxes are *ad valorem* (a percentage of the selling price) and not *specific* (so much per physical unit). The revenue from taxes on incomes and profits will increase after a time lag. Expenditure which is fixed in terms of money, such as interest on the national debt, pensions, and—at first—the salaries of civil servants, will remain the same.

I turn to the effects on output. At first, these will be favourable. Prospects of profit will be bright, and therefore firms will tend to produce to full capacity. Unemployed labour and other resources will be absorbed into employment unless prevented by obstacles to mobility.

But once full employment has been attained, rising prices cannot bring about any further increase in total output. What is likely is an increase in investment. All on fixed incomes will be forced to consume less, and this will free labour and other resources to move from the consumption industries into the investment industries. Entrepreneurs will wish to increase their capacity, and this will lead to greater investment.

It is when prices stop rising that there will be trouble. Some enterprises will have to close down; they paid only because their selling prices were rising faster than their costs. Some of the new assets, such as plant to make capital goods, may be redundant; they were designed to support a volume of investment greater than the community can afford. And it may well be that some entrepreneurs, anxious to make hay while the sun shone, have not properly maintained their fixed capital and have allowed their stocks to run down.

Must prices stop rising? If they rise so fast that there is a runaway inflation, this must come to an end. How can economic activity go on at full speed when prices double or more than double from one hour to another? We have had no experience of this in Great Britain, but other countries have. The best-known example is the inflation in Germany which reached its climax, and collapsed, in 1923. The most fantastic example is the jet-propelled inflation in Hungary in 1944. When the inflation stopped, the new currency unit, the florin, was equal to 40,000 quadrillions of the old pengo: this is a figure with twenty-nine noughts. A runaway inflation must stop. People cease to accept the currency as a measure of value and there will be chaos until a fresh start is made with a new and stable currency.

But would it not be possible to maintain a gentle and continuous fall in the value of money? I suspect that a number of economists believe in their hearts that this would be the ideal policy, reducing the burden of fixed charges, providing a constant stimulus to business, and thus maintaining full employment.

I doubt whether such a continuous mild inflation would be possible. I think that as soon as people realized that the Government was following this policy, they would anticipate the coming rise in prices, bringing it about more quickly, and to a greater extent, than was planned.

Let us suppose, however, that the inflation goes according to plan. It might lead to a deficit in the balance of payments, but we can ignore this possibility: we can suppose, for example, that other countries too are inflating at the same rate.

Would the result be to maintain full employment? The view that it would rests on the belief that trade unions would accept lower real wages, giving larger profits to the entrepreneurs, provided that their money wages were not reduced. Keynes tended to hold this belief. But surely all recent experience contradicts it. Once the trade unions realized that inflation was under way, they would not be fooled. On the contrary, they would be likely to demand wage increases that not merely kept real wages constant but increased them. Instead of a mild inflation which increased profits at the expense of wages, the inflation would have to be speeded up in order to keep profits at their normal level by passing on wage increases in the form of higher prices.

As for the rentier, he has been milked often enough in the past. But he is beginning to revolt, and nowadays the problem is how to induce people to save more. A continuous inflation would make people reluctant to save in order to lend at fixed interest, unless rates of interest were high enough to compensate them for the fall in the value of their money.

Hence, in my opinion, the profits of inflation would soon melt away, and the supposed benefits of inflation, except in the earlier stages, are illusory.

On the other hand, a sharp fall in prices, such as took place during the Great Depression, may cause heavy unemployment and numerous bankruptcies.

There is something to be said for a policy of stabilizing money incomes. If we suppose that productivity will continuously increase, owing to technical progress, such a policy would mean a continuous mild deflation. The fruits of economic progress would be shared by all in the form of a gently falling cost of living. No unemployment would be created, for by hypothesis the increase in physical marginal products would offset the fall in their prices. But I fear that such a policy would be quite impracticable in the modern world, where most sections of the community expect and demand increases in their money incomes as time goes on.

The effects of a rise in the value of money on the distribution of wealth are just the opposite of those of a fall. All on fixed money incomes gain, including those workers who keep their jobs; the total real incomes of British workers as a whole were greater during the Great Depression than at any former time. Profits, on the other hand, tend to fall unless the productivity of labour increases enough to offset the fall in prices. Governments tend to incur deficits, their revenue falling more than their expenditure if most of the latter is fixed.

The reader may perhaps conclude that the best policy is to keep the value of money stable. This would safeguard the purchasing power of all savings and fixed incomes and would encourage saving and lending.

But there may be times when monetary expansion is needed to increase employment, and it is often difficult to prevent some rise in prices as a by-product of the expansion. Again, there may be times when some deflation is needed to check a boom before it goes too far. And if it is desired to keep the exchange value of the currency stable in terms of gold, or of American dollars, some inflation or deflation may be needed from time to time for this purpose.

4. THE QUANTITY THEORY OF MONEY

Whenever and wherever there has been a large increase in price levels it has been associated with a large increase in the supply of money.

Public opinion, however, has often failed to realize the connection, and has attributed the rise in prices to some other reason, such as "profiteering." The quantity theory of money has rendered a useful service by showing that money is no exception to the general rule that an increase in the supply of anything tends to reduce its value, and a decrease to raise its value.

The best-known version of the quantity theory is that put forward by Professor Irving Fisher and embodied in the equation:

$$MV = PT.$$

In this equation, M stands for the quantity of money, V for its velocity of circulation, P for the price level, and T for the volume of goods exchanged against money.

The *velocity of circulation* of money is the average number of times a unit of money is spent during the period—say, a year—under consideration. A £1 note that changes hands ten times during the year, buying £1 worth of goods each time, is equivalent to ten £1 notes each of which changes hands only once. The total value of all the cheques drawn during a year is many times greater than the total of bank deposits. We must therefore multiply the quantity of money by its velocity of circulation in order to find the total money expenditure.

The Fisher equation is an "equation of exchange." A flow of money exchanges against a flow of goods, and the money spent must equal the value of the goods bought.

Suppose that 1s. 6d. exchanges against 3 loaves at 4d. each and a pint of milk at 6d. The cost of this collection—3 loaves and a pint of milk—is 1s. 6d. If at some later date 3s. exchanges against this same collection, its cost has doubled. The prices of bread and milk may each have doubled, a loaf costing 8d. and a pint of milk 1s., or one price may have more than doubled and the other less than doubled— for example, bread may have risen only 50 per cent, to 6d. a loaf, and milk 200 per cent, to 1s. 6d. a pint—but what is certain is that the price level of this collection has exactly doubled, for it now costs exactly twice as much. Or it may be that 9d. now buys this collection, 1s. 6d. buying 6 loaves and 2 pints of milk; in that event the cost of the collection, the price level, has halved.

Clearly the principle is just the same when we consider not just two items, bread and milk, but the whole volume of retail sales on the one hand and the amount of money spent on them on the other hand.

The moral is that a change in the total money expenditure (MV), week by week or year by year, will cause the same percentage change in the price level—provided that T remains the same. And a change in the volume of goods sold (T), week by week or year by year, will cause a corresponding (but opposite) change in the price level—other things (M and V) remaining the same. A bigger flow of money tends to raise prices and a bigger flow of goods to reduce them.

This is all very well, as far as it goes. But it does not go very far.

Its first defect is that if we consider the total money expenditure, the price level is a hotch-potch which covers everything bought with money. By far the greater part, in value, of all money transactions, in a country such as Great Britain, are purchases and sales of securities and other assets. I argued at the beginning of this chapter that such a conglomerate price level is not a useful concept. Yet if we consider only retail sales, the connection between the total amount of money in existence and the flow of money expenditure on retail sales is remote. It is quite possible for the total amount of money to increase while money expenditure on retail sales falls, or conversely; and even if both increase, or decrease, together, one may change by a larger proportion than the other.

Its second defect is that other things do not remain equal.

A change in M may affect T. For example, an increase in the amount of money during a period of unemployment may increase employment and therefore output, giving an increase in T with little or no increase in the price level, P.

A change in T may affect MV. For example, a general increase in output may not lead to a general fall in prices. As a rule, during a boom, output and prices both increase. The increase in T leads to an increase in V, and possibly in M, and owing to the increase in MV the price level P rises, rather than falls, despite the increase in T.

A change in M may affect V. As we have noted earlier, during an inflation people are anxious to get rid of money, which is depreciating in value, and its velocity of circulation increases. They expect that prices will go on rising, so they buy quickly, making prices rise still faster. This was well illustrated during the German inflation after the 1914–18 war. The volume of the note issue increased from 81 milliard paper marks in December, 1920, to 116,000 milliard in August, 1923, but prices rose about forty times more than the increase in the quantity of money; the value of the note issue in gold marks fell from 4,800 million at the former date to 116 million at the latter date.

It is not correct, therefore, to assume that other things remain equal. A change in M may cause a change in V or T, or both; a change in any of the four terms in the equation of exchange may cause a change in one or more of the other three.

The third defect of the quantity theory is that the real causes of a change in the value of money may lie right outside its field of vision. For example, the real cause of a rise in the price level may be the growth of population, leading to a fall in output per head in a country where land and other resources are limited in amount; or it may be a general rise in money wages without a corresponding increase in output; or it may be a series of budget deficits arising from a war. It is, of course, always possible to show that changes in the price level must be accompanied by changes in M or V or T, but in order to understand what has happened, and to follow the chain of causation, we must know the reasons why M or V or T have changed.

The conclusion is that the quantity theory is not very helpful. But it is useful in showing that when a marked inflation takes place there is a causal connection between the large increase in the quantity of money and the large fall in its value, and in pointing to the corollary that the way to stop the inflation is to stop increasing the quantity of money—although in practice this is often easier said than done.

5. THE DEMAND FOR MONEY

There is a story that a Chinese war lord once disproved the quantity theory of money. He wanted to increase the volume of paper money he issued, in order to pay his soldiers and others. So he asked his bankers what would happen if he did. They explained that a bigger amount of money would exchange against the same volume of goods and that therefore prices would rise. He replied that he was going to issue a lot more notes and that, if prices rose by as much as 5 per cent, banker A and banker B would have their heads cut off; if by 10 per cent, then C and D would also have their heads cut off, and so on. He did issue more notes; and prices did not rise.

What happened, of course, was that the bankers held a corresponding amount of money as idle balances. The quantity theorists would say that this did not disprove their theory; the bankers kept money out of circulation, thus offsetting the increase in M by a decrease in V. But an alternative form of explanation is that the bankers increased their own demand for money to offset the increase in supply.

The demand for money is the demand for money to hold, the demand for money balances. It is the inverse of the velocity of circulation; we can say either that the demand for money has increased or that the velocity of circulation has diminished, or conversely. The former expression is perhaps preferable, for we can then explain the value of money in the same way that we explain the value of other things, in terms of supply and demand, without introducing a new concept, the velocity of circulation.

Some money balances, notably those held on deposit account at banks, are normally idle. Others are active, payments-in and payments-out being made frequently. Apart from hoarders, people hold very different amounts of money at different times. Wage-earners paid on Fridays have more money on Friday nights than on Thursday nights. Nevertheless every person or firm holds on the average, taking one day with another, a certain sum of money. What determines the amount of money which, on the average, he wishes to hold?

We have come across this question before, when we considered the monetary theory of interest. It is rather confusing, because if the total amount of money in a country is given, then at any moment all of it must be somewhere—in pockets, in tills, in the vaults of banks, and so on. The total amount of money, no more and no less, must be demanded, in the sense that all of it must be held somewhere by somebody. But the value, or purchasing power, of this amount—the demand for money in terms of other things—may change.

An increase in the demand for houses, the stock of houses being given, shows itself in an increase in the value of houses. In the same way, an increase in the demand for money shows itself in an increase in the value of money—that is, in a general fall in price levels. This happens during a depression. The output of goods falls off, the quantity of money may remain the same, yet price levels fall. Why? Because the demand for money has increased. For the demand for money is a demand to *hold* money rather than other assets. When people think that the prices of other assets, such as securities or real estate or goods, are likely to fall they will prefer to hold money rather than to spend it in buying such assets. The velocity of circulation of money falls; in other words, the demand for money increases.

A change in the habits of the community may alter the demand for money. Suppose, for example, that more wage-earners are paid by cheque, and open banking accounts. They would keep some of their money in the form of bank deposits and not of cash, whereas before they kept it all in cash. This would be a decrease in the demand for cash by the public; it would enable the banks to increase the volume of bank credit without reducing their percentage reserve of cash against deposits. Again, an increase in the practice of offsetting book-entry debts due from A to B by debts due from B to A (a process which is carried to the limit when firms engaged in different stages of producing the same commodity amalgamate with one another), will reduce the demand for money.

The amount of money which people or firms want to hold in order to make current payments will tend to vary with their money incomes: the bigger the income, the bigger the balance needed. It will also tend to vary with the price level of commodities. What usually happens is that a rise in incomes and prices is accompanied by an increase in the quantity of money, which makes possible larger money balances. When an inflation is under way, a further increase in the supply of money seems inevitable to enable business to carry on. Firms have to meet larger wages bills and to pay more for materials; households need more money to pay for a week's shopping. Nevertheless, if it were possible to hold this "inadequate" supply of money constant, the inflation would stop. Incomes and prices would adjust themselves downwards, perhaps at the cost of unemployment and bankruptcies, until the existing supply of money became "adequate." To that extent, the quantity theory is correct.

Given the habits of the community and the general level of incomes, what determines the amount of money a person (or firm) wishes to hold?

If he did not hold money, he could either spend it or invest it. It is easy to understand why people prefer holding money to holding large stocks of goods that may deteriorate in quality. The question is why they do not invest this money and get interest on it until the time comes when they want to spend it. One reason is that it is costly and troublesome to invest small sums for short periods. Another reason is that people are not sure how much money they will need in the near future, and like to keep a certain amount of cash or bank deposits as a liquid reserve against possible unforeseen contingencies. Finally, they may fear that the prices of securities will fall. Thus people and firms keep a certain proportion of their assets in the form of money.

An increase in their liquidity-preference, and therefore in their demand to hold money rather than other assets, will tend to reduce the price-level of bonds—that is, to raise the rate of interest. A decrease in their liquidity-preference will do the opposite; it will push up the prices of bonds, which people are now more eager to hold.

A change in the demand for money may also lead to a change in the price levels of commodities. Suppose, for example, that people think the rate of profit is rising. They will want to keep a smaller proportion of their assets in the form of money, since investment is now more profitable than it was before and their need for liquidity is no greater. Investment will increase. Purchases by entrepreneurs and others who get command of the new capital will increase, and this will tend to raise prices. Although the total amount of money may remain the same, its value will fall. Thus the desire of the public to hold a smaller proportion of their assets in the form of money will be fulfilled. Each may hold as much money as before, but its value will be less.

6. Why Does the Value of Money Change?

In order to explain any particular change in the value of money we should study all the relevant circumstances.

For example, during 1950 and 1951 most materials rose in price. It was feared that the war in Korea might soon lead to a world war. Consequently there was increased public and private stock-piling and bigger rearmament programmes. When this fear abated, stock-piling fell off, the pace of rearmament was reduced, and the prices of materials came down again.

Changes may take place simultaneously in the supply of money, the demand for money, and the levels of output and stocks of goods. It is not enough to know, for example, that the supply of money has increased by so much. We must know also how and where the new money was injected and what happened to it. Perhaps it passed into idle balances, and had no effect. Perhaps it was created by the banks and used by them to buy securities: the first effect will be a tendency to raise the prices of securities, or in other words to reduce the rate of interest. Perhaps it was advanced to firms who had to pay higher wage rates; in that event, it will soon be spent by the wage-earners and will tend to raise retail prices—unless, we must add, the higher wages are accompanied by an increase in output large enough to prevent prices from rising despite the increased money expenditure.

Inflation has been described as "too much money chasing too few goods," a description which is in harmony with the quantity theory. We can perhaps go a little further. "A man's reach must exceed his grasp," says Browning. A country's reach often exceeds its grasp. It wants to spend so much on maintaining or raising standards of living, so much on social services, so much on investment, so much on defence. It has not the labour and other resources to do all that it wishes. If an attempt is made to carry out all the programmes, in terms of money expenditure, something has to give. What gives is often the price level; prices rise so that the money programmes do not mean as much in real terms; the grasp of the country is restricted to what the available labour and other resources can produce (plus any aid from abroad), but its reach, in terms of money, can be as long as it wishes.

A *budget deficit* is often inflationary. But not always. Public expenditure, from money borrowed or created by the Government, may succeed in bringing unemployed workers and other resources into productive activity; the increased money expenditure may be matched, after a time, by a greater flow of output; and the value of money may fall only slightly, or not at all.

But often a budget deficit is incurred during a period of full employment, or is much greater than is needed to bring about full employment. For example, a Government may need money to fight a war, and may raise most of the money not from taxation but from borrowing. In so far as it borrows from the public, the question is what they would have done with the money had they not lent it to the Government. If money balances become more active when they are turned over to the Government, Government borrowing is inflationary. In practice, the Government will probably create new money. In some countries it might simply print more notes and use them to pay for its expenditure. Nowadays, in a country such as Great Britain, the Government would borrow from the banks, printing more notes to enable the banks to maintain their cash reserves. The way to stop such an inflation is for the Government to cut down its expenditure (if it can!) and to increase taxation, so that it can pay its way without creating more money and without inflationary borrowing.

A *budget surplus* is deflationary or disinflationary if it takes away money from taxpayers who would otherwise have spent it, and if the Government then keeps the money fairly idle—for example, by using it to repay public debt. Should the Government spend the money on, say, a development programme, the budget surplus is not deflationary; it merely transfers that amount of expenditure from consumption to investment. In the long run, however, greater public investment will lead to a larger volume of output, and this will tend to keep down prices.

In Great Britain after the war we often heard of *the inflationary gap*. This was the sum by which, it was calculated, money incomes had to be reduced in order that the expected volume of output (plus imports less exports) could be bought at prevailing prices. More narrowly, it was the amount by which voluntary saving would fall short of planned investment, including public investment. This amount, therefore, had to be taken in the form of increased taxation in order to prevent a general rise in prices. The flow of money expenditure on consumers' goods would then equal, and not exceed, the flow of consumers' goods, without any general rise in their prices.

An *export surplus* tends to be inflationary. A country has exported more than it has imported. The exporters have received more money than the importers have paid out, so that total money expenditure may increase, whereas the flow of goods on which the money can be spent has been reduced, for more exports have left the country than the imports received in exchange for them. Conversely, an *import surplus* tends to be deflationary.

Fluctuations in investment are often a major cause of changes in the value of money. Greater investment, as we have seen earlier, tends to reduce the value of money if it is financed by an expansion of bank credit. Higher prices impose "forced saving," for the benefit of the entrepreneurs, on all with relatively fixed incomes. Conversely, a reduction in investment tends to reduce prices. We must not forget, however, that changes in investment may be associated with changes in employment and therefore in output. I have also mentioned *changes in wage rates*. A general rise in wage rates that is not matched by a corresponding increase in output will be inflationary, and conversely.

I have made a number of tentative generalizations, but the main impression I would like to give the reader is that we should not rely on generalizations or formulas or equations, but should study each particular case in the light of all the relevant facts.

PART VII

INTERNATIONAL TRADE

CHAPTER XXXIV

THE THEORY OF INTERNATIONAL TRADE

1. WHY HAVE A SEPARATE THEORY FOR INTERNATIONAL TRADE?

ALL trade arises from specialization between districts, which was discussed in Chapter VI. National boundaries in no way change the differences between districts, such as differences in climate and in natural resources, which make specialization by districts advantageous. The trade between the various Australian States was international until their federation into a Commonwealth in 1901, since when it has been domestic or internal. The trade between Southern Ireland and Great Britain was domestic until Southern Ireland became a separate republic, since when it has been international. But clearly such changes in boundaries do not alter the facts of economic geography. Why, then, should we take account of national boundaries by having a separate theory of international trade?

The reason, in two words, is national governments. The remaining chapters of this Part all deal with monetary aspects of international relations. They discuss the various systems—free exchange rates, fixed exchange rates, and exchange control—under which a country may tackle the problem of maintaining equilibrium in its balance of payments with the rest of the world. No such problem arises between, say, Yorkshire and Devon, or even between England and Wales. For they share the same money, the pound sterling; they form part of the same monetary and banking system. A separate country usually has its own separate money and its own separate monetary and banking system. It therefore has its own balance-of-payments problems.

The subject of the present chapter is the theory of international trade. The traditional reason for a separate theory of international trade is that labour and capital move far less freely between countries than within a country.

Workers are often reluctant to go to a different country, especially if the language and ways of living are different, despite the attraction of higher wages. Even if they are willing to go, and can find the fare, they may not be allowed to enter. Many national governments restrict immigration.

Private owners of capital often will not take the risks of foreign investment and national governments often restrict the export, and sometimes the import, of capital.

Within a country, labour and capital tend to combine with the various natural resources and to distribute themselves among districts in such a way that real wages and the rate of return on capital are the same throughout the country. Between countries, the situation is very different. Some countries are heavily overpopulated relatively to others, and partly for this reason there are large differences in real wages between countries. Some countries have much less capital, relatively to other factors, than other countries, and their rates of profit and interest therefore tend to be higher.

As a first broad generalization, we can say that it is the different proportions in which the various factors, including natural resources, are present in different countries that governs the pattern of international trade. A country exports goods that embody a high proportion of those factors in which she is relatively abundant. Tropical countries export tropical products. Countries with large deposits of minerals tend to export those minerals. The United States, where capital is relatively plentiful and therefore cheap, specializes in mass-produced manufactures requiring a large amount of capital. Australia, where grazing land is relatively abundant, exports wool. Countries with groups of workers with special skills tend to export their products; for example, Great Britain exports engineering products and worsteds, Switzerland exports watches, and Germany chemical products.

This generalization must be qualified. Some products are produced, and perhaps exported, by countries with very different proportions between their factors. For example, rice is produced both in the East, where labour is abundant, and in the United States, where labour is much scarcer relatively to capital. The difference in factor-proportions here shows itself not in the product, but in the method of production. In the East, rice is produced by methods involving much labour relatively to capital, whereas in Louisiana and California rice is produced by highly-mechanized methods employing far less labour per ton.

Again, we must remember also the influence of demand. For example, both the United States and Russia have large deposits of oil, but they need all their own output and more; they are importers, not exporters, of oil.

Nevertheless it is helpful, as a first approximation, to assume that if a good embodies a high proportion of a certain factor, it is likely to be exported from countries where that factor is relatively abundant and therefore relatively cheap.

The traditional or classical theory of international trade assumes, to begin with, that factors of production cannot move between countries, whereas goods can move freely between countries. This assumption is realistic enough for a first approximation. In practice there is some movement of labour and capital between countries (which tends, as far as it goes, to make wages and the return to capital less unequal between countries),[1] and national governments often restrict imports of goods: there is some discussion of the effects of such restriction in the present chapter.

2. THE GAIN FROM INTERNATIONAL TRADE

I think that no argument is needed to show that a country gains by importing goods, such as tropical products or minerals, that she could not produce for herself. If she did not import them, she would have to do without them. If they are consumers' goods, her consumers prefer to spend a certain amount of money on them rather than on domestic products. If they are producers' goods, such as raw materials, they make possible domestic industries that otherwise could not exist.

The gain to the exporting countries is also clear. The export demand widens the markets for their products and tends to keep up their prices. How could Northern Rhodesia have a flourishing copper-mining industry if all the copper had to be used within her own borders and could not be exported in any form? How much wheat would Canada grow, and how low would its price be, if she had to consume it all herself?

I shall therefore discuss only international trade in goods that the importing countries could produce for themselves. Why should they import them when they themselves could produce them?

If the whole world were one country, it would be easy to see how consumers gain by different goods being produced in different places. They would tend to be produced where their costs of production plus marketing are lowest. Any other arrangement would raise costs and prices, giving a smaller total output from the available resources. In the same way, the advantages of specialization between districts within a country are usually recognized. It is only when goods cross national boundaries that the advantages of specialization and trade are questioned.

What these advantages amount to is that two countries can produce a greater combined output, from the same factors of production, if each specializes on those products that it can produce best, than if each tries to be self-sufficient. I shall now illustrate this point by an arithmetical example, which I shall use throughout the chapter. This example, like the similar example given in Chapter VI, Section 5, assumes that people produce and consume only two commodities, and for this and other reasons it will no doubt strike the reader as very unrealistic. But it greatly simplifies the task of exposition, and the conclusions drawn from it are fundamentally valid; as we shall see, it can readily be modified to fit the facts of the world we live in.

[1] See Chapter XXV, Section 5.

Suppose that two countries, *A* and *B*, each has the same number of workers, the same amount of land and capital, and, in short, the same quantity of factors of production. In isolation, each uses half its factors to produce tea and the other half to produce linen. Owing to some difference (in climate, for example), the same factors in *A* can produce twice as much tea as in *B*, but only half as much linen. So *A* produces, say, 100 units of tea and 50 units of linen, while *B* produces 100 units of linen and 50 units of tea.

Now suppose that trade takes place between *A* and *B*, *A* specializing entirely in tea and *B* entirely in linen. *A* produces 200 units of tea and *B* 200 units of linen, whereas formerly their combined output was only 150 units of tea plus 150 units of linen.

The manner in which this gain—a gain of one-third in their combined real income—is divided, between the two countries, will depend on the terms of trade—on the rate at which tea is exchanged for linen. Suppose that this rate is 1 unit of tea against 1 unit of linen. Then *A* might exchange, for example, 80 units of tea (per week or year) against 80 units of linen, so that *A* would now have 120 tea and 80 linen, while *B* would have 80 tea and 120 linen.

Since the same factors in *A* could produce either 2 units of tea or 1 unit of linen (in other words, since I have chosen "units" which correspond to a certain amount of factor-services), it follows that when *A* was isolated, a unit of linen cost twice as much as a unit of tea. Say that a unit of tea cost £1. Then a unit of linen cost £2. In *B*, when *B* was isolated, the position was exactly the opposite. If a unit of linen cost £1, then a unit of tea cost £2, because it needed twice as many factors to produce it. Now that the two countries trade freely with one another, the price of tea is the same in both (namely, £1 a unit, its cost of production in *A*), and the price of linen is the same in both (also, as it happens, £1, its cost of production in *B*).

It is possible that some people might object to the consequences of trade between the two countries. For example, some people in *A* might complain that their country has "lost an industry"—namely, the linen industry. It has been destroyed by competition from *B*; all its workers have had to transfer to the tea industry. *B* is "dumping" linen on *A* at £1 a unit; its cost of production in *A* is £2 a unit. Why not have a "scientific" tariff that equalizes costs of production, in this case by an import duty of 100 per cent, £1 a unit, on linen imported from *B*? Clearly such a "scientific" tariff would abolish all international trade, for international trade takes place just because costs of production *are* different. Nevertheless, this so-called "scientific" tariff was accepted in principle, at one time, by the Government of the United States.

It is true enough that *A* could produce linen for herself, but she could do so only at twice the cost, in terms of factors, of *B*. She can get twice as much linen from a given amount of factors by using them to produce tea, and exporting the tea in exchange for linen, as she could get by using them to produce linen directly. In fact, A now gets both more tea and more linen, simply by specializing on tea. She used to get 100 tea + 50 linen; she now gets 120 tea + 80 linen, without any extra effort.

This arithmetical example is, to repeat, highly simplified. But it brings out the fundamental point, the gain from specialization and trade, and this point remains valid despite the modifications that must be made to bring the example into harmony with the real world. I will now discuss briefly the modifications which must be made to take account of (a) transport costs, (b) many countries, and not only two, (c) many commodities, and not only two, and (d) changing, and not constant, opportunity-cost ratios.

(a) Transport costs reduce the gain from international trade. The importing country has to pay costs of transport as well as the price received by the exporter. (Thus the price of linen in A, and the price of tea in B, would exceed £1 by the costs of transport.) In some cases, transport costs may more than offset differences in production costs, so that no trade takes place.

Reductions in transport costs, and improvements in methods of preserving goods (e.g. refrigeration and canning), make possible more specialization and trade. Some things, such as services and perishable commodities, cannot be transported; but tourists can come to the country and buy them on the spot.

(b) There are many countries, not only two. The whole of the rest of the world provides a country with potential foreign markets and foreign sources of supply. Trade is multilateral. There is no need whatever for the value of trade between two countries to balance. To take a simple example, West Africa sells cocoa to the United States for dollars, with which she buys engineering products and textiles from Great Britain, who can then use the dollars to buy cotton and tobacco from the United States.

If we take Great Britain as country A in our example, we can group the rest of the world together as B. (We must of course substitute British exports for "tea" and British imports for "linen," but the general reasoning still applies.)

(c) There are many commodities, and not merely two, that enter into international trade. In our example, tea represents all the different goods which are exported from country A, and linen represents all the different goods which are imported into country A.

In addition to export goods and import goods, a country will produce various goods, such as bread and liquid milk, and services, such as inland transport services, which are domestic, being neither exported nor imported.

Exactly which goods, and how much of each, A will export and import will depend on the world demand for the various goods as well as on their comparative costs of production. Owing to changed conditions, a country may import some quantities of goods which she formerly exported (as the United States now imports some timber) or may export some quantities of goods which she formerly imported (as Japan now exports steel). We can be sure, however, that A will have a greater comparative advantage in any good that she exports than in any good she imports, and will therefore obtain a larger real income by specializing and engaging in international trade than she could obtain if she were self-sufficient. Great Britain, for example, obtains a much greater quantity of foodstuffs and raw materials by using part of her labour and other resources to produce engineering products and other goods for export, and importing foodstuffs and raw materials in exchange, than she could obtain if she closed down her export industries and used the factors now employed in them to produce foodstuffs and raw materials at home.

(*d*) My arithmetical example assumes that a given collection of factors in A will always produce either 2 units of tea or 1 unit of linen, however much tea (and, therefore, however little linen) is produced. In other words, it assumes a constant opportunity-cost ratio between tea and linen of 2 to 1. Conversely for B.

In practice, this assumption is not true. Labour and land and other factors are not homogeneous. There are bound to be some factors in A (for example, some areas of land) which are unsuitable for tea production and some factors (perhaps the same ones) which are relatively suitable for linen production. Hence, if A goes on expanding her output of tea, and reducing her output of linen, the opportunity-cost ratio will change. As she transfers less and less suitable factors to the tea industry, by giving up an additional unit of linen output, she does not obtain an extra 2 units of tea but only, say, $1\frac{3}{4}$, then $1\frac{1}{2}$, then $1\frac{1}{4}$, and so on. The economic problem for A is to make the best use of her factors. If she has some factors which yield her more linen by producing linen directly than by producing tea to export in exchange for linen, then it will pay her to employ them in producing linen.

This explains why, even under complete free trade, a country may produce for herself some output of a commodity she mainly imports. Great Britain, for example, has about a million acres of land very suitable for wheat-growing. Although Great Britain is a large importer of wheat, this land can produce wheat more cheaply than any imported wheat can be bought, and (unless alternative crops that this land could produce instead should yield a higher net return than wheat) will continue to do so.[1]

[1] In fact, Great Britain assists her wheat-growing in order to maintain a larger acreage—over two million acres, including less suitable land—under wheat.

I must add, however, that there may be other reasons why a country produces, or even exports, goods of a type she imports. A country may be a large area, and one part may import a commodity that another part exports. Thus Hamburg may import coal from Great Britain, while the Ruhr produces coal not only for home consumption, but also for export. The cost of transporting coal by sea from Great Britain to Hamburg is considerably less than the cost of transporting coal from the Ruhr to Hamburg. Again, the commodity imported may differ from the commodity produced at home, although both bear the same name in popular speech. Thus France imports a far greater quantity of wine than she exports, but the wines she exports are of a finer quality, on the whole, than those she imports; and the British cars imported by the United States are of different types from those the United States produces and exports. Again, a country may deliberately encourage the production of certain goods at home, although she could obtain them more cheaply from abroad. Thus Great Britain subsidizes the home production of beet sugar, although she can and does import sugar much more cheaply than she can produce it.

3. The Principle of Comparative Costs

There are three types of cost: money cost, factor cost, and opportunity cost.

The *money cost* of producing a commodity is normally lower in a country that exports it than in a country that imports it. Why, then, do we bother with the kind of theory we have been discussing? Why not simply say that goods will be produced where their money costs of production (and marketing) are lowest?

The reason is that this statement, although true, is merely superficial. Money costs of production are made up of prices paid to various factors. These prices are different from what they would be if there were no international trade. The existing factor-prices, and therefore the existing money costs, in a country are partly the *result* of international trade. We therefore need a more fundamental explanation of why trade takes place.

By the *factor cost* of producing a commodity I mean, in the present context, the *quantity* of labour and other factors needed to produce it. It is not true that commodities are normally produced where their factor-costs are lowest. As we saw in Chapter VI, a community makes the best use of a factor by employing it for that task where its contribution is most valuable. A doctor who is a first-class typist is more useful as a doctor. France could produce more wine for herself, instead of importing it from North Africa and elsewhere, and could perhaps produce it with a smaller amount of labour and land. But this would mean putting under vineyards some land which is at present employed in more valuable tasks, such as growing wheat. The land of the French wine-growing districts renders a more valuable contribution by growing grapes, but other land, owing to differences in soil and climate, is better employed in other ways. It might grow more or better grapes per acre than land in North Africa, but it yields a higher net return producing something else.

The *opportunity-cost* of producing a unit of one commodity is the amount of the next-best commodity that the same factors could produce instead. *The fundamental explanation of why trade takes place is that opportunity-costs are different in different countries.*

In my example, the absolute factor-cost of producing tea was less in A than in B, and conversely for linen. Only half as many factors were needed to produce a unit of tea in A as were needed in B. A had an "absolute advantage" over B in the production of tea, and B had an "absolute advantage" over A in the production of linen.

The principle of comparative costs, or comparative advantage, points out that two countries will gain by specialization and trade, provided that each has a comparative advantage—lower comparative costs—in the commodities it exports.

Suppose that A and B both have the same number of workers. Suppose that in A they could produce either 200 units of tea or 200 units of linen, or 100 units of tea + 100 units of linen, and so on, an extra unit of tea "costing" a unit of linen and an extra unit of linen "costing" a unit of tea. In other words, the opportunity-cost ratio is constant at 1 unit of tea to 1 unit of linen. Suppose that in B the workers could produce either 80 tea or 160 linen, or 40 tea + 80 linen, and so on, an extra unit of linen "costing" half a unit of tea and an extra unit of tea "costing" 2 units of linen. In other words, the opportunity-cost ratio is constant at 1 unit of tea to 2 units of linen. Both countries will gain by specialization and trade, because their opportunity-cost ratios are different.

Suppose, for example, that in isolation A produces 150 tea + 50 linen, and B produces 40 tea + 80 linen. Suppose that A specializes entirely on tea, producing 200 units, and B entirely on linen, producing 160 units, and that the terms of trade are 1 tea against $1\frac{1}{3}$ linen. Suppose that A exchanges 45 tea against 60 linen from B. A now has 155 tea + 60 linen, and B 45 tea + 100 linen. Clearly both countries have gained by specializing and exchanging.

By hypothesis, a worker in A can produce 25 per cent more linen than a worker in B. Yet it pays A to import linen from B. For every unit of tea exported from A obtains $1\frac{1}{3}$ units of linen in exchange. If A had used her labour to produce linen, instead of importing it, she would have obtained only 1 unit of linen with the labour that produces 1 unit of tea.

This is sometimes expressed by saying that A's absolute costs (factor costs) are lower than B's for both tea and linen, but that A's comparative advantage lies in tea; her comparative costs are lower for tea.

There is a concealed ambiguity here. If workers in A can produce everything more efficiently than workers in B, then they are better workers, or they are aided by more natural resources or by more capital, or they use better methods. It is rather misleading to imply that the "quantity of factors" is the same in the two countries if they produce more of everything in A.

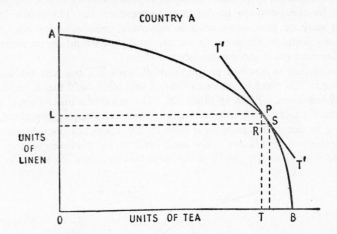

COUNTRY A

UNITS OF TEA

In order to explain the gain from international trade we need only point to differences in opportunity-cost ratios. It is true that these ratios are not constant. But the amounts of different goods produced will be such that the opportunity-cost ratios equal the relative prices. For example, A will produce some linen for herself. She will expand her output of tea up to the point at which further factors, transferred from the linen industry, would yield just 1 unit of tea for every $1\frac{1}{3}$ units of linen forgone. The price of 1 unit of tea is the same as the price of $1\frac{1}{3}$ units of linen. It pays better for factors to produce $1\frac{1}{3}$ units of linen than anything less than 1 unit of tea, and it pays better for factors to produce 1 unit of tea than anything less than $1\frac{1}{3}$ units of linen. Exactly the same applies to B. In equilibrium, the relative opportunity-costs will equal the relative prices of the alternative amounts of products.

The above diagram shows the production possibilities of country A. She can produce either OB tea and no linen; or OA linen and no tea; or any combination of tea and linen represented by any point on the curve AB.

The curve AB is humped, and not a straight line, showing that the amount of linen output that has to be forgone in order to produce an extra unit of tea increases as the output of tea increases (moving along the curve AB towards B).

When international trade enables country A to obtain $1\frac{1}{3}$ units of linen for each unit of tea she exports, she will expand her output of tea and therefore will reduce her output of linen. But as she moves along AB towards B, she will come to a point P at which she has to give up $1\frac{1}{3}$ units of linen output to produce yet a further unit of tea. And beyond P she would have to give up an increasing quantity of linen (rising to 3, 4, or more units) to produce still more tea. This is shown by the steepness of AB as it approaches B. The underlying reason may be that some land is relatively unsuitable for tea, but especially suitable for linen; this is the land that would be transferred from linen to tea if she moved beyond P.

Equilibrium is reached at the point P, with OT tea and OL linen produced. To produce an extra unit of tea, RS, would mean producing PR less linen. PR is $1\frac{1}{3}$ times RS. The price of a unit of tea is the same as the price of $1\frac{1}{3}$ units of linen. There is no object, therefore, in moving, in either direction, away from P. The opportunity-costs (shown by the slope of T^1T^1) are in the same ratio to one another (namely $1\frac{1}{3}$ to 1, or 4 to 3) as the prices of the marginal products RS and PR.

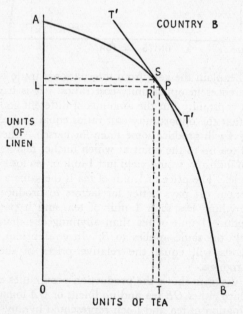

The above diagram shows the production possibilities of country B. She is in equilibrium at P, producing OL linen and OT tea. To produce a further unit of linen, *RS*, she would have to use land and other factors that could produce *RP* tea, and if she moved still further towards *A*, she would have to give up larger and larger quantities of tea to produce extra units of linen. She is therefore in equilibrium at *P*. *RS* is 1⅓ times *RP*; the opportunity-costs, shown by the slope of T^1T^1 (the same, 4 to 3, as in the previous diagram), are in the same ratio to one another as the prices of the marginal products *RP* and *RS*; the price of 1 unit of tea (*RP*) is the same as the price of 1⅓ units of linen (*RS*).

4. THE TERMS OF TRADE

I have already mentioned the terms of trade, in Chapter V, Section 1. In our example, the terms of trade are the price ratios between tea and linen. If the price of tea rises and the price of linen remains unchanged (or if the price of tea rises more, or falls less, than the price of linen), the terms of trade have become more favourable to the tea-exporting country *A* and less favourable to the tea-importing country *B*.

If opportunity-cost ratios are constant—for example, 1 tea to 1 linen in *A*, and 1 tea to 2 linen in *B*—the terms of trade must lie somewhere between them. *A* will want more than 1 unit of linen in exchange for a unit of tea, for she could produce linen for herself by producing one unit less of tea for each unit of linen she produced. *B* will want to give less than 2 units of linen for a unit of tea, for she could produce tea for herself by giving up 2 units of her linen output for each unit of tea she produced.

The terms of trade will depend on the combined demand schedules of the two countries for tea and linen. In fact, opportunity-costs are not constant. Equilibrium will be reached when, at the prices ruling for tea and linen, nobody would rather buy more of one and less of the other, and when, as we saw in the above diagrams, opportunity-cost ratios are the same in both countries and are the same as the terms of trade.

Countries both export and import a wide range of commodities. The terms of trade of a country, or rather changes in them, are measured by the change in the price level of its exports relatively to the change in the price level of its imports. This raises the problem of how to measure these price levels. One way is to take some year—say, 1950—as the base date and to value the exports of, say, 1953, at their 1950 prices. We can then say: the exports of 1953 actually sold for so much, say 105; at 1950 prices they would have sold for, say, 100; the export price level is therefore 5 per cent higher than in 1950. We can then do the same thing for imports. Suppose the price level of imports is only about 2 per cent higher. It follows that the terms of trade are nearly 3 per cent better than in 1950; a unit of exports buys nearly 3 per cent more imports than in 1950.

But when there are considerable changes, over a period, in the composition of exports and imports, in the proportions of the totals formed by different categories of goods, and perhaps also in their qualities, such comparisons cannot provide an accurate measure. For this reason, the Board of Trade changes its base date every few years. Recent figures for the United Kingdom are as follows—

(BASE: 1954 = 100)

Year	(1) Import Prices	(2) Export Prices	(3) Terms of Trade [(1) ÷ (2)]
1955	103	102	101
1956	105	106	99
1957	107	111	96
1958	99	110	90
1959	98	109	90

The terms of trade of a country are the relation between two sets of world prices: the prices of the kinds of goods she exports and the prices of the kinds of goods she imports. Most countries are not important enough, either as suppliers or as markets, to change world prices in order to turn the terms of trade in their favour. If, however, a country is the main supplier of a commodity, it might restrict exports of it in order to raise its price. Or a number of countries, who between them supply most of the exports of a commodity, might combine for that purpose. I discussed this question under the heading of commodity control schemes in Chapter XVI, Section 7. In the same way, a country may be such an important buyer of some commodity that by buying less it can force down its price. The United States did force down the price of tin, by restricting her purchases, during the latter part of 1951. But cases of this kind are rare.

Even if a country could improve its terms of trade in such ways, it may be against its interest to do so. For example, at the moment Great Britain needs to export all she can. How absurd it would be to restrict her exports of steel in the hope that she would thereby push up the world price! She might succeed in raising the price a little, but at the cost of cutting down her exports and losing markets to her competitors. Again, Great Britain might force down the price of wheat a little, for the time being, by buying less. But it would be folly to make her people go short of bread, and to antagonize wheat-exporting countries, for a small and temporary "gain" in the terms of trade.

A change in the terms of trade is the consequence of some change in the conditions of demand or supply. We must consider the signi-

ficance of this underlying change before we can decide whether the
new situation as a whole is more favourable or less favourable to any
particular country. An improvement in the terms of trade may reflect
a change that on balance is unfavourable, and conversely. I will
consider a few cases.

An increase in the world demand for certain products benefits the
countries exporting these products. For example, Australia has
enjoyed a large rise in her real income owing to the post-war increase
in the demand for wool. No doubt a large rise in the national income
creates problems of adjustment, and if export prices fall back, it may
be difficult to reduce money wages from their prevailing high levels.
But there can be no question of the net benefit to a country of such
an improvement in its terms of trade. On the other hand, the countries
that import these products, and have to pay more for them, are in that
respect worse off than before.

The very favourable change in the terms of trade of Great Britain
after 1929 was due to the Great Depression, which was a general
misfortune. The prices of most foodstuffs and raw materials fell heavily,
and the countries exporting those products suffered severely from the
large adverse swing in their terms of trade. But Great Britain was at
the receiving end, and cheap imports enabled the bulk of her population to achieve a higher standard of living than ever before. On the
other hand, she suffered a large increase in unemployment, especially
in her export industries. Overseas countries, receiving much less for
their products, could not buy as many manufactures as before.

The discovery of artificial nitrates, providing cheaper fertilizers, was
a benefit to the world as a whole. But it was a great blow to Chile,
who depended largely on her exports of nitre. Their price fell, the
terms of trade moving against her, and she had to adjust her economy
in order to produce other exports (notably copper) in place of nitre.

On the costs side, a favourable change in the terms of trade of a
country may arise from changes adverse to her economy. For example,
one of her main exports may be some mineral, the deposits of which
are becoming worked out. The fall in its output may lead to a rise
in its price, but this will not compensate for the decline of the industry.

A fall in the export prices of a country may be due to technical
improvements that reduce both real and money costs of production.
Output per worker or, more generally, output from a given amount
of factors, has increased. The net effect will probably be to raise the
real income of the country, despite the worsening of her terms of trade.

5. INTERNATIONAL TRADE AND PRICES

Goods that enter into international trade have a world market, and
therefore their price at any port tends to be the same after allowing

for costs of transport. Once they enter another country, their prices
may be increased by import duties and importers' profits.

With a rate of exchange of £1 = $2·80 we should normally expect
that any good exported from the United States and costing $x there,
would cost £x ÷ 2·80, plus costs of transport, on arrival in Great
Britain. During the post-war period, however, Governments in the
sterling area have restricted purchases by their citizens from the
dollar area, and in consequence some internationally-traded goods
have been appreciably dearer in sterling than in dollars.

A Government may make a long-term contract with another country
to buy stated quantities of a commodity at a price that is fixed, or
fixed within certain limits, in advance; and this price may turn out,
as time goes on, to be either above or below the prevailing market
price. Thus the British Government has agreed to buy sugar at a fixed
price (which may substantially exceed the market price) from the
Commonwealth; and under the International Wheat Agreement
(of which the United Kingdom is once again a member) the importing
countries undertake to buy, and the exporting countries to provide
them with, stated supplies of wheat at not less than a certain minimum price and not more than a certain maximum price. A firm could
make similar contracts for raw materials, but this is usually too risky,
as the selling prices of the firm's products may fall.

Again, a monopolist (for example, a steel cartel) may charge higher
prices at home than for its exports. But the general rule is that a world
market means a uniform price. In our example, if a unit of linen
costs £1 in B, we can assume that it costs £1 (or the equivalent in A's
currency of £1) in A also.

The real income per head of a country depends mainly on its output
per head and partly on its terms of trade. Let us take wages to
represent incomes. Suppose that wages in B are £1 a day. Then
they will be higher in A, for a worker in A produces 150 per cent more
tea (200 to 80) and 25 per cent more linen (200 to 160) than a worker
in B. We can say exactly how much higher they will be by looking
at the terms of trade. The terms of trade, we assumed, are 1 unit of
tea to $1\frac{1}{3}$ units of linen. The price of tea is therefore £$1\frac{1}{3}$ a unit. Our
example assumed that the amount of labour required to produce a
unit of linen in B could produce $1\frac{1}{4}$ (i.e. $\frac{200}{160}$) units of tea in A. Therefore if wages in B, which produces linen, are £1 a day, wages in A,
which produces tea, will be $1\frac{1}{4} \times 1\frac{1}{3} \times$ £1, or £1 13s. 4d. a day.

Of course any country can make its money incomes, in its own
currency, as high as it likes. But it cannot raise real incomes by doing
so. Suppose, for example, that money wages in B are raised to £3 a
day. Then the local price of linen will go up to £3 a unit, for its
money cost of production will have trebled. And as the terms of trade
are $1\frac{1}{3}$ linen for 1 tea, the price of tea in B will rise from £$1\frac{1}{3}$ to £4 a

unit. Money incomes will treble and so will the cost of living. If prices and incomes remain the same as before in A, the rate of exchange between the two currencies will now be 3 B pounds against 1 A pound.

Suppose now that A decides to prohibit imports from B because B is a "cheap labour" country. A is back where she was, self-supporting. Instead of getting, by specialization and trade, 155 tea + 60 linen, she has only 150 tea + 50 linen. And B also is worse off. Deprived of her export market, she gets only 40 tea and 80 linen instead of 45 tea and 100 linen. Real wages must fall. The way to help workers whose wages are relatively low is to buy their products, not to ban them. British workers would be injured, not helped, if the United States were to ban imports of British cars on the ground that wages are so much lower in the British motor-car industry than in the American.

The general effect of international trade is to raise the price, in any country, of any factor that is relatively abundant and cheap. For the exports of that country are likely to contain a high proportion of the services of that factor. The export industries increase the demand for that factor. For example, in countries where land is plentiful, exports of agricultural products, whether foodstuffs or raw materials, tend to raise the price of land—although it remains lower than in more densely populated countries. In the same way, in countries where labour is relatively plentiful, exports embodying a high proportion of labour services tend to raise wages.

The prices of "domestic" goods and services, not entering into international trade, may vary widely between countries. Rents in a particular district, as I noted in Chapter XXVIII, Section 3, may be a special case. House rents in New York may be much higher than in Canada. Again, public utilities tend to be local monopolies; the charges which they are allowed to make depend partly on public policy, and may vary considerably between countries.

As a general rule, however, there is a link—although not always a close one—between international prices and domestic prices. The link is that factors of production can move between export industries and domestic industries. The earnings of workers in the export industries tend to vary with the world prices of their products; and similar workers in domestic industries are not likely, for long, to earn either very much more or very much less than their comrades in the export industries. The same applies to other factors also.

An expansion of international trade tends to raise real incomes all round. Some groups in a country may be temporarily injured by competing imports; they may have to transfer to other fields, as in our example the tea producers in B had to transfer to the linen industry. But the country as a whole will gain.

There is a situation, however, in which a country as a whole may lose by an expansion of international trade. This is the situation known to economists as *two countries competing in a third*. Suppose, for example, that Great Britain has been selling cotton goods to Australia and that now Japan appears upon the scene, offering similar goods more cheaply. Japan will gain and Australia will gain, but Great Britain will lose. She will be forced to cut her prices, accepting less favourable terms of trade, and even so she will have to reduce the volume of her exports.

There may be some compensation. The emergence of Japan as a supplier means that she emerges also as a buyer; the more she exports, the more she will import. She may not import much directly from Great Britain, but trade is multilateral; if British exports in general remain competitive, some of the money spent by Japan on imports will come to Great Britain, via some other countries, in the form of an increased demand for some of her exports. She will have to adapt herself, however, to the new situation, producing fewer cotton goods, in which her comparative advantage is now small, and more exports of a type in which her comparative advantage is greater.

What Japan does to Great Britain in the field of cotton textiles Great Britain may do to Japan, or to another competitor, in some other field. Where competition is the rule, as in international trade, somebody is bound to get hurt from time to time. It is the price that must be paid for economic progress. The great rise in western standards of living over the past hundred years was made possible by the vast expansion of world trade. Great Britain, or some other country, may suffer a set-back from time to time owing to foreign competition, but in the long run every country, and certainly Great Britain, is bound to gain from a large and expanding volume of international trade.

6. Free Trade and Protection

The general argument of this chapter favours complete freedom of trade. Free trade enables the maximum advantage to be gained from specialization between countries. It compensates, to some extent, for the unequal distribution of factors of production. Factors of production cannot move freely between countries, but if their products —goods—can move freely, then exports and imports are a substitute for the movements of factors, each country exporting goods that embody a high proportion of the factors which it has in relative abundance and importing goods embodying a high proportion of the factors in which it is relatively scarce.

Yet in practice nearly every country has always imposed restrictions on at least some of its imports. These restrictions take various forms. Taxes known as duties or tariffs (the whole schedule of duties being known as the *customs tariff*) may be imposed on certain imports, some being taxed more heavily than others. The quantity of a certain good that may be imported may be restricted to a stated maximum known as a *quota*; import quotas were discussed in Chapter XIX, Section 4. Nowadays the most powerful and effective method of restricting or prohibiting certain imports from particular countries (notably the dollar area) is exchange control, which I discuss later. Further, all kinds of administrative regulations may constitute what has been called an "invisible tariff." For example, unnecessarily severe rules imposed on the alleged grounds of health and hygiene may keep down imports of live animals and other goods; public authorities may favour local firms as against foreign firms in placing their contracts; tariff regulations may be unduly complicated and subject to change without notice, thus creating risks for importers; railway rates on inward movements of goods may be higher than on outward movements.

Why do countries place these restrictions on their imports? They may believe that protection—the protection of their local industries against the competition of imports—is desirable as a long-term policy on economic grounds. Before turning to such arguments, however, I will say a little about four other possible reasons for restrictions on imports. They may be imposed to yield revenue; or to protect the country's balance of payments; or as an emergency measure; or on non-economic grounds.

Most Governments levy import duties on imports of goods such as tobacco, drink, and petrol, in order to raise revenue. If the country itself does not produce such goods or if any it does produce are taxed at the same rate (as cigarettes, etc., are taxed in Great Britain) by what are known as *excise duties*, then the primary purpose of such duties is to raise revenue and not to protect local industries. They may, however, have some protective effect on substitutes produced within the country and not subject to corresponding excise duties; for example, import duties on petrol may incidentally tend to protect the local coal-mining industry. Again, if imports of the taxed commodities are considerably curtailed by the duties on them, fewer factors of production will be employed in the export industries, for in the long run to curtail imports is to curtail exports. But as a rule Governments select for such "revenue duties" commodities for which the demand is fairly rigid, and therefore the consequent diversion of resources (away from the export industries) is not very great.

I explain the meaning of the balance of payments in the next chapter, and I discuss exchange control, which consists largely of restrictions on imports imposed in order to prevent a deficit in the balance of payments, in Chapter XXXIX. All I need to say here is that most countries of the free world are pledged, as members of the International Monetary Fund, to aim at the reduction and eventual abolition of such "exchange restrictions" as rapidly as they can.

Protection is often advocated as an emergency measure against a general depression of trade. There may be heavy unemployment. Money spent on local products directly creates local employment, whereas money spent on imports does not. Fuller employment may be deemed worth the rise in the cost of living due to protection. Increased activity in the protected industries, it may be argued, might even stimulate investment and promote recovery.

It was on such grounds that most countries considerably increased their protection at the outset of the Great Depression in the early 1930s. In particular, countries such as France and Germany greatly restricted their imports of foodstuffs in order to protect their farmers against imports whose prices had fallen to around half of what they had been in 1928.

But the imports of one country are the exports of another, and restrictions on them create unemployment and distress in the exporting countries. The latter will have less to spend (since their own export earnings are reduced) on imports from their customers, and they are very likely to follow suit by protecting their own local industries against them. This is what happened during the Great Depression. For example, the overseas agricultural countries protected and stimulated their own manufacturing industries, and bought fewer manufactures from Western Europe and other exporters of manufactures.

In my view, the general increase in protection during those years was in fact a short-sighted and beggar-my-neighbour policy which deepened and prolonged the Great Depression. I think it is generally agreed that if another world depression should threaten, it would be very desirable to find some means of inducing every country to maintain, and not to reduce, the volume of its imports.

Some arguments for protection are based mainly on non-economic considerations. Thus a country may stimulate its iron and steel industry in order to be better prepared for war, or may protect its agriculture because it wants to have a larger agricultural population. An economist can only point out the sacrifice, in the form of a standard of living lower than it would otherwise be, entailed by such policies, leaving statesmen and citizens to decide whether the sacrifice is worth making.

I turn now to economic arguments for protection as a deliberate policy.

Some arguments which carry much weight with the general public are mainly fallacious. A leading example is that imports from countries with low wages should be taxed in order to prevent the standard of living of workers in the home country from being reduced. I tried to show the fallacy of this contention in Section 5. Cheap imports, whatever the reason for their cheapness, tend to raise, not to reduce, standards of living in the importing countries.

Those concerned with a particular industry may urge that protection against competing imports would enable that industry to expand, or would prevent it from declining. Nobody disputes this. But is it desirable to penalize the whole consuming population for the benefit of the workers and shareholders in that industry? If it is, then why should not the same argument be applied to every industry that faces foreign competition? Such all-round protection would no doubt enable money wages to be maintained, but it would lead to a substantial rise in the general cost of living, reducing real wages.

The protection of home industries always tends to affect adversely employment and earnings in the export industries, for the less a country spends on imports, the less purchasing power it provides for foreigners to spend on its exports.

We are driven back to the general theory of international trade set out in this chapter. The fundamental question is how the factors of production can best be distributed between export and other industries in order to provide the greatest real income for the country as a whole. Unemployment is a separate problem, best tackled, in my view, by measures other than restrictions on imports.

Some arguments for protection are based on sound economic analysis. For example, if a country is an important buyer of a commodity, it may be able, by placing an import duty on it, to reduce its world price, thus turning the terms of trade in its favour and in effect making the foreign suppliers pay part of the import duty. As the foreign suppliers lose at least as much as the importing country gains, this argument for protection rests on a national, and not an international, outlook.

Even if it is considered perfectly moral to impose losses and hardships on other countries, there is always the possibility that they may retaliate. This possibility applies equally to restrictions on imports that would increase employment in the restricting country—provided that other countries were not thereby provoked or forced into restricting their own imports.

Another argument for protection is the famous "infant industry" argument. It is urged that certain industries would be quite suitable for a country, and could eventually stand on their own feet, provided they were protected for a period during which they could get a start despite the competition of similar imports. Whatever the theoretical merits of this argument, in practice these infants seldom grow up; we can look around the world today and see the infant industries of one or two generations ago still assisted by a substantial measure of protection, and mostly clamouring for more. This suggests that the best way to give an infant industry a start may be to subsidize it from general revenue; the taxpayers can then see how much it is costing, and can review the position from time to time.

Most of the popular arguments for protection merely assert, without any proof, that a country ought to be more self-supporting. There are several arguments, however, which are accepted by some (but by no means all) who understand and appreciate the benefits of international specialization. The difficulty is that once protection is introduced, economic analysis often fades out of the picture, giving way to political pressure, propaganda, log-rolling, and, in some countries, graft and corruption. The commodities that are in fact protected, and the amount of protection that each receives, may bear little resemblance to the pattern that would have resulted from the strict application of the theoretical arguments. There may be a valid theoretical case for a limited degree of protection in certain circumstances, but on practical grounds the best course is usually free trade.

CHAPTER XXXV

BALANCES OF PAYMENTS

1. How Payments are made between Countries

DIFFERENT countries have their own currencies. We must not be misled by the use of the same name for different currency units. There are quite a number of pounds, dollars, francs, and so on—all different. For example, Australian pounds are quite different and separate from British pounds, Malayan dollars from American dollars, Belgian francs from French francs.

As a rule, the currency of one country is neither legal tender nor generally acceptable in another. We cannot pay our debts in France with Bank of England notes, nor can Frenchmen pay their debts here with notes of the Banque de France. Broadly speaking, the currency of a country stays in that country all the time, and is not used to make payments in other countries.

Nearly all payments between countries are made through banks. Clearly if a bank operates both in country A, where it holds balances of A's currency, and in country B, where it holds balances of B's currency, it is a simple matter for it to receive a sum of money in A and to pay out an equivalent sum, in B's currency, in B, or conversely.

Great Britain has a large and widespread international trade, and London is a leading financial centre. Most payments between Great Britain and other countries, and some payments between other countries, are settled through London.

The chief foreign and Dominion banks have offices in London and hold sterling balances in London. They can therefore make payments in sterling, either to British banks or to one another, and they can receive sterling in London, paying out an equivalent amount in their own currencies in their own countries. British banks have some branches overseas, but for the most part they use local banks which act as their agents and will pay out local currency on their behalf. The balances of foreign currency held overseas by British banks are very small compared with the sterling balances held by overseas banks in London.

Suppose, for example, that a British resident wishes to pay 10,000 francs to a creditor in Paris. He goes to his bank, pays it the corresponding amount in sterling, and obtains a draft, on either its Paris branch or the French bank that acts as its agent in Paris, for 10,000 francs. He sends this draft to his creditor, who presents the draft (or gets his own bank to present it for him), and collects his 10,000 francs.

If a particular bank is running short of, say, sterling, it can usually buy sterling from another bank, paying in its own currency. So long as payments from one country to the rest of the world about equal payments by the rest of the world to that country, over a period, no real difficulties will arise. But if a country is continuously paying out more than she receives, there will be difficulties. The chief alternative methods of dealing with such difficulties—in other words, of correcting an adverse balance of payments—are discussed in subsequent chapters.

At present about half all international transactions are made in sterling, and therefore most countries keep sterling balances. But a considerable volume of international transactions is carried out in terms of (United States) dollars, and a number of countries hold their foreign exchange reserves mainly in dollars.

2. The Balance of Trade and the Balance of Payments

The balance of trade of a country is the relation, over a period, between the value of her exports and the value of her imports. If the former exceeds the latter, the difference is her *export surplus*; if the latter exceeds the former, the difference is her *import surplus*.

Some countries, notably the United States, Canada, and South Africa, value their imports f.o.b. (free on board)—that is, at their value when they leave the country from which they are sent. Most other countries value their imports c.i.f. (cost, insurance, freight)— that is, at their value on arrival. Clearly the former method shows a larger export surplus, or a smaller import surplus, than the latter; and the difference, which may amount to 10 per cent or more, should be allowed for when making comparisons between a country that values its imports f.o.b. and another that values its imports c.i.f.

Countries also differ in what items they include in imports and exports. They may either include or exclude items such as gold and silver, parcel post, ships' bunkers and stores, armaments, second-hand ships, and fish. I will not discuss these details, for all items are included in a balance of payments, which is comprehensive.

A country has to make payments abroad for other transactions as well as for imports. She may have to pay for shipping services and other services rendered by foreigners; her citizens spend money while travelling abroad for pleasure or business and may remit money to relatives or friends abroad; she may have to pay royalties on foreign films; her Government may make grants to its colonies or to international bodies such as the International Refugee Organization. Foreigners may own property or other investments in the country, on which they receive rents or interest or dividends; her Government may have to pay interest on a loan from another Government or from an organization such as the International Bank or the International Monetary Fund. And there are many other types of transactions that may involve payments abroad.

All such transactions may have their counterpart on the other side of the account. Countries receive payments for services of all kinds— from foreign tourists, as income on their foreign investments, and so forth—as well as for their exports.

For many years Great Britain has had a large excess of imports. This is mainly because some of her residents have received considerable sums as interest or dividends on their overseas investments, while British firms have rendered shipping, banking, insurance, and other services to people abroad. These payments have been received, in effect, in the form of goods: hence the surplus of imports.

Clearly we can get a complete picture only by taking account of all transactions, and not restricting ourselves to imports and exports. Such a comprehensive account is given by the balance of payments.

The balance of payments of a country is a record of its monetary transactions, over a period, with the rest of the world. I take the United Kingdom as an illustration. Any transaction, such as the purchase of imports, that involves a payment to somebody outside the United Kingdom by a person or Government or firm or other body in the United Kingdom is known as a *debit* item. Any transaction, such as the sale of exports, that involves a payment by the rest of the world to somebody in the United Kingdom is a *credit* item. The criterion is whether sterling is used to buy other currencies or whether other currencies are used to buy sterling. The nationality of the persons concerned is not relevant; for example, a payment by a foreigner living in the United Kingdom to a Britisher living overseas is a debit item.

There is no reason whatever, on the face of it, why the total debits of all these multitudinous and separate transactions should exactly equal the total credits. If there is a substantial and continuing discrepancy, one way or the other, the Government may be constrained to take some action to bring the two sides closer together. I discuss later the different measures it may take. My present point is that there is no reason why the debits should equal the credits.

It is customary, however, to divide a balance of payments into two parts: into transactions on current account and transactions on capital account. The current account will show a credit balance or a debit balance, as the case may be. The capital account will show how this balance was financed. As a matter of book-keeping, therefore, the capital account must show a balance equal and opposite to that of the current account.

Suppose, for example, that the current account of the United

Kingdom shows a debit balance of £x. How have these payments been met? Very likely they have been met by a corresponding increase in sterling balances: foreign and Dominion banks have in effect advanced the money; the short-term indebtedness of the United Kingdom has increased to the extent of £x. The capital account therefore shows "Increase of Sterling Liabilities" £x as a credit item. The two sides of the balance of payments, taking the current account and the capital account together, must always equal one another because every transaction must be financed by somebody—if the seller provides the goods or services on credit, he is making a short-term loan that will be included as a credit item in the capital account.

3. THE UNITED KINGDOM BALANCE OF PAYMENTS, 1958

The following provisional summary of the United Kingdom balance of payments for 1958 is adapted from Cmd. 700 of 1959: United Kingdom Balance of Payments, 1956 to 1958.

CURRENT ACCOUNT

Debits £ million

1.	Imports (f.o.b.)	3,309
2.	Government	272
3.	Shipping	343
4.	Interest, Profits and Dividends . . .	285
5.	Travel	152
6.	Migrants' funds, legacies, and private gifts (net)	28
7.	Total Debits	4,389

Credits

8.	Exports and re-exports (f.o.b.) . . .	3,429
9.	Government	56
10.	Shipping	510
11.	Interest, Profits and Dividends . . .	338
12.	Travel	137
13.	Other (net)	374
14.	Total Credits	4,844
15.	Surplus on Current Transactions . .	+455

CAPITAL ACCOUNT

Overseas Investment	−190
Increase in overseas sterling holdings . .	+54
Increase in gold and dollar reserves . . .	−284
Other items	−35
	−455

It will be seen that transactions are grouped into a few broad categories. Most of them are self-explanatory, but a few remarks may be helpful.

It will be noted that in the table imports are valued f.o.b. (in British trade statistics they are valued c.i.f.). In so far as they are carried in British ships, the freight payments by the British importers to the British shipping firms are internal payments. In so far as they are carried in non-British ships, the freight payments (or charter payments) are included in item 3 (except that oil freights are included with other oil transactions in item 13). Item 3 covers the disbursements abroad (e.g. for bunkers and ships' stores) of the British shipping industry. The corresponding payments by foreigners for the use of British shipping, and their disbursements in British ports, are shown in item 10. It will be seen that item 10 exceeds item 3; there was a net credit (of £167 million) on shipping.

Expenditure abroad by the British Government (item 2) was mainly military (£183 million). Other items were Colonial grants (£34 million), Relief and other grants (£14 million), and expenditure on pensions (£11 million), diplomatic posts, and so forth. The corresponding credit item (item 9) covers receipts by the British Government—for example, from the United States Government under certain financial agreements. It will be seen that the disbursements of the British Government substantially exceeded its receipts; there was a net debit of £216 million.

Interest, profits, and dividends on foreign investments in the United Kingdom and interest on loans made to the United Kingdom are shown in item 4. This item includes interest on the credits made by the United States and Canadian Governments shortly after the war (£39 million) and interest earned on sterling balances owned by non-residents. The corresponding credit item—interest, profits, and dividends on British investments and loans made abroad—is item 11, which exceeded item 4 by £53 million.

British tourists and business representatives spent £152 million on foreign travel (item 5), £15 million more than the corresponding expenditure by foreigners on travel in the United Kingdom (item 12). These travel items do not include fares: fares to shipping companies are included in Shipping and fares to airlines in item 13.

Migrants' funds, legacies, and private gifts is an item (item 6) of which only the net balance (corresponding to the net balance of £15 million on travel) is shown.

Item 13 shows the net debit balance on a wide range of transactions. The largest component is the overseas transactions of the United Kingdom oil companies. Other components include the earnings of the City of London on banking, insurance, and similar transactions performed for non-residents (a credit item), payments and receipts in

R

respect of civil aviation, film royalties (a net debit of about £10 million), and the expenditure of United States and Canadian forces in the United Kingdom (a credit of £70 million).

On all these current transactions there was a large net surplus of £455 million.

Cmd. 700 gives more details than I have shown under "Capital Account" of how this surplus was disposed of. The main items, however, were the increase in gold and dollar reserves of £284 million (much larger than in 1957, when it was only £13 million, or in 1956, when it was only £42 million) and overseas long-term investment of £190 million (corresponding to £270 million in 1957 and £200 million in 1956). Both these are "debit" items because they involve the purchase of other currencies to the values shown.

During 1959, the volume of British exports increased by nearly 5 per cent, but the volume of imports increased by over 6 per cent, the price-levels of both exports and imports remaining fairly stable. The surplus on current transactions was probably a little below £250 million.

4. The Significance of the Balance of Payments

A credit balance of payments, or surplus, on current account is commonly called "favourable," and a debit balance, or deficit, "unfavourable" or "adverse." But we must examine the causes of a credit or debit balance before we can judge whether the situation as a whole is favourable or unfavourable to the country.

Clearly every country cannot have a surplus. The surpluses of some countries will have their counterpart in the deficits of others. And sooner or later balances due between countries must be settled, and settled in goods (including gold), for one country will not accept the paper money of another in payment. Over a period, therefore, the receipts of any country will tend to equal its payments; if it has a deficit for some time, this will be followed by a surplus when it pays its debts, and conversely.

International investment gives rise to surpluses and deficits. Consider a country that is borrowing heavily from abroad in order to carry out capital development, either under the Government or under private enterprise. Her imports will increase, taking the form either of capital goods for the new projects or of consumers' goods (in effect, for the workers employed on the projects). For the time being, the country will have a large deficit, offset by the inflow of capital.

There is nothing unhealthy about this. The deficit is not in any way unfavourable or adverse to the country. If all goes well, the capital formation will expand output and enable the country to increase her exports. When she is repaying the foreign loans, she will have a surplus on her balance of payments on current account.

A lending country, on the other hand, will have a surplus while she is lending and a deficit while she is being repaid. Here again the terms favourable and unfavourable are meaningless; clearly there is nothing unfavourable about having one's debts repaid.

It will be noted that the only way in which a country can receive capital from abroad is by a deficit—other items being equal, an import surplus—equal to the amount of foreign investment received. But this does not mean that a country needs "external aid" (grants or loans from international bodies or from other countries) only if her balance of payments is in deficit. A country which, by prudence and restraint, maintains equilibrium in her balance of payments may both be poorer and have richer investment opportunities than another which spends more than her income and thereby develops a deficit.

Consider now a country which is not receiving an inflow of investment capital, but which nevertheless tends to have a continuous deficit in her balance of payments on current account. In order to simplify the wording, let us suppose that credit items other than exports equal debit items other than imports. Then the country is importing more than she can pay for by her export earnings. She is overspending her income, living beyond her means.

Importers pay in full, in their own currency, for the goods they import. So do the final consumers of imports. They are living within their incomes. What is wrong?

The banking system must provide the importers with foreign exchange, and the export earnings of the country are not large enough to provide all the foreign exchange required. There is a gap, the deficit in the balance of payments, to be filled. And any method of filling it, so long as the deficit continues, is only a temporary expedient which can be used for only a limited period.

The gap may be filled by "disinvestment." The Government or private individuals may sell some of their foreign assets. This will provide some foreign exchange at the moment. But in the long run it will make the situation worse, for it will reduce the investment income received by the country from abroad. It is a course likely to be adopted by the Government only in grave emergency. (For example, in the early months of the war, the British Government mobilized and sold American securities owned by British residents, in order to obtain dollars.)

Again—another form of disinvestment—the Government may part with some of its reserves of gold and foreign exchange. But the reserves owned by most Governments, including the British Government, are smaller than are needed to provide an adequate cushion against a temporary deficit. In such a case, a deficit can be covered in this way for only a short time.

Another method of filling the gap is for the Government to borrow abroad. There is an international institution, the International Monetary Fund, which was created mainly to make loans for this purpose—but loans of limited amounts for limited periods. Some friendly Government may be induced to lend, to help the country over a bad period, but it will be unlikely to go on lending if the country continues to live beyond her means, for in that event how will she be able to repay?

The conclusion is that a continuous deficit in the balance of payments will have to be corrected, sooner or later. No doubt it can be argued that while a country is living beyond her means, she is better off. It is the imports we receive, not the exports we part with, which enter into our standards of living. Exports are a means of obtaining imports, not an end in themselves. All this is very true. But it is equally true that a country cannot go on indefinitely living above her income—unless she is permanently subsidized by another country, as Albania was subsidized by Italy in the 1930s. Sooner or later she will be forced to cut her coat according to her cloth; and the longer she delays, the more drastic and unpleasant will be the subsequent adjustment.

What is it, exactly, that requires adjustment? Apart from international borrowing and lending (which temporarily increase or reduce a country's spending power) the claim of any country on the world's output, including her own, is the value of what she produces.[1] Apart from grants made to her by other countries, she cannot get something for nothing. It is when a country consumes and invests more than she earns by her output that she is living beyond her means and runs into difficulties. A deficit in her balance of payments is only a symptom. The fundamental cause of the disequilibrium is that she is consuming (and investing) more than she produces.

The fundamental remedy, therefore, is for her to increase her production relatively to her consumption; in other words, to save more. The most acceptable solution would be for her to increase her output and not to increase her consumption correspondingly. It is not a solution if she increases her consumption as much as she increases her production; her disequilibrium will remain. If she does not increase her production sufficiently, then some means must be found of reducing her consumption—a reduction in money incomes, or a rise in the cost of living, or rationing.

This is the key to the problem discussed in the following chapters. On the surface, the remedy for a deficit in the balance of payments is to restrict imports and promote exports. But this is not the only possible remedy, and restriction of imports is a bad remedy because it adversely affects other countries. Even so, it will work only if it leads

[1] Plus any investment income received from abroad, and minus any investment income paid abroad.

to a fall in consumption relatively to output. The better course is an adequate increase in output, relatively to consumption.

5. BILATERALISM

If different currencies are freely convertible into one another, the balance of payments between country A and any other country B, or any group of countries, is of no significance. Country A can cover her debit balances with some countries by her credit balances with others. All that matters is the balance of payments between country A and the rest of the world as a whole.

Under bilateralism, country A tries to balance her payments with country B. This reduces the benefits of specialization by countries. The greatest advantages are derived from international trade if each country is free to sell where it pleases and to buy where it pleases. Bilateralism is like barter. It requires a double coincidence of wants before any trade can take place. It reduces the total volume of trade and prevents it from flowing freely in the directions indicated by relative advantages in production.

Suppose there are four countries. A specializes in the production of coffee, B of cotton, C of sugar, D of wheat. A wants to buy wheat, B coffee, C cotton, and D sugar. If A, buying wheat from D, insists that D should buy as much from her as she buys from D, what will happen? D does not want coffee—perhaps she grows some herself, or perhaps her citizens prefer some other beverage which they produce for themselves. But D does want sugar. How can she get it? She could get it from C. But C does not want wheat, which D exports; C wants cotton, which D does not export. The insistence of A on bilateralism in her trade with D will kill a four-cornered trade from which all four countries would benefit. For A could sell coffee to B, B could sell cotton to C, C could sell sugar to D, and D could sell wheat to A.

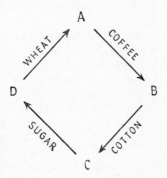

This is, of course, an extreme and hypothetical example. A great deal of international trade can and does continue under bilateral arrangements. But its total volume is kept down, and its pattern somewhat altered, by the restrictions imposed under bilateralism.

The advantages of international trade are bound to be reduced, more or less substantially, if people are not free to buy the types of goods and services which they prefer, and to buy them where they can get the best value for their money.

Why, then, does a country ever follow a bilateral trade policy? One reason may be that she hopes in this way to expand her exports, or at any rate to secure sheltered markets, at a good price, for some of them. For example, during the 1930s Great Britain used her bargaining power as the chief importer of, for example, Danish butter and bacon and Argentine meat, to make a number of trade agreements. "You buy so much of our coal, or steel, or machinery, and we will buy so much of your butter, or bacon, or meat." Germany also made a number of such trade agreements with Balkan and other countries.

Whether such bilateral trade agreements are an advantage to a particular country depends on the circumstances. If A, because she is the chief buyer of B's products, can obtain an agreement from B which gives her favourable terms of trade, this is an advantage for A but not for B. Other countries, finding themselves largely excluded from B's market, may play the same game themselves, and A may find that her increased exports to B are offset, or more than offset, by her decreased exports to other countries. The increase in British exports during the 1930s to the Scandinavian and Baltic countries and to the Argentine can certainly be attributed partly to her trade agreements with those countries, but it is probable that British exports to other non-Empire countries would have expanded more if these agreements had not been made. A further point is that such bilateral agreements tend to create international bitterness; even if both parties to the bargain are satisfied, and often the weaker party is not, other countries resent their exports being largely excluded from those markets.

Since the war, the main reason for bilateralism, carried out by means of exchange control, has been that currencies have not been freely convertible into one another. In particular, there has been a general shortage of United States dollars.

6. Methods of Restoring Equilibrium in the Balance of Payments

It will be remembered that if country A is making long-term investments in the development of country B, for the time being A will have a surplus and B a deficit. Such surpluses and deficits are a necessary accompaniment of international investment and raise no problems of disequilibrium. (If the investment is a failure, B may be faced with a difficult problem of how to repay, but that is another story.)

International disequilibrium has two complementary aspects—the surpluses of some countries and the deficits of others. I shall consider mainly the latter, for it is when a country is in deficit that she is compelled to make some kind of adjustment in her economy. But countries with persistent surpluses can help the deficit countries to restore equilibrium more quickly and easily by taking suitable measures to reduce their surpluses: measures such as following a more liberal import policy or expanding their money incomes.

The connecting thread between the last three chapters of this Part is that they discuss alternative methods by which a country can maintain or restore equilibrium in its balance of payments.

Let us revert to the case of a country living beyond her means, meeting the difference by drawing on her reserves of gold and foreign exchange. What methods can she employ to correct this situation, to make her deficit disappear, and to stop the drain on her reserves?

The direct and obvious method is to restrict her imports and other debit items (for example, by placing limits on the amount of foreign exchange allowed to her residents travelling abroad) and to expand her exports and other credit items (for example, by granting concessions to foreign tourists). This method has been employed by many countries since the war through the machinery of exchange control. This is discussed in Chapter XXXIX.

Instead of, or in addition to, such a direct attack on the symptoms, a country can attempt a more fundamental adjustment. Such an adjustment will involve a change on the monetary side. There are two broad alternatives. On the one hand, she can let the exchange value of her currency fall. Here the expectation is that less foreign exchange will be spent on imports (and other debit items), which now become dearer in local currency, whereas more will be earned by exports (and other credit items), which now become cheaper in foreign currencies. I discuss this method in the course of Chapter XXXVII.

On the other hand, she can maintain the exchange value of her currency but reduce her national income in terms of money. Here the expectation is that her people will not be able to afford as much as before for imports, while cost reductions may stimulate exports. I discuss this method in the course of Chapter XXXVIII.

An intermediate course is to devalue the currency. The exchange value of the currency is reduced to a lower but fixed level, where it is intended to keep it. Chapter XXXVIII also discusses devaluation.

It must always be remembered, however, that the fundamental need is for the country to expand her output relatively to her consumption (or, less satisfactory, to reduce her consumption relatively to her output).

As a prelude to these discussions, the following chapter outlines the chief relevant features of the post-war world.

CHAPTER XXXVI

THE POST-WAR SITUATION

1. THE SHORTAGE OF DOLLARS

THE damage and dislocation due to the war left most countries very short of real capital. They needed imports of equipment, raw materials, and foodstuffs well in excess of their normal peace-time requirements, in order to rehabilitate their industries. The chief source of such imports was the United States, which had emerged from the war with an output much greater than before. But the chief way in which they could earn dollars was by exporting goods to the dollar area. Their exports industries had suffered from the war, and most countries could not export anything like as large a volume of goods as they did before the war. They suffered, therefore, from an acute shortage of dollars.

The United States came to their assistance. Under the Marshall Plan she provided European countries with $13,000 million (of which the U.K. share was $2,780 million) over four years, mostly by grants and partly by loans. The purpose of the Plan was to hasten the economic recovery of European countries: to enable them to increase their output and exports and eventually to stand on their own feet. The Marshall Plan came to an end about 1951, but it was in effect replaced by "defence aid": grants given by the United States towards the cost of building up armaments by European countries for the defence of the free world.

The United States has given large grants to other areas also, notably the Far East, during the post-war period, and has also made long-term loans and investments in Canada, Latin America, and elsewhere. The total amount of dollars she has made available to the rest of the world in these ways has exceeded her export surpluses, and she has had to part with gold, especially recently, to make up the difference. Excluding military supplies provided under grants, during 1948–57 her exports of merchandise averaged $13,900 million a year and her imports only $10,500 million. But she made Government grants averaging $2,600 million a year, and Government and private long-term loans and investments averaging $1,900 million a year.

Nevertheless most countries outside the dollar area [1] have been

---

[1] The members of the dollar area (in addition, of course, to the United States and, Canada) are named in the following doggerel, which I composed during the Commonwealth Finance Ministers' Conference at Sydney, in January, 1954—

short of dollars throughout the post-war period, and still are. Despite the considerable economic recovery made by Europe and some other areas, their demand for dollars exceeds the supply. In other words, their citizens want to acquire more dollars, for such purposes as the purchase of American goods, than are available. Their demand for dollars is therefore restricted by exchange control. It is the shortage of dollars (despite U.S. grants and loans) that is the chief reason for exchange control.

It follows that in order to do away with exchange control and to make sterling and other currencies freely convertible into dollars, it is first necessary to overcome the shortage of dollars. How can this be done?

Some writers think that it cannot be done. They say that the industries of the United States employ so much more capital per worker, and are so far ahead of the rest of the world in their knowledge and application of modern techniques, that it is impossible for other countries to compete with them effectively. They conclude, therefore, that the United States will inevitably continue to have a large export surplus, and that we must reconcile ourselves to the permanent need for exchange control as the only practicable method of coping with a permanent shortage of dollars.

This view is directly contrary to orthodox economic theory. In

---

Salute to the Dollar Area

Ecuador has dollars galore.
San Salvador
Has even more.
Colombia too
Can do, can do,
While little Liberia
Is no way inferior.
Honduras and Guatemala,
Mexico and Panama,
Venezuela, Nicaragua,
Bolivia and Costa Rica,
Cuba and the Philippines,
Not forgetting Haiti and the Dominican Republic,
All are part of this scenaria,
Members of the dollar area.

What have they got that we haven't got?
Maybe it's rubber, maybe it's oil,
Maybe a fertile tropical soil.
Perhaps it is merely, sad to relate,
That they have not heard of the Welfare State.
Perhaps it is just that they wear sombreros
And never drink champagne at Ciro's.

Brothers, this is very sad,
Let us all export like mad
Until we reach a state of grace
And look the dollar in the face.

R2   B.E.

Chapter XXXIV I explained the principle of comparative costs, which shows that one country may produce everything more efficiently than another and yet find it to her advantage to specialize on those industries where her superiority is greatest.   There is no reason why such a country should not have a substantial foreign trade, with its balance of payments in equilibrium.   Yet it is true that when we examine the various ways in which the dollar shortage might, theoretically, be overcome, most of them present serious political difficulties.

I will consider first three types of measures which other countries might take—namely, deflation, exchange depreciation, and greater productivity—before I turn to measures the United States might take.

In general terms, the problem for countries outside the dollar area is how to prevent their citizens from spending more freely on imports, foreign travel, and other "debit" items when exchange control is removed.   They must somehow be prevented from increasing their consumption, unless their output increases correspondingly.   Otherwise their expenditure of foreign exchange will exceed the supply, and their reserves of gold and foreign exchange will be drained away until they are confronted with a balance-of-payments crisis and have to take some drastic action, probably the reimposition of exchange control, to stop this drain.

One possible course is deflation.   This would reduce their money incomes and therefore their demand for imports in general, including imports from the dollar area.   It would reduce their costs and thereby enable them to compete more effectively with dollar goods in all markets (including their own and that of the United States).   If their imports (and other debit items) and their exports (and other credit items) remained about the same, they would be in the same position as at present, but free from exchange restrictions.   If their imports were reduced and their exports expanded, they would be consuming less (and saving more) and therefore building up their foreign exchange reserves.   But this solution is widely opposed, as it is believed that deflation would create considerable unemployment.

An alternative solution might be for other countries to depreciate the exchange value of their currencies against the dollar, as Great Britain did when she devalued the £ (from $4·03 to $2·80) in September, 1949.   This would restrict imports from the dollar area by raising their prices in local currencies.   But it is doubtful whether this would provide a permanent solution.   The consequent rise in the cost of living would probably lead to a rise in wages and other money incomes; this would mean higher costs and therefore higher prices; and the dollar shortage might soon reappear.

By far the best course would be for other countries to increase their productivity.   This would be a solution, however, only if they refrained from increasing their consumption more than their output.   If they increased their expenditure on imports by more than the increase in their export earnings, they would have a deficit in their balance of payments despite their greater productivity. But there are grounds for expecting that a substantial increase in productivity might overcome the dollar shortage. At present, output per worker in most countries is much lower than in the United States, and it is quite possible that for that very reason they might diminish this difference, increasing their productivity at a faster rate than the United States. This would mean that American goods would no longer be so attractive compared with their own, which would tend to fall in price, or to rise less (if there were a general upward movement in prices) than American goods. If such a movement went far enough (as it has done already in some countries, such as Western Germany), the demand for dollars by the rest of the world might keep within the limits of its dollar earnings, without any need for either deflation or exchange depreciation or exchange control.

I turn to some of the ways in which it has been suggested that the United States might help. If other countries abolish their exchange restrictions, they will tend to spend more dollars. There are several ways in which the United States might make more dollars available to them.

One suggestion is that the United States should increase the grants and loans she makes to other countries sufficiently to bridge the whole of the *dollar gap* (the difference between the amount of dollars the rest of the world wishes to spend and the amount it earns). This would enable other countries to abolish their discriminatory restrictions against payments to the United States for goods and services.

This proposal is based on the view that the poorer countries should not be expected to live within their means. The richer countries, mainly the United States but also others including Great Britain, should help them to increase their means by further assisting their economic and social development through grants made by a Special United Nations Fund for Economic Development (SUNFED) and loans (for long periods and at low rates of interest) made by an International Development Association. The consequent improvement in their standards of living, it is believed, would promote peace and prosperity everywhere.

But to provide an adequate amount of aid would place a heavy burden on American and other taxpayers and would encounter the objection that the money ought to be spent, instead, in relieving poverty at home. It seems most unlikely that such a scheme will be adopted, on a large enough scale, in the near future.

Another suggestion is that the United States should take steps to raise her prices, in order to wipe out or reduce the comparative attractiveness of American goods, which is the root cause of the excessive demand for dollars. The general trend of American prices has been upward since the war, but the same is true of other countries also. The proposal implies, therefore, a fairly rapid and considerable inflation in the United States. Such an inflation might well unsettle the American economy, besides causing hardship to all on fixed incomes. If it should lead to an American depression, and a consequent heavy reduction in American imports and American aid, it would be a bad policy from the standpoint of the rest of the world, as well as for America herself.

Linked with this suggestion is the proposal, strongly advocated by South Africa, that the United States should raise her buying price for gold, which is still at the prewar level of $35 an ounce. This would tend to raise the general level of prices in the United States; and it would directly benefit gold-producing countries, who would receive more dollars for their gold.

Opponents of this proposal either dislike inflation or point out that if the United States wishes to inflate, she can do so without raising the price of gold; they consider that the latter course would be merely making a present to gold producers, who are not the people most in need of aid.

Another proposal is that the United States should make a large "stabilization loan" to the sterling area. This would strengthen the dollar reserves of the sterling area and might enable the pound to be made freely convertible (that is, without exchange restrictions— except possibly on transfers of capital) into dollars. Such a loan would clearly be desirable to facilitate the free convertibility of sterling. But it would be worse than useless if it were drained away over the next year or two. The fundamental need is to ensure that the sterling area (or, more broadly, the rest of the world outside the dollar area) can earn, year by year, as many dollars as it spends.

This need might be met by a more liberal American policy towards imports of goods and services, enabling the rest of the world to earn more dollars. This is the meaning of the slogan "trade, not aid."

At present, American restrictions on imports take various forms.

First, there is the tariff itself. The general level of import duties is now much lower than it was in 1930–34 (although it has been reduced little, on balance, during the last ten years) and since then the volume of imports has doubled. At present, half, by value, of all merchandise imports enters free of duty. The other half pays an average rate of only 12 per cent (a third paying 10 per cent or less, another third between 10 and 20 per cent, and the other third 20 per cent or more). Nevertheless there would be a considerable expansion of American imports of certain commodities if the relatively low duties on them were removed.

There are also import quotas. These restrict, and in some cases keep out altogether, imports of various agricultural goods. At present, quantitative restrictions are applied to imports of wheat, wheat flour, sugar, raw cotton, linseed oil, butter, rice, peanuts, flax-seed, cheese, live cattle, and dressed beef. Import quotas have recently been imposed also on petroleum products and on lead and zinc.[1]

Under the Defence Production Act of 1933, imports of certain products are subject to quantitative restriction; for example, for some time there has been a complete prohibition of imports of butter into the United States.

The "Buy American" Act of 1933 means that a foreign firm cannot obtain a contract (e.g. for constructing a power station or a dam) from the Federal Government unless its tender is 25 per cent below the lowest tender of an American firm. Many States and municipalities have similar legislation.

Within the field of services, the main restriction on competition from other countries is on their shipping. The coastal trade is reserved entirely for American ships, and subsidies are paid also to enable American shipping companies to compete with foreign ships. American ships now carry over 50 million tons of cargo a year; before the war they carried less than 20 million tons.

Some liberalization of American policy has taken place. Since 1934, a number of import duties have been reduced, in return for equivalent concessions by other countries, under the Trade Agreements Act of 1934. But this Act, several times renewed and amended, contains loopholes and "escape clauses." How much further it will be possible to go, in the face of opposition from American manufacturers and other protected interests, remains to be seen.

Other possibilities include a further expansion of American public and private investment in other countries and a further increase in American tourist expenditure.

If the United States avoids any depression more severe than the minor ones of 1954–5 and 1957–8, pursues a somewhat more liberal import policy, and continues to make grants for military and economic aid, and if other countries increase their productivity more than their consumption, there is a good possibility that the dollar shortage will disappear. Indeed, substantial progress has already been made. At the close of 1958, most countries of Western Europe, including the United Kingdom, made their currencies convertible (into dollars) for current earnings by non-residents and have now removed exchange-control restrictions on imports of most goods from the dollar area.[2]

[1] See "United States Import Policy," by Gardner Patterson in *Lloyd's Bank Review*. April, 1959.
[2] Part of the sterling-area dollar deficit arises from transactions with Canada and other dollar-area countries. To restore complete convertibility between the pound and the dollar it would be necessary to achieve equilibrium between the sterling area as a whole and the dollar area as a whole.

2. THE STERLING AREA

The sterling area consists of the British Commonwealth minus Canada and a few other countries, mainly some major oil-producing countries in the Middle East (such as Iraq, Kuwait, and Quatar), and the Irish Republic. It is a voluntary association that any country is free to leave (but not to enter).

Sterling is the currency of the United Kingdom only. Other members of the sterling area have their own currencies. But these are linked to sterling at fixed rates; for example, the Indian rupee is kept equal to 1s. 6d. and the Australian pound to 16s.

Sterling is used, however, by the countries of the sterling area (and by some other countries too) to settle most of their international transactions. The countries of the sterling area therefore keep sterling balances in London.

But some payments—notably payments to the dollar area—have to be made in gold or dollars. The United Kingdom holds the reserve of gold and dollars for the whole of the sterling area.

Apart from special arrangements for the gold produced by South Africa, all the gold and dollars earned by any country in the sterling area are paid into the common pool—the U.K. reserve of gold and dollars—in return for the equivalent amount of sterling. And any sterling-area country which wishes to make payments in gold or dollars can and does make them out of the common pool, paying the Bank of England out of its sterling balance and receiving the gold or dollars in exchange.

The sterling area is thus a huge banking system, for which the United Kingdom keeps the central reserve of gold and dollars. But it is more than that.

It is a group of countries who consult together and work together towards a common economic policy. One aim of this policy is to build up the gold and dollar reserves of the sterling area. They are still too low; at the end of 1959 they were only £1,000 million, enough to pay for only two months' imports by the sterling area from the rest of the world. In pursuit of this aim, each member country tries to earn more dollars and to save more dollars, for the benefit of all.

Naturally those countries whose exports happen to sell in the dollar area tend to earn more dollars than they spend, and to be net contributors to the common pool. Australia with its wool, South Africa with its gold, Malaya with its rubber and tin, West Africa with its cocoa, are in that position. But other countries enable the sterling area to save dollars: for example, the West Indies provide sugar which otherwise might have to be bought, for dollars, from Cuba. The important thing is that every country should do all it can to help. This means that they should all follow sound internal policies, trying to expand their output more than their consumption and avoiding inflation (which is bound to lead to a drain on the dollar reserves).

During recent years the stress has been laid more on the positive aspect of expanding output and exports, by sound economic development, rather than on the negative aspect of restricting dollar expenditure. The ultimate aim is a general expansion in world trade. Building up the dollar reserves is a means to that end; only as sterling becomes stronger can exchange restrictions on dollar expenditure be further relaxed.

Meanwhile, trade and payments within the sterling area itself can be, and are, comparatively free. Some import duties are considered essential to protect local industries, but they are kept to the minimum. Every country in the area will accept payment in sterling from other member countries. There is no need for exchange-control restrictions against one another. Hence the sterling area is a great area of multilateral trade. Within this area, goods move freely between countries; there are no restrictions on other transactions, such as tourist expenditure; and even capital moves quite freely from one country to another.

3. Sterling Balances

About half all international transactions are now settled in sterling. This is the main reason why countries hold sterling balances in London.

There are other reasons too. Some Commonwealth countries keep all or part of their reserve against their local issue of currency notes in the form of sterling. An overseas bank may temporarily increase its sterling balance because for the time being short-term rates of interest are relatively high in London. Or firms may hold sterling rather than, say, francs, if they fear that the franc may soon be devalued.

During the war, the British Government bought goods and services, such as local supplies for her armed forces, from a number of countries, paying in sterling. In this way, the sterling balances of such countries (India, for example) were considerably increased.

Before the war, the total of sterling balances belonging to non-residents (mainly Governments or central banks) was between £600 million and £700 million. After the war, it was between £3,000 million and £4,000 million and has remained around that level ever since. When the export earnings of a sterling-area country increase faster than it spends them, its sterling balances rise; in the opposite case, they fall.

In September 1959 the total (excluding holdings of £705 million by non-territorial organizations, such as the International Monetary Fund was £3,434 million, of which £2,674 million was held by sterling area countries.[1]

---

[1] *Monthly Digest of Statistics*, November, 1959.

What is the significance of these sterling balances? They are not, except for a small amount, lying on deposit in London banks. They are invested in various securities: long-term gilt-edged securities, Treasury bills, and so forth. But most of them could readily be withdrawn, and if they were, the gold and dollar reserves would fall. Even if they were spent on British exports, no current payment would be made for such exports: they would be what are called *unrequited exports*, representing the repayment of a debt by Great Britain.

Most of these sterling balances are likely to stay where they are, unless a new devaluation of sterling is feared. They are needed as working balances or currency reserves. Moreover, some countries have agreed, in order not to impose too big a strain on the British economy, to a maximum limit on the annual amount which they may withdraw. Nevertheless the large total of these short-term liabilities underlines the need for a reserve of gold and dollars adequate to cope not only with a temporary deficit in the balance of payments of the sterling area, but also with possible withdrawals of sterling balances for other reasons.

4. THE EUROPEAN MONETARY AGREEMENT

The European Monetary Agreement, like its predecessor, the European Payments Union, which it replaced at the close of 1958, comes under the Organization for European Economic Co-operation. It consists of the seventeen countries of the O.E.E.C.—namely, Austria, Belgium, Denmark, France, Western Germany, Greece, Iceland, Ireland, Italy, Luxembourg, the Netherlands, Norway, Portugal, Sweden, Switzerland, Turkey, and the United Kingdom. A country includes its associated monetary area; hence United Kingdom transactions with the E.M.A. cover the whole of the sterling area.

The E.P.U., which began operating in July, 1950, was a regional clearing system. All transactions between member countries were offset against one another, only the net debit or credit balance of each country being paid or received. Under the E.P.U., trade greatly expanded between its member countries, but they all (except Switzerland and West Germany) discriminated against imports from elsewhere, notably from the dollar area. A regional arrangement of this kind is far better than general bilateralism, but a world-wide system of multilateral and non-discriminatory trade would be much better still.

A move towards this goal was made at the close of 1958. All the O.E.E.C. countries (except Greece, Iceland, and Turkey) then made their currencies convertible for current earnings by non-residents. France devalued by $17\frac{1}{2}$ per cent, but the other countries felt that their currencies were strong enough relatively to the dollar to take this step without devaluation.

The E.P.U. was therefore no longer needed, and came to an end. It is expected that most transactions will now take place through the ordinary mechanism of the world market. But the E.M.A. was created, largely as a stand-by arrangement should anything go wrong.

It provides clearing facilities for its members, but all net balances must be settled entirely in gold. Under the E.P.U. they could be settled partly in credits provided by creditor countries such as West Germany.

Each member puts a certain amount of its currency at the disposal of the E.M.A., and this enables the E.M.A., within limits, to underwrite rates of exchange between member countries, but with appreciable margins which make it cheaper for them to use the market. For example, it will accept sterling from non-sterling member countries at the clearing but at only $2·78 to the £, and it will provide them with sterling, but charges $2·82 to the £.

It has a European Fund of $600 million,[1] from which it grants lines of credit (at present, at $3\frac{1}{2}$ per cent a year, for up to two years) to member countries in difficulties with their balance of payments owing to their efforts to comply with the trade liberalization programme of the O.E.E.C.

This programme aims at the progressive removal of quantitative and other restrictions on imports. Under the E.P.U. it had already done much to liberalize and expand inter-European trade. It is being continued under the E.M.A.

5. The International Monetary Fund

The establishment of an International Monetary Fund was agreed upon at the Bretton Woods Conference in July, 1944. This Conference made plans to promote world recovery after the war. It set up an International Bank for Reconstruction and Development, which would assist countries to get on their feet and develop their economies by means of long-term loans. It proposed an International Trade Organization in order to reduce and simplify tariffs and other restrictions on imports, but this organization has not come into existence.[2] The Fund was designed to promote multilateral trade by helping countries to keep the exchange values of their currencies stable. It was hoped that there would be a general return to the gold standard and that exchange restrictions, except possibly on capital movements, would be abolished.

Each member country has a quota, governing both its subscription to the Fund and the extent to which it can draw on the Fund. It contributes 25 per cent of its quota (or 10 per cent of its gold reserve, whichever is smaller) in gold and the rest in its own money.

[1] 45 per cent inherited from the E.P.U. and the rest guaranteed, in gold, by member countries ($86 million by the United Kingdom).

[2] There is, however, a General Agreement on Tariffs and Trade (G.A.T.T.) between a number of countries, which serves the same purpose.

The aggregate of the forty-four countries' quotas, agreed on at Bretton Woods, was $8,800 million, the largest being those of the United States ($2,750 million), the United Kingdom ($1,300 million), and the U.S.S.R. ($1,200 million). The U.S.S.R., however, has not joined the Fund (or the Bank), while a number of additional countries have, bringing the total membership up to nearly seventy.

It was thought that five years, at most, would be long enough for member countries to decide, perhaps after a period of experiment, on firm gold parities for their currencies. Each member had to declare the gold parity of its currency within five years, and was expected to try to maintain it.

The Fund will help a member in temporary deficit on its balance of payments by selling it foreign currency, up to 25 per cent of its quota in any one year.[1] The object is to give the country a breathing space during which it can take whatever measures are needed to restore equilibrium in its balance of payments. Not much use has been made of these facilities; most countries have needed more than temporary and limited assistance to cope with their shortage of dollars, and have relied on exchange restrictions.

A country is permitted to change its gold parity if it is plain that otherwise it would be continuously in difficulties. Should some such change be inevitable, devaluation was considered a much better alternative than imposing exchange restrictions. But consultation and agreement were desirable; there should be no return to the competitive beggar-my-neighbour exchange depreciations of the 1930s. A devaluation of over 10 per cent can be made only to overcome a "fundamental disequilibrium," and requires the consent of other members of the Fund.

It is a weakness of the present rules of the Fund that delicate questions of policy, such as a proposed devaluation, must in theory be debated by the full Board of Directors. There would be a much better chance of agreement, perhaps on some suitable compromise, and less danger of leakage of information on which speculators might act, if preliminary negotiations were carried out in secret by a small group acting for the Fund as a whole.

Other measures the Fund may take include formally declaring a particular currency to be "scarce" and permitting members (after consultation with the Fund) to impose exchange restrictions on its use; and arranging for all members to inflate together (should they so wish) without disturbing exchange stability, by all reducing their gold parity by the same percentage.

---

[1] The Fund levies a service charge of ¾ per cent a year, and in addition (after the first three months) an interest charge of ½ per cent a year; the interest charge rises (by ½ per cent a year) after the first year and, moreover, an additional ½ per cent a year is charged for each additional 25 per cent of its quota which a country may purchase as time goes on. When the total charge reaches 4 per cent a year, the country must consult the Fund on ways and means of repurchasing its currency.

In fact, the consultation of countries with the Fund has often been only formal. A leading example was the decision of the United Kingdome to devalue sterling in September, 1949. A full-dress debate in the Fund, with all its risks of publicity, before reaching a decision was considered out of the question. Again, the Fund has never formally declared the dollar to be "scarce," but member countries (outside the dollar area) have taken independent action, each imposing its own restrictions on the use of dollars, and varying them from time to time.

The Fund has not fully played the part for which it was set up, of easing temporary balance-of-payments difficulties against a background of firm exchange-rates. This is because most countries have not felt in a position to make their currencies convertible. At the close of 1958, however, as mentioned in the preceding section, sterling and most European currencies were made convertible if earned on current transactions by non-residents.

The Fund needs a large increase in its capital, for the total value of world trade has doubled since 1950. Some revision of the relative quotas of different countries is also needed. Both these needs are now being met. So, incidentally, are the similar needs of the International Bank for Reconstruction and Development.

CHAPTER XXXVII

FREE EXCHANGE RATES

1. EXCHANGE RATES AND THE BALANCE OF PAYMENTS

THE British Government at present keeps the exchange value of the pound sterling at $2·80. It therefore restricts the demand for dollars, by permitting only a limited amount of imports from the dollar area and only a limited amount of dollar expenditure by British tourists and others. It watches carefully the state of its gold and dollar reserves, for should it authorize the expenditure of more dollars than are received, it has to make good the difference from its reserves.

Suppose that the Government were to change its policy and to leave the exchange value of sterling entirely free, to be determined from day to day by the market, without attempting to exercise any control over it. All the special measures to restrict dollar expenditure and to protect the reserves could be swept away. The dollar shortage, for Great Britain, would vanish overnight. Instead of dollars being rationed they would be available for all—at whatever price restricted the demand for them to the amount offered by people who wanted to buy sterling, giving dollars in exchange.

Suppose, for example, that the value of sterling fell to $2·00. This would mean that all dollar imports cost 40 per cent more—that would contract the demand for them. British tourists abroad would find that it now took £1 8s. to buy what £1 bought before. Similarly with all debit items. £1 would no longer buy $2·80 worth of goods and services, but only $2·00 worth. The demand for all debit items would fall, except for those (such as interest payments to the dollar area) which could not be reduced. On the other hand, at least to begin with, the export of British goods and services would expand, for every British export that had formerly cost $2·80 would now cost only $2·00.

I took $2·00 merely as an illustration. It may be that equilibrium would be attained around the present rate of $2·80; or it may be that a much lower rate than even $2·00 would be needed. In any event the rate would fluctuate, like any other free price, from time to time. But, through these fluctuations, it would equate the demand for dollars with the supply of them. The free price would replace the present apparatus of exchange restrictions.

It is theoretically possible that a country could never attain equilibrium by a fall, however great, in the exchange value of its currency. Its supply of exports and its demand for imports might both be very inelastic. For example, a South Sea island might export only copra. It could not appreciably expand its output of copra, for newly-planted coconut trees do not begin to yield until after six years. Its imports might be mainly essential foodstuffs. Hence any reduction in the dollar price of its exports would yield fewer dollars, for the volume of exports would not expand, while its volume of imports would fall very little, despite a sharp rise in their prices in local currency.

In such a situation, the theoretical solution would be to raise, not to lower, the exchange value of its currency. But I do not believe that such a situation exists in any country in the world. A higher price for any export nearly always succeeds, in one way or another, in calling forth a larger supply: more labour is attracted to the export industries, more is produced from the interior of the country and sent to the coast for export, and so on. Moreover, a country usually has quite a range of *potential* exports: goods normally produced only for domestic consumption, or perhaps not at all, but which would be produced for export if their prices were high enough. The export of services might expand also; for example, more tourists might be attracted if local prices were cheaper in terms of their own currency. Similarly with imports: if their prices rise high enough, people will do without some of them, perhaps using local substitutes instead.

I shall assume, therefore, that in practice equilibrium will always be attained by a sufficient fall in the exchange value of the currency, the increased volume of exports more than compensating for any reduction in their dollar prices, and so on.

I have taken the dollar to represent all foreign currencies. If the exchange value of, say, sterling were completely free, there would be a definite relation between the value of sterling in dollars and its value in any other currency, say francs. Suppose, for example, that £1 = $2·00 and that $1·00 = 500 francs. Then £1 must equal 1,000 francs. If it were worth more (say, 1,100 francs), then it would pay anybody with dollars to buy sterling, use the sterling to buy francs, and change the francs back into dollars, making a profit (of 10 per cent). Such transactions, which take place when quite small differences in cross-rates appear, are known as *arbitrage* transactions. Hence such differences are at once smoothed out, provided that such transactions can be carried out legally. When they are forbidden, as they are under exchange control, there may be appreciable differences in cross-rates.

A small country can attain equilibrium, through free exchange rates, more easily than a big one. If Lilliput has its own pounds, and their value falls from $2·80 to $2·00, its exporters will get nearly the same price as before in dollars (and 40 per cent more in their own currency), for a greater volume of their exports will do little to reduce their world prices. But Great Britain is different. She is such a large exporter that when her volume of exports expands, their prices will fall, and exports formerly sold for $2·80 may now sell for appreciably less. They will sell for well over $2·00, or the stimulus to exports would disappear. But suppose they sell for about $2·40. The exporters will now get £1 4s. instead of £1, but the country as a whole will lose by the adverse change in its terms of trade (unless the dollar prices of its imports fall to the same extent, which is unlikely).

Great Britain is a large exporter, and a fall in the exchange value of the pound is therefore likely to turn the terms of trade somewhat against her. Moreover, a number of other countries, outside as well as inside the sterling area, would probably keep more or less in step with sterling, as they did in the 1930s. If sterling depreciated, they would depreciate their own currencies to about the same extent, partly through fear that otherwise British exporters would be able to undersell their own exporters in the world markets. This would further expand the volume of exports of the types exported by Great Britain (or other members of the sterling area), and would tend to reduce their prices in terms of other currencies, such as dollars. This is a point, as far as it goes, against the use of free exchange rates by Great Britain as a method of balancing her payments.

2. Influences Affecting Exchange Rates

Most dealings in foreign exchange are carried out through banks Suppose that sterling were quite free to vary in exchange value. When foreign banks thought that their sterling balances were becoming too big, they would charge a higher rate for foreign currencies (offering sterling, therefore, at a lower rate) in order to increase payments-out from their sterling balances (to persons buying sterling) and to decrease payments-in (by persons buying foreign currencies). Conversely, when their sterling balances were becoming too small, they would raise the exchange value of sterling, charging a lower rate for foreign currencies.

They will wish to keep a certain minimum of sterling balances, enough to enable them to carry on their exchange business. How much they will wish to keep above this minimum will depend partly on their views about the future value of sterling—the more sterling they hold, the greater will be their loss if its exchange value should fall. It may depend partly also on relative rates of interest in London and elsewhere; other things being equal, higher rates of interest will attract larger balances. But it will depend partly, too, on their assets and liabilities in their own countries.

When a bank in, say, France accepts sterling from a customer (who may have received it in payment for his exports to Great Britain), its sterling balance goes up and so do its deposits in France. For the customer is not paying in a cheque received from another Frenchman; the bank itself is creating an additional amount of deposits, against sterling in London. Hence an excess of such payments, for exports and other credit items, will increase the total of bank deposits in France. If the French Government does not increase the supply of cash (corresponding to the inflow of gold which would take place if both countries were on the gold standard), then there will be no more cash available to the French banks and their cash ratio to deposits will fall because their deposits will have increased. Their remedy will be to give fewer francs for sterling than before.

What are the underlying forces that govern the demand to buy sterling, with foreign currencies, and the supply of sterling offered to buy foreign currencies?

Relative prices may be of dominating importance. Other people want sterling mainly in order to buy British goods and services. If British prices were twice as high, they would be prepared to give only about half as many dollars or francs as before for £1 sterling; provided, of course, that prices in other countries remained the same. Exchange rates tend to vary with relative price levels; I discuss this point in the following section.

Capital movements take place, in normal times, largely because short-term interest rates are higher in one centre than in another. Funds may be transferred, for example, from New York to London if they can earn 4 per cent in London as against 2 per cent in New York. The exchange risk can be overcome by a *forward exchange* transaction, probably with a bank. If *A* transfers a million dollars to London now, he can arrange to transfer them back in, say, three months' time, at a rate fixed now, by buying a million dollars three months forward. Other people will be wanting to arrange now to buy sterling with dollars in three months' time, so that a "forward" market is possible.

During the 1930s, however, large speculative movements of "hot money" took place. These movements were not governed by relative interest rates, but by the fear that some currencies would fall in value. They were movements out of those currencies and into others which it was hoped would remain stable or rise in value. Before sterling left the gold standard, in September, 1931, there were large speculative movements out of sterling. When sterling had fallen considerably, and it seemed likely that some other currencies would follow it, there were heavy movements out of these currencies and into sterling. It was largely for the purpose of offsetting such movements, in either direction, and of preventing them from causing violent temporary fluctuations in the exchange value of sterling, that the British Government established the Exchange Equalization Fund.[1]

Changes in the *terms of trade* may lead to changes in exchange rates.

[1] See Chapter XIX, Section 5.

Should the demand for a country's exports increase, so will the demand for its currency.

Suppose, to give a simple hypothetical example, that the only transactions between Great Britain and France are the export of British coal in exchange for French wine. Great Britain exports 10 tons of coal a day at £5 a ton and imports 20 gallons of wine a day at 2,500 francs a gallon; £1 = 1,000 francs. Now suppose that the French demand for coal increases. They can get more coal only by exporting more wine. But the British demand for wine remains the same; to get more sterling they must offer their wine more cheaply. A new equilibrium may be reached with, say, 36 gallons of wine (90,000 francs) a day exchanging against 15 tons of coal (£75). The new rate of exchange will be £1 = 1,200 francs. The French need sterling only to buy coal; their demand for coal and, therefore, for sterling has increased; the terms of trade have become more favourable to Great Britain by one-fifth (2⅖ gallons instead of 2 gallons of wine against 1 ton of coal), and the increase of one-fifth in the exchange value of sterling exactly reflects this improvement, provided that other things, notably money costs, remain the same.

3. The Purchasing-Power Parity Theory

This theory was used after the first world war to demonstrate that the fall in the exchange values of the German, Polish, and other currencies was due mainly to inflation in those countries. This was quite true. If we start from an equilibrium situation, and prices in country A rise, say, a hundredfold, while they remain stable in country B, we should expect people in B to want 100 times as many units of A's currency as before in exchange for 1 unit of theirs, for 100 units of A's currency now buy only as much as 1 unit bought before. If B's prices have, say, doubled, then we should expect a unit of her currency to exchange for 50 times as many units of A's currency as before, and so on; in general, we should expect changes in the exchange values of different currencies (as compared with a previous position of equilibrium) to reflect the changes in their price levels.

This would not happen, however, until price levels had settled down. While A was inflating, and her prices rising, we should expect the exchange value of her currency to fall faster. For there would be speculative capital movements out of A's currency and into more stable currencies.

Subject to this proviso, the purchasing-power parity theory does explain the dominant reason for changes in exchange rates over a period during which large movements have taken place in the relative price levels of different countries. It is not satisfactory, however, as a general explanation of exchange rates.

It may be presented in either of two forms. In its narrower form it relates only to the relative prices of internationally-traded goods; in its wider form it relates to the relative price levels of all goods and services.

It is quite true that internationally-traded goods have a world market and therefore tend to be the same price (after allowing for transport charges) at any port. For example, if a bushel of wheat costs $1·40 at a United States port, and £1 = $2·80, then it will cost 10s. (plus transport charges) at a British port. But this does not throw much light on the chain of causation. The two prices, $1·40 and 10s., do not determine the exchange rate. The price in the exporting country often determines the price in the importing country, taking the rate of exchange (£1 = $2·80) as given. The rate of exchange itself is determined by all the forces affecting the demand for the two currencies. True, the greater part of the demand is usually a demand to pay for imports. But the fundamental reason for a change in the exchange rate, and therefore in the relative prices of goods such as wheat in the two currencies, may be a change in the terms of trade, or it may be movements of capital, or it may be a heavy demand for one of the currencies in order to meet any of the "debit" items (e.g. interest payments or tourist expenditure) entering into the balance of payments. The mere fact that the price of a good in A equals its price in B at the prevailing rate of exchange does not fully explain how the latter is determined.

In its narrower form, therefore, the theory is a truism. In its wider form it is not true. There is not a close and firm relationship between the prices of a country's exports and imports and the prices of its domestic goods and services, which do not enter into international trade. If £1 equals $2·80 or 1,380 francs, it by no means follows that the purchasing power of £1 in Great Britain is the same as that of $2·80 in the United States or of 1,380 francs in France.[1]

Some exponents of the theory have tried to avoid this objection, and also the difficulty of directly comparing price levels between countries, by relating *changes* in exchange rates to *changes* in price levels. Start from some base date when exchange rates are more or less in equilibrium. Call the price level in A 100 and the price level in B 100, at the base date. If at some subsequent date the price level in A is, say, 150 and in B, say, 300, then 1 unit of A's currency should then exchange for twice as many units of B's currency as before, for that is the purchasing-power parity between the two currencies as compared with the base date. In general, if at any date the price level in A is X and

---

[1] As a matter of fact, in 1955 £1 bought about 48 per cent more (on the British expenditure pattern, although only 12 per cent more on the American expenditure pattern) in the United Kingdom than $2·80 bought in the United States. See *Comparative National Products and Price Levels* by Milton Gilbert and Associates.

in $B\,Y$, then the rate of exchange between the two currencies will tend to be $\dfrac{X}{Y}$ of what it was at the base date.

The price level within a country may change owing to changes in its indirect taxes. Suppose, for example, that A imposes import duties of 100 per cent. The internal prices of her imports would about double, but the effect would be to raise, rather than to lower, the exchange value of A's currency, for her demand for imports and therefore for foreign currencies would be reduced. The exponents of this version of the theory say, therefore, that allowances must be made for changes in indirect taxes. The same applies to transport costs.

Applied in this way, the theory does provide some indication of how exchange rates might be expected to move. But it can be a treacherous guide. Other factors, such as speculative movements of capital, may make exchange rates diverge sharply from their purchasing-power parities, calculated in this way. For example, in April, 1933, the United States devalued the dollar. As between December, 1932, and December, 1933, retail price levels in Great Britain were stable, and in the United States they increased by only about 3 per cent. But the rate of exchange was £1 = \$3·28 in December, 1932, and £1 = \$5·12 in December, 1933.

4. The Advantages and Disadvantages of Free Exchange Rates

The great advantage of free exchange rates, as compared with the gold standard, is that they leave a country quite free to follow its own independent monetary policy. It can stabilize its price levels or its money incomes, or it can expand the supply of money to secure fuller employment or contract it to check a boom; in short, it can do whatever it pleases. Under the gold standard, as we shall see in the following chapter, this is not so. A country has to adjust its incomes and prices to those of other countries, whether such adjustments are in harmony with the needs of its economy or not, and whether they agree or conflict with the monetary policy it would prefer to follow. It has to make these adjustments in order to keep its exchange rates stable.

Under exchange control, a country can follow its own monetary policy, at any rate within wide limits, but only by imposing controls over its exports and imports and, indeed, over all aspects of its economic life in so far as they may affect its balance of payments. Under free exchange rates this whole apparatus of direct controls can be swept away; equilibrium in the balance of payments will be maintained simply and solely by changes in the exchange value of the currency.

The great disadvantage of free exchange rates is that they tend to reduce the volume of international trade and investment by making them more risky. Anybody who contracts to make or to receive a payment in another currency runs the risk that the exchange value of that currency may rise or fall before the payment is made. A profit of 20 or 30 per cent on exports to Ruritania is turned into a severe loss if the currency of Ruritania halves in value before the payment is made. It is not always possible to guard against such losses through an off-setting forward exchange transaction; there may be no forward exchange dealings in that currency, or if there are, a general belief that its value will fall will force down its future value well below its present value. Again, an exporter or lender may try to cover himself by selling or lending in terms of his own currency. But the other party, in the other country, then runs the risk that he will have to pay more, in his own currency, when the time for payment comes.

It is true that this risk is present under any system. If Ruritania is on the gold standard, there is always the danger that she will leave the gold standard, and that the value of her currency will fall heavily overnight. The same applies to exchange control. And if she does run into difficulties which make her take such action, it may well be that money due to foreigners (including profits on their own direct investments in the country) may be "blocked" for the time being. But all these risks are greater when a country's exchange rates are permitted to fluctuate than when that country is following a policy of keeping them stable.

An argument against exchange depreciation as a method of correcting an adverse balance of payments is that it may involve an adverse change in the terms of trade. As we saw, such an adverse change is likely to be greater for a country (or for a group, such as the sterling area) that is an important exporter.

I have assumed that exchange depreciation does not lead, to begin with, to any increase in local incomes and domestic prices. In that event, costs in the export industries will rise only to the extent that they use imported materials which have increased in price owing to the rise in the exchange value of foreign currencies.

But, in practice, exchange depreciation may be followed by an increase in money incomes and domestic prices, supported by an increase in the quantity of money; in other words, it may lead to inflation. Should this happen, costs in the export industries will rise, and the demand for imports will revive because people have more money to spend and the prices of local substitutes are now higher. The exchange value of the currency will fall further, and there will be speculative movements of capital away from it. A continued movement of this kind can easily accelerate and culminate in a runaway inflation. Unless a country can check consequent increases in its money incomes and prices, this danger is an additional argument against free exchange rates.

CHAPTER XXXVIII

THE GOLD STANDARD

1. FIXED EXCHANGE RATES

A COUNTRY is on the gold standard when its Government keeps the purchasing power of a unit of its currency equal to the purchasing power of a definite weight of gold. There are various ways of achieving this result.

The simplest way is to use gold coins with a gold content equal to their face value. The Government is prepared always to provide an unlimited number of such coins in exchange for a corresponding weight of gold. Conversely, the Government is always prepared to sell any amount of gold bullion, in exchange for its own currency, at the same fixed rate. And gold can be freely exported or imported.

For example, before 1914 Great Britain used gold sovereigns. The sovereign was a definite weight of gold. One-twelfth was base metal, of negligible value, to make the coins harder and more durable, and therefore the sovereign was said to consist of gold "eleven-twelfths fine." It contained $113\frac{1}{623}$ grains of pure gold. This meant that $4\frac{1}{4}$ sovereigns contained one ounce of pure gold, and that the price of gold bullion on the London market was always within a fraction of £4 5s. an ounce, or £3 17s. 10½d. per ounce eleven-twelfths fine. The Mint was always prepared to buy or sell gold at that price.[1] Hence British currency was virtually equivalent to gold; it was linked to gold at the rate of £4 5s. an ounce.

The United States, France, Germany, and the other countries on the gold standard all had their own currency units—dollars, francs, marks, and so on—but they, too, were linked to gold in the same way. And because they were all linked to gold, they were all linked to one another. Since £1 and $4·866 were both kept equal to the same weight of gold, the rate of exchange could not vary appreciably—the limits being set by the relatively small cost of shipping gold—from this *gold parity* of £1 = $4·866. Rates of exchange between gold standard countries were virtually fixed.

The same result can be achieved without the use of gold coins. It can be achieved, as it was by Great Britain between 1925 and 1931, by the so-called *gold bullion standard*, under which the Government is

---

[1] Actually the rate was about £4 4s. 11½d. per ounce, and the Mint gave £3 17s. 9d. per ounce 11/12th fine, charging 1½d. for expenses.

always prepared to buy and sell gold bullion at a fixed price, and places no restrictions on its import or export. Again, a country can adopt an *exchange standard*. If its economic relations are mainly with Great Britain, it can adopt a sterling exchange standard, always being prepared to buy or sell sterling at a fixed rate; if with the United States, it can adopt a dollar exchange standard; and so on. If the planet country is on the gold standard, then the satellite country is on the gold standard at one remove.

We often hear somebody ask why some genius cannot invent an international currency. It would be intolerable if every British county had its own separate and independent currency, yet that is the situation in the world as a whole. If it is clearly desirable for a country to have a single currency, why not the world, or at any rate a large part of it?

Those who ask this question do not realize that the gold standard did virtually what they want. In effect, the countries on it were sharing a common currency, for their currencies were all linked to gold and thereby to one another. It hardly mattered whether a person held pounds or dollars or francs or marks, for they were all freely exchangeable for one another, and at rates that were virtually fixed.

But these days have gone, maybe for ever. It is the fashion nowadays to denigrate the gold standard. Let us see why.

2. ADJUSTMENTS OF NATIONAL INCOMES

We know that the balance of payments of a country can be in equilibrium with a permanent excess of imports if the difference is made up by receipts from other items, such as interest on overseas investments or payments by tourists. The reader can allow for this point in what follows, where for brevity I write only of imports and exports.

In the long run, a country must restrict her imports to the volume she can pay for with her export earnings. In the short run, she can import more, meeting the difference by loans or gifts from other countries or by parting with some of her assets (including her gold reserves). But these are only temporary expedients. If she is to stand on her own feet, her exports must pay for her imports.

Suppose that the imports of a country are continuously exceeding her exports. With a free exchange rate this can soon be stopped by a fall in the exchange value of her currency: imports will cost more, and so fewer will be bought, while exports may be stimulated by reducing their prices in other currencies. But this solution is ruled out under the gold standard. The whole point and purpose of the gold standard is to maintain fixed rates of exchange. What, then, can be done?

If nothing is done, then sooner or later the country will be driven off gold. Her Government has undertaken to sell all the gold demanded, at a fixed price; gold will be demanded continuously, to fill the continuous gap in the balance of payments; the gold reserves will become more and more depleted until finally the Government is no longer able to keep its undertaking to provide gold, because it has no more gold to provide. In order to prevent this from happening, in order to check and indeed to reverse this continuous outflow of gold and to stay on the gold standard, the Government must take some action.

This action, to be effective, must lead to *a reduction in the money national income*. With less money to spend, people will not be able to afford so many imports. Moreover, a fall in local incomes, including wage rates, is a fall in local costs. The prices of locally-produced goods will fall, and they will therefore be bought, to a greater extent than before, instead of imports. And lower costs may stimulate exports.

A major criticism of the gold standard is that such action, such measures of deflation, may do great harm to the economy of the country. The classic method is to raise the Bank rate, and thereby other rates of interest, and to reduce the quantity of money. But if the trade unions refuse to accept reductions in money wages, labour costs do not fall. Instead, there is unemployment, maybe heavy unemployment. The fall in the money national income is indeed brought about, but not by a fall in wage rates. It is brought about by unemployment. With total spending power reduced, fewer workers can be employed; and higher rates of interest check investment. A depression is created, in order to stay on gold. This is tragic nonsense, say the critics. Away with the gold standard! Let each country follow its own monetary policy, and thereby maintain full employment.

It should be noted that the extent of the fall in national income required to restore equilibrium in the balance of payments will depend largely on the kinds of goods imported. Should they be mainly luxuries and semi-luxuries, a small fall in national income may lead to a much larger percentage fall in imports.[1] But should they be mainly goods such as essential foodstuffs, not easily replaced by local products, a large fall in national income may be needed to bring about a fall of, say, 10 per cent in imports. In such a case the argument against deflation is especially strong; and British imports, on the whole, are of this nature.

Nevertheless there is no escape from the brute fact that in the long run a country can import only what she can pay for. Suppose that there is a large fall in the world prices of the chief exports of a country, but not of her imports. The terms of trade have moved against her. She is worse off than before. In one way or another, her real income

---

[1] This happened in the United States in 1938, when a fall in her total consumption of 4 per cent was accompanied by a fall in her total imports of 25 per cent. (But the fall in U.S. imports during the U.S. recessions of 1953–54 and 1957–58 was very slight.)

must fall; and if 75 to 80 per cent of her national income goes to labour, the real income of her workers, taken as a whole, must fall. They will not like it, but they cannot avoid it. The problem is how to avoid making matters worse by creating unemployment.

The solution of this problem depends mainly on the attitude of the trade unions. One assumption is that they will not agree to any cuts in money wages, but will accept a rise in the cost of living without demanding a corresponding increase in their pay. On this assumption, equilibrium could be achieved through a rise in the prices of imports. A free exchange rate would avoid unemployment, for the exchange value of the currency would fall and import prices would rise, thereby contracting the demand for imports, money incomes remaining the same. Exchange control also would avoid unemployment, for imports could be restricted directly and either their prices would rise or they could be rationed, money incomes remaining the same. It might even be possible to stay on the gold standard by imposing a general duty on all imports (and perhaps a general subsidy on all exports) and thereby equating imports and exports without reducing money incomes.[1]

But this assumption is hardly supported by the evidence. The evidence indicates that "trade unions have been as willing to strike for advances in wage rates when the cost of living has risen by more than a small percentage as to strike for the maintenance of a wage rate when threatened with a reduction."[2] This means that free exchange rates or exchange control might not solve the problem any better than the gold standard.

If we assume that trade unions will always insist on maintaining "real" wage rates, no solution is possible. Whenever there is a substantial fall in the real income of a country, there is bound to be heavy unemployment, under any monetary system, for the goods will simply not be available to provide all the workers with the same real wages as before. Those who keep their jobs will maintain their real wages, but only at the cost of unemployment among their comrades.

A third assumption, however, is possible. It is that workers are open to argument and persuasion and will agree to reductions in money wages (as they did in Holland) provided they are convinced of the need for them. On this assumption, a country could reduce its money income in order to stay on the gold standard without thereby creating unemployment.

It may well be that each of these three assumptions contains a certain amount of truth, and that the attitude of the workers will vary with time and place and circumstance.

[1] This was proposed by Keynes in the Macmillan Report, as a means of enabling Great Britain to stay on the gold standard, in 1931.

[2] J. S. Dunlop: "The Movement of Real and Money Wage Rates," *Economic Journal*, September, 1938.

I return to the point that the gold standard involves adjustments from time to time in national incomes. These adjustments are governed by the need to equate imports and exports, and fundamentally they rest on the principle that a country's share in the world income should reflect its share in world output.[1] Its claim on the world's goods, including those which it produces itself, is measured by the value of its own contribution to world output. The same principle applies to districts within a country. If Lancashire produces 5 per cent of the output of Great Britain, her income will be 5 per cent of the national income.

Should there be a relative increase in the output of one district, owing to an influx of workers, or to greater efficiency in production, or to a greater demand for its products and a consequent rise in their prices, then the relative income of that district will increase, and in the opposite circumstances it will fall. The same applies to countries. Under the gold standard, each country has a fairly definite ratio between its gold stock and its money income. If the total amount of gold remains the same, then a country whose relative output is increasing will tend to acquire gold and to increase its national income, and a country whose relative output is falling will tend to lose gold and to reduce its national income.

The general rule that national incomes reflect the values of national outputs is modified by international loans and gifts. Country A can spend more than she produces (and B less) if she receives a loan or gift from B. During the fourteen years since the end of the war, the United States made loans and gifts to other countries amounting to over 70 milliard dollars; this exceeded her export surplus and she therefore exported some of her gold reserves.

3. PRICE LEVELS UNDER THE GOLD STANDARD

When a number of countries are on the gold standard, they are all virtually sharing a common currency. Their rates of exchange with one another are fixed and stable. If the price of an internationally-traded good rises or falls x per cent in dollars, it will rise or fall by x per cent in pounds, dollars, francs, marks, and all other gold-standard currencies. This does not mean that the purchasing power of money is the same in every gold-standard country. One country can have a higher internal price level than another if it has higher import duties and other taxes on commodities, provided that despite its higher level of internal prices (and therefore, if the amount produced per worker is the same, of money incomes) it manages to restrict its imports to the value of its exports. But it does mean that the price levels of all gold-

[1] Plus its net receipts (or minus its net payments) of interest, profits, and dividends from abroad.

standard countries tend to rise and fall together, for their currencies are all firmly linked to the same commodity, namely gold, and their purchasing power therefore varies with the purchasing power of gold.

In the preceding section I discussed the changes in national incomes that must be made from time to time by gold-standard countries in order to correspond to changes in relative national outputs and to enable each country to equate its imports and exports while keeping the value of its currency fixed in terms of gold. These changes are all relative changes—changes in national incomes relatively to one another. I now turn to a different question. What determines the purchasing power of gold? In other words, what determines the absolute level of prices throughout the gold-standard system?

In the absence of any regulation and control, price levels would depend on the supply of gold and on the demand for money. Increased supplies of gold due to the discovery of new gold-mines or to cost-reducing technical improvements in methods of gold-mining would tend to send price levels up. An increased output of goods would tend to send them down. A general increase in the demand for money (a fall in its velocity of circulation), such as occurred during the Great Depression, would lead to a general fall in prices.

One of the advantages sometimes claimed for the gold standard is that its takes monetary policy out of the hands of politicians who, if they had full control, might well yield to the pressures of various groups for higher incomes and to the temptation of creating more money (instead of following the unpopular course of raising taxes) to provide their Governments with more revenue, and might in this way bring about a runaway inflation. A currency firmly wedded to gold, it is argued, is a currency in which everybody will have full confidence; it is a "sound" currency because it is tied to other gold standard currencies and is not subject to local manipulation.

It is quite true, whether one regards it as an advantage or as a disadvantage, that a country on the gold standard cannot do whatever it likes in the sphere of monetary policy. It shares a common price level with the other gold-standard countries, and has to keep more or less in step with them. But it is not true that changes in this common price level are left to blind chance. The various gold-standard countries, between them, control and regulate their common price levels. Gold is their servant, not their master. The gold-standard system as a whole has a monetary policy.

The snag lies in the words "between them." The more countries there are on the gold standard, the wider the area of fixed exchange rates, the better. As with a telephone system, the more members there are, the more useful is the system to everybody on it; there is little point in being the sole subscriber. But it is difficult for a large number of countries continuously to agree on a common policy. In practice, monetary policy will inevitably be determined mainly by the most important countries, and the others will have to follow their lead.

Should Great Britain return to the gold standard, or at any rate make sterling freely convertible into dollars and abolish exchange restrictions, no doubt there would be constant consultation between the United States and Great Britain, and so far as possible with other countries, on the most appropriate policy. But although there would probably be agreement on the general aims—namely, to prevent undue inflation while maintaining employment and avoiding slumps—there might be marked differences of opinion from time to time on the best method of attaining these aims.

That is why some people are opposed to a general return to the gold standard. They fear the dominant position of the United States. She has a very large national income; she is far and away the biggest source of capital for foreign investment; she owns most of the world's gold reserves. Other countries on the gold standard, it is argued, would in effect be tying their currencies to the dollar.

Suppose, the argument continues, that there should be a severe slump in the United States. Under any monetary system, this would be a disaster to the rest of the world. Her imports are small relatively to her own output, but they form a large and important proportion of the exports of other countries. If she had a severe slump, her imports would fall, and she might also cut down her loans and gifts to other countries, creating unemployment and hardship throughout the world. But how much worse matters would be if the currencies of other countries were tied to the dollar under the gold standard! They would lose gold to the United States and would be compelled to deflate; the United States would "export unemployment" to them, whereas if they were independent in their monetary policy, they could freely expand credit in order to try to maintain employment.

Up to date, however, the United States has succeeded admirably in expanding her output and maintaining employment, and at the same time assisting the rest of the world to the tune of around 5 milliard dollars a year, without any sign of a serious slump. It might well be urged that if a return to the gold standard is desirable on general grounds, the problem of how to deal with an American slump can be faced if and when it arises.

I return to the point that the gold-standard system as a whole can control the general price level. Suppose, for example, that it was generally agreed that some inflation was desirable. Each country could expand the volume of its bank credit, on the basis of its existing gold reserves. They could all inflate together, and provided they kept in step, no country would lose gold to any other, and rates of exchange would remain stable.

They could inflate together. But should one country go ahead on its own, inflating much more than the others, it would soon be pulled up short by the loss of gold and forced either to keep in step or to leave the gold standard. This happened, for example, to France in September, 1936. Under the "Blum experiment," wages were sharply raised. Local prices rose also. France lost gold and was forced to devalue.

The gold standard thus imposes a discipline on the member countries. A country cannot increase its money income, without a corresponding increase in its output, unless other gold-standard countries are doing the same. Nor can it maintain its money income if there is a substantial fall in the value of its output. A country that insists on doing so may stay on gold for a time by borrowing from abroad or by selling some of its assets (such as its foreign investments), but if this situation continues, it will be forced eventually to leave the gold standard and go its own way, or to impose restrictions on its imports, or to devalue.

4. Devaluation

A country devalues when it reduces the gold parity of its currency, making the unit of its currency equal to a smaller weight of gold than before, and therefore raising the price of gold in terms of its own money. Devaluation usually takes place overnight, but a country may leave the gold standard and return to it after an interval at a lower parity: thus the United States left gold, at $20·67 an ounce of gold, in the spring of 1933, and returned, at $35 an ounce, early in 1934. The devaluation of sterling in September, 1949, was expressed in United States dollars; its exchange value was reduced overnight from $4·03 to $2·80.

Devaluation may seem a marvellous solution to the problem of a country that is importing too much (or exporting too little) and is therefore tending to lose gold, but dare not deflate for fear of creating unemployment. At one stroke, the prices of her imports are raised, and therefore the volume of imports is reduced, while her exports can be offered at lower prices in other currencies, and therefore their volume will expand. The outflow of gold is at once stopped, and instead gold flows in. Her balance of payments, which had been in deficit, at once begins to show a surplus. And yet the advantages of fixed exchange rates are retained, for she is still on the gold standard, although at a lower parity than before.

This is all very fine, provided that wages and other money incomes do not rise so much that they completely offset the effects of the devaluation. If they do, then the demand for imports will revive, because people have more money to spend, and the competitive advantage which devaluation gave to her export industries will be counteracted by the rise in their costs. After a time, the country will be back where it was before, faced with the same balance-of-payments problem.

Devaluation is thus either a once-for-all solution or no solution at all. It is not a remedy that can be adopted again and again. If a country makes a practice of devaluing, confidence in her currency will be destroyed. Whenever she is getting into balance-of-payments difficulties, it will be thought that she may once more resort to devaluation. Her own citizens, as well as others with balances in the country, will seek to transfer their capital out of her currency and into other currencies that they consider safer. This flight of capital will increase her outflow of gold and may well force her off the gold standard, or compel her to devalue, whereas with a better record she might have succeeded in weathering the storm.

5. The Advantages and Disadvantages of the Gold Standard

The great advantage of the gold standard is that it provides practically fixed rates of exchange between the countries on it. This is a very real boon to traders and investors, for it removes the risk of loss from fluctuations in exchange rates. Hence it greatly facilitates international specialization and trade, and international investment. The gold-standard system as a whole gains by having virtually a common currency, in the same way that a country gains by having a single currency instead of a separate currency for each of its various local areas.

Of course, any international standard would achieve this result. Indeed, it could be achieved simply by an agreement amongst the various Governments to keep exchange rates fixed at a given level. But under such an agreement one particular currency, possibly the dollar, would have to serve as a standard. The only common standard likely to be accepted by most important countries is the gold standard; gold is the traditional monetary reserve, people prefer their currency to be backed by gold, and gold movements between countries provide tangible evidence of changes in balances of payments and of the need to adjust incomes upward or downward.

The gold standard, however, loses most of its virtue if traders and investors fear that it may not be maintained. The stimulus that it gives to foreign trade and investment depends on their confidence that exchange rates will in fact remain stable. When a currency is devalued three times in two years, like the French franc during 1936–38, it not unnaturally becomes distrusted. If a country wishes to enjoy the benefits of the gold standard, it must be willing to follow the rules —to expand its income when it is receiving gold, and to reduce its income when it is losing gold.

The modern tendency is to regard deflation as an evil to be shunned, and it is true that if money wages are rigid, deflation will cause unemployment. Yet what are the alternatives? If every time a country suffers a loss in real income (for example, from a drought or from a fall in the prices of its exports) it retreats behind a barricade of import restrictions or depreciates the exchange value of its currency, all hope of stable conditions for world trade are destroyed; we are back to the chaos of the 1930s. The country itself does not escape the loss of real income by such measures; it may indeed maintain its money income, but only by a higher cost of living, which imposes burdens on those least able to bear them.

The "good neighbour" policy is to make every effort to stay on gold without injuring other countries (and perhaps provoking retaliation) by import restrictions and exchange depreciation. Other countries will help. The Fund has money to lend for this purpose. The system as a whole may be willing to inflate to some extent to help countries that are in difficulties. But there are limits to this. Inflation still has its dangers, even if exchange rates remain fixed. The amount of inflation needed to float such countries up into equilibrium may be so great that it would lead to a general slump.

The great disadvantage of the gold standard, therefore, is that a country is not free to follow the monetary policy it considers best for itself. In particular, it may be compelled at times to reduce its money income, and this may create unemployment. For this reason, some countries may prefer to remain independent rather than to share a common currency.

On the other hand, a large and expanding volume of world trade creates employment, while restrictions on imports by one country create unemployment in the export industries of the countries that provide her with imports. Stable exchange rates, with relative freedom from import restrictions or at any rate from sudden increases in them, are clearly a great benefit to the world as a whole; but in order to maintain such a system countries may be required from time to time to take measures, notably deflationary measures, which they consider would be too harmful to their economies or would be politically impossible.

CHAPTER XXXIX

EXCHANGE CONTROL

1. Why Countries Adopt Exchange Control

I HAVE discussed various methods by which a country can control its balance of payments. These methods, or their opposites, can be applied to correct either a persistently favourable balance or a persistently adverse balance. I have stressed the latter, because it is a chronic deficit rather than a chronic surplus that plunges a country into difficulties. But a country with a chronic surplus can and should expand its loans to other countries, or reduce its restrictions on imports, or expand its money income, or allow the exchange value of its currency to rise, perhaps revaluing it (the opposite of devaluing it) at a higher level; by taking such measures it will help those countries that are in deficit and will play its part in restoring general equilibrium.

Exchange control, however, is not a two-way method. It is a method of preventing a deficit, rather than a surplus, in the balance of payments. It is a method that by its nature applies to relatively weak currencies and not to strong ones, for its purpose is to maintain, at least nominally, a higher exchange value for a currency than the exchange value it would have in a free market. In other words, foreign currencies (or some of them) are priced lower than they would be in a free market. Therefore they must be rationed. They are rationed by means of exchange control.

A country may adopt exchange control as a method of correcting an adverse balance of payments because she is unwilling to adopt any of the alternative methods I have discussed, or any combination of them, while some of them may not be within her power: a country cannot command a constant stream of loans or grants from other countries, and some are restrained by international agreements (e.g. under G.A.T.T.) from increasing their import duties as and when they wish.

Thus deflation may seem unwise, or politically impossible. Yet exchange depreciation also may seem ruled out. A country may wish to maintain the exchange value of her currency for reasons of prestige, or to keep down the prices of imports and thereby the cost of living, or because she realizes that a fall in its exchange value may turn the terms of trade against her, or because (as in most European countries) her citizens would interpret a fall in its exchange value as a sign of coming inflation, and would upset the economy by acting on that assumption.

Under such conditions, exchange control offers a tempting way of escape. The exchange value of the currency is maintained. But there need be no reduction in money incomes; indeed, they may even increase. Instead of deflation, there is direct restriction of imports and other debit items in order to keep the balance of payments in equilibrium.

Exchange control was adopted by a number of countries during the Great Depression and retained throughout the 1930s. Nazi Germany in particular, had a very complete system of exchange control, covering all her transactions with other countries. Great Britain, however, did not adopt this system; she restricted herself to smoothing out fluctuations in the exchange value of sterling, and offsetting the effects of speculative movements of capital, by means of her Exchange Equalization Fund.

After the war, many countries, including Great Britain and the rest of the sterling area, adopted exchange control as a means of rationing dollars and other "hard" currencies (such as Swiss francs). No doubt they hoped that the dollar shortage would disappear after a time, when they had recovered from the effects of the war, but in the meanwhile exchange control seemed the least undesirable method of keeping down their demand for hard currencies.

2. THE CONSEQUENCES OF EXCHANGE CONTROL

A currency under exchange control is not freely convertible into foreign exchange. Individuals and firms cannot buy as much foreign exchange as they wish for whatever purpose they wish. They must apply to the central bank, which allots only limited amounts and only for approved purposes.

Nor can exporters and others keep the foreign exchange they acquire. They must surrender it all to the central bank and they will be paid, of course, only the official rate.

There are many variants. For example, in some countries exporters are allowed, as an inducement, to keep a proportion of their foreign exchange. In Great Britain, since the end of 1958, sterling earned by non-residents has been freely convertible into any other currency. But the broad principle is that foreign exchange (or certain kinds of foreign exchange, notably dollars) is scarce and is rationed by the Government, through the central bank.

Since the demand for foreign exchange exceeds the supply, its value would be higher—in other words, the exchange value of the local currency would be lower—in a free market. There are nearly always, therefore, attempts to evade the regulations. For example, exporting firms may agree with their foreign buyers to invoice their exports below their value and thereby to acquire for themselves, unknown to their Government, balances of foreign exchange. In the same way, importing firms may arrange with their suppliers to invoice their imports at more than their cost, in order that they may retain the difference in the form of foreign exchange. Hence Governments imposing exchange control are constrained to check export prices and import prices. They usually impose heavy penalties on attempts to evade exchange control either by false invoicing or by other methods, such as smuggling gold or jewels or currency notes out of the country. Their object is to keep control of all foreign exchange earned by residents in order to ensure that the limited amounts available are used in the ways they consider most beneficial to the country as a whole.

All transactions involving foreign exchange will be subject to control. Consider imports, for example. Nobody will be allowed to import anything unless he gets the approval of the Government, in the form of an import licence. Imports may be confined to certain types of commodities, those considered essential. There may be discrimination between countries, a larger volume of imports being permitted from some countries than from others. Quotas may be fixed by the Government, laying down the amount or value of each commodity that may be imported from each country during, say, the next three months. Or the Government may not commit itself beforehand; every proposed import may be considered separately on its own merits and either approved or disapproved. Particular industries, or even particular firms, can be favoured, rather than others, in the distribution of import licences.

Clearly such a system gives great power to the Government. It can decide exactly what shall be imported, and from where, and by whom, without being bound by any general rules and without having to give any reasons for its decisions. It can continuously adjust its tactics to meet changing conditions, permitting some imports it had formerly prohibited, or conversely, or allowing more from some countries and less from others. It can thus ensure that the limited amount of foreign exchange available is spent in the ways it considers of the greatest advantage to the country as a whole. The close and detailed control of imports, together with a similar control of exports and of other transactions involving foreign exchange, goes a long way towards enabling the Government to direct the economic activities of the country into those channels it considers most desirable.

Exchange control, therefore, can be a powerful instrument of central planning. It can give the Government a flexible and far-reaching control over all aspects of the economy affected by international transactions.

Exchange control, however, has serious disadvantages.

In the first place, it creates risk and uncertainty in international trade. Other countries do not know where they stand. Country *A*, practising exchange control, may be one of their chief customers. She may import certain commodities from them and then suddenly stop importing them at all, or she may switch her purchases from one country to another overnight. Or she may be an important supplier (of certain raw materials, for example), and suddenly cut off her supplies or divert them from one country to another. Country *A* will suffer in the same way in so far as she trades with countries that themselves practise exchange control.

In the second place, if the economic system of the country is based mainly on private enterprise, exchange control will make it very difficult for firms to plan ahead. They cannot be sure they will receive adequate supplies of imported materials, or what their prices will be. They therefore cannot quote firm delivery dates, or firm prices. They cannot even plan for a certain volume of output. In so far as their exports are controlled, they cannot be sure that they will be allowed to supply a customer in a particular country; they may be ordered to divert their exports to other countries, whose currencies are needed more badly.

In the third place, exchange control needs a host of administrators if it is to be effective. This not only ties up manpower which might be used more productively. In some countries it has led to considerable corruption (for example, in granting import licences). And it has often lowered the standards of business morality: firms have shown great ingenuity in inventing methods of evading the regulations.

3. PAYMENTS AGREEMENTS

Suppose that two countries are both practising exchange control, but that their restrictions are directed mainly against a third currency—say, dollars. They may be prepared to trade fairly freely with one another, provided that neither of them thereby loses any dollars. Their two Governments may therefore make a *payments agreement* under which current transactions between them are permitted freely, each Government undertaking to try to maintain equality in the current balance of payments between them.

They may go farther, by drawing up a detailed list of quantities of different goods that each expects to export to the other during the coming year. The values of the two totals will be the same, unless provision is made for other net payments (for example, interest payments) from, say, *A* to *B*, in which event the forecasts will provide for an export surplus of that value by *A*.

There will be some restriction, however, on the types of goods exchanged. For example, A may export certain goods that could be sold for dollars or that are "in short supply." She will not be prepared to sell more than a limited amount of such goods to B and, as a rule, she will do this only if B promises not to re-export them (for example, to the dollar area) and makes concessions to her of equal value.

The Agreement on Trade and Payments of June, 1949, between the Government of the United Kingdom and the Argentine Government [1] will serve as an example. The preamble recognizes "that it is to the mutual advantage of the contracting Governments that commercial and financial transactions should be encouraged in such a manner as to achieve balance of payments at the highest possible level" and "that it is expedient to take appropriate measures to ensure the continuity and expansion of the traditional exchange of goods and services of the two countries." The Agreement contains schedules listing the amounts and values of different goods to be exported (as a minimum) each year for the next five years from each country to the other, the totals being £129 million for Argentine exports and £121 million for British exports (the difference covering interest payments, etc., by the Argentine). The Argentine was to provide stated quantities of meat at agreed prices (subject to review for future years), as well as maize, hides and skins, and other commodities. The United Kingdom was to supply a long list of goods, including £29 million of petroleum and petroleum products, £8·5 million (1,500,000 tons) of coal, and £7 million of iron and steel and manufactures thereof.

Such a payments agreement may go wrong. It may be upset by unforeseen changes in world conditions or world prices. Or country B may in fact buy much more from A than A buys from her, so that A acquires a large and growing balance of B's currency. What happens then? One possible solution is for the exchange value of B's currency to be reduced in terms of A's. Or the Government of A may take special measures to divert purchases to B. Or the flow of goods from A to B may be restricted either by A or by B. Under the payments agreement between Japan and the sterling area, Japan acquired a growing sterling balance which by 1952 exceeded £100 million, and restrictions were imposed on purchases from Japan by the sterling area. Two years later Japan was short of sterling. [2]

Under the various British payments agreements, payments are normally made in sterling. This means that the other country must keep a working balance of sterling. It was agreed that the working balance of the Argentine should be £20 million; should it exceed that amount, the Argentine could convert the excess into dollars. This

<hr />

[1] Cmd. 7735 and Cmd. 8744 of 1949.

[2] The post-war British payments agreements with Brazil provide another example. Brazil bought more from Great Britain, and sold less to Great Britain, than had been expected. She therefore accrued commercial debts of over £60 million. The last Payments Agreement makes provision for her gradual repayment of these debts.

Agreement also (like several others) provided a guarantee against "revaluation"; countries enjoying such a guarantee on their sterling balances were compensated when the pound was devalued.

A payments agreement usually permits freedom of payment for current transactions only, capital movements remaining under strict control. But one country may owe debts to the other. She probably is not in a position to repay them at once. The payments agreement may state an agreed rate at which she will repay. Thus a number of British payments agreements state at what rate limited amounts of sterling balances can be released and used to pay for current transactions.

A payments agreement between only two countries implies that they must balance their trade with one another. In the absence of any restrictions, A would probably have a considerable export surplus or import surplus with B. The advantage of the payments agreement between them might be enhanced if they could include C. A might then run, say, an import surplus with B, covered by her export surplus to C, while C balanced the triangular trade by her export surplus to B. The greater the number of countries, the higher the level at which their total trade with one another will balance.

From this standpoint, the sterling area is a huge multilateral payments agreement, for payments within the area are comparatively unrestricted. It is true that the area as a whole discriminates against dollars, earning all the dollars it can, but restricting its dollar purchases, and that the various members buy from one another, as far as possible, rather than from the dollar area. But within the area transactions are relatively free. The same applied, to some extent, to the European Payments Union.

The United Kingdom has separate payments agreements with each of a number of countries outside the sterling area. Multilateralism used to be provided by the *transferable accounts* system, by which countries outside both the sterling area and the dollar area could make payments in sterling to one another. Since the close of 1958, however, this system is no longer needed, for currently-earned sterling can now be converted (by non-residents of the sterling area) into any currency, including dollars.

Payments agreements are a means of expanding trade by escaping from the rigours of exchange control. But they are themselves a consequence of exchange control. They exist only because there is discrimination (at present, mainly against the dollar area). They divert trade: a country buys from another with which it has a payments agreement, rather than from a third country that could satisfy its requirements better or more cheaply but has a harder currency. If exchange control could be abolished, payments agreements would not be needed, and world trade would expand, perhaps very considerably, and would follow the pattern indicated by comparative costs.

4. CONVERTIBLE STERLING

At the close of 1958, sterling currently earned by non-residents of the sterling area, and sterling balances held by them in bank deposits or Treasury bills, were made freely convertible into gold or any currency, including dollars.

As I wrote in Chapter XXXVI, Section 4, most European countries took similar measures at the same time, and the European Payments Union came to an end.

In practice, non-residents of the sterling area have been able to convert sterling into other currencies for nearly four years. The sterling which they have currently acquired has been known as "transferable sterling," and the United Kingdom has supported the rates at which it could be exchanged for other currencies, keeping them within about 1 per cent of the official rates. However, making such sterling formally convertible does give holders of it some assurance that its convertibility will be maintained, and no doubt some exchange business formerly transacted (in transferable sterling) in such markets as Zürich and New York will now be carried out in London.

Imports from almost anywhere outside the sterling area are now just as much a potential drain on our gold and dollar reserves as imports directly from the dollar area. This was recognized in May, 1959, by removing restrictions on imports from the dollar area of a wide range of consumers' goods which already entered freely from Western Europe. Some discriminatory restrictions (for example, on textiles and clothing and pharmaceutical products) still remain on imports from the dollar area, and there is still a quota on dollar motor-cars (but it has been raised from £600,000 to £1,500,000) and quotas on dried fruit, fresh citrus fruit, and certain canned fruits (but they have been raised from £1,500,000 to £7,700,000). The main purpose of convertibility is to free international trade from restrictions. No doubt it is hoped that the liberalization of imports from the dollar area will help to bring about a more liberal import policy by the United States and other dollar countries.

Sterling is still by no means fully convertible. Residents of the sterling area are still subject to restrictions on their right to obtain dollars and other currencies and are still limited on the amount they may spend on foreign travel. There are still restrictions on movements of capital from sterling into other currencies even, to some extent, for non-residents (although, as the various balance-of-payments crises demonstrated, they are subject to large-scale evasion).

It may take a long time before sterling can be made fully convertible by residents of the sterling area (and some restrictions on capital movements may remain indefinitely).

In order to bring this about, the sterling area must be able to earn enough foreign exchange, month by month and year by year, to cover its payments to the rest of the world and to build up its comparatively small reserves of gold and dollars. This implies that the sterling area must have an export surplus (or, more generally, a surplus of credits over debits in its balance of payments on current account). Increased export earnings must not all be spent on imports. The sterling area must expand its exports relatively to its imports, which means that it must increase its output relatively to its consumption, thereby increasing its savings. This is quite possible for a country such as Great Britain, which has already made considerable progress in this direction. It is a hard course, however, for underdeveloped countries such as India and most British ex-colonies. They need foreign capital to help implement their programmes of economic and social development. They are more likely to make economic progress if their own efforts and saving are supplemented, possibly on a still more generous scale than in the past, by economic aid from the richer countries such as the United States and Great Britain.

PART VIII

POST-WAR POLICY

CHAPTER XL

BRITISH ECONOMIC POLICY SINCE THE WAR

1. The Loss of Capital due to the War

The purpose of this chapter is not to give a year-by-year account of the economic history of Great Britain since the war, but merely to point out some of the leading features and trends.

During the war, destruction and damage to property, although on nothing like the scale suffered by Russia and Germany, were caused by enemy action; buildings and other installations were bombed, and ships were sunk. Nearly half a million houses were destroyed or rendered uninhabitable, and another half a million had to be replaced owing to age and neglect. The merchant fleet was reduced from 22 to 16 million tons deadweight. Moreover, the maintenance of various assets, not essential to the war effort, was kept down to a minimum; many branches of industry and trade made do with more or less worn-out plant and equipment in order to free labour and materials for war purposes. Stocks had run down and personal durable assets had deteriorated.

Hence Great Britain came out of the war a good deal worse-equipped, for peace-time activities, than she went into it.

Moreover, Great Britain emerged from the war with greatly reduced external assets and greatly increased external liabilities. She had parted with some gold (£150 million) and with a substantial part (£1,100 million) of her overseas investments in order to pay for goods needed during the war from the United States (before lend-lease was introduced) and elsewhere. Her war expenditure overseas had led to a large accumulation of sterling balances belonging to other countries: £3,680 million as against less than £700 million before the war. Soon after the war ended, she was assisted by loans of £937 million from the United States and £312 million from Canada, on which she is now paying interest.

Before the war, Great Britain had been a great creditor nation. The value of her overseas investments and gold reserves was much greater than her external liabilities (sterling balances, external public debt, and overseas private investment in Great Britain). By now, her external assets may again exceed her external liabilities, but by much less than before the war.

The difference shows itself in the balance of payments in the net receipts from interest, profits, and dividends. Before the war, this was about £200 million a year: equivalent to more than £700 million at present import prices. In 1958 it was only £53 million. Owing to this heavy fall, and to the fall in other receipts (such as those from shipping) and less favourable terms of trade, Great Britain has had to expand her volume of exports very substantially in order to pay for her imports.

The internal national debt increased during the war from £7 milliard to over £23 milliard (and is now over £25 milliard). This, however, is not a burden in the sense that an external debt is a burden. The interest-payments on external debt go to non-residents, whereas those on internal debt are merely transfers of money between residents, from taxpayers to debt-holders. It is true that large transfer-payments on the internal debt may require relatively high taxation, which may weaken incentives to work and invest; but the payments are not in themselves a net burden on the community.

At present, interest on the internal national debt amounts to little more than £700 million a year. This is only about 4 per cent of the national income, as compared with nearly 5 per cent in 1938, and of course a considerable part of the interest is recovered in income-tax on the recipients. Moreover, the whole of the debt is not "dead-weight"; part of it has been invested in assets which yield the Government nearly £250 million a year.

2. Some Post-War Trends

The years immediately following the end of the war were years of comparative hardship. There were of course no bombings or black-outs but in other respects the conditions of civilian life were not much less austere than during the war. Average levels of personal consumption were considerably lower than before the war, and the range of choice was limited. There were still shortages and queues, and rationing and a number of other war-time restrictions remained in force. As time went on, conditions gradually improved and restrictions were gradually relaxed or removed; from about the close of 1951 onwards there was continuous and substantial progress in these directions.

In 1946 the total volume of output was nearly as great as in 1938 and over the next five years it increased (owing largely to fuller employment than before the war) by nearly 15 per cent. Why, then, did personal consumption remain considerably below pre-war levels?

One reason is that a larger proportion of the output than before the war was exported. Over the period 1946–51 the average volume of exports was more than 40 per cent greater than in 1938, while the average volume of imports was nearly 20 per cent smaller.

Another reason is that the Government took a larger share of the output than before the war. The services provided by the Government are for the benefit of the community, but they do not enter into personal expenditure.

Another reason is that part of the output during the immediate post-war years was devoted to making good the loss of capital—housing, for example—during the war.

The main reason, however, is that the terms of trade were much less favourable than before the war. In 1946 about 9 per cent more exports were needed than in 1938 to buy a given volume of imports. In 1951, owing to the marked rise in the prices of many foodstuffs and raw materials due to the Korean war, about 39 per cent more were needed than in 1938. Throughout this period, 1946–1951, the terms of trade became increasingly less favourable. The average prices of imports doubled while those of exports rose only by 60 per cent.

After 1951, this trend was reversed. Between 1951 and 1958 import prices fell by 16 per cent while export prices rose by 10 per cent. In 1958 only about 6 per cent more exports were needed than in 1938 to buy a given volume of imports.

As Great Britain exports about a fifth of its output, these changes in the terms of trade account to a considerable extent for the comparative hardship of the early post-war years and the growing prosperity after 1951. Although the volume of output increased at a fairly steady rate throughout the whole period (indeed, slackening-off during the last four years) real national income rose much faster after 1951.

Another important trend has been the marked increase in saving during recent years.[1] The estimates of personal savings are subject to a considerable margin of error; and the amount which should be deducted for depreciation, to reduce gross saving to net saving, is to some extent a matter of opinion. Nevertheless there can be little doubt that total net savings have more than doubled, in real terms, since the earlier post-war years. This has been due largely to the great increase in personal savings, which are estimated to have shot up from £229 million (gross) in 1951 to £665 million in 1952 and £1,341 million in 1958. This in turn has probably been due mainly to the growth of personal incomes after tax, from less than £11 milliard in 1951 to over £17 milliard in 1958, a rise of about a quarter in real terms, affording larger margins for saving.

Finally, I may mention again the trend during recent years towards greater economic freedom, giving more play to the price-mechanism and more scope to business decisions and consumers' preferences.

In the early post-war years there were Government controls over many economic activities. Imports were severely restricted. The Government itself continued for some time to be the sole importer of

---

[1] The figures for 1956–58 were given in Chapter XXVII, Section 4.

most foodstuffs and raw materials. Scarce materials, such as steel, were allocated to firms, and some types of investment (e.g. private house-building) were restricted. A number of consumers' goods continued to be rationed. Efforts were made to check rising prices by subsidies on foodstuffs and housing, price-fixing, rent restriction, and other devices.

As time went on, many Government controls were gradually removed. Monetary measures came to replace direct controls as the main weapon against inflation; here, too, the latter part of 1951 was a turning-point. Private enterprise replaced Government trading, and the whole economy gradually became more free, although rationing was not finally abolished until 1954 and rent restriction remained until 1958.[1]

It can certainly be claimed that Government controls were necessary during the dislocation and shortages of the immediate post-war years and that their removal was made possible by the growing prosperity of recent years, due largely to the improvement in the terms of trade since 1951. At the same time, I share the view, as the reader is aware, that their removal has itself made a substantial contribution to our recovery. They distorted the price-system, diverting efforts and investment into less productive channels, and they considerably increased the risks of industry and trade.

3. How Far have Economic Aims been Achieved?

(a) Full Employment

The dominant economic aim throughout the post-war years has been the maintenance of full employment. And this aim has been very fully achieved. Until very recently, the total number of unemployed has been consistently below, and usually well below, half a million.

It has been achieved partly by devices such as controlling the location of new establishments,[2] but mainly by expanding the amount of public and private expenditure on consumption and investment. The expansion in the amount of money has somewhat overshot the mark and has produced, throughout the post-war period, an inflationary situation, discussed in Section 4.

(b) Higher Standards of Living

I have already pointed out that levels of consumption were lower than before the war during the earlier post-war years but rose appreci-

---

[1] The Act of 1957 removed control from all houses except those with a rateable value (on 6th November, 1956) of only £30 a year (£40 in London) or less. The rents of the latter remained controlled but may be increased quite substantially—to between 1⅓ and 2⅓ times their gross annual value (as assessed for rating).

[2] See Chapter XXI, Section 5.

ably after 1951. Personal expenditure on consumers' goods was £14·9 milliard, at market prices, in 1958, as against £4·4 milliard in 1938, and population was nearly 9 per cent greater. It is difficult to make a good comparison of retail prices over an interval of twenty years, but it is officially estimated that consumers' expenditure, at constant prices, was over 20 per cent greater in 1958. This is equivalent to an increase, in real terms, of 11 to 12 per cent per head of population.

It must be remembered, however, that personal saving was much higher in 1958 than in 1938. Real personal income per head (after tax), which includes saving as well as consumption, was over 20 per cent higher in 1958.

Moreover, the above calculations omit a very important element: namely, the improvement in the health and education of the people due to the great expansion in "free" social services provided by the State.

(c) Less Economic Inequality

Even before the war, economic inequality was less in Great Britain than in many other countries. Since then, it has been reduced considerably more. Great Britain today is one of the most egalitarian communities in the world.

The above calculation of an average increase in real personal incomes of over 20 per cent conceals substantial changes in the distribution of the national income. The real incomes of most wage-earners have risen by 40 to 50 per cent, while the real incomes of most property-owners and of some professional persons and highly-paid salary-earners have fallen.

The following table gives a general picture, but it should be treated with caution. The numbers in the various groups have changed, there were more unemployed before the war, and the incomes of self-employed persons are gross (before depreciation).

INCOME BEFORE TAX (£ million)

	1938	1948	1958
Income from Employment . . .	3,022	6,766	13,413
Farmers	69	301	439
Professional Persons . . .	118	209	290
Other Sole Traders and Partnerships .	460	810	1,107
Rent, Dividends, and Interest . .	1,134	1,189	2,191
National Insurance Benefits, etc. .	275	705	1,488
Total Personal Incomes .	5,078	9,980	18,928
Index of Retail Prices . .	100	175	272

Average weekly earnings in manufacturing and certain other industries were four times as high in October, 1958, as in 1938. This is a rise of nearly 50 per cent in the real incomes of manual workers. It is true that the industries from which the Ministry of Labour obtains its statistics of earnings cover only 7 million workers. Earnings in the industries not covered (agriculture, coal-mining, transport and distribution, and various service industries) rose less, owing to less overtime, but they probably increased, in real terms, by at least 40 per cent.

Earnings rose more than wage-rates (which only trebled) owing to the movement of workers towards the higher-paid occupations, to the increase in overtime (due largely to reductions in the standard working week, often by abolishing Saturday morning work, to give a 44-hour five-day standard working week for most males), to high piece-rate earnings, and to payments above trade-union rates.

There is also less inequality than before the war among wage-earners themselves. The lower-paid workers have improved their relative position; the rates for more highly-skilled jobs exceed theirs by a lower percentage than before the war.

The real incomes of most salary-earners have also risen, but by considerably less than those of most manual workers. For example, the range of pay for male non-graduate qualified teachers was £168 to £408 a year before the war and is now, since the increases made in 1959, £520 to £1,120 a year. Moreover, large groups of salary-earners, such as teachers and civil servants, have had their salary scales revised only at intervals of several years, while most wage-earners have obtained increases every year.

Some of the more highly-paid salary-earners are now receiving less, in real terms, than before the war. For example, the pre-war range for a male Principal in the Civil Service (London area) was £800 to £1,100 a year, and in 1959 it was £1,500 to £2,120 a year. Increases in the salary scales of many civil servants are now being made, but most of them will be less than 10 per cent.

Among the self-employed, farmers seem to have improved their position most and professional persons least. For example, before the war over half the general medical practitioners earned more than £1,000 a year; the comparable figure today is about £2,500 a year.

The total of personal incomes from rent, dividends, and interest is less than twice what it was before the war, although the amount of capital is much greater. Within this group, those who have fared worst are holders of fixed-interest securities and (until 1958) landlords of rent-controlled properties.

People living on annuities or pensions which are the same, in money terms, as before the war are bearing the whole burden of the subsequent increases in the cost of living. Government-paid non-contributory old-age pensions were 10s. a week before the war and are now 28s. 4d. a week (18s. 4d. for married women).

The above table gives incomes before tax. Income-tax and surtax take a larger proportion from present-day incomes than they took from the corresponding smaller pre-war incomes. Consider, for example, a married man with two children under 11 whose income (all earned) is twice what it was before the war. If it has risen from £1,000 to £2,000, his net income after tax has risen from £897 to £1,624 (in 1958, it was only £1,586). If it has risen from £2,000 to £4,000, his net income after tax has risen by only two-thirds, from £1,672 to £2,786 (in 1958, it was only £2,690). The higher the income, the greater is the proportion taken in tax.

There has thus been a marked trend towards greater equality. This shows itself in various ways. For example, the children of the lower-income groups are better fed and cared for and are therefore healthier than before the war. Many working-class households today are better housed, own durable consumers' goods such as television sets or refrigerators, and spend more on holidays. On the other hand, the number of resident servants in private homes fell from 707,000 in 1931 to 178,000 in 1951 (the date of the last census); many can no longer afford to keep servants and have to do their own housework.

This trend has been accentuated by the growth of public expenditure on such purposes as health and education, retirement pensions and other national insurance benefits, housing subsidies, and family allowances. Total public expenditure on these purposes was about £500 million in 1938 and is over £2,500 million today.

It must be remembered that the social services are paid for to a considerable extent by the mass of the people. The great majority of manual workers pay no income-tax or pay at low rates, but they all (except married women who choose not to join the scheme) pay national insurance contributions; and taxes on consumption (for example, on tobacco and beer) form a considerable part of public revenue. Nevertheless the Welfare State does involve a substantial transfer from the relatively rich to the relatively poor.

(d) Social Security

In this field there has been great progress. In addition to greatly increased public expenditure on such social services as health (now about £650 million a year) and education (now about £600 million a year) we have had since the war a very comprehensive system of social insurance. This has its defects,[1] but it does provide a national minimum income (adjusted for needs) for all; it covers self-employed persons, such as shopkeepers, as well as employees.

A very important post-war innovation is the provision of pensions for (insured) retired men over 65 and retired women over 60. At present the rate for retirement pensions is 50s. a week for men and

[1] See the last paragraphs of Chapter II, Section 5.

women insured in their own right, plus additions for dependants—30s. a week for a wife, 15s. a week for the first child, and 7s. a week for other children. It was decided to start paying these pensions forthwith, without waiting until the contributions had built up an adequate fund. The Fund will therefore continue to be subsidized, to a growing extent, from general revenue unless the rates of contribution are increased or the retiring ages raised.

The national insurance scheme also provides sickness benefit (of unlimited duration) and unemployment benefit (of limited duration, but subject to possible extension). The present rates are 50s. a week for men, single women, and widows, 34s. a week for married women, and 28s. 6d. a week for young persons under 18, with the same additions for dependants as those made to retirement benefits. Other benefits under the scheme include widows' benefits, guardians' allowances, maternity benefits, death grants, and benefits for injuries and disablement.

The normal weekly rates of contribution (which include contributions, e.g. 1s. 10½d. for men employees, towards the cost of the National Health Service) are at present 9s. 11d. for men employees and 8s. for women employees, their employers contributing 8s. 3d. and 6s. 9d. Rates of contribution for young persons are somewhat lower and for self-employed persons somewhat higher.

Family allowances are paid for all children except the first in each family, who gets no allowance, at the rate of 8s. a week for each child.

For persons outside the national insurance scheme, and for those whose insurance benefits are inadequate to provide them with a minimum level of subsistence there is, in the last resort, national assistance. This is subject to a "means test." At the close of 1959 over 1·7 million persons were receiving national assistance grants, mostly to supplement retirement and old-age pensions and sickness and unemployment benefits.

It is clear from the above details that some measure of social security is now provided in Great Britain from the cradle to the grave.

(e) A Stable Pound

The aim of maintaining a pound that is stable in purchasing-power has not been achieved. Ever since the war, until 1958 and 1959, we have had a more or less continuous inflation. Retail prices have risen almost continuously and are now some 175 per cent above their pre-war level and nearly 80 per cent higher than at the end of the war.

4. INFLATION

Sufficient public and private expenditure on consumption and investment may prevent slumps and maintain fairly full employment. On the other hand, too much expenditure will lead to inflation. This is what has happened in Great Britain since the war. We have had very full employment accompanied by almost continuous inflation.

The root cause of inflation is overloading the economy with more demands than it can fulfil. The manpower and other resources of the community cannot, or at any rate do not, provide all the goods and services that public authorities and enterprises and individuals set out to buy, and have the money to buy, at current prices. So prices rise, restricting what people actually get to what can be produced, or imported in exchange for exports, plus any income received from abroad. It is also possible for a country to live beyond its means, for a time, by raising loans to cover its balance-of-payments deficits or by running down its reserves of gold and foreign exchange or by selling its foreign assets.

Until the last year or so, the British economy has been overloaded. The real national income has been too small for us to carry out all the investment we wished, to devote about 40 per cent of public expenditure to social services and over a quarter to defence, to make loans and grants overseas, and at the same time to increase our consumption.

The best measure of the extent of inflation is the rate at which the national money income is rising faster than the national real income. This need not involve an actual rise in commodity prices, but it usually does; and for Great Britain we can use the more familiar index of retail prices, or the cost of living, as a rough measure.

The real national income depends mainly on the level of output, but it is also affected by the terms of trade. Between 1948 and 1951 the terms of trade considerably worsened, so that while output rose by an average of some $3\frac{1}{2}$ per cent a year, real national income rose by only about 2 per cent a year. From 1952 to 1958, on the other hand, the terms of trade became more favourable, so that while output rose by an average of only 2 to 3 per cent a year, real national income rose on the average by about $3\frac{1}{2}$ per cent a year.

Throughout the post-war period, the cost of living has risen almost continuously. It is now nearly 80 per cent higher than at the end of the war; the average increase has been 4 to 5 per cent a year.

This is much less than the increase which has taken place in some countries. Some South American countries, for example, have had increases in their cost of living of 20 to 30 per cent or more, year after year. Nevertheless it has had serious disadvantages and may well be a handicap to our economic progress should it continue.

It resembles a general tax on consumption imposed on all, including the poorest, irrespective of their ability to pay. Only those with sufficient economic power to obtain a compensating increase in their money incomes can escape this growing burden.

The expectation of continued inflation tends to keep up rates of interest. People are reluctant to lend at low rates of interest if they think that their money will buy 4 or 5 per cent less in a year's time. They have the alternative of investing in "equities" (ordinary shares) and probably reaping a capital gain: the general price-level of British equities has risen nearly as much as the cost of living since 1938, and between 1952 and 1958 it doubled. High rates of interest tend to divert investment away from assets (such as buildings, ships, and plantations) which take a long time to construct or which have a long life (so that interest-costs are high relatively to depreciation) or which take some years before they begin to yield a return, and towards assets which yield quick profits. Houses and flats tend to be built to be sold outright (which reduces the mobility of labour) rather than to be let on leases at fixed rents.

In so far as inflation means that costs in Great Britain rise more than in countries which compete with her, it will become increasingly difficult to sell British exports. This is already happening. Some countries, in Western Europe for example, have managed to maintain fairly full employment without much increase in their prices and costs; in Western Germany the cost of living towards the close of 1958 was less than 20 per cent, and in Belgium it was less than 15 per cent, above the 1948 level. Great Britain devalued the pound in September, 1949. If inflation continues, she may eventually be forced to devalue again. This would be bad for the reputation of sterling as an international currency, and for the income which is earned by London as an international financial centre and commodity market. If devaluation is averted by increasing exchange control, this will be a reversal of our recent progress towards greater freedom of international trade, from which, as a leading trading country heavily dependent on imports, we have so much to gain.

Many factors may play a part in accentuating or checking inflation; some of them were discussed in Chapter XXXIII, Section 6. Among the factors likely to check inflation are an increase in output, an improvement in the terms of trade, an increase in saving, either voluntary or (for example, through higher taxes and budget surpluses or increased National Insurance contributions) compulsory, reductions in public expenditure, and measures which keep down the expansion of money and credit. The influence of any particular factor depends on to what extent it affects the ratio of national money income to national real income.

A widely-held view is that the dominant influence in bringing about inflation during the post-war period has been the success of the trade unions in forcing up wages year after year. An opposing view is that excessive money incomes have been due to the "demand-pull" of continuous increases in the amount of expenditure rather than to the "cost-push" of higher wages.

Since inflation is due to a general overloading of the economy, in which many factors play a part one way or the other, the search for a single dominant "cause" is perhaps somewhat fruitless. But if a verdict has to be given between the above two views, it must be in favour of the latter.

In most years wage-rates have increased considerably less than actual earnings. This has happened partly because many employers have been paying wages above the trade-union scale. They could afford to do so because they knew that they could pass on their increased costs in the form of increased profits. On the whole, company profits have been rising, at times faster than wage-rates. Moreover, in most years the number of vacancies registered at employment exchanges has exceeded the number of unemployed.

All this suggests that inflation has been due to excessive monetary demand, leading employers to compete for scarce labour, rather than to the pressure of higher wage-rates.[1]

The Government has been trying, especially since 1951, to check inflation by keeping down the quantity of money. It has restricted the volume of "liquid assets" available to the banks (which the banks try to keep at not less than 30 per cent of their deposits) by funding Treasury bills, at the close of 1951 and subsequently. It has raised the Bank Rate whenever monetary demand seemed increasing too fast or the exchange value of sterling seemed threatened; from September, 1957, to March, 1958, the Bank Rate was 7 per cent. It has at times asked the banks not to increase their advances, or to restrict them for hire-purchase finance. Recently, assisted by more favourable terms of trade and increased saving, this policy has been successful. From April, 1958, to December, 1959, the retail price index remained fairly stable. How long it will keep stable, in face of further demands for increased wage-rates, remains to be seen.

At present, the banks have been freed from restrictions on their lending. Most of them have absorbed or taken shares in hire-purchase finance companies and are making "personal loans" not backed by collateral securities. It may be that if considerable restrictions of credit are needed in the future the Government will not again impose limitations on bank advances but will instead reintroduce something like the war-time system of Treasury Deposit Receipts; it has already taken powers to do this.[2]

To return to the "cost-push" versus "demand-pull" argument, while it is true that the evidence supports the latter rather than the former, it is also true, in my view, that more moderate wage demands, if combined with appropriate monetary and public-finance measures, would have resulted in much less inflation. To put the same point in another

---

[1] On this whole subject see "Inflation in the United Kingdom, 1948–57," by F. W. Paish, (*Economica*, May, 1938).

[2] They will be called "Special Deposits" and will bear interest based on the current Treasury bill rate; they will not form part of the banks' "liquid assets."

way, suppose that post-war Governments had set out (as the Government of Western Germany did) to follow adequate anti-inflationary policies. Would any Government have been firm enough to carry them through in the face of trade-union demands for higher wage-rates than were warranted by increases in the real national income? The attempt to do so might have involved nation-wide strikes, growing unemployment, and consequent loss of output.

This dilemma may very possibly present itself in reality in the not too distant future. If so, it remains to be seen how the Government, whatever its political complexion may be, will cope with it.

5. EXTERNAL TRADE

Great Britain has a population of over 50 million on an area of less than 89 million square miles (of which Scotland has over 30 million). She imports well over half her food and most of her raw materials in exchange for exports, mainly of manufactured goods. Her comparatively high standards of living are maintained by her external trade.

Before the war, Great Britain, or rather the United Kingdom, had a large excess of imports over exports, the difference being made up mainly by net income from overseas investments and net receipts for shipping and other services. After the war, owing to the marked fall in these "invisible" items, it was clear that she would have to keep down imports and to expand the volume of exports very substantially.

Imports were greatly reduced, especially from the dollar area, and although restrictions have been relaxed as economic conditions improved, the volume of imports is still not much greater than before the war. The volume of exports expanded fairly continuously and is now about twice the pre-war volume. The figures are given below.

The expansion of exports was promoted in the early post-war years by direct Government controls. It was assisted by the devaluation of sterling in September, 1949. During recent years exports have taken place under the free play of the price-mechanism, but the Government can promote exports relatively to home sales by restricting credit and imposing or increasing indirect taxes (including purchase taxes) or can promote home sales relatively to exports by doing the opposite.

Since the war, special assistance has been given to British farmers. One reason for this was that it was thought unlikely that exports would expand sufficiently to pay for all the imports we should need, and that therefore it would be desirable to expand agricultural output. The British arrangements are less open to objection than, for example, those of the United States, under which farmers are guaranteed prices much above world prices for most of their products, and American consumers have to pay these high prices while their Government has to carry very large stocks which cannot be sold at the prices fixed. In Great Britain, farmers receive "deficiency payments" to make up their incomes to what they would have been had prices been at certain agreed levels (revised from year to year) instead of at their actual levels; and prices to consumers are not raised. Nevertheless the policy is expensive; it is now costing some £250 million a year, divided among 300,000 full-time and 50,000 part-time farmers. Nor does it seem really necessary on economic grounds. It is doubtful whether it makes agricultural output greater than it would otherwise be by more than a small percentage, and in 1958 we were able to pay for our imports and still have a surplus of £455 million on current account.

In 1959 exports of U.K. produce were £3,326 million (of which 85 per cent were manufactures) and re-exports were £130 million. If exports of shipping and other services are added, we export about a quarter of our output. Imports (c.i.f.) were £3,993 million in 1959. It is clear, therefore, that any substantial change in the terms of trade will have a significant effect on national real income.

An improvement in the British terms of trade implies a worsening in the terms of trade of countries exporting primary products. Some of these countries are relatively poor and on general grounds an increase in their export earnings should be welcomed. It is also true that such an increase provides them with more purchasing-power to buy British and other exports. At the same time, it is absurd to argue that therefore we gain by high import prices and lose by low import prices. The result, from the purely British standpoint, is the exact opposite.

I mentioned earlier that the terms of trade moved adversely to the United Kingdom after the war until 1952 onwards, when this movement was reversed. The year-by-year figures are given overleaf.

The share of the United Kingdom in world exports of manufactured goods has fallen progressively from about 21 per cent in 1953 to about 18 per cent today. This could be a danger signal. In fact, however, it reflects mainly the general expansion of world trade (especially among the countries of western Europe) over that period. In so far as the absolute volume of British exports is at least maintained, and the terms of trade do not significantly worsen, there is little cause for alarm.

As a leading trading nation, the United Kingdom is almost certain to gain by the general removal or relaxation of restrictions on imports and the general expansion of world trade on a multilateral and non-discriminatory basis. By her membership of G.A.T.T. and O.E.E.C. she is pledged to promote these aims. Even if a general expansion of world trade is accompanied by a moderate fall in her percentage share, it is very likely to increase the absolute amount of British trade. The opposite policy, of attempting to provide "sheltered markets" for British exports by bilateral agreements, Commonwealth preferences, and similar measures would be likely to lead, as it did in the 1930s, to retaliation by other countries and a contraction of British trade, even if it increased her percentage share.

U.K. External Trade 1946-1958

	1938 = 100					Net Surplus (+) or Deficit (−) on Balance of Payments on Current Account £ million
	(1) Volume of Imports	(2) Volume of Exports	(3) Import Prices	(4) Export Prices	(5) Terms of Trade (3) ÷ (4)	
1946	67	99	213	196	109	− 298
1947	76	109	258	222	116	− 443
1948	78	137	288	244	118	+ 1
1949	85	151	291	250	117	+ 31
1950	85	174	333	267	125	+ 300
1951	96	174	443	319	139	− 403
1952	88	166	430	333	129	+ 247
1953	95	169	383	324	119	+ 188
1954	96	177	381	318	120	+ 230
1955	107	190	394	323	122	− 73
1956	106	201	397	334	119	+ 258
1957	110	205	403	349	116	+ 272
1958	110	197	371	350	106	+ 455

Source: London and Cambridge Economic Bulletin in *The Times Review of Industry*, March, 1959.

These considerations should be borne in mind in connexion with British policy towards such arrangements as the European Common Market. The first measures to implement this were taken at the beginning of 1959. It is part of a plan to promote integration among the six countries—France, Germany, Italy, and the three Benelux countries: the Netherlands, Belgium, and Luxembourg—who have joined together to form the European Economic Community. The broad plan is to move towards political and social as well as economic integration: for example, to allow migration freely among themselves and to have parallel social legislation on such subjects as equal pay for women. As part of this broad plan, the six countries have formed a customs union, or Common Market, and will gradually reduce their import duties and other restrictions against one another, until in twelve to fifteen years' time, it is hoped, the Common Market will become a free-trade area (except, probably, for agricultural products).

The most important question to ask is whether the European Common Market is likely to promote a general expansion of world trade or merely to divert some of the present trade with other countries into regional trade among the Six. If the Common Market gradually reduces its present import restrictions against other countries (as it well may), the answer is that it is likely to promote a general expansion of world trade just as the German Zollverein did in the latter part of the nineteenth century. It should therefore be welcomed.

At the same time, it would be a great advantage to the United Kingdom and other countries if their exports could enter the Common Market on the same terms as those of the Six themselves. The best solution, of course, would be a world-wide system of free trade, but many countries are too committed to protecting their own industries or agriculture for this solution to be a practical possibility. Great Britain, Sweden, Norway, Denmark, Switzerland, Austria, and Portugal have formed the "Outer Seven" and over the next ten years will reduce barries to trade in industrial goods with each other until none remain. But clearly this is only a partial solution; it is to be hoped that it will lead to a much wider free-trade area.

6. Balance-of-Payments Crises

In a country such as the United Kingdom, which exports a substantial part of its output, the effects of inflation will show themselves in its balance of payments. Unless other countries are inflating also, at about the same rate, the rise in money incomes will expand the demand for imports and the rise in costs will check the growth of exports. Labour and other resources will tend to be diverted from the production of commodities which enter into world trade (that is, from the export industries and from industries producing goods that compete with imports) and towards the production of "domestic" goods and services which are more sheltered from external competition and can therefore rise more in price. The result will be a growing deficit in the balance of payments and a growing drain on the country's reserves of gold and foreign exchange. The first thing to "give" under the strain of inflation may be the ability to pay for imports; the first crisis to develop may be a balance-of-payments crisis.

Despite direct controls, which restricted imports and promoted exports, this happened in the United Kingdom after the war.

There was a serious balance-of-payments crisis in the summer of 1947. In July sterling was made convertible, for all current transactions, in accordance with our agreement with the United States. In fact, large amounts of capital, held in sterling, were also converted into dollars. This led to such a drain on our gold and dollar reserves that convertibility had to be abandoned after only five weeks.

In 1949 reserves began to fall again, owing partly to the American recession and the consequent reduction in the dollar earnings of the sterling area. Speculators believed that the pound would have to be devalued. Sterling area importers paid quickly, to forestall a fall in the value of the pound, while foreign importers of sterling-area products delayed their purchases and payments. (These practices are known as "leads" and "lags.") Consequently the reserves fell further, and the pound was devalued in September.

The extent of the devaluation, from $4·03 to $2·80, was greater than had been expected and perhaps greater than was needed; indeed, one or two leading economists claimed that there should have been no devaluation at all. As things turned out, it provided elbow-room for continued inflation.

After devaluation, reserves rapidly recovered. But in 1951, owing to the rise in the prices and volume of imports, and other factors, they fell again, and there was another crisis around the close of the year.

The gold and dollar reserves rose from $1,685 million in the summer of 1952 to over $3,000 million in June, 1954. By that time, retail prices had been stable for fifteen months. Thereafter, investment (including the building-up of stocks, which had fallen very low) tended to outrun saving; retail prices resumed their upward trend; imports increased sharply; reserves fell (to $2,120 million at the end of 1955); and the autumn of 1955 witnessed yet another balance-of-payments crisis.

In 1956 personal savings again rose sharply and despite the Suez affair the United Kingdom had a substantial balance-of-payments surplus on current account. Nevertheless, Suez led to heavy speculative sales of sterling, and the United Kingdom had to borrow £200 million from the International Monetary Fund.

In the late summer of 1957 fresh speculative sales of sterling, together with heavy withdrawals of her sterling balances by India, caused a heavy drain on the reserves and another balance-of-payments crisis, despite a loan of £89 million from the U.S. Export-Import Bank. The drastic rise in the Bank Rate to 7 per cent in September marked the turning of the tide. Since then, the international status of the pound sterling has greatly improved.

The gold and dollar reserves, which had fallen to $1,850 million in September, 1957, were $977 million at the close of 1959.

The fundamental reason for these balance-of-payments crises has been inflation and the fundamental reason for the recent improvement is that inflation has been kept in check. The fight against inflation has been going on, at first mainly by direct controls, then by budgetary means, and since 1951 mainly by monetary measures, ever since the collapse of the "cheap money" experiment of 1946, but to meet each balance-of-payments crisis anti-inflationary measures, such as restricting credit and investment, have been accentuated for the time being.

Within the general balance-of-payments problem there has been the special problem of the dollar shortage (discussed in Chapter XXXVI, Section 1), and until recently each crisis has been followed by further cuts in dollar expenditure, throughout the sterling area, and by renewed efforts to earn more dollars. Recently, however, the dollar has been no stronger than a number of other currencies; this has been recognized by most countries of Western Europe, and the United Kingdom, in making their currencies convertible (to non-residents) and by ending the European Payments Union.

The United Kingdom surplus or deficit, year by year, in its balance of payments on current account has been set out in the Table in Section 5. This, however, does not tell the whole story. Sterling has been especially vulnerable owing to the low level of its gold and dollar reserves and the high level of sterling balances.

Even at £1,000 million, the gold and dollar reserves do not provide an adequate cushion against temporary adverse movements in the balance of payments. They are equivalent to only three months' total imports into the United Kingdom, as against ten months' before the war. Moreover, since the war they have served as the central reserve not only for the United Kingdom but for the whole sterling area, and have thus been subject to a drain from any sterling country that has incurred a dollar deficit.

Overseas sterling holdings are over £4,000 million.   Some £700 million are held by "non-territorial organizations" such as the International Monetary Fund, and an appreciable part of the rest serves as currency reserves for various countries or as working balances, and is not likely to be withdrawn. But very large sums can be withdrawn immediately if the holders fear that the value of sterling may fall.

Nevertheless there will be no speculative drain on sterling balances, and the reserves will prove adequate, if the Government has the will (as it has the power) to continue holding inflationary tendencies as firmly in check as it has done during 1958 and 1959.

7. The Present Position and Outlook

At the moment, in the first weeks of 1960, the United Kingdom has never before been so prosperous. With few exceptions, such as Northern Ireland and the Lancashire cotton industry, there is everywhere full employment; the total number of unemployed, which rose for a short time to over 600,000 a year ago, is back to just over 400,000. Levels of consumption are high, and so are personal savings. The average earnings of men employed in manual work are over £13 a week, and further increases in pay and reductions in hours are on their way; and most salary-scales have been appreciably raised. Yet the cost of living has remained practically stable since April, 1958.

I have left the section on the dollar shortage (Chapter XXXVI) virtually unchanged, as I think it is of historical and general interest, but for the moment the dollar gap has been closed. It is now the

T   B.E.

United States which has been running short of other currencies. The deficit on her balance of payments was over $3 milliard in 1958 and probably nearly $4 milliard in 1959. During these two years she parted with more than $3 milliard of gold, although her gold reserves are still very large—about half the world's total.

It is true that during 1959 the gold and foreign exchange reserves of this country fell by some £100 million. But the Government paid out more than twice that amount in repaying the Export-Import Bank loan and part of the International Monetary Fund loan (both borrowed during the Suez crisis) and in increasing its subscription to the latter body. Sterling is at present strong. At the same time, we should try to raise our gold and foreign exchange reserves well above their present size of about £1,000 million. This would mean increasing further our present level of saving.

At present, savings are large enough to cover investment—there has been no inflation for nearly two years—and probably amount to at least 11 or 12 per cent of the national income. This is a fairly high proportion for a country with a very low rate of population increase; some countries have to use a large part of their savings merely to provide capital assets (such as houses, schools, and factories) for their large annual growth in numbers. Nevertheless still more should be saved in order to keep sterling strong, especially if we wish to increase substantially our overseas investment and our aid to underdeveloped countries.

The Government has constantly to decide whether to damp down expenditure on consumption and investment in order to check inflation or whether there is sufficient slack in the economy to follow policies which stimulate home demand and output. In his April 1959 Budget, the Chancellor took the latter view. He felt it was safe to reduce the standard rate of income-tax from 8s. 6d. to 7s. 9d. in the £ and to reduce all purchase taxes and the duty on beer by a sixth. He announced an accelerated programme of public investment in the nationalized industries, and he reintroduced "investment allowances" to stimulate private investment.

In fact, the economy at the time was poised for renewed expansion. Over the previous four years its rate of growth, damped down by anti-inflationary restrictions on credit and expenditure, had been very slow. The index of industrial production (1954 = 100) was only 107 in the first quarter of 1959 as compared with 106 in the first quarter of 1955. This index covers about half our total output. The other half consists of transport, distribution, other services, and agriculture. This half had been expanding slightly, so that total output had been rising, but at a rate of under 1 per cent a year.

Nevertheless these four years of relative stagnation in industrial output were a period during which increased and improved capacity was being created. Investment in industry continued, and so did technical progress; some 4,000 patents a year were applied for. Obsolete assets, such as some old plant and machinery and ships, were replaced by new and more efficient ones; plans were implemented to improve the designs and quality of products and to give a greater output per worker.

Stimulated by the Budget, a striking expansion took place. By the end of 1959 the index of industrial production had risen by over 10 per cent. (This was accompanied by a rise in the price-level of British equities which, accentuated by the Conservative majority of 100 at the October general election, rose by a further 50 per cent during 1959.)

Whether output will continue to expand at a substantial rate, as full capacity is approached, and without renewed inflation, remains to be seen. It will depend on whether increases in hourly wage-rates are matched by increases in output per worker, on whether saving increases, and on the fiscal and monetary policies of the Government. The Chancellor will be under great pressure to reduce taxation in his 1960 Budget, but he may decide that it would benefit the economy more to aim at a larger budget surplus, and to keep interest rates fairly high. His decision will be known by the time these lines appear in print.

The factor which has contributed most to our improved economic position over the last few years—apart from the recent spurt in industrial output—is the favourable trend in the terms of trade. In 1959 they remained almost unchanged. They may become a little less favourable during the next few years, but there seem no grounds for expecting any marked adverse trend.

If this forecast proves correct, it will be satisfactory for the United Kingdom (provided that it can continue to expand its volume of exports, as it did in 1959) and for other industrial countries, but it will be less satisfactory for countries which rely largely on their exports of primary products. The latter include a number of underdeveloped countries, which have been increasing their real incomes per head at a much slower rate than the more advanced countries during recent years. There seems a general feeling at present that more should be done to provide them with economic aid. It seems clearly desirable that they should be assisted to increase their output per head and to obtain larger export earnings (in some cases by selling more at lower prices, made possible by greater reductions in cost due to technical progress) thereby raising their very low standards of living.

Among the industrial countries, some have been expanding their output and real income per head of population at a considerably faster rate, until just recently, than the United Kingdom. For example, since 1953 Western Germany has expanded her total output by over 60 per cent, has doubled her volume of exports, and has built up her foreign exchange reserves to over $6,000 million. We cannot afford to be complacent. At the same time, it remains true that our real incomes are among the highest in the world—higher than in Western Germany and much higher than in the Soviet Union. Unless there should be a marked downward trend in the value and volume of British exports, there is no cause for alarm.

I now give my personal views on some measures which I think would strengthen our economy. The subjects which I want to discuss are trade-union restrictive practices, reform of the income-tax, over-full employment, and inflation.

In some industries, output per worker could be greatly increased if the trade unions gave up their opposition to labour-saving devices or their "go-slow" policy of limiting the amount of work performed by each worker. These attitudes spring mainly from the fear of unemployment. But there is most unlikely to be another Great Depression. Heavy and widespread unemployment can and no doubt will be prevented, although in a progressive economy there must always be some movement away from contracting industries and towards expanding ones. By far the most important factor in making possible higher standards of living and shorter working hours is the growth of output per worker; and it is very much in the interests of the workers themselves, as well as of the community as a whole, to increase output instead of keeping it down.

Some restrictive practices, such as limiting unduly the number of apprentices to a trade or insisting on an unnecessarily long period of apprenticeship, and the strict demarcation of functions between different trade unions, are designed to improve the position of certain sections of workers relatively to others. But they also keep down output and are therefore against the public interest. For example, in 1959 the Birkenhead shipyard of Cammell Laird was kept idle for seven weeks entirely to a dispute between two trade unions about which should make the chalk-marks for riveting. We have, very properly, a Restrictive Practices Court to prevent restrictive practices by industries and firms. Why not apply similar measures to restrictive practices by trade unions if they are clearly against the public interest?

Our "progressive" system of income-tax and surtax is very well administered, but it has great defects. As I have pointed out at the close of Chapter XXIX, it discriminates against saving and against risk-taking; this could be partly remedied by imposing an annual (and progressive) tax on the capital value of all the assets which a taxpayer owns instead of taxing the income from them. Another great defect is that the present system discourages increased effort by taking a progressively larger slice of the consequent increased earnings. This could be prevented, at little cost to the Exchequer, by fixing in advance the weekly amount of tax which each worker had to pay, based on normal weekly earnings for his occupation and grade. If he earned more through working overtime or (under piece-rates) working harder, he would not be taxed at all on these extra earnings, and if he earned less through voluntary absenteeism he would still have to pay the fixed amount of tax. This system could be applied also to salary-earners and professional persons. It would completely remove the present "disincentives" to extra effort.

If we are to avoid stagnation, everybody continuing to do the same job in the same place until he dies or retires, there must be mobility of labour. This implies a certain amount of unemployment. Provided that those unemployed (except for the unemployables) will soon find another job, there is no reason for alarm if the numbers of unemployed are as great as, say, 500,000. The Government, however, might do still more than it is doing now to facilitate the movement of workers between occupations, industries, and places. Its present plan to spend a considerable sum in assisting the cotton industry during its contraction, and helping it to improve its efficiency, is intended to achieve this aim.

The growth of output per head is due mainly not to greater exertions by the workers themselves but to increased investment and technical progress. The new plant, machinery, and other capital assets make possible a larger output from the same amount of labour. The workers are entitled to their share in the general increase in output, but so also are the owners of the capital which brought it about. If output increases by, say, 3 per cent a year and the workers demand a considerably greater increase in their wages, the consequence will be either inflation or unemployment.

The Government itself is a large employer; there are over $2\frac{1}{2}$ million workers in the nationalized industries. If the Government stands firm against excessive wage-claims by its own employees, and keeps down the volume of bank deposits sufficiently to prevent private employers from passing on excessive wage-increases in the form of increased prices, there will be no inflation. This course, however, may call for considerable courage by the Government and may lead to large-scale strikes if the trade unions refuse to give way.

It is possible that large groups of private employers may decide under pressure to give increases in wages which run well ahead of increases in productivity (or that arbitration tribunals may award such increases) even if the Government follows an anti-inflationary policy. In that event, there will be considerable unemployment, for the volume of money expenditure will remain too low for the same amount (or a slightly increased amount) of goods and services to be sold at appreciably higher prices.

With or without inflation, excessive wage-increases are likely to cause most difficulty in the export industries (and in industries meeting keen competition from imports), for they are in the most exposed position and are the least able both to raise their prices and to maintain their volume of sales.   Such a situation might lead to another balance-of-payments crisis.

Clearly the best course would be for the trade unions to co-operate whole-heartedly in measure to increase output per worker-hour.   This would give them greater real incomes, and a shorter standard working week.   Money wages could be raised, quite substantially as time went on, without any rise in the cost of living.   The basic truth that in the long run standards of living depend on the volume of output is the most important lesson which economics has to teach.

SOURCES OF STATISTICAL INFORMATION

I HAVE kept the following list to a minimum.

The United Nations Statistical Year Book contains annual statistics for practically every country in the world on nearly all economic subjects.

The Economist (weekly) publishes banking and other financial statistics for the United Kingdom and contains economic statistics both for the United Kingdom and other countries; it covers different subjects in different weeks.

The Annual Abstract of Statistics publishes annual statistics for the United kingdom on nearly every subject for which there are regular and reliable figures.

The Monthly Digest of Statistics is less comprehensive but contains up-to-date monthly figures for the United Kingdom on most economic subjects.

The Blue Book on National Income and Expenditure is published annually, usually in the summer. *The Economic Survey*, published annually about March, appraises current trends. Two White Papers a year are published giving comprehensive statistics on the *United Kingdom Balance of Payments*.

All the above except the first two are published by H.M. Stationery Office, Kingsway, London, W.C.2.

The Quarterly *Bulletin of the London and Cambridge Economic Service* is now published in *The Times Review of Industry*. It contains 90 leading series of statistics, with "long runs" (usually back to 1913).

INDEX